Hobbes: War among Nations

Edited by
TIMO AIRAKSINEN and MARTIN A. BERTMAN

Avebury

Aldershot · Brookfield USA · Hong Kong · Singapore · Sydney

Published by

Avebury

Gower Publishing Company Limited
Gower House
Croft Road
Aldershot, Hants GU11 3HR,
England

Gower Publishing Company
Old Post Road
Brookfield, Vermont 05036
U S A .

Printed and Bound in Great Britain by
Athenaeum Press Ltd., Newcastle upon Tyne.

ISBN 0 566 05769 7

Contents:

Introduction and Acknowledgements

Timo Airaksinen and Martin A. Bertman

At the University of Helsinki, in May of 1987, scholars from various nations met to discuss the question of whether World Government can be justified on the basis of the principles of Thomas Hobbes.[1] The papers collected in this book reflect the discussion of the question on that occasion.

It was our intent to offer these proceedings of the Hobbes Conference as a book to the general public in 1988, on the 400th anniversary of the birth of Hobbes. In the academic world, interest in the work of Hobbes is not only strong but if anything increasing, as evidenced by the large number of books and articles devoted to him, the recent founding of an International Hobbes Association with a *Hobbes Newsletter* and journal, *Hobbes Studies*, and at least a dozen conferences, throughout the world, devoted to some aspect of his thought during this anniversary period.

It was our particular concern to focus the discussion of Hobbes's political thought on the question of international relations, since it has been given relatively scant attention. One reason for that scantness is that Hobbes himself considered states to be in a "state of nature" or war, one with the other. With the impossibility of a World-State in the seventeenth century, and, consequently, without a sovereign entity to both create and enforce laws, Hobbes viewed the treaties that states made with one another mere fragile conveniences to be followed or not as a state understood its own interests. Political stability is created when a large number of persons contract to give their individual wills to a public person or sovereign. His great power assures peace. Hobbes believed, however, that states, with their individual sovereign wills intact formally, and with the existence of a material condition of competition without lawfulness, that is, an enforceable law, are in a condition of war. This is true whether or not hostilities are declared or, even, when allied states embark on mutual ventures. For fortune might for a time bring profit in this, as wandering plunderers unite but then disband as circumstance makes that more profitable. Therefore, as Gershon

Weiler put it, 'relations between sovereigns exercised Hobbes's mind only as afterthoughts in rounding off what he had to say about the correct structure of a municipal political system'.

There is no disagreement among Hobbes scholars about Hobbes's viewing a World-State an absurdity and international relations proceeding in a condition of war, where force and fraud are the great virtues. Nevertheless, the question of whether a World-State can be justified at present on Hobbesian principles causes disagreement. The majority of the scholars represented herein believe a World-State cannot be so justified.

Whether or not the majority is right, the question that caused disagreement served its intended purposes. It accomplished the following: it provoked thinking about which doctrines in Hobbes were more and which less important; it tested the applicability of Hobbes to the political realities of our own time; and it focused attention on the possibility of a World-State and the problems of international relations.

We will briefly present some of the main lines of controversy. First, the case for those who believe that World Government is justified on Hobbesian principles. The present world has arrived at or is close to allowing the possibility of destroying all human beings through weapons of war. Further, the economic interdependence of the world makes prosperity a substantially international problem. Hobbes's fundamental doctrine is that the state is formed primarily in the interest of individual self-preservation and also for the sake of prosperity. Where as in the seventeenth century, particular sovereign states ensured in good measure these values they at present do not. Since it was rational for individual persons to enter the state then, it is parallelly reasonable for individual states to join together now and form a World-State. Indeed, since the purpose of the individual state is to protect the lives of its members, the real possibility of world destruction through instruments of war erodes the ability of states to fulfil that purpose and increasingly makes them an anachronism.

There is much opposition to this justification represented in the collected papers. It takes various forms of attack. One approach is tangential to Hobbes, except perhaps to invoke his spirit of realism in political analysis. It is an appreciation of national forces, which Hobbes does not consider except in the parallel ideological manifestation of religious sectarianism. It is argued that a state also has a national identity and, often indeed contending national identities, so that it is unrealistic that the states, or those groups that wish to form or gain state power, will allow the creation of a World-State. It is implied that such a hope is as utopian as Hobbes's call for caesaropapism in his religiously divided England. Besides, some of the scholars argue for the value of nationalism and assume that a World-State would not allow for it.

Another sort of argument against the impracticality of World Government has a psychological aspect. It is argued that since states achieve a substantially immediate and concrete protection of their citizens, it is psychologically difficult in the extreme to give up that good for the ideational possibility of danger by way of world destruction. Formally, it is argued that states as artificial persons have no right, in some sense, to enter into a yet greater artificial World-State since the line of authorisation is only available for persons. This is argued in the face of such historical examples as the American colonial states merging, under a constitution, to become the United States.

The most central attack against the justification on the basis of Hobbes relies on the admitted fact that Hobbes himself considered World-State an absurdity and international relations as a sort of warfare. This attack, therefore, either undercuts the danger of the present situation or, if it concedes the danger, it argues that Hobbes has not provided a mechanism to create a World-State.

Of course this brief and selective presentation does not do justice to the range, learning, and argumentative skill of the papers. Neither does it suggest the contents of a number of papers that focus less on the main question than on the Hobbesian doctrines that are a background to it, e.g., his legal theory, methodology, ethics, and theory of man. Our intent was merely to prepare the reader in a most general way.

Our penultimate task is a sad one. Our colleague and great contributor to Hobbes scholarship, Isabel C. Hungerland, Emeritus Professor at the University of California at Berkeley, died just before the appointed time of the presentation of her paper, which was read on her behalf. With great respect, it is to her that we dedicate this book.

This conference has been sponsored by the Philosophical Society of Finland, International Hobbes Association, the City of Helsinki, the University of Helsinki, the Finnish Cultural Foundation, and the Ministry of Education. We are grateful for their help which made this conference possible. We also extend our thanks to all those who helped in the various stages of this meeting, especially Ms. Päivi Lehikoinen and Ms. Maija-Riitta Ollila.

Tampere Peace Research Institute (TAPRI) and its director Dr. Vilho Harle provided valuable assistance in the editing and publishing of the proceedings of the conference.

Notes

1. In his opening words, Professor Ilkka Niiniluoto, Chairperson of the Philosophical Society of Finland, said the following:

    'Political philosophy in the wide nonacademic sense has, of course, a long history in the life of Finland, even though our country gained its independence only 70 years ago. It is worth mentioning especially the legendary career of the Finnish Marxist Otto-Ville Kuusinen, who, after studying aesthetics at the University of Helsinki moved to the Soviet Union in the 1920's and ended his career in Moscow as an academician and as a member of the Presidium of the Central Committee of the Communist Party.

Political philosophy in fact had an important academic position already at the first Finnish university which was founded in Turku in 1640 (and which was later moved to Helsinki). The Faculty of Philosophy had chairs in theoretical philosophy (logic and metaphysics) and practical philosophy (morality and history). Thus, the first professor of political philosophy at our university, Michael Wexionius, was a contemporary of Hobbes: he wrote his main works on the genesis, nature, and relative value of political systems in the decade preceding the appearance of *Leviathan* (1651). One of Wexionius' successors, Andreas Wanochius, was probably the first of the Finnish Hobbes scholars: in his *De radice, causis et vinculis societatis humanae* (1690) Wanochius argued, against Hobbes, that man is indeed social by his original nature.

The most significant of all Finnish political philosophers has been Johan Vilhelm Snellman, whose statue can be seen in front of the Bank of Finland in Helsinki. Snellman was a Hegelian philosopher who is usually regarded as our "national philosopher": he had a decisive influence on the rise of the national — cultural, economical, and political — life in 19th century Finland. Snellman published his influential *Läran om staten* (in Swedish) in 1842; it was the first extensive *Staatslehre* based upon Hegelian principles, with a special emphasis on the historical role of the "national spirit" which expresses itself dynamically through nations by their language and literature. In 1856 Snellman became professor of "ethics and the system of sciences" at the University of Helsinki. The title "philosophy" could not be used, since a little earlier, in 1852, the Emperor had closed all chairs of philosophy in the whole Russian Empire. He suspected that they spread revolutionary ideas in politics and religion.

Snellman's successor Thiodolf Rein, who founded the Philosophical Society of Finland in 1873, was a political liberal, a representative of the nobility in Parliament. After Rein the Chair of Philosophy was again divided into Theoretical and Practical — the latter was occupied since 1906 by the famous philosopher and sociologist Edward Westermarck. One of Westermarck's successors, Professor Jussi Tenkku, is the author of a monograph *Oikeus ja elämän arvo* (Justice and the Value of Life) (1962) on the history of 17th century political philosophy — a work which initiated modern study of Hobbes in Finland. — I hope that these brief introductory remarks give you some idea of the background and the position of those philosophers who now cordially welcome you to start the Hobbes Conference in Helsinki.'

What is Alive in Hobbes

Martin A. Bertman

Georg Henrik von Wright, the eminent Finnish philosopher, in his *Explanation and Understanding* (1972), distinguishes two traditions: the Aristotelian and the Galilean. The former focuses on a teleological approach for understanding and the latter, as von Wright puts it, 'runs parallel with the advance of the causal mechanistic point of view in man's effort to explain and predict phenomena.' Hobbes, who considered his older contemporary, Galileo, to be the first founder of a new science since Euclid, obviously belongs to the Galilean tradition. In this paper, I will contrast Hobbes to the other tradition which takes seriously the possibility of metaphysics, that is, that the teleological explains as well as provides an understanding of reality.

In his article on teleology in *The Encyclopedia of Philosophical Sciences* (Part I, 204), Hegel writes:

> The distinction between the End or *final cause*, and the mere *efficient cause* (which is the cause ordinarily so called), is of supreme importance. Causes properly so called, belong to the sphere of necessity, blind, and not yet laid bare. ... The End, on the other hand, is expressly stated as containing the specific character in its own self — the effect, namely, which in the pure causal relation is never free from otherness. ... By End, however, we must not at once, nor must we merely, think of the form which it has in consciousness as a mode of mere mental representation. By means of the notion of INNER DESIGN Kant has resuscitated the Idea in general and particularly the idea of life. Aristotle's definition of life virtually implies inner design, and is thus far in advance of the notion of design in modern Teleology which has in view finite and outward design only.

1

Hegel's remark notes a tradition which excludes Hobbes and most modern, and especially empiricist, philosophers between Galileo and Kant. The crucial distinction here turns on whether teleological explanation has an "inner design" which depends on final causality or an external one which depends on efficient causality alone. This difference opens and closes variant possibilities for the ontological description of nature and also human nature. I submit that Hobbes's view of causality, both in nature and in the construction of the state, is more clearly understood by his opposition to the metaphysical inner design viewpoint.

But, before turning to Hobbes, I will develop the inner design viewpoint. To do this, instead of locating the discussion in Aristotle, as Hegel suggests, I turn to the magistral Plotinus. His platonism is less problematic, and, in its doctrinaire format, more clearly confrontational. To start, Plotinus provides a clear statement of his opposition to explanations merely from efficient causality. Freedom in action, which for Plotinus, like for Kant and for Hegel, is essential to our humanity, cannot be aptly posited, or explained, on the basis of an outer design or external perspective; and so, it cannot be conceptualised by efficient causality. Plotinus says:

> How can a compelling imagination, an appetite drawing us where it will, leave us masters in the ensuing act? Need, inexorably craving satisfaction, is not free in face of that to which it is forced: and how at all can a thing have efficacy of its own when it arises from an external, has an external for its very principle, thence taking its being as it stands? It lives for the external, lives as it has been moulded: if this is freedom, there is freedom in even the soulless. (Plotinus, VI, 8.)

This statement strikes the same note as Hegel in limiting the power of explaining action by efficient causes because such explanations are unable to capture the freedom of the individual. By specifically focusing on the efficacy arising from imagination and appetite, Plotinus might well have in mind his opposition to materialism, conspicuously to the atomic tradition, and especially to the Epicureans. (Cf. Hobbes, EW, V, 313: 'For I said not, the will is not moved, but we are not moved: for I always avoid attributing motion to anything but body.')[1] In taking pleasure and pain as the basis of action and by reducing this phenomenal experience, it seems, ultimately, to matter in motion, Hobbes as well as Epicurus is challenged by Plotinus.

In the following selection of quotes, Plotinus provides a view of action where the rational aspect of the act is timeless. This is self-conscious and reflexive since man is essentially rational; indeed, because Plotinus also holds that reason controls rather than arises from matter, contemplation is the supreme self-assertive act. Further, freedom is an aspect of a voluntary act involving knowledge and, in the fullest sense, self-unifying knowledge is in the contemplation of the Good. This Good is not conditional, just as our essential nature in its reliance on the Good is not materially conditioned. Consequently, to be free

2

or to actuate our essence, means a readiness to prefer the Good to any circumstantial or conditional value: one's biological life, country, children, etc. By acting in time in frienship with the Good, one achieves something of the quality of timeless reality. In Plotinus' own words:

> Act, we aver, is timeless. (Plotinus, IV, 1:16.)

> Action, thus, is twofold: there is that which occurs in the external, and that which does not. The duality of Action and Passion, suggested by the notion that action always takes place in the external, is abandoned. (Plotinus, VI, 1:19.)

> Thought itself need not be an action, for it does not go outward towards its object but merely attends to it. It is not always an activity; for all Acts need not be definable as activities, for they need not produce an effect: activity belongs to Act only accidently. (Plotinus, VI, 1:22.)

> ... ignorance is not compatible with real freedom: for the knowledge necessary for a voluntary act cannot be limited to certain particulars but must cover the entire field. Why, for example, should killing be involuntary in the failure to recognize a father and not so in the failure to recognize the wickedness of murder. (Plotinus, VI, 8:1.)

> Effort is free once it is toward a fully recognized good; the involuntary, precisely, motion away from a good. (Plotinus, VI, 6:4.)

> Virtue and the Intellectual-Principle are sovran and must be held the sole foundation of our self-disposal and freedom. Virtue does not follow upon occurences as a saver of the imperilled; at its discretion it sacrifices a man; it may decree the jettison of life, means, children, country even; it looks to its own high aim and not to the safeguarding of anything lower. Thus our freedom of act, our self-disposal, must be referred not to the doing, not to the external thing done but to the inner act, to the Intellection, to virtue's own vision. (Plotinus, VI, 8:16.)

> Being accompanies the Act in an eternal association: from the two (Being and Act) it forms itself into the Good, self-springing and unspringing. (Plotinus, VI, 8:7.)

By considering the Act categorically, as timeless, and action as something else, that is, as only accidentally belonging to Act, Plotinus offers two ontological schema. And, consequently, two frameworks for the explanation of things in time. One is the provisional calculation from experience, here the explanatory are external, finite, and limited. The probabilities of sense experience and the idiosyncratic aspects of personal and cultural values are such. When this sort of explanation is interrogated, Plotinus, like Plato's Socrates, finds it unsatisfactory because of its limited vision of the human condition and, at the least, a tendency to logical incoherence and so an incapacity to generate systematic organisation. The other explanatory approach, from eternal principles, proposes to accomplish much of what the first cannot. Plotinus indeed claims finite, contingent oriented methodologies, like those that are in induction from sense experience, point beyond themselves to the Good, that is, to the source and sustaining condition of reality.

It is precisely against such dual ontological schema — just even the less bold platonism of Descartes, who did consider the *res extensa* mechanistically — that Gilbert Ryle levies the charge of a 'ghost in the machine'. Ryle, like Hobbes, who often likens man to a machine, opposes the inner design explanation. Though their language must be somewhat adjusted, Ryle, at least by implication, and Hobbes consider the will — that aspect of man most like God for Descartes — ontologically reducible to a material condition and, also, the will is assertable of animals as evidenced by their external behaviour. What they oppose, as Ryle puts it, is the theory where the workings of the body are motions in space so that

> the causes of these motions must then be *either* other motions of matter in space *or*, in the privileged case of human beings, thrusts of another kind. In some way which must forever remain a mystery, mental thrusts, which are not movements of matter in space, can cause muscles to contract. (Ryle 1949, 63-4.)

The will, then, is a convenient term but it is shorthand for the material processes, observed and on the basis of observed experience.

The following quotes from Hobbes show the sharp contrast between his outer design viewpoint and the inner design one of Plotinus:

> For the nature of good and evil follows from the nature of circumstances. (On Man, XI, 4.)

> A body is said to work upon or act, that is to say, to do something to another body, when it either generates or destroys some accident in it; and the body in which an accident is generated or destroyed is said to suffer, that is, to have something done to it by another body; as when one body putting forwards another body generates some motion in it, it is called the AGENT; and the body in which motion is so generated, is called the PATIENT... (De Corpore, EW, I, Ch. 9.)

> I conceive that nothing taketh beginning from itself, but from the action of some other immediate agent without itself: and that therefore when a man first hath an appetite or will to something, to which immediately before he hath no appetite or will, the cause of this is not the will itself but something else in his own disposition. (Liberty, Necessity, and Chance, EW, V, 372-3.)

> For will itself is an appetite; and we do not shun something because we will not do it, but because now appetite, then aversion, is generated, by those things desired or shunned, and displeasure necessarily follows from those same objects. (On Man, XI, 1.)

> Lastly, I hold that the ordinary definition of a free agent, namely, that a free agent is that, which when all things are present to produce the effect, can nevertheless not produce it, implies a contradiction, and is nonsense; being as much as to say, the cause may be sufficient, that is necessary, and yet the effect not follow. (Liberty, Necessity, and Chance, EW, V, 385.)

> ... voluntary presupposes some precedent deliberation, that is to say, some consideration and mediation, of what is likely to follow, both upon

4

the doing and the abstaining from the action deliberated of. (On Liberty and Necessity, EW, IV, 243.)

This ensemble of quotes evidences Hobbes's reduction of will to the action of appetites which is the spring of behaviour: the will and the appetite is for Hobbes the very same thing (see EW, V, 93). Further, in contrast to Plotinus, Hobbes's free agent need not be a rational or, even, a living agent. He defines freedom as action without external impediments (Cf. EW, IV, 273-4). Freedom is merely considered in terms of the ontologically equivalent notions of sufficiency and necessity. All things therefore have liberty or freedom for Hobbes for he takes this to be the very movement or the assertion of capacity of the thing itself. Of Hobbes's position, his contemporary appointment, Bishop Bramhall says, 'This is brutish liberty, such a liberty as a bird hath to fly when her wings are clipped' (EW, V, 40). Clearly, Hobbes's notion of freedom is not only consistent with compulsion but discusses the same circumstance, though from a different modal perspective. For to say a thing is free or has sufficient power to say it can do what it can do and to say a thing is compelled or necessitated is to say it must do what it does, that is, it has no more power than it has to do otherwise than it does.

Bramhall notices Hobbes's externalist approach and complains, 'It is not inconsistent with true liberty to determine itself, but it is inconsistent with true liberty to be determined by another without itself' (EW, V, 32). Unlike the inner design tradition, the use of the word "action" by Hobbes does not demand self-consciousness. Indeed, voluntary action, the action resulting from deliberation or calculation of possible circumstances as action also motivated by desire, is neither more nor less free than the motions of inanimate things. Nevertheless, the particular way that will is reduced to desire, for Hobbes, is clearly emphasised in his understanding of deliberation:

> ... deliberation is nothing else but so many wills alternatively changes, according as a man understandeth or fancieth the good and evil sequels of the thing concerned which he deliberateth whether he shall pursue it... So that in deliberation there be many wills, whereof not any is the cause of voluntary action but the last. (EW, V, 401-2.)

Unlike Plotinus, Hobbes's outer design approach does not use "voluntary" for the process itself of deliberating; by calling the last appetite or consideration of the process leading to an act the will, he places emphasis on the change the individual causes outside himself. Indeed, when pressed by Bramhall that he calls even spontaneous acts deliberate, Hobbes says, 'there may be a difference between what may be deliberation and that which shall be construed as deliberation by a judge' (EW, V, 350). This avoids a contradiction for Hobbes and it shows us again his inclination to and outward or public credential for names or attributes which are used to describe human action. Further, the process of deliberation, since it must be ultimately explained by matter in motion, the physical processes to which Hobbes never attaches value in themselves, is thereby aside from the having of value. Thus, when speaking of value, Hobbes locates efficient causality in relation to the man and not to the matter from which his individuality arises. Because in terms of value, the efficient cause is the man, and not some part or physical condition of him, Hobbes, unlike Plato in his *Laws*, and consistent with nominalism's referential orientation to individuals, finds it hard to speak of warfare within a man. A man may indeed be mad or foolish but he, and not some part of his inner motions, acts; and, he acts always under conditions. Conditions, as they fulfil desires, make for pleasure and pain. Since desire always has an object acting on the individual, in this sense, man is neither pleased nor pained by his own self.

Also in the deliberation to construct a state, outward design expresses itself in the emphasis on conditions for the welfare of the individual. But since the state is an artificial individual, the notion of cause in reference to it is also artificial. Hobbes says, 'To make a law, is therefore to make a cause of Justice, and to necessitate justice' (EW, IV, 253). Not only is justice — the outer design to contain and socialise desire — reduced to a calculation about the conditions for pleasure and pain but, most interestingly, by speaking about justice, which is artificially created by human arrangements, in causal terms, Hobbes enters into the realm of rhetoric. Now the use of "cause" and "necessity" is different from their use in physics, in terms of referential force, because here Hobbes speaks about conventions.

Granting Hobbes's assumption that a properly made civil law alone in fact creates justice, rather than in the yet undetermined sense of the laws of nature, nevertheless, the obedience to it depends on both an individual's knowledge of it and his desire to comply. Consequently, the natural characteristics of man are of course not destroyed; man's welfare depends on the proper civil procedure but obedience to it depends on natural man, as indeed Spinoza pointed out and consequently added that this was his main disagreement with Hobbes (Letter 50, to Jelles). When Hobbes argues that the citizen has given up his freedom to disobey a law by transferring his liberty to the sovereign, obviously freedom here is being used in an artificial and different way than capacity to act in the world. It opens a space for rhetoric just because the citizen must be *persuaded* to obey. Therefore, when one makes a promise or a covenant, such as the covenant which forms the state, one provides the cause for obedience, which then is necessary, but here "cause" and "necessity" are artificial and, consequently, defeasible; it has a prescriptive force but not a descriptive or predictive force. When Hobbes says, 'I understand how a cause can be necessary, and the effect not be necessarily produced,' (EW, V, 296) he is not aptly thinking of the civil laws which he sometimes calls a "cause of justice." Indeed that Hobbes adds that the law without the sword is useless, the point is clear: man's natural fear

6

of death, and not merely his promise, is needed for the state's continuance.

But, to repeat, the point is that even under threat of the sword, natural man can, because sometimes he does, disobey. Consequently, Hobbes's use of the world "cause" here is slippery, sliding between those capacities of the state to effect the material welfare of a human being and that which one might properly call the "reason" for one's obedience to it.

That the discussion of causality is sometimes of the basal physical analysis and sometimes of an associated but, nevertheless, different mode — the artefacted — is most important. Hobbes, like Kant, faced by the conclusion of nature mechanised, ordered by efficient causes, chooses also a realm where final causes emerge. But, instead of a separate practical reason, with the free will in an ethical realm (with its ensuring consequence of moving toward the familiar dualism both in the conception of reason and of ontology), Hobbes locates value in desire: wanting and not wanting. This however, has the following consequence: desire, like all bodily processes, being ontologically reducible to matter and motion suggests that human values are, like secondary qualities, an illusionary condition of human perspective: 'the variety of things perceived in sense experience, such as color, sounds, odors, and so on, have no cause other than motion, concealed partly in objects acting and in objects sensing' (De Corpore, EW, I, Ch. 6). Perhaps, this can be put more positively by simply saying that value exists where nature creates a material condition for complex sensibility, values thus arise from natural forces but are only present in a particular creature's desires.

For Hobbes science and philosophy are epistemologically the same:

> Philosophy is the knowledge, acquired through correct reasoning, of effects or phenomena from the conception of their causes or generations, and also of generations which could exist through the knowledge of their effects. (De Corpore EW, I, Ch. 1,2.)

Metaphysics or "philosophia prima" merely has an ultimate generality by defining the names involved in the generation of any object whatsoever that might then be investigated by a specific science. Plotinus, however, and the inner design tradition, try to separate at least provisionally, the ontological commitments of science and metaphysics; and, thereby, to allow science to focus on finite, mutable, and temporal material entities while, nevertheless, providing value ultimately for these by metaphysics. Thereby, Plotinus seeks to rescue the external or, even, the functional explanations of efficient causality from valuelessness by subordinating them to the final causality of essences. For Hobbes this is absurd. He writes:

> The writers of metaphysics reckon up two other causes besides the efficient and the material, namely the ESSENCE, which some call the formal cause, and the END, or final cause; both of which are nevertheless efficient causes. (EW, I, 123.)

7

Hobbes's reduction of formal and final causality to material and efficient causality, means that action, as a possibility of aliveness, is a condition of matter in motion. Hobbes, however, does not hint that he is a hylozoist; on the contrary, life for him, is an emergent quality of complex sensate individuals. That mere matter and motion is not *per se* alive, seems to have an explanatory gap for the eventual emergence of life from it.

Whether this is an apt argument against Hobbes, matter in motion is not life as Hegel understood it — of a rational principle or Geist organising reality — when, on his suggestion, I distinguished between Hobbes and the inner design tradition. Though efficient causality can describe the norms of materially complex individuals, that is, functional purpose, the question remains if, when purpose is missing from the material processes at the ground of these norms, which is the case in Hobbes, (excluding his consciously honorific ultimate reference to God,) value exists beyond the conditional. Perhaps it is Hobbes's point that it does not; he seems comfortable with God's answer to Job, that is, God's unquestionable and unexplainable power as the source of the good. Bramhall would incline to Plato's argument in the *Euthyphro* that the good is recognised by the divine. Hobbes choice seems to be between a fideist piety and an inability to explain value on ultimate rational grounds.

The classic presentation of seeking value beyond mere physical explanations, which are open to the charge of the relativity, if not the charge of an ultimate intellectual incoherence, is found in Plato's *Phaedo* when Socrates points out that he is in jail not because his body is in a certain physical condition but because he made certain decisions. To reduce Socrates's decisions to matter in motion is to make of the a bare fact of reality without a ground of purposive value for that fact. Though Hobbes would also find Socrates's decisions the source of value, Plato would accuse Hobbes of contradicting himself by ultimately reducing those decisions to matter in motion. Hegel on this ground, I believe, does not consider Hobbes to have a conception of life: the brute fact of existence even when expressed as the functioning of a physical system — but without mind — does not have life. And pleasure, as an end in itself, Hegel discounts as even capable of meaning much less of generating value, since it is, as Plato puts it in the *Philebus*, 'formless and cannot give form'.

Hobbes's notion of life, and value, is on the contrary determined by objects providing pleasure and pain, calculated in relation to the desires: 'whatever is the object of any man's Appetite or Desire; that is what he calls Good: And the object of his Hate, and Aversion, Evil: And of his contempt, Vile and Inconsiderable' (Leviathan I, Ch. 6). Of course the reduction of good to desire does not deny the emergence of a public good through the civil laws. The civil laws provide a safe, though constrained, condition for a man; instrumentally, they foster the primary desire to exist, and, as well, the hope of prospering. The civil laws are demanded or necessary just because all the desires of a man can scarcely be fulfilled; a man cannot have felicity especially under a condition of competition for objects by individuals whose desire structure (though not always the objects of his desire) are the same as his. So experience shows a man that he cannot obtain all that he desires and his pleasures are therefore conditional or limited. Hobbes writes:

> The greatest good, or as it is called, felicity and the final end, cannot be obtained in the present life. For if the end be final, there would be nothing to long for, nothing to desire, whence it follows not only that nothing would itself be a good from that time on, but also that man would not even feel. For all sense is conjoined with some appetite or aversion; and not to feel is not to live. (On Man, XI, 15.)

Returning briefly to Plotinus, though Plotinus finds the desires or the "duress of human nature and the needs of individual existence" important, it is interesting to compare him to Hobbes on actions oriented by desire:

> When, on the contrary, the agent falls in love with what is good in those actions, and, cheated by the mere track or trace of the Authentic Good, makes then his own, them, in his pursuit of the lower good, he is the victim of magic. For all dalliance with what wears the mask of the authentic, all attraction towards the mere semblance, tells of a mind misled by the spell of forces pulling towards unreality. Contemplation alone stands untouched by magic; no man self-gathered falls to a spell; for he is one, and that unity is all that he perceives, so that his reason is not beguiled but holds due course, fashioning its own career and accomplishing its task. In the other way of life, it is not the essential man that gives the impulse, it is not reason; the unreasoning also acts as a principle, and finds its premises in emotion. (Plotinus, IV, 4: 44.)
>
> The essential man is beyond harm. (Plotinus, IV, 43: 43.)

For Plotinus and the classical tradition, much, if not all, of our existence as animals takes external circumstance as the medium to express our humanness. But our continued existence is not the fundamental value. Action, then, in the fullest sense, is the establishment of our rationally unconditioned essence in this conditional medium. It may be said, acting self-consciously is a thinking despite the constraints of the world: thinking is the action and, the rearranging of the world is the shadow of action. The accusation against Hobbes's viewpoint is that he takes the shadow for the only action. Hobbes's outward design never loses its conditionality, for him that is evidenced in just this: a man wishes to supersede any particular desire as it is satisfied. A moving finger of finitude, the unity of the individual is in this way not in-and-for itself. The aliveness of self-awareness is reduced to the matter-of-factness of desire where wants, by being met or not, by providing pleasure and pain, in their degrees, are the very organisation of individuality. But, in opposition to the classical tradition, this individuality is rather unelevated. Hobbes says:

A wooden top is lashed by the boys, and runs about sometimes to one wall, sometimes spinning, sometimes hitting men on the shins, if it were sensible of its own motion, would think it proceeded from its own will, unless it felt what lashed it. And is a man any wiser, when he runs to one place for a benefice, to another for a bargain, and troubles the world with writing errors and requiring answers, because he thinks he doth it without other cause than his own will, and seeth not the lashings that cause his will? (EW, V, 55.)

The fundamental principle of matter in motion itself does not have, so to speak, an inside, it does not have essential value; thus, Hobbes's value is always self-oriented and perspectival. Its bedrock, from which arises a rational perspective, is in maintaining the organisation of complex individuals. This argument seems to present an amphibolous division. On the other hand, we are here tempted to say, "man is the measure," his continuance and pleasure sets the agenda, whereas, on the other hand, since man himself is reduced to the more general analysis of matter and motion, we can, without denying the necessity of the former, relate to it with pessimism.

Hobbes writes:

Whatever accidents or qualities or senses make us think there be in the world, they are not there, but are seeming and apparitions only: the things that are in the world about us, are those motions by which these seemings are caused. (EW, I, 102; EW, IV, Ch 1, 10.)

But one cannot leave the matter here because there is an ironic twist in Hobbes's position. The cognitive status of the fundamental physical principle is less secure than the value perspectival one of man discoverable by introspection. Needing stable principles, he says:

Civil philosophy is demonstrable for we make the commonwealth ourselves. But because natural bodies we know not from construction, but seek it from effects, there lies no demonstration of what the causes be we seek for but only what they may be. (EW, VII, 184.)

It is civil philosophy, a science of which Hobbes claims to be the founder, that is certain for it relies on the construction from principles found equally in all human beings. Thus, Hobbes proceeds to introspection, of which he says:

He that governs a whole nation, must read in himself, not this or that particular man: but mankind; which though it be hard to do, harder than to learn any language or science; yet when I shall set down my own reading orderly, and perspicuously, the pains left another, will be only to consider, if he also find not the same in himself. For this kind of doctrine admitteth no other demonstration. (Leviathan, Preface.)

If 'this doctrine admitteth no other demonstration' is to be taken at face value, Hobbes's civil philosophy depends on the reliability of introspection. (Though, more precisely, the civil philosophy needs the products of introspection, *viz.*, that greed and glory seeking are "desire structures" so great that they must be checked by the yet greater desire for preservation.) Hobbes's admission of the difficulty of introspection, in itself provides doubt about the certainty of any particular introspection. Considering the further difficulty of the epistemological assumption that a (properly done) introspection would provide knowledge not only of some other man but of all mankind added doubt arises. However, as a check on the probity of an introspection, Hobbes always suggests experiential verification; that is, the general behaviour of man can be explained by the principles arrived at by the introspection; indeed, in *Elements of Law* and *De Cive*, experience alone is mentioned and seems sufficient for Hobbes's political theory. Yet since Hobbes considers principles derived from sense experience only probable, to use the experiential to check the putatively certain method of introspection is limited. Limited all the more, in that such a check needs the sorting out of ''manners'', that is, those cultural and educational causes of outward behaviour, from those which would present themselves as expressions of a universal structure of desire. Of course, the same problem arises as well in introspection. A further difficulty is the possibility that, even if all men have the same desires, the degree and relationship among the desires are different for various men. Indeed, behavioural evidence presents such differences. Hobbes's task, in consequence of this, is to discount the behaviour of some men. Not only because such are conditionally based on different objects of desire (though, also, they might be based on an improper calculation), but, especially, just when behaviour suggests a structure of desires other than that Hobbes finds in himself or, if not simply other, than desires different in intensity and/or intrastructural relation. He, for example, is forced not only to call suicides insane but even those models of heroism, like Achilles, who would nobly sacrifice their lives because his own introspection finds the avoidance of violent death fundamental and, consequently, this is generalised as mankind's most powerful desire.

Hobbes at the start of his literary career translated Thucydides, at the end, Homer. The lesson of Thucydides against war, as or leading to madness, was to be taken, apparently, more seriously than the virtues of a homeric warrior culture. If Hobbes is right, he implies that cultures can drive one to insanity. They propose ideals which are in opposition to our basic desires and, therefore, one must face ideologies with a sober assessment based on physical needs. That suicidal ideals are accepted, itself shows rhetoric: black rhetoric. On the other hand, that one is sometimes surrounded by social madness, demands white rhetoric. Indeed, the professed purpose in Hobbes's ''Introduction'' to his translation of Thucydides and his *De Cive* and *Leviathan* is to persuade his countrymen of the benefits of peace and the obligations they have to preserve the commonwealth.

But this persuasion is hinged to a debatable epistemological point. Hobbes,

11

though claiming that introspection brings a universal certainty, and that behaviour confirms the kinds, intensities, and order of mankind's desires, nevertheless, when faced with what men actually do and what men say about their motivations, he must find excuses; and, indeed, relying simply on experience, as in the De Cive, he is even in a worse position. He must try to bring men to the result of his introspection though they call him a "monster". Hobbes, like the Protagoras that Plato paints, seems to wish to persuade all men that his self-measure is also mankind's. This is strange indeed since, in principle, the good is reduced to desire and one cannot quarrel with desire for then one would find the good somewhere else; each man must know his own good in this sense, as Hobbes sometimes notices: 'one cannot speak of something as being simply good; since whatsoever is good for someone or another' (De Homine XI, 4). Hobbes's rhetoric, then, if it is presented to men that have different fundamental desires, not merely different objects of desire, thereby, loses its *raison d'être*.

Hobbes's ability to convince, however, is in stressing the functional aspect of the state; this subtly engages the *usual* though hardly universal desires for continued existence and prosperity. Hobbes often remarks, 'he who wants the end must also want the means.' The commonwealth is the means to continued existence.[2] Yet, even by clarifying the mine and thine by artifice's creating a *measure* for value, it does not fundamentally create value, which is constant to human nature. Convention's relation to nature, then, is to present the opportunity but not the source of value. So for example, when Hobbes says, the sovereign is the source or font of all honor, he is not denying that in human nature there is a desire for ascendency over one's fellowman. Instead, he seems to make the very interesting point that conventions not only secure those objects desired in the state of nature, like food and sex, but they as well create new objects for the desires peculiar to civil society. After all connoisseurship is hardly possible in the state of nature. Nevertheless, the values of natural man, are in the unchanging sub-structure of value. Despite the variance of the objects of this desire structure, due to experience, reason, and circumstance the structure is putatively unchanged by gender, period of life, culture and education. Such matters, like the state itself, are conditional: they provide, in some sense, both the objects and the capacity for the desires. Convention, thus is also an outer design for achieving value, for it provides the objects that move the appetite or will.

Yet, Hobbes must convince us that the fundamental desires he would find in his reading of himself do not change from man to man and that they provide more than an ephemeral basis for value. It is his need for a stable foundation to construct his political recommendations that makes Hobbes posit his dubious doctrine of the desires. Bereft of a metaphysics that emphasises teleological

12

reason that is ontologically linked to the order of nature, Hobbes looks at man's desires: preservation and prosperity are rational, that is, in the sense of an opposition to the suicidal as irrational. It is hard to quarrel with this as a usual human view and that disguises the ungroundedness of these values and their perspectivalism.

The rhetorical posture of Hobbes is always primarily related to the preservation of the individual's existence and, then, to "common living" (cf. Leviathan, Part I, Ch. 13). One hopes to fulfil this under those conditions which would allow one to exist, that is, to exercise power. So, the question of whether world government, today, is reasonable on Hobbes's principles depends on the single matter of whether present conditions are calculated to endanger existence and hamper commodious living. The latter is obviously hampered by the condition of competing states. Resources spent on armament erode the powers of most men to live more commodiously. The fundamental matter, however, is whether the condition of technical advance in weaponry, in the hands of competing states, has arrived at or is approaching the point where every individual's survival is clearly jeopardised. If one finds that the conditions of armament (as well as the technology of world communication, transportation, and economics) endanger the preservation of states and, consequently, each human member of those states, I think world government is justified on Hobbes's principles.

In sum, the line of Hobbes's argument is that just as the logic of the state allows for different actual civil laws of particular states so, too, the conditions for their existence affect not the nature but merely the particular character of the political organisation. Since the 400 years from Hobbes's birth in 1588, the conditions for our preservation and commodiousness have indeed changed so that what Hobbes considered inappropriate for his own time, world government, is now appropriate on essentially his same basis for state formation: self-preservation.

The considerations of this paper were too complex to bring us simply to this point. Some of the abstracts for this conference, remarked, in various ways, that the title of the conference is ambiguous. Ambiguity was taken differently than in this paper: I find the notion of world government itself problematic because the notion from which it arises, *viz.*, the individual's ability to govern himself — what it means to act as a human being — is not clear. This is not a matter of not recognising Hobbes's intuitions, but rather of questioning their plausibility. I have suggested that the ground of this difficulty is a metaphysical issue or, rather, it is the issue of the possibility of metaphysics which discloses an essential inner design for man as a guide.

Notes

1. References are made to the following works and editions of Hobbes: *The English Works of Thomas Hobbes* (EW), ed. by W. Molesworth, John Bohn, London 1841, (Reprint: Scientia Aalen, 1962); *De Homine* (On Man) in *Man and Citizen*, ed. by Bernard Gert, Doubleday, New York 1972; *Leviathan*, ed. by C. B. Macpherson, Penguin, London 1968.

2. For Hobbes, the civil condition qualifies individuality; it is just the social or political position of a man that is his value. Position, important to the outer design of a mechanistic description, is the condition for the exercise of power. Hobbes says: 'The *Value*, or *worth* of a man, is as of all other things, his Price; that is to say, so much as would be given for the use of his Power: and therefore is not absolute but a thing dependent on the need and judgement of another.' (Leviathan Part, I, Ch. X). The civil law binds citizens: but this binding is artificial. Hobbes says, 'So when we *speak freely*, it is not the liberty of voice, or pronunciation, but of the man, whom no law hath obliged to speak otherwise than he hath' (Leviathan Part II, Ch. XXI). But, in the very same paragraph, above this, Hobbes had said, 'when the words *Free*, and *Liberty*, are applied to anything but *Bodies*, they are abused; for that which is not subject to motion is not subject to Impediment' (ibid.). This provides us with a very significant instance of Hobbes understanding of political rhetoric: the political condition — law as a cause of justice — impersonates nature. For the sake of existence, the citizen seemingly binds his natural capacity, his freedom: both the state's threat of retaliation and the wisdom of having a commonwealth obliges him to the fictive condition of the state. If you will, this is Hobbes's Golden Lie because man cannot live in nature without restraining conventions.

14

The Unity of Hobbes's Philosophy

Peter Machamer and Spyros Sakellariadis

I

It is a commonplace of the literature to say that Hobbes is concerned to show the dependence of his civil philosophy upon his natural philosophy. Yet the form of this dependence has been the subject of much controversy. Hobbes himself writes in *De Corpore*[1] that the principles of natural philosophy must be fully understood before the principles of civil philosophy can be demonstrated:

> ... he that teaches or demonstrates any thing (should) proceed in the same method by which he found it out; namely, that in the first place those things be demonstrated, which immediately succeed to universal definitions (in which is contained that part of philosophy which is called *philosophia prima*). Next, those things which may be demonstrated by simple motion (in which geometry consists). After geometry, such things as may be taught or shewed by manifest action, that is, by thrusting from, or pulling towards. After these, the motion or mutation of the invisible parts of things, and the doctrine of sense and imaginations, and of the internal passions, especially those of men, in which are comprehended the grounds of civil duties, or civil philosophy; which takes up the last place. And that this method ought to be kept in all sorts of philosophy, is evident from hence, that such things as I have said are to be taught last, cannot be demonstrated, till such as they are propounded to be first treated of, be fully understood. (De Corpore, 87.)

Again, in the Dedication to *De Homine* (1658), Hobbes claims that political and natural philosophy are necessarily interrelated:

> Having completed this section, *De Homine*, I have finally fulfilled my promise. For you now possess the prime elements of my philosophy in all its divisions and subdivisions. Moreover, it happens that the two parts

15

whereof this section consists are very dissimilar. One is very difficult, the
other very easy; one consists of demonstrations, the other of experience;
one can be understood by few, the other by all. They are therefore
somewhat abruptly conjoined; but this was necessary, granted the method
of my work as a whole... For man is not just a *natural* body, but also a
part of the state, or (as I put it) of the body *politic*; for that reason he had
to be considered as both man and citizen, that is, the first principles of
physics had to be conjoined with those of politics, the most difficult with
the easiest. (De Homine, 1.)

Critics have tended to view these claims in either of two ways: first, that Hobbes is simply wrong to think that natural philosophy is in the least way relevant
to politics, or, second that Hobbes, in principle, thinks he can, and, in fact, attempts to, reduce politics to physics. In this paper we will try to show what truth
there is to both these claims. We shall argue that neither is completely correct.
Attempting to reconcile the insights behind these two positions will involve laying out the architectonic of Hobbes's philosophy and examining the interconnec-
tions of its various levels. In particular, we will show how Hobbes's version of
a nominalistic theory of language acts to unify the various parts of his
philosophy.

II

Traditionally, the claim has been made that any theory of man, whether ethical,
psychological or political, is not derivable from, nor reducible to, natural
philosophy. The *logi classici* of this position in Hobbes's commentators are A.E.
Taylor's 'The Ethical Doctrine of Hobbes' (1938) and Warrender's *The
Political Philosophy of Hobbes: His Theory of Obligation* (1957). On their view,
Hobbes's theory of moral obligation must be separated from his natural
philosophy and psychology on logical grounds. They claim that it is logically impossible to derive an account of how men should act (a moral theory, incorporating a normative claim) from an account of how they do act (a psychological
theory incorporating a descriptive claim.)

In particular, Warrender argues that:

A moral obligation to obey the civil law cannot logically be extracted from
a system in which man has no moral obligations before and apart from the
institution of the law. Any view that assumes otherwise, contains a hiatus
in the argument that cannot be surmounted, and if, in fact, this is
Hobbes's position, he must be held to have failed in his main enterprize.
(Warrender 1957, 6.)

The argument is that Hobbes cannot assert the existence of a moral obligation
to obey the civil law, the will of the sovereign, unless some basis for this moral
obligation exists prior to the coming into existence of the law, i.e., the creation

16

of the Sovereign. It is said to follow that if Hobbes is to have a tenable theory of moral obligation, the moral obligation must exist in some form prior to the creation of the Sovereign. Warrender holds that Hobbes satisfies this condition by implicitly assuming that a moral obligation exists in the state of nature prior to the existence of the civil state. He attempts to give an account of Hobbes's conception of laws of nature which supports this contention. Warrender and Taylor argue that to make sense of the claim that laws of nature are obligatory, they must interpret them as being divine commands. Taylor puts this as:

> I can only make Hobbes's statements consistent with one another by sup-posing that he meant quite seriously what he often says, that the natural law is the command of God, and to be obeyed *because* it is God's com-mand. (Taylor 1938, 417.)

If we equate natural laws with commands, then they must be the commands of someone who commands by a right present before the existence of the civil state, than is, by divine right. Only God could be in the position to provide a bridge between the state of nature and the subsequent civil state.

There is some text in Hobbes's work to support this claim. In the *Elements of Law* (1640), Hobbes claims:

> They are called the laws of nature, for that they are the dictates of natural reason; and also moral laws, because they concern men's manners and conversation one towards another; so are they also divine laws in respect to the author there of, God Almightly; and ought therefore to agree, or at least, not to be repugnant to the word of God revealed in Holy Scripture. (Elements, 111.)

Here Hobbes does equate laws of nature with divine commands, and, thus, seems to support Taylor's claim that human beings obey the natural law even in a state of nature because it is God's command. This reading also would sup-port their thesis that the hiatus between the moral philosophy of Hobbes and his political philosophy can be bridged by reference to God.

There are problems, however, with any interpretation of Hobbes's argument which makes an appeal to God central. First, there is the fact that Hobbes himself seems to place very little weight on this strand of the argument. When Warrender and Taylor claim that Hobbes can only derive a moral obligation from a consideration of natural philosophy be appealing to God, they are making cen-tral an argument which Hobbes deems peripheral and making peripheral Hob-bes's central argument, namely the argument relating obligation to self-interest.

Second, Hobbes makes it clear that the laws of nature function in three ways as ''dictates of natural reason'', as ''moral laws'', and as ''divine laws''. In the above passage, and in *Leviathan,* Chapter 31, God is only brought in as a source of authority and power to assure that the laws of nature are consistent with what is written in Scripture, not to justify the claim that moral or natural laws are to be obeyed *because* they are consistent with Scripture. Hobbes's talk of God does not support Taylor's claim that human beings obey the natural law *because* it is God's command. Rather, it does not appear to address itself to that issue, but only to the claim that the natural law which is obeyed *is* God's command.

If our reading of Hobbes is right, there is no good argument to the effect that Hobbes bridges the gaps between moral, political, and natural philosophy by reference to God's commands. One of the aims of this paper is to show that a proper understanding of the overall structure of Hobbes's whole philosophy is necessary in order to understand the relation of the laws nature to natural, moral, and political philosophy. In that overall structure, arguments that focus on God's power are really peripheral.

Third, Warrender and Taylor, in claiming that Hobbes can only deduce a theory of moral obligation from a theory of man's actual actions by reference to God, separate Hobbes's theory of moral obligation from his natural philosophy. But, if the two theories are logically separate, then they need independent justification, for it would be logically consistent to hold that one while rejecting the other. This would make problematical the claims Hobbes makes, as in the passages first quoted, to the effect that a full understanding of the principles of political and moral philosophy (and, hence, its justification) requires a knowledge of his natural philosophy. Warrender and Taylor could even be right in claiming that Hobbes is wrong in supposing that the knowledge of the former requires a knowledge of the latter, but they do not give an adequate account of why Hobbes thought this was so. This they must do if they are to give an interesting and historically viable interpretation of Hobbes.

III

In contrast to the attempts of Warrender and Taylor to separate what Hobbes takes to be interrelated parts of his thought, there have been attempts to show that these strands are really connected. In *Hobbes's System of Ideas* J.W.N. Watkins (1973) argues that the essential theses of Hobbes's political theory are implied by his more general philosophical doctrines. Watkins agrees with Warrender that, had Hobbes derived a set of categorical moral imperatives from factual premises, then he would have committed a serious logical error, but, Watkins claims, Hobbes does not do this. Instead Hobbes derives a set of hypothetical imperatives (involving prudential ''ought'' statement) that are based upon the presupposition that any man will naturally seek to preserve himself from a violent death:

> My thesis is that Hobbes did derive his prescriptions from factual premises, but without committing a logical fallacy; for his prescriptions are

18

not *moral* prescriptions — they are more like "doctor's orders" of a peculiarly compelling kind. A medical regimen may assume something of the appearance of a stern moral code. It may require painful sacrifices. To live in accordance with it may require great determination. Lapses may be followed by remorse. But its sanction is not moral. It is prescribed in the patient's own interest. (Watkins 1973, 76.)

These imperatives or prescriptions have a peculiarly compelling character because they rest upon facts of human nature and its constituent passions. These in turn are nothing but motions of the corpuscles making up a human body. Expanding on this, Watkins argues that the is/ought argument of the *Leviathan* (Ch. 12) is valid when interpreted in terms of a psychologistic theory of human nature, and that this fits with Hobbes's reductionist position whereby all theories reduce, ultimately, to natural philosophy. Therefore, on Watkin's view, *contra* Warrender and Taylor, Hobbes's political and natural philosophies do not need independent justification. On standard reductionist views, if Hobbes's natural philosophy is justified, then *a fortiori* anything derived from it, for example political philosophy, is also justified.

On the standard view, for a reduction to be accomplished, every primitive terms appearing in the reduced theories (political and moral philosophy) and not in the reducing theory (natural philosophy) must "be associated with" terms in the reducing theory by way of correspondence rules. Then, if a theory (e.g. natural philosophy), together with a set of correspondence rules logically entails another theory (e.g., political philosophy), we say that the latter theory has been reduced to the former. Reduction so specified has the consequence that the reducing theory can do all the work of explanation (in a deductive-nomological sense) and schematisation of data which the reduced theory used to do, without remainder.

Though Watkins avoids the problems that face Warrender and Taylor by treating Hobbes as some sort of reductionist (ontological or philosophical), his view generates problems of internal coherency and historical and textual adequacy.

First, in accepting the seemingly intuitive distinction, used by Warrender and Taylor, between the moral and the prudential "ought", Watkins is taking certain liberties of interpretation. In order to state his reductionist claim, Watkins separates the different levels of Hobbes's philosophy (moral, natural and political). He then suggests that, for Hobbes, the claim that someone ought do something does not involve a moral "ought" in any traditional sense, but rather a prudential "ought". A person X ought to do Ø means that if X is to act in his own interest (towards self-preservation), then X will do Ø. And for Hobbes, men have a natural tendency to act so as to preserve themselves. Thus, Watkins likens Hobbes's ought's to doctors's prescriptions, where the patient observes them in order to preserve himself. Given the prudential/moral distinction,

19

Watkins, Warrender and Taylor all agree that Hobbes can derive a prudential "ought" from his natural philosophy, but they differ on the consequences of this. Where Warrender and Taylor say that Hobbes confuses the two ought's, Watkins claims that Hobbes is concerned only with prudential ones.

It is, however, anachronistic to analyse Hobbes's text in terms of the prudential/moral distinction. By accepting this distinction, Watkins is committed to claiming that the "ought's" of the different levels of Hobbes's system function differently. In order to support the attribution of the distinction to Hobbes, Watkins would have to show how these different functions are manifest at each level in the system. Watkins produces no text for this, and in addition, it seems that there is no such text that will support the attribution of this distinction to Hobbes. Hobbes in his own way denies that "ought's" used at different levels are actually distinct. Obligations, on each of the levels, are not treated differently, and are, in fact, defined identically. In the absence of such text, Watkins's interpretation of Hobbes's normative claims derives its support from the fact that it brings the rest of Hobbes's system into a coherent whole. It is, however, highly dubious methodologically to claim that Hobbes was really talking only about prudential "ought's" in spite of Hobbes's explicit claims about moral obligations solely in order to vindicate his interpretation of the interrelation of the levels of Hobbes's system.

The second problem with Watkins's interpretation concerns not its historical and textual adequacy, but its internal coherence. Watkins wants to claim that Hobbes is a reductionist. He attempts to spell out Hobbes's reductionism in two different ways. On each way Watkins starts his argument by speaking of Hobbes's system of ideas. First, he attempts to show how it might be that Hobbes could say that a philosophical theory entails a political conclusion. He grants, with Warrender and Taylor, that the content of a political theory cannot strictly be entailed by philosophical premises. This leads him to claim a weaker sort of reductionism for Hobbes:

> A philosophical proposition cannot by itself entail a proposition having a political content which the former lacks. But the introduction of a philosophical theory a into an existing circle of statements b may make it possible to derive a new political conclusion c; in which case a implies that if b then c. Moreover, if c is controversial, whereas b consists of uncontroversial background assumptions (for instance, that men live in proximity to one another, that their resources are scarce, that it is physically possible for one man to kill another), then the philosophical idea bears the chief responsibility for the political conclusion, and the latter may be said, by a pardonable ellipsis, to be an implication of the philosophical idea. (Watkins 1973, 10.)

Watkins's point is that a theory with political content can only be derived from premises with political content. Thus, in order to derive a political conclusion

20

c from a philosophical theory *a*, we must conjoin *a* to a set of statements *b* which have political content. Watkins says, furthermore, that if *b* is uncontroversial, it can be suppressed: *b* has the effect of a tautology (and therefore is suppressible) so consequently we can say that *a* entails *c*.

The ellipsis, however, is not pardonable. For *b* cannot both have political content and be suppressible: if it is suppressible (has the effect of a tautology) than *a fortiori* it must be (in effect) *content-less*, and conversely, if it has political content it is not suppressible. If *b* is suppressible, it cannot give any content to *c*. Again, if *b* is only "pardonably" suppressible, then any political content of *c* is "pardonably" suppressible, that is, the political content of *c* would have to be effectively tautologous. But if *c* is effectively tautologous, then presumably anything entails it, and by a "pardonable ellipsis" anything may be said to bear the chief responsibility for *c*.

Given that this weak sort of reductionism is quite problematic, we ought to try to find a stronger interpretation of Watkins's assertion 'I shall argue that some of his political ideas are implied by some of his philosophical ideas...' (Watkins 1973, 8). He ought to be claiming that he will show that there is some strict reduction of political content to philosophical content in Hobbes's master plan. But this he admits cannot be done without introducing premisses with political content; and these, just because of the role they play, are not innocuous.

On the second way of making out his reductionist claim, Watkins distinguishes the different levels of Hobbes's system and the correspondence rules linking them. These correspondence rules he identifies with Hobbes's laws of nature. Watkins wants laws of nature to function as correspondence rules in a traditional reductionist schema. For example, to derive the proposition, that men act so as to preserve themselves, from statements about the sub-visible particles, etc., one needs to invoke the laws concerning motion and interaction of the small particles, etc. Thus, the claim goes, *via* the laws of nature we can derive an "ought" from Hobbes's natural philosophy. The person's inner constitution (describable in terms of natural philosophy) causes him to have this desire for self-preservation. So Watkins can say that, in a sense, Hobbes's theory of natural philosophy entails the essentials of Hobbes's theory of moral obligation.

The problem with this approach is fundamental. In Hobbes's system the laws of nature are used as basic explanatory principles embodying causal principles which underpin his whole philosophy. Philosophy, we recall, is the ascertaining and stating of such causes (De Corpore, 3). Laws of nature thus capture causal content and are not simple meaning postulates. Given such non-supressable content, they cannot be used in the manner necessary to be correspondence rules in a reductionist schema. Consequently, Watkins's reductionist interpretation of Hobbes is internally incoherent; laws of nature cannot function as correspondence rules, since in Hobbes's system they represent causal claims. For Hobbes these causal principles are the most philosophically interesting parts of his theory. The problem of interpretation, then, is how to make sense of these causal claims whilst linking the various levels of Hobbes's philosophy. As we shall see later, the reason why laws of nature can function thus for Hobbes lies in Hobbes's theory of meaning. His version of nominalism will be seen to unify the various levels of his system in a way which dispenses with the need for correspondence rules.

So far we can say the following. On the one hand, the Warrender-Taylor claim involves a misrepresentation of Hobbes's use of the term ''ought'' that is, they claim that Hobbes makes an unjustified equivocation on the meaning of the word ''ought''. On the other hand, though, a reductionist claim, if construed with the laws of nature functioning as correspondence rules, is inconsistent with Hobbes's theory concerning the nature of philosophy. We will show later how Hobbes avoids the reductionist issue, and does not equivocate on the meaning of ''ought''.

IV

Hobbes never actually states that political philosophy can be reduced to natural philosophy, the nearest he comes to this is the claim that an understanding of the former cannot be achieved without a clear understanding of the principles of the latter. This has lead Spragens (1973) to reject the reductionist interpretation of Watkins, and to give a different model in terms of heuristic analogy of the relation of politics to natural philosophy in Hobbes's work. We quote at length from Spragens's argument, because an analysis of it will raise many interesting points which will lead us to a clear statement of Hobbes's position. Spragens argues as follows:

> Even where one theoretical model cannot properly produce a theoretical model appropriate to another realm of reality by a process of logical deduction, it may have a profound influence on the other area of theory by means of analogy. Theory developed to explain one area of reality — the motion of physical bodies, for example — may have a persuasive structuring impact upon a second theoretical model directed toward understanding of another area of reality — the emotions of human beings, for example. The formulations of one theory do not govern the other theory in a direct, deductive way; they have their impact by analogically shaping perceptual patterns used to relate and tie together the raw data of the area in question. Models and metaphors which were developed to conceptualize one set of data, especially if they are seen as properly relevant to another set of data, may serve to establish the conceptual patterns which are used to understand the other set of data... While it is true that Hobbes's natural

philosophy cannot provide the content of his political theory, then, it serves as a source of heuristic models which shape and limit his political theory analogically. (Spragens 1973, 166.)

Earlier Spragens had rejected Watkins's reductive model on the grounds that a proposition with political content cannot be deduced logically from a philosophical theory without such content. In the passage quoted, he argues that theories which cannot be related deductively may still be significantly related by analogy, basing his discussion on a set of (what he calls) Kuhnian insights.

Spragens's claim seems to be essentially psychological: One has a theory applicable, say, to natural philosophy. The mind is then disposed to look for theories with the same structure that apply to other levels, such as, the political. Accordingly, the new theory is 'analogically shaped' (Spragens 1973, 166), or 'shaped and tailored' (p. 176) by the old theory, or the mind is 'conditioned by' (p. 169), 'suggested to' (p. 170), or 'formatively influenced by' (p. 171) the structure of the old theory. For example, in natural philosophy we may have a conception of a body as an entity that undergoes interactions as an organised whole. In this sense our theory explaining natural phenomena uses such an entity as a fundamental unit, e.g., a corpuscle. Spragens's claim is that if we hold such a theory of natural philosophy, and attempt to work out a political theory, we would do so first by trying to see if we can individuate an analogous body in the realm of political phenomena. This analogous body then may be used to analyse political events. In our hypothetical natural philosophy, events would be explained in terms of motion of bodies, defined in terms of change of the relative positions between themselves. Analogously, in the political realm, we would try to invididuate bodies such that we can explain political phenomena in terms of the motion of these bodies, motion being defined in terms of the change of relative political positions. It may also be the case that other concepts receive different, though analogous, definitions. For example, position may be no longer defined spatially, but, we might talk of political power. The claim so far is at least relatively clear: We have a theory of natural philosophy whose structural characteristics may be abstracted and applied to other phenomena as potential organisers of new phenomena, and that the mind of a theoretician actually acts in this way.

Though relatively clear, Spragens's proposal is still quite vague and loose. In addition, it fails to do justice to the historical Hobbes. The first problem becomes apparent if one considers his notion of what it is for a theory to "fit" the phenomena. Spragens claims that in order for a theory, which has been developed by projection or abstraction from another, to be able to organise and explain a new realm of phenomena, there must be some perceived compatibility between the theory and the phenomena.

23

Spragens seems to be talking about the logical or psychological character of theory construction. What he fails to notice is that in order to establish that there exists a "resonance" between two *prima facie* different domains of phenomena he assumes that there already extant, usable criteria for the adequacy of explanation. He assumes we know when a given analogy yields a satisfactory theory and when it does not:

> In order for perceptual models of natural philosophy to become influential in shaping perceptions of political order, it is necessary for them to achieve what might be called *resonance* with some patterns found in the realm of politics. That is, the theorist must perceive, or believe he perceives, political realities which are relatively isomorphic with the model which has developed from a consideration of natural realities. (Spragens 1973, 169.)

For example, if we grant that, at the level of natural philosophy, a corpuscular theory is adequate, then Sprangens's claim is as follows. We abstract the structural characteristics of the corpuscular theory and try to apply these to, say, political phenomena. We may find that the theory provides "good" explanations of these political phenomena if we assume that the basic "body" of political phenomena is the sovereign. Alternatively we may find that the best explanations are produced if we take the basic political body to be nation-states, rather than humans, or families, or political parties, or whatever. In each case, though, if we think that "good" explanations have been given of the new phenomena by the structure abstracted from the theory of natural philosophy, then, says Spragens, we think that there is a "resonance" between the realms, that the realms are relatively isomorphic. Manifestly, Spragens has given us only a very vague notion of what it is for a theory of "fit" the phenomena. Couched in vague language about "resonance", etc., the criterion is also very simple: for a theory to "fit" phenomena it must provide adequate explanations. Spragens, however, gives no machinery for evaluating the utility or value of explanations, other than psychological satisfaction with the theory.

This leads to the biggest problem of Spragens's proposal. Having claimed that theories can be applied to different sets of phenomena if they are resonant with each other, he goes on to argue that we can identify isomorphic theories of natural philosophy and politics in Hobbes's work. He then claims that this isomorphism is itself evidence that Hobbes is psychologically induced to look for a political theory isomorphic to his natural philosophy:

> In the case of Hobbes, as I shall argue, the determinative models in his interpretation of nature do have resonance in some fundamental components of politics — especially in the area of human passion and motivation. In human vanity, egocentricity, appetitiveness, desire for power, and self-preservation Hobbes found aspects of human behaviour which lent themselves readily in his view to conceptualization by the same basic models that had proved so fruitful in the understanding of natural phenomena. (Spragens 1973, 169.)

Thus there were certain things about the phenomena (the actual ways that humans acted) which allowed Hobbes, according to Spragens, to create an isomorphic theory to his theory of natural philosophy. In outline then, Spragens is going to try to show that there is a certain structural similarity between Hobbes's natural and political philosophies. He claims that this similarity can be explained in terms of a psychological hypothesis.

Although Spragens identifies his position as Kuhnian, in acknowledging only psychological influences in his model, he deals with only a part of the Kuhnian mode. By relying on analogy as an undefined psychological factor, Spragens avoids some of the traditional criticisms of "orthodox" Kuhnianism, but end up relying too heavily on untested and unexplicated assumptions concerning the nature of psychological influence. The problems relating to the construction of a satisfactory theory of psychological influence are legion, and Spragens makes no attempt to deal with any of them in a general way. He does, however, try to deal with two instances of this problem, in his discussion of Hobbes on the law of inertia and on the nature of motion.

Spragens says that it is not possible to demonstrate beyond doubt that Hobbes's political thought is influenced by his natural philosophy. He does, however, try to argue for the influence claim by highlighting some of the 'very striking parallels' that are present between the conceptual forms fundamental to Hobbes's natural philosophy and the conceptual forms operative in his depiction of the political order. He takes Hobbes's theory of motion as developed in his natural philosophy and shows that the analogous concept of motion can be applied in political philosophy, even though the content of the theory is completely different. Hobbes defines "motion" as 'the privation of one place, and the acquisition of another' (De Corpore, 70). Natural bodies move according to the law of inertia:

> What so ever is at rest, will always be at rest, unless there be some other body besides it, which, by endeavouring to get into its place by motion, suffers it no longer to remain at rest... In like manner, whatsoever is moved, will always be moved, except there be some other body besides it, which causes it to rest. (De Corpore, 115.)

This relentless motion of natural bodies, viewed by Hobbes as subvisible particles, causes all change: 'all mutation consists in motion' (De Corpore, 70).

In natural philosophy, Hobbes sees observed phenomena as the result of motions caused by the interaction of bodies in inertial motion. Spragens claims that this model of interaction can be seen to be involved in Hobbes's political philosophy as well:

> The analogical carry-over into the interpretation of human, political phenomena of the new motion model leads Hobbes to a profoundly significant assumption from which his political theory must begin: men, too move inertially. Not physical motions alone, but human emotions as well

25

move endlessly, restlessly. Human motives are not specific finite desires which may be terminated by their fulfillment. Human life is not the quest of definite ends whose attainment brings the quest to a satisfied conclusion. Instead, as motivationally inertial creatures, like all the world, men move endlessly and insatiably. Therefore Hobbes postulates "for a general inclination of all mankind, a perpetual and restless desire of Power after power, that ceaseth only in death". His fundamental psychological model, that is, is a human equivalent of the law of inertia. (Spragens 1973, 177.)

In natural philosophy, physical bodies move inertially in that they maintain their state of motion unless hindered by another physical body, so too in moral philosophy, human bodies move (pursue) inertially in that they maintain their state of motion (pursuit). The perpetual desire of power after power is an example of the inertial movement of man.

Furthermore, Spragens argues, one can give a similar explanation of why men seek to preserve their own life:

> All nature fundamentally desires its self-preservation; it wishes, inertially, to preserve in its established path. Man, as a natural creature, is no different. He is possessed by an overriding natural tendency to seek his self-preservation. (Spragens 1973, 175.)

Again, self-preservation is an expression of the humanised law of inertia. Exactly parallel to the explanation given for corpuscular bodies, human beings strive to preserve their own existence. Thus, Spragens concludes, the conceptualisation of the desire for self-preservation of humans is isomorphic with the conceptual pattern of inertia for physical bodies.

It may be granted that Spragens has shown that some isomorphic patterns are found in Hobbes's natural and political philosophies. However, this fact does not support the claim that 'the fundamental paradigm of inertia as the pattern of "natural action" has a profound shaping influence upon the basic motivational psychology from which Hobbes begins his consideration of the nature and tasks of political order'. In order to justify this claim it is not sufficient to demonstrate the isomorphism: that the end products (the patterns) are as they are does not show that the method which produced them is of a particular kind.

A great deal of additional historical work would have to be done before one would be in a position to claim that psychological influence of analogical reasoning is the cause of the observed patterns. For example, it would have to be established that the theory of natural philosophy was temporally prior than the theory of politics, that there was some conscious formative influence, etc. This is an almost impossible historical task. More directly, in the face of no explicit pronouncements by Hobbes of psychological and generative influences, it would be very precarious to claim that the influence was conscious. Spragens would be reduced to arguing for some form of unconscious influence. This claim would be quite unenlightening and fail to take into account Hobbes's written statements concerning the connection of natural and political philosophy.

The "formative influence" theory fails to explain the claim which Hobbes occasionally makes, that a knowledge of the principles of natural philosophy is necessary even for political philosophy. If the connection between the two theories is purely psychological, then the political theory actually could be understood completely without any reference to natural philosophy. For on Spragens's theory once the analogous theory is generated, its adequacy and intelligibility lie strictly within its own domain. His is a theory of heuristics of psychological influence, not the logical conditions for understanding phenomena. A knowledge of natural philosophy would possibly facilitate the learning of political philosophy, but this does not make it necessary.

Spragens does attempt to show how this model of psychological influence works in the particular case of the concept of motion:

> The extension of this model of behaviour from the realm of natural philosophy to the realm of political philosophy was not merely a possible theoretical assumption which Hobbes happened to make. He was instead positively lead to take this step by the framework of the Aristotelian cosmology which he tacitly accepted... (and which) depicted all natural motion as manifesting the same basic pattern of the actualization of potentiality... therefore, it was a natural assumption for Hobbes to make that the transformed conception of motion possessed universal applicability... (and so) it was easy for him to presume that human behaviour should be perceived and interpreted in fundamentally the same manner as the behaviour of other constituents of nature. (Spragens 1973, 167-8.)

The claim is that Hobbes is influenced by Aristotelianism to the extent that he is conditioned to think that all objects in the universe move in the same manner. It is, therefore, "a natural assumption" for Hobbes to make, that his laws of motion as developed in natural philosophy, have applications in other realms of phenomena. Thus, Spragens claims, the fact that Hobbes applies his definition of motion to human beings is explained by a vague reference to his Aristotelian background. This explanation is not very helpful either. Spragens admits that Hobbes readily rejects a large portion of Aristotelianism, so we need to explain why Hobbes rejects certain portions and not others, and how the doctrines he selectively accepted all fit together. In particular, to support Spragens's claim one would have to show that Hobbes tacitly subscribes to a certain portion of this putatively Aristotelian methodology (of the universal applicability of the concept of motion) though in fact Aristotle had no conception of this universal applicability that even remotely resembles Hobbes's.

This specific claim of Spragens's argument is no less problematic than the general claims we saw earlier; it does not begin to cogently establish psychological influence (or even explain what this influence would amount to). It only indicates an area where this might have taken place. In addition, it raises

27

a methodological problem of *ad hocness*; the claim that Hobbes accepts the universal applicability of the concept of motion because Aristotle did, explains no other fact whatsoever. It, thus, stands isolated and cannot be either verified nor falsified by reference to other parts of Hobbes's work. At best such a claim could be loosely used in a general discussion of Hobbes's indebtedness to Aristotle.

Spragens makes the situation worse, however, by claiming that Hobbes is able to make this judgement of the universal applicability of the concept of motion because his main attack on Aristotelianism was directed against its concept of substance. This, he suggests, necessitated only a "drastic metamorphosis" of the Aristotelian cosmology, not its "outright abandonment" (Spragens 1973, 168). Hobbes's attack on the Aristotelian concept of substance is, according to Spragens, spearheaded by his philosophical nominalism (pp. 86-7). Unfortunately, Spragens does not enlarge upon this theme, and it is hard to tell exactly what his views are on the connection of nominalism and universal applicability. Contrary to Spragens's apparent position, we will try to argue that it is this very nominalistic theory that accounts for the applicability of concepts like motion to the various realms of organisation in Hobbes's philosophy. Further, this nominalism is responsible for (what Spragens calls) the isomorphism between the natural and political levels.

V

We have claimed that the only way to achieve a viable understanding of Hobbes's philosophy is to look at the structure of his system as a whole. The unsatisfactory traditional interpretations arise out of an insistence that the relation of the different levels of Hobbes's system can be understood in terms of the levels themselves, without regard to Hobbes's theories of causes, language and so forth. Our proposal is to show that only if we take into account Hobbes's theory of philosophy and language, especially his version of nominalism, do we get an adequate account of what Hobbes is trying to do.

Hobbes's theory of language arises from the logical tradition present at Oxford during his training (Walton, mss). This Ramist logical tradition incorporated much of the nominalism of earlier periods (Jardine 1974). It is this nominalistic theory of meaning that provides Hobbes with the bridge between the levels of his philosophy. It functions to unify his system into a reasonably coherent causal structure.

Our argument will be structured as follows. We give a summary of Hobbes's nominalism, showing how it is, in Hobbes's view, that terms acquire their meaning. Most important of all are the universal terms, like "body", "law", "motion'', etc., which are used *with the same meaning* throughout Hobbes's system. The doctrine will be illustrated by use of the examples of ''motion'', ''obligation'' (''ought''), and ''endeavor'' (''*conatus*''), showing how the words are used in natural, moral and political contexts. The way these terms are used creates the ''resonance'' between the levels and structural patterns that Spragens notices. Finally, this theory of meaning will be seen to justify Hobbes's claim that knowledge of the principles of natural philosophy must be fully understood before the principles of civil or political philosophy can be understood, and *vice versa*. We start, then with an exposition of Hobbes's theory of meaning.

For Hobbes, the name is the fundamental linguistic unit. Names are assigned arbitrarily to ideas or conceptions of objects, subject only to the constraints of internal coherence of the language (De Corpore, 16-28). Hobbes takes names to refer primarily to the utterer's conceptions or ideas. As these conceptions are caused, normally, by objects, the names derivatively can be said to be applicable to objects in the world. Though there are complex issues raised by such a theory, in what follows we shall ignore such complexities and proceed, as Hobbes himself does, to speak of names referring to objects (thus, leaving out the always intervening mind).

Propositions are formed when names are joined together with words like ''is'', etc., (copulatives). To these constructions truth values apply. A proposition is true when the entities picked out by the subject of the proposition (a name) are the very same entities, or are included in the set of entities, picked out by the object of the proposition (another name). Truth and falsity belongs to speech,not to things (De Corpore, 36).

For Hobbes the purpose of forming propositions by conjoining names by copulatives is to 'make us think of the cause for which those names were imposed on that thing' (De Corpore, 31). Thus to 'seek what it is *to be* anything, as *to be moveable, to be hot,* etc., (is to) seek in things the causes of their names' (p. 31). For example, if we see an object and call it ''moved'', 'the cause of the name is that it *is moved,* or the *motion* of the same' (p. 32). The causes of names, though, 'are the same with the causes of our conceptions, namely, some power of action, or affection of the thing conceived, which some call the manner by which any thing works upon our senses, but by most men are called accidents' (p. 32).

Hobbes defines the concept of accident as those parts of an object which constitute its nature:

> Now, by parts, I do not mean here parts of the thing itself, but parts of its nature; as, by parts of man, I do not understand his head, his shoulders, his arms, etc., but his figure, quantity, motion, sense, reason, and the like; which accidents being compounded or put together constitute the whole nature of man, but not the man himself. (De Corpore, 67.)

29

He then argues that the general cause of anything is motion. Given any object or event, once its parts and their causes have been analysed, Hobbes can utilise the machinery of composition or synthesis in order to gain knowledge about the event or object. Specifically, composition or synthesis can begin by examining causal relations in an aggregate of the several bodies party to an interaction.

In the light of their general discussion, Hobbes discusses how we can acquire knowledge of the principles of civil and moral philosophy:

> *Civil and moral philosophy* do not so adhere to one another, but that they may be severed. For the causes of the motions of the mind are known, not only by ratiocination, but also by the experience of every man that takes the pains to observe those motions within himself. And, therefore, not only they that have attained knowledge of the passions and perturbations of the mind, by the *synthetical method,* and from the very first principles of philosophy, may by proceeding the same way, come to the causes and necessity of constituting of commonwealths and get the knowledge of what is natural right, and what are civil duties; and, in every kind of government, what are the rights of the commonwealth, and all other knowledge appertaining to civil philosophy; for this reason that the principles of the politics consist in the knowledge of the motions of the mind, and the knowledge of these motions from the knowledge of sense and imagination; but even they also that have not learned the first part of philosophy, namely *geometry* and *physics*, may, notwithstanding, attain the principles of civil philosophy by the analytical method. (De Corpore, 73.)

He is claiming here that there are two ways by which we can have knowledge of the principles of civil philosophy; by the synthetic method, which proceeds from the first principles of natural philosophy and then from moral philosophy, or by the analytic method, which proceeds by intuitively grasping the motions of the mind, and then using them as principles for civil philosophy. It is this synthetic method which has been the subject of the controversy concerning reduction to which we have addressed ourselves in this paper. The analytic method, however, is generally glossed over, but is extremely important for the reduction issue.

Hobbes is claiming that we can have knowledge of the principles of moral philosophy by introspection, and this introspection is the process of *observing the motions of the mind*. If one held a strict reductionist position with respect to motion, these motions of the mind would be taken to be literally motions of objects in the mind. Hobbes would be then claiming that, with sufficient introspection, one could become aware of tiny corporeal objects changing their spatial positions in the brain. (This, of course, assumes his materialism.) This is, in itself, ridiculous. It is also clearly not what Hobbes meant, since he claimed that a knowledge of the motions of the mind would enable someone to determine the principles of civil philosophy even if he did not know any physics or geometry. The motions of the mind which Hobbes is discussing are not to be conceived as the motions of invisible corporeal objects, but rather as "parts of its nature", i.e., not physical parts but the natural parts he spoke of when defining "accident". The reductionist problems arise from treating all motion as a physical determination of physical objects, for then talk of motions of the parts of the mind has to be regarded as analogical or metaphorical. This is, however, to misunderstand Hobbes's conception of motion and in general his conception of the function of names in language.

Hobbes talks of many different kinds of bodies, for example, inanimate, animal and political or artificial (Leviathan, Ch. 9). In order that he can justify calling each of these differing aggregates with their different qualities by the same name "body" (so that he can then analyse them in terms of the causes and principles governing bodies), Hobbes supplies a theory of meaning for universal terms like "body", "motion", *"conatus"*, etc. According to Hobbes, there are no universal ideas or objects:

> ... this word *universal* is never the name of anything existent in nature, nor of any idea or phantasm formed in the mind, but always the name of a word or name; so that when a living *creature, a stone, a spirit*, or any other thing, is said to be *universal*, it is not to be universal, but that only these words, *living creature, stone* etc., are *universal names*, that is names common to many things; and the conceptions answering them in our mind, are the images and phantasms of several living creatures, or other things. And therefore, for the understanding of the extent of a universal name, we need no further faculty but that of our imagination, by which we remember that such names bring sometimes one thing, sometimes another, into our mind. (De Corpore, 20.)

Hobbes claims that a universal term gains its meaning from the various particular objects it supposits, from the particular conceptions it signifies or objects it names. Thus, for example, a body, whether natural or artificial, is that which is independent of our thought and extended in space (De Corpore, 102).[2] Given this definition it becomes proper to speak in physics of corporeal bodies moving or endeavoring to move of human beings moving or so endeavoring, or of the Sovereign or Commonwealth undergoing motion or endeavoring to do so. In this latter case the Commonwealth, in the person of the Sovereign, by the actions of consent and authorisation, becomes an artificial body capable of motion, e.g., of suppressing or endeavoring to suppress rebellion. The meaning of the term "body" employed in any particular realm (e.g., politics) is determined not only by that realm itself, but also by the other realms in which it applies (e.g., natural philosophy).

The effects of this nominalism are readily seen in the case of the concept of motion. "Motion" is a universal term and therefore as our knowledge of it 'we have in the first place (its) definition' (De Corpore, 70). Thus, though its application in different realms we come to know about motion. For example, in the case

31

of natural philosophy, motion is the endeavor or motion of corporeal objects, defined as the continual relinquishing and acquiring of places of the objects. In moral philosophy, the motions are the endeavors or motions motions of the mind, namely 'appetite, aversion, love, benevolence, hope, fear, anger, emulation, envy, etc.' (De Corpore, 71). The fundamental law of motion, for example, refers both to the fact that corporeal objects continue to endeavor to change their places unless hindered, and to the fact that human beings continue to have appetites and aversions (both endeavors), and, unless hindered, will change their place in order to accomplish the goals of those motions.

In political philosophy, motion refers primarily to the actions of the Sovereign. (Remember that all action is motion of some form or another.) Specifically, the Sovereign will move to establish laws by which peace will be preserved unless hindered (Leviathan, Ch. 19, sects. 7, 8, 9). In doing so, the Sovereign is moving inertially, compelled by the necessity of his office. *Qua* Sovereign, e.g., he can no more fail to make rules, than he can forfeit his own power (Ch. 18, sect 2). The form that the inertial motion of the Sovereign must take is mandated by the circumstances of creation of this artificial body that is personified in the office of the Sovereign.

A more complex case than motion is that of the significance of "obligation". Much of the controversy over whether Hobbes can derive an obligation from an empirical theory, an "ought" sentence from an "is" sentence, centers about the ambiguity of the word "ought" in traditional analyses. Spragens, for example, claims that Hobbes can be saved from the accusation that he committed the logical *faux pas* of deriving a categorical imperative from naturalistic premises, by distinguishing carefully the different senses of obligation involved (Spragens 1973, 115). What Spragens and other critics fail to realise is that the very same concept of law (and nature) is being used in all cases, but its application in different realms of phenomena makes it appear that the word "law" is used with different meanings. In actual fact, the term "law" is being applied with the same meaning to the physical, moral, and political levels. It does different work at each level, just as in the case of the concept of motion. Spragens is willing to claim that there is only one real concept of motion, which has universal applicability, but will not go so far as to say that there is only one real concept of law. Spragens draws this distinction between the uses of the concepts of motion and law because he justifies the universal applicability of the concept of motion on grounds of psychological influence, and it is not clear that a parallel justification could be made for the universal applicability of the concept of law. Once, however, one sees how concepts and their corresponding names function for Hobbes, the two cases are perfectly parallel and the grounds for distinguishing between them vanish.

The laws of motion in physics, the laws of nature that drive human beings, and the "laws" that determine and specify the actions of the Sovereign are all laws in the same sense. In each case it is part of the nature of that kind of body to move and act in certain ways. In the political case, this nature has been created by covenant. This is why the Commonwealth is an artificial body. The obligations that attach to each sort of body are to be explicated by explaining the laws that each kind of body must follow. In all cases, the obligation stems from natural necessity (or the necessity of that *kind* of body's nature).

Confusion arises concerning the nature of obligation in Hobbes from focusing discussions of the problem of obligation upon the obligation of the subjects to obey the laws made by the Sovereign. This is not the proper focus. The obligation of subjects derives from the covenant that creates the Sovereign and authorises his actions or motions as their own. They are obliged to act in certain ways as constituent parts of the Commonwealth, just as corpuscles that are constituent parts of a natural body are obliged to move in patterns that preserve the unity of that natural body.

Finally, it is clear that the universal name "endeavor" ("*conatus*") is of prime importance for Hobbes. This concept of endeavor is used to specify the causal power of an agent or acting body at an instant. It is always specified by reference to a future state that the agent will achieve or actualise by virtue of its nature. At the physical level, the endeavor of bodies is an explanatory concept that explains (or describes, if you will) the future actions of the body in terms of its immediate past history. In the realm of human actions, endeavors are the beginnings of motions of the mind toward an object or goal that is set by the causal force of its past history (habit) or by its natural constitution (vital motions). In political philosophy, the endeavors of the Sovereign are those rights he is created with in accord with the covenant. The endeavor specifies the Sovereign's causal powers as authorised by the constitutive act that created the Sovereign's nature, i.e., created the Sovereign.

At all levels, *conatus* is that which describes the power of the basic unit of that level (the "body") to change its state in certain specifiable law-like ways or along certain directions, whether the state is physical, moral, or political motion. Again, as in the cases of "motion" and "obligation", "*conatus*" denotes the very same thing (in this case, a causal function) at every level of Hobbes's philosophy. At each level, or for each kind of body, it refers to the powers appropriate to that body as a cause of its own motion and of motion in other bodies. Though it is an idealised, universal concept, its very universality (universal applicability) provides Hobbes with a naturalistic theory of motions that is applicable to all things. Any attempt, therefore, to analyse Hobbes's philosophy that fails to take into account *conatus* distorts the causal picture of philosophy that Hobbes takes to be essential in every domain of thought. The concept is central in Hobbes's unified philosophy.

We are now in a position to understand the relation of Hobbes's theories of political and natural philosophy. Though there is no reduction of the one level to the other, the two levels are connected by a theory of meaning which entails that the universal terms used in both levels depend on each other for their meaning. The meaning of a term is given by its use in the whole system. The system itself has a "structure" that can be, and is, specified by causal connections, natures, and powers that are codified in the definitions of the terms used to describe these systems.

Hobbes's claim, quoted at the beginning of the paper, that an understanding of civil or political philosophy cannot be achieved without a prior understanding of natural philosophy, is to be taken literally. To understand the principles of political philosophy requires knowing the meanings of the terms employed in those principles since they refer to the specific causes of political phenomena, but the meanings of the terms employed are determined not only by the realm of political entities and phenomena, but also by the realm of physical bodies. Consequently, without a knowledge of natural philosophy and its causes, it is impossible to acquire a complete knowledge of the principles and causes of political philosophy. The converse also applies, that without a knowledge of political philosophy, it is impossible to have a complete knowledge of the causes and principles of natural philosophy. Without both, it is impossible to have a causally coherent theory of the world including mankind and its institutions. To develop such a theory is, for Hobbes, the proper business of philosophy and is what he attempts to do.

Notes

1. References are made to the following works and editions: *De Corpore*, in The English Works of Thomas Hobbes (EW),Vol.1, ed. by W. Molesworth, John Bohn, London 1839; *Decameron Physiologicum*, in EW, Vol. 7; *Elements of Law*, in EW, Vol. 6; *De Homine*, in *Opera Latina*, Vol. 2, ed. by W. Molesworth, John Bohn, London 1839; *Leviathan*, in EW, Vol. 3.

2. Also: 'anything that hath a being, without the help of sense.' (Decameron..., 81).

Hobbes and the Concept of World Government

Isabel C. Hungerland

I

Hobbes's supposition of the state of nature (in his application of it to nations) obviously leads to the conclusion that a strong and effective government is needed for our survival. My main thesis is that the Hobbesian argument, properly understood, is convincing, especially today when nuclear weapons abound. As an introduction to the proper understanding of the argument, I make, in brief form, the following points which on other occasions, I have developed in detail. The state of nature supposition may be viewed as a game theory model, but it is *not* as often supposed a ''prisoners' dilemma'' model, one in which a cooperative solution is ruled out. To understand the supposition, one must examine Hobbes's notion of geometrical analytics (as set forth in the *De Corpore*) along with the analogy he draws between geometry and political science. It then becomes evident that the supposition is a model in the sense of an *interpretation* of a theory, and hence constructed so as to be analytically true of it. It follows that one must distinguish between the analytically true interpretation of a theory and the application of a theory (so interpreted) to the real world. Such applications involve probable hypotheses, e.g., in the analogous application of geometrical theory, interpreted for lines without breadth, etc., to the problems of engineering.

I devote the main body of the paper (sections IV, V, VI, VII) to such problems which I have hitherto mentioned but not explored. These problems, if they are to be solved in a Hobbesian spirit, require us to regard man in the context of other animals, and turn to the various biological studies of the evolution and genetic predispositions of homo sapiens. Recent developments in sociobiology and in neuroscience provide new evidence that the Hobbesian picture of homo sapiens was on the right track. In developing these points, I argue that unrealistic sentimental approaches to the question of what humans are like (approaches that I think have long dominated philosophical moral theory) only compound the dangers that threaten us today.

II

It has become fashionable to consider Hobbes's supposition of the state of nature as a so-called game theory model of the prisoner's dilemma sort. Such models deal in general with strategies which ideally rational persons would adopt in certain sorts of social situations, i.e., more than one player is involved.[1]

The situations are "models" in that they are depicted so as to illustrate certain consequences of the theory — rationality is idealised and a multitude of possible real life details are omitted. The following is the well-known prisoner's dilemma situation. Two prisoners are isolated from one another — no communication is possible. Both know that if one confesses and the other doesn't, the non-confessor will be let off, and the confessor will get 10 years. If both confess, each gets one year. If neither confesses each gets five years. The matrix below represents the imagined situation with the pay-offs for strategies 1 (confess) and 2 (don't confess) for players A and B. Strategy 1 is termed the cooperative strategy and Strategy 2 the non-cooperative one.

		B	
		1	2
A	1	(1,1)	(10,0)
	2	(0,10)	(5,5)

This model has been attributed to Hobbes's state of nature and the conclusion drawn that once in that state humans can't get out by cooperating.

The following features of the state of nature model should make it plain that it is not a prisoner's dilemma one — i.e., a condition in which the cooperative strategy cannot be used:

1. The players are able to communicate and hence to bargain with one another. (Hobbes supposes that realising what the state of nature is like, they get together to form the ideal commonwealth.) Moreover, not only are they aware of the laws of nature as the rational strategies for all members of homo sapiens, but as rational, they observe the laws always, *in foro interno*. And Warrender has shown convincingly, I believe, that this observance amounts to much more than a silent wishing. It requires friendly gestures and cooperative overtures and proposals, so long, of course, as the individual is not endangered by

36

these.

2. The human players are ideally rational in the following ways. (a) They can calculate the consequences of war and see immediately that peace is far better for them. (b) They can figure out means to the desired end. (c) In willing an end, they also will the means to it.

3. Each player has the ability in "reading" his own nature, to 'thereby read and know, what are the thoughts and passions of all other men, upon the like occasions.'[2] (In brief, they have "mutual knowledge" of one another, i.e., each know that p and that the other know that each knows that p.) Being able to do this produces the realisation that mutual distrust and a state of war will prevail, *unless* a commonwealth is established. So, they proceed to do so. (There are no suckers, so cheaters have no chance to succeed.)

To ask of the model questions like the following is analogous to confusing engineering problems with geometric ones: 'How long did it take them to realise that cooperation was the best policy?' 'How, before enforceable regulations were instituted, could they decide to cooperate?' The transition from state of nature to social organisation is properly taken as instantaneous. The point made in the model is that ideally normal, rational persons, were all social authority removed from their world, instantly realise the consequences and, bargaining reasonably, institute the required means to restore it. (Here again, to ask how long the bargaining would take, is irrelevant.) The bargaining, of course, requires some giving up on the part of each so that everyone alike may benefit.

If now we look back at the matrix of the prisoner's dilemma model, the differences between it an Hobbes's supposition are striking. The A_1B_1, cooperative strategy for each, has as consequence, a life worth living for both. The A_2B_2, a non-cooperative strategy, has as consequence, a life not worth living for either. Moreover, the A_1B_2 and A_2B_1 combinations do not represent viable alternatives. Since the players are evenly matched in relevant respects and none are suckers, any attempt on the part of either to deceive or default would put both back into the intolerable state of nature. Hobbes, in effect has so set up his supposition as to make the choice basically one between life and death, thus "demonstrating" what today is describable as the connection between inclusive fitness and sociality. As Lorenz has pointed out homo sapiens is one of the very few species that has not in the course of evolution acquired a prohibition against the killing of conspecifics. So, what Hobbes's model suggests is that humans' big brains might do for them what evolution has not been long enough to accomplish for the species.

So much for the currently fashionable interpretation of Hobbes's supposition of the state of nature as a prisoners' dilemma model. To fully correct this mistake we must look at the general concept of a model closely. Both Ernest

Nagel and Karl Popper in their impressive works in the methodology of the sciences, have carefully defined and illustrated the role of a model in the sense of an *interpretation* of a theory, one that is so constructed as to be *analytically true* of it (Nagel 1961, 90-3 and 95-7; Popper 1959, 73). To be properly understood, Hobbes's supposition must be seen as a model in this sense, and his well known analogy between geometry and political philosophy throws light on this point. It was not of course till modern times that geometric systems were conceived and treated as abstract axiomatic systems with spatial models functioning as interpretations of them. Hobbes, of course, had no explicit concept (no terminology for) the distinction in question. But we can see that his abstracted and idealised motions, productive of abstracted and idealised entities, like lines, points, planes, constitute an interpretation in the sense in question of Euclidean geometry. The "exposition to sense" of shapes drawn by compass and ruler (like circle or triangle and explicitly defined by means of the primitive terms) are not applications via coordinating definitions of geometry to the perceptual world. Such drawn shapes represent the idealised objects only in so far as they have the requisite Euclidean properties. Any divergence and of course there are some, are not at issue — they are disregarded. But in an *application* of Euclidean geometry in physics or in engineering, the matter is different. Suppose we decide to link, by a coordinating definition, the Euclidean concept of straight line with the path of rays of light. Here various physical hypotheses must be considered concerning the nature of light, and how it travels in different media as well as hypotheses about the physical material and surrounding conditions of measuring instruments. Such hypotheses, as Hobbes was well aware, are matters of probable reasoning, not of demonstration. In engineering, for example, in casting metal into Euclidean shapes, the distinction between an interpretation as analytically true and an application is even more obvious. Depending upon the practical requirements of the engineering job, we accept a higher or lower degree of approximation to Euclidean properties.

III

As an introduction to my attempt to deal with the problems involved in applying Hobbes's model to the real world, it will be useful to give a summary account of the role of the supposition in Hobbes's derivation of his moral principles, the laws of nature. The supposition is, of course, a contrary-to-fact conditional. Once Hobbes has established it on the basis of various definitions and principles of his system he adds to it the following "unless" clause: unless men were to establish by contract the civil state, i.e., civil authority. Now this clause contains concepts — those of *contract* and *civil state* — which cannot be defined solely in terms of natural science concepts, or correlated with them as in non-homogeneous reduction. What Hobbes roughly deduces is the *need* of humans for constraints on their natural appetites. He then tries to show that certain legal institutions (defined in non-natural science terms) are the only workable constraints. (In brief, what Hobbes tries to show is that if men didn't have civil society, they would have to invent it in order to survive!) And, in a well known passage in the *Leviathan* he says that nations with their weapons pointing at each other are in a state of war (i.e. a state of nature) thus implying that his argument holds for nations as well as for individuals. In brief, only a world civil government can prevent international wars and a global state of nature.

One more important point before turning to the problems of applying Hobbes's model to the real world. The model, I have shown, is *not* a prisoners' dilemma one because of the mutual knowledge and communication among the "players." As we shall see, it is the absence of such conditions and the lack of striving to fulfil them, along with some basic features of human nature and stand in the way of world peace.

IV

In the Hobbesian model, or supposition, men are, as I have said presented as having a highly idealised rationality, but also described, though in abstract form, as having the tendency to aggressiveness under certain general conditions. It is of importance to note that in giving his account of human nature Hobbes contrasts and compares homo sapiens with other creatures. He seems to have been (with the possible exception of Aristotle) the only philosopher even though he lived before Darwin to look at us as animals not as in the Christian view as creatures midway between the animals and the angels, but leaning a little nearer the latter. (Today philosophical moral theories still seem to operate under the shadow of Church dogma in this respect.)

In order, then, to deal with the problems of applying Hobbes's model to the real world, I propose to show how his account of human nature, given only in abstract outline in the supposition, can be appropriately filled out by material from contemporary sociobiology and neuroscience. When that is done, I shall argue, the need for a world government, after *adequate preparation* for it, can be convincingly shown. The adequate preparation consists in increasing mutual understanding and communication among members of different nations and religions, and this in turn requires the fostering of a variety of international organisations, that include some devoted to raising the level of education and the ending of starvation among the less "advanced" nations.

In examining Hobbes's account of humans before filling it out with material from contemporary science, we should remember that Hobbes said we have "passions" that drive us towards peace as well as "passions" that drive us towards war and in addition, the faculty or reason to show us how to avoid the "nasty" condition of war.

When the *De Corpore* is carefully studied on such matters as vital motion and pleasure, Hobbes's principle of death-aversion (or self-preservation) turns out to be strikingly similar to Cannon's formulation of the principle of constancy for organisms, homeostasis, widely interpreted.

Otto Fenichel, for example, is able to state the so-called constancy principle for organisms — their tendency to maintain homeostasis — in such a way that all behaviour can be subsumed under it. Fenichel, in arguing against Freud's notion of a death instinct, in addition to a life-seeking one, writes, quoting from Cannon's formulation:

> The word... (homeostasis) "does not imply something set and immobile, a stagnation;" on the contrary, the living functions are extremely flexible and mobile, their equilibrium being disturbed uninterruptedly, but being re-established by the organism equally uninterruptedly... It seems more appropriate (than taking the constancy principle as one of Nirvana-seeking) to see the ultimate goal for all these equalization tendencies as the aim of maintaining a certain level of tension characteristic of the organism, of "preserving the level of excitation", as Freud put it very early. (Fenichel 1945, 12; see also pp. 58-81.)

Fenichel is, of course, very much aware of the diversity of human behaviour. His thesis is that this diversity will not be understood scientifically,

> ... if an attempt is made to differentiate a "homeostatic instinct" from other "nonhomeostatic instincts." Homeostasis (interpreted as in the above passage) is, as a principle, at the root of all instinctual behaviour; the frequent "counter-homeostatic" behaviour must be explained as a secondary complication, imposed upon the organism by external forces. (Fenichel 1945, 13.)

In order to avoid the common misunderstanding of Hobbes's death aversion principle I have coined the terms self-All, self-Other, and self-Own to characterise the various interests human display. In selecting from a menu a meal I particularly enjoy, I am displaying self-Own interest; in giving needed medicine to my child, self-Other; in working for rules that are for the good of everyone alike in a community of which I am a member, I display self-All interests. Such interests for Hobbes are the moral one. They are not "unselfish", for they include my own. The moral point of view, then, according to Hobbes is that of a member of community who works for the good of everyone alike, including himself, and does so because, provided others do so likewise, that course is rationally dictated by his Self-Own interests. In brief, according to Hobbes, it is rational to be reasonable, provided others are so likewise.

Fenichel and Cannon, from whom I quoted above, wrote before the recent developments in sociobiology and their accounts of "instinctive" behaviour needs modification and additions. So, in my filling in of the outline of the Hobbesian picture of homo sapiens, I turn to current sociobiology.

A good introduction to the relevant material is provided in a book *The Selfish Gene* by Richard Dawkins, intended for the general educated public as well as for colleagues. Dawkins employs metaphors (later carefully unpacked) and simplifications (noted carefully) in expounding sociobiology. In a vein reminiscent of Hobbes in both style and substance he writes as follows. We are, he tells us, 'survival machines... programmed by our genes', those molecules called 'replicators', that is, molecules that 'make copies of themselves' (Dawkins 1976, 36-7). It should be noted that genetic programming does not and could not entail the determination of every move in every environmental circumstance, but just the operation of dispositions to respond in certain general ways to certain general conditions, such general behavioural "rules" being modifiable by environmental forces including, in the case of humans, the cultural.

Fortunately, sociobiologists by inventing the concept of a *predisposition* have ended the earlier extremely aggressive disputes among scientists about whether aggression and other widespread patterns of behaviour are innate or acquired through culture. The answer, of course is neither exclusively. Edward Wilson has a clear account of this, but since he writes in a way that seems to irritate some philosophers and fellow scientists, I shall, in what follows quote mainly from the zoologist Desmond Morris and the sociobiologist David P. Barash.

Morris selects in his detailed account of what a predisposition is, the interesting example of snake aversion among humans. Morris starts by convincingly refuting the notion that this aversion is explained by the snakes' being a phallic symbol, a "poison penis" as it were. He points out that the peak of snake aversion in children comes long before prudery, that there is little difference between the sexes in the aversion, and that our closest living relatives, the chimpanzees, the gorillas and the orang-utans exhibit a similar aversion. (Presumably, prudery is unknown among these primates!) In young apes, the aversion appears, not at birth, but as they are reaching the stage of making brief sorties away from their mother. 'For them' he writes 'an aversion response clearly has an important survival value and would also have been of great benefit to our early ancestors' (Morris 1967, 192-3). Morris proceeds to criticise effectively various experiments on chimpanzees supposed to support the purely "cultural" explanations. He concludes with the following account of predisposition as inborn responses which do not mature in encapsulated forms irrespective of the outside environment. ... they should be thought of more as 'inborn susceptibilities' (ibid., 193).

Edward O. Wilson, from whom I shall quote only briefly, begins an extraordinarily well documented chapter on aggression with the kind of statement that infuriates the tender minded and certain sorts of Marxists. He asks the skeptical question 'Are human beings innately aggressive?' and replies 'The answer to it is yes' (Wilson 1978, 99). However, Wilson goes on to develop the concept of a predisposition along the lines of the Morris account, and proceeds to point out that humans, though 'markedly predisposed to aggressiveness' are 'far from being the most violent of animals. ... I suspect that if the madryas baboons had nuclear weapons, they would destroy the world in a week'(ibid., 103-4).

To the above accounts of aggressiveness as a predisposition should be added the following points. Aggressive animal behaviour is a broader concept than that of fighting to kill. It includes, in the mating season of many animals, various displays of male prowess that have a high value for the survival of the genes of the displayer. For example, male red deer, equipped with antlers that make battles between evenly matched males dangerous, engage in "battles" of roaring before choosing to attack or flee. The outroared male, unwounded, retreats. Unfortunately, homo sapiens' big brain has led him to invent artificial weapons of greater and greater deadliness, culminating in the nuclear weapons of today. The time of our evolution has not been long enough for us (as I pointed out earlier) to acquire as most species with naturally dangerous weapons have (e.g. the rattlesnake) a prohibition against killing conspecifics. So, while the predisposition to aggression, widely understood, can work in some species for the preservation of the genes of the fit individual and so, derivatively benefit the species, in homo sapiens, unless we use reason to control it, it becomes, as Hobbes saw, the kind of passion that may drive us towards the extinction of our species. In brief, our basic self-preservation predisposition unguided by clear reasoning may drive us to wars under the false impression that we are acting in self-defence. The Vietnam war is a good example of this and the repudiation of the notion by the American people that it was a war of self-defence is a good example of the triumph of reason. Let us not forget though, that before we withdrew, many young lives were lost and that American soldiers massacred women and children.

Before I turn in the next section to the "passions" that drive us towards peace, I want to conjure up for you cruelties to conspecifics of which homo sapiens is capable. Historians write about wars in general terms, embellished by statistics. Only literary persons, I believe, help us to see what human wars are. Edith Sitwell, in the following passages, makes us face what in recent history as far as the human race goes, Protestants and Catholics, both preaching love of fellow men did to one another in the religious struggles in 16th century England:

> The horrors of the Maryan reign in no wise excelled those of King Henry's. The crowds might well have remembered the cry of a Catholic

saint in that earlier reign, as his heart was torn from his living body... In thinking of the frightful cruelties enacted in the Maryan Age, we are apt to forget two things. The first is that (monstrous and unpardonable as is the cruelty) it is no more cruel to burn a living being in the name of a travesty of Almighty God... endowed with our own cruelty... than it is to commit the unspeakable obscenity of disembowelling, emasculating, and tearing the heart from a living being in the name of another travesty. ... This last, Henry sanctioned, Elizabeth sanctioned ... The cruelty on each side was responsible for that in the other. "The villainy you teach me I will execute," said a creation of the greatest man ever born in England "and it shall go hard, but I will better the instruction". (Sitwell 1962, 36-8.)

Walter Scott, Dickens, and Tolstoy have also given us vivid accounts of man's wartime cruelty to man.

I should like to end this account of the "passions" that, unless controlled by reason, drive us towards the killing of conspecifics, with some speculation on my part, suggested by my readings in sociobiology and anthropology. Could we, in our evolutionary history, beginning with our emergence from the forests onto the savannahs of Africa, have acquired along the way a predisposition to antagonism towards creatures that strongly resemble us, but differ in one or several respects? Homo Sapiens coexisted with similar forms of primates, now extinct. Could it have in that past benefited us to acquire such a susceptibility? I find it interesting that the Neo-Nazis in the USA call blacks "monkeys", and that in World War II the Japanese were often so-called. and I have had occasion to note that even children from liberal families, unexposed till they enter school to persons with different colors of skin, etc., tend to show prejudice. On the other hand, children from wealthy families who have servants from various ethnic groups, *provided* that these servants are treated as an extension of the family, show no prejudice. Such examples conform to the notion of a predisposition (Barash 1979, 31 ff.).

V

In this section I shall consider the "passions" that drive us towards peace. Here we should recall that Hobbes listed "solitary" as one aspect of the "nasty" life in the state of nature. The sociobiologist Barash has given a clear and cogent account of how (to employ the technical jargon) "sociality" constributes in many species to "inclusive fitness" and shows how the morality of many religions in their doctrine of the "brotherhood" of man, may be credited with pointing the way today to our survival. (In the section following this I shall consider another aspect of dogmatic religions, illustrated in the preceding quotations from Sitwell, that works in the opposite direction.)

The misleading contrast (selfish-generous or altruistic) is so firmly engrained in our general western Christian outlook that even sociobiologists have been puzzled by the terms. However, being scientists, not philosophers, they have gone ahead (noting that their use of the terms diverges from the common one) to make the very sort of distinctions in animal behaviour that have concerned me in elucidating Hobbes. Since, as I have shown earlier, Hobbes foreshadows certain features of sociobiological theory, the coincidences here are not surprising.

Barash, in discussing the theory about certain forms of what is termed "altruism", succinctly describes it as an expanded view of evolutionary fitness (he is well aware that the sociobiologists' use of the term, "altruism" is at variance with common usage):[3]

> The upshot of kinship theory is an expanded view of fitness, recognizing gene frequency as reflected in all relatives, rather than simply the production of offspring. *Inclusive fitness* is the term used to incorporate the summed consequences of both personal fitness (via offspring) and fitness derived via the representation of genes in relatives. Behavior, whether altruistic of not, will evolve if and only if it is mediated by genes whose effect is to increase the inclusive fitness of the bearer relative to the consequences of inclusive fitness of alternative behavior mediated by alternative genes. It provides a coherent theory for the biology of nepotism among living things.

What I have termed self-other interest (recognised by Hobbes in his account of *benevolence, good, will,* and *charity*), is classified by Barash as a special kind of altruism, namely *reciprocity*:

> A major alternative (to kinship theory in explaining altruistic behavior) is reciprocity, an appealing notion that can select for altruism with no assumptions whatever concerning genetic relatedness... The basic requirement for altruism to evolve via reciprocity is that... the return to the altruist must be greater than the decrement in inclusive fitness imposed by the original altruistic act. (Barash 1979, 94.)

Barash goes on to list various conditions which would have to be met in order for reciprocal altruism to be a viable system, and after considering them concludes: '... reciprocity is most likely to evolve among intelligent, closely integrated social species in which the opportunities for reciprocity and individual recognition would be greatest' (Barash 1979, 95.)

Here, there is an obvious application — with suitable modifications — to homo sapiens. The extremely wealthy who establish universities, foundations, art galleries, and so on, do so without impoverishing themselves, and gain what (as Freud and others have shown us) is of enormous importance to humans, social approval which bolsters self-esteem. (Also, if the university or art gallery is named in memory of a close kin, one sees the reinforcement provided.)

In saying this, I wish in no way to suggest that the benevolent person has no

44

identification with and hence sympathy for the recipients of his generosity. Hobbes's account of the passions, and present-day sociobiological explanations of "altruism" are *not* "nothing but" forms of reductionism. They represent possible scientific explanations which establish certain connections between our large-scale social behaviour and certain genetically determined pre-dispositions modified by our environment, including, of course, the cultural one.

In the previous section, we saw that we need to restrain our aggression when it takes the form of killing conspecifics. In this section we have seen that reason is needed to extend our limited sociality from the national community to the international, that is, to complete the slow progress from tribal communities to the community of conspecifics. As Barash writes at the end of his book; after discussing the "discrepancy between our biology and our culture": 'we are riding a fearsome tiger on a one way trip. Maybe we can slow it down a bit, at least so we don't fall off and get eaten, and perhaps someday we might even succeed in mastering the beast after all' (Barash 1979, 324).

It will be fitting to close this section with the following summation of Hobbes's moral theory as I see it. For a person A to see him or herself as one member among others of a community X is essential to morality *provided* that, if X is less inclusive than the human species, A does not see other humans just as *non-members* of X — the basic species membership must be always there for us, in the background if we are to act morally.

VI

In this section, I propose to consider the harm done by unrealistic views of human nature — such views exhibited not only in most religious but also in most philosophic moral theories. The text for my argument is supplied in the following quotation from Watkins,

> A man's natural appetites are not sinful. What is objectionable is his moralized projection of them in the form of pseudo-commandments to which other men are vainly expected to submit. This inflates conflicts of interest into ideological hostilities... (Watkins 1973, 110.)

What Watkins calls "realism," can, I suggest, be further elucidated in the following way. As I have indicated earlier, Hobbes based (in an appropriate sense of the word) moral theory on the best available evidence about the nature of humans, and such evidence is appropriately described as "scientific".

Unfortunately, most religions have been unrealistic in the sense in question. Such religions are usually fanatic in their doctrine that this leader of this religion is *The* Way, *The* Truth, *The* Light. The tragic results of such fanaticism were presented in the quotation from Edith Sitwell. From one side of the mouth of such religious leaders issues the command to love or like all our fellow men; from the other, issues the command to slaughter the infidels, the blasphemers and so on. Hobbes does not ask us to love or even like all our fellow men, but to treat them fairly. For non-scholars, he sums up the laws of nature in the negative version of the Golden Rule. In this connection, it is of interest to note that the zoologist Morris offers the following plausible account of the origin of religion. He suggest that when we emerged from the forests and the savannahs of Africa and took up hunting, 'the old style monkey tyrant had to go and in his place there was a more tolerant, cooperative naked ape leader... This change (he writes) left a gap. From our ancient background there remained a need for an all-powerful figure... and the vacancy was filled by the invention of a God' (Morris 1967, 147). Such an invention unfortunately serves our predisposition to aggression. Each side, in human warfare believes God is on his side.

Philosophers of the West in their moral theories, though God is no longer involved, unfortunately appear still to operate under the unrealistic "Love one another" admonition of Christianity. As an example, I cite the position I recently heard expounded, namely that a Hobbesian world government would guarantee mere coexistence. If the "mere" in that statement had been employed in its Latin sense of "undiluted," I would have no quarrel with the position. But it was obviously employed in the non-Latin derogatory sense. On this interpretation I regard the view as mistaken and harmful.

Let me start by asking a few rhetorical questions. Would not pure or undiluted coexistence of the various groups in Beirut that have been slaughtering one another for years, be a valuable step forward? The same sort of question might be asked of Forsyth county in the American state of Georgia, where no blacks dare to live and where race prejudice once again after the progress of the 60's, has reared its ugly head. Coexistence under a competent government implies common interests and promotes some kind of cooperation. In Georgia, for example, it would be to the common interest of both blacks and whites, should they be able to coexist there, to have good roads, efficient use of taxes, adequate transportation, and so on. Analogous considerations would apply to the inhabitants of Beirut, should they be able to coexist and thus emerge from their almost state of nature situations and if Caucasian Germans under Hitler had been able to coexist with Jews, the greatest cruelty in all our history ever inflicted by humans on humans would have been avoided.

Here, I should pause and sketch out my interpretation of Hobbes's account of the nature of a civil government or state.

I follow the late Howard Warrender and my Berkeley colleague, Joseph Tussman, in taking Hobbes's account of an effective civil state as not to be essentially a hard and brutal rule of dictatorial sovereign power. Those who so interpret it forget that Hobbes in expounding his theory is usually concerned

46

with an *ideal* sovereign power, whether embodied in one man, or a group, or all citizens. And an ideal sovereign shapes civil laws with the laws of nature as guide. Now Hobbes is (understandably) criticised for identifying *legal* and *just*, but if we interpret "just" as "presumed just" then, in a reasonably ideal state, the laws should be so presumed. And we should note that *equity* as treated by Hobbes was to assure fairness in the operation of laws in case the presumption was not so.[4]

An allied error occurs when political scientists do not distinguish between Hobbes's theory and his opinion, based on history up to his time, that monarchy would work better than democracy. Here we should remember that the authority of the sovereign, according to Hobbes, rests on the consent of the governed, and hence all three possible forms of government have a democratic basis. The citizens (the *demos*) *are* the Leviathan.

Another unwarranted criticism of Hobbes's theory of sovereign power arises from superficial analyses of existing political structures which, of course, do not as clearly exhibit certain features as does the model.

Sovereign power in Hobbes's theory by definition must be undivided. Richard Peters, voicing a frequent criticism of the doctrine writes, 'it is possible for a constitution to be framed, as in the U.S.A., with the express intention of there being no overall sovereign in Hobbes's sense' (Peters 1950, 224-5). But Professor Robert P. Kraynok, Colgate University, in correspondence with me on this topic has written, illuminatingly, as follows:

> This separation of powers, however, does not mean that sovereignty is divided. Sovereignty is absolute because the people are the sole and final source of authority for the three branches and the Constitution.
>
> Officials in all three branches are "representatives" of the people, chosen either directly or indirectly ... Moreover, the Constitution derives its authority from "we the people." And it cannot be changed by the normal legislative process, but must be amended by extraordinary procedures involving the states and may even involve the calling of a "constitutional assembly".

Again, arising from the same source, are the rhetorical questions (in this country raised most often by students): "When did I ever sign a contract?" "Why am I obliged to obey the laws of the U.S.?" Joseph Tussman, in a work in political philosophy that has many Hobbesian features, gives the following account of the distinction (also clearly made by Hobbes) between "express" and "tacit" consent:[5]

> The difference between express and tacit consent is not ... the difference between two kinds or degrees of consent. It is a difference in the way in which consent is given. There is really little point in insisting that the only way in which consent can be indicated or given is by the express utterance of "I consent" or "I pledge allegiance". Not only may there be other verbal acts which can be interpreted as the giving of consent, but there may

be non-verbal acts (failure to act is also included) which have the same force.

Perhaps the most persistent misreading of Hobbes by political scientists is the *might is right* one. Howard Warrender, in the following passage, succinctly exposes the errors in this reading:

Irresistible power obliges according to Hobbes, but we discover later that only God has such power, and that less power does not oblige, which puts a different complexion upon the whole situation.

Similarly, it is not conquest itself that gives the right to govern, but on Hobbes's submission it is the covenant of the vanquished and then only if he is trusted and not kept imprisoned or shackled. And so it is at every turn. Hobbes's State of Nature is not a moral vacuum; not *all* covenants are void in this condition ... Nor is the sovereign absolute. As against the constitutionalists it may be appropriate enough to speak of Hobbes's sovereign in this way, but it is only a relative or approximate description. For a true theory of absolutism it is necessary to look earlier to the divine right and legitimist philosophers, or later to Rousseau and Hegel. In Hobbes, the absolutism of the sovereign is qualified; by the individual's right to self-defence, to run away in battle, not to kill his father not even the sovereign if commanded so to do; it is further qualified by the subject's right when (in his own opinion) the sovereign has lost the power to protect him to contract himself under a new political agency, or qualified perhaps even by the *duties* of the sovereign (— though owed to injunctions of the civil law, political obligation depends ultimately upon an obligation to obey a law beyond this, the natural law (as interpreted by the individual). (Warrender 1979.)

To this statement by Warrender, I wish to add, as a reinforcement of his line of argument, the following quotation from Hobbes, which should be read with the Hobbesian account of the motive for taking on the social contract in mind:

The obligation of subjects to the sovereign, is understood to last as long, and no longer, than the power lasteth, by which he is able to protect them. For the right men have by nature to protect themselves, when none else can protect them, can by no covenant be relinquished. (Leviathan, 114; EW, Vol. III, 208.)

VII

How are we to implement our need for mutual understanding and communication, so as to avoid nuclear war between nations? For more than a generation the lack of such understanding and communication has persisted between the so-called (depending on who is speaking) democracies and Marxist dictatorships or between capitalism and communism. Bertrand Russell once remarked that it appeared as if something very like old religious Protestant vs. Catholic conflicts were going to be repeated in the case of dogmatic political philosophies,

48

with the same fanaticism and disregard for human welfare in general.

Of late, there are promising signs on both sides of progress, not in mutual love or even liking, but in mutual understanding and tolerance of cultural and political differences. Here, as a Californian I am proud to point to my state where extreme differences in "life-style" and political outlook coexist with no uncontrollable conflicts. My fellow Californians range, in their life-styles, from Hippies (now aging) and young Punks, to Yippies (young upwardly mobile persons); also from the traditional nuclear family to Dinks (double income, no kids couples). In religion we range from Humanist churches that reject the notion of God, and far-out Guru communities, to the fundamentalist who reject the theory of evolution. (Only the latter are intolerant, but they are a minority tolerated by the others.) And all of us want our tax money wisely spend, all of us want to be protected from environmental pollution, and so on. As members of a community, we do have common needs.

To return to the international scene — what both sides should be aware of are the following facts. In the United States, our laws now contain social welfare provisions that in the days before President Roosevelt, were recommended only by the socialist, Norman Thomas, then regarded by many as a dangerous "radical." Also, of late, members of both of our major parties have recommended, because of the "locking into" the welfare cycle of most of our poor, the imposing of requirements on the recipients to take job training, etc. In brief, their "liberty" to continue poor and unemployed will be restricted, and our government will take less permissive, more fairly stern parental role towards its citizens, thus turning more in the direction of socialism. On the other political side, in China for some years now a certain amount of capitalism has been permitted and there has been talk of more democracy. Also, today in Russia, the words "democratic socialism" are beginning to be heard, as well as talk of introducing limited amounts of "capitalist" incentives. And perhaps most importantly, protesters against the regime are beginning to be released from confinement and allowed to speak out. On our side, it was, I believe, a very good thing for fanatic Americans to see on their TV the voluntary exodus from the United States of recent immigrants from Russia, who chose to return, after being exposed to some of the "freedoms" in our big cities, for example, the freedom to be poor and homeless, to be attacked by criminal gangs and so on.

Abstractly considered, (i.e., apart from cultural background, and so on) a democratic socialism that allows a certain amount of capitalism, would seem to be the ideal society, embracing what is best in other forms. However, democracy works well only if the vast majority of citizens have a fairly high level of education. To bring an undeveloped, backward nation to such a condition in a fairly short time requires some kind of dictatorship. (Let us not forget that it took England about 600 years to achieve democracy, and we branched off from that long development.) Moreover, ardent democrats should remember that for Marx, the dictatorship of the proletariat was *not* the final ideal condition of society. Granted that his vague utopian dream of what would be is unrealistic, still the dictatorship is supposed to "wither away."

Since then, from each side of the political dichotomy, we seem to be approaching one another, there is hope that we may end up in a condition of communication and mutual understanding of a sort that guarantees coexistence.

In conclusion, I wish to say that I do not think an effective world government can be achieved in a few year. The United Nations must first slowly but surely be strengthened, and the various kinds of cooperative efforts now being made from both sides encouraged. These cooperative efforts now include work in ecology, science, medicine, the arts, and even some American businessmen are interested. Birth control in countries like Africa is of paramount importance if we are to avoid starvation among large portions of the world's population. Dogmatic religions should stop opposing such efforts. Once we achieve more similarity in fairly high educational level and well-being throughout the world, while preserving some cultural diversity, we should, I believe, be ready for an effective world government.

Notes

1. See Jeffrey 1983, 16-8 and 20. It should be noted that Jeffrey first presents the so-called Bayesian framework for deliberation in terms of (subjective) probabilities and desirabilities in a way familiar to gamblers and actuaries (pp. 5-6). He later substitutes the notion of *preference*, employed today by Harsanyi and others in social welfare theories. See Jeffrey 1977, 318-43.

2. *Leviathan*, Oxford edition, p. 2; EW, Vol., III, p. xi. In referring to the *Leviathan*, I use the pagination of the first Oxford edition.

3. Barash 1979, 88. It should be noted that these conclusions are reached only after careful calculations with mathematical models. Also, the definition of "inclusive fitness" is as follows: '... the term used to incorporate the summed consequences of both personal fitness (via offspring) and fitness derived via the representations of genes in relatives.'

4. In a paper, 'Hobbes on Equity and Justice', presented at the Hobbes Tercentenary Congress (University of Colorado, Boulder, 1979), Larry May writes, '... Hobbes clearly distinguished between what I will call the "thin" role of justice and the much wider role of equity (Hobbes's term for fairness in his political and legal writings).' After a carefully documented support of his thesis, May concludes, 'There must be some visible limits to the sovereign's power in order that the subjects see the legal system as both (1) necessary for their safety *and* (2) fair, that is, not arbitrary and not without appeal when the laws excessively interfere with the subject's liberty.' Another paper correcting misinterpretations of Hobbes as a legal philosopher is Stanley L. Paulson 1983.

5. Tussman 1968, 35. Much of what Tussman has to say on the basic issues of political philosophy agrees with my interpretation of Hobbes: see pp. 19f. and 51f.

The Whiteness of the Whale: Thomas Hobbes and a Paradox of War and Fear[1]

Timo Airaksinen

> 'And now we rushed into the embraces of the cataract, where a chasm threw itself open to receive us. But there arose in our pathway a shrouded human figure, very far larger in its proportions than any dweller among men. And the hue of the skin of the figure was that of the perfect whiteness of the snow.' Poe: *A. Gordon Pym*
>
> 'This elusive quality it is, which causes the thought of whiteness, when divorced from more kindly associations, and coupled with any object terrible in itself, to heighten that terror to the furthest bounds.' Melville: *Moby-Dick*

1. A Paradox of Fear, or "Loomings"

The Pequod, Captain Ahab's whaling ship, sails the vast expanses of the southern seas killing whales and, after the long trip, processing their oil for sale. The crew and their captain are living in a small world of their own. The captain has sovereign power over everybody during their journey; the design and execution of their plans and goals depend on his will only. The responsibility is his. The Pequod meets other ships and that creates a second level social network: the captains meet without a command relation to each other. In this way, the crews and their captains form a stratified social system, in which the relations between ships constitute a second level network.

Through their meeting, something new and surprising is revealed: the ships are innocently chasing a prey they should know cannot be caught, nonchalantly licking their wounds, miraculously lucky in their efforts, or desperately trying to recover what is forever lost; some are shamefully retreating or heading straigth to their doom. In fact they are after a mythical and deceptive image, regardless of what they experience, observe and learn. There is something wrong with all the ships. Everyone of them relates a twisted narrative about life, its goals, and destiny. They all want the ultimate bounty, the exlusive great Leviathan — but only Ahab knows the real nature of their prey. Ahab's virtue is that he, and only he, has courage to see the truth about whaling.

The sea, a battleground of the isolated ships vigorously endeavoring towards the satisfaction of their apparent desires, represents a source of motivational mystery. The surface conceals the truth, which happens to be a deadly monster. The White Whale itself is a platonic form of destruction and violence, or a parody of the denial of such a negative form. The whaling project does not promise much in terms of 'felicity,' or the 'continual success in obtaining those things which a man from time to time desireth' (Leviathan, 129).[2] Ahab himself is a perfect example of Hobbes's proud man. His only passion is glory, to wage war against the White Whale. He cannot win. Therefore he is also the very antithesis of the prudent man. He knows he will not succeed, but not even this can stop him because his pride is far greater than his care for his own survival. And there is no one else but himself he can rely on, as no greater power will support and help him. When he finally charges against his foe, he will perish with everyone he commands and everything that he rightfully owns. Only a life-buoy, a coffin, and a boy Ishmael, a perfect outsider, are left floating at the site of the ultimate battle.

If one does not interfere, if one does not want to kill, such outsider's innocence may still save the person. But the revengeful and vainglorious desire to get even with the enemy is going to destroy one's powers. Within the bounds of this allegory, one may say that the sovereign Ahab sacrifices law and peace at home for what he thinks will be the final war effort abroad; alas, he cannot win. His enemy will always stay there ready to make battle. Therefore, the sovereign will never attain to "felicity" and final peace.

Herman Melville writes in *Moby-Dick*:

> They were bent on profitable cruises, the profit to be counted down in dollars from the mint. He was intent on an audacious, immitigable, and supernatural revenge.

Hobbes's sovereign may have goals which are other than and even opposed to those of the citizens. Their peace of mind and sense of security also depend on foreign policy that may be outside their own competence and knowledge. War is closer than they tend to think. And citizens will be drafted into the king's army. Such is the fate of Hobbes's man. Peace and security at home will vanish because of the foreign enemies one cannot repel. One is forced to fight again and again, and to risk one's life in a never ending combat both at the borders and in foreign lands. The foreigners are from far away, their culture is strange, and their numbers and powers are unknown. No one can reasonably expect to control all of his foreign foes — not even to know them. International war is a veritable Pandora's Box. Hobbes never explicates these conditions that are so obviously related in his political theory.

Therefore, the *paradox of fear* is this: Hobbes's man achieves peace and security at home but only by creating at the same time the necessary conditions of a new type of war. The sovereign pacifies his own realm, although there is no organised warfare without him. And a foreign war is no less destructive than a civil war is, as I shall argue. The domestic tranquillity is, therefore, based on collective self-deception of the citizens — except if safety is based on some natural geographical borders, like in the case of Hobbes's England. Let us try to see why this is so and why the various possibilities to found a super-state world government on Hobbesian principles will fail.

Now, even if the sovereign controls his own territory with ultimate efficiency — his word and sword are the law — whenever he turns around and focuses on other sovereigns, he will notice that they are not dissimilar to him. The sovereign cannot command and control other sovereigns. As Hobbes thinks, he therefore assumes a proud and glorious intent and seeks his chance of getting the better of his potential enemies. The effort is like Ahab's mad charge against the whale. The enemy will not vanish. In this respect the case is like that of the state of nature, which it, of course, cannot be. A sovereign does not exist in the state of nature.

In their own way, Hobbes's sovereign powers must ultimately understand that their typical 'state and posture of Gladiators' (Leviathan, 187) and the alleged state of nature among them (Leviathan, 394) are ultimately going to cost the citizens their most cherished value: their safety. Hobbes defines *war* in such a way that the absence of the conditions of peace is already war, and thus the typical relations between sovereign powers constitute war:

> So the nature of War, consisteth not in actuall fighting; but in the known disposition there to, during all the time there is no assurance to the contrary. (Leviathan, 186.)

War is like bad weather, Hobbes says, it need not actually rain. The key idea refers to an anticipated threat so that the result is a kind of dispositional theory of war. When war is possible, war exists — and it may lead to actual fighting and killing.

Hobbes's view of safety is also very broad: a person wants to protect his total welfare, including private property and all other similar amenities. Such safety will remain fragile and easily disturbed. Safety is a kind of general stability of

53

life and other desirable things and conditions. Hobbes writes,

> But by Safety here, is not meant a bare Preservation, but also all other Contentments of life, which every man ... shall acquire to himself (Leviathan, 376.)

War and safety are related in complex ways: safety entails at least the absence of war, which means a basic guarantee of one's life and goods. But perhaps not all lack of safety is war? One may lack some "contentments of life" without a "known disposition" to fight.

2. An Unlimited Commonwealth, or "The Pequod Meets the Virgin"

From the empirical point of view, Hobbes does not recognise any historical, national, religious, class-related, or racial boundaries which would appropriately create the borders between countries. Hobbes's commonwealth may be a state but is not a country, and neither do its citizens constitute a nation. What I mean is that a commonwealth is defined simply by the range of the efficient domestic power exercise. A nation is constituted also by its language, culture and history. And a country is a political unit which is defined in some natural way, for example, by means of a "nation". The notion of a country seems to presuppose some unifying principle which is not merely power. In this case a citizen is firmly tied to his country and fellow countrymen with, say, blood relationship, friendship, education, conventional duties, shared culture and history, and patriotism. A natural man knows nothing of such ideals and emotions. Hobbes writes,

> If a Subject be taken prisoner in war; ... and hath his life and corporall Libertie given him, on condition to be Subject to the Victor, he hath Libertie to accept the condition. (Leviathan, 272-3.)

Considerations of nationality and patriotism create moral boundaries against such a treason. But Hobbes's prisoner of war may change sides without a second thought, as if the only boundaries were those established by efficient power exercise. Once the sovereign power loses its grip, the prisoner is again unconditionally free. There is no loyalty.

It follows, as I shall argue, that all Hobbesian commonwealths are as large as their communication technology and other similar empirical limitations will allow. No emotional, historical or ideological factors are taken into account. Let me explain this idea. Given that there is a source of sovereign power, it is limited by those practical and technological factors which make, say, communications and travel too difficult over long distances. When the sovereign cannot know about the developments in the further reaches of his realm, and when he cannot exercise his power because he is unable to send weapons and soldiers to stop a civil war, one must say that the borders of the commonwealth are drawn accordingly. Certainly the borders must be drawn somewhere, because peace or the citizens' safety have their own geographical limits.

Actually the power wielder must, in order to qualify as a sovereign, control a *maximally* large geographical territory. Otherwise a perpetual civil war could rage within his territory — as I shall maintain — and he cannot be a sovereign. Therefore, only if he controls such a piece of land where all wars will be international wars, is he a sovereign. The problem is, simply, that if the maximality condition is not granted to the would-be sovereign, we could as well think that all fathers have their own commonwealths, and any one person or coalition who can dominate over a couple of his weaker fellows is also a monarch. This is clearly against Hobbes's intentions. Small coalitions cannot protect their members against other *similar* coalitions.

A sovereign must possess *efficient power* over a *maximally large* geographical territory (cf. Leviathan, 364 concerning a discussion of "Want of Absolute power" as a serious political disease). The second point is normally overshadowed by the first, without any good reason, except that Hobbes himself concentrates on it. Nevertheless, both conditions are necessary for domestic safety and, accordingly, the existence of a commonwealth.

We find a hidden counterfactual clause here: a strong person who dominates over his neighbours is not a sovereign if it were possible for him to control a larger area. If the person were more determined and resourceful he could rule over all of the neighbourhoods. In other words, if the power wielder can in principle control the whole area, but he does not, this lack of control entails that the wars are in fact civil wars: his power is challenged in such a way that the unrest concerns his realm.

My point is that it is not enough to control the area one happens to control, because that fact alone does not guarantee anybody's safety. If the realm is not maximal, there can be other similar power-centers within this same area, just like there are many families. We need a sovereign power which covers the whole area and which is, therefore, unique. Certainly a permanent civil war, which would result from the competition between many non-unique power centers, is an impossibility, given Hobbes's definition of a sovereign. The would-be sovereigns could not pacify their own realms and this is an anomalous situation. Of course a sovereign is a person or a coalition who exhibits exactly an ability to control the citizens and guarantee their safety.

The creation of the maximal territory can also be understood as follows. Take a geographical area where people make a covenant to establish a sovereign power. There can be no reason to think that some groups of people are left out if they could join in. Everyone is afraid, everyone needs a sovereign to protect them, and if people disagree on the sovereign, they are still engaged in civil war. What they must be able to do is to choose *one* sovereign who represents them *all*. The problem concerns the question of how the limits of "all" are actually drawn. This is an empirical question and its answer depends on technology and communications — as I already suggested. It also follows that the borders of the state may change. When technology and, say, roads develop, the sovereign is able to control a larger piece of land. The borders tend to fluctuate.

Our unqualified counterfactual clause above is too strong, as can be seen as follows. Let us consider a counterargument to the effect that the area of an established sovereign power may be limited by another sovereign, that is, by foreign policy and not only by technology. This idea may be taken to show that one sovereign power is restricted to its sub-maximal geographical area — which was said to be impossible. Suppose now a sovereign S who rules over his (maximal) geographical area A. Suppose further that S' rules over the adjacent area A', and that S' (but not S) has all the technical means to rule over A + A' (or, area A' is sub-maximal), except that he cannot repel S from area A. According to my unrestricted argument above, in such a case S' is not a real sovereign because he will be engaged in a civil war against S.

S' is in a position where he does not yet have unchallenged power over his maximal area; thus the actions of S must be taken, from the point of view of S', to constitute a civil war. But S was a sovereign power who therefore is not engaged in a civil war. This is an absurd result. There either is or there is not a civil war.

It is indeed easy to imagine a situation where sovereigns are capable of ruling over each other's territory and subjects, and yet no civil war exists. If we say that their non-maximal territories do not entail a civil war because real sovereigns are engaged only in foreign wars, we have a problem.

The line of thought above indicates that the borders of a commonwealth are also drawn in reference to some competing sovereign power, and not only to technological factors. We can then see a real problem in Hobbes's political theory: it is unacceptably vague talk to refer to a sovereign power that is limited by another sovereign power, given that their mutual situation is such that at least one of them could rule over the other's territory. Why should we not call this a civil war? And if it is a civil war, the alleged sovereigns are not real sovereigns.

The lesson to learn is that only a thin red line separates a civil and an international war. If S maintains his perfect control over area A, he looks like a sovereign in war; but if S' could rule over A, the same situation looks like a civil war. And let me repeat the root of such an ambiguity: the idea of perfect power should be applied only to geographical areas and groups of people which are large enough — but we do not know what "large" means in the present context.

We can make a simple stipulation which allows us to avoid this Hobbesian ambiguity: we say that if S' can in principle control a geographical area, and this control is challenged for any reason whatsoever, the result is a civil war. (It

56

follows that S in our example above is not a sovereign power.) And if the civil war is permanent, the sovereign status of S' duly collapses.

England and Scotland provide an example (see Leviathan, 251). Fighting between these two constitutes a civil war in Hobbes's time, although both are 'Kingdomes'. An island has its natural borders so that the main threats to peace may be expected to come from inside, geographically speaking. Such life in isolation tends also to create an implicit feeling of ethnic self-sufficiency. One's home is the whole world where the only possible war is a civil war. What is outside need not be taken into consideration. One need not worry about any foreign enemies and therefore one pretends that there are no foreign wars. And furthermore, one accepts the falsehood that one is alone and self-sufficient in the world. Any foreign enemy will stay behind the natural borders. Most people are savages anyway and their lands will be used for the purposes of emigration in order to pacify some social disturbances caused by the dispensable classes (see Leviathan, 387). Perhaps Hobbes is short-sighted in this case. He seems to think that foreign war is only a secondary source of worry. But this may be based on a false inference from the isolation of the British Isles and his reluctance to accept the importance of national boundaries between different countries.

Ironically, it seems that the chasing of the whale is in vain. Peace will come automatically to all those innocents who dare to wait until its time has come. The Earth will become a single global technological village. A unique power base emerges at the moment when the maximal area of power exercise is the whole wide world. For a while an international war looks like a civil war. After this era one sovereign will rule over all the people of the world, so that the world government will come about. The people of the world will make a covenant with one king — this is now the only way to avoid a civil war. After they have signed it there is just one sovereign in the whole wide world. The original contract knows, in principle, no inherent limits. There are only empirical limits which may be expected to fade away when the technological culture advances.

A real sovereign rules over a maximal area, but only the Earth itself is the ultimately maximal realm. It seems as if sovereignty were a process leading towards a global state. And this entails world peace. Such is the Hobbesian argument from the virgin innocence of citizens.

In this way, if the communications work well enough and there are no nations and countries, it follows from Hobbes's own principles that ultimately one commonwealth will cover the global village. All the frightened inhabitants will make a pact with only one sovereign. As Hobbes says, men are like 'mushrooms, come to full maturity, without all kind of engagement to each other' (Man and Citizen, 205). The commonwealth is the first and the last form of their ''engagement to each other''. Therefore they are able to live together regardless of how the state borders are drawn and, say, racial groups distributed. The citizens do not care. Under ideal technological conditions, the whole earth can be dominated by a single sovereign power. This is peace.

However, as it is, every country is only relatively isolated, although it may look to its citizens like the whole world, like Hobbes's England. Such an original state of innocence is then destroyed by cruel facts. Beyond the sea and the mountains one sovereign has already, perhaps unbeknown to the other, seized power — and then those two suddenly meet. What happens?

3. Sovereign Powers and the State of Nature or "Leg and Arm. The Pequod, of Nantucket, Meets the Samuel Enderby of London"

It is interesting to notice that Hobbes's political rhetoric clearly suggests that a sovereign is a unique individual. Moreover, Leviathan the biblical beast is the king of all sea — certainly a unique creature who rules all the waters without competition. As God shows Job, no one can even imagine such a challenge. And it is true that the power of a sovereign looks absolute to the citizens, as the original front page picture of the king so aptly shows — the human figure, encomposing in his body many other human beings, much larger than any dweller among men. Yet any sovereign must recognise others. There are many similar leviathans.

Let us look at the following new argument. If the state of nature and international politics were truly and strictly analogous to each other, we would already have a super-state world government. The sovereigns, when they meet, would be frightened enough to make an authorising contract in favour of one superpower. Hobbes grants the sovereigns full rights to give away their own power in favour of another sovereign, if they think such a decision to be fit to advance safety, or 'to dispose of the Succession by words of Contract, or Testament' (Leviathan, 250). Our key characterisation is that if sovereigns behave like natural persons in the state of nature, they are in need of a state-founding covenant.

Can we plausibly argue that the sovereigns themselves are sick with fear so that in order to protect themselves they will agree, among themselves, and independently of their subjects, to authorise one super-sovereign? This would be an easy way of getting rid of the whale of war: we decide that the beast should not exist.

The point is as follows: Suppose there are two or more genuinely Hobbesian sovereigns whose mutual geographic and economic relations are such that they cannot fail to recognise each other as they actually are. No self-deception is possible. It is clear that there are no lawful contracts open to them. As independent powers, they are bound to stay in the state of nature and perpetual war, as Hobbes maintains. This fact motivates them to do something about their mutual condition. They surrender their powers in favour of one sovereign. The gladiators decide against fighting. Is this correct?

Now, if the sovereigns are tied to the state of nature they will indeed make a contract to stop the war, according to Hobbes's political master argument applied to the present case. They can do this only by establishing a super-sovereign. However, we know that no such super-power exists; therefore, the sovereigns as natural persons are not locked into a perpetual war in the state of nature. The analogy to individual men and the situation of natural persons somehow does not work. Some crucial differences between the state of nature and foreign policy must exist.

Let me suggest first that sovereigns (as natural persons) need not experience too much fear. Next we shall turn to a more important point: a sovereign is also an artificial person. The second point, seemingly, has more explanatory value.

My first point is that if every commonwealth is geographically maximally extensive, no super-commonwealth creating covenant is possible because any larger unit would then be too large to survive. The maximality condition should be taken seriously. Therefore, war is a natural, necessary, and perpetual relation between all genuine sovereigns. This also means that when one sovereign is destroyed by another, the winner may yet be unable to establish his permanent rule over the vacant territory: his area was already maximally large and cannot be enlarged simply by means of a new conquest or covenant.

Perhaps a conquering sovereign cannot expect to profit much. He is sometimes unable to acquire new subjects. Therefore, the sovereigns need not try to destroy each other, even when they try to solve their border disputes violently. Accordingly, they need not be afraid, and no contract by means of which a super-sovereign would be created will ensue. A maximally extended sovereign power is a self-sufficient person who need not cope with any overwhelming problems or try to acquire radically more benefits than what he already has. Border disputes and other similar disagreements will lead to wars, of course, but the fellow sovereigns need not commit themselves to any suicidal military efforts because of them. The point is that sovereigns are not really unsafe or afraid. Only total destruction defeats the sovereign while even the most limited military adventures kill citizens. We cannot find anything in foreign policy and wars which a sovereign as a natural person would find too frightful. His personal safety is not in question, except in some extraordinary circumstances.

My conclusion is that Hobbes's reference to the state of nature in international affairs is a rhetorical trick based on an imperfect analogy. A sovereign as a natural person need not be afraid in the same way as persons generally are. His fear is limited. Even if 'the Law of Nations, and the Law of Nature, is the same thing' (Leviathan, 394), it does not follow that the sovereigns need to found a super-commonwealth to protect themselves. We now turn to our second problem, namely, sovereigns as artificial persons and the implications of this.

4. Fake Peace at Home, or "The Pequod Meets the Bachelor"

Hobbes describes a king as a private person whose desires include 'Fame from new Conquest' as well as 'ease and sensuall pleasure' and who, like any real individuals, may kill (Leviathan, 161). However, this is just an illustration of human disposition and cannot be read as applying especially to kings and perhaps even less to all other types of sovereign power: to a multiple personed sovereign. Hobbes deals with this same subject matter in several contexts. First, he writes:

> A Person, is he whose words and actions are considered, either as his own, or as representing the words or actions of an other man, or of any other thing to whom they are attributed, whether Truly or by Fiction. When they are considered as his owne, then is he called a Naturall Person: And when they are considered as representing the words and actions of an other, then is he a Feigned or Artificiall person. (Leviathan, 217.)

Second, Hobbes maintains that 'it is the Unity of the RepresEnter, not the Unity of the Represented, that maketh the Person One,' thus emphasising the unitary nature of that artificial condition he calls the sovereign (Leviathan, 220). He returns to these questions again when he discusses 'Publique Ministers' (ibid., 289). Moreover 'in Monarchy, the private interest is the same with the publique' (ibid., 241) so that the sovereign king is largely dependent on the strength and success of his subjects. This provides him with a motive to further their security — presumably an ideal political state of affairs where duty and interest merge.

The real nature of the sovereign is a moot question in Hobbes's philosophy. The problem is familiar from the modern view of political and coercive authority. Here we have a kind of balancing act between the ruler's personal "*an* authority" and his positional "*in* authority". The president of Finland, for example, is a living person whose actions and decisions can be explained by means of his individual psychology. But he is also the president and, so to speak, a place-holder at the top of the pyramid of power. Much of his ability and influence can be explained through his position and its structural characteristics.

The relations between in and an authority are complex and certainly beyond the scope of the present paper. What is important, however, is that the sovereign is not unambiguously an individual natural person. Therefore, his fears, goals, and dangers may be qualitatively different from those of individual

60

persons in the state of nature. The sovereign who loses his war may destroy his commonwealth, and this is a source of fear: it endangers his position, status, glory and power. It is not however clear what kind of fear it is. This is not true of an individual in the state of nature: such a psychological state of anxiety and fear is familiar to every person because his life will be short and dangerous. But the artificial person is different. Perhaps we can say that his fear is not psychological but political.

Any sovereign power, an artificial person, endeavors to protect its power base; such a typical motivation certainly exists — this is almost an axiomatic truth in the Hobbesian science of politics. Nevertheless, of course the sovereign in its artificial sense does not experience natural fear. As a kind of structurally defined function the sovereign can be identified with the force and might which guarantee the civil laws. For this reason it, by definition, controls its own environment. And it need not care for anything else. It is safe: it has the power over the domestic environment, indeed its laws, to a certain extent, create that environment, and the foreign policy need not really threaten it as a person. War may certainly threaten the throne but the consequences of that threat must be very different from those which are against one's personal security. The artificial person may disappear but the fate of the natural persons — who once were the power wielders — is now strictly irrelevant. We are interested only in artificial persons and their typical motives.

Hobbes himself seems to think that once the home front is pacified the rest of the military business is just pretending and playing war games. The sovereigns are seeking for glory. Splendid posing, in gladiator outfits, is what sovereigns do *vis-a-vis* each other, as Hobbes says. The domestic front, on the other hand, is important in a different way, because it serves one's real interests.

We have seen that Hobbes's sovereign, even if it is a monarch, need not be timid and weak in the same sense as any natural person is. We already called its fears "artificial", too. It may be afraid of losing its power but this is not the same motive as the anxiety and terror experienced by natural persons. However, the sovereign may lose power and the corresponding motivational state can be called "artificial fear". This construct embodies the simple truth that power bases are typically protected. An artificial person is afraid of losing its power, which also means the destruction of the commonwealth. But such an artificial emotion is different from the natural fear which is experienced by natural persons.

Now, artificial fear does not lead the sovereign towards the world government, even if fear leads natural persons towards the commonwealth. No sovereign power really needs the world government: it need not protect its life, and the protection of the structural power base is best done by assuming a proudly threatening position against all other sovereigns. Artificial fear brings about war. Natural fear leads us to peace.

For this reason, it seems that Hobbes's political theory does not formulate the real problem of foreign politics and international war: this is misrepresented as a fake state of nature which is neither too scary or dangerous — which sounds like a flat contradiction. In other words, to call international law a law of nature does not explain anything, even if the "state of nature" is Hobbes's *explanans par excellence*. No interesting conclusions can be drawn from the view that international politics is a state of nature and its principles mere laws of nature.

I shall try to show next why such a happy state of affairs is deceptive from the point of view of natural persons. Their sovereign, the artificial person, will not protect them against the foreign enemy.

5. The Return of Civil War, or "The Pequod Meets the Rachel"

Hobbes writes: 'But in vain do they worship peace at home, who cannot defend themselves against foreigners' (Man and the Citizen, 177). When a foreign war is lost, political anarchy may return. This is the case when the protective (domestic) power base vanishes: all its help is denied and the homeless citizens struggle to find new guarantees for their vital security. The loss is enormous but no one can help. A foreign war can destroy the sovereign power, understood as a legally constituted in-authority. In fact we only need think that one geographical part of the state is surrendered to the conqueror. A commonwealth may always have the maximal extension but civil war is often only local.

War may detach a part from the whole commonwealth. The fate of this lost part of the commonwealth is an open question. If such a catastrophe takes place and the winner is either unable or unwilling to have a new contract with the people, lawlessness will reign again. And to those who live in that area this is a serious problem and a source of fear.

Let us keep in mind that the conqueror may decide to exterminate or totally to enslave the former subjects of the defeated sovereign. Actually the conqueror may have a good reason for deciding to exterminate the population. If his rule is already maximal, he cannot accept the defeated people as his new subjects. The logic of my "maximal area of sovereignty argument" yields some grim prospects. We realise that when technological and social change is slow while wars still go on, the motive for exterminating a vanquished people is quite predictable. The losers become a mere burden to the winner who cannot wield permanent power over them, that is, make them either slaves or citizens. The borders of his state cannot be changed. The vanquished people can also be left

62

alone but, then, they will make a new covenant with another sovereign. Exactly this state of affairs can be prevented by means of the extermination of the whole population.

Four different possibilities obtain: (1) the losers are killed, (2) they are enslaved, (3) they are left alone in the state of nature, or (4) they sign a treaty with the conqueror. The very worst possibility, killing, is an open option but it need not be realised, for instance, when the state borders can in the new situation be drawn differently. The borders are never quite definite but they can be changed. The winner may indeed be able to accept the losers among his subjects. This is the happiest possibility. According to Hobbes, no harm at all ensues to the population because of such a change of sovereigns.

The most terrifying alternatives have been made actual even in the 20th century Europe. The early history of America illustrates the case, too. Most of the Indian population was erased when it became evident that they were unable to work as slaves and they continued to defend their land. Slaves were brought from Africa instead. Yet another example is the Thirty Year War (17th century) which created an absolute chaos in Europe. Because of the war Germany was depopulated in the end.

Hobbes certainly recognises the citizens' need to defend the sovereign power and also to serve in the army, because it is one of the main duties of the sovereign to protect the borders. Unpredictability of life and political terror are factors which demand solutions for avoidance before they emerge, say, from the ruins of a lost foreign war. After that people are left alone, like the children of the captain of the Rachel, who are lost at sea. The captain cannot find his children after their battle against the White Whale. He and his ship are safe but his children are gone.

6. An Anatomy of Losers, or "The Pequod Meets the Delight"

Any war can lead to civil war and consequently to the ultimate evil. I mean that war may destroy the political machine and bring about anarchy. Certainly civil war can do it more quickly. Nevertheless, the other side of the coin is that the conqueror may decide to exterminate the whole population. This is to say that harm and losses must be expected. Hobbes's principles entail that any commonwealth, however peaceful domestically, experiences a kind of potential state of nature because of the perpetual foreign war in the international theatre. However, such a conclusion is not what Hobbes himself was after.

A case of domestic powerlessness is provided by the African kings south of Sahara and their kingdoms before the era of colonialism. I do not think these facts of political anthropology are well known in spite of their inherent interest.

Let us review some aspects of successful African despotism.

Elias Canetti's *Crowds and Power* (*Masse und Macht*)[3] is a rich source of narratives about many aspects of power and powerlessness. As Canetti explains, certain ancient African kingdoms had peculiar rules which regulated the inheritance of the crown. The new king had to be elected, and for that reason a state of anarchy was declared. Anyone could do whatever one wanted, kill, rob, and maim. A new king was elected, and all potential competitors were put to death.

The king assumed the role of the ceremonial lion, a living guarantee of the civil and religious laws. He also divinely influenced the fertility of his nation's women and the people's sources of food. He killed as he pleased in order to exhibit his divine powers, to send messages to other gods, and to keep his power base intact. In some cases, he was closely observed for any signs of weakness: gray hair or symptoms of illness meant a death sentence to the king. A powerless monarch was useless and his vitality and virility were symptoms or criteria of his divine powers. The monarch represented a totem and was an artificial father of all his subordinates, just like Captain Ahab has his totemic features. Moreover, the White Whale is the totem animal and therefore taboo: the White Whale is the emblem of all things that are forbidden, frightening and destructive.[4] The African kings combined these aspects, positive and negative, as they both protected and destroyed. Their actions were both beneficial and baneful. The African kings were fighting that supernatural foe, inevitable weakness and death, as well as the possible famine and slavery of their own people in the hands of their enemies. People also knew what civil war means: the change of a sovereign ruler involved a period of anarchy.[5]

Such was the bloody and violent rule, also involving excessive human sacrifices, but it was as well a lawful system of government. It shows a deeply ironic analogy to the Hobbesian commonwealth. We can say that such despotism achieves everything an Hobbesian sovereign should achieve, expect that the African kings used very strange methods. But this is a question of political style, better than of substance. The system was, indeed, designed for keeping the subjects safe — except against the king — alive and fertile, gods happy, foreign enemies out of the country, and crops good. The citizens may have had little reason to rebel. And it worked for hundreds of years making Africa probably a better place to live then than it is now, after the rule of the great imperialist powers, their pet ideologies, and their exploitations, naked or hypocritical.

The most important fact in this story of the African kings is the periodic anarchy between two kings' rule. A foreign war or a revolution has similar effects. When the earlier power base is gone, everything is permitted for a while when the revolution is eating its own children. People return to their natural condition. The rule of law may be established quickly, but if people are afraid of violent death even a short period is enough to fill their hearts with terror. They should be ready to do something to avoid the recurrent state of lawlessness.

Certainly such social unrest and its anarchic conditions are not quite the same as the state of nature. One should say that the original state of nature is a hypothetical *explanans*, some features of which are applicable to civil wars and, analogously, also to foreign wars. In international politics both the vainglorious postures assumed by sovereigns and their perpetual condition of war are indicative of the state of nature in such a derivative and limited sense, as I shall argue next.

The question is: is it true that the state of nature never was and cannot be realised in our social world? The answer seems to be in the affirmative. All the calamitous states of affairs, as we know them, are mere approximations and analogical descriptions of the hypothetical original social condition. As Hobbes writes:

> There had never been any time, wherein particular men were in a condition of warre one against each other-; yet in all times, Kings, ... are in continuall jealousies. (Leviathan, 187.)

In spite of his very loose definition of 'Warre', Hobbes is perhaps committed to the view that the original and perfect state of nature never really existed. Let us study this problem more closely.

In the context of the above quotation, Hobbes suggests that some savages actually live in the state of nature, but he also claims that they have families and a kinship structure. This seems to entail that some kind of social order prevails along with these social ties. Hobbes then produces a counterfactual argument to the following effect:

> Howsoever, it may be perceived what manner of life there would be, where there were no common Power to feare; by the manner of life, which men that have formerly lived under a peacefull government, use to degenerate into, in a civill Warre. (Leviathan, 187.)

It is important to see that the original war in the state of nature is only a fictional entity whose nature must be understood in the counterfactual way and in terms of an analogy to civil war; or by comparing the situation with a change from peace to war. We are first invited to consider the counterfactual case of a total lack of power base, and this then illustrated by the (undesirable) characteristics of the change of peace into war. The change teaches us the crucial lesson.

We may also try to argue as follows. The impossibility of the original state of nature follows from the psychological impossibility to live, as a person, without ever applying any moral notions at all. One needs only to recall Hobbes's definition of a person (quoted above) in order to verify this point: a Naturall Person is he whose words and actions are his own (Leviathan, 217). The concept of ownership is a normative idea, at least *prima facie*. But such an argument cannot be successful.

We have suggested an argument to the effect that no aspect of human action is without its moral controls and implications. Whatever you do or think, wherever you are, you already presuppose some features of morality to be sanctioned and, thus, a motive for you. Morality motivates, perhaps imperfectly in its force, but it motivates. I am proud of myself, I regret some things, and I am at social goals — even independently of the sovereign sword and the law. The fact is that the phenomenology of morals points to the direction of non-original social conditions. If anarchy prevailed, everybody would know it as something which *should* be superseded by the law and order. But this presupposes that one knows what morality is. Certainly some moral truths will be learned in family life under parental rule — and we have parents and family.

Now, the problem is that Hobbes's own concept of morality is unusual and difficult. The question is whether Hobbes's man is an egoistic natural creature who always aims at his own private good disregarding other people, or whether he is capable of altruistic actions, too. The view that Hobbes's man is not a thoroughgoing egoist is quite plausible. Its acceptance rests on the observation that man may well be an altruist, but in the state of nature the conditions are such that he has not many chances to realise his kind dispositions. The world is so cruel that a person must be an egoist in order to survive. In this way, we can say that the state of nature contains moral agents. But we did not want this conclusion.

Another and more successful argument for the thesis that the original state of nature never really existed can be extrapolated from Hobbes's remarks on family. Hobbes writes:

> A son cannot be understood to be at any time in the state of nature, as being under the power and command of them to whom he owes his protection as soon as ever he is born. (Man and Citizen, 117, footnote.)

Moreover, he writes,

> that the precept of *honouring our parents*, belongs to the law of nature, not only under the title of *gratitude*, but also of *agreement*. (Man and Citizen, 215.)

Hobbes also says that all men are born ''unapt for society.'' This does not mean that at any moment of time they would live in natural conditions. The correct interpretation is again counterfactual: if a child lived alone after his birth, he would live in the state of nature. But because he cannot survive alone, he never lived in the pure state of nature. He lives in family which is a contractual organisation of power and authority. Therefore, no perfect state of nature ever existed and whatever might happen it will not exist. It is a theoretical fiction.

It follows from the above that there cannot be any final and ultimate difference between a civil and a foreign war — their difference is a matter of the relative distance from (hypothetical) total anarchy. Both types of war are similar when compared to anarchy as the standard. The sole difference between them concerns empirical facts and historical circumstances, though it may be easier to dramatise the perils of domestic conflicts than those of foreign wars. If one is lucky the sovereign is competent, his wars seem justified and they stay away from home, and none of one's friends or relatives is drafted so that a sweet victory will fill the heart with patriotic pride and bliss. It is time to celebrate new invasions, better business in the future, and most of all, the glory of the sovereign and that great land of ours. A good example is Great Britain's Margaret Thatcher's successful war in the Malvinas/Falkland Islands. Despite loss of life, it can be held, it brought a feeling of national glory and pride.

And then Hobbes's argument from vainglory bites again. Once the citizens of the commonwealth are ready to believe that they are fit and powerful enough to live a life greater than anything they knew before, they are also ready to destroy a great state. The positive advice derived from history is ambiguous exactly in the same way as a famous answer by the Delphic oracle: cross the river and you will destroy a great state. Ultimately that great state is your own glorious commonwealth.

My conclusion is that all war is alike in the sense that it can be described in terms of the model of the war in the state of nature. All war is destructive. Accordingly, it is a logical mistake to maintain that civil war belongs to the state of nature although foreign war does not. Civil and foreign wars are not as different as Hobbes may sometimes suggest. He may have supposed that only civil war takes people back to the state of nature. I have argued that also foreign war does the same.

Here we must recognise the following corollary of what I said above, namely, if a sovereign cannot guarantee his subjects' safety against the dangers of the type ''war in the state of nature'' — including dangers of a foreign war — the sovereign is no better than some coalition that deters the threats issued by another one. A family, clan, corporation, or a protective agency which can use violence and force is also able to step out of the (hypothetical) original state of nature. People are no longer absolutely isolated although there is no state. Total protection is only a dream anyway.

The sovereign's achievement is, therefore, not the elimination of the state of nature. His achievement is the enforcement of safety across certain social circumstances and domestic institutions. But if a foreign war is like a civil war and international politics nothing but temporarily suspended warfare, the subjects need not consider the sovereign power to be too successful. The sovereign is always in principle relatively unsuccessful, although his existence creates some additional distance from the original state of nature — but so do your parents, friends and business partners, too.

My conclusion is that a world government is justified, even if it does not exist, because it is needed for the protection of the citizens — exactly in the same way as the domestic sovereign power is justified. But, of course, we do not have actually enforced international laws and justice since there is no sovereign's sword. In this sense justification is an empty word in the present context. There is a Hobbesian dilemma of the international law and order. The original social contract creates a political situation which can neither bring about lasting peace nor guarantee safety, simply because the contract itself creates a possibility of a new type of war. The limited nature of such a contract is the source of trouble. We need an unlimited contract, one that covers all countries and peoples and creates one super-state, instead of many geographically limited states.

7. The Logic and the Facts of War, or "The Symphony"

Here is another analogy to the whiteness of the whale: glory and destruction go hand in hand. In the state of nature people dream of glory and acquisition; also, for a civil man, foreign wars look glorious. They lure the sovereigns to risk their power through threatening their neighbours. And just like Ahab first refuses to listen to and help the desperate captain of the Rachel, only to hastily pass the ruined Delight in pursuit of the whale, sovereign powers act without realising that the real enemy is the war itself. They may win over any given enemy, but they cannot win the war. Captain Ahab could kill any given whale but the White Whale.

Human powers and organisations are limited so that the ultimate idea of the white enemy itself is unconquerable. Alas, the fact that we know this, and we have always known it, means almost nothing. This is a Hobbesian feature of the nature of fear. Once again, the fearful person cannot find a way to destroy the sources of his fear. How could that happen? Fear is a weak and timid attitude that drives one away from its source. But where ever one goes, the same terror will be there.

As Hobbes, the nominalist, puts it: man's appetites and desires drive him forward where ever he does not find a psychological barrier, such as pain and death. The laws of nature, visible to his uncorrupt reason, are largely supervenient on these limits. Also the sovereign domestic power is limited in his drive to protect the life and property of his subjects. If the sovereign were a natural person, he might even surrender to a super-sovereign. But as far as it is a sovereign power, a structural in-authority is not interested in such an international covenant. The commonwealth can subsist in the state of an international perpetual war. But the subjects will be left without the protection they need most. (Why wouldn't they refuse to sign such a contract which does not promise peace between nations?) They were unable to establish a sovereign power base which is geographically so extensive that no foreign conflicts could ever emerge. They were, however, able to establish a guarantee for law and morality, but this was not enough. They still miss the greatest prize they expected to win by means of their surrender to sovereign power — the freedom from the hunt of the White Whale. They succeeded only in creating some distance to the hunt. Their only hope is now placed in the broader and broader social contracts that will ultimately lead to an efficient world-government in the future. In the end of time they will be safe, but neither a utopia nor a savior will emerge earlier. Meantime they fight and wait.

Notes

1. I am grateful to Professor Martin A. Bertman (Ben-Gurion University, Isreal) for his detailed criticism and to Professor E. M. Adams (Chapel Hill, North Carolina) for his comments.

2. All references to Hobbes's *Leviathan* (1651) are to C.B. Macpherson's edition, Penguin Books, Harmondsworth, 1968. Herman Melville''s *Moby-Dick* (1851) is also available as a Penguin Book edition, 1972. I shall also make references to *De Cive*, in *Man and Citizen*, ed. by Bernard Gert, Peter Smith, Gloucester, Ma, 1978.

3. Canetti 1973, 441 ff. See also Lenski 1966, 154 ff., and the wonderful philosophical novel by Bamber Gascoigne (1986) who provides a fictional account of a sexual and religious kingship in Brazil.

4. See Freud 1950. Freud writes: 'Any violations of the taboos that protect the totem are automatically punished with severe illness or death', and 'His attitude towards his totem animal was superlatively ambivalent: he showed both hatred and love to an extravagant degree' (pp. 104 and 130), as if referring to Ahab.

5. Hobbes in *Leviathan* (p. 346) anticipates David Hume's famous argument from the lacking circumstances of justice. Hobbes says that floods and other natural catastrophes make the civil laws void. This is a stronger theory that the one which only allows war to make laws void. Is it not strange that laws do not protect society under such circumstances in which they are needed most? In actual fact this may be true, but laws were supposed to guarantee the moral laws of nature. — On Hume, see Mackie 1980, 84 ff. It is questionable, however, whether Hobbes was a proto-Humean or Hume a crypto-Hobbesian in questions concerning the missing circumstances of justice.

Death, Identity and the Possibility of a Hobbesian Justification for World Government

Paul J. Johnson

The Possibility of Justifying World Government on Hobbesian Principles suggests two quite different, though possibly related questions. One is "Are there Hobbesian principles which we could use now to justify forming a world government?" Or put somewhat more precisely, "Is the justification Hobbes gave for civil government adaptable or convertible in a way that would now justify a world government?"

The second, and quite different question suggested by the title is, "Could we justify, on some set of principles, not necessarily Hobbesian principles, a world government constructed on the model of the civil government that Hobbes constructs on his principles?" Or, perhaps more clearly, "Can we justify forming a world government on Hobbesian principles of government?" So the ambiguity of the title possesses the virtue of exhibiting two of the important questions which must be addressed in thinking about world government; "Can it be justified?" and "What kind of world government could we justify?" To answer these questions with reference to Hobbesian principles, of course, we first need to know what Hobbes's justification for civil government was and how he justified the sort of civil government he approved. In this paper I will concern myself with Hobbes's justification of government and whether it is applicable to the current world situation.

On what might be called the traditional reading of Hobbes, unfortunately still too common, the sort of government Hobbes justifies follows as a corollary from the justification he is seen as giving for forming a civil government. The traditional story goes like this. Men naturally fear death and an early death above all. Men also have a vicious, aggressive and wolflike nature. Consequently, men living individually without any common power over them to restrain their natural viciousness would be constantly at war with one another and no one could be safe or expect to live out a natural term of life. What emerges from this situation is a logic of fear. The only way innately vicious men can be prevented from attacking one another is to render them afraid of doing so; and the only way of doing that is to set up a sufficiently terrifying power so that men's fear of it will outweigh their natural urges to attack one another. Setting up such a power is the process of forming a civil government. To be sufficiently terrifying, the holder of this power, the sovereign, must be unlimited or absolute. On this view then, civil government is justified and its form is determined by the same set of considerations.

Now I have argued at length that this reading of Hobbes is mistaken (Johnson 1982). Hobbes does indeed rest his justification of civil government on certain features of human nature, but it is not part of Hobbes's view of human nature that men are naturally vicious. There simply are no texts in Hobbes's writings to support this view. The texts that appear to do so and which are ordinarily cited to support this notion, on careful reading, turn out to have nothing at all to say about human nature. Moreover, Hobbes explicitly denies that humans are evil by nature in the "Preface to the Reader" of *De Cive*.[1] And, in his discussions of the state of nature he regularly makes references to men with modest and generous dispositions. The existence of such men is, of course, inconsistent with supposing some innate wolflike human nature. If there are "temperate" men even in the state of nature who would 'according to the natural equality which is among us, permit as much to others, as he assumes to himself' as Hobbes describes them in *De Cive*[2] then, clearly enough, the war of all against all in the state of nature cannot be generated by innate human viciousness. But if men are not innately vicious, then absolute government does not follow as a necessary corollary from the justification of government itself, but requires a separate and independent justification.

The fact that men do not have an innately wolfish nature, however, makes no difference to Hobbes's justification for forming a civil government. For in a hypothetical non-social state the logic of fear will still operate so long as all men are not modest and generously disposed. So long as some men are, or are thought to be, vainglorious, competitive or vicious, all men are thrust into a state of uncertainty and reason will suggest to each a first-strike defensive strategy. So long, then as the nature of men is not uniformly modest or generous, the war of all against all is on in the state of nature.

Now Hobbes did not suppose that men generally ever lived in such a state, though not knowing much about native Americans, he suggested that they lived in something like that brutish state. So, for Hobbes the state of nature was not a historical condition that men at some time were in and then had to reason their way out of. It is important to remember that Hobbes's argument is not addressed to men in the state of nature, but to men living in troubled times, men in societies broaching on or already engaged in civil war. And civil war raises the possibility of a total disintegration of society. What has split once may split again or the devastation become so complete that social forms could no longer be maintained and each person would be forced to fend for himself. So the state of nature was not, for Hobbes, a condition out of which men had to climb, but one into which they might slide. The purpose of Hobbes's argument, then, is to dissuade social men from destroying the social order on which their lives and welfare depend.

It is for this reason that the famous description of the state of nature in *Leviathan*[3] becomes a litany of all the advantages men would lack without social organisation. Autochthonous men, 'sprung out of the earth, and suddenly, like mushrooms, and come to full maturity, without all kind of engagement to one another', as Hobbes in one place (De Cive, 117) describes the inhabitants of the state of nature, could not appreciate such considerations. But Hobbes knew that men in society wanted not only to live, but to live well and so he reminds them of those goods their lives would lack without social order. Nonetheless, since living itself is the necessary precondition of living well, it is on man's instinctive fear of death, that 'terrible enemy of nature' (Elements of Law, 71), that Hobbes rests his justification of government.[4] And so, he points out, while 'every man is desirous of what is good for him, and shuns what is evil'', they fear ''chiefly the chiefest of natural evils, which is death'.[5] Death itself is, however, inescapable. And consequently, the chief evil which it is practically possible for men to prevent is early, violent death.

Given this then, Hobbes's justification of government takes the form of what he calls a 'regulated train of thoughts' (EW, III, 13) where some strong desire provokes a chain of means-ends calculations. Since the potentially preventable evil which men most instinctively shun is early death, that which they most instinctively desire is to live a natural term. In anything like the state of nature, their chances of doing this would be, at best, very poor, because in that situation a war of all against all is inevitably generated. Since men by natural necessity try to preserve their lives, they have the right to do anything they think may preserve it including killing or enslaving anyone else. However, given that men are effectively equal when it comes to the ability to kill one another, for even the weakest can kill the strongest by stratagem, the war of all against all would be self-perpetuating. It could not be ended by victory for 'in this state the conqueror is subject to so much danger, as it were to be accounted a miracle, if any, even the most strong should close up his life with many years, and old age' (De Cive, 49). The means to the end of living a natural term is then for every one to give up his natural right to all things, thereby creating a sovereign entity strong enough to create and maintain order and hence provide security. Government is justified because it sharply reduces the possibility of an early, violent death.

Before we can answer the question of whether this line of justification can be applied to our current world situation, it is important to notice several features of the practice of justifying. First, strictly speaking, we always justify retrospectively or prospectively; that is, when we justify actions we are always referring to actions already done or actions we are contemplating doing. Secondly, we justify an act by showing that it is either in some sense good or innocent. Thirdly, we show an act to be good or innocent by demonstrating that the act either falls under or fails to violate, some generally accepted rule of behaviour or we may show that the results of the act in question are better than would be (or would have been) the case without the act or, in cases of justification by innocence, that the act would make (or made) no significant difference. The fourth and final point about the practice of justifying that we need to note here is that when we justify acts by showing that things would be better if the act were done, the person constructing the justification normally does this in terms of values that he or she actually holds. So by showing that the action maximises values actually held, the justifier ends with a motive for doing the act in question.

Now I say normally this is the case because it is possible for us to justify acts that we know are, in the present situation, impossible and it is also possible for us to work out justifications in terms of values we do not hold, as when we try to understand the puzzling actions of someone else. So in both these ways, justification can be theoretical rather than practical, in the sense of not providing us with motivations to act. But someone in normal circumstances who made a first person prospective justification in terms of ''it would be better if...'' and who then said, ''I think this act is justified, but I have no motivation to carry it out,'' would be saying something puzzling which would require explanation, perhaps in terms of logically irrelevant psychological factors such as extreme depression. Or, failing this, it would have to be taken as an expression indicating that the original justification was faulty in having overlooked some relevant factors which should have been considered and which effectively counterbalance those actually considered. In this latter case, the assertion of no motive to act is tantamount to denying that the act in question is in fact justified.

It seems clear that Hobbes's justification of government is meant to operate as a first person prospective justification, to be carried out by men in society imagining that they are individuals in a state of nature. Imagining themselves in such a condition, Hobbes believes, men would see that they would have the strongest possible motive for forming a government which could provide them with order and security. Hobbes assumed that members of society, having run this thought experiment, would transfer this reasoning to their own present social situation and conclude that they should accept any inconveniences of their present government rather than risk bringing about a state of nature in which their lives would be in danger. Hobbes's reasoned justification of government is intended to motivate men to peaceful compromise by invoking each individual's fear of early death.

In putting Hobbes's argument in this way I am taking it for granted that Hobbes thought of himself not as a detached theoretician of politics, but as an engaged actor in practical political life.[6] By creating what he took to be a science of politics he hoped to influence peoples' behaviour, to render them more willing to accept the inconveniences of government and to make them more peaceful. If we are to think about our own predicament in the spirit of Hobbes, we should ask whether Hobbes's justification of government will actually work; that is, will it actually provide human beings with motivating reasons to form a world government? Answering this question focuses our attention on human psychology. Here the important questions would seem to be: "Do human beings naturally fear death?" and, if they do, "Will that provide them with an overriding motivation for forming or accepting some effective form of world government?"

Though there are a few modern theorists who have held that the fear of death is a cultural construct,[7] the vast weight of authority supports Hobbes's view that humans naturally fear death. This dispute is probably not amenable to definitive resolution, but for my purposes it makes no difference, for I am going to argue that even if Hobbes is right and the fear of death is natural to humans, that in the vast majority of situations that fear in socialised humans is not sufficiently powerful to carry the justificational and motivational load Hobbes places on it.

Part of Hobbes's originality lay in denying the classical view that man was by nature a social animal. The outcome is that human beings are seen by Hobbes as being first and foremost individuals (Johnson 1982). These notions constitute an important advance in political thought. For now political arrangements are clearly seen as open to rational criticism and reconstruction and the central probblem of social life, the problem of mediating the inevitable tensions in social arrangements between the demands of group life and the needs and desires of individuals is brought into clear focus. What Hobbes importantly failed to notice, however, is the way in which the epistemological and characterological individuality he correctly attributes to human beings works together with their fear of death and other anxieties to cause them to create and adopt ideologically supported social identities. These group identities in turn often act not only to reduce or eliminate the fear of biological death in individuals but simultaneously to provide them with powerful motives for sacrificing their biological life.

As we have seen, Hobbes's justification for government, finds its natural environment in the hypothetical state of nature where men's lives are not only poor, nasty and brutish, but solitary and, in prospect, short. By hypothesis, in the state of nature men could not form social identities supported by ideologies. As they are solitary they can only think of themselves as individuals and it is as individuals that they must confront the likelihood of their biological death. In such a situation they could not mask this inevitable event from themselves by adopting a trans-individual ideological identity. So, from the point of view of the individual in the state of nature, submission to a government is justified because any government that can maintain order reduces the possibility of early death.

Within a social context, however, Hobbes's argument loses force. For, though the establishment of civil government can reduce the fear of early violent death, the fear of death itself remains to be dealt with. In societies humans demonstrate a nearly universal tendency to identify with one another on the basis of perceived traditional, ethnic, linguistic, cultural, racial or national likenesses and to then develop an ideology asserting and justifying the superiority of "us" over "them".[8] The more fervently the individual identifies with an ideological group, the more the group comes to be perceived as the bearer of values which will survive so long as the group survives. And, as the values of the group are perceived as superior to all others, they easily become thought of as "natural" and "eternal". Sinking one's individuality in the comforting identity of the group thus provides a potent method of overcoming the fear of death. Further, in providing meaning and significance to the individual's life, this identification also provides a powerful justification for dying. For if the ideological group is the bearer of eternal values, then one may justly die to preserve them. To the extent one has identified with the group, the less significant does one's own life seem unless it is an expression of the values of the group. And so, the less significant does one's own biological death come to seem. Indeed the best thing one may do with one's insignificant individual life is to sacrifice it heroically for the group and gain a kind of immortality. For so long as the values of the group survive, one has escaped death.[9]

In *De Cive* (p. 46), Hobbes noted that 'there are no wars so sharply waged as between sects of the same religion and factions of the same commonweal'. He attributes this to the damaged sense of individual self-esteem which occurs when one's views are gainsaid. Here Hobbes's emphasis on the individual misleads him. For someone who has adopted an ideological identity something much more serious than injured pride has occurred when my group divides. My very sense of who and what I am is threatened. And worse by traitors; people who once shared with me the correct interpretation of the world and the eternal values with which I identify. It is not just my pride that is hurt. My life as I conceive it is threatened. It is no wonder such battles are so ferocious.

The problem for Hobbes's justification of government then, is that a person who has adopted an ideological identity is no longer in a position to be motivated by a rational argument resting on the possibility of his own biolocigal death as he is more concerned with his psychological life and the preservation of the values around which it is structured and of which, indeed, it may primarily consist. For such persons Hobbes's arguments can have little if any force.

I would suggest, finally, that the modern world is typified by forces which propel people into ideological identifications. An ideology in George Bernard Shaw's felicitous phrase is 'something between a theory and a religion' (Eriksson 1960). Ideologies function by replacing the full complexity of the world with a simplified and highly schematised view of reality. By reducing the confusing complexity of the real world and placing what is left into an architectonic structure of values, ideologies clarify for the person his place in the world, ensure his value, and finally, and most importantly for problems of world peace, provide him with an explicit or implicit plan of action.

Ideologies with their power to simplify by structuring perceptions, of course, serve not only to reconcile men to their biological death, but to resolve other anxieties as well. Besides the anxieties generated since the end of the Second World War by the increasing possibility of an earth-encompassing nuclear holocaust, developments in economics, technology and communications have made it increasingly difficult for the person to maintain a sense of individual unity and integrity. The development of a truly international economic system has at the same time spread technological change ever more rapidly throughout the world. Modern communications not only force us to respond to events worldwide but spread ideas for change and action to the most remote corners of the world.

The result is that throughout the world traditional ways of life have been subjected to disruptive, disorganising forces.[10] Village life has been increasingly replaced by a world mass community where the cultural diversity characteristic of earlier times is gradually, though at an ever quickening pace, being flattened and homogenised into a world culture. The impact on individuals is disorienting to say the least. No longer can a person readily find his identity in a way of life that, if restricted in its options, was as natural as breathing, where he would live as his father lived and as his son would live after him. Paradoxically, as the diverse traditional ways of life are being worn away and replaced by a common world culture, the individual finds himself subject to a greatly increased and diversified number of cultural forces and stimuli. Though this presents the individual with a greater variety of opportunities and possibilities for ways of life than perhaps have ever before been available to humans, this variety is also confusing and frightening in its fastpaced complexity. The individual, deprived of the certainties of traditional ways and more or less forced into an unfamiliar and uncertain future, is strongly motivated to convert the traditional way of life into an ideology with which he can safely identify.[11] In the United States the two most recent manifestations of this tendency, in my opinion, have been the success of Reaganism and the (related) development of political evangelicalism.[12] In a variety of ways this process may be seen going on around the world as tribal, linguistic, sectarian and other groups clamor, and often go to war, for what they call freedom and independence, but which often is only the psychological security of relative simplicity.

With such powerful psychological forces at work, one can hardly be optimistic about the prospects for some workable world government. When an ideological identification has been adopted, a person is no longer in position to respond to reasoned accounts of possible dangers to his biological life. What is feared is destruction of the ideology which would constitute for the person a kind of psychological death, a death all too often 'harder to contemplate than biological death' (Frank 1968, 131). Where biological death is no longer the dominant fear of human beings, it would seem that no Hobbesian justification of government could occur. Unfortunately, it would appear that our contemporary world is one beset by forces rendering a Hobbesian justification for world government less and less likely and, though I regret such a pessimistic conclusion, any other effective reasoned justification.

Notes

1. References are to the following works and editions: *De Cive*, English version, ed. by H. Warrender, The Clarendon Press, Oxford 1983; *The Elements of Law Natural and Politic*, ed. by F. Tönnies, 2nd ed., Barnes and Noble, New York 1969; *Leviathan*, in *The English Works of Thomas Hobbes of Malmsbury*, Vol. III (abbreviated EW, III in references and footnotes), 2nd printing, Scientia Verlag, Aalen 1966.

2. *De Cive*, 46. (Spelling modernised in this and all further quotes.)

3. EW, Vol. III, 113. All references in this form are to the second reprinting (1966) of the Molesworth edition of *The English Works of Thomas Hobbes*.

4. *De Cive*, 47. The instinctiveness of the fear of death is indicated in the continuation of this passage: men fear death by a certain impulsion of nature, no less than that whereby a stone moves downward.

5. As we shall shortly see, in the state of nature, other men are the greatest danger anyone faces. So Hobbes concludes that 'the original of all great and lasting societies, consisted not in the fear they had towards one another, but in the mutual fear they had of each other.' (De Cive, 44).

6. This is increasingly evident as we move from Hobbes's earlier to his later political works, and is especially so in the *Leviathan*, which is highly rhetorical. This has recently been argued at length by Johnston 1986. See also my *'Leviathan's* Audience' forthcoming in a volume to issue from the Nante Conference of June 1987.

7. See Becker 1973, especially Chapter Two, "The Terror of Death", the best account of this debate with which I am familiar.

8. 'Ethnocentrism, the overvaluation of one's own group in comparison with other groups, especially those perceived as rivals, is virtually universal. Membership in a group is an integral part of an individual's concept of himself. The group's success is his success and its failures damage his self-confidence; its friends and enemies are also his. Many people's group identification is so much a part of their personal identity that they would rather die than be absorbed into an alien group (Frank 1968, 104. See *passim*. but esp. pp. 97-113).

9. 'An individual human life is a momentary flash of experience squeezed between two oblivions in a universe that appears indifferent to human existence... Since the full recognition of one's utter insignificance is intolerable, everyone has some way of shielding himself from the awful truth. Most people accomplish this by identifying with some enduring and larger group and, beyond this, by viewing their lives as being in the service of some more or less permanent abstraction...' (Frank 1968, 109) Curiously, Arnold Toynbee, in his survey of the ways in which people have dealt with death, missed this most common way. See Toynbee 1968, 59-94.

10. For a valuable study of this process in the United States see Wheelis 1958.

11. This process is similar in important ways to the identity crisis suffered by adolescents at that point where they are no longer willing or able to identify themselves as members of a family. For an interesting account of such crises which contains interesting reflection on ideological identities see Erikson 1960, pp. 37-87. For a recent study of the way in which such identifications were significant in the formation and life of nations see Smith and Brass 1985.

12. Perhaps the most tragic instance of this sort of development in the United States took place in the seventies, when the doors were open widest for blacks to move into the mainstream of American life. They failed to take full advantage of these opportunities, many of which have now disappeared. It is perhaps significant that it was at that time that the "black is beautiful" movement began. Alex Haley's *Roots* was published in 1974.

Hobbes and the Concept of International Law

Robinson A. Grover

Thomas Hobbes holds contradictory views concerning the state of nature applied to nations and the possibility of international law. On one hand, his complete neglect of the topic of international law makes it appear that he considers international law either uninteresting or useless or impossible. On the other hand, his constant references to nations being in a state of nature with regard to each other raise the obvious question: why shouldn't nations, like individuals, use reason and prudence to get out of this state of nature by appointing a "super-sovereign"? Curiously, Hobbes never retracts his claim that nations are in a state of nature towards each other, nor does he ever deal with the full implications of this claim.

Hobbes argues for the similarity of the state of nature between individuals and between nations in *De Corpore Politico* (1640), *De Cive* (1642) and *Leviathan* (1651).[1] In all cases his argument is a simple appeal to history and current events. He argues that forts, city walls, standing garrisons, and spies all prove the mutual suspicion and fear that nations have for each other, and he implies that this national fear is similar to the fear that individuals have for each other in the state of nature.

In fact, Hobbes could have also made a semantic argument as well, and one that would be completely consistent with his arguments about justice in the state of nature. This argument would be that international law is "an absurdity" since, by definition, there can be no law where there is no sovereign and, again by definition, *inter*-national law must be between separate nations which have no common sovereign. Therefore, "International Law" is a contradiction (an absurdity). What we have is either not law or it is not international (cf. Leviathan, Ch. 14).

So far, the thrust of Hobbes's position is clear: nations stand to each other as do individuals in the state of nature/war. But, at this point, Hobbes's analysis of nations in the state of nature is completely different from that of individuals in the state of nature. Hobbes goes on to assert that individuals do have a method of getting out of the state of nature despite their self-centered fears. This method involves mutual promises and the creation of a sovereign to enforce these promises. However, he says nothing about treaties between independent nations and about the creation of a supra-national sovereign to enforce such treaties. By this omission he gives the impression that there is no way out of the state of nature for individual nations.

So we have a paradox. Hobbes treats two similar states of nature differently. One leads to promises, the sovereign, and civil society. The other, apparently does not. Why not?

One obvious reason is to be found in the fact that Hobbes is a seventeenth century Englishman, and to Tudor and Stuart Englishmen an appeal to a supra-national sovereign would sound suspiciously like an appeal to the Pope or to the Holy Roman (Spanish) Emperor. As an Englishman, and particularly as an Englishman who spent all his life as a servant of one of the great Tudor families, even the hint of an appeal to such Catholic, imperial powers would be unthinkable. Sixteenth and seventeenth English history would set Hobbes's mind in the direction of national power and independence, not supra-national sovereignty.

This bias towards national sovereignty would be strengthened by the French and English Civil Wars. The great problem for Hobbes and for most of his contemporaries was not lack of international government but the lack of effective national government. The immediate political fact of anarchy or near anarchy in England focused his attention on national issues to the virtual exclusion of international ones.

However, giving historical reasons why Hobbes was primarily interested in national sovereignty and uninterested in international authority, is not sufficient. Indeed, the historical bias for his failure to discuss international law is a weakness and not a strength in his theory unless this bias is supported by philosophical arguments as well. Therefore, we must look to his philosophical account of the development of civil society to see if it can be applied to nations as well as to individuals.

The general problem for Hobbes, as for all contract theorists, is to explain why we always ought to keep our promises. Hobbes's contract theory rests on making a promise to refrain from doing certain acts in the future. The initial promise can be justified on selfish or prudential grounds. The subsequent keeping of the promise can usually be justified on the same selfish or prudential grounds. However, suppose that we later find that our reasoning was in error and that keeping the promise will be seriously disadvantageous to us. If we made a stupid promise, how can we reasonably argue that we must be twice stupid and keep it? Alternatively, suppose that circumstances have changed and our originally reasonable promise has become seriously disadvantageous. In a world without a coercive sovereign, am I not irrational to perform an act that I would never knowingly have promised to perform in these new circumstances? In short, can any contract theorist who tries to justify contractual obligation on self-interested grounds ever claim that we always have a (self-regarding) obligation to keep our contracts? To do so implies that keeping contracts is always in our best interest. This is a contingent, factual claim which cannot be established *a priori*. Moreover, it is a claim that our experience contradicts.

The most tempting answer to this contractual *conundrum* is that we must keep our promises or the sovereign will punish us. This is a bad answer. First, when we have only just made promises, there is no sovereign yet to enforce them. Second, it destroys the contractual nature of Hobbes's theory. If the justification (and not just the motive) for keeping our promises is our fear of the sovereign, then we have a legal positivist and not a contract theory. Even in *Leviathan*, where Hobbes comes closest to legal positivism, he discusses our obligation to keep promises as part of the law of nature and not as part of the rights of the sovereign.

Moreover, the answer that we must keep our promises or the sovereign will punish us is a bad answer philosophically because it confuses the reason that justifies our doing something with the causes that incites us to do it. Our fear of the sovereign's power may cause us to keep our promise, but that fear alone is not the justification for promise-keeping. The fact that Hobbes treats contracts and promise-keeping first and only then moves to the powers of the sovereign is clear proof that he was aware of this distinction.

This leaves us with three questions: First, does Hobbes think the state of nature between nations is the same as the state of nature between individual human beings? Second, is his justification for getting out of the state of nature between individuals adequate? That is, is Hobbes's argument about the obligation to keep our promises in a state of nature a good argument? Third, does this argument apply equally well to nations in the state of nature?

Hobbes argues that several conditions are always present in the state of nature which make it an undesirable state. Individuals, motivated by averice, fear, or pride, are always likely to attack each other. This analysis seems to be basically the same whether the individual is a natural person or an artificial person such as a sovereign or a state, However, there do seem to be some differences in emphasis. When he considers nations in a state of nature, Hobbes comes to emphasise fear more than the pride or averice.

In *De Corpore Politico*, Hobbes argues that vain-glory and appetite cause men to provoke each other or to encroach on each other. Fear is only mentioned as mutual fear caused by the competition for glory:

> Further, since men by natural passion are divers ways offensive one to another, every man thinking well of himself, and hating to see the same in others, they must needs provoke one another by words, and other signs of contempt and hatred, which are incident to all comparison, till at last they must determine the pre-eminence by strength and force of body. Moreover, considering that men's appetites carry them to one and the same end; which end sometimes can neither be enjoyed in common, nor divided, it followeth, that the stronger must enjoy it alone, and that it be decided by battle who is the stronger. And thus the greatest part of men, upon no assurance of odds, do nevertheless, through vanity, or comparison, or appetite, provoke the rest, that otherwise would be contented with equality. (De Corpore Politico, Ch. I, 4-5.)

There is very little discussion of the causes of war between nations. What little Hobbes says on the matter is part of his discussion of the duties of sovereign. These duties include avoiding unnecessary war:

> The last thing contained in that supreme law, *salus populi*, is their defense; and consisteth partly in the obedience and unity of the subjects, of which hath been already spoken, and in which consisteth the means of levying soldiers, and of having money, arms, ships, and fortified places in readiness for defense; and partly, in the avoiding of unnecessary wars. For such commonwealth, or such monarchs, as affect war for itself, that is to say, out of ambition, or of vain-glory, or that make account to revenge every little injury, or disgrace done by their neighbors, if they ruin not themselves, their fortune must be better than they have reason to expect. (De Corpore Politico, Ch. IX, 9.)

Again, the chief reason for war seems to be pride or vain-glory on the part of the sovereign. Fear may be there as well, but other than mentioning the need for money, armies, and forts of defense, Hobbes does not discuss any source of conflict beyond princely ambition for glory.

In *De Cive* he sums up his analysis of why human beings enter into society: 'All society therefore is either for gain, or for glory' (De Cive, Ch. I, 2). It is only with section 3 of Chapter I that he goes on to discuss fear, moreover in sections 4-6 he returns again to 'vain-glory' and 'appetite' as the worst and 'most frequent reason why men desire to hurt each other' (De Cive, Ch. I, 6). Fear of a pre-emptive attack is not mentioned. However, when discussing nations in the state of nature, he stresses the need for security rather than pride or gain:

> There are two things necessary for the people's defence; to be warned and to be forearmed. For the state of commonwealths considered in themselves, is natural, that is to say, hostile. Neither if they cease from

82

fighting, is it therefore to be called peace; but rather a breathing time, in which one enemy observing the motion and countenance of the other, values his security not according to the pacts, but the forces and counsels of his adversary. And this by natural right, as hath been showed in chap. II. art. 11, from this, that contracts are invalid in the state of nature, as oft as any just fear doth intervene. (De Cive, Ch. III, 7.)

On this basis Hobbes goes on to argue that the use of spies, a war treasury and a standing army are essential steps for any sovereign:

We must therefore, for fear of war, in time of peace hoard up good sums, if we intend the safety of the commonwealth. Since therefore it necessarily belongs to rulers, for the subjects' safety to discover the enemy's counsel, to keep garrisons, and to have money in continual readiness; and that princes are, by the law of nature, bound to use their whole endeavour in procuring the welfare of their subjects: it follows, that it is not only lawful for them to send out spies, to maintain soldiers, to build forts, and to require monies for these purposes; but also not to do thus is unlawful.

To which also may be added, whatsoever shall seem to conduce to the lessening of the power of foreigners whom they suspect, whether by slight or force. For rulers are bound according to their power to prevent the evils they suspect; lest peradventure they may happen through their negligence. (De Cive, Ch. XIII, 8.)

In *De Cive* Hobbes explicity puts nations in a state of war with each other, but he cites only fear as a cause of this state of war. When he discusses human beings he puts more emphasis on pride or greed than on fear as a cause of war.

In a footnote to *De Cive* added five years later in 1647 Hobbes makes an interesting, detailed analysis of what he means by fear:

I comprehend in this word fear, a certain foresight of future evil; neither do I conceive flight the sole property of fear, but to distrust, suspect, take heed, provide so that they may not fear, is also incident to the fearful. They go to sleep, shut their doors; they who travel, carry their swords with them, because they fear thieves. Kingdoms guard their coasts and frontiers with forts and castles; cities are compact with walls, and all for fear of neighbouring kingdoms and towns; even the strongest armies, and most accomplished for fight, yet sometimes parley for peace, as fearing each other's power, and lest they might be overcome. (De Cive, Ch. I, 2, footnote.)

From this time onward "fear" assumes a much more prominent and a much more positive function in Hobbes's thought. Correspondingly, the Renaissance or Elizabethan concepts of pride and glory became less important. In *Leviathan* Hobbes cites his famous three 'causes of quarrel: first, competition; secondly, diffidence; thirdly, glory' (Ch. XIII). It is noteworthy that here the stress is on fear rather than ambition or glory as the cause of war.

Curiously, Hobbes had very little to say about nations in a state of war in *Leviathan*. One passage on the subject is also from Chapter XIII:

But though there had never been any time wherein particular men were in a condition of war one against another, yet in all times kings and persons of sovereign authority, because of their independency, are in continual jealousies and in the state and posture of gladiators, having their weapons pointing and their eyes fixed on one another — that is, their forts, garrisons, and guns upon the frontiers of their kingdoms, and continual spies upon their neighbors — which is a posture of war. But because they uphold thereby the industry of their subjects, there does not follow from it that misery which accompanies the liberty of particular men.

What is interesting here is that Hobbes simply asserts that nations stand in a posture of war toward each other, but he does not give a specific reason why this is so. Second, he asserts that although this is a state of war, it is not as serious to the individual citizen as internal civil war would be. Moreover, he does not mention the duty to avoid unnecessary wars as a specific duty of the sovereign as he does in *De Cive* (Leviathan, Ch. XXX).

Therefore, it seems that there is a slight evolution of Hobbes's thought on the state of war in these three works. The evolution takes two forms. First, Hobbes goes from what could be called a Renaissance view of man which emphasises pride and ambition to what could be called a modern view which stresses man's fearful nature.[2] Secondly, he seems to suggest a distinction between harmful and harmless states of war or states of nature. He never drops his claim that nations are inherently in a state of war with each other, but he does come to argue that this is not so serious in the case of nations (McPherson 1962, 104.) The reason he gives for this argument is that states at war with other states nevertheless 'upheld the industry of their subjects'. This sounds very like the claim of some modern historians that warfare, or at least the preparation of warfare, has been one of the chief spurs to modern economic development (cf. McNeill 1982). Hobbes's claim is more modest: that preparation for war does not harm economic development. Nevertheless, it is an interesting insight for a political thinker at the very beginning of the modern era.

Since Hobbes clearly believes that nations as well as individuals are in a state of nature regarding each other, what are his arguments about getting out of the state of nature? These arguments all depend on proving that we have an obligation to keep our promises in the state of nature. The sovereign obliges us to keep our promises by supplying the necessary motivation, but the source of our obligation comes from the fact that keeping promises (such as our promise not to attack others unprovoked) is always justified. Hobbes gives four arguments that are intended to justify the proposition that we should always keep our promises.

First he argues that there are limiting conditions that invalidate many of promises that we might be inclined to break. Specifically, a promise not to defend our lives is invalid. 'A covenant not to defend myself from force is always void.' 'A covenant to accuse oneself, without assurance of pardon, is likewise invalid.' Since this class of promises is always invalid, the resulting obligation will be null. Therefore, these promises, which we would have an overwhelming temptation to break, are invalid. Similarly, prior promises invalidate later promises. This means that we can never be caught on the fork of two valid, contradictory promises. Finally, we must have some sign of assent from the party with whom we contract. Therefore, we can not make promises to animals or to God. However, we can make unilateral vows (Leviathan, Ch. XIV).

The effect of these limitations on the use of promises is to eliminate some categories of promises that would be difficult or impossible to justify on prudential grounds. The invalidity of promises to abstain from self-defence is the most obvious example. However, these limitations on promises are more a matter of logical form than content. They do not eliminate all difficult cases.

Second, Hobbes argues that to promise to do a thing and then to fail to do it is a contradiction:

> He who through weakness of mind does nor omits that which before he had by contract promised not to do or omit, commits an injury, and falls into no less a contradiction than be in the schools is reduced to an absurdity. (De Cive, Ch. III, 3.)

This is not a very good argument. First, it is not strictly true, because a contradiction arises when a proposition and its negation are asserted at the same time. In the case of broken promises, we have a promise and an act, not a proposition and its negation. Moreover, the promise and the promise-breaking happen at different times. Secondly, the defect in a contradiction is that it allows false propositions to be asserted as true. The defect in the broken promise is that it allows us to do something that we promised not to do. But what is wrong with that if the doing of the act aids in our self-preservation? After all, it is self-preservation, not truth, that is the goal of the original promise.

Third, in *Leviathan* Hobbes uses the argument that no rational person can break a promise and expect to be able to continue living in civil society. He makes a brief use of a similar sort of argument in *De Corpore Politico* when he argues that sovereigns who engage in unnecessary wars 'if they ruin not themselves, their fortune must be better then they have reason to expect' (De Corpore Politico, Ch. X, 9). In *Leviathan*, Hobbes adopts this argument from sovereigns in a state of nature back to individual human beings in a state of nature:

> He, therefore, that breaks his covenant, and consequently declares that he thinks he may with reason do so, cannot be received into any society that unite themselves for peace and defense, but by the error of them that receive him; nor, when he is received, be retained in it without seeing the danger of their error, which errors a man cannot reasonably reckon upon as the means of his security; and therefore if he be left or cast out of society he perishes and if he live in society, it is by the errors of other men,

which he could not foresee nor reckon upon, and consequently against the reason of his preservation. (Leviathan, Ch. XV.)

Again, this is not a very satisfactory argument because it tries to establish a universal proposition about promise-keeping on the basis of individual psychological or prudential reactions. Moreover, much of Hobbes's historical account in *Behemoth* is about individuals breaking their promises and expecting to get away with it. Many people in Hobbes's immediate experiences had broken their vows or oaths to the Stuarts or to the Commonwealth and had been forgiven, which makes his argument rather ineffective.

Finally, in *De Corpore Politico*, there are passages in which Hobbes appears to argue that universal obligation to keep our promises is based on an objective standard such as 'what all men by reason' understand to be beneficial, rather then 'what every man in his passion' calls beneficial:

> Every man by natural passion, calleth that good which pleaseth him for the present, or so far forth as he can foresee; and in like manner, that which displeaseth him, evil. And therefore he that foreseeth the whole way to his preservation, which is the end that every one by nature aimeth at, must also call it good, and the contrary evil. And this is that good and evil, which not every man in passion calleth so, but all men by reason. And therefore the fulfilling of these laws is good in reason, and the breaking of them evil. (De Corpore Politico, Ch. IV, 14.)

This appears to be an attempt to establish an objective rather than a subjective standard for deciding when to keep promises. The individual's subjective will, based on his passion of the moment will often tend to ignore the long-term effects of promise-breaking in favour of the short-term benefits. However, the appeal to all men relying on reason and not on individual emotion, provides a better, more objective standard. This argument is very interesting because of its shift away from Hobbes's usual subjective standard. But, as interesting as this shift may be, it is a difficult argument for Hobbes to sustain because it contradicts his doctrine of natural rights:

> Also, every man by right of nature is judge himself of the necessity of means and of the greatness of the danger. (De Corpore Politico, Ch. I, 8.)

Hobbes cannot consistently argue that all persons should be their own judges and also appeal to some universal, rational standard that judges us not by what we now think necessary, but of what "all men by reason" would think necessary. He will have to abandon either his doctrine about natural right or his tentative doctrine about the objective standard of good and evil.

In fact, Hobbes keeps his doctrines of natural rights; it re-appears in both *De Cive* and in *Leviathan*. Except for one footnote in *De Cive* (Ch. I, 10, footnote) nothing further is heard of Hobbes's suggestion of any standard of good or evil other than our individual judgement.

Therefore, none of the four arguments that Hobbes suggests to justify the claim that we ought always keep our promises is really successful. The argument about the invalidity of promises not to defend ourselves is excellent, but does not cover enough of the promises we are tempted to break. The argument about the self-contradiction of promise-breaking is wrong. The argument based on the suggestion of an objective standard of good and evil contradicts Hobbes's other, more important doctrines. Only the argument that we have no logical justification for expecting to be forgiven for promise-breaking has any real power. This is doubtless why Hobbes makes it the main argument to justify promise-keeping in *Leviathan*. But even this argument is defective because it turns on each individual making a rational analysis of the consequences of promise-keeping or promise-breaking each time that he or she is tempted to break a promise and each time coming up with the conclusion that in the long run promise-breaking won't pay. By Hobbes's own account, human beings are too weak and too emotional to make that calculation all the time. Nor are circumstances such that all promise-breaking will always be bad for the promise-breaker. Thomas Hobbes has not proven that we are always justified, on prudential grounds, in keeping our promises in a state of nature.

The situation then is that Hobbes's justification of promise-keeping is weak and he needs that justification to get individuals out of the state of nature and into civil society. Does this same problem apply to getting nations out of the state of nature and into civil society?

It appears that the same problem does apply. First, Hobbes argues that 'the law of nations, and the law of nature, is the same thing' (Leviathan, 342). In *De Cive* he argues in more detail for similar origins and similar nature of the law of nature that applies to individuals and the law of nations:

> Again, the natural law may be divided into that of men, which alone hath obtained the title of the law of nature, and that of cities, which may be called that of nations, but vulgarly it is termed the right of nations. The precepts of both are alike. (De Cive, Ch. XIV, 4.)

Since Hobbes asserts that natural law and the law of nations are the same, we could reasonably expect that any difficulties in one would also occur in the other. Hobbes does not discuss promise-breaking by nations directly, as he does promise-breaking by individuals, but the same problems are obviously present.

The argument that there are limiting conditions that invalidate many of the promises that we might be inclined to break is true for nations as it is for individuals. However, as with individuals, it does not exclude all foolish or dangerous treaties. A nation may be prohibited from making a treaty because an earlier treaty pre-empts the subject, but it can make a treaty that turns out to be against its self-interest to keep. If the law of nature and the law of nations are one, and if the law of nature obliges self-preservation, why should the destructive provisions of the treaty be kept? But if there is no justification for treaty-keeping beyond current self-interest, what is the use of making them at all?

Likewise, the absurdity of promise-making and promise-breaking is no better an argument for nations than it is for individuals. If breaking a treaty will preserve the country, the fact that promising and then reneging on the promise is "contradictory" is irrelevant for that country, just as it would be for an individual.

Likewise, the appeal to an objective standard of some sort will not work if each nation is expected to consult only its own judgement of its own interest. If the law of nature for individuals dictates that each individual is the sole judge of 'necessity of the means and the greatness of the danger', and if laws of nations are similar to laws of nature, then nations too must be the sole judge of their needs. And if they are to be sole judges in their own cause, they cannot appeal to some "objective" standard based on what all nations would agree was in that country's interest. The argument concerning individuals applies to nations as well.

Finally, the argument that a known promise-breaker will never be trusted to keep treaties will not work as a deterrent to treaty-breaking. First, nations have broken treaties and been allowed to make further treaties. Second, even if nations would always suffer, some nations under stress (like some individuals under stress) will act irrationally.

Granted then that Hobbes's justification for getting out of the state of nature is weak both for nations and for individuals, is the failure of his justification argument as serious in the case of nations as in the case of individuals? Probably not. Because of the limited effects of most international anarchy, Hobbes does not appear to think that the state of nature is as serious for nations as it is for individuals. International anarchy can still leave us with a strong national government to protect our interests. National anarchy (civil war) is bad because it affects us directly and adversely. International anarchy may actually benefit the nation by strengthening the citizens' motives to obey the sovereign and by strengthening the national economy. With luck, the adverse effects of international anarchy may never be felt by individuals.

The crucial difference in the two cases is the shielding effect of national institutions which interpose themselves between the international anarchy of sovereign nations and the solitary citizen. I suspect that Hobbes never wrote about the evils of the state of nature that exists between nations because he never thought that the evils were all that serious. And he never thought they were serious because he thought that the national state could and would maintain internal civic order despite the international state of nature in which it existed.

But, if Hobbes did implicitly rely on the nation to shield its citizens from the consequences of the international state of nature, this very device suggests two forceful arguments against all of Hobbes's political philosophy.

First, Hobbes consistently tries to eliminate all institutions that stand between the individual and the sovereign. Thus, the law and the church are made subordinate to the sovereign, while the family is made into a temporary grouping of individuals. But, if the analysis of this paper is correct, it is precisely the ability of the state to interpose itself between the individual and international anarchy that makes the lack of a super-national sovereign tolerable. If this mechanism (the interposition of the state) will work for the individual in one case, why not in other cases? Why not remedy the ordinary state of nature by interposing other institutions such as the law or the church or the family to mitigate the effects of the state of nature on ordinary individuals? Why always go directly and only to a national absolute sovereign?

Secondly, why insist that the first promise that we must make and keep is the one to give up our right of nature? This is the most important right we have and giving it up is the most difficult political act we can do. Psychologically it would be the last act to be performed by an individual, and then only after a long train of successful experiences of having others make and keep promises about events of lesser importance. And yet, Hobbes makes it the first act. Since Hobbes's brief analysis of the international state of nature implies that some states of nature are relatively tolerable, this suggests further that we can start to get out of the international state of nature by making partial treaties about items of lesser importance. We do not have to give up the right of national self-defence to some supra-national absolute sovereign because the state of nature that nations are in is not all that bad. We have the moral and practical space, Hobbes seems to think, to pause before we commit ourselves to a supra-national sovereignty.

But once again, if this argument works for nations in a state of nature with each other, why won't it work for individuals as well? Why can't both individuals and nations develop limited covenants on specific matters until they develop an effective, if limited, national and super-national sovereignty? In short, Hobbes has got himself back in a bind. If he argues that nations stand to each other in a state of nature as do individuals, and that individuals in a state of nature are in a wholly undesirable condition, then he should argue that nations in a state of nature are in that same undesirable condition. Any move Hobbes makes to argue that the condition is not all that undesirable for nations can only backfire because it can always be turned around and used to argue that the state of nature is not all that bad for individuals either.

In the long run, Hobbes chooses not to discuss the problem. Given the difficulties of his position, that is an understandable response. It is not an adequate philosophical solution.

Notes

1. The references are made to the following works and editions of Hobbes: *De Corpore Politico*, in R. A. Peters (ed.), *Man, Body, and Citizen, Selections from Hobbes's Writings*, Collier Books, New York 1962; *De Cive or The Citizen*, ed. by S. P. Lamprecht, Appleton-Century-Crofts, New York 1949; *Leviathan*, in *The English Works of Thomas Hobbes*, Vol. III, ed. by W. Molesworth, John Bohn, London 1839-1845.

2. Cf. Machiavelli's *The Prince*; or Shakespeare's *Henry V*.

Hobbes on International Relations

Tommy L. Lott

1. Introduction

Hobbes's name is frequently mentioned in discussions of international politics, but unfortunately his own remarks concerning international relations have been generally overlooked. (See, for instance, Beitz 1979; Cohen 1984; Kavka 1983; Schiller 1972.) Interpreters bent on applying Hobbes's doctrines to international relations tend to focus on his account of the state of nature, although usually without saying much about what he had in mind when he presented this idea. Hobbes's state of nature can be assimilated to several different paradigms, and, as some interpreters have noted, he seems to employ different conceptions of it for different purposes (Wernham 1965). He sometimes suggests that the state of nature is a presocial condition, such as the situation of "savages" in seventeenth century America, or the inhabitants of early Germany.[1] On this model of the state of nature we are to 'consider men as if but even now sprung out of the earth, and suddainly (like Mushromes) came to full maturity without all kinds of engagement to each other' (De Cive, Ch. VIII, sec. 1, 117). The chief characteristic of this paradigm is that humans are ruled largely by their passions. Hobbes seems to be only slightly committed to using this paradigm because his central model is based on his view of the dissolution of society during a civil war.[2] Because their condition is the result of the *removal* of government, on this dissolution model of the state of nature, agents are socialised, i.e. they are capable of being rational. This paradigm, more than any other, guides Hobbes's thinking about the grounds of political authority.

91

Interpreters have sometimes been led by their own emphasis on Hobbes's presocial paradigm to believe that his state of nature was only meant to be hypothetical, i.e., a construction derived from his account of the passions. (See e.g., Goldsmith 1966, Ch. 4; Johnson 1982, 42.) On this interpretation, his frequent references to certain facts about the world with regard to the state of nature are to be taken as nothing more than his drawing upon common experience to confirm his hypothesis regarding human nature. While this reading fares well with regard to Hobbes's presocial paradigm it fails to make clear how he intended his remarks regarding the state of nature to apply to international relations. If Hobbes's idea of the state of nature is to be understood strictly as a heuristic device that serves to make clear his contractarian justification of absolute sovereignty, then, in the case of international relations, it should similarly serve to make clear his contractarian justification of an absolute international sovereign. But in none of Hobbes's remarks regarding international relations does he indulge his argument for absolute sovereignty. Instead, we discover upon reading Hobbes that his international relations paradigm of the state of nature functions mainly to bolster up his argument for an absolute *national* sovereign. I propose to give an account of Hobbes's remarks on international relations that reconciles his political theory with his reluctance to state the case for an international sovereign.

2. The Law of Nations

Although civil war was Hobbes's favourite illustration of the state of nature, he sometimes uses the case of international relations to verify his claims regarding the warlike conditions that obtain in the state of nature (EW, Vol. III, 115 and 200). To the extent that there has never been a world government this model is similar to the presocial paradigm.[3] However, unlike either the presocial paradigm or the civil war paradigm, in the case of international relations, there does not even seem to be the likelihood of establishing a civil society (i.e. world government), yet Hobbes weakly suggests that when sovereigns follow the laws of nature the result will be peace among nations (EW, Vol. III, 342-3; De Cive, Preface, 29; De Cive, Ch. XIV, sec. 4, 171; EL, Part II, Ch. X, sec. 10, 190). But can Hobbes's remarks concerning war and peace be applied to the case of war between nations, as well as to the case of civil war?

In the case of civil war Hobbes maintained that there will not be a lasting peace without a sovereign to overawe all parties to the conflict. In the case of international relations, however, he seems to have believed that if there is peace it will be the result of the deterrent capabilities of sovereign states.[4] When we understand the purpose of Hobbes's political principles to be only to justify political authority in a domestic context, they seem inconsistent at times with his view of international relations. He has to fit into his political theory both the claim that there will be perpetual war, in his dispositional sense, in the state of nature, and the claim that, when the laws of nature are observed by everyone, peace will eventuate. The tension between these two claims is alleviated in the case of state government by his argument for absolute sovereignty. He never extends that argument, however, to the case of international relations to justify world government. This raises the question of whether Hobbes saw the two cases as entirely parallel.

Some of Hobbes's remarks indicate that he did think of the two cases as parallel. In *Leviathan* he claims:

> Concerning the offices of one sovereign to another, which are compre-
> hended in that law, which is commonly called the law of nations. I need
> not say anything in this place; because the law of nations, and the law of
> nature, is the same thing. And every sovereign hath the same right, in pro-
> curing the safety of his people, that any particular man can have, in procur-
> ing the safety of his own body. And the same law, that dictateth to men
> that have no civil government, what they ought to do, and what to avoid
> in regard of one another, dictateth the same to commonwealths...(EW, Vol.
> III, 342.)

Hobbes seems to speak here equally of both the law of nature and the right of nature. In other places he shifts the emphasis towards the right of nature (De Cive, Ch. XIV, sec. 4, 171). The reason Hobbes sometimes places greater em-phasis on the right of nature is because he believed that security is necessary for the *exercise* of the laws of nature and, since this is lacking in international affairs, sovereigns will be more inclined to exercise their right of nature. The law of nations will, under conditions of insecurity, in effect become more like the right of nature than the law of nature.

When we consider the right of nature in the international context it appears to be a skeptical doctrine that is amenable to the position of the fool. Hobbes alleges that the fool's skepticism derives from false principles. In a voice similar to the fool's he presents this erroneous reasoning as follows,

> ... justice is but a vain word: that whatsoever a man can get by his own
> industry, and hazard, is his own; that the practices of all nations cannot
> be unjust... (EW, Vol. III, 282.)

It is worth nothing that Hobbes admits here that nations practice injustice towards each other, although he wants to argue against the skepticism this fact implies. There is some evidence which suggests that, with regard to interna-tional relations, Hobbes may very well be committed to the skepticism he claims is grounded on false principles (Dialogue, p. 57; De Cive, Epistle 2, 24).

Hobbes did not believe that nations (i.e., sovereigns) will follow the laws of nature to any great extent.[5] Indeed, he saw the illicit behaviour of nations as an additional reason for subjects to more willingly obey their sovereign. A weakened commonwealth is vulnerable to an invading conqueror. Hence, absolute sovereignty resulting in domestic peace is required to strengthen a nations's ability to engage in war.

Given that in the case of international relations the state of nature will be a state of war, the fool's position can be sustained on Hobbes's principles which specify that when peace cannot be attained, the agent 'may seek and use all helps and advantages of war' (EW, Vol. III, 117). According to the laws of nature an agent is never required to give up her right to self-defence, and is only obligated *in foro interno* when it is unsafe to perform. Hence, any obligations incurred while endeavoring peace that jeopardise an agent's self-preservation are understood, by the right of defence, to be invalidated. The position of the fool accords with these stipulations such that the skepticism Hobbes attributes to that position seems to be implicit in his own view. The skeptic is claiming that, in general, one should only keep covenants when it is advantageous to do so, and, in particular, that if one can escape detection, or better advance one's interests through force or fraud, then one can justifiably do that also.

On Hobbes's view (Leviathan, Ch. XIII) force and fraud are justified under conditions of war. When Hobbes's fool questions whether prudence dictates covenant-breaking the point is stated in terms which appear to be an offer Hobbes cannot refuse:

> ... he questioneth, whether injustice... may not sometimes stand with that reason, which dictateth to every man his own good; and particularly then, when it conduceth to such a benefit, as shall put a man in a condition, to neglect not only the dispraise, and revilings, but also the power of other men. (EW, Vol. III, 132.)

In his example of the usurping heir Hobbes argues against the agent seeking the advantage of dominance by pointing out that such actions only invite similar conduct by others. He does not, however, confront the possibility that, in international relations, the quest for primary could prove to be the best strategy of defence.[6] If covenant-breaking proved to be advantageous in this particular way, Hobbes does not have any ground on which to condemn it. His endorsement of force and fraud under conditions of war suggests that, in the case of international relations, he must also endorse covenant-breaking that will enable one nation to gain dominion over another. Such covenant-breaking would then be justified by the right of nature.

Given the pervasive influence of his doctrine concerning the right of nature it is rather surprising that Hobbes even raises the question of whether prudence dictates violating an agreement when doing so is advantageous. Although he seems to recommend against the use of both force and fraud when he tells us that in the state of nature 'there is no man who can hope by his own strength, or wit, to defend himself from destruction', his exchange with the fool is directed primarily at those who would take his principles to allow the practice of deceit (EW, Vol. III, 133). Indeed, Hobbes was prone to condemn the fool for wanting to make the case for the use of fraud. If, however, by the right of nature, a person always has an inalienable right to use force to defend herself against force, why wouldn't she also have an inalienable right to use fraud to defend herself?

3. Can Sovereigns Seek International Peace?

With regard to international relations Hobbes's view of the role of force and fraud is far from clear. It is noteworthy that in some of his remarks regarding the state of nature Hobbes makes an important distinction between the international and domestic contexts. The exchange between his philosopher and the lawyer in the *Dialogue* gives us a vivid display of how he wanted to distinguish them:

> Ph. What hope then is there of a constant Peace in any Nation, or between one Nation, and another?
> La. You are not to expect such a Peace between two Nations, because there is no Common Power in this World to punish their Injustice: mutual fear may keep them quiet for a time, but upon every visible advantage they will invade one another, and the most visible advantage is then, when the one Nation is obedient to their King, and the other not... (Dialogue, 57.)

Hobbes's claim that international peace is not to be expected amounts to an acknowledgement that the situation of international relations will always be a state of nature. When he shifts his focus to the fact that a nation that has civil disorder is at a disadvantage *vis-a-vis* other nations that have domestic peace his aim is to connect the sovereign's protection with the subject's obedience (EW, Vol. I, xiii).

Although there can be temporary leagues among nations, in which case sovereigns can enter into defence pacts with each other, Hobbes maintained that there can be no expectation of a *constant* peace between nations. Readers must be wary of Hobbes's use of the term ''peace,'' for he uses it almost exclusively with reference to the sovereign's duty to prevent civil strife.[7] Hence, when he claims that there can be no expectation of a constant peace between nations his point seems to have been that there can be no expectation of a world government. The sovereign's duty in international affairs is mainly to see that the commonwealth is properly defended against foreign enemies.

Because international relations is a permanent state of nature involving frequent hostility, nations have an absolute liberty to pursue their self-interest (De Cive, Ch. XIII, sec. 13, 163; EW, Vol. III, 201). Given the tendency of nations to behave like arrant wolves toward each other, sovereigns are obligated by natural law to do 'whatsoever shall seeme to conduce to the lesning of the power of forreigners whom they suspect, whether by sleight, or force' (De Cive, Ch. XIII, sec. 9, 160).[8] Here Hobbes's view of international relations seems to accord with his *Leviathan* (Ch. XIII) account of the state of nature, for he speaks of the sovereign's use of force and fraud to defend the state against potential foreign enemies. One important difference between the behaviour of sovereigns in international affairs and individuals in the state of nature, however, is that a sovereign is *obligated* to provide for the defence of the commonwealth, whereas individuals simply have a right to defend themselves. The question this raises is whether the special duty sovereigns have to defend the commonwealth constrains their actions with regard to seeking peace.

Hobbes moves very quickly from speaking in terms of the sovereign's duty to provide defence and security, in the sense of subjects 'being preserved from forraign and civil warres', to speaking in terms of the sovereign's duty to provide for the welfare and benefit of subjects. He lays great stress on the fact that the chief difference between the state of nature in the domestic and international contexts is that the safety of subjects under domestic government renders the international situation less miserable (EW, Vol. III, 115; De Cive, Ch. XIII, sec. 6, 159). His notion of safety includes, in addition to 'bare preservation', the acquisition of wealth (EW, Vol. III, 322). This rather expanded notion of safety, which he claims a sovereign is obligated by the law of nature to provide, entitles a sovereign to invade, conquer and colonise other nations.[9]

In his description of the generation of a commonwealth in the presocial state of nature Hobbes shows little reluctance to endorse the use of force and fraud. His *Leviathan* version of this account yields a fairly explicit anthropology:

> And as small families did then; so now do cities and kingdoms which are but greater families, for their own security, enlarge their dominions, upon all pretences of danger, and fear of invasion, or assistance that may be given to invaders, and endeavour as much as they can, to subdue, or weaken their neighbors, by open force, and secret arts, for want of other caution, justly; and are remembered for it in after ages with honour. (EW, Vol. III, 154.)

Hobbes was aware of the possibility that sovereigns could always justify invasion, conquest and colonialism on the pretense that such actions are a necessary pre-emptive measure required for defence. Moreover, he held, as a simple fact about human nature, that those sovereigns whose power is greatest have a restless desire to acquire more, by engaging in war and conquest, in order to assure their present power (EW, Vol. III, 86).

Hobbes's remarks concerning international relations do not always make clear the role of force and fraud in international affairs. Although he seems to have believed that the right of nature is absolute in the international context there is an important sense in which he also wanted to introduce certain limitations.

I have already noted that his reply to the fool is mainly an argument against the use of fraud.[10] I now want to similarly consider his doctrine regarding the validity of coerced contracts as an argument against the use of fraud.

In his discussion of the ransom case Hobbes maintains that agreements extorted by intimidation and threats are binding.[11] But Hobbes's claim that force and fraud are the cardinal virtues of war is at odds with his claim that extorted promises are valid, for it seems counterintuitive to allow a conqueror to use the threat of violence to gain dominion over a neighbouring state and not allow the vanquished sovereign to make a false promise to escape dominion. Hobbes even recommends promising, with the addition of oath-taking, as a remedy to a sovereign's need to use force against another sovereign (De Cive, Ch. V, sec. 15, 193). What seems to be urging Hobbes in this direction is the fact that his contractarian notion of obligation requires trust as a condition for performance. Hence, by assenting to be governed (i.e., choosing not to die) the vanquished *authorise* the dominion of the conqueror and thereby incur an obligation to obey her commands. Unlike the vanquished sovereign who is enslaved, or tortured, and who can by natural right do whatever is necessary to escape, once an agreement is made with the conqueror the vanquished sovereign must fulfil it:[12]

> ... if a weaker prince, make a disadvantageous peace with a stronger, for fear; he is bound to keep it; unless, as hath been said before, there ariseth some new, and just cause of fear, to renew the war. (EW, III, 126.)

One way to get Hobbes's claim that force and fraud are the cardinal virtues of war to fit with his claim that extorted promises are valid is to view his ransom case as the best illustration of his idea of the social contract. Hobbes acknowledges that sovereignty by conquest is widespread (EW, Vol. III, 706). He provides a characterisation of an historical process of small groups of families growing into larger kingdoms as an account of the origin of the state. Force is given a central role to play in this account and sovereignty by conquest (and in some cases even sovereignty by rebellion) are treated simply as extensions of the historical process Hobbes describes.[13]

If Hobbes's law of nations is tantamount to the sovereign's exercise of the right of nature, given his assessment of the hostility and potential conflict in international relations, it would seem that a sovereign can never be obligated to pursue peace with other nations, whenever this poses a threat to national security. Rather, the first law of nature obligates sovereigns to adopt a defensive posture toward each other. Hobbes's conflation of the notions of security (of safety) and self-interest could very well be understood to entitle sovereigns to seek hegemony as a defensive strategy against any *potential* threats to national security. Hence, according to Hobbes's political principles, international sovereignty by conquest could eventually produce a world government. (See EW, Vol. III, 335; cf. Polin 1972, 298; Pangle 1976, 339.)

Notes

1. The Elements of Law (EL), Part I, Ch. XIV, sec. 12, 73; De Cive (DC), Ch, I, sec. 8, 49; Leviathan (EW, Vol. III), pp. 114 and 224. The references are made to the following editions: *De Cive*, ed. by H. Warrender, Clarendon Press, Oxford 1983; *A Dialogue between a Philosopher and a Student of the Common Laws of England*, by J. Cropsey, University of Chicago Press, Chicago 1971; *The Elements of Law*, ed. by F. Tönnies, Barnes and Noble, New York 1969; *Leviathan*, in *The English Works of Thomas Hobbes*, Vol. III, ed. by W. Molesworth, John Bohn, London 1841; *The Questions Concerning Liberty, Necessity, and Chance*, in EW, Vol. V., John Bohn, London 1841. Subsequent references to Hobbes's works will be given in parentheses in the text as follows (when appropriate), title, part number, chapter number, section number and page number.

2. See Hobbes's reply number XIV in *The Questions Concerning Liberty, Necessity, and Change*, in EW, Vol. V, 184.

3. Hobbes does not admit that a league of nations counts as world government because 'there is no human power established, to keep them all in awe' (EW, Vol. III, 223).

4. The deterrent capability of a particular state depends, of course, on the strength of its military, but also, according to Hobbes, on the extent to which it is free from civil discord. See J. Cropsey 1971, 57; and EW, Vol. III, 164, 166, 170 and 174.

5. Hobbes points out that 'in the warre of nation against nation a certain mean was wont to be observed' (De Cive, Ch. V, sec. 2, 86).

6. Hobbes claims that 'Nature gave a right to every man to secure himself by his own strength, and to invade a suspected neighbor, by way of prevention...' (EW, Vol. III, 276). See also EW, Vol. III, 88.

7. With regard to international relations Hobbes does sometimes speak of a 'peace between enemies' (EL, Part I, Ch. XV, sec. 13, 79) and a 'disadvantageous peace' (EW, Vol. III, 126), but upon close examination we can see that he is really speaking in terms of his dispositional sense of *war*. See especially EW, Vol. III, 666.

8. See also *De Cive*, Epistle, p. 24 and Ch. 13, 163-4.

9. Hobbes claims that it is a sin if the sovereign does not consult his experts before rashly making war and risking the safety of the commonwealth. He, nonetheless, maintains that 'Necessity and security are the principle justifications, before God, of beginning War' (Dialogue, 159).

10. In *Leviathan* XXX Hobbes reiterates his argument against the fool and recommends against the use of *either* force or fraud. His focus, however, is on the rebel who would violate faith (EW, Vol. III, 324).

11. See EL, Part I, Ch. xv, sec. 13, 79; De Cive, II, Ch. VIII, sec. 3, 118; EW, Vol. III, 189-90. Apparently this case (especially the prisoner of war example), as well as the image of the lion (force) and the fox (fraud), is an allusion to Cicero's *De Officiis*, pp. 43-45.

12. See EL, II, iii, 3, p. 128; De Cive, VIII, 3, p. 118; EW, Vol. III, 189-90.

13. Although Hobbes gave a contractarian justification of conquest by distinguishing the *motivation* for entering into an agreement from its *justification*, he, nonetheless expresses a moral concern about this practice when he tells us that 'there is scarce a commonwealth in the world whose beginnings can in conscience be justified' (EW, Vol. III, 706).

Force and Fraud

Gershon Weiler

Let me begin by following the advice of the late J.L. Austin. When asked for "tips" to get through the ordeal of schools, he said 'Above all, answer the question'. Well, having been set the question, whether world government is justifiable on Hobbesian principles, allow me to begin by a firm answer in the negative. It seems to me clear, beyond all reasonable doubt, that not only would Hobbes not have sanctioned a world-government, even under conditions of the present nuclear menace, but also that there is nothing in his doctrine to warrant, by derivation and inference, support for the opposing view.

I shall first state my thesis, as clearly as I can, and after that I shall offer textual and other arguments in its favour. When we speak of justification, at any rate within the context of Hobbesian politics, I think it is barely disputable that what is meant is nothing but rationality. I cannot think of any other meaning that could be attached to the notion of justification. Hobbes's resolute and pioneering confrontation of the pretensions of theological politics, to which no less than half of *Leviathan* is devoted, rules out any possible dissension from so linking justification and rationality. Taking this much for granted, our question is now reformulated to read, whether it is rational, in the context of Hobbesian political philosophy, to demand of a nation-state to transfer its natural rights to a world-government, in a way that is analogous to the rational demand made upon individuals that they renounce their natural rights in favour of a law-making, and thus peace-assuring, municipal sovereign.

Individuals deal with each other, in the insecure Hobbesian state of nature, by relying, as occasion and opportunity allow or suggest, upon the twin devices

99

of force and fraud. Hobbes's argument in favour of sovereignty rests upon showing that, on balance and in the long run, the objectives pursued by force and fraud, chief among these being security, can be better attained by abandoning the road of force and fraud in favour of civil law. In terms of international relations this translates into the question, whether it is the case that a nation state which wishes to behave rationally, ought to abandon its natural right to use force and fraud for the sake of making itself secure. Force and fraud, in the language of international politics, are called war and diplomacy. These are the two usual ways in which states relate to each other (Aron 1966).

A world-government, if it means anything, means at least the renouncing of war and diplomacy. For indeed, if there were a world-government, then there would be no entities left to conduct war or to engage in diplomacy. My negative thesis, then, asserts that it is not true that a nation, any nation, that wishes to act rationally, ought ever to give up its natural rights to the use of force and fraud to some other body. The qualification of *any* nation is, of course, highly important, for it is always possible to find some nation-states which would find it convenient if there existed a world-government, because they could reasonably expect to dominate it and exploit it for their own interests. This, however, would fall very short of the standards set by the Hobbesian theory of individuals, which, squarely and forcefully, rests upon the assumption of the equality of men. Indeed, Hobbes begins Chapter XIII of *Leviathan*, where the first step toward a rational political condition is taken, by the grand pronouncement, 'Nature has made men so equal...'

Nations, of course, are not at all equal in power, and therefore, this should make us wary of any possible thesis that asserts or entails that it could rational for a nation to renounce its natural rights, and what is often taken as equivalent with this, that it is (always) irrational for a nation to resort to force. There is a large dose of healthy utilitarianism in Hobbes's ideas about rationality: it clearly follows from acting rationally that one's situation is improved. The Fundamental Law of Nature makes this abundantly clear:[1]

> And consequently it is a precept, or generall rule of Reason, *That every man, ought to endeavour Peace, as farre as he has hope of obtaining it; and when he cannot obtain it, that he may seek, and use, all helps, and advantages of Warre*. The first branch of which Rule, containeth the first, and Fundamentall Law of Nature; which is, *to seek Peace, and follow it*. The Second, the summe of the Right of Nature; which is, *By all means we can, to defend our selves*.

The statement could not be clearer: *under some conditions* the most rational thing for a person is to use all the means of violence at his disposal. The sovereign's chief role is to affect a change in the possibility for these conditions. But in the absence of such a change, in a state of nature, the use of force remains eminently rational. The question, translated again into the idiom of international relations, becomes whether it is true that there are some conditions conceivable in which it would be irrational *for each and every nation* to resort to war. Surely, this could be the case only if it were demonstrably true of some condition that, within its context, the use of force would make the situation worse for *each and every* nation, while refraining from it, by implication, would make it indisputably better. The core of the argument for the negative thesis is that not only is such a demonstration not available but, on the contrary, the very opposite is true. To put it differently: I am arguing that, unless things in the world change radically, there can be no conditions in which it would be rational for *all* states to give up their liberty and compact a world-government.

Now I would like to make here a point that is of some, though not decisive, significance for our topic. I think that Hobbes was wrong when he described the condition 'where every man is Enemy to every man' (Leviathan, Ch. XIII, 96), as a condition of war. This cannot be considered right, precisely on the basis of Hobbes's definition, in the same place; '...the nature of War, consisteth not in actual fighting but in the known disposition thereto, during all the time there is no assurance to the contrary'. Clearly, the condition indicated is not that of war in the ordinary, reasonable sense but of an unstructured violence which is never far from the surface and is thus likely to erupt at any time. War, by contrast, is a highly structured affair (and there is no need to go to Clausewitz for support on this point). Indeed, it makes sense to argue that, historically speaking, political sovereignty grew from the needs of war, from just the necessity to organise, in an effective way, large numbers of people for a single purpose. The Hobbesian state of nature has nothing of this and, beyond bare necessities, is characterised by a typical randomness of ends, to use an expression of Talcott Parsons (1968, 59-60). These are pursued by uncoordinated individuals who are capable of calculation. The point is of some importance in the light of what has been said before. If it is rational *not* to give up one's capability of using ''plain'' violence as an individual, unless some conditions are first satisfied, how much more rational it must be not to renounce the right of *war* in the case of nations which, by the very fact of being nations, already provide a measure of security to the individuals which compose them.

Indeed, a great deal, even if not all, that is of importance here turns upon and depends on our understanding correctly the true nature of the relationship that exists in Hobbes between individuals and groups, say nations organised in states. It is not for nothing that the first of the four parts of Leviathan is entitled *Of Man*. For Man is indeed both the matter and artificer of the state, as it is so succinctly put in the programmatic introduction to *Leviathan*. Hobbes derives all *oughts* of political science from the *is* of human nature. Contrary to the premodern tradition which attached no political meaning to the notions of *anthropos* or *homo*, Hobbes's theory of politics is naturalistic precisely because it

101

is built upon a true political knowledge from the implications of human nature. For Hobbes, the fact that someone is human is politically significant because this very humanity answers the twin questions: who is politics *for* and who *institutes* political arrangements. In this sense man is both the matter and artificer of politics. Humanity — the fact of being a human being — is *status*-generating.

One of the questions we must note, and which needs to be answered in any attempt to establish a parallel between the rationality of municipal sovereignty and that of a would-be world-government, is whether nations are natural, or at least natural-like, in the *status*-generating sense in which Hobbes says individuals are. The question is whether the opening words of the Fundamental Law of nature, quoted above, *'That every man...'*, can be transposed, *salva veritate*, into the idiom of international relations. It is a further part of the negative thesis of this paper that such transposition is not possible. Nations or states are not natural entities like human individuals. We need here to take seriously the repeated *dictum* of Hobbes that the Leviathan is *artificial*. The artifice of the state is rationally justifiable because it rests upon something which is *not* artificial but natural, *viz.*, human individuality and, especially in its chief characteristic to preserve itself and to prosper. Consequently, an artifice like a world-government which rests only upon entities that are themselves artificial, could have, at best, only a much lower possibility of justification.

To establish that nations are not at all like individuals, not like *every man*, we must turn to the passage in *Leviathan* which, because its unique reference to Hobbes's conception of international relations, I regard as the major source for any possibly acceptable answer to the question. The passage occurs at the very end of Chapter XXX (*Office of the Sovereign Representative*). The chapter is not a little problematic on account of its attribution of duties to the sovereign who is meant to be, on Hobbes's own theory, nothing less than *legibus solutus* (Weiler 1970). This passage, to which I shall henceforth refer as the *Leviathan*-passage, deals with the office, *viz.* obligations, of the sovereign in international affairs: and, it might well be that Hobbes's brevity here suggests a discomfort he may have felt by disputing, even if obliquely, royal prerogative of war and peace. Doctrinally, this was enunciated, for example, by James I, in his eloquent *Speech in the Star Chamber* in 1616, where he declared that 'as for the absolute Prerogative of the Crowne, that is no Subject for the tongue of a lawyer, nor is it lawful to be disputed' (James I, 332-3; see also Wormuth 1939). By making war and peace between sovereign princes subject to rational constraints, Hobbes removed them, in one single passage, from among the putative mysteries of state, those *arcana imperii*, which James I regarded as his private reserve. Here is the *Leviathan*-passage:[2]

> Concerning the Offices of one Soveraign to another, which are comprehended in that Law, which is commonly called the *Law of Nations*, I

need not say any thing in this place; because the Law of Nations, and the Law of Nature, is the same thing. And every Soveraign hath the same Right, in procuring the safety of his People, that any particular man can have, in procuring the safety of his own Body. And the same Law, that dictateth to men that have no Civil Government, what they ought to do, and what to avoyd in regard of one another, dictateth the same to Commonwealths, that is, to the Consciences of Soveraign Princes, and Soveraign Assemblies; there being no Court of Naturall Justice, but in the Conscience onely; where not Man, but God raigneth; whose Lawes, (such of them as oblige all Mankind,) in respect of God, as he is the Author of Nature, are *Naturall*; and in respect of the same God, as he is King of Kings, are *Lawes*. But of the Kingdome of God, as King of Kings, and as King also of a peculiar People, I shall speak in the rest of this discourse.

This is a curious passage. On the one hand, the reader might well say that Hobbes reaffirms the absolutist doctrine regarding international relations. There is no judge in these matters but the conscience of the God-fearing prince, a piece of fiction to which Hobbes seems to have been rather badly addicted, if one is to take at face-value the testimony of his *Behemoth*: 'Curia enim justititae naturalis prater conscientiam nulla est, quam regit solus Deus...'[3]

All the same the reference to conscience and the practical advice as to what to do and what not to do, bring war and peace into the orbit of ordinary human affairs where reason does have a decisive say. Indeed, the advice to the sovereign not to make unnecessary wars readily echoes the doctrine of Grotius in his *De jure Belli et Pacis* (1625). Since, although only the sovereign can make war, yet even he is in need of justification for making it, *viz.* either to prevent the invasion of his territory and/or the rights of his subjects or in order to punish such invasions or violations perpetrated in the past. The whole of Chapter XXX of *Leviathan*, which advises the sovereign to make only laws that are good, necessary and perspicuous, thus ends with the admonition to the sovereign not to make unnecessary wars. Of course, the decision about the particular cases is left solely to the conscientious deliberations of the sovereign.

In matters that concern the relations between sovereigns, there are no rules, no theorems suggested by reason, but only judgements which, by definition, involve an element of uncertainty. The idea of a "scientific" politics has always been highly problematic, so the notion of a scientific *international* politics is bound to be even more so. On this aspect of the *Leviathan*-passage, Goldsmith rightly comments 'There are no absolutely valid rules, either moral or prudential, for conducting foreign policy'.[4]

Before discussing the *Leviathan*-passage in more detail, I wish to quote a few more passages from Hobbes, the import of all of which being that the most basic characteristc of international relations is extreme insecurity:

We see all countries, though they be at peace with their neighbours, yet guarding their frontiers with armed men, their towns with walls and ports and keeping constant watches. To what purpose is all this, if there be no fear of the neighbouring power. (EW, Vol. II, p. 15.)

And here is another passage to the same purpose, in more detail:

> The last thing contained in that supreme (i.e. natural) law, *salus populi*, is their defence; and consisteth partly in the obedience and unity of the subjects... and in which consisteth the means of levying soldiers, and of having money, arms, ships, and fortified places in readiness for defence; and partly, in the avoiding of unnecessary wars. For such commonwealths, or such monarchs, as affect war for itself, that is to say, out of ambition, or of vainglory, or that make account to revenge every little injury, or disgrace done by their neighbours, if they ruin not themselves, their fortune must be better than they have reason to expect. (EW, Vol. IV, 219-20.)

This passage again relates to international affairs, giving the impression that relations between sovereigns exercised Hobbes's mind only as afterthoughts in rounding off what he had to say about the correct structure of a municipal political system (cf. EW, Vol. IV, 228).

By this roundabout tour we come back to the Fundamental Law of Nature quoted above and to a need for a thorough examination of what is involved in Hobbes's identification of *jus naturale* with *jus gentium*. This is our next task and once it is properly executed, it will also be clear why there can be no justification of world-government on Hobbesian grounds. In order to get the foundations of this examination well and truly laid, it is, however, necessary to begin with Hobbes's classic distinction between *lex* and *jus*, which occurs in a passage at the opening of Chapter XIV of *Leviathan*. It comes just before, and as an introduction to, the Fundamental Law of Nature:

> A LAW OF NATURE, (*Lex Naturalis*,) is a Precept, or generall Rule, found out by Reason, by which a man is forbidden to do, that, which is destructive of his life, or taketh away the means of preserving the same; and to omit, that, by which he thinketh it may be best preserved. For though they that speak of this subject, use to confound *Jus*, and *Lex, Right* and *Law*; yet they ought to be distinguished; because RIGHT, consisteth in liberty to do, or to forbeare; Whereas LAW, determineth, and bindeth to one of them: so that Law, and Right, differ as much, as Obligation, and Liberty; which in one and the same matter are inconsistent. (Leviathan, Ch. XIV, 99.)

The above passage ought to be read in the light of the lines closing Chapter XV, where the meaning of law is further elucidated:

> These dictates of Reason, men use to call by the name of Lawes; but improperly: for they are but Conclusions, or Theoremes concerning what conduceth to the conservation and defence of themselves; whereas Law, properly is the word of him, that by right hath command over others. But yet if we consider the same Theoremes, as delivered in the word of God, that by right commandeth all things; then are they properly called Lawes. (Leviathan, Ch. XV, 122-3.)

Now the plain meaning of all this seems simple enough. The law of nature is the instruction that nature herself gives us to guide our conduct through the medium of reason. The object of this instruction is the preservation of human beings. In the light of this, by way of centre-piece of our whole discussion, our next question must be: can one derive from Hobbes a theorem about the supreme reasonability of a world-government as the best means to preserve ourselves. Needless to say, our question is *not* whether the commands of a world-state, if already in existence, would be law, for it obviously would be. However, to derive from this that the world-state itself would be rational is to beg the question. For our question is no less than whether there *ought* to be a world-state; a world-government where the *ought* of law is to be derived from its powerful *is*. To put the same slightly differently, I am asking whether it can be argued that, given the present condition of the world, it follows from the text of Hobbes that the establishment of a world-government would be in accordance with, and prescribed by, the Fundamental Law of Nature. I believe, it is readily seen that in the Fundamental Law of Nature the transition from *jus* to *lex* is immanent and that the Fundamental Law executes the transition from *is* to *ought*. The condition in which *every man* is formally though not actually unlimited in every way, suggests, if not to every man, at least to the *rational* man, that something is radically wrong with this condition: no man is limited by anything except by his actual capacity to grab whatever he wants. This perception, clear to all in the course of experience, is how peace *follows* from war; this is how from the unbridled *jus naturale* emerges the restraining rationality of the *lex naturale*. Does this natural inference obtain with respect to world-government, given the Hobbesian thesis, which is crucial here, *viz.* that *jus naturale* is the same as *jus gentium*?

It is worth noting that Hobbes's identification of the two kinds of *jus*, while not uncontroversial, is well founded in tradition. Tradition provided Hobbes with a choice of possible interpretations here and he chose, one presumes, the one that suited his general theory best (d'Entraves 1951, 26). The most likely explanation for his adoption, then, of this interpretation is that according to it *natural* is to be understood as *normal*, and, in this meaning, natural law is just a rule 'corresponding to the nature of things, to a concrete situation of fact and life' (ibid., 29). But this interpretation of *natural*, while plausible, gives us much less than we need. For it does not help us to answer our chief question to be told that in international affairs the right of nature prevails, that this is in fact how things really are. What we want and need to know is if the Fundamental Law of Nature is applicable here so that there is a transition analogous to the one Hobbes applies to *every man*: so, from the state of nature of international relations to a rational inference for a *law of nature*, i.e. to the theorem of world-government. We might be inclined to say, *prima facie* at least, that there is no reason why the analogy should not hold. 'Nam *jus gentium* et *jus naturae* idem sunt...' (LW, vol. III, 253). If there is a transition and, thus, an escape, from *jus naturae* in the one case, why should there not be one in the other case, when *jus naturae*, for Hobbes, is the same as *jus gentium*? Indeed, if international affairs could be conceived as merely the relationships of sovereigns, where the legitimacy of each sovereign and the territorial limits of his sovereignty were uncontroversially agreed upon, then it would make very good sense to argue that nature herself dictates, though the rationality of sovereigns, that they find a way of desisting from fighting each other, since they would obviously be better off not fighting than they could hope to be through fighting. This would be compellingly true in our own time, when fighting could be no less dangerous for victors than for the vanquished. But, and this is the most important of *buts*, there is no such an agreement and there cannot be such an agreement: what is to count as *gens* for the purposes of *jus gentium*, is not only not uncontroversial, but it is *essentially* controversial. It is the very stuff of international affairs to permanently reshuffle the pack, not of cards, but of the players themselves. Who is playing and who is entitled to play the game of international politics? These are the questions which block the road to a world-government though Hobbes concerned himself little with the matter. It is sufficient to cast a brief glance at Chapter XI of *Leviathan*, entitled 'Of the differences of Manners', to realise how little sensitivity and reflection Hobbes had for national differences. Hobbes disappoints one here, he is indeed a true individualist (Macpherson 1962).

But, the central matter is this, Hobbes is not making light with words when he calls the Fundamental Law of Nature *fundamental*. It is truly the *fundamentum* of the whole system, that solid rock about which the roots of fact and norm are inextricably interwoven with each other. Having accounted in a scientifically adequate manner for the nature of man, Hobbes finds with the truth about man the very norm, that fundamental norm, which is enjoined by that truth itself. There is no truth more fundamental about man than that peace is better for his *life*, its preservation and prosperity, than war. Yet, there is no wisdom more easily flowing from this truth than that no behaviour is as irrational, because it is destructive of life, as peaceful behaviour which is unilateral. This linkage between truth and norm (''Do not be a lone pacifist!'') is the *fundamentum*, a kind of analytic proposition, rather akin to that other famed proposition, *pacta sunt servanda*. It is at this most basic point that the analytic-compositive method of Hobbes is at its best. By analysis we descend to the most basic item conceivable, *viz.* a man, and this item is indisputably basic for if we descend further than it by analysis (dismembering), than the items so obtained cannot be put together again, by way of synthesis.

For the analytic-compositive method to work for international relations, it should be possible to do something analogous. It should be possible to descend to the rock of a basic notion, a *nation*, a *state*, a non-controversial *sovereign*. But Hobbes knew that there was no such *fundamentum* available for international relations. Within the commonwealth, like Plato before him, he wished to put an end to politics and to replace it by something else, a sort of scientific rulership. This I take to be the import of his repeated insistence upon the theorem that *justice* is what the sovereign says it is. For a world-government to be possible on Hobbesian principles, it should be possible to order, in an analogously scientific manner, the basic marbles of the game. But given that there is no analysis possible that would yield such basic international marbles, the identity of the basic objects, the very players in the international game, must remain systematically disputed and controversial. In other words, international relations are hopelessly and perhaps tragically just international *politics*. For *gentes* are not given, they cannot be rationally coordinated once and for all. There is no escape for them from the state of nature, the rules governing their interrelationships are just nature herself. They are doomed to speak politically to each other, until they go under and are replaced by new players; and this is the language of war and diplomacy, force and fraud.

It is the hallmark of every known attempt to establish a world order that it has some rule to designate who the players are. Those who seek a non-war-like world order, indeed, must be conservatives; they must not allow for the possibility that new players will replace old players, for such a replacement is typically executed by force and that is certainly war-like. By contrast, realists try to take the world as it is. Hobbes was certainly a realist. This is why he took *natural* to mean *usual* or *normal*. The classic author of vision here, of course, is Polybius: the historian who was exercised by the very phenomenon of old players being replaced by new players in the international game. What makes empires and kingdoms strong and what makes them later weak, and ultimately go under? Polybius is the permanent antidote against the delusions of programmatic conservatism. Also it was Machiavelli who, under the inspiration of Polybius, posed the question about the dialectic of *virtú* and *fortuna*, a dialectic that taught that the state was mortal, that it can just cease to exist due to events which are quite irrational. That *fortuna* sometimes gets the better of *virtú*, Hobbes learned this lesson well. The great Leviathan 'is mortal, and subject to decay, as all other Earthly creatures are' (Leviathan, 246; cf. Pocock 1972 and 1975). And Hobbes knew, of course, his Polybius: at the end of the introduction to his translation of Thucydides he left a lapidary statement of his appreciation of Polybius. After quoting approvingly Justus Lipsius in praise of Thucydides, he adds only this: 'Next to him is Polybius' (EW, Vol. VIII, 31-2).

Polybius looked for some causal explanation for this decline and rise of players in the international arena, seeking some factor that lies deeper than the surface of violent confrontation, for example, "corruption". Hobbes too had no illusions about the possibility of initial condition that could be relied upon to speak the sweet words of reason forever to the surviving players. He knew that the instability of the international scene was not accidental but essential. We can readily convince ourselves of how right he was here if we just consider that to this day there remains a systematically grey area in the concept of aggression. The League of Nations attempted in 1933 to define this troublesome concept; the task was assigned to the famed Politics-committee. This had no trouble in listing standard cases of aggression, such as invasion, bombardment, etc., but its efforts ultimately foundered on a paragraph which was to have defined as aggression the tolerance of a state or groups actively hostile to a neighbouring state. The UN General Assembly Resolution (3314) on the Definition of Aggression (1974) is wisely silent on this point. It is apparently "good" international conduct to be both against aggression and to support national liberation movements. Sometimes it is even said that the "real" aggressor is the force that just stands in the way of such movements. The old player becomes an aggressor by simply refusing to quit.

Looked at from this vantage, Hobbes's lack of appreciation of the power of nationality is, in a way, a testimony to the sharpness of his vision. He was thinking basically in terms of sovereigns standing in natural relations to each other. Given that sovereignty was an artifice, it must be rationally justified. The ruler, in the last resort, is justified in his rulership by the will of the ruled. The impersonal state, independent of both ruler and ruled, is just on the horizon of Hobbes; his Leviathan is still the prince magnified (Shennan 1974, 111). However, with the advent of the nation state a much stronger ideological justification is demanded of rulership. Not since the era of theological justification has there been such a demanding criterion for legitimacy. In fact, this principle of nationality is so strong that people are ready to forego their individual, rational, Hobbesian interests and lay down their lives for the nation (Berlin 1958). Perhaps Hobbes was saying to us that rationality stops at the individual; only an individual can have rational interests. International affairs are doomed to irrationality.

It is a principle of international law that the existence of a state is constituted by the recognition granted to that state by other states. It is a fact of international life that recognition, typically in those cases where confrontation by force is most likely, is a matter of controversy. Such controversies, about the legitimacy of this or that state, or about the demand of some group or other to have a state of its own, are the very stuff of international politics. A world-government could arise only after the elimination of such conflicts. It is an important fact in this context, that there always *must* be some group or state which will be requested to make a sacrifice for the sake of world-stability. And this sacrifice might well mean not only compromising some vital national interest but even the end of the very existence of the state. Of course, great nations have no such fears. But Milan Kundera, the great Czech writer, knew what he was about when he defined *small nation* as one the very existence of which is endangered at any time. History supplies with countless examples of what can happen to really small nations. The latest of these cautionary tales, as far as I know, is East-Timor, where a whole nation is slowly tortured out of existence. It is quite clear that the voluntary adoption of such a role of self-sacrifice could never be justified within the constraints of Hobbesian rationality. Much of the attraction that Hobbes has for our time comes from his being the first and still the greatest philosopher of non-ideological security. Instead of pursuing ideals, he instructs us to concentrate on the essentials, most importantly upon staying alive. It was in the process of working out the consequences of security, uppermost on the scale of rational values, that he was ready to concede to the fugitive, whose only prospect is death at the hand of his sovereign, the repossession of his full *jus natural*, that self-defence which is limited only by physical capacity. What on earth could justify, robbing a nation of that right of self-defence *in extremis* which the philosopher was ready to recognise as inalienably belonging to any individual whose life is directly threatened?

It could be objected at this point that I am not taking seriously enough, in terms of method, the radical individualism of Hobbes. It could be argued that I am wrong in demanding a valid analogy between what Hobbes says about individuals and nations or states. According to this possible line of criticism, all that matters is that the individual should ensure his physical safety, irrespective of any irrelevant consideration about the identity of the sovereign who grants him that safety. In support of this way of looking at things, it would be possible to mobilise all that Hobbes says against regarding religious interests, such as salvation, as a *true* interest. It could be said, in parallel, that pride and other benefits which follow from national self-determination and the possession of a nation-state, are not true interests. Therefore, they should be given up for the sake of the safety of individuals. Now, without going into questions of political theology and group-psychology, both of which are highly relevant here, there is a very simple refutation of this criticism. Consider the proposition ''better red than dead'', in the widest possible sense, not merely by reference to communism. Those who assert it imply that submitting to the conqueror one automatically assures one's individual physical safety. Hobbes used to speak of submission in this vein. But, despite Hobbes, we are a much wiser and much sadder generation: we know that the conqueror sometimes butchers those who submit. No, submission is no guarantee of safety in our times. To derive the possibility of justifying world government on the basis of Hobbes, would require that we interpret him in a way that would overlook his magnificent feel for the

109

reality of the human condition and turn him into the kind of utopian he detested. A Hobbes today who would endorse a world-government would be rather like the Gandhi who advised the Jews under Nazi-rule, in his famed letter to Martin Buber, to follow, under the circumstances the totally idiotic strategy of non-violence.[5]

A world-government could, of course, still come into being, roughly like the United Nations, as a coalition of states in which a few strong "partners" dominate the rest. It is not inconceivable that the interests of these strong partners may converge. The United States, the Soviet Union and the People's Republic of China, if they really meant business, should not have much difficulty in jointly controlling the world. They may even pool administrative resources and call the result a "world-government". I do not think for a moment that a world governed by this sort of a sovereign agency would be a better world. I am fairly confident that I am not saying this because I come from a country whose citizens regard themselves, not without justification, as an endangered species. But there are others as well and not only the people of East-Timor. I cannot think of a single good reason why they should voluntarily assent to jeopardising their chances of survival, even as individuals, for the sake of peace that will reign ever after in a world cleansed of their peace-disturbing presence. Not that there is much chance even of that. It would certainly be a distortion of his deepest intentions to attribute to Hobbes an endorsing of this sort of a prospect *qua* rational objective worthy to be pursued.

To sum up: the stuff of international relations is the constant reshuffling, qualifying and disqualifying of players in the game of international politics. This accords with Hobbes's theory that states and nations are artificial, and not natural entities. To interpret this in a reductionist spirit and to argue that there *ought* to be no states or nations, but only individuals united in one commonwealth where their safety would be guaranteed by a world-sovereign, runs too much against the realism pervading the whole of Hobbes's political philosophy. A reductionist interpretation of this sort makes an unnatural demand on the rationality of individuals, *viz.* that they realise that their true interests are always individual and never group-interests. This, indeed, would go against all we know about how people understand themselves. Since people are not likely to adopt such reductionist individualism spontaneously, the alternative is to put it into effect by force. Forcing people to be "free" of their group "delusions". Presumably this would cause even more wars than those brought about by sovereign states, whose interactions follow the dictates of the cruel logic of *jus naturale*.

Given the essentially contested nature of the identity of players, it is impossible to formulate, in the context of international relations, a principle that is logically analogous to the Fundamental Law of Nature, valid in the individual domain. Similarly, it is impossible to construct, within the context of Hobbes, and for the same reason, an introduction to the philosophy of international relations that would perform the same task as the first part of *Leviathan,* 'Of Man', performs for the doctrine of municipal sovereignty. In the absence of such foundation, it cannot be held that a justification for a world-government can be derived from the principles of Hobbes's political philosophy. So until group endeavour passes into oblivion, whether by nature or miracle, there is no substitute for force and fraud, for war and diplomacy, in the governance of the world.

Notes

1. *Leviathan*, Ch. xiv, 100. References to this work are according to the Oxford edition (Clarendon Press).

2. *Leviathan,* Ch. xxx, 273. Cf. also *Philosophical Rudiments,* in *The English Works of Thomas Hobbes* (EW), Vol. II, ed. by W. Molesworth, John Bohn, London, 1839—1845, 186-7.

3. I cannot resist quoting a line from the Latin version of the Leviathan-passage, Ch. xxx, in *Latin Works* (LW), Vol. III, pp. 253-4, ed. by W. Molesworth, John Bohn, London, 1839—1845.

4. Goldsmith 1966, 191. In Goldsmith's rather lengthy discussion of the Leviathan-passage, the possibility of a world government is not even mentioned. Cf. also Hood 1964, 4. Hood's emphasis on the obligatoriness of conscience does nothing to remove the essential uncertainty which is the hallmark of judgement.

5. I discuss these problems in greater detail in my Hebrew book, *On War* (Tel Aviv, 1984), a philosophical essay which grew out of the acrimonious controversy in Israel generated by the Lebanon War.

Hobbes on World Government and the World Cup

Arthur Ripstein

Since Plato, one of the dominant metaphors of political philosophy has treated the state as a person writ large.[1] Although Hobbes makes the comparison between the quarrels of nations and those of persons only in passing, his account of the origins and costs of conflict between people is perhaps most fruitful when extended to conflicts between states. Yet most developments of Hobbesian analyses of international relations focus only on one half of Hobbes's account of conflict, and treat nations as rationally self-interested acquisitive agents (e.g. Gauthier 1969, Appendix). My aim is to focus on the neglected half of Hobbes's account, and consider those conflicts between nations that are the outcome of their concern with glory and prestige. I shall also offer the beginnings of what I take to be a Hobbesian solution to the resulting conflicts. When transferred to international relations, Hobbes's treatment of glory fails to provide a justification for world government. But it does provide something of a justification for the World Cup.

1. The State of Nature and the State of War

Hobbes suggests that three factors 'render men apt to invade'. First is the competition for those scarce goods necessary for 'commodious living'. Second is diffidence, the fear that others will invade, which leads to preemptive attack. Third is glory, which leads to invasion for the sake of reputation:

112

The first use violence, to make themselves Masters of other mens persons, wives, children and cattell; the second, to defend them; the third, for trifles, as a word, a smile, a different opinion, and any other sign of undervalue, either direct in their Persons, or by reflection in their Kindred, their Friends, their Nation, their Profession, or their Name. (Leviathan, 185.)[2]

Diffidence is the least deep seated of the three sources of conflict; whatever importance it might have in explaining actual fighting, it is parasitic upon competition and glory in the order of explanation. Diffidence leads those that are not disposed towards war to become so. Hobbesian person only stage pre-emptive attacks when they believe, for whatever reason, that others are apt to invade them.[3] If a commonwealth can be instituted in circumstances in which nobody fears invasion based on acquisitiveness or glory, there is no problem for diffidence to exacerbate. A stable commonwealth with a ruling sovereign entirely removes diffidence as a source of conflict, for it removes the grounds of such fear and distrust.

The other two sources of conflict are more significant to Hobbes's project for two reasons. First, they lie at the very root of conflict. Second, unlike diffidence, they can at best be controlled, but not eliminated by the institution of a sovereign. The institution of a sovereign does not make the appetite for goods or for glory disappear.

For both individuals and nations, the solution to conflict over material goods is straightforward and plausible: the costs of conflict, measured in terms of the goods it is waged over, are higher than the expected value of victory. The conflict resulting from competition over scarce goods insures that none will devote sufficient effort to productive activities that would make them more plentiful. The risk to life is increased by the struggle over the means to life. Thus making and keeping peace is to the advantage of all the same grounds that lead them to invade in times of war.[4] Hobbes's laws of nature allow peace to be made and kept; thus it is to the advantage of each to obey them and submit to the arbitration of the sovereign that enforces them so long as each is assured that all will.[5]

Diffidence also has a role to play in motivating and justifying peace: just as fear leads to premptive attack in the state of nature, the fear of violent death finally convinces Hobbesian persons to accept an absolute sovereign. Like appetite, fear both leads to conflict and points to its solution.

When reckoned in terms of appetite and fear, the rationality and advantages of making and keeping peace are apparent. The laws of nature create an artificial common good of peaceful interaction; if it is to the advantage of all, why is any form of coercion needed? Part of the answer is that the sovereign's power both increases the cost of violating the laws of nature and decreases the likelihood of successful violation. As a result the expected gain from invasion is diminished considerably. But the sovereign is needed for another reason as well: the advantages peace brings do not guarantee peace because of the second source of conflict, glory. Unlike appetite and fear, glory generates conflict in the state of nature, but is not better served by commonwealth and sovereignty. In *De Cive*, Hobbes says that 'We do not therefore by nature seek society for its own sake, but that they may receive some honor or profit from it' (De Cive, 111). Yet as we shall see, although all may receive profit from society, most must necessarily fail to receive honour.

2. Glory

Hobbes's account of conflict stemming from the human passion of glory is independent of his account based on appetite. Glory, for Hobbes, is the 'joy arising from a man's own power and ability' (Leviathan, 124), grounded in either his own past actions or, more significantily, in his reputation among others.

Hobbesian Glory involves a number of related motivations and reactions. All are alike in resting on an agent's conception[6] of his or her own powers in relation to the powers of others; they differ in the particular powers that are at issue. Specific objects of glory include the ability to rule, membership in a prestigious family or profession, and the importance of one's friends and one's wisdom. Each of these is a possible grounds for quarrel, for they are all factors about which different opinions of people can be held than those people hold of themselves.[7]

Glory and conflict

The place of glory in Hobbes's account of the generation of conflict is clear. He suggests six reasons why people come to blows while other gregarious creatures able to live together in peace (Leviathan, 226). The first five involve only desire to be preeminent and rule; the sixth, that animal society is natural rather than artificial is nothing more than a summary of the previous five. Each of the reasons reveals the importance of the glory account, for Hobbes's conception of what the lives of bees must be like is very close to his conception of life among people kept apart only by their incompatible appetites. Appetite and scarcity are not only sources of conflict. For Hobbes 'Man is then most troublesome when he is most at ease', scarcity alone leaves people too busy to regularly come to blows. Unlike other social creatures, such as bees, people are in constant competition for honour and dignity; eminence surpasses comfort as the object of desire; no bee supposes itself more able to rule than its fellows; nor do bees have language to offend or insult each other; and bees, unlike peo-

114

ple, lack ambition. Bees are able to cooperate because they can all pursue a common good; having only a common benefit, their cooperation is natural, requiring neither contract nor enforcement; bees live together "naturally" because their interests are in harmony (as are the interests of people) and there is nothing to keep them apart.

Unlike bees, people will attack each other over "trifles", and even attack each other for fear of being attacked over trifles. Because of the desire to be better than others, left on their own people cannot even have an artificial common good.

The glory account: an objection

A supposedly devastating objection has been levelled against Hobbes's account of glory and its place in his science of politics. The objection originates with Rousseau's *Discourse sur l'origine de l'inegalite parmi des hommes*. Rousseau points out that *amour propre*, the desire to think well of oneself, and be thought well of by others, is a *comparative* desire, one that can only be had by social creatures able to make such comparisons. Like diffidence, it can only arise in a social setting. As such, it is a passion inappropriate to presocial persons in a Hobbesian state of nature. Presocial creatures have only what Rousseau calls *amour de soi-meme;* each is concerned only with his or her own needs, and if any regard is payed to others, it is only as competitors or possible objects of use. Rousseau's natural persons do not think of others as judging them at all; hence they cannot worry about the esteem in which they are held (Rousseau 1964, 219, note 15). Rousseau's point is simple: presocial beings have no interest in the esteem of others; Hobbesian natural persons are just such beings.[8]

Two replies are in order on Hobbes's behalf. First, even if glory requires a social setting in which to emerge, it may nonetheless be a natural passion. Hunger only motivates behaviour in the presence of food. Sexual desire is a natural drive, but only emerges and takes its specific form in a social setting.

Second, nobody seriously supposes that it is Hobbes's intent to give a natural history of the human race. Indeed, he explicitly concedes that the state of nature probably never occurred as he describes it. The *Leviathan* aims to display the need for, and legitimacy of, absolute sovereignty by showing what is apt to become of a society of creatures like us in its absence. Thus Hobbes can reply to Rousseau that glory renders men apt to invade, whatever its origins might be.

3. Four Features of Glory

The differences between people and bees display four ways in which glory leads to conflict: *first*, it is sometimes useful as means to other goods; *second*, it is a positional good, which it is impossible for all to enjoy simultaneously; *third*, the esteem of others, or lack thereof, is easily misperceived; *fourth*, and most important, it is typically pursued in a non-rational manner. I examine these points in order.

Power and glory

The esteem and respect of others is often useful as a means of increasing one's own comfort and security. The more powerful one is taken to be, the more seriously one's threats will be taken, and the more easily will one entice others into alliances. Thus, in one sense, glory is a typical Hobbesian "power": a present means to some future apparent good. As a power, it is an object of interest that all will do what they can to acquire and maintain, for the respect of others protects one's position.

Hobbes sometimes seems to want to treat glory as simply another "power", a useful means of securing future goods: 'For riches, knowledge, and honor are but several sorts of power' (Leviathan, 226). If glory were nothing more than an instrumental end, the solution to conflicts brought on by glory would be straightforward: like the laying down of arms, the demonstrable advantages in terms of the very goods it is meant to secure would lead each to put glory aside on the condition that all do so. But glory is not only a power, and so cannot be so easily brought under control.

Position

Unlike most other powers, glory is not something everyone can have a share of: 'Because that glory is like honour; if all men have it, no man hath it, for they consist in comparison and precellence' (De Cive, 112). Glory is what economists refer to as a "positional good": each wants not simply to be thought well of by others but to be valued as highly by others as by him or herself.

> Further, since men by natural passion are divers ways offensive to one another, every man thinking well of himself, and hating to see the same in others, they must needs provoke one another by words, and other signs of contempt and hatred, which are incident to all comparison, till at last they must determine the preeminence by strength and force of body. (EW, Vol. IV, 182.)

116

Since Hobbesian persons value themselves above all others, each wants to be "eminent" valued by others above themselves. Needless to say, this is a condition that cannot be satisfied for all.

This positional feature of glory leads to pointless quarrel and invasion, and the fear thereof, because, at bottom, to be concerned with it is to be concerned more with relative position than with absolute position. There are two ways of improving one's relative position: improving one's own absolute position and lowering that of one's competitors. Hobbesian glory makes that latter course as appealing as the former. In battle, this leads to greater concern with victory than with its fruits. When Hobbesian persons invade for the sake of glory, it is because they care for victory over and above the spoils it can be expected to bring.

Misperception

Third, the disrespect of others is easily misperceived. The thirst for glory will only lead to conflict if everyone notices that they are being denied their share. Sadly, this condition is all too easily satisfied, whether or not they are being so denied. Unlike scarcity, disrespect is almost entirely in the eye of the beholder; an imagined slight leads to conflict as easily as a real one can. Glory can lead to invasion over "trifles" because almost anything that can be interpreted as a sign of disrespect; such signs are most easily righted by a demonstration of power and ability. Successful attack is the most decisive form that such a demonstration can take; it is decisive both in reassuring the agent and silencing the person taken to have doubted him.

Irrationality

Persons far-sighted enough to recognise that the costs of competitive war outweigh its benefits might still lose control of themselves in attacking for glory. 'The understanding is by the flame of the passions never enlightened, but dazzled' (Leviathan, 242). It is precisely because glory is an *irrational* motivation that it is so dangerous. In calling certain motivations "irrational", I mean simply this: the resources that an agent is willing to expend because of that motivation are not proportional to the expected value to be gained by acting on it.[9] If people only "quarreled" when they had good reason to suppose something was to be gained, life in the state of nature would not be 'solitary poor, nasty, brutish, and short':

> Moreover, considering that men's many appetites carry them to one and the same end; which end sometimes can neither be enjoyed in common nor divided, it followeth that the stronger must enjoy it alone, and that it

be decided by battle who is the stronger. And thus the greatest part of men, upon no assurance of odds, do nevertheless, through vanity, or comparison, or appetite, provoke the rest, that would otherwise be contented with equality. (EW, Vol. IV, 83.)

The sense in which glory is an irrational motivation can be brought out by noticing an important feature of rational desires. Rational desires are pursued on the basis of their expected value. The expected value of an action has two components: the desirability of the outcome, and the likelihood of its achievement. A rational motivation only leads to action when the agent believes that there is some reasonable probability that the action will bring about the desired result. The Hobbesian person who desires wealth, for example, will only invade for its sake if she supposes that there is a good chance of victory. To be sure, such probabilities are easy to misestimate, and diffidence leads those in the state of nature to error when they consider the likely outcome of not attacking.

But still, the pursuit of normal desires at least approximate rationality. That is why an absolute sovereign is so effective in preventing conflicts engendered by appetite: a sovereign increases both the cost and probability of unsuccessful attack. Thus a rational agent will not suppose that there is anything to be gained by attacking others.

Hobbesian glory, on the other hand, is not pursued rationally. It resembles ordinary desires in that it has an external object, namely the respect and admiration of others. Like other desires, the desire for glory reveals itself in its consequences: it is satisfied when one gains that admiration and respect. But unlike ordinary desires, the effort expended in its pursuit is not proportional to the agent's estimation of the probability of gaining it. When Hobbesian persons invade for glory, they do not typically act on the basis of an estimate of the likelihood of earning the respect of others.[10] Instead, they act because they wish to right what they take to be an egregious wrong, whatever the consequences.[11]

It is worth noticing that this non-rational or irrational feature of glory is shared by a number of other motivations. Although he focuses on glory as a source of conflict in his political works, in *Behemoth*, his history of the English Civil War (which in many ways served as his model of a state of war) Hobbes points to religious factionalism and fanaticism as a primary source of conflict. Like glory, religious fanaticism leads to attack without regard for probability of outcome.[12] Merely raising the costs of conflict and lowering the likelihood of success is not enough to prevent it.

Although the costs of invading for glory are genuine material costs, they are not reckoned as such in leading to invasion. The costs and expected benefits of attack cannot be calculated in units of glory. Failure to attack when slighted has costs in glory, but attacking normally does not have costs in glory that can be measured against them. That is why it is a dangerous passion, far more likely to lead to the war of each against all than competition alone would.

The role of glory in producing pointless conflict is illustrated by a simple game called ''the dollar auction'' in which two people bid for a dollar bill (Teger 1978). More akin to the state of nature than an ordinary auction, both the winner and the loser must pay whatever they bid; wherever the bidding stops, *both* parties pay whatever they have bid, with the dollar going to the highest bidder. Studies of actual dollar auctions reveal that bids often escalate well beyond the dollar point. As bids go higher, the desire to minimise one's losses leads to increasing bids; raising one's bid from $1.40 to $1.65 when an opponent has bid $1.50 cuts one's loss from $1.40 to only $.65. And so both bidders reason, leading to steady escalation. Each seems blind to the fact that the other is reasoning in a strictly parallel fashion, and devotes increasing resources without paying attention to the fact that the expected value of success is steadily *decreasing*.[13] Once one has started to bid in the dollar auction, each additional bid is in some sense rational. But to get involved in the first place, and to continue playing when one can at best minimise one's loss is foolish.

Why do players allow the escalation to get so quickly out of hand? In studies of actual subjects who had played the game, A. Teger found that many subjects reported that they felt a desire to win, over and above the advantages of winning. This very Hobbesian desire to outwait, outwit, and outwill one's opponent for the glory that it brings lies at the root of conflict in the state of nature. Other subjects claimed they had 'too much invested to quit'. This motivation is Hobbesian glory in its paradigmatic form — the willingness to engage in increasingly foolish behaviour to avoid the need to admit that one has behaved foolishly in the past.[14]

How realistic an account of human motivation and conflict has Hobbes given? Has he exaggerated the irrational role of glory and its ability to lead to conflict? Hobbes need not, and does not suppose that all natural persons are driven by glory, whatever the odds. His point is rather that given that some 'taking pleasure in contemplating their own power in acts of conquest, which they pursue further than their security requires; if others, that otherwise would be glad to be at ease within modest bounds, should not by invasion increase their power, they would not be able, long time, by standing only on their defence, to subsist' (Leviathan, 185).

Not all Hobbesian persons are ''naturally'' concerned with glory.[15] But once conflict has begun, diffidence and glory feed on each other to produce total war among seekers of glory. In times of peace, such 'naturall powers' as strength and prudence are advantageous to all who have them, for they aid in the appropriation of nature. And instrumental powers, such as riches and friends, are valuable to all who possess them, even if others possess more, for they aid both in the appropriation of nature and the other parts of 'commodious living'. But in times of war, all powers are directed at defence and preemptive attack. Unless one has more than others do, those resources are of no use; power is nothing, balance of power everything. Because diffidence may lead others to attack, and the only power worth having is eminent power, all are forced to strive for eminence whatever the odds of success. The only alternative is certain defeat. Thus even if glory is not an original motive of all Hobbesian persons, conflict in the state of nature ensures that it will become one.[16]

It is because the pursuit of glory outstrips its rational basis that it is central to Hobbes's political theory. Leviathan is 'king of the proud' (Leviathan, 362) rather than 'king of the appetitive' because creatures that are merely appetitive can recognise the advantages of peace, and so do not need constant reminders to keep them in line. The material costs of conflict are high enough to make an absolute sovereign unnecessary for beings who are merely rational and appetitive. The second through fifth laws of nature, enjoining peace and the keeping of contracts are self-reinforcing once accepted by a sufficient number; only a 'foole' could fail to see their advantages. The 'king of the proud' is needed to enforce the sixth through tenth laws of nature: the prohibitions of retributive and vengeful punishment, pride, and arrogance. Each of these is justified in terms of its advantages in acquiring goods and avoiding fear. Each thus requires a power to overawe because no other ''advantage'' can convince us to hold them in check. Because glory is pursued without regard to the costs of that pursuit, mere material advantages cannot hold it in check. The sovereign must be all powerful to be able to raise the only threat that is *guaranteed* to hold even glory in check: that of life itself.

Diverting glory

The striving after glory cannot be expected to simply disappear in times of peace; the best the sovereign can hope to do is divert it to harmless avenues. The very factor that makes glory a potential source of conflict allows it to be so diverted. Because those who seek glory seek eminence and victory for their own sake rather than for the sake of the results they bring, the struggle to outdo others can take place without being a struggle over scarce goods. Thus glory can be deprived of its fatal object. Hobbes is not entirely explicit about the means he advocates, but his remarks allow us to reconstruct a proposal in keeping with the spirit of his view of politics. Part of Hobbes's solution is to let the sovereign simply *decide* who will be respected in the commonwealth. Among the rights and powers of the sovereign is the right to decide which honors will be bestowed, and on what grounds. Hobbes does not discuss how this bestowal is to be done, but his purposes make only one solution plausible. Positions of glory must be bestowed in such a way that individuals will not suppose that they will

120

be able to gain or recover glory by destructive means.[17]

If glory cannot be eliminated, it must not be allowed to be divisive. The purpose of laws is 'not to bind the People from all voluntary actions; but to direct and keep them in such a motion, as not to hurt themselves by their own impetuous desires, rashnesse, or indiscretion, as hedges are set, not to stop travellers, but to keep them in the way' (Leviathan, 388). Hobbes is not explicit about the mechanisms he intends, but it is clear that the mechanism must minimise the consequences of the four factors that make glory divisive in the first place. Glory must not be attainable by lowering the status of others. It must be made (comparatively) useless as a means to future goods[18]; it must be allocated in a public way so that it cannot be easily misperceived, and the resources that can be devoted to its pursuit must be limited so that one cannot have too much invested to quit.

We shall look at these mechanisms more carefully when we turn to international relations. The striking thing to notice for now is the extent to which Hobbes treats glory as *purely* comparitive: Hobbes presumes that the desire for eminence can attach itself to any dimension of comparison. Only on such an assumption could we expect that the desire for glory could be satisfied by allowing the sovereign to allocate it at will.

Hobbes's treatment of glory shows an important dimension to his view of conflict. The successful Hobbesian sovereign deals with the two sources of conflict among his or her subjects by separating them: mutually advantageous laws of nature commanding justice, equity and mercy ensure that reason and appetite will never lead to violent conflict; careful allocation of honours and control over contests of honour guarantees that the pursuit of glory will take place in a harmless way. The all powerful sovereign ensures that none will suppose that violence will bring glory or material gain, or right any wrongs to either. Glory does not disappear; it is simply deprived of its fatal object.

4. National Glory and International Conflict

I begin this section with an apology. Any attempt to develop a Hobbesian account of international relations carries with it an inherent danger. There are perils involved in taking the metaphor of nations as persons writ large too seriously; those perils are particularly apparent in the case of endowing entire nations with an emotional life and concern for their own esteem and the respect of others. The glory that Hobbes sees at the root of conflict has a conscious component to it that we cannot suppose to be a property of nations. The visceral element of glory, vain-glory, and fear cannot be readily attributed to social entities lacking viscera.

121

Having apologised, I hasten to add that there is no greater peril involved in speaking of nations pursuing glory than is involved in attributing interests and desires to them more generally. Nations no more have consciously avowed interests than they have conscious self esteem; a nation as a whole has no mind in which to consider alternative means to "future apparent goods". Nor are national goals distributive properties, consciously entertained by all of the people of a nation.[19] A state's "national interest" whether it is in territorial expansion, stable commerce, or cultural integrity, need not be shared by all nationals. Rather, national goals are emergent properties, the attribution of which is to be judged on the basis of its explanatory power.[20] So long as the nation consistently pursues those goals in changing circumstances, their attribution serves to shed light on its behaviour, even if the mechanism by which they are incorporated changes. The nation's overall goal might be the vector sum of indefinitely many factors; the particular factors involved may change while the goal remains unchanged.[21]

Something similar can be said for the passions of nations, including glory. They need not be viscerally distributed among all of the individuals in the nation. Rather, they are motives that allow a consistent pattern to be found in a nation's changing behaviour. A nation's concern for glory, in such forms as avenging an imagined wrong, or showing its force, might not be a concern of all of the people. Yet it can serve to move the nation to act. The attribution of passions to groups, like the attribution of desires, can only be vindicated by its fruitfulness.

The state of nature that exists between nations is not a state of constant violence; a Hobbesian analysis of international relations need no more make that supposition than Hobbes himself need suppose that individuals in a state of nature are constantly coming to blows. The state of nature is a state of war because of what Hobbes calls the 'lack of assurance to the contrary'; it is the wastefulness of constant preparation, and the fear that accompanies it, that make the state of nature "incommodious" as much as the actual risk of violent death do. It is important to keep this in mind in looking at the role of glory in international relations: even if it does not lead directly to violent death, the constant threat of "quarrel" and all that that entails is detrimental enough to make its costs too high. From Hobbes's perspective, national glory is unacceptable less because it directly causes conflict than because it leads to wastefulness and exacerbates ongoing conflicts.

National glory

Both Hobbes and Rousseau suppose that a well governed society whose members are at peace may go to war for the sake of its own glory. Part II of *Leviathan* includes an extended discussion of good citizenship and the means

122

of promoting it; the result is a nation with pride. Even if we take Rousseau's criticism of Hobbes seriously and suppose that nations are not made up of Hobbesian persons, we can see why as nations they would behave like them. Rousseau claims that *amour-propre* can redirected to yield a love of one's community rather than competition with one's fellows. For such redirection to be possible, one must be a member of a free people. A well governed society of the sort Rousseau envisions will bear all of the marks of glory because it will attach positive value to carrying out the threats it has made, even when there is nothing to be gained by carrying them out.[22] It will also attach positive value to its own customs, and avoid advantageous agreements with nations it disapproves of.

Both Hobbes and Rousseau offer philosophical theories of the state; there is also some empirical evidence that groups will behave very much more like Hobbesian persons than the individuals that comprise them do. Teger found that teams were far less willing to cut their losses in playing the dollar auction game. Instead, each member of the team was unwilling to be seen by cohorts as ready to back down. The mutual reinforcement of irrational behaviour is just what we would expect: whether groups are made up of Hobbesian or Rousseauian persons, the groups themselves will behave very much like Hobbesian persons. The unwillingness to admit that one's past behaviour has been irrational is reinforced by the unwillingness to admit it to one's compatriots.

National glory leads to conflict, and preparation for conflict in each of the four ways individual glory does: first, it is sometimes useful in gaining allies and making one's threats plausible; second, it is a positional good that not all can have; third, reputation among others is easily misperceived; fourth, it is all too often pursued irrationally.

The long term political gains that come from being thought powerful are sufficiently obvious that I pass over them without example; the positional status of glory and this risks of misperception I also pass over, for they are strictly analogous to the case of individual glory. The irrationality of glory, and the dire consequences thereof, deserves more attention.

A nation concerned with its own glory will be unwilling to back down from disagreement and conflict even when it has no reason to expect anything in the way of gain from continuing, and even when the costs of continuing to fight or arm are high. One of the incommodious results of national glory is the need to assure oneself of the ability to win wars one does not seriously expect to fight. Both the United States and the Soviet Union have more than enough nuclear weapons to destroy the entire world many times over, yet each continues to arm, not simply for fear of attack, but for fear of falling behind.

In a society less well-ordered than those Hobbes and Rousseau envision, glory has if anything, a more substantial role to play. If the individuals in the society do not share ends to a substantial degree, or are unwilling to accept economic restraint, national glory can bring them together and make all sorts of incommodious arrangements agreeable. Sacrifices can be demanded for the sake of a war effort that could not be justified in any other way, including the largest sacrifice of all, laying down one's life for one's country. The promise of gain, if promised at all, is secondary. The willingness to go to war is a property of a nation as an aggregate; it depends on the willingness of those who must individually bear the costs of war, either by actually fighting and risking attack, or by diverting resources that could be used for other purposes. Even those analyses of foreign policy that reveal economic motives under every action cannot ignore the fact that those who fight often take themselves to be fighting on more noble grounds. Just as Hobbesian persons each suppose themselves better able to rule than others, so do nations take themselves to have a better way of life and way of regulating intercourse between nations. And just as there may be self-serving motives underlying this confidence among individuals, so may like considerations underlay it in the case of nations. But in either case, those self-serving interests would not have their day in the form of conflict without the ennobling power of glory; nations and individuals are more ready to ignore the excessive costs of struggle so long as they suppose that struggle to have a point beyond the material advantages it is supposed to bring.

The earlier example of how Hobbesian glory creates conflict in the form of "dollar auction" situations has direct application to the arms race. Barry O'Neill has argued that the escalation of the arms race over the past four decades has followed precisely this pattern: the desire to win for the sake of winning outweighs the expected value of victory (O'Neill 1986, 33-50). O'Neill points out that in the international arena there is a further source of conflict in that parties often make verbal commitments about their future moves which it is politically difficult for them to back down from. This is, of course, precisely what proud Hobbesian persons, whether writ large or small, would be expected to do: announcements about one's power and determination continue to motivate even when flaunting that power and determination is no longer advantageous.[23] The costs are high:

> The subjects of those kings who affect the glory, and imitate the actions, of Alexander the Great, have not always the most comfortable lives, nor do such kings usually very long enjoy their conquests. They march to and for perpetually, as upon a plank sustained only in the midst; and when one end rises, down goes the other. (EW, Vol. VI, 12.)[24]

5. The Solution

That nations behave like Hobbesian persons is apparent; we have seen why it is plausible to suppose that their motives are not unlike those of Hobbesian persons. If so, we must look for a Hobbesian solution to the conflicts that result.

Although his analysis of the problem is illuminating in the case of international conflict, Hobbes's own solution cannot be transferred intact to the case of nations. In the international as in the individual arena, the sovereign body must be able to do two things: raise the risks and costs of war to a point where no party will suppose there is anything to be gained by invasion, and "overawe" all so that the cost of invasion is so high that even glory will not lead to conflict. The first task is one that can be fulfilled, however incompletely, by such international bodies as the United Nations. By providing peacekeeping forces, and censuring aggressors, some control can be exercised over the risks and costs of appetitive war. By decreasing the likelihood of successful attack, and increasing its cost, nations can collectively make peace more appealing.[25] But the second role of the sovereign is much harder to fill in the international arena. For there is no way to raise the stakes in international conflict to the point where glory *must* be outweighed. There is no equivalent of the fear of violent death to compel nations to not invade for glory. Or, rather, if there is such an equivalent, such as a world government with a nuclear monopoly, it is not an alternative that the nations of the world can be expected to seriously entertain. The risks of empowering a single agency with the power of life and death over entire nations may be more than any nation will allow. What is needed instead is a way of keeping glory under control.

We have seen that Hobbes's solution to the problem of individual conflicts brought on by glory involve depriving glory of its fatal object, power over others. Glory is not eliminated, but merely rendered harmless by allowing the sovereign to control its pursuit and allocation so that it will not lead to violent conflict.

What international analogue to this might be available? A direct generalisation of Hobbes's own solution for individual glory and conflict to the international arena would not work. An all powerful distributor of honour acceptable to the nations involved is unrealistic. But the root idea underlying Hobbes's solution is workable when extended to international affairs. Even if a single agent cannot be depended upon to distribute glory in a way acceptable to all, a way can be found to allocate so that its pursuit does not lead to conflict.

If there is such a way, it involves depriving glory of its fatal object, and allowing it to vent itself in a forum in which victory can be valued for its own sake, over and above whatever results it might bring. If Hobbes is right about the independence of glory from its particular object, any sort of contest will do so long as it can be kept in control. One such forum is international sport, using the soccer arena as proxy for the global arena. The glory and self esteem of both entire nations and the individuals that make them up can depend on the outcome of contests in which the loser loses only glory, and none loses their life.

Transferring conflicts over glory to sporting contests reduces the force of the four ways in which glory leads to conflict. Glory is no longer especially useful as a means to other goods; it might sell T-shirts and souveniers, but it will not bring material property where there was none. Second, success is only gained by playing well, not by harming others.[26] Third, the criteria of success are explicit and do not lend themselves to misperception. It is also all but impossible to have "too much invested to quit"; every contest has a well-defined end, so cannot continue to escalate simply because both parties have committed so much in the past. And the diversity of sports makes it possible even for those losing on some fronts to win on others.[27] The net effect of these is to divert glory from its fatal object by neutralising its positional aspect.

It is sometimes supposed that international sport is desirable because it allows nations to learn to get along. The obvious applicability of a Hobbesian account of individual conflict to international relations points to an unnoticed aspect of international sport. As a forum in which non-rational national passions can be vented, it serves to deprive them of their fatal object. While it is doubtful that the battle of Waterloo was really won on the playing fields of Harrow and Eton, it may be that the best hope of avoiding a thermonuclear holocaust takes place every four years on the playing fields of Milano and Mexico City.[28]

Notes

1. Hobbes made a fundamental contribution to the development of one side of this doctrine is with his notion of Leviathan as an "artificial person" with a single will.

2. References to *Leviathan* are to C.B. Macpherson's (1968) edition. References to *De Cive* are to Bernard Gert's (1978) edition *Man and Citizen*. References to all other works are taken from Molesworth (1840), *The English Works of Thomas Hobbes* (EW).

3. In the introduction to *De Cive*, Hobbes notes that diffidence explains why the state of nature becomes a war of each against all, even if relatively few people are morally childish enough to attack without provocation. So long as a few do attack, all must become warlike defensively; thus each must be prepared against all.

4. It may be that fear of violent death is what drives people to make peace; but the rationale for peace comes from its advantages.

5. I explore the contrast between Hobbes's acceptance of social motivations in accounting for conflict and his idealised view of persons motivated solely by appetite in justifying institutions in Ripstein 1987.

6. That the focus is on the way things seem rather than the way things are is crucial to the place of glory in the genesis of conflict.

7. For Hobbes, glory also is the source of laughter, which he defines as 'sudden glory arising from some sudden conception of some eminence in ourselves, by comparison with the infirmity of others.' (EW, Vol. IV, 46).

8. Hampton (1986), makes the same point in terms of peaceful interaction being the precondition of reputation in the first place. Glory can only lead to conflict after a peaceful period of comparison.

9. Perhaps "non-rational" would be a better term; I do not mean to characterise all motivations that lead to actions independently of the expected value of their outcomes negatively. Some of the noblest of human motivations display this feature: love, loyalty, and moral commitment. I choose the slightly pejorative epithet "irrational" both because Hobbesian glory is decidely less than noble and because contemporary defenders of Hobbes tend to treat Hobbes as an ancestor of game theory.

10. Of course people seldom make conscious estimates of the probablity of successful action; the distinctive feature of Hobbesian glory is that they do not even act "as-if" they make such estimates.

11. I do not mean to suggest that it is impossible to assimilate Hobbesian glory to any decision theoretic model. Perhaps by attributing a sufficiently intense preference for the respect and admiration of others, the calculations can be made to come out right. Hobbesian glory is a source of conflict because it is not sensitive to ordinary changes in probabilities; thus it cannot be treated as a preference on a par with those generated by appetite.

12. I ignore the possibility that religious fanaticism has for its primary motivation the promise of eternal salvation. The important point for Hobbes's purposes is that fanaticism leads to attack and unwillingness to compromise without regard to the prospects of victory.

13. The expected value decreases because the probability of success remains at one-half, while the distance between the value of the two possible outcomes decreases as the bidding escalates beyond the dollar point.

14. Teger points out that the classic case of this comes with owners of old cars. Having bought a new muffler, one spends hundreds of dollars on a new transmission, just so that the money spent on the muffler will not have been wasted.

15. The relative numbers involved vary throughout Hobbes's works: in *De Corpore Politico*, most are held to seek glory, and thus carry the rest along; in *De Cive*, only a minority cause trouble but provoke diffidence in others; in *Leviathan* Hobbes is not explicit about numbers.

16. David Gauthier suggests that this is the only source of glory. Without insecurity, glory would disappear. As we have seen, this is not Hobbes's view.

17. Part of the solution involves making loyalty itself the source of glory, as Hobbes suggests in *De Cive* (Ch. XIII, sec. 12). This ensures that glory-seeking will be at worst harmless, at best

127

beneficial. In Chapter VI (sec. 11 n.) Hobbes suggests a less substantial solution to the tendency to quarrel over questions of worship and the human sciences: 'Neither doth this happen by reason of the falseness of the principle, but of the dispositions of men, who, seeming wise to themselves, will needs appear such to all others. But though such dissensions cannot be hindered from arising, yet may they be restrained by the exercise of the sovereign power, that they prove no hindrance to the public peace.' Let people quarrel, Hobbes suggests, so long as they do not come to blows over it.

18. Hobbes is explicit that positions of honour, however allocated, must not lead those who occupy them to suppose that they are in any way above the laws of nature (Leviathan, 386).

19. The notion of distributive properties is introduced in Massey 1976.

20. This is not to say that the question of how those goals are embodied is unimportant; simply that it is extrinsic to a Hobbesian analysis of international relations.

21. Compare this to the point that Peter French has made about corporations: a corporation can be a locus of agency, the behaviour of which is describable in terms of its beliefs and goals, without being identical to the individuals that make it up, for any action a large corporation makes typically takes enough time that some employees and shareholders change in the interim. See French 1979, 207-17.

22. By 'nothing to be gained' I mean nothing. It is often supposed that nations lose credibility, and thus the future power of threat, by failing to carry out threats. Though this is doubtless sometimes true, it is not always. Some threats are so specific to the situation in which they are raised that backing down from them fails to show anything about the threatening party's underlying dispositions.

23. O'Neill also notes that something like Hobbesian diffidence serves to exacerbate the situation: nations tend to misperceive each others motives, and so to escalate further.

24. This quotation is from the Lawyer in *A Dialogue between a Philosopher and a Student of the Common Laws of England*. The Lawyer cannot usually be taken to express Hobbes's views, but the Philosopher (who acts as Hobbes's mouthpiece) says in the next sentence: 'It is well.'

25. It may be that a more powerful body, perhaps a world government, would be more effective towards this purpose; I leave that question to others.

26. Although one might win a game by breaking the opposing goalkeeper's arm, one does not gain glory by so doing.

27. Sometimes international sport will have the opposite effect, and a defeat on the playing field will lead to a desire for revenge off the field. Some critics of international sport comdemn it precisely because it is an expression of national glory at its ugliest. Thus George Orwell (1968) suggests that far from displacing it, international sport gives fuel to animosity between nations. If Hobbes is right, animosity is unavoidable, and any expression of it short of outright war is to be sought. Yet Orwell is no doubt right that there is a point at which tensions between nations run so high that sport can only exacerbate them; the solution I propose on Hobbes's behalf is meant only to limit the risks inherent in national glory, not to eliminate them entirely.

28. I am grateful to Leon Galis and Robert Shaver for helpful comments on an earlier version of this essay.

World-State or State-World:
Thomas Hobbes and the Law of Nations[1]

Bernard Willms

Introduction

Preliminary remark 1: Asking Hobbes

Written around the muzzles of old Prussian field guns one sometimes finds the inscription: *Ultima Ratio Regis*. The putting the field guns into action, the language of arms, was viewed to be a means of political reason. At the beginning of the nineteenth century Clausewitz held this view.

Everyone knows that even at the present time there are military authorities who regard nuclear warfare as a matter of rational planning, who think a nuclear war might end with their own side as the winner. Today this is essentially a problem of the superpowers and of the territories "dominated" by them. The present disarmament negotiations would have quite a different character if the superpowers did not have the potential battlefield outside their own territories. That possible battlefield is the center of Europe — a place where the greatest potential for destruction can be found which has ever been available to that unchained *ultima ratio*. Still to look at these capacities of destruction as an *ultima ratio* might be reasonable to some Dr. Strangelove in the Pentagon or elsewhere. For us, the inhabitants of central Europe, the matter looks different. The French author Régis Debray puts it like this:

> To the United States the loss of European outpost would mean that they had lost a battle, for us it would be war with the most likely outcome of complete destruction. ... the United States are interested in believing it to be possible to confine the conflict to Europe. The best outcome for them would be such a limited conflict — for us Europeans it would be the worst thing that could happen to us. (Debray 1986.)

That quotation should serve to remind us, that Europeans in fact have the best reasons to search for a more rational theory of war and peace than that of the old Prussians. The capacities of destruction have through quantitative increase gained a new quality. And there are good reasons to doubt whether our political thinking is prepared for the level of that new quality, in spite of all those mighty efforts of our peace research.

The professional attitude of the historian of political ideas is to look in a new situation for advice from the past. And as, since R.G. Collingwood, we know, that in Thomas Hobbes's works we have 'the world's greatest store of political wisdom' it makes good sense to turn to him. Indeed, Hobbes made peace the very essence of his thinking.

Leviathan is, as we all know the ''artificial body'', the mortal God. Anything that Leviathan does or has to do is directed to one end: peace. In his own time of civil war and religious strife Hobbes was first of all concerned with the foundation and preservation of internal peace, of civil order as such; but we also find in his works many arguments about international politics and about the law of nations.

Hobbes research until today has not given too much attention to that point. One does find some remarks about it in Tönnies, Goldsmith, Dietrich Braun and Reinhard Koselleck. Certain aspects of Hobbes's thinking about foreign politics are described by Carl Schmitt, Erich Cassirer and Christian von Krockow. The literature of international law mentions Hobbes mostly as purely denying the possibility of something like international law. Such gross misunderstanding can even be found in such famous works as those by Friedrich Berber, G.A. Walz, Arthur Nussbaum and Alfred Verdross (Tönnies 1896; Goldsmith 1966; Braun 1963; Koselleck 1959; Schmitt 1950; Cassirer 1919; Krockow 1962; Berber 1960; Walz 1930; Verdross 1963). A more detailed analysis of Hobbes's theories of international politics and international law is to be found in David P. Gauthier's *Logic of Leviathan* and in Ernst Reibstein's *History of the Ideas of International Law.* In his *Appendix on international relations* Gauthier sketches a general interpretation which starts from Hobbes's characterisation of international relations as state of nature. Reibstein presents Hobbes's laws of nature as rules of international law, but without further examination.[2]

Preliminary remark 2: Is justifying the business of Minerva's Owl?

Searching for justification often seems nothing but the recourse of weakness. Guilt and weakness may try to restore their miserable position by ''justifying'' themselves. A successful justification could indeed be able to turn one's position into a more glorious one. Justification can consist in denying responsibility — a war criminal may urge, as an excuse, the authority of orders. In such a case justification keeps the flavour of misery. Justification may take place if controversial action is referred to uncontroversial higher norms: this is the very point of using "justification" in juridical way.

Justification may take place if — perhaps with the help of "Fortuna" — some fault, which normally is to be condemned, can be turned into a success. In the battle of Zorndorf (1758) General Seydlitz, neglecting the orders of King Frederick, retarded his attack. But this plain disobedience was justified in that it led to victory. This is an example of "glorious justification" and philosophy might learn from it — in spite of the example's military background. But for the present, philosophy seems to be quite remote from the persuasive power of a victorious cavalry general. The problem of justification is put in a way which shows decisive weakness. In a position of weakness philosophy runs after justification in two kinds: philosophy tries to justify something or it tries to justify itself.

The field which philosophy thus tries to order itself with is theology — which, of course, cannot strengthen its position as philosophy. Protestant theology has, taking up parts of Roman law, developed a doctrine of justification. Justification here comes close to the doctrine of final atonement. Its import is the idea of the restoration of the lost adoption by God, a restoration only depending on God's grace. Justification in this way is a very typical figure of religious belief — and one may easily comprehend that the philosophical position cannot be strengthened by taking over theological concepts.

Since Job's wife and friends tried to find some justification for the evil Job received, philosophers again and again have been fascinated by the trivial attempt to justify evil, harm and injustice in the world. But already the God of the Bible rejected such an attempt to rationalise his creation in that trivial way by answering: 'Where wast thou when I laid the foundations of the earth?' (Job. 38:4). Any philosophical attempt regarding theodicy must fail — as Kant and Voltaire have shown, each in his own way. Philosophy need not justify something or even justify its own existence or practice. It doesn't stand in need for that. It makes no sense to tell contemporaries how important or how useful philosophy can be. Philosophy shall try to do its job, that is, attempting the truth, and thereby asserting humanity and freedom. To think over how the work of philosophy is to be sold — e.g., by showing its ability to "justify" — is not the job of philosophers. Anything may be sold in a society like ours: this is just a question of marketing. Philosophy should not join this business. If it succeeds in getting into supermarkets, it will share the fate of those displays of the Athenian market of which Socrates said: 'How numerous are the things I don't need.'

Can world government be justified on Hobbesian principles? — The answer is No!

I'm not trying to give a systematic outline of Hobbes's theory of the "Law of Nations". I'll concentrate on the question which is put to Hobbes with the intention to actualise him against the background of the present situation of a world which considers the new quality of war and peace. Avoiding the word "justify" according to my preliminary remark 2, I put the problem in the following way: Are we able to draw from Hobbes's construction of Leviathan the model of some Super-Leviathan, who could bring the state of nature among the states to an end and thus bring us a world peace? If 'the world's greatest store of political wisdom' is to be put to good use for us in the present time then potential benefits depend on putting forward the adequate question. And I have doubts whether any benefit will be gained if we ask for the possibility of a world-state or world peace be it in the way the question is considered by Immanuel Kant or in the way it is suggested by the United Nations.

My thesis is that the idea of a world-state, a Super-Leviathan, which meets the task to create world peace — as Leviathan creates internal peace — can in no way be drawn from Hobbes. And not only because Hobbes himself says nothing about such a consequence but because this idea — which doesn't deserve the name "idea" because it's a mere fiction — is philosophically absolutely impossible. And I try to explain this by the following four points.

1. The General Philosophical Impossibility of the Concept of a World-State

Constitutive for any political subject (state) as for any individual subject is the quality of a "person". To act as a subject (or person) presupposes the necessity to recognise one's own limitations in space and time. Thus it is fundamental for the political subject to be aware of what he is and what he is not, what lies inside of his boundaries and what not, who belongs to him and who does not. So the mere condition of any self-conscious political reality implies negativity, or as Carl Schmitt put it: the very substance of political existence is the discrimination between friend and enemy. There are just no "natural boundaries" and the result of that negativity among the states is war. And, thus, it becomes not too unreasonable to call war an *ultima ratio*. But *vis-à-vis* the actual and disastrous developments of nuclear warfare the problem to overcome war as a result of political negativity reaches a new dimension. Regarding this problem, two models are predominant: that of a world-state and that of a world-society. (I do not deal with the problems of the latter.)

Nothing seems to be more plausible than to transfer the achievements of the modern state, especially in establishing and preserving internal peace, into the model of a state containing the whole world. In such a fictious state the sphere of all politics will become domestic politics. The simplicity of such thinking lies openly opposed to any dialectical reasoning. Negativity being the unavoidable

133

part of being a (political) subject one necessarily destroys the character of the subject by cancelling all negativity. One single subject is no subject at all. If the state loses its quality as subject, it cannot be conceptualised as realising the quality of man as subject, i.e., as realising freedom. A world-state would be, in an exact sense, a fundamentally inhuman construction. As a model it can only be plausible in containing nonphilosophical assumptions, which, in a trivial way, belong to mere fiction. And, of course, it is not accidental, that such a world-state is often conceived in science fiction. But even here, as a single political system, *terra* can only be conceived as a political subject by confronting it with extra-terrestrian opponents and, consequently, as involved in "Star Wars".

In a world-state world politics is replaced by world police. Without alternatives one can think of that possibility only as being one of the most totalitarian police systems man could create. As far as states are acting political subjects they have been — and are — the subjects of warfare. But the disasters of warfare do not result from the existence of states as such, not from their negativity as such, but from the non-recognition of the rights of other political subjects — domestic or foreign. The strict philosophical argument for the impossiblity of a world-state can be summarised with Hegel who, in paragraph (*Zusatz*) 92 of the *Encyclopedia*, says:

> Die Negation ist im Dasein mit dem Sein noch unmittelbar identisch und diese Negation ist das, was wir Grenze heißen. Etwas ist nur in seiner Grenze und *durch* seine Grenze das, was es ist. Man darf somit die Grenze nicht als dem Dasein bloß äußerlich betrachten, sondern dieselbe geht vielmehr durch das ganze Dasein hindurch.

This unavoidable negativity is made clear by Charles Taylor in the following way:

> But bodily reality is external reality, is *partes extra partes*, extended in space and time. Hence for consciousness to be it must be located, it must be somewhere, sometime. But if a consciousness is somewhere, sometime, it is not somewhere else, sometime else. It thus has a limit between itself and what is not itself. It is finite. (Taylor 1975, 89.)

2. Hobbes's Reality as a Pluriversum of States

The rise of a modern international law is linked to the recognition of sovereign states, the Leviathans, which exist side by side. A consequence of the existence of a plurality of states, each of them existing in his own right, is that those political bodies have and recognise mutual relations. A world-state or an universal monarchy, like the Roman Empire or the *Reich* of the middle ages is not reconcilable with that kind of international law. In the *Encyclopedia of International Law* (*Wörterbuch des Völkerrechts*) by Strupp and Schlochauer that historical fact is put like this:

International law was generated by the *"divisio regnorum"*, the decentralization of the *Sacrum Romanum Imperium uno actu* with the rise of the territorial state. After the vanishing of the community international law developed as juridical tie of a plurality of sovereign states. (Kunz 1962, 611.)

Now the theory of sovereignty from the beginning shows two sides: domestic and foreign. Sovereignty means that the power of the Leviathan is unlimited and that it is independent of any foreign power, secular or religious. And these presuppositions make home affairs subject to rational, planned action. This point is at the heart of sovereignty and until today it is one of the most important parts of theory of state and in international law. In the international law the three essential attributes of a state or commonwealth — according to the *Inter-American Convention of Rights and Duties of States* (Montevideo, 26 December 1933) are: state power, state territory and state people. The state-power must be sovereign and able to enter into international relations. The territory has to show the extension of sovereignty and to be delimited by other state-territories.[3]

In his theory of the commonwealth, Hobbes supposes that the delimited territory for his sovereignty only makes sense if it is clear where it ends. Furthermore, he supposes the destruction of the unity of a Christian Europe. In *Leviathan* he says, in discussing the theories of Bellarmin:

> In which argumentation there be two gross errors: one is, that all Christian kings, popes, clergy and all Christian men, make but one commonwealth. For it is evident that France is one commonwealth, Spain another, and Venice a third etc. And these consist of Christians; and therefore also are several bodies of Christians; that is to say several churches: and their several sovereigns represent them, whereby they are capable of commanding and obeying, of doing and suffering of a natural man. (Part III,42.)

In the same way *Leviathan* speaks about ''the people'' as a unified community of subjects obliged to a certain sovereign in a delimited territory. The community of the subjects consists of those who transferred their natural rights to the sovereign. So we can see that Hobbes always presupposes a real commonwealth and, according to him, to construct a World-State is just as impossible as to insist on a *Respublica Christiana*. In his theory of the commonwealth Hobbes always acts according to the political reality which unavoidably demands us to 'discriminate between friend and enemy'.

So, to come to the conclusion: I think that to enlarge the rational construction of the Leviathan to a world-wide range in order to get world-wide peace would be a ''very gross error''. Leviathan is not a model which can be applied as one likes. Here we are confronted with concrete political thinking, the foundations of which, in Hobbes, are nominalistic. To the nominalist, the concrete, the reali-

135

ty is always individual. The Leviathan, i.e., the modern commonwealth is a political person. And to think or to talk of a person presupposes the existence of other persons. A conception of one world-state makes no sense. For Hobbes world is unavoidable a "pluriversum" of states. There is no possibility of imagining a single world-state. That would be a fiction in the worst meaning of the world, a utopia — and not even a nice one — substituting world politics by world police.

Of course one may conceive anything, but a "strict" philosophy like that of Hobbes has nothing to do with fiction. Hobbes's answer to the question of world peace is in his *dictamina rectae rationis* related to the political persons, the pluriversum of Leviathans as actors. This theory of political reason excludes any imperialism as well as a world-state.

The belief of coming to world peace by erecting a world-state is as foolish as the belief that the Leviathan could make all harm disappear completely — a thought, whose foolishness is only surpassed by the fiction that some changes in the social system make crime disappear. To this foolishness is sometimes added the belief that changing of all social systems in a certain, for example, the socialist way, would bring about world peace. Thomas Hobbes saves us from such foolishness.

3. The Political Person and Its "State of Nature"

In Hobbes's theory of Leviathan — and also in international law afterwards — we find the analogy between the sovereign state and the individual person. The commonwealth is thought of as a person, and those persons find themselves in a state of nature without any power placed above them. In *Leviathan* we read:

> And in him consisteth the essence of the commonwealth; which, to define it, is one person, of whose acts a great multitude, by mutual covenants one with another, have made themselves everyone the author, to the end he may use the strength and means of them all, as he shall think expedient, for their peace and common defense. And he that carrieth this *person*, is called sovereign... (Part II, 17.)

And in *De Cive* (V, 9): 'Civitas ergo, ut eam definiamus, est *persona una...*' The individual as such having a natural right to everything, transfers this right to the sovereign in order to get protection for his life, his safety, his work and his wealth. Also we must say that civilised man is created in that act of transferring his inefficacious or abstract right to everything. So the commonwealth becomes a political person. The Leviathan looks after the rights of all its subjects, first of all, to protect them against foreign enemies.

The commonwealth is the person whose acts unify the wills, rights and forces of the subjects, The commonwealth as a person is represented by the person of the sovereign. The commonwealth as *persona moralis* or as "political person" exists under the same conditions as the self-conscious individual person. A person becomes a person by delimitation and by recognising the difference between himself and the rest of the world, including any other individual. The concept of person cannot be universalised; a person is always and necessarily a person among other persons. And Leviathan, being a political person, can only be thought of as a delimitated individual, finding itself to be different from others — and finding itself in a state of nature.

I think a further step can be taken. What I intend is to rethink the character of Leviathan as a political person. This character makes the state of nature among nations at least a little different from the original state of nature. Leviathan as a political person is not, as is often said, the last wolf. It is a work of art. It is constructed for a certain purpose, to solve a certain problem. And this purpose is the very reason of its existence. The very reason of Leviathan as artificial — not natural — person is *salus populi*. And, to quote from *De Cive*:

> (Salus populi in quo consistat?) Primum, ut ab hostibus externis defendantur. Secundum, ut pax interna conservetus. Tertium, ut quantum cum securitate publica consistere potest, locuplectentur. Quartum ut libertate innoxia perfruantur. (XIII, 6.)

The sovereign's first business is the security of the subjects. And by security is not only meant the bare preservation of life, 'but also all other contentments of life, which every man by lawful industry, without danger, or hurt to the commonwealth, shall acquire to himself' (Leviathan, XXX). The sovereign cannot content itself with seeking or keeping peace, it must create and generate peace. Peacemaking is the end of its very existence. As it is the creator of civil peace and order, it also is obliged; or better, it realises itself in creating external — as well as internal — peace by its action. Peace for Hobbes is something which must be produced. This view of politics is part of his technical approach to the world. And this technical approach demands a "person" to execute the political circumstance.

Hobbes's starting point was not some ideal or visionary view of the relations between states, but the analysis of foreign relations as reality presented them to him. And those relations were the unavoidable result of the behaviour of free, sovereign and independent commonwealths in a state of nature. He characterises this real behaviour in *Leviathan*:

> In all times, kings and persons of sovereign authority, because of their independency, are in continual jealousies, and in the state and posture of gladiators; having their weapons pointing, and their eyes fixed on one another; that is, their forts, garrisons, and guns upon the frontiers of their kingdoms; and continual spies upon their neigbours, which is a posture of war. (Part I, 13.)

137

Hobbes studied the actions of state relations in order to find out how to consider political action on the basis of practical science. 'True knowledge is always gained from natural reality' — as Horkheimer put it. The Leviathans act for the self-preservation of their own commonwealths. And Hobbes — seeing that the utmost aim of Leviathan's existence, the creation and preservation of a civil state, depends on state authority, self-assertion and independence — concludes that there is no alternative to the state of nature among commonwealths. War is not always avoidable, nevertheless the misery of the people will not be as great as in civil war, i.e., state of nature. Indeed, in war among states the public wealth may even increase. Yet warfare must be reduced to a minimum. And to achieve that rational advice can be given, from which a corpus of *dictamina* can be drawn and may form a law of nations. It makes no sense to look for theories of justice and injustice here, there is no place for ideals. Action is what is needed, realistic to the concrete situation. Politics becomes part of Hobbes's 17th century technical view of the world. World, also the world of politics, is the field of the individual political person to create and preserve himself.

The difference between the individual in the state of nature and the political person in the state of nature is that the former, *bare* state of nature between individuals is nothing else but a practical impossibility, since it is the very destruction of them. But the state of nature among political persons is compatible with the real existence of individuals in a civil order. Yet peace remains the utmost aim of Hobbes's political theory. Leviathan, for him, has without doubt a right to everything, but this right is linked with the reason of its very existence, which is peace. So politics of security are necessary for any political person. Leviathan having created the civil order has, according to the reason of its very existence, to establish its continuance and security.

4. Law of Nature — Law of Nations

I am not willing to remain simply negative. I intend to show that Hobbes, as far as international relations are concerned, doesn't leave us with a pure *bellum omnium in omnes*. And not only because his laws of nature — *dictamina rectae rationis* — really are rules for peaceful relations among states, but, also, because the Leviathans in the international state of nature show a different quality than human beings in their miserable state of nature.

According to *Leviathan* (Ch. XXX) the law of nations is identical with the law of nature. These laws of nature are, as Hobbes himself concedes, only 'improperly' called laws. Nevertheless they are the law of nations and we have to make the best of it. Reason, i.e., the attribute which makes a man man, at first sight makes for depravity in the state of nature, because it is used by man to overcome his fellow man. But together with fear and the desire of self-preservation it becomes the very means to end the disastrous state of *bellum omnium in omnes*.

A sovereign, being a person in state of nature, is subject to the law of nature. It is his very first aim to seek peace and keep it. More than the individual person the sovereign is obliged always to think about the worst possible case. Seeing other sovereigns trying to extend their power, he cannot show humility and a peaceful mind — which an individual might do — but must prepare for war to guarantee the safety of his people. In current literature on the law of nations the problem of war-prevention plays a dominating part. To quote only one author: 'The ultimate goal of the law of nations is an international state of peace, which enables all people and all nations to exist in orderliness with and beside each other' (Sauer 1955, 189).

Hobbes's law of nature are properly interpreted as commandments for the prevention of war. Of course the foundation of the law of nature/nations are the first and the second (Leviathan I, 14). Another fundamental presupposition for international relations and the peaceful coexistence of nations is the fifth law of nature/nations: 'that every man strive to accommodate himself to the rest'. In accordance with that, modern law of nations states: 'A nation which does not accommodate itself to the generally recognized rules of international relations falls into mistrust, isolation and aversion' (Lammasch 1930). Here as well as for the other laws, I see no need to give examples from today's international politics. It simply would take too much space. In this case I only like to remind the readers of the problem of the disintegration of the law of nations caused by the existence of the socialist nations and the (so called) Third World.

In order to reduce mistrust leading to war for reasons of security we need the forth and sixth law of nature/nations:

> ...that a man which recieveth benefit from another of mere grace, endeavour that he which giveth it, have no reasonable cause to repent him of his good will. For no man giveth but with the intention of good to himself. ... that upon caution of the future time, a man ought to pardon the offences past of them that repenting desire it.

Ambition, which leads to war on behalf of reputation and recognition is limited by the seventh and the eighth law. According to the latter, it 'should be avoided to declare hatred or contempt of another ... by deed, word, countenance, or gesture ... because all signs of hatred, or contempt provoke to fight...' The seventh law states, 'in revenges, that is retribution of evil for evil, men look not at the good to follow. ... Besides, revenge without respect to the example, and profit to come, is a triumph, or glorying in the heart of another, tending to no end ... contrary to reason...' (Here I cannot help to make a political remark: there are few examples which show so horribly the truth of Collingwood's statement that the disasters of the 20th century make men see Hobbes's true value than the peace dictated at Versailles. It was nothing else but one of the main causes of World War II.)

The tenth law commands, regarding to the conclusion of peace: '... that at the entrance into conditions of peace no man require to reserve himself any right, which he is not content should be reserved to every one of the rest.'

These few examples are sufficient to show that Hobbes holds a reasonable theory — *dictamina rectae rationis* — of a law of nations and of the behaviour of states among states.

Conclusion: 'The Sciences, are Small Power'

All wise and rational *dictamina* are not able to exclude irrational conduct. For the citizens the sword of the Leviathan enforces their observance to the civil law; without changing the *conditio humana*, that is, men are neither fundamentally good nor fundamentally evil. They are free, which beside all else, means they always have the possibility to act irrationally, even in a crazy way. What is the possibility in international politics to enforce the observance of these laws? When looking at this question we must always take into account that there are "crazy nations" as Dror (1963) titled his interesting study on this problem.

My argumentation about the impossibility of a world-state guaranteeing world peace together with the *small power* of the *dictamina* seems to be a rather poor result of examining Hobbes on this problem. Science can provide advice, *dictamina rectae rationis* but science, which in Hobbes includes philosophy, being of small power, cannot put an end to war. Peace is the result of the Leviathan's daily work, which is politics. I take it for one of Hobbes's most important political insights that there is no natural peaceful living. Peace cannot be regarded as a gift of heaven. The world of human life does not rest in the hands of the Almighty. Politics is something to be worked on, a result which is to be extracted from very obstinate and stubborn "material" — namely man.

The sovereign must remain a political person to be fit for its job. And its work, politics, remains — at home and abroad — a work which Max Weber, another great realist in politics, formulates as follows: 'Politics always is a drilling of very hard wood with patience and perceptiveness' (Weber 1971, 560).

Notes

1. For several references in this paper I owe much gratitude to an unpublished MS by Miss Monika Baumann, Bochum.

2. Gauthier 1969; and Reibstein 1958-63. As to current discussion: In a general way R.J. Vincent (1981) examines *The Hobbesian Tradition in Twentieth Century International Thought*. Vin-

cent's result is that Hobbesian tradition gets more and more 'moribund': 'undermined by the decline of the state and the rise of international government' (p. 91). It seems to me, however, that this statement is more concerned with the current discussions going on in political science than with the reality of actual politics. Cornelia Navari (1982) is absolutely right in encountering Vincent's argument showing that, looking at any international order whatsoever, one cannot deny that it deserves its existence to those great Leviathans. International order is depending from their existence. They had to "generate" or to create it — as well as internal peace and order. Quite close to the argument of the necessity of a "pluriversum" of Leviathans is Murray Forsyth (1979). Forsyth looks at that "pluriversum" as irrevocable and for him the rationality of behaviour among states is — as far as Hobbes is concerned — indeed prescribed in the "law of nature". Seeing any international relation determined by power, Hobbes's theory for Forsyth remains "realism". Hedley Bull (1981) sees Hobbes as the founder of the realist tradition, which in 20th century is held e.g. by Morgenthau. Yet for Bull, Hobbes is 'the philosopher of peace'. Hobbes's theory of international anarchy for him keeps its actuality; in a very interesting way he describes the nuclear deterrence as the institutionalisation of the Hobbesian "fear". (For the latter argument see also already B. Willms 1974.) Donald W. Hanson (1984) discussing also the concepts of Walzer, Beitz and Stanley Hoffmann, tries to show Morgenthau's meaning of "realism" can in no way get applied to Hobbes. But this approach takes Hobbes's individualism in an abstract way. Neither its rationality, the laws of nature, nor its idea of a person are treated by Hanson.

3. First put in this way by G. Jellinek (1900).

141

Hobbes's Logic of Law

Eerik Lagerspetz

1. Hobbes's Problem

The question of the foundations of legal systems might be regarded as the basic problem of legal theory. An adequate account of the foundations should provide an answer to the following questions: (1) What are the identification criteria for rules belonging to a legal system? (2) When does a legal system exist? (3) What makes the rules belonging to a system binding? The answers to these questions must be found outside a system itself. A legal system can, of course, include norms which provide identification criteria for other norms, or criteria for the existence of the system itself, or prescriptions concerning the normative force of the rules belonging to it. But we cannot answer these questions simply by pointing these norms, for these norms themselves are parts of their system. In order to answer the questions we must move into the meta-level. The analogy between the question of ultimate foundations in jurisprudence and the distinction between object-languages and meta-languages in logic has been noticed by Ivor Wilks (1955, 342-47) and by Julian Freund (1965, 119-20).

Thomas Hobbes was one of the first theorists who clearly saw the problem of the ultimate foundations. I will start by presenting a logical reconstruction of Hobbes's influential solution; then, I try to show how other theories in jurisprudence can be seen as attempts to solve the dilemmas arising from Hobbes's classical solution. My reconstruction is in the spirit of Hobbes's general approach: it is well known that Hobbes believed that the proper method of political philosophy is "geometrical", i.e. deductive.

Hobbes defines all laws as commands:[1]

Law in general, is not Counsell, but command; nor a Command of any man

142

to any man; but only of him, whose command is addressed to one formerly obliged to obey him. (Leviathan, Ch. xxvi, 40)

Therefore, we can define:

(1) N is a valid norm for x →there is some y whom x ought to obey and y has commanded N.

Hobbes's analysis is based on pragmatics of commanding. Commands are addressed by a superior to a subject; therefore, the following principles are natural:

(2) If in matter m, x ought to obey y → it is not true that y ought to obey x, in m.
(3) No one ought to obey oneself.
(4) If in matter m, x ought to obey y and y ought to obey z → x ought to obey z, in m.

These principles express *asymmetry, irreflexivity* and *transitivity* conditions for authority relations. The first two conditions are explicitly stated in *De Cive*:

> Neither can the city be obliged to her citizen; because, if he will, he can free her from her obligation; and he will, as oft as she wills; for the will of every citizen is in all things comprehended in the will of the city; the city therefore is free when she pleaseth, that is she is now actually free. (Ch. vi, 80.)
>
> Nor can he be obliged to himself, for the same part being both the obliged and the obliger, and the obliger having the power to release the obliged, it were merely in vain for a man to be obliged for himself, because he can release himself at his own pleasure; and he who can do this, is actually free. (Ch. vi, 79.)

Other authorities ought to be obeyed because they are also authorised by a sovereign; the authority of the sovereign, on the contrast, is not based on positive norms (commands) but on the social contract and natural law. Therefore, our obligation to obey a sovereign is prior to any specific legal obligations:

> For since our obligation to civil obedience, by virtue whereof the civil laws are valid,is before all civil law, and the sin of treason is naturally nothing else but the breach of that obligation, it follows, that by the sin of treason, that law is broken which precede the civil law, to wit, the natural, which forbids us to violate the covenants and betrothed faith. But if some sovereign prince should set forth a law on this manner, thou shalt not rebel, he would just effect nothing. For except subjects were before obliged to obedience, that is to say, not to rebel, all law is of no force. Now

143

the obligation which obligeth to what we were before obliged to, is superfluous. (De Cive, Ch. xiv, 170.)

Consequently, we can define the concept of sovereignty as follows:

(S) y is the sovereign for x $\rightarrow$ x ought to obey y, and there is no valid norm that x ought to obey y.

If there are any valid norms, there must also be a sovereign satisfying the definition. Suppose that for every y who must be obeyed by some x there were a valid authorising norm with that effect. Because of (1), even an authorising norm must be a command issued by some authority z. If this z were identical with y, the norm would be superfluous, as Hobbes says. If z were somebody else, the question about the source of authority would reappear. And because infinite regress is obviously excluded, there must be an ultimate authority which satisfies the definition (S).

According to Hobbes, sovereign power is *illimitable*. This follows from the postulate (1) that all valid norms are commands, and from the supposition that power can be limited only by norms:

(L) Some possible commands of y are not valid norms for x $\rightarrow$ there is a valid norm N for y that some of her possible commands are not valid norms for x.

If some of the possible commands of y are not valid norms, we say that her authority is limited. Now, let us make the counterassumption: For every y, the authority of y is limited. By (L), the limitation is always based on some valid norm N, which, by (1), is a command of some z of whom y ought to obey. Because of irreflexivity, z cannot be identical with y, and because of asymmetry, it is not so that z, in turn, must obey y; there cannot be any "loops" in the chain of commands. But, according to our counterassumption, there must then be a further authority w who sets limits for z, etc. The counterassumption leads into infinite regress, and therefore:

(5) There exists an authority y such that all his possible commands are valid norms (or, his power is illimited).

Clearly, such a y is a sovereign in the sense expressed by (S). All his commands are binding, thus all other authorities of the system based their power on his commands, and therefore, there cannot be a separate authority authorising him. Hobbes himself formulates the argument in this way:

For if his power were limited, that limitation must necessarily proceed from some greater power. For he that prescribes limits, must have greater

144

power than he who is confined by them. Now that confining power is either without limit, all is again restrained by some other greater than itself, and so we shall at length arrive to a power which hath no other limit, but which is *terminus ultimus* of the forces of all citizens together. (De Cive, Ch. vi, 84.)

Hobbes's conclusion can also be supported by his theory of interpretation. It is an essential part of his general doctrine that the monopoly to interpret the Scriptures is in the hands of the sovereign power. This is important, because the power to interpret a norm is actually a power to command the norm's subjects. His doctrine of legal interpretation is similar:

And therefore the Interpretation of all Lawes dependenth on the Authority Soveraign; and the Interpreters can be none but those, which the Soveraign (to whom only the Subject oweth obedience) shall appoint. For else, by the craft of an Interpreter, the Law may be made to beare a sense, contrary to that of the Soveraign; by which means the Interpreter becomes a Legislator. (Leviathan, Ch. vi, 146.)

This doctrine can be formulated as a principle:

(6) x ought to obey norm N and y has the power to interpret N $\rightarrow$ x ought to obey y.

Now, if there are norms constraining the power of a sovereign, and if, for every norm there must be someone with the power to interpret it, we are back in the regress. From (6) and from the irreflexivity condition it follows that the sovereign itself cannot have the power to interpret these norms; from (6) and from the asymmetry condition it follows that the interpreter cannot be any of subjects. Thus, there cannot be such norms:

But those Lawes which the Soveraign himselfe, that is, which the Common-wealth maketh, he is not subject. For to be subject to Lawes, is to be subject to the Common-wealth, that is to the Soveraign Repre-sentative, that is to himselfe; which is not subjection, but freedome from Lawes. Which errour, because it setteth the Lawes above the Soveraign, setteth also a Judge above him, and a power to punish him; which is to make a new Soveraign; and again for same reason a third, to punish the second; and so continually without end, to the Confusion, and Dissolution of the Common-wealth. (Leviathan, Ch. xxix, 173.)

For these reasons, there cannot be constitutional norms constraining the power of a sovereign. Neither can there be any International Law in the proper sense.

A legal system is, for Hobbes, a set of persons united by authority relations; in modern terms it is a partially ordered set with a maximal element, a sovereign. However, I have not proved yet that there must be a single maximal element. This would mean that sovereignty is *indivisible*. In order to prove it, we need an additional postulate.

For Hobbes it is essential that "ought" implies "can". This follows directly from his attempt to merge the requirements of the law of nature with individual rationality. Therefore, it is clear that the following condition holds:

(7) The set of norms valid for x is consistent.

Suppose that sovereignty is divided so that both y and z are sovereigns of x. Then, either y and z can give mutually inconsistent commands for x or they can not. If they can, the condition (7) is not satisfied. Therefore, their power to give commands must be limited. But, by (L), the limitation is possible only through valid norms. If these norms are issued by one or the other of the two sovereigns, then either this sovereign is limiting its own power, which is impossible, or it is limiting the power of the other sovereign, in which case the other cannot be a sovereign. On the other hand, if the limiting norms were issued by some third party, neither y nor z could be a sovereign. Consequently, sovereignty is indivisible.

The consistency argument is presented in *Leviathan*, when Hobbes speaks about the powers of religious and civil officials:

> For seeing the *Ghostly* power challengeth the Right to declare what is sinne it challengeth by consequence to declare what is law... and again, the *Civil* Power challenging to declare what is law, every subject must obey two Masters, who both will have their Commands be observed as Law, what is impossible. Or if it be but one Kingdome, either the *Civill*, which is the Power of the Common-wealth, must subordinate to the *Ghostly*, and then there are no sovereignty but the *Ghostly*, or the *Ghostly* must be subordinate to the *Temporall*, and then there is no Supremacy but the *Temporall*. (Leviathan, Ch. xxix, 173.)

Contrary to what is sometimes asserted, the indivisibility of sovereignty is a necessary consequence of the Hobbesian theory of law.

As we have noticed, it is a theorem of the theory that if there are valid norms, a legal sovereign must exist. Therefore, there necessarily is *a rule of succession* in every continuous legal system, i.e. a rule of the following form:

(C) If x ceases to be the sovereign, y becomes the sovereign.

If there were no rule of succesion, it would be impossible to identify the successor of a sovereign, and after the death of x, the system would disappear. The rule of succession is a valid norm and must be based on the existing sovereign's expressed or tacit command:

> For the death of him that hath the Soveraign power in propriety, leaves the Multitude without any Soveraign at all; that is, without any Representative in whom they should be united, and be capable of doing any action at all: And therefore they are incapable of Election of any new Monarch, every

man having equall right to submit himselfe to such as he thinks best able to protect him... Therefore, it is manifest, that by the Institution of Monarchy, the disposing of the Successor, is alwaies left to the Judgement and Will of the present Possessor. (Leviathan, Ch. xix, 103.)

Indivisibility, illimitability and continuity are the essential properties of a Hobbesian sovereign. The conceptual role of a legal sovereign is very similar to that of the omnipotent God in theology. As it is sometimes noticed, the concept of omnipotence is ambiguous in both cases. (See Hart 1972, 144-50.) Can a necessarily omnipotent being voluntarily give away some part of its omnipotence. Both affirmative and negative answers seem to be inconsistent with the idea of necessary omnipotence. In imperative theories of law, this problem (which is analogous to the Stone Paradox in theology) can be formulated as follows. Suppose that a Hobbesian sovereign gives an order to his subjects:

(O) x ought not to obey any commands of the sovereign concerning the matter m.

Has the sovereign succeeded in limiting his own power over the subjects? If (O) establishes a valid norm for x, then the commands of the sovereign concerning the matter m are not valid norms for x. On the other hand, if (O) does not establish a valid norm, then there is at least one valid command of the sovereign which is not valid. Both conclusions seem to be against the theorem that the sovereign is necessarily omnipotent.

Hobbes's solution to this problem is, that in spite of its form, (O) does not constitute a real command. By expressing (O), the sovereign has not performed a meaningful speech act:

> If the monarch promise aught to any one, or many subjects together, by consequence whereof the exercise of his power may suffer prejudice, that promise or compact ...is null. ...he who sufficiently signifies his will of retaining the end, doth also sufficiently declare that he quits not his right to the means necessary to that end. Now he who hath promised to part with somewhat necessary to the supreme power itself, gives sufficient tokens, that he no otherwise promised it than sofar forth as the power might be retained without it. Whensoever therefore it shall appear that what is promised cannot be performed without prejudice to that power, the promise must be valued as not made, that is, of no effect. (De Cive, Ch. vii, 98.)

Hobbes seems to have thought that when a sovereign tries to give command like (O), he actually intends to use his power concerning the matter m, and the validity of the command is dependent on that power. The command produces a paradox of self-reference; the command is valid only if it is not valid. A sovereign can give his power away only by resigning. This interpretation of illimitability is fatal for all attempts to base the International Law on valid norms. The sovereign is equally unable to make contracts with other sovereigns, for that would limit his powers, too. Agreements between sovereigns cannot be but mutual declarations of intentions, without any normative impact.

2. Other Theories

In his theory, John Austin adopts the main points of Hobbes's theory of law. For Austin, as for Hobbes, laws are commands addressed by a political superior to a subject. At the top of the legal system there is a supreme authority, the sovereign, who is habitually obeyed by the rest of the population of a political society, but who himself does not obey anyone. The sovereign's power is illimitable (Austin 1954). Hobbes's infinite regress-argument reappears in Austin's works:

> The power of the superior immediately imposing the restraints (for a sovereign, EL) or the power or some other sovereign superior to that superior, would still be absolutely free from the fetters of positive law. For unless the imagined restraints were ultimately imposed by a sovereign not in state of subjection to a higher sovereign, a series of sovereigns ascending from infinity would govern the imagined community. Which is impossible and absurd. (Austin 1954, 254.)

This proof is valid only if Hobbes's conditions of irreflexivity and asymmetry are accepted. Otherwise authority x could be able to limit the power of another authority y and *vice versa*, or x could limit its own power.

The conditions (2)-(4), however, seem to be incompatible with Austin's attempt to reduce the legal authority relations to facts about habitual obedience. As Austin himself recognises, empirically observable habits of obedience are not necessarily a symmetric (Austin 1954, 25). For example, a legislature may habitually obey the prescriptions of a supreme court in certain matters, while the court may accept the superiority of the court in other matters. It is possible that a system in which the supreme authority is divided among several agencies controlling each others may generate inconsistencies in some situations. If such an inconsistency emerges, so that the decisions of the legislature and the court conflict, it may be only the happenstances of the political situation which determine who has the last say. It is not necessary that the solution is somehow predictable from the present habits of obedience existing among the legal organs.

There are other difficulties in the theory. For Austin, all constitutional as well as international law is merely "positive morality". This is problematic, because the source of this morality is often the same as the source of laws, namely the supreme legal authorities. And even if constitutional norms are only a part of morality, it must be admitted that it often effectively constrains the activities of legal authorities. Contrary to Austin and Hobbes, sovereigns seem to be able to limit their own power. Here, it is the irreflexivity condition which creates problems (cf. Morawetz 1980, 20-1).

Another difficulty comes from the asymmetry condition and from the Hobbesian doctrine of interpretation. It is deeply rooted in modern political theory, that although a legislature uses the highest legal power in a society, the ultimate power belongs to the electorate, which, as the *pouvoir constituant* controls the legislature and other legal authorities. The modern democratic theory supposes a symmetrical relation between the sovereign and the subjects as a whole; this is the doctrine of popular sovereignty. A great part of the history of modern political thought can be seen as an attempt to accommodate the symmetrical relation between legal authorities and their subjects implied by the democratic doctrines into the hierarchical picture of law in Hobbes, and others.

Examples of these difficulties are Filmer's and Kant's denials that the people can ever have a legal right to depose their sovereign. They deny this for the Hobbesian reason that such a right would presuppose an authority entitled to interpret such and to exercise such. Since that authority isn't the sovereign itself (for then the right would be empty), and it cannot be the people (for that would leave the sovereign powerless), or a third party (for that would either make the third party a sovereign, or lead into infinite regress). On the other hand, Hunton and Locke accepted that the people have a right to step outside the legal system ("appeal to Heaven") and remove rulers which surpassed the constraints of constitution.

The supposed symmetricalness of authority-relations is a real problem. Although we noticed that authority relations can well be symmetrical in the sense that x and y have authority over each other in some different issues, this symmetricality is still restricted in the sense that they cannot have complete authority over each other's *exercise of that authority*. If the people, for example, have an effective right to throw out their otherwise omnipotent rulers, the rulers cannot have a right to control the people's exercise of that right.

The German sociologist Niklas Luhmann has, interestingly, formulated the problem in quite similar terms as I have here. In his rather difficult article, Luhmann (1980) describes the development of modern political doctrines as a progress from an a-symmetrical two-position -idea (sovereign → subject) to a symmetrical three-position -idea (people → politics → administration → people). The necessity of the third mediating position comes from the fact that a fully symmetrical authority system would be indeterminate (Luhmann 1980, 70-1). This implies that the relations between authorities must be intransitive: from the fact that the electorate exercises control over politicians, and the politicians, in their turn, over administration, does not follow that the people can control the administration.

Austin tried to accommodate the idea of popular sovereignty by suggesting that in democracies, the electorate is the sovereign. But Austin agrees with Hobbes that no-one can command himself (Austin 1954, 284). Austin's solution is that the sovereign body can impose obligations for its individual members. The members of a sovereign body can collectively, and in their official capacities, command all the members distributively and each in their personal capacities. (This looks quite like Rousseau's solution to the same problem.) But there is still a problem, noticed (among many others) by David Lyons (1984, 50): 'we cannot identify the members of the electorate without having recourse to those legal rules that establish voting priviledges'. One of the problems appearing in Austin's theory is the difficulty to identify the legal authority which is supposed to be the source of all laws without referring back to these laws. Again, this problem is by no means unique for Austin. A similar problem arises from the Realist doctrine that all law is created by courts.

The form of legal positive adopted in Germany during the 19th century responded to the last problem in the following way: Law is the will of the State, and the State is identifiable as a social fact, without recourse to legal norms. The problem raised by constitutional and international law was solved by supposing that the State was capable of self-limitation (Selbstverpflichtung) (see Jellinek 1921, 367-79). This is the other possible answer to the omnipotence dilemma created by the commands like (O).

This version of positivism was the starting point for the theory of Hans Kelsen. There are almost no references to Hobbes in Kelsen's main works. Nevertheless, the basic logic of their theories is similar, and they both shared the ''geometrical'' conception of method (Kelsen 1911, 92-5). A comparison between Kelsen and Hobbes is made by Gentile (1986, 44-59). Gentile, however, is stressing other aspects in their works than I here.

Kelsen rejects the idea of the State's self-limitation (Kelsen 1970, 312-3). He also rejects Austin's and the German Positivist's attempt to find a non-normative foundation for law. For Kelsen, sovereignty and the State were normative concepts. His way to formulate the question about the ultimate foundations of legal systems is epistemological: How is it possible to conceive something as a normative order?

Kelsen's theory is normative and ''pure'' in two senses. It is supposed to be purified from all factual considerations. It is also normative in the sense that relations inside the legal system are relations between norms, not between persons in different positions.

For Kelsen, the predicates ''higher''and ''lower'', or ''superior''and ''inferior'' refer to the properties of norms. Lower norms are derivable from the higher norms in the sense that higher norms *authorise* the creation of lower norms. The following passage is typical for Kelsen:

The reason for the validity of a norm is always a norm, not a fact. The quest for the reason of validity of a norm leads back, not to reality, but to another norm from which the first norm is derivable... (Kelsen 1949, 111.)

Thus, we can formulate the following:

(1') N is a valid positive norm $\rightarrow$ there is a norm N' such that it authorises the creation of N, and N is created according to N'.

It is this relation which compels a legal system into a hierarchical structure:

> To the question why a certain act of coercion — e.g. the fact that one individual deprives another individual of his freedom by putting him in jail — is legal act, the answer is: because it has been prescribed by an individual norm, a judicial decision. To the question why this individual norm is valid as part of a definite legal order, the answer is: because it has been created in conformity with a criminal statute. This statute, finally, receives its validity from the constitution, since it has been established by the competent organ in the way constitution prescribes. (Kelsen 1949, 115.)

Ultimately, norms belong to one and same legal system because their validity can be traced back to the first constitution which established the legal order in question (Kelsen 1949, 115). In order to create this kind of unified hierarchy between various norms, Kelsen must accept the normativist counterparts of the Hobbesian conditions (2)-(4):

(2') Norm N authorises norm N' $\rightarrow$ it is not true that N' authorises N.

(3') No norm authorises itself.

(4') N' authorises N and N'' authorises N' $\rightarrow$ N'' authorises N.

These principles are not sufficient to guarantee the *unity* of legal systems supposed by Kelsen. They do not imply that all the chains of authorisation have a common starting point: the fact that every lower norm is derivable from some higher norm does not imply that there is a higher norm from which all lower norms are derivable. This is a point made by Munzer (1972, 48; cf. a similar point against sovereignty made by Lucas 1966). However, the unity requirement follows from the Kelsen's idea that a legal system is necessarily a consistent system of norms. Kelsen supposes that a legal system itself must provide means to solve conflicts between alleged norms: when two legal requirements seem to be mutually inconsistent, there must either be a third norm saying which of the two norms is valid, or an organ authorised to solve the dispute. This organ must base its competence on some norm belonging to the same system. Thus, Kelsen has a principle of indivisibility of normative systems comparable to Hobbes's principle of indivisibility of sovereignty. In order to avoid contradictions, only one normative system can be considered as the binding one:

> If one assumes that two systems of norms are considered as valid from
> the same point of view, one must also assume a normative relation be-
> tween them; one must assume the existence of a norm or order that
> regulates their mutual relations. Otherwise insoluble contradictions be-
> tween the norms of each system are unavoidable and the logical principle
> that excludes contradictions holds for the cognition of norms as much as
> for the cognition of natural reality. (Kelsen 1949, 115.)

The principle of consistency leads into the principle of unity:

(5') N and N' are valid positive norms $\rightarrow$ there is a norm N'' such that it
authorises both N and N'.

The principles (1')-(5') and the exclusion of infinite regress imply the conclusion
that for every system of valid positive norms there is a unique maximal element
which is not authorised by any positive norm but which itself authorises all other
norms of the system. This is Kelsen's famous Grundnorm or the basic norm.
The proof is exactly the same as Hobbes's and Austin's proof of the existence
of a sovereign:

> The norm which represents the reason for validity of another norm is call-
> ed, as we have said, the "higher" norm . But the search of the reason of
> a norm's validity cannot go on indefinitely like the search for cause of an
> effect. It must end with a norm which, as the last and the highest, is
> presupposed. It must be *presupposed*, because it cannot be "posited",
> that is to say: created, by an authority whose competence would have to
> rest on a still higher norm. This final norm's validity cannot have derived
> from a higher norm, the reason of its validity cannot have questioned. Such
> a presupposed higher norm is referred in this book as a basic norm.
> (Kelsen 1970, 195.)

We notice the parallelism between the arguments of Hobbes and Kelsen. And
similar *regressus ad infinitum* arguments do appear in other philosophical contexts. Every chain of justification must ultimately either to go *ad infinitum*, or
to refer back to itself, or to stop at some point. A common solution in philosophy
is to stop the regress to a justificatory ground which is supposed to be
qualitatively different from the earlier steps of the argument: The Immovable
Mover, statements which are beyond doubt, and so on. Kelsen's basic norm has
a comparable function.

As compared with the Hobbesian notion of sovereign, the basic norm has certain advantages. It solves the problem of self-limitation, and it makes possible
to base the highest authority on law, not only on the pre-legal fact of sovereignty. However, the ghost of *Leviathan* is still haunting in Kelsen's normative conception of legal system. Kelsen could not ignore the fact that legal organs often
seem to break the rules regulating their conduct: legislatures can enact norms

which are apparently inconsistent with the limitations prescribed by constitutions, courts can refuse to apply ostensively valid norms, and so on. And such unauthorised actions can have their intended effects. Kelsen was ultimately unable to avoid the fatal conclusion: if a legal organ decides to act as a Hobbesian sovereign with unlimited powers, and to ignore the restrictions posed by constitutional or international laws,and if its actions are politically successful, the organ has created new legal facts by breaking the law. This conclusion is especially damaging for his theory of international law.

Several legal theorists, from Harold Laski and Leonard Nelson to H.L.A. Hart have argued that the Hobbesian conception of sovereignty is either theoretically inadequate or politically dangerous or both. They may be right. Nevertheless, the Hobbesian conception still penetrates a great part of contemporary thinking in international affairs. One reason for the persuasiveness of this doctrine is certainly found in its exceptional logical clarity.

Notes

1. References are made to the following works and editions: *De Cive*, in *Man and Citizen*, ed. by Bernard Gert, Peter Smith, Gloucester 1987; *Leviathan*, Dent's Everyman Library, London 1973.

Agreements with Hostage-Takers

Martin P. Golding

I

The topic of this paper is an old problem that has contemporary relevance. We may well use Hobbes's formulation. 'It is a usual question,' he says,[1]

> whether compacts extorted from us through fear, do oblige, or not: for example, if, to redeem myself from the power of a robber, I promise to pay him 100 £ next day, and that I will do not act whereby to apprehend and bring him to justice, whether I am tied to keep promise or not (De Cive, Ch. II, 16.)

Hobbes's example of a promise made to a robber, or the promise of a ransom to an enemy (as he puts it in *Leviathan*, 14), is of course just an instance of a current global problem, namely agreements with hostage-takers, hijackers, and terrorists. Are such agreements binding?

This issue is discussed by many other 17th-century writers, most notably Grotius and Pufendorf. Its oldest statement, however, might be that found in Cicero, who has no doubts about how it should be answered. 'Suppose', says Cicero,

> that one does not deliver the amount agreed upon with pirates as the price of one's life, that would be counted no deception — not even if one should fail to deliver the amount after having sworn to do so; for a pirate is not included in the number of lawful enemies, but is the common foe of all the world; and with him there ought not to be any pledged word or oath mutually binding. (Cicero, 107.)

As is well-known, Hobbes disagrees with Cicero. 'Covenants entered into by fear, in the condition of mere nature,' Hobbes writes, 'are obligatory... And even in commonwealths, if I be forced to redeem myself from a thief by promising him money, I am bound to pay it till the civil law discharge me' (Leviathan, 14).

Pufendorf, on the other hand, agrees with Cicero's conclusion, though, as we shall see, he rejects the latter's rationale.

It may seem that the contemporary problem is somewhat removed from the one posed by Hobbes, for it arises, not in connection with a promise made by some individual to another, but rather in connection with promises made by a government or an agent of the sovereign. And in the latter case, it arises both in the international context (e.g., an agreement made between the Italian government and Lebanese hijackers situated in a boat off the cost of Egypt) and the domestic context (e.g., an agreement made by the Governor of New York State with prison inmates who have taken guards as hostages). It seems to me, however, that as far as Hobbes is concerned there may be little or no difference of principle among these cases, for they all can be considered instances of state-of-nature promises, in some respects. They are all, in any event, coerced promises, promises extorted by intimidation or threats, whose bindingness, under certain conditions, is affirmed by Hobbes.

In this paper, I want to examine Hobbes's grounds for maintaining that extorted promises can be binding. It is quite clear that this is an important matter for him, as is shown by the continuation of the quotation given above from *De Cive*, Ch. II, 16:

> But though such a promise must sometimes be judged to be of no effect, yet it is not to be accounted so because it proceedeth from fear. For then it would follow that those promises which reduced men to a civil life, and by which laws were made, might likewise be of none effect; (for it proceeds from fear of mutual slaughter, that one man submits himself to the dominion of another)...

This argument is not repeated in the *Leviathan*, perhaps because it amounts to no more than begging the question of the validity of his own theory of the political contract. Still, it is plain that the general binding force of coerced promises remains strategically important for Hobbes. While I think that there is no difference in principle, for Hobbes, between agreements extorted by kidnappers from governments and those extorted from individuals, toward the end of my discussion I shall return to the question of governments' agreements with hostage-takers.

II

Since much of this paper is concerned with Hobbes's theory of the obligation of promises, some preliminary, general remarks on promise and contract-making are in order. The first point that deserves notice, I think, is that promise or contract is, as Hobbes maintained, a form of social ordering. There are, of course other such forms. Ordering by domination is one that is recognised by

155

Hobbes, and other possibilities are suggested by Sir Henry Sumner Maine's status-contract distinction and Tönnies's *Gemeinschaft-Gesellschaft* continuum.

But there are important differences, which Hobbes overlooks, between the "one shot" agreement of the sort being considered here and contracts that set the conditions of long-term collaboration, for example, a labour-management agreement. Both kinds, of course, involve the future, and in each sort the cleverness and the bargaining power of the parties are significant factors in setting the terms of an agreement, as is obvious in the case of coerced promises. Yet the complexities involved in negotiating the long-term agreement seem, on average, to far exceed those of the one-shot affair. In the former, the parties will come to the negotiations with many "anticipatory expectations." And, as Lon Fuller points out in an excellent discussion of ordering by contract (1968, 110-132), it carries a cost as well as advantages: an explicit contract may prove to be too inflexible, especially when future contingencies cannot be foreseen, as is often the case. (This is the trouble with the detailed marriage contracts that are popular in some circles.) There also are some relations that do not readily admit of long-term ordering by contract: relations between intimates, between hostile parties, and between superior and inferior, where the agreement will impinge upon the authority of the superior.

Hobbes overlooks these considerations in his tendency to view the political contract as just one other sort of contract, though he does try to take one of them into account by his unrealistic postulation of equality in the state of nature. These considerations must be kept in mind, I think, in any attempt to extend Hobbesian thought to the question of international order. Few of these considerations, however, seem to have any bearing on the problem of coerced promises, where the inequality of the bargaining power of the parties is evident. Nor do they seem to be of equal relevance to the case of one-item contracts between individuals.

Two other preliminary points should be noted. Though the expression "I promise" sometimes is used to affirm a fact, promise-making concerns the future (*pace* Professor Patrick Atiyah). But how is promise possible? How does — to put the matter somewhat dramatically — that which is not, but will be, get transformed into the "now," a present obligation? This is an important question because reciprocity and mutuality depend on the idea of the future, an idea that, as an anthropologist has argued, also underlies the very notion of kinship (see Wilson 1983). Justice Oliver Wendell Holmes thought that the origins of promise were a mystery: 'to explain how mankind first learned to promise,' he says 'we must go to metaphysics, and find out how it ever came to frame a future tense' (Holmes 1923, 251). The futurity of promises is central to Hobbes's discussion. (A promise, he says, uses such words of the future as "I will give, I will grant"; a promise in fact is "a promise of the act of will to come" — see

Leviathan, 14.) It is this feature of promises which raises the problem of trust — can I trust you to do tomorrow what you have today promised to do tomorrow? — and trust is needed to get us out of the state of war.

A second aspect of the question "How is promise possible?" turns on the fact that promises impose obligations where none existed before. But how do we get committed to a course of conduct that, absent the promise, is morally neutral? Aside from the considerations mentioned above regarding how the terms of a contract are negotiated there must be some ground or principle on which the obligation of promises is based. Whatever this ground may be, many thinkers would hold that coerced or extorted promises will contravene it. How can Hobbes, for whom the issues of trust and the obligation of promises are so intertwined, hold otherwise?

III

It is necessary to keep in mind the sort of promise or contract situation that is at issue: it is, first of all a *bargain* contract, and more precisely what Hobbes terms a covenant, though his use of the word is not always consistent. We have to imagine a dialogue between the hostage-taker or hijacker and victim which has the following form:

(1) Kidnapper: I will do X, if you will do Y.
(2) Victim: I will do Y, if you will do X.

The order in which the statements are made does not seem to matter. "Do X" and "do Y" function as place-holders, and may be respectively filled in by such expressions as "let you (me) go" and "send back $100." I don't think we should exclude a bargain in which the kidnapper or hostage-taker offers the victim a drink of water in return for the victim's promise to send back $100 should he ever manage to escape. The next step in the situation is that the kidnapper X's, that is, performs. The victim now has a covenant with the other party. Is the victim morally obliged to Y, that is, keep this covenant? Hobbes's answer, unlike Cicero's and Pufendorf's is affirmative. Why so?

Before we consider this question, let us note that if the occurrences of "will" are eliminated and the place-holders are filled in with "promise to let you (me) go" and "promise to send back $100," we have what Hobbes calls a covenant of mutual trust. In the condition of "mere nature" such a covenant is void. 'He should play the fool finely,' says Hobbes, 'who should trust his captive covenanting with the price of his redemption' (De Cive, Ch. II, 16). 'For he that performs first has no assurance that the other will perform after, because the bonds of words are too weak to bridle men's ambition, avarice, anger, and other passions without the fear of some coercive power...' (Leviathan, 14).

There are, it appears, many possible theories of the obligation of promise and contract, and I think we shall not find it easy to fit Hobbes under any one rubric. If we were considering a general basis for the *legal enforcement* of promises, we could note that it is approachable from two extremes. It might be held, on the one hand, that promises should generally be unenforceable, but exceptions should be made for those it is desireable to enforce; on the other hand, it might be held that promises should generally be enforceable, but exceptions should be made for those whose enforcement is undesirable. The adoption of one or the other of these approaches by a legal system is likely to influence how its law of contracts develops (see Farnsworth 1969).

Now while Hobbes is not directly dealing with the legal enforcement of promises and contracts, we might speculate for a moment on which alternative represents, as it were, the Hobbesian approach. The third law of nature, in *Leviathan* (Ch. XV) 'that men perform their covenants made,' or as it is put in *De Cive* (Ch. III, 1) 'to perform contracts, or to keep trust,' suggests something like the second option, namely, that there is a general moral obligation to keep all promises. An exception exists, however, for the gratuitous promise, the promise of a "free gift," whose enforcement, as it were, would be undesirable. The basis of this exception, as stated in *De Cive* (Ch. II, 8) is that 'it is (not) suitable to reason, that those who are easily inclined to do well to others, should be obliged by every promise, testifying their present good affection.' Furthermore, a man should have the opportunity to change his mind, especially since the person to whom he made the gratuitous promise 'may alter his desert.' When a promise is morally binding, the promisor is not generally allowed to change his mind.

The second alternative is also suggested by the apparent fact that, in the state of nature, one who renounces a right cannot recover it without some action on the part of others. The underlying principle here seems to be that surrendering a moral permission (if a Hobbesian natural right genuinely is a *moral* permission) amounts to placing oneself under a moral constraint (see Kavka 1986, 303).

There are, however, many passages that suggest the first alternative, namely, that there is no general moral obligation to keep promises in the state of nature, but rather that any such obligation arises only under very specific conditions and for specific reasons. Since I shall be going into these conditions in some detail, I shall mention only the invalidity of covenants of mutual trust as evidence for the first option. The crucial matter in settling this issue of alternatives is Hobbes's view on how promises get made, and it has a significant bearing on the question of agreements with hostage-takers, that is, coerced promises. In my opinion it is not easy to settle the question of which of the two positions Hobbes maintains, because he seems to have more than one account of the obligation of promise-keeping.

IV

It is obviously impossible to consider here the entire gamut of theories of contractual obligation. Instead, let us speak of paradigms of obligation. These fall into three rough and partially overlapping groups: (1) consent theories, (2) benefit-reliance theories, and (3) commitment theories. The first group contains those accounts that stress the role of the "will" in founding an obligation and accord respect for individual autonomy and the capacity for rational, voluntary choice. The second group includes theories that ground obligation on benefits received or detriments suffered. Loosely speaking, if I receive a benefit from you I have a duty to reciprocate it; and if I act in reliance on your word or deeds (which presumably costs me something) you should see to it that I have no cause to regret that reliance. The third group is perhaps the least well-defined. It covers commitments based on group membership, citizenship, loyalty, friendship, or concern for others. Although in the end it might be the most important of all, I think we can put it aside in this discussion. While the remaining paradigms have implications beyond the issue of the obligation of promise-keeping, our treatment will be confined to it.

It is worth noting that the adoption of one or the other group of theories of contractual obligation could be legally significant. Many countries have no enactment empowering people to bind themselves contractually, and the agreements and promises that will be enforced are likely to depend implicitly on a preferred theory.

Hobbes's position seems to contain elements of both of the remaining paradigms of obligation. A statement in *Leviathan* (Ch. XXI) suggests something like a consent or "will" theory of contract. 'There is no obligation on any man, which ariseth not from some act of his own,' he says. All obligation, then, has its source in self-obligation. Mutual promise-making, as Kant might have said, is a way of enlarging the scope of one's will; it makes the future one's present possession, so to speak. When two parties voluntarily obligate themselves to each other, a bond is created; it is entirely a matter of the intention of the parties that their words be effective. Furthermore, there is a passage that seems to assert that the first party in a covenant of mutual trust may be required to perform his part of the bargain. 'Covenants which are made in contract of mutual trust, neither party performing out of hand, if there arise a just suspicion in either of them, are in the state of nature invalid' (De Cive, Ch. II, 11). He adds in a footnote that the suspicion must be the result of 'some new cause of fear ... for the cause which was not sufficient to keep him from making compact, must not suffice to authorize the breach of it, being made.' Absent a new cause of fear, then, the first party has a duty to perform. (The difficulty with this proviso, however, is that each individual is his own judge of when such

159

a cause has arisen.) These considerations lead to the conclusion that Hobbes sees promise as an independent basis of obligation. The gratuitous-promise exception was explained above.

There are, however, reasons for thinking that Hobbes was aware of the possibility of reliance-type paradigm. In discussing the expression "I will give it you tomorrow," he says that the words "I will" signify 'a promise of an act of the will to come,' and being of the future, they 'transfer nothing.' Nevertheless, he goes on to say:

> But if there be other signs of the will to transfer a right besides words, then, though the gift be free, yet may the right be understood to pass by words of the future: as if a man propound a prize to him that comes first to the end of a race, the gift is free; and though the words be of the future, yet the right passes; for if he would not have his words so be understood, he should have not let them run. (Leviathan, 14.)

This somewhat obscure argument rests on Hobbes's view that 'the bonds of words' are too weak to bridle men's passions. The expression of an intention to will something in the future, or perhaps of an intention to have an intention, cannot create an obligation. The mere promise of a prize doesn't obligate the promisor. How, then, does the obligation arise? Arguably, the answer is that because the runner justifiably relied on the promisor's words — after all, no effort was made to stop the race — there is an obligation to pay up (Atiyah 1983, 12). I am not suggesting, of course, that Hobbes vividly has in view the protection of the "reliance interest" (as Anglo-American lawyers call it) as a basis of promissory obligation. Such an outlook, though, would have provided him with another possible justification for the validity of the victim's coerced promise in some cases: for instance when the hostage-taker charged tickets for a vacation on his credit card, in reliance on a promise to send back $100.

Still other passages, most notably that of our case of the covenanting captive, suggest a benefit-type paradigm. The general problem of the obligation of state-of-nature promises is similar to that of the "prisoners' dilemma," namely, the problem of trust. But when the first party to a covenant has performed his side of the bargain, the problem obviously is overcome. 'It holds universally true,' says Hobbes, 'that promises do oblige when there is some benefit received, and when to promise, and the thing promised be lawful' (De Cive, Ch. II, 16). A reason, in addition to the one mentioned earlier, as to why a gratuitous promise imposes no obligation is that it is not made in return for a benefit already received or to be acquired (see De Cive, Ch. II, 8).

Each of the above paradigms of promissory obligation has difficulties that we need not go into (see Fried 1981). If any theory is at all successful, it probably combines elements of all of them. The root of the difficulty in identifying Hobbes's position stems, I think, from his holding, on the one hand, that a promise is an act of self-obligation through the declaration of an act of the will, that is, a declaration made with intention of becoming bound, and, on the other hand, that 'words alone are not sufficient tokens of the will' regarding the future. It seems clear, at any rate, that if Hobbes has a simple consent or will theory of promissory obligation, it is difficult to understand how he could regard a coerced promise as valid. More about this soon, however.

V

In order to grasp Hobbes's position we have to look more closely at his account of promise-making. It is necessary, first, to go behind this account and consider the treatment of the renouncing and transferring of rights through a *present* act of will. Hobbes makes a great deal of the language used in declaring one's will or intentions (Leviathan, 14): I give, I grant, I have given, I have granted, I will that this be yours (which refer to the present or the past); I will give, I will grant (which refer to the future, and are the language of promise):

> The way by which a man (he says) either simply renounces or transfers his right is a declaration or signification by some voluntary and sufficient sign or signs that he does so renounce or transfer, or has so renounced or transferred, the same to him that accepts it. (Leviathan, 14.)

When these sufficient signs refer to the present or past, the act of will, it appears, is irrevocable. For as Hobbes writes:

> And when a man has in either manner abandoned or granted away his right, then he is said to be OBLIGED or BOUND not to hinder those to whom such right is granted or abandoned from the benefit of it; and that he *ought*, and it is his DUTY, not to make void that voluntary act of his own; and that such hindrance is INJUSTICE and INJURY as being *sine jure*, the right being before renounced or transferred. (Leviathan, 14.)

These consequences of appropriately expressing one's will are supported by Hobbes with the following argument:

> ... *injury* and *injustice* in the controversies of the world is somewhat like to that which in the disputations of scholars is called *absurdity*. For as it is there called an absurdity to contradict what one maintained in the beginning, so in the world it is called injustice and injury to undo that which from the beginning he had voluntarily done. (Leviathan, 14.)

This strange argument might be correct as a report of usage, but it is hardly convincing from a normative perspective. One might as well say that once you make up your mind, you are no longer permitted to change it! There are, I think, various ways in which the argument can be filled out, but none of them (e.g., that by going back on one's declaration of will, one frustrates the reasonable expectations that have been aroused in others) is in the spirit of Hobbes. (We shall soon encounter, from *De Cive*, another appeal to absurdity, where the argument seems better.)

Hobbes's doctrine, which here seems to be that a man can bind himself merely by intending to bind himself, can be understood, I think, if we link it with his discussion of deliberation and will in *Leviathan* (Ch. VI). He defines ''deliberation'' as 'the whole sum of desires, aversions, hopes, and fears continued till the thing (a contemplated act or omission) be either done or thought impossible.' The will, he holds, simply is 'the last appetite in deliberation,' 'the last appetite or aversion immediately adhering to the action or to the omission thereof.' Any act preceded by (caused by?) an appetite or aversion is a voluntary action.

Now it is in this discussion that Hobbes makes a rather interesting remark. He explains why ''deliberation'' is so called. 'It is called *deliberation* because it is a putting an end to the *liberty* we had of doing or omitting according to our own appetite or aversion.' In other words, we *un*liberate ourselves. About all this one may ask whether Hobbes is serious or joking. For this is phony etymology, as Hobbes, a good classical scholar, must have known. (''Deliberate'' comes from ''liberare,'' to weigh in the mind; think of Libra, the zodiacal sign represented by scales.) But Hobbes seems to be serious. The idea expressed here is actually used in *De Cive* (Ch. II, 10), where he explains that when words are sufficient tokens of the will, that is, of the last act in deliberating, 'the liberty of non-performance is abolished, and by consequence are obligatory. For where liberty ceaseth, there beginneth obligation.'

What we have, then, is a *psychological* explanation of how it is that a man can bind himself merely by intending to bind himself, when a present act of will is involved. But Hobbes also apparently thinks that he is giving a normative rationale of obligation (i.e., a rationale for moral obligation). His argument, however, is an equivocation on the terms ''obligatory'' and ''obligation,'' something like the confusion of being obliged and having an obligation which H.L.A. Hart attributes to Austin's theory of law.

Now Hobbes makes an important point immediately after the discussion of deliberation (Leviathan, 6). He is surveying the forms of speech by which the passions are expressed, for instance, ''I deliberate,'' ''I will,'' ''I command,'' etc. He concludes as follows:

> These forms of speech, I say, are expressions or voluntary significations of our passions; but *certain* signs they be not, because they may be used arbitrarily whether they that use them have such passions or not. The best signs of passions present are either in the countenance, motions of the body, actions, ends or aims which we otherwise know a man to have. (Emphasis added.)

If it is the case that we might need signs other than words to determine a man's present passion or act of will, how much more so when a promise of a future act of will is involved. In fact Hobbes continually insists on the necessity of 'tokens of the will' other than mere words when promises are made, since a promise refers to a future act of will. These signs are needed to establish that

162

a man means what he says.

Benefit and reliance supply these signs, these other tokens of the will. As Hobbes writes in *De Cive* (Ch. II, 10):

> But the covenant made by the party trusted (e.g., the released captive) with him who hath already performed (e.g., the hijacker), although the promise be made by words pointing at the future, doth no less transfer the right of future time, than if it had been made by words signifying the present or time past. For the other's performance is a most manifest sign that he so understood the speech of him whom he trusted, as that he would certainly make performance also at the appointed time; and by this sign the party trusted knew himself to be thus understood, which, because he hindered not, was an evident token of his will to perform.

It is clear, then, that the obligation to keep a covenant depends on the *mutual understandings* of the parties, on how each party interprets the words and behaviour of the other party *and* on each party's understanding of the other's interpretation of his words and behaviour. The difficulty with this approach is obvious, however. If one cannot be sure of whether a man means what he says at the first level, it seems that one should not be able to be sure of what he means at this more complicated level. In these passages, Hobbes is, in effect, trying to reduce a promise, a statement about a future act of will, to an expression of a present act of will, and the reduction doesn't work. If this claim is correct, then Hobbes needs benefit and reliance as contributory bases of contract and promise over and above their role as fixers of meaning, as is suggested by some of the passages referred to earlier.

In any event, it remains to ask how all this serves to bind the released captive to send back the $100. Even if the hostage-taker's 'performance is a most manifest sign that he so understood the speech' of the victim, and by this sign the victim 'knew himself to be thus understood,' why should that make a difference? For these considerations are not incompatible with the captive's making the promise with *mental reservations*. More than this, these considerations can themselves be used in an explanation of how it is possible to deceive other people and make false promises. I suspect that Hobbes was moving toward an "objective" or "formal" theory of contract and promise, in which the parties' understandings of their transaction may be less important than the community of speakers' understanding of it. Other aspects of his political theory, however, prevented him from reaching this position.

VI

Hobbes's position, as it has thus far emerged, seems to be that a man who has received a benefit in exchange for a promise, or who has allowed his promise to rely on his promisee, (logically or conceptually) *cannot* make a false promise.

163

At the same time he also holds that it would be unjust to make a false promise. These considerations apply as much to a promise made to a hostage-taker as to anyone else. In an odd footnote to *De Cive* (Ch. III, 27) Hobbes states that 'he that doth all things against those that do all things, and plunders plunderers, doth equity.' Apparently, the released victim of kidnapping for ransom is not permitted to "plunder" the wrongdoer if he has promised not to.

Making a false promise is not only impossible and unjust (under certain conditions), but it is also irrational. Hobbes writes:

> He who through weakness of mind does or omits that which before he had by contract promised not to do or omit, commits an injury, and falls into no less a contradiction than he who in the Schools is reduced to an absurdity. For by contracting for some future action, he wills it done; by not doing it, he wills it not done: which is to will a thing done and not done at the same time, which is a contradiction. (De Cive, Ch. III, 3.)

(This argument, interestingly, presages Kant's notion of pragmatic contradictions, contradictions in the will.) Unless it is impossible for a contractor to change his mind, or unless it is the case that one always carries about one's prior intentions, it is hard to see how the contractor is willing 'a thing done and not done *at the same time*.'

Something like this argument, however, can be more easily made regarding a false promise, but in order to do so some very important ideas have to be added to Hobbes's exposition. Sorely lacking in Hobbes is an account of how the social practice of promise-making comes into existence. Now, the historical origins of the practice or institution may be lost to us in the depths of the past, as Justice Holmes suggested. Still, it seems that individual promise-making presupposes that a convention about promises, and the language of promise, are already in place. As Hume pointed out, we need not suppose that the convention is explicitly adopted. The institution of promise-making is undoubtedly important to any social group or social relationship that "deals in futures," as it were. On the economic level, promise is necessary for people who deal in an established market; it is not needed for barter. The enforcement of promises and contracts protects the parties against fluctuation in prices. As Roscoe Pound maintained, it is a presupposition of economic order that promises will be kept (for Hobbes it is a presupposition of peace), because the expectation created by a promise has value in the market (if it is enforced, it should be added). But promise (and commitment) has importance for human relations beyond the economic sphere, which we cannot go into here (see Wilson 1983).

Once a convention of promise-making is already in place, we can understand why there is something like an "absurdity" in making false promises. The "contradiction" consists in invoking the convention or institution, which presupposes that promises generally will be kept, while *at the same time* excluding oneself from its operation. It is in this way that we have to understand Hobbes's

164

claim that making a false promise is to will and to not will the performance of a future act. Unfortunately, the social conditions which are themselves presupposed by the convention are ruled out by Hobbes's theory.

In any event, it is far from clear that Hobbes's position on the binding force of a promise made to a hostage-taker or kidnapper is helped by the above considerations. For in order to hold that the released victim is bound by his having invoked the convention or institution of promise, it is necessary that he be drawn into the convention in an acceptable or fair way (see Fried 1981). But this was not the case, for the promise was extorted from him by threats.

Hobbes of course insists that a promise made under fear is voluntary. He refers to the ancient example of the man who throws a cargo overboard to save a ship from sinking; the act in question is voluntary, for after all the man wanted to do it. The example comes from Book III of the *Nichomachean Ethics*, and Hobbes brings only half of what Aristotle says. The act is what Aristotle calls a "mixed" action, voluntary from one point of view and involuntary from another.

Assuming that the promise was voluntary, though, why then call it coerced or extorted? Isn't it the hostage-taker's offer just like any other innocent offer? No it is not, as Pufendorf points out:

> Contracts into which a man is unjustly forced by the very person to whom he gives the promise, or with whom he contracts, are invalid. For the injury which he inflicts upon me by inspiring an unjust fear, renders him incapable of claiming his rights against me under the agreement... (Pufendorf 1927, 52.)

The key phrase in this quotation is "unjust fear." In a more extensive treatment of the question in his *Of the Law of Nature and Nations (De jure naturae et gentium)* (III, vi, 11 and 12) Pufendorf argues that although the lesser evil that is chosen by the captive is, in the situation, the object of his desire, 'as things stand, it is not enough to found an obligation.' The kidnapper's abstaining from inflicting a greater injury on the victim is not equivalent to the conferring of a benefit.

Pufendorf rejects Cicero's view that any promise made to a pirate is invalid and should not be kept because, as Cicero says, pirates are enemies of mankind. According to Pufendorf, such a promise is invalid only if made through compulsion of fear. Pufendorf agrees with Hobbes's statement 'that what I lawfully covenant, I cannot lawfully break' (Leviathan, 14), but he adds, '*provided* the other party can lawfully demand it of me.' Now, the notion of fear, he says, is ambiguous. It has two senses: plausible suspicion and great terror arising from the threat of grievous harm. It is imprudent to make a contract with someone we suspect to be a cheat, but it is not made void by that sole cause. On this he agrees with Hobbes. But the case of a threat of grievous harm is different. Here, there is an "imperfection" in the other party that 'renders him incapable of acquiring a right.' That imperfection is the result of having inspired in the victim an "unjust fear," a fear he had no right to inspire.

Plainly, the root of the disagreement between Hobbes and Pufendorf is their contrasting views of natural rights. I think Pufendorf is perfectly correct in regarding the Hobbesian "right of nature" as a phony right:

> ... not every Natural License, or Power of doing a Thing, is properly a *Right*; but such only as includes some Moral Effect, with regard to others, who are Partners with me in the same Nature... For "tis ridiculous Trifling to call that Power a *Right*, which should we attempt to exercise, all other Men have an *equal right* to obstruct or prevent us. (Pufendorf 1917, Bk. III, 48.)

It is, in any case, a strange situation that a hostage-taker should have a right to kill his captive, because in the state of nature each man has a right to the other's body, while the captive has no right to break an extorted promise.

VII

I want to conclude this paper with a few words on agreements with hostage-takers made by governments. As far as I can tell, this issue is nowhere discussed by Hobbes. It is hard to imagine, however, that he would have held that the sovereign power of a particular territory should be bound by a promise made to someone within its own domain. For this would entail that the sovereign could be sued in its own courts by the hostage-taker to have the promise enforced. Moreover, it does not seem desirable that such promises should be legally enforceable, for it would lower confidence in the legal system (see Attiyah 1981, 47).

The case of ransoms promised by governments to governments, however, may be different. Unfortunately, Hobbes does not have a discussion of international relations on the order of Grotius's and Pufendorf's, or even Cicero's. Cicero does hold that agreements with legitimate, declared enemies are binding (1968, 108). Still, Hobbes seems to regard agreements between governments as binding, even to the extent that 'if a weaker prince make a disadvantageous peace with a stronger, for fear, he is bound to keep it; unless, as has been said before, there arises some new and just cause of fear to renew the war' (Leviathan, 14).

I don't know what can be extrapolated from this statement about a government's agreements with hostage-takers, hijackers, and terrorists who are outside the sovereign's domain. Such individuals often claim to be legitimate, declared enemies of the government in question. It would seem that governments should be at least as cautious in conferring legitimacy on an enemy as they should be in picking their friends.

Notes

1. References are made to the following works and editions: *De Cive*, ed.by S. P. Lamprecht (modernised spelling), Appleton-Century-Crofts, New York, 1949; *Leviathan*, Parts I and II, ed. by Herbert W. Schneider (modernised spelling), Bobbs-Merrill, Indianapolis 1958.

The Hobbesian Structure of International Legal Discourse

Martti Koskenniemi

I

There are two ways of arguing about order and obligation in international affairs. A *subjective* argument traces them back to the subjective consent or the subjective interests of the State. An *objective* argument bases order and obligation on non-subjective sources, justice, common interests, "progress" or the nature of the world community, for example. These arguments seem both exhaustive and mutually exclusive. A point about world order or obligation is either subjective or objective and seems unable to be both at the same time.[1]

In this paper I shall defend a view according to which classical and modern discourse about international law constantly oppose subjective arguments with objective ones without being able to fully accept either. I shall argue that international legal discourse proceeds so as to reconcile subjectivism and objectivism within itself. This will, however, render legal discourse indeterminate because of contradictory assumptions. In other words, by attempting to make subjective and objective arguments compatible with each other international law becomes unable to carry out a coherent project for world order and allows conflicting answers to problems of international lawfulness.

I shall proceed in the following way: first, I shall show how lawyers have, since Hobbes, moved within a system which allows, indeed demands, the production of subjective and objective arguments. Second, I shall demonstrate how attempts to pursue a fully subjective or a fully objective discourse about international lawfulness seem unacceptable because they are vulnerable to the criticism of being apologist or utopian. Third, I shall outline some of the strategies which lawyers have used to make subjectivism and objectivism seem compatible. Finally, I shall briefly expose the manner in which disputes about international law remain incapable of principled (material) solution as each such solution would require making a choice between subjectivism and objectivism, a choice which cannot be made within prevailing assumptions of what it is that distinguishes law from politics.

II

Justifying world order on Hobbesian premises is usually held to be a problem because those premises seem so subjective. From Hobbes we learn that there is no such thing as an objectively constraining natural law. All that natural law does is point the way to the attainment of individual objects of desire (Leviathan, Ch. XIV).[2] What earlier thinkers, such as Aquinas, for example, held as an objective natural law was merely a camouflaged statement of their subjective, and in that sense, arbitrary desires. There is no justification to apply such desires to persons who do not share them.[3] When this view is transposed from inter-individual to international relations we seem at a loss when trying to defend a conception of international order. If there is no material code which is objective in the sense that it can be justifiably asserted against recalcitrant States, how can an effective (binding) world order be argued for? How can a statement about world order oppose the view that States have the right to do whatever they desire?[4]

But the Hobbesian argument is not fully subjective, indeed it cannot fully be so. This is easiest to see if we contrast it with the views of later, democratically-minded, liberal theorists. Why could Hobbes not have held, along with later liberals, that different subjective desires involve the same object and become in this sense "objectified"? As the circumstances in which people live seldom differ radically, why did Hobbes not believe that they are bound to have the same ("objective") desires? He did not because he shared a different conception of the objective nature of man. His moral subjectivism is grounded on an objectivist argument from human psychology. For Hobbes, man is "an automated machine", to borrow Macpherson's expression.[5] His objective condition is one of being possessive. He is ruled by what Freud was to call the "pleasure principle". Objective forces, that is forces *beyond him*, drive him to minimise pain and maximise pleasure. It is this objectively asocial, or antisocial, nature in man which makes it impossible for Hobbes to construct social order in a fully subjective way and it is this which distinguishes him from later liberals. The sovereign is needed as an external force, to keep in check the disruptive forces in man. The justification of the sovereign is non-subjective — a matter of objective (and non-political) causality.

In short: Hobbesian discourse assumes that morals and obligation are subjective in the sense that they emerge from the subjectivity of the speaker. But this view is received as an assumption concerning man's objective nature. While morals and law are an *a posteriori* consequence of the Hobbesian discourse, man's possessive nature is an *a priori* condition thereof. The Hobbesian argument *reconciles* subjectivism with objectivism. The subjective argument relies on an objective one while the content of the objective position can make itself known only in a subjective way (that is, in individual behaviour or by introspection of one's own inclinations towards antisocial behaviour, generalised).

III

Let us now look at why international lawyers have, since Hobbes, shared this manner of reconciling objectivism and subjectivism. Why have they been unable to accept either a fully objective or a fully subjective international order?

Early internationalists such as the Spanish theologians Vitoria and Suarez, or the Dutch protestant Grotius, shared what post-enlightenment lawyers understood as an attempt to create a fully objective argument about world order. For them, the core of the law of nations was something aprioristic, anterior to States and effectively controlling what States could legitimately will. The problem, as later lawyers saw it, was how such objective norms could be argued for. Mere references to revelation or to *recta ratio* seemed insufficient. How could one know whether one man's faith or his reason really grasped the pretended objective norms in their authenticity? Quite the contrary, attempts to argue about objective justice were understood either as utopian constructions which presupposed the existence of conditions which they purported to create or simply as attempts to impose the speaker's political views on others. As religious faith was lost, attempts to argue about the justness of war, for example appeared either as moralist fiction or *post hoc* rationalisation of subjective policy.[6]

The unacceptabily of pure objectivism lies in the fact that it remains without reference to what States actually will or how they conduct themselves. As it lacks such connection with State practice it seems *utopian* and unverifiable. Consequently, it cannot ground a reliable world order. These criticisms of natural law are well known and shared by virtually all modern international lawyers. If naturalist argument still persists, it is defended by reference to State practice and, to that extent, it has lost its objective character.[7]

But the problem is that defending norms by reference to subjective acceptance, will, or interests tends to collapse into full subjectivism and to become unacceptable because it is merely *apologist*. Whether we associate the subjective argument with State belief, will or interest, it seems incapable of grounding a *binding* international order, that is, an order which could be applied against non-accepting States. To be sure, the original argument against objectivism was epistemological: we cannot know norms without looking at what States *believe* to be valid norms. But there seems little difference between saying that the law is what States believe and what they will to be law. States — just like people — tend to present what they will as objective norms. This, of course, was the very basis of the Hobbesian criticism of natural law. On these same assumptions, there is no justification for an external observer to say that although this is what you say you *believe* to be law, it is really what you *will*. On this matter each person (and State) remains himself the ultimate authority. Though epistemological, the Hobbesian criticism tends to become ontological. In other words, it tends to make subjective experience *constitutive* (instead of merely declaratory) of the norm: it becomes indistinguishable from pure voluntarism, i.e. the view which holds law as identical with State will.

Now, pure voluntarism cannot of course justify the imposition of a standard against non-accepting States. For the contrary to be possible, it must be allowable to argue that this norm is binding because it is what you will (or willed at some earlier stage) although you have now come to deny your will. But the argument from "knowing better" is excluded by our previous argument against natural law. For it entails theory of "objective interests", distinguishable from articulated wants. To be able to impose an argument about interests against actual wants presupposes the possession of a non-subjective theory of interests. But such theory is vulnerable to the original criticism against a fully objective natural law.[8] In other words, each of the subjective arguments will either contradict the presumptions on which they were based or remain apologist and so incapable of being used against non-accepting States. To be binding, the argument about world order needs, at some point, to include an objective argument within itself.

There is a simple, well-known logical reason for why this is so. Most classical and modern lawyers think that law arises from State will. But why should a State be bound by the will it has sometimes expressed? *Pacta sunt servanda* — agreements must be kept — we say. But unless we argue in a circle, we cannot base this norm on a further State will. The *pacta* norm needs to be argued as a structurally or logically "necessary" natural law norm.[9] A "pure" subjectivism has no leg to stand on. Just as Hobbes based his system on an objective psychology, the modern lawyer needs to ground binding force on an objective argument about, for example, legal logic, social necessity or the like.

I will conclude by saying that discourse about world order needs to incorporate an objective and a subjective strand within itself. It must assume consent to remain binding because of the "nature" of law, some theory of community interest or the like. But to know the content here we must refer back to subjective acceptance.

171

IV

Let me now illustrate some of the strategies whereby lawyers have attempted to reconcile subjectivism and objectivism in order to avoid the accusation that their system is either apologist (non-binding) or utopian (incapable of demonstrating its content in a reliable fashion).

A first example is provided by the Swiss jurist Emer de Vattel. His influential work, published in 1758, contained three kinds of law: necessary natural law, voluntary law and positive law (Vattel 1758, XIV, XIX-XX and § 7-21). Later lawyers have been unable to appreciate the point of this classification (Wheaton 1936, 310; Woolsey 1879, par. 26; Corbett 1951, 30-1). They have presented Vattel as either a positivist or a naturalist in disguise. Consequently, they have criticised him of utopianism or apologetics. But this does injustice to the coherence of the internal structure of his work. Vattel attempts to reconcile natural and positive law by means of his "voluntary law" which can be manipulated so as to appear both objective and subjective at the same time. What is this law? It is said to consist of the interpretations and modifications which States have introduced into universal natural law in order to apply it in their own historical situation. It partakes in the objective and subjective. It is not utopian in being responsive to what takes place in practice. But it is not apologist either as it is still natural law and maintains its connection with an objectively constraining morality (see also Ruddy 1975, 111-9.) The problem with it is, however, that it seems so elusive. Therefore, later lawyers have been incapable of using it as their mediating strategy.

A second example is provided by the German jurist Georg Jellinek. In his work, published in 1880, he outlines the content of his *Selbstverpflichtungslehre*, or "autolimitation" theory. Modern lawyers have criticised this theory as apologist. They have thought that holding international law as "external municipal law" deprives it of constraining force. (See e.g. Brierly 1958; Lauterpacht 1933, 410-12; Verdross 1926, 12-20.) But they have failed to grasp how Jellinek — along with the German historical school of law — have really attempted a reconciliation between subjectivism and objectivism. Jellinek admits that if the law were really dependent on the subjective will of the State, it would fall into simple apology. But this is not what he claims. On the contrary, normative State will is neither free nor arbitrary. Not all will can create *Selbstverpflichtung*. Only that can which is in harmony with the *Staatszwecke*, the objective purpose of the State as it enfolds itself in the nations's history.[10] For the historical school, the needed binding force is received from history, which is assumed to direct itself towards constantly higher forms of culture and organisation. Jellinek's system escapes the criticisms of utopianism and apologism by its subjective-objective structure. Law is subjective and concrete as it is based on will. But will is constrained by the objective — and social — process of history. This solution seems successful only when the (optimistic) assumption about history's progressive social character could be held. Not surprisingly Jellinek's system began to look apologist after the experience of the first world war.

The third example takes us to the modern conception of *jus cogens*. This is assumed to be the hard core of modern international law. It consists of peremptory norms, that is, norms which cannot be deviated from by States even by agreement. To that extent it seems fully objective. It binds States irrespective of their behaviour, will or interests. But how can one know which norms actually are such? According to the definition of *jus cogens* in the 1969 Vienna Convention on the Law of Treaties, a peremptory norm is:

> A norm accepted and recognized by the international community as a whole as a norm from which no derogation is permitted.

In other words, we are in the presence of yet another attempt at reconciliation. Peremptory norms are norms which States subjectively accept as such. As the Article speaks of the international community *as a whole*, it seems to assume that every State's consent is needed, not just the consent of some representative part of States. Indeed any other solutions would seem to violate sovereign equality. *Jus cogens* is objective as it overrules State will. But it is subjective in that its content can only be known through what States will. But the reconciliation fails. Each State remains capable of avoiding the constraining force of *jus cogens* by denying that it has consented to any particular *content*. For to say that one can know its content without reference to State will is vulnerable to the objection of utopianism. On the other hand, to say that its content can be known through what other States will violates sovereign equality. And sovereign equality — that is, the equal right to have one's will determine the content of one's obligations — follows from adopting the perspective which denies the binding (legal) character of substantive natural law.[11]

V

I shall now move to the effect of the subjective-objective character of international legal argument in the practice of dispute-settlement. My contention is that disputes about the lawfulness of particular State acts remain incapable of material solution because each dispute looks to be a dispute between subjectivism and objectivism. Since a preference between the two cannot be made, a dispute-solution proceeds to hide the contradiction.

In the practice of legal dispute-solution the contradiction between subjectivism and objectivism appears in the following way: the position expressed by one's opponent is interpreted to be either a subjective or an objective one and, on either ground, unacceptable. This occurs because each position must be capable of both subjective and objective support. The dispute soon appears to require making a preference between subjectivism and objectivism. As such a preference cannot be made, the dispute-solver's recourse is to strategies of evasion; for example, the proceduralisation of the dispute or the reinterpretation of the parties' positions so as to seem compatible and to point towards the same solution.[12]

Take, for examle, a dispute about the binding force of a treaty provision. State X argues that State Y has breached its obligations by not carrying out a provision included in a treaty between them. This position can be interpreted as a *subjective* one: States must carry out treaty provisions because treaties express consent and consent binds. But it can also be expressed as an *objective* one: treaties are binding because justice, good faith or legitimate expectations require this. State Y now chooses either one of these to interpret its opponent's claim. Let us say Y chooses the subjective interpretation. State X can now develop an objective argument to counter this: the provision is not binding because it is inequitable, or unjust. A State may rely on the *rebus sic stantibus*, or changed circumstances, rule to express this. From the problem-solver's perspective it now looks as if he had to prefer subjectivism or objectivism. He needs to decide whether treaties bind because they express consent or because they express justice. It is important to notice that the situation would be the same had State Y chosen to interpret State X's position as an objective one and, therefore, to develop a subjective point to counter this. It might have denied that the provision (or the interpretation of it by State X) really expressed what was consented to. The position of State X would in such case appear as an objective point about declared intent and legitimate expectations instead of what the parties had originally, authentically agreed.

In both cases a decision seems to require taking a stand on the relative superiority between subjectivism and objectivism. Such superiority cannot, however, be upheld.

If one chose a purely subjective explanation of why treaties bind, then one must look at the parties' original intent. But original intent cannot be opposed to a party denying such intent unless one accepts an objective position: intent binds as it is declared. Reliance on declared (instead of actual) will is objective: its point is not to give effect to real will but to the legitimate expectations of *other* States to whom the declaration was made. It is a standard of justice (Müller 1971). Thus subjectivism will either result in denying the provision's binding force or it will result in objectivism, i.e., holding the provision to be binding in order, say, to protect other States.

If one chose a purely objective explanation of why treaties bind then one seems to have to look at the content of justice, equity, the "legitimate" character of created expectations and so on. But the content of such standards cannot be known without looking at what States themselves regard as just, equitable or legitimate. Reliance on such standards will therefore, once again become subjective. If not subjective, then the assumption should be accepted that written provisions can be opposed to a State's will regardless of whether they express consent or not. But this loses the identity of a treaty as a consensual undertaking and goes against accepted doctrines concerning the vitiating effect of error, or duress, for example. Thus preferring objectivism will either result in holding the State bound irrespective of its will, in which case the problem-solver will lack criteria for justifying the adopted standard, or it will result in subjectivism, the view that the standard is binding to the extent that it expresses real consent. And this latter strategy will either result in apologism or refer one back to some objective argument about justice, once more.

Whichever standard the problem-solver chooses, he will always remain vulnerable either to the objection of apologism or the charge of utopianism. How, then can legal problems be solved? Let me now illustrate one way in the functioning of the "strategy of evasion". By the argument from tacit consent the problem-solver will be able to make the contentious difficulty of a standard for the material dispute to disappear. He will be able to propose that there was no dispute at all as the parties had already agreed. Sovereign equality is preserved as both States' consent is rendered effective.

The point about tacit consent is a typical strategy for mediating the contradiction between subjectivism and objectivism. Vattel's voluntary law has such a point. The whole body of modern customary law can also be used for this. Custom is posited between the fully objective natural law (or "general principles") and the fully subjective treaty. It partakes in the character of both. It is subjective in that it is regarded as binding because it expresses the *opinio juris,* or the will to be bound. It is objevtive in that proof of *actual* will is unnecessary and presumptions are made on the basis of general and consistent behaviour.[13]

The difficulty with modern doctrines about custom is that they are circular. If we wish to avoid apologism, we shall have to think of the *opinio juris* as presumed rather than a "real" consent to be bound. This is so because we cannot plausibly argue that "we know better" what the State had consented to. But if the *opinio* is merely presumed, then we cannot know which conduct can be so interpreted as to allow this presumption. For not *all* behaviour creates norms. Binding and non-binding usages must be distinguished from each other. This distinction is made by the *opinio juris* construction.

Only such conduct binds which expresses one's subjective will to be bound. But this presupposes that we can know subjective will *independently* of the behaviour under scrutiny. And this possibility was excluded precisely by the attempt to avoid apologism by the presumed consent construction.

Let us take the imaginary dispute between State X and State Y once more. State Y has referred to the changed circumstances rule to free itself from the treaty provision. This looks like an objective point and, indeed, was presented as such by Y itself. The problem is that accepting it would violate the subjective consent of State X. It would become bound by a non-consensual standard, as interpreted by State Y. But the changed circumstances doctrine can be interpreted also from a subjective perspective. It may be presented as an implied condition in the treaty.[14] On such an interpretation the parties are assumed to have consented to its application. The problem-solver frees State Y. But as it is freed through the operation of the changed circumstances rule as an implied condition which the parties were assumed to have accepted, then, after all, State X's consent remains unviolated. Instead, the material dispute between the two States is wiped away by assuming that they agree to the framework for decision making. The solution gives effect to both States' consent. As taking account of changed circumstances also counted for justice, objective considerations were also satisfied.

Such a decision comes about as a strategy of evasion. It is not produced nor justifiable by reference to legal argument. It leaves unexplained why the interpretation of the content of the *rebus* rule by Y was given preference to its interpretation by X. To be sure, it was argued that X had tacitly consented. But how do we justify the point against X itself that its conduct was such as to allow this presumption? This could be done if there existed a rule to the effect that certain conduct, namely that adopted by X during the negatiations, is deemed to express consent. Quite apart from the fact that no such rules exist — indeed no such rule can exist as the same conduct might have different meaning in different circumstances — even if it existed it would still have to receive subjective justification from both Y and X. But X might now deny that it had consented to this rule. The problem-solver would then need to construct tacit consent also behind this rule — which could again be challenged. And so on *ad infinitum*.

The decision in this imaginary — but in fact often occurring — problem rested on an interpretation of the meaning of the parties' behaviour and of the *rebus* rule. During the argument, both were interpreted alternatively in a subjective and an objective way. But none of the interpretations could remain permanent as we could always develop a further subjective or objective point to challenge the previous one. Discourse remains open-ended. Any adopted solution will inevitably appear as a violent cut, a closure by means of authority. It will seem capable of being challenged by precisely the sort of arguments which were used to arrive at it. In other words, legal argument does not only remain powerless to justify the adopted solution, it also provides the means whereby the solutions can be considered unacceptable. The practical consequence is that international law appears weak and incapable of producing solutions which are convincing to people who do not *already,* by non-legal criteria, accept them (see also Kennedy 1980, 353 *et seq.*, 376).

VI

The Hobbesian legal mind is suspicious of, and even hostile to political solutions to legal questions. This leads the Hobbesian approach to incorporating both subjectivism and objectivism into its arguments. Law is not utopian because it is based on (concrete) State will. It is not apologist, either, because it is binding regardless of such will. As a matter of legislation, law is subjective; as a matter of adjudication, law is objective. But the two strands constantly threaten each other. A purely subjective theory of legislation will ultimately lose the law's binding force: no standard can be opposed to a State unless that State accepts it at the moment of application. A purely objective theory of law-ascertainment will necessarily entail overriding State will. This is natural as subjectivism and objectivism *define themselves* so as to exclude each other. For the point of the subjective argument is that will is superior to, or overrides, any ideas about natural justice. And the assumption behind the objective argument is that justice is better than, or overrides, actual will. If this contrast between objectivism and subjectivism is lost in an attempt at reconciliation, then both points become nonsensical: justice becomes not only equivalent but identical with will.

Notes

1. "Subjective" and "objective" are, of course, loaded notions. I shall here refrain from defining them in any other way apart from their relationship of mutual exclusion. This is also the only permanent manner in which the terms are used, or implied, in standard discourse about international law or obligation. For a useful recent discussion of how the two notions organise discourse in different ethical, philosophical and psychological issues by constantly entering into opposition and claiming priority *vis-à-vis* each other, see Nagel 1985.

2. References are made to *Leviathan*, ed. by C. B. Macpherson, Penguin, Harmondsworth, 1982.

3. 'For one calleth wisdom what other calleth fear; and one cruelty what another justice... and therefore such names can never be true grounds for any ratiocination' (Leviathan, Ch. IV, 109-10).

4. Conventional legal consciousness regularly contrasts a "Hobbesian" conception of the international order with a "Grotian" one, the latter being in some sense more "objective" than the former. See e.g. Brierly 1958, 23-5; Bull 1977, *passim.*

5. Macpherson 31-2 and *passim.* For a useful discussion on Hobbes's view of human nature, see e.g. Goldsmith 1966, 48-83.

6. For a criticism of the "arbitrary" character of early objectivism, see, in particular, Kaltenborn von Stachau 1847, 11, *et seq.*, 24-5 and *passim*. A. von Bulmerincq (1858, 14-68) points out that the early writers neglected the crucial distinction between law as it is and as it ought to be and were for this reason unable to ground a "scientific" study of international law. In a similar vein, T.A. Walker 1983, 91) believes that the scientific nature of international law lies in that it '... must take as its foundation *facts* as they are.'

7. For the way in which positivism and natural law become indistinguishable during argument, see e.g. Boyle 1985, 327 and 337-8.

8. On the impossibility of justifying a theory of objective interests, dissociable from articulated wants, under the assumptions behind liberal political theory, see e.g. Levine 1981, 49-70.

9. This point was noted by Grotius, Hugo in *De Jure Belli ac Pacis*, Bk. II, Ch. XI. For modern discussion, see e.g. Hart 1961, 42-3 and 189-95. The *pacta sunt servanda* norm has been characterised by international lawyers alternatively as a natural or a moral norm, a logical or structural "hypothesis" and a social "necessity". See e.g. Anzilotti 1929, 42-5; Verdross 1926, 28-33; Lauterpacht 1933, 418-9; O'Connell 1962, 8.

10. Jellinek 1880, 38-9. He points out that will cannot be arbitrary ("Willkür"). If it were, no binding obligation could be created. He points out:'...die letzte Grunde des Rechts nur in einem objektiven Principe gefunden werden könne' (p. 43).

11. For a conventional discussion on *jus cogens* in international law, see e.g. Sztucki 1974.

12. On these strategies, see Koskenniemi 1987, 71 *et seq.*, 93-105.

13. For an exposition and perceptive criticism of the "two-element theory" of customary law, see Haggenmacher 1986, 5-125.

14. Vamvoukos 1985, 5 *et seq.*, 48-9 and *passim*. On the problems created by strategy of reading non-consensual obligations as "implied conditions" in contracts under standard legal practice, see also Atiyah 1981, 23-4 and 89-90.

Hobbes and the Problem of Rationality[1]

Noel E. Boulting

"Something being rationally justified on the basis of something else" provides the focus for this paper. In it attention will be given to what approaches there are in contemporary philosophical circles to the problem of the grounding of rationality itself (see Bartley 1984). Given that a number of approaches to this problem can be identified, it seems fair to inquire how far Hobbes's philosophy can be related to any of them. Subsequently it may prove possible not only to speculate on how any principles might be justified upon which World Government could be based, but to suggest whether or not Hobbes's own philosophical approach itself provides a warrant for such a justification.

A remark of Karl Popper will help to distinguish at least two approaches philosophers have taken to the grounding of rationality problem: 'The "world" is not rational, but it is the task of science to rationalize it' (Popper 1971, Vol. 2, 357). He identifies his own approach with this position, calling it Critical Rationalism, opposing it to what he calls an uncritical rationalism where the world is regarded as rational and discovered rather than invented through scientific theorising. I propose to call Popper's uncritical rationalism Substantive Rationality.[2]

Substantive Rationality

Karl Popper attacks Platonic philosophy in responding to the question "What is there?" because Platonism postulates a set of forms which are distinct from but originate the particularity of everyday existence. This essentialism

179

developed in two directions which led to an opposition between religious and rationalistic traditions as to the authoritative base of faith, whether in God, as "author of the play" imposing order upon the temporal world akin to that exercised by Platonic Forms or in reason itself. More recently the rationalistic tradition has often been associated with a kind of naturalism which holds that the nature of things or the order in nature, at least, can be discovered by a philosophic mind without invoking God-talk or referring to Revelation. These two traditions, in the multiplicity of their particular assertions and methodological orientations, however, were in 'complete agreement regarding the existence of a reality about which such insight could be gained', as Max Horkheimer (1974, 17) once made the point, even though the grounds for this insight into the nature of things were denied by two other intellectual currents at the time — Calvinism and Empiricism.

Even modern philosophers have tied the pursuit of reason to the notion that it is in the ultimate nature of things for them to lie together in what might be called some aesthetic harmony. For example, Whitehead's philosophy exhibits what he calls a faith in the order of nature (Whitehead 1926, Ch. I, last paragraph). He claims that the fact that immediate experience is capable of providing the deductive superstructure required by scientific theorising must mean immediate experience "itself has certain uniformity of texture" (Whitehead 1926, 246). His speculative philosophy attempts to provide a rationale for this claim.

A like quest may be seen in the concern for discovering a "logic of the world" present in the philosophy of Maurice Merleau-Ponty (1966, 326). For him, rather than that ontology being ascertained through what we know or seem to learn about the world scientifically, it is revealed through our bodily awareness, through a phenomenology of feeling (ibid., 408). But for neither Merleau-Ponty nor Whitehed is reason beyond nature as it was for both Plato and for the religious tradition, but rather it is hidden within nature. Science is, in relation to immediate experience, but "a second-order expression" (ibid., 41 and p. viii).

Now at least three central features of Hobbes's philosophy are incompatible with this way of grounding the rational enterprise suggested by these examples of Substantive Rationality. Firstly, for Hobbes we can only have reliable knowledge of what men make, and since geometry and the commonwealth in their different ways are human creations they are demonstrable. This qualification does not apply to nature since we do not know how the objects were constructed and thereby we can only speculate on their natural causes (Watkins 1973, 45). Since we have no certain knowledge of nature, talk about an order imposed on nature, or present within nature itself or even as emerging through the activities of men working upon nature, is pure speculation even if it does yield a politically useful myth (Merleau-Ponty 1964, 130 and 1973, 33). Hobbes, then, does not provide a basis for grounding the rational enterprise itself in a way proponents of a Substantive Rationality would require.

Secondly, in Christianity, in Whitehead's aesthetic naturalism and in Merleau-Ponty's philosophy, man is regarded as "species being", as the young Marx (1977, 67) once put it. His existence is understood necessarily with a social presumption that is undetachable from his individuality: man is constituted by social relations. For Hobbes, on the other hand, man is lonely, isolated and essentially self-interested rather than other-regarding.

Thirdly, Hobbes's extravagant claim that the value of something is its price emphasises that nothing in nature has a value in itself (Leviathan, Ch. X, par. 16). Indeed, outside society, that is to say within the condition of mere nature, 'notions of right and wrong, justice and injustice, have there no place' (ibid., Ch. XIII, par. 15). Good and evil merely pertain to our appetites and aversions (ibid., Ch. VI, par. 7) and do not arise out of nature, nor are they created necessarily, since they signify nothing about reality at all until the civil realm is instituted.

Let us now turn to a philosophy which has proved as hostile to the claims of a Substantive Rationality today as was Hobbes's philosophy in his own time — Critical Rationality itself.

Critical Rationality

According to a proponent of Critical Rationality, the rational attitude, that of seriously considering what we learn from experience or by argumentation, is simply adopted. In as far as it is so adopted a commitment to the use of reason is irrational since it is merely a matter of "faith in reason". Accordingly, since no logical grounding can be provided for engaging in the rational enterprise itself, we either choose to adopt Critical Rationality or we are left with choosing what Popper calls "comprehensive irrationalism" (Popper 1971, 230).

Critical Rationality is closely associated with what can be called an epistemological fallibilism. One of the most important features of this doctrine lies in its optimism. That optimism is grounded in the promise science supposedly holds for solving problems by means of theories which tell us more and more about our world — not that this progress in finding what can be accepted as descriptions of natural or even social states of affairs guarantees their truth. Critical Rationality, then, adopts a procedural sense of rationality involving a methodology of critical testing and critical discussion guided by the ideal of approaching the truth. Indeed, science is a highly rational activity because it satisfies the requirements of this procedural approach (Watkins 1967).

For the Critical Rationalism there is no way of being rational in the social and political realms other than by arriving at decisions, and by being critical of them reflecting — as they may do — our desires, or in terms of their efficaciousness in satisfying our desires. Thus, whereas factual statements, pertaining to what is the case with regard to states of affairs in the world, are open to be *accepted*, standards or values that emerge from social decision-making, and value claims or statements pertaining to ethical principles or standards, are considered as *created* by us.

In opposition, then, to the value naturalism invoked in the different forms of Substantive Rationality, an advocate of Critical Rationality asserts that ethical principles or statements involving standards cannot be derived from factual ones: no bridge can be found logically to close the gap between *is* and *ought* statements. Nonetheless some of our ethical principles might be thought worth holding onto because they sustain criticism better than others even if they cannot be ultimately justified. When a question does arise about the applicability of some ethical principle, all we can do is to exercise our imagination in an attempt to evoke a sympathetic understanding of the likely effects of the application of the principle, that is by trying to universalise it upon the ground that in committing ourselves to it we are to be understood as prescribing it for *anyone* in a like situation. An appreciation of the need for such *formal* universalisability carries with it, of course, an awareness of how the application of such principles generally are circumscribed by the desires of others (Hare 1965, 37ff, 180ff. and 195).

Before examining how far Hobbes can be regarded as a precursor in the tradition of Critical Rationality, reference must be made to two other forms of rationality, Constitutive and Qualitative Rationality. Issues pertaining to the latter will not be raised here, since it contends no rationale can be found for engaging in the rational enterprise itself, nor can a faith in reason offer a solution since, as Adorno put it, 'a thought that is purely consistent will irresistibly turn into an absolute for itself.' Proponents of a Qualitative Rationality stress the insight that the unique particularities of our experience so often seem to be non-susceptible to rational structuring.[3] Given that we can't say *what* exists, even our attempts to *say* what there is appear to fall short or run counter to what we feel presences itself to us.

Since Hobbes would not have much time for an approach which attempted to de-institutionalise rationality in its ''mythologisation'' of experience, I may perhaps be forgiven for dismissing Qualitative Rationality in so few words without, I hope, belittling it. Yet this very dismissal paves the way for introducing another form of rationality, Constitutive Rationality, for it does try to provide a rationale for grounding rationality itself by drawing attention to the way language is employed in critical discussion in our attempts to say what there is.

Constitutive Rationality

According to a proponent of Constitutive Rationality, submitting to rational discussion and critical argument presupposes, as an empirical fact, that, as Habermas puts it, 'we always find ourselves in a communication which is intended to lead to agreement' (Habermas 1976, 215). The idea that genuinely engaging in rational discussion and critical argument can, in communications, lead to agreement, at least renders explicit, however, an obscurity within the problem of grounding rationality itself. This can be drawn out in at least two ways.

Firstly, if it was the case that in communication we did intend to arrive at inter-subjective agreement, then this would constitute a transcendental way for grounding debate. This kind of grounding arises out of reflecting on the conditions which make possible a genuine critical argument or serious debate in the first place. The question arises, however, as to whether or not *engaging* in critical argument and debate of itself *does presuppose* and therefore *can provide* a transcendental ground for engaging in such forms of communication.

Secondly, reflection on the conditions underlying discussion or argument calls our attention to a significant feature of Critical Rationality itself. A proponent of Critical Rationality seems to presuppose that a human being can stand as an isolated individual, outside the community's influence on engagement in rational argumentation and critical communication, in order to make a decision about whether to engage in such activities or not. One cannot imagine what kind of a decision that would be if the rules which made such discussion or argument possible and the value claims — speaking the truth, being impartial yet sincere and so on — were not acknowledged, at least implicitly by such a person. Nonetheless this solitary isolation, presupposed by considering such a decision-making position externally, and referred to by Karl-Otto Apel as "methodological solipsism",[4] is reminiscent of the natural condition of mankind, which Hobbes so graphically relates to us in Chapter XIII of the *Leviathan*. More needs to be said, however, about Constitutive Rationality before the possibility that his philosophical approach bears some resemblances to that of Constitutive Rationality is dismissed, especially as some scholarship in Hobbes's philosophy over the last twenty years has taken place within this tradition (see e.g. Weiler 1970, 210ff.; Herzog 1985, 52-61).

To claim that a proponent of Critical Rationality commits methodological solipsism, makes a shift in the level of argument concerning the response of a Constitutive Rationalist to the grounding of the rationality problem, for the Critical Rationalist can be challenged as to whether such a methodological solipsism is a real possibility. If it is not, then the Critical Rationalist's decisionism is undermined and he has to make room for the claims of a Constitutive Rationality (Apel 1980, 269). It would be almost universally accepted that people have to engage in communicative interaction at some stage to sustain a community at all (Habermas 1980, 159).

It might appear, however, that Hobbes does consider just this possibility when he considers under what circumstances a man may be excused for standing outside the realm delimited by civil law even if it is only because he doesn't think that this realm can satisfy what he sees as his basic needs or things 'necessary for his life' (Leviathan, Ch. XXVII, par. 26). Even if such a stance amounts to rejecting a certain quality of life, which the civil realm might sustain either for himself or for others, the question still arises as to whether such a stance amounts to rejecting any kind of civil life whatsoever (Radnitzky 1970, 375).

Justification on Hobbesian Principles

Can a case yet be made for saying that anything resembling a Constitutive Rationality can be found in Hobbes's philosophy? In beginning to answer this question it is worth pointing out that Constitutive Rationalists are neutral as to whether or not man is to be regarded ultimately as a social creature or as an isolated, lonely individual. Such a conclusion is hardly surprising in view of the fact that Constitutive Rationalists are not concerned with saying *what there is* but rather with those human efforts which are made to *say* what there is. Attention, then, is paid to the way language is employed in critical discussion. The significance which is thus attached to the role of language can be illustrated by examining briefly the way attempts have been made to claim that there are obligations in what Hobbes called 'the Natural Condition of Mankind' (Leviathan, Ch. XIII).

Some fifty years ago, A.E. Taylor argued that Hobbes held that there were obligations by nature to which the formation of a state would add no new kind. These had the imperative of moral law, so that Hobbes thus anticipates Kant's contribution in moral philosophy, for obligations are discovered by reason, perhaps in a manner akin to the discovery of mathematical theorems. According to this position, then, it is the dictates of reason which properly give rise to moral obligation possessing an immutable and eternal character (see e.g. Taylor 1969, 35ff.). It was perhaps but a small step to equate these obligations with natural laws, thereby providing a route to theism (Warrender 1969, 67ff.).

Assuming the correctness of Taylor's view of Hobbes and given that a Constitutive Rationalist might accept the commendatory force of such obligations in Hobbes's 'Natural Condition of Mankind', their force for him would not derive from an obligation to obey the laws of nature, the word of God or even the intuitive insight provided by attending to the dictates of reason. Rather the notion of obligation would be defined in terms of renouncing or transferring a right, and that renunciation or transfer would be *expressed in language* (Barry 1968, 127).

Could Hobbes be interpreted as a Constitutive Rationalist in this way? Examination of certain passages in the *Leviathan* are necessary to settle the issue.

The first thing to be said is that Hobbes distinguishes between covenants proper and "promises mutual" (Leviathan, Ch. XV, par. 5) or what he refers to as 'covenants of mutual trust' in the pagination of Chapter XIV (par. 17). In the case of the latter 'there is no security of performance on either side' since 'there is no civil power erected over the parties promising' (ibid., Ch. XV, par. 5). Indeed, earlier in the pagination to Chapter XIV he refers to these 'covenants of mutual trust' as 'invalid' and within the text as 'void' specifically in 'the condition of mere nature' (ibid., Ch. XIV, par. 17).

Yet, can't we ask "According to what Hobbes writes, can there be obligations, in the sense of renouncing or transferring a right, in the condition of mere nature?" Brian Barry is at first doubtful as to whether there is an obligation to perform some action in this condition, an obligation created on the basis of any form of renouncing or transferring rights, doubtful because reasonable suspicion can always be harboured as to whether the other person will fail to keep the other side of the bargain (Barry 1968, 123). Though this suspicion seems valid it does not go far enough, since, for Hobbes, not only are we always in a state of fear with regard to what others might do in such a situation, 'wherein every man to every man, for want of a communal power to keep them all in awe, is an enemy' (Leviathan, Ch. XVI, par. 5), but, in addition, some unanticipated occurrence might make such an obligation strike against any benefit to the promiser.

Brian Barry's own first doubts are relinquished on finding Hobbes writing:

> ... if I covenant to pay a ransom or service for my life, to an enemy; I am bound by it. For it is a contract, wherein one receiveth the benefit of life; the other is to receive money or service for it; and consequently, where no other law (as in the condition of mere nature) forbiddeth the performance the covenant is valid. (Leviathan, Ch. XIV, par. 26.)

Unfortunately, this passage is not about covenants of mutual trust at all, but about what Hobbes refers to in the pagination as 'Covenants extorted by fear'. So Barry's doubt ought not to have been relinquished. In addition, even the sustaining of these covenants is hedged with qualifications if the paragraph as a whole is examined. So Hobbes speaks of the possibility of 'some new and just cause to fear' which might lead to the undermining of even these kinds of covenants 'in the condition of mere nature'.

In addition, Barry is unsure whether Hobbes thought, in the case of covenants of mutual trust, that since there can be no assurance the other person will keep his side of the bargain if the originator of the agreement performs first, there is no obligation to perform first, since reasonable suspicion makes the covenant void. In addition the performer could simply betray himself to a possible assailant. Barry tries to overcome his doubts even here by quoting this text:

> The cause of fear, which maketh a covenant invalid, must be always something arising after the covenant made; as some new fact, or other sign of the will to perform: else it cannot make the covenant void (Leviathan, Ch. XIV, par. 19.)

Unfortunately at least two considerations undermine any weight that could be attached to this stipulation. Firstly, in its context, this paragraph follows one in which the condition of civil estate has been referred to where 'fear is no more reasonable' since a power has been set up 'to constrain those that would otherwise violate their faith' (Leviathan, Ch. XIV, par. 18). So, such covenants can be held to be valid, prudentially, in the civil estate. But can such covenants hold in the condition of mere nature? This question leads us to a second consideration, since new causes of fear continually arise in this condition. Such covenants of mutual promise, then, could not be sustained; they would always be subject to what Karl-Otto Apel calls 'a criminal reservation.'[5]

Such a conclusion, however, should not surprise us in view of Hobbes's remarks about what can be expressed in language generally.[6] For him speech is distinguished by its sheer arbitrariness, for, like the commonwealth, it is constructed by men, and what men have made can be unmade.[7] The artificiality of language is expressed in such sentiments as 'For words are wise men's counters, they do but reckon by...' (Leviathan, Ch. IV, par. 13). This simply adds to the impression that there is nothing binding in what is said.

This impression of arbitrariness is deepened when Hobbes's account of the nature of argumentation is examined, for he remarks 'No man can know by discourse, that this or that is, has been, or will be' (Leviathan, Ch. VII, par. 3). The whole point of discourse is to increase knowledge for some unspecified end (ibid., Ch. VII, par. 1). Yet without some arbitrator or judge between two discoursers in dispute 'to whose sentence they will both stand their controversy must come either to blows, or be undecided, for want of right reason constituted by Nature; so it is also in all debate of what kind so ever' (ibid., Ch. V, par. 3). Even if a reader is shocked upon reading this for the first time, he may thereby not be surprised to read later that such words as ''good'', ''evil'', ''vile'' and so on simply signify something about the person employing them, since there is no 'common rule of good and evil, to be taken from the nature of the objects themsélves' (ibid., Ch. VI, par. 7) to guide the appropriate employment of such words. We can see, then, why R.S. Peters, for example, can write that 'Hobbes treated argument rather like a wrestling bout in which the point was to throw the other fellow and glory in his discomfiture' (Peters 1967, 164), rather than reaching intersubjective agreements in the way a Constitutive form of Rationality would require.

Hobbes as a Critical Rationalist

Despite the fact that Critical Rationalists might attack Hobbes either for his brand of essentialism, instrumental in his attempt to establish a demonstrable science for political life, or for overlooking the dangers of totalitarianism in his desire to avoid the horrors of Civil War, it can be argued that family resemblances exist between his position and that of Critical Rationality, sufficient for his philosophy to be regarded as a precursor or a pioneer, at least, in the tradition of Critical Rationality itself (Watkins 1973, 123-6). Consider, for example, the stress Critical Rationalists place on the avoidance of conspiracy theories, their attack on "ideological factors" in philosophy, their claim of subjectivity with regard to such factors and, also, in the making of moral judgements, as well as the stress they place on the doctrine of methodological individualism itself (Watkins 1973, 125 and 130). Indeed it is just this latter doctrine which Watkins admits may suffer from adverse implications as a result of confessing that Hobbes's individualistic theory of language is inadequate, an admission which I think goes hand in hand with Hobbes's "methodological solipsism".[8]

In addition, consider two further similarities between those who advocate Critical Rationality as a policy and the views of Hobbes. Hobbes wrote, 'Men that distrust their own subtlety, are, in tumult and sedition, better disposed for victory than they that suppose themselves wise or crafty' (Leviathan, Ch. XI, par. 16). Isn't this exemplary of the critical attitude itself?

Second, consider the focus of that last remark of Hobbes: it concentrates attention neither upon what we find in experience, nor upon how language can be used to describe that experience, but, instead, upon our conjectures, thoughts or theories in relation to what has been experienced. Hobbes provides us with a reason, if one were needed, to show why men should indeed do this.

In addition to emphasising the centrality of the critical attitude and the importance of theorising about experience, however, Hobbes adopts another very important tenet which is also central to Critical Rationality — a decisionalistic "faith in reason". The Critical Rationalist arbitrarily adopts, as a matter of faith in reason, the rational attitude as opposed to what is lumped under the general heading of irrationalism. This sense of the arbitrary seems to haunt Hobbes's philosophy too. For him, as we have seen, there is no way of deciding between competing moralities, competing interpretations of the Bible or even competing ways in which rational discourse may be employed. His sense of rationality arises out of what can be called an "artificial" reason, originating from an ultimate desire for self-survival, so that, as Watkins points out, when it comes to matters concerning the civil state 'an arbitrarily chosen system must be imposed and accepted *as if* if it were the "true" one' (Watkins 1973, 129).

If it be the case that the philosophy of Thomas Hobbes can be understood as heralding or pioneering the tradition of Critical Rationality, then we can see that the answer to the question "Can something be rationally justified on Hobbesian Principles?" must be in the negative, for nothing can be justified in terms of Critical Rationality itself. This same conclusion applies to the question of World Government. Of course a form of World Government might arise in the interest of pursuing Hobbesian Principles, so as to avoid what Colleen Clements calls 'the anarchic pattern of stasis collapse'.[9] But Hobbes's philosophy, in principle, could not be invoked to *justify* any such institution.

It might be objected to my thesis that, even if Hobbes cannot be read as providing a rationale for justifying principles upon which World Government could be based, since he does not show how such principles can be perspicuously derived, nonetheless he could be regarded as providing a case for a contextual justificatory argument. By this is meant that some principle, institution or proposal is taken as relatively "justified" when it survives criticism more satisfactorily than its competitors. Although this suggestion would be in the spirit of a Critical Rationality, it would not do the job required here. For even if it was admitted that Hobbes could be understood 'as defending the "bourgeois" life by showing its preferability' to other forms of social life, it would still have to be shown that this kind of interpretation did represent the focal point of his political theory (Herzog 1985, 26). In other words, such an interpretation could show only that the "bourgeois" form of life could be *legitimated*, never *justified*.

Notes

1. I am indebted to Peter Dews of the Extra-Mural Department of the University of London for drawing my attention to these four possible approaches to the "grounding of rationality" problem outlined in the work of Jürgen Habermas, though neither are to be credited with the misleading way in which these approaches may have been developed in this paper. I am also indebted to Cyril Hodgkinson, Margaret Cashin and Professor Martin Bertman for helpful suggestions in the writing of this paper. The contents of it are based on Chapter 12 of the author's *Technology and Training*, a book edited by Cyril Hodgkinson.

2. Jürgen Habermas (1977, Ch. 7) draws attention to the distinction between a substantive concept of rationality as opposed to Popper's "decisionalistic" one.

3. Jürgen Habermas (1971, 86) identifies this form of rationality by saying it involves a mysticism associated with what he calls 'the resurrection of fallen nature'. The quotation is from Adorno 1979, 382.

4. Popper 'believes that one can think and take meaningful decisions before one has acknowledged, even *implicitly*, the rules of argumentation as those of a critical communication community; or — and this amounts to the same thing — that one can philosophize about critical communication from a standpoint outside it' (Apel 1980, 269).

5. Apel 1982, 14. I am indebted to him for making this article available to me after his reading of an earlier version of my paper.

6. For a more extended discussion on whether such obligations can hold in a state of nature, see Farrell 1984, especially pp. 308-11.

7. Hobbes does not distinguish speech from language nor, evidently, do Isabel C. Hungerland and George R. Vick 1973. Hobbes does not make the move that Merleau-Ponty (1964) makes in distinguishing second-order expression or empirical language from authentic or first-hand speech. See also Peters 1967, 117.

8. Methodological individualism implies the doctrine that 'the "behaviour" and the "actions" of collectives, such as states or social groups, must be reduced to the behaviour and to the actions of human individuals'. See Popper 1971, 91 and also 324. Watkins's admission that the social nature of language has adverse implications for methodological individualism occurs in the second note of his 'The Human Condition: Two Criticisms of Hobbes', in Cohen 1976.

9. Different kinds of World Government are suggested by Clements 1978, 2 ff.

Bibliography

Adorno, T. (1979), *Negative Dialectics*, Seabury Press, New York.

Anzilotti, Dionisio (1929), *Cours de droit international*, tome I, Sirey, Paris.

Apel, Karl Otto (1980), *Towards a Transformation of Philosophy*, tr. by Glyn Adey and David Frisby, Routledge and Kegan Paul, London.

Apel, Karl Otto (1982), 'Normative Ethics and Strategical Rationality', *Graduate Faculty Philosophical Journal*, Vol. 9.

Aron, Raymond (1966), *Peace and War*, Krieger , Malabar.

Atiyah, P. S. (1981), *Promises, Morals, and Law*, Clarendon Press, Oxford.

Austin, John (1954), *The Province of Jurisprudence Determined and the Uses of the Study of Jurisprudence*, ed. by H. L. A. Hart, Weidenfeld and Nicolson, London.

Barash, David P. (1979), *The Whispering Within*, Harper & Row, New York.

Bartley III, W. W. (1984), *The Retreat to Commitment*, Open Court, La Salle.

Becker, Ernest (1973), *The Denial of Death*, The Free Press, New York.

Beitz, C. (1979), *Political Theory and International Relations*, Princeton University Press, Princeton.

Berber, F. (1960), *Lehrbuch des Völkerrechts*, Beck-Verlag, München.

Berlin, Isaiah (1958), *The Concepts of Liberty*, Oxford University Press, Oxford.

Blumering, A. von (1858), *Die Systematik des Völkerrechts von Hugo Grotius bis auf die Gegenwart,* Karow, Dorpat.

Boyle, James (1985), 'Ideals and Things: International Legal Scholarship and the Prison-House of Language', *Harvard International Law Journal*, Vol. 26.

Braun, D. (1963), *Der sterbliche Gott oder Leviathan gegen Behemoth*, Zurich.

Brian, Barry (1968), 'Warrender and his Critics', *Philosophy*, Vol. XLIII.

Brierly, James (1958), *The Basis of Obligation in International Law*, Clarendon Press, Oxford.

Bull, Hedley (1977), *The Anarchical Society*, Columbia University Press, New York.

Bull, Hedley (1981), 'Hobbes and the International Anarchy', *Social Research*, Vol. 48.

Canetti, Elias (1973), *Crowds and Power*, Continuum, New York.

Cassirer, E. (1919), *Natur- und Völkerrecht im Lichte der Geschichte und der systematischen Philosophie*, C.A. Schwetkse und Son, Berlin.

Cicero (1913, 1968), *De Officiis*, tr. by W. Miller, Loeb Library Edition, Harvard University Press, Cambridge, Mass.

Clements, Colleen (1978), 'The New Patterns of World Government', *Journal of Social Philosophy*, Vol. 9.

Cohen, M. (1984), 'Moral Skepticism and International Relations', *Philosophy and Public Affairs*, Vol. XIII.

Cohen, R. S. et al. (eds) (1976), *Essays in Memory of Imre Lakatos*, Reidel, Dordrecht.

Corbett, P. E. (1951), *Law and Society in the Relations between States*, Havecourt
& Brace, New York.

Dawkins, R. (1976), *The Selfish Gene*, Oxford University Press, Oxford.

Debray, R. (1986), *Die Weltmächte gegen Europa*, Rowolth, Reinbek.

Dror, Y. (1963), *Verrückte Staaten*, Frankfurt-am-Main.

d'Entrèves, A. P. (1951), *Natural Law*, Hutchinson, London.

Erickson, Eric H. (1960), 'The Problem of Ego Identity', in Stein, Maurice et al. (eds), *Identity and Anxiety*, The Free Press, Glencoe.

Farnsworth, E. Allen (1969), 'The Past of Promise: an Historical Introduction to Contract', *Columbia Law Review*, Vol. 69.

Farrell, David M. (1984), 'Reason and Right in Hobbes's Leviathan', *History of Philosophy Quarterly*, Vol. 1.

Fenichel, Otto (1945), *The Psychoalytic Theory of Neurosis*, Norton, New York.

Forsyth, M. (1979), 'Thomas Hobbes and the External Relations of States', *British Journal of International Studies*, Vol. 5.

Frank, Jerome D. (1968), *Sanity and Survival*, Random House, New York.

French, Peter (1979), 'The Corporation as a Moral Person', *American Philosophical Quarterly*, Vol. 16.

Freud, Sigmund (1950), *Totem and Taboo*, tr. by James Strachey, Norton, New York.

Freund, Julian (1965), *L'Essence du politique*, Sirey, Paris.

Fried, Charles (1981), *Contract as Promise*, Harvard University Press, Cambridge, Mass.

Fuller, Lon L.(1968), *Anatomy of the Law*, New American Library, New York.

Gascoigne, Bamber (1986), *Cod Streuth*, Ballantine, New York.

Gauthier, David (1969), *The Logic of Leviathan*, Clarendon Press, Oxford.

Gentile, Francesco, 'L'obligation politique: Hobbes et Kelsen', in Hart, H. L. A. (ed.), *The Concept of Law*, Clarendon Press, Oxford 1972.

Goldsmith, M. M. (1966), *Hobbes's Science of Politics*, Columbia University Press, New York.

Grotius, Hugo, *De Jure Belli ac Pacis Libri Tres*, Clarendon Press, Oxford. Reproduction of the edition of 1646 and tr. by F. W. Kelsey, Carnegie

Endowment for International Peace, Washington D.C.

Habermas, Jürgen (1971), *Towards a Rational Society*, Heinemann, London.

Habermas, Jürgen (1976), 'A Positivistically Bisected Rationalism', in T. Adorno et al. (eds), *The Positivistic Dispute in German Sociology*, tr. by G. Adey and D. Frisby, Heinemann, London.

Habermas, Jürgen (1977), *Theory and Practice*, Heinemann, London.

Habermas, Jürgen (1980), *Legitimation Crisis*, tr. by T. McCarthy, Heinemann, London.

Haggenmacher, Peter (1986), 'La doctrine des deux elements du droit coutumier dans la pratique de la Cour internationale', *Revue generale de droit international public*, Vol. 90.

Hampton, Jean (1986), *Hobbess and the Social Contract Tradition*, Cambridge University Press, Cambridge.

Hanson, W. (1984), 'Thomas Hobbes' Highway to Peace', *International Organization*, Vol. 38.

Hare, R. M. (1965), *Freedom and Reason*, Oxford University Press, Oxford.

Hart, H. L. A. (1961), *The Concept of Law*, Clarendon Press, Oxford.

Hegel, G. W. F. (1964), *Logic*, tr. by William Wallace, Oxford University Press, Oxford.

Herzog, Don (1985), *Without Foundations*, Cornell University Press, Ithaca.

Holmes, Jr., Oliver Wendell (1923), *The Common Law*, Little, Brown, and Co., Boston (1881).

Hood, F. C. (1964), *The Divine Politics of Thomas Hobbes*, Clarendon Press, Oxford.

Horkheimer, Max (1974), *Eclipse of Reason*, Seabury Press, New York.

Hungerland, Isabel C. and George R. Vick (1973), 'Hobbes's Theory of Signification', *Journal of the History of Philosophy*, Vol. XI.

James I (1918), *The Political Works of James I*, ed. by C. H. McIlwain, Harvard University Press, Cambridge, Mass.

Jardine, L. (1974), *Francis Bacon: Discovery and the Art of Discourse*, Cambridge University Press, Cambridge.

Jeffrey, Richard C. (1983), *The Logic of Decision* , 2nd ed., University of Chicago Press, Chicago.

Jeffrey, Richard C. (1977), 'Advances in Understanding Rational Behavior', in J. C. Harsanyi (ed.), *Foundational Problems in the Special Sciences*, Reidel Dordrecht.

Jellinek, G. (1900 and 1921), *Allgemeine Staatslehre*, Springer, Berlin.

Jellinek, G. (1880), *Die rechtliche Natur der Staatenverträge*, A. Hölder, Wien.

Johnson, Paul J. (1982), 'Hobbes and the Wolf-Man', in J. van der Bend, (ed.), *Thomas Hobbes: His View of Man*, Roldopi, Amsterdam. (Reprinted in C. Walton and P. J. Johnson (eds), *Hobbes's Science of Natural Justice*, Martinus Nijhoff, Dordrecht 1987.)

Johnston, David (1986), *The Rhetoric of Leviathan*, Princeton University Press, Princeton.

Kaltenborn von Stachau, Carl (1847), *Kritik des Völkerrechts nach dem jetzigen Standpunkte der Wissenschaft*, G. Mayer, Leipzig.

Kant, Immanuel (1970), *Kant's Political Works*, ed. by Hans Reiss, Cambridge University Press, Cambridge.

Kavka, G. S. (1983), 'Hobbes's War of All against All', *Ethics*, Vol. 93.

Kavka, G. S. (1986), *Hobbesian Moral and Political Theory*, Princeton University Press, Princeton.

Kelsen, Hans (1911), *Hauptprobleme der Staatsrechtslehre*, Mohr, Tübingen.

Kelsen, Hans (1949), *General Theory of Law and State*, Harvard University Press, Cambridge, Mass.

Kelsen, Hans (1970), *The Pure Theory of Law*, University of California Press, Berkeley.

Kennedy, David (1980), 'Theses on International Legal Discourse'', *German Yearbook of International Law*, Vol. 23.

Koselleck, R. (1959), *Kritik und Krise*, Suhrkamp, Frankfurt-am-Main.

Koskenniemi, Martti (1987), 'Sovereignty. Prolegomena to a Study of International Law as Discourse', *Kansainoikeus-Jus Gentium*, Vol. 4.

Krockow, Ch. von (1962), *Soziologie des Friedens*, Gaatersloh.

Kunz, J. L. (1962), 'Völkerrecht allgemein', in Strupp and Scholochauer (Hersgbr.), *Wörterbuch des Völkerrechts in drei Banden*, Band III, Berlin.

Lammasch, H. (1930), 'Die Lehre von der Schiedsgerichtsbarkeit in ihrem ganzen Umfange', in Stier-Somlo, *Handbuch des Völkerrechts*, I. Band, 1. Abteilung, Stuttgart.

Lauterpacht, Hersch (1933), *The Function of Law in the International Community*, Clarendon Press, Oxford.

Lenski, Gerhard (1966), *Power and Privilege*, McGraw-Hill, New York.

Levine, Andrew (1981), *Liberal Democracy*, Columbia University Press, New York.

Lucas, J. R. (1966), *The Principle of Politics*, Oxford University Press, Oxford.

Luhmann, Niklas (1980), 'Selbstlegitimation des Staates', *ARSP Beiheft* 15.

Lyons, David (1984), *Ethics and the Rule of Law*, Cambridge University Press, Cambridge.

Mackie, John (1980), *Hume's Moral Theory*, Routledge and Kegan Paul, London.

Macpherson, C. B. (1962), *The Political Theory of Possessive Individualism*, Clarendon Press, Oxford.

Marx, Karl, *Economic and Philosophic Manuscripts of 1844*, Lawrence and Wishart, London.

Massey, Gerald (1976), 'Tom Dick, and Harry and all the King's Men', *American Philosophical Quarterly*, Vol. 13.

May, Larry (1979), 'Hobbes on Equity and Justice', paper presented at the Hobbes Tercentenary Congress, University of Colorado, Boulder.

McNeill, William (1982), *The Pursuit of Power*, University of Chicago Press, Chicago.

Melville, Herman (1972), *Moby-Dick*, Penguin Books, Harmondsworth (1851).

Merleau-Ponty, Maurice (1964), 'Indirect Language and the Voices of Silence', in *Signs*, Northwestern University Press, Evanston.

Merleau-Ponty, Maurice (1966), *Phenomenology of Perception*, tr. by Colin Smith, Routledge and Kegan Paul, London.

Merleau-Ponty, Maurice (1973), *Adventures of the Dialectic*, Northwestern University Press, Evanston.

Merleau-Ponty, Maurice (1978), *Sense and Nonsense*, tr. by H. Dreyfus and P. A. Dreyfus, Northwestern University Press, Evanston.

Morawetz, Thomas (1980), *The Philosophy of Law*, Macmillan, New York.

Morris, Desmond (1967), *The Naked Ape*, Crown, New York.

Muller, Jörg P. (1971), 'Vertrauenschotz im Völkerrecht' in *Max Planck Institut für ausländisches Recht und Völkerrecht*, Beiträge 56, Carl Heymanns, Köln-Berlin.

Munzer, Stephen (1972), *Legal Validity*, Martinus Nijhoff, The Hague.

Nagel, Thomas (1985), 'Subjective and Objective', in Rajchman and West (eds), *Post-Analytic Philosophy*, Columbia University Press, New York.

Nagel, Ernest (1961), *The Structure of Science*, Harcourt, Brace and World, New York.

Navari, Cornelia (1982), 'Hobbes and the ''Hobbesian Tradition'' in International Thought', *Millenium*, Vol. 11.

O'Connell, D. P. (1962), *International Law for Students*, Macmillan, London.

O'Neill, Barry (1986), 'International Escalation and the Dollar Auction', *Journal of Conflict Resolution*, Vol. 30.

Orwell, George (1968), 'The Sporting Spirit', in *In Front of Your Nose*, Harcourt, Brace and World, New York.

Pangle, T. L. (1976), 'The Moral Basis of National Security: Four Historical Perspectives', in K. Knorr (ed.), *Historical Dimensions of National Security Problems*, University of Kansas Press, Lawrence.

Parsons, Talcott (1968), *The Structure of Social Action*, Free Press, New York.

Paulson, Stanley L. (1983), 'Reassessing Hobbes as Legal Philosopher', paper presented at the APA Eastern Division meeting, December 1983.

Peters, R. S. (1950 and 1967), *Hobbes*, Penguin, Harmondsworth.

Plotinus (1958), *Enneads*, McKenna edition, Basic Books, New York.

Pocock, J. G. A. (1972), *Politics, Language and Time*, Atheneum, London.

Pocock, J. G. A. (1975), *The Machiavellian Moment: Florentine Political Thought and the Atlantic Republican Tradition*, Princeton University Press, Princeton.

Polin, R. (1972), 'Force and Its Political Uses in Hobbes', *Philosophical Forum*, Vol. 3.

Popper, Karl (1959), *The Logic of Scientific Discovery*, Basic Books, New York.

Popper, Karl (1971), *Open Society and Its Enemies*, Vol. 2, Princeton University Press, Princeton.

Pufendorf, Samuel (1927), *On the Duty of Man and Citizen*, tr. by Frank

Gardner, Oxford University Press, Oxford (*De Officio hominis et civis*, 1675).

Pufendorf, Samuel (1717), *Of the Law of Nature and Nations*, tr. by Basil Kennet, London, 3rd ed. (*De jure naturae et gentium*, 1672).

Radnitzky, G. (1970), *Contemporary Schools of Metascience*, Henry Regnery, Chicago.

Reibstein, E. (1958-63), *Völkerrecht. Eine Geschichte seiner Ideen in Lehre und Praxis*, Verlag Karl Allen, Freiburg/München.

Ripstein, Arthur, 'Foundationalism in Political Theory', *Philosophy and Public Affairs*, Vol. XVI.

Rousseau, Jean Jaques (1964), *Discourse sur le origine et les fondaments de le inegalite parmi des hommes*, Gallimard, Bibliothèque Pleiade, Paris.

Ruddy, R. Francis (1975), *International Law in the Enlightenment. The Background of Emmerich de Vattel's ''Droit des Gens''*, New York.

Sauer, E. (1955), *Grundlehre des Völkerrechts*, Heymann, Köln und Berlin.

Schiller, M. (1972), 'Political Authority, Self-Defense, and Pre-emptive War', *Canadian Journal of Philosophy*, Vol. I.

Schmitt, C. (1950), *Der Nomos der Erde im Jus Publicum Europaeum*, Greven, Köln.

Shennan, J. H. (1974), *The Origins of the Modern European State 1450-1725*, London.

Sitwell, Edith (1962), *The Queens and the Hive*, Little, Brown and Co. Boston.

Spragens, T. A. (1973), *The Politics of Motion: The World of Thomas Hobbes*, University Press of Kentucky, Lexington.

Sztucki, Jerzy (1974), 'Jus Cogens and the Vienna Convention on Treaties', *Österreichische Zeitschrift für öffentliches Recht*, Suppl. 3, Springer, Wien.

Taylor, A. E. (1938), 'The Ethical Doctrine of Hobbes', *Philosophy*, Vol. 13.

Taylor, A. E. (1969), 'The Ethical Doctrine of Hobbes', in B. H. Baumrin (ed.), *Hobbes' Leviathan: Interpretation and Criticism*, Wadsworth, Belmont.

Taylor, C. (1975), *Hegel*, Cambridge University Press, Cambridge.

Teger, A. (1978), *Too Much Invested to Quit*, Pergamon, New York.

Toynbee, Arnold (1968), 'Traditional Attitudes Toward Death', in Toynbee et al. (eds), *Man's Concern with Death*, MacGraw-Hill, New York.

Tussman, J. (1968), *Obligation and the Body Politic*, Oxford University Press, Oxford.

Tönnies, F. (1896), *Thomas Hobbes, Leben und Lehre*, Stuttgart.

Vamvoukos, Athanassios (1985), *Termination of Treaties in International Law: The Doctrines of rebus sic stantibus and desuetude*, Clarendon Press, Oxford.

Vattel, Emer de (1758), *Droit des gens ou principes de la Loi Naturelle appliquaes à la conduite et aux affaires des Nations et des Souverains*, Londres.

Verdross, A. (1926), *Die Verfassing des Völkerrechtgemeinschaftes*, Springer, Berlin.

Verdross, A. (1963), *Abendländische Rechtsphilosophie* Springer, Wien.

Vincent, R. J. (1981), 'The Hobbesian Tradition in Twentieth Century

International Thought', *Millenium*, Vol. 10.

Walker, T. A. (1983), *The Science of International Law*, London.

Walton, C. (mss.), *The 'Prima Philosophia' of Thomas Hobbes*.

Walz, G. A. (1930), 'Das Wesen des Völkerrechts und Kritik der Völker-rechtsleugner', in Stier-Somlo, *Handbuch des Völkerrechts*, I. Band, 1. Abteilung, Stuttgart.

Warrender, H. (1957), *The Political Philosophy of Hobbes: His Theory of Obligation*, Clarendon Press, Oxford.

Warrender, H. (1969), 'Hobbes's Conception of Morality', in B. H. Baumrin (ed.), *Hobbes' Leviathan: Interpretation and Criticism*, Wadsworth, Belmont.

Warrender, H. (1979), 'Hobbes and Macroethics: The Theory of Peace and Natural Justice', paper presented at the Hobbes Tercentenary Congress, University of Colorado, Boulder.

Watkins, J. W. N. (1967), 'Decision and Belief', in Robin Hughes (ed.), *Decision Making*, BBC, London.

Watkins, J. W. N. (1973), *Hobbes's System of Ideas*, 2nd ed., Hutchinson, London.

Weber, M. (1971), 'Politik als Beruf', in *Gesammelte politische Schriften* Mohr, Tübingen.

Weiler, Gershon (1970), 'Hobbes and Performatives', *Philosophy*, Vol. XLV.

Wernham, A. G. (1965), 'Liberty and Obligation in Hobbes', in K. C. Brown (ed.), *Hobbes Studies*, Basil Blackwell, Oxford.

Wheaton, Henry (1936), *Elements of International Law*, Carnegie Endowment for International Peace, Washington D.C. (Reproduction of the edition of 1866).

Wheelis, Allen (1958), *The Quest for Identity*, Norton, New York.

Whitehead, A. N. (1926), *Science and the Modern World*, Cambridge University Press, Cambridge.

Wilks, Ivor (1955), 'A Note on Sovereignty', *Philosophical Quarterly*, Vol. 5.

Willms, B. (1974), 'Ist weltpolitische Sicherheit institutionalisierbar?', *Der Staat*, Band 13.

Wilson, Edward O. (1978), *On Human Nature*, Harvard University Press, Cambridge, Mass.

Wilson, Peter J. (1983), *Man, the Promising Primate*, 2nd ed., Yale University Press, New Haven.

Woolsey, T. D. (1879), *Introduction to the Study of International Law*, 5th edition, Sampson Low, London.

Wormuth, F. D. (1939), *The Royal Prerogative*, Cornell University Press, Ithaca.

Wright, Georg Henrik von (1975), *Explanation and Understanding*, Cornell University Press, Ithaca

About the Authors

Timo Airaksinen,
Professor of Philosophy, University of Helsinki, Unioninkatu 40 B, 00170 Helsinki, Finland.

Martin A. Bertman,
Professor of Philosophy, Department of Philosophy, Ben-Gurion University, Box 653, Beer-Sheva, Israel.

Noel E. Boulting,
University of London, home: 36 Crosier Court, Upchurch, Nr. Sittingbourne, Kent ME9 7AR, England.

Martin Golding,
Professor of Philosophy, Department of Philosophy, Duke University, Durham, North Carolina 27708, USA.

Robinson A. Grover,
Professor of Philosophy, Department of Philosophy, University of Connecticut, University Drive, Torrington, Connecticut 06790, USA.

Isabel Hungerland (†),
Professor of Philosophy, University of California, Berkeley, California, USA.

Paul J. Johnson,
Professor of Philosophy, Department of Philosophy, California State University, San Bernardino, CA 92407, USA.

Martti Koskenniemi,
Academy of Finland and the Ministry for Foreign Affairs of Finland, home: Korkeavuorenkatu 15 B, 00130 Helsinki, Finland.

Eerik Lagerspetz,
Department of Philosophy, University of Turku, 20500 Turku, Finland.

Tommy L. Lott,
Professor, Department of Philosophy, University of Massachusetts, Boston, Harbor Campus, Boston, Massachusetts 02125, USA.

Peter K. Machamer,
Professor of Philosophy, Department of History and Philosophy of Science, University of Pittsburgh, Pittsburgh, PA 15260, USA.

Arthur Ripstein,
Professor, Department of Philosophy, University of Toronto, Toronto, Ontario, Canada M5S 1A1.

Gershon Weiler,
Professor, Faculty of Humanities, Tel Aviv University, Ramat Aviv, Tel Aviv 420111, Israel.

Bernard Willms,
Professor, Department of Political Science, Ruhr-Universität Bochum, Box 102148, 4630 Bochum 1, BRD.

To Andrew

O star, (the fairest one in sight),
We grant you loftiness, the right
to some obscurity of cloud –
it will not do to say of night,
Since dark is what brings out your light.
Some mystery becomes the proud.
But to be wholly taciturn
In reserve is not allowed.
Say something to us we can learn
By heart and when alone repeat.
Say something! And it says, "I burn."
But say with what degree of heat.
Talk Fahrenheit, talk Centigrade.
Use language we can comprehend.
Tell us what elements you blend.
It gives us strangely little aid,
But does tell something in the end.
And steadfast as Keats' Eremite,
Not even stooping from its sphere,
It asks a little of us here.
It asks of us a certain height,
So when at times the mob is swayed
To carry praise or blame too far,
We may choose something like a star
To stay our minds on, and be staid.

– Robert Frost, "Choose Something Like A Star",
from *Steeple Bush* (1947)

Contents

Editor's Preface

Jean Hampton died on April 2, 1996, three days after going into a coma induced by a massive brain hemorrhage. The main intellectual project she was actively engaged on just before her death was the completion and revision of a draft of a book with the working title *A Theory of Reasons*. The draft she was working from contained nine chapters and a preface, introduction, and preliminary material. She had significantly revised the first three chapters in the weeks prior to her unexpected and premature death, which prevented her from completing her work on the rest of the manuscript.

Jean thought of this as her most important work, and had asked me to ensure its publication in the event she was unable to do so herself. With the encouragement of Terry Moore of Cambridge University Press, I have undertaken to honor her request. The book is closely based on computer files of the most recent versions of the preface, introduction, and preliminary material, and nine chapters of *A Theory of Reasons* as they were left at Jean's death.

The material has been lightly edited to remove obvious typographical and other minor errors. More substantial editorial interventions are noted explicitly, mainly in footnotes and appendices – the words of the editor in the text are enclosed in brackets. When difficult editorial decisions arose, I have tried to make them in such a way as to preserve the original material even when it was repetitious or lacking in continuity. Additions and modifications were made solely to make the book as independently intelligible as possible. At the head of each chapter is the date of the author's last revision of the computer file containing that chapter. These dates make it clear that while the material up to Chapter 3 was revised just before Jean's death, the rest of the chapters had not been revised since up to a year earlier.

Had Jean lived, she would certainly have extensively revised the material in Chapters 4 through 9, including completing Chapters 6 and 9, which are here merely outlined. Since it was her custom to go through several drafts before publishing any work, I consider it very likely that even the revision she was working on when she died would not have resulted in the final draft of the manuscript. Jean compared her creative philosophical work to the art of sculpture. Just as the sculptor strives to reveal what he or she sees already present at least in its rough outlines in the unworked clay, so too the philosopher first sees the truth, if only in broadest outline, and then seeks to reveal it in detail by analysis and the construction of arguments. This is a process that has no natural termination. In the case of this book, it is a process that was far from complete at the time of its author's death.

As Jean says in her preface, this work is intended to stimulate its readers to rethink its questions for themselves rather than to present them with a definitive resolution. Especially in light of its unfinished state, such rethinking must start from a sympathetic reading and refashioning of the arguments it contains. Jean herself often used to say that to convince a philosophical opponent, it is not sufficient to refute his or her arguments as these are presented. To carry conviction, one must first understand and develop these arguments into their strongest form, and only then show why even this improved form of argument fails to justify the intended conclusion. She would certainly have hoped and expected that those critical of the ideas presented here, as well as her more sympathetic readers, would strive to provide those ideas with the best possible justification before attempting to evaluate their worth.

A number of people joined me in the task of editing the manuscript. Ron Milo and Christopher Morris carefully read lightly edited drafts of the entire manuscript and made many detailed suggestions about additional editing, most of which I followed. I have David Silver to thank for compiling the bibliography and for detailed discussions on the structure of arguments in Chapter 8 against the Resolution Strategy, and Cindy Holder for compiling the index.

Preface and Acknowledgments

[computer file 2/10/96]

Israel Scheffler once told me that every time he wrote a book, he would swear it would be his last. Any author knows the feeling – books take too long to write, the arguments and the prose never seem good enough, and when one is all done, the enormity of all that is still wrong with the final product hits home. Still, authors are ever hopeful that their contributions will be of *some* use, and I am no exception. I have aimed to write a book that does not so much attempt to persuade, as to dissuade – I wish to shake readers loose from the grip of a conception of the world that threatens our ability to act both rationally and reasonably.

In the process of constructing a work that attempts to rattle those who read it, I have been the recipient of much help, often from people who are quite opposed to this project. I am very grateful for their generous support and probing criticisms. In particular, I would like to thank Julia Annas, John Broome, Tom Christiano, David Copp, Ron Milo, Ken O'Day, John Pollock, Joseph Raz, John Roemer, Robert Sugden, and Bruno Verbeek. I also owe much to the graduate students attending my seminars at the University of California at Davis and the University of Arizona, in which portions of this book were presented. Their persistence in demanding more clarity and better arguments was invaluable in revising the final product. Finally, I am indebted to the audiences who heard portions of this book presented at lectures, conferences, and seminars at Oxford University, Texas Tech University, the University of Western Illinois, Yale Law School, Chicago Law School, CREA and the École Polytechnique (Paris), The European University Institute in Florence, the University of North Carolina at Chapel Hill, the University of Notre Dame, Calvin College, Dalhousie University, Pomona College, the University of Sussex, and the University of East Anglia. Special thanks goes to the

Philosophy Department at the University of Bristol, where I gave a series of lectures on topics in this book in January 1996 as a Benjamin Meaker Visiting Scholar, for their very helpful discussions and comments.

Thanks also goes to the National Endowment for the Humanities, to the American Council of Learned Societies, and the Pew Charitable Trusts for providing me with fellowship support that has given me the time I needed to write and finish the book. I am particularly grateful to the Pew Foundation for granting me a three-year Pew Evangelical Scholarship, by way of supporting the work of someone who is committed to being a Christian analytic philosopher. I hope that this book will seem to them to have been a good investment.

In February and March 1996 I was a research fellow at CREA (Centre de Recherche en Epistemologie Appliquée) of the École Polytechnique. I am very grateful for the marvelous research environment, and would like to particularly thank Pasquale Pasquino and Jean-Pierre Dupuy. I am also grateful to the Social Philosophy and Policy Center at Bowling Green State University for providing me with a warm and supportive research environment during the summer of 1993.

I am grateful to my husband Richard Healey for many things, including the tactful way in which he phrased his criticisms of portions of this book and for getting me up in the morning and making my tea. I am also grateful to my son Andrew Hampton-Healey for all his questions about my project. This book is dedicated to him and honors his thoughtful pursuit of the truth, of which his parents are very proud.

Introduction

[computer file 3/24/96]

Theology and Absolute Ethics are two famous subjects
which we have realized have no real objects.
                                    – Frank Ramsey[1]

THE PROJECT

For many years now, an interesting conflict has raged within contemporary philosophy. On one side of the conflict are "objectivist"
moral and political philosophers, who believe in and accept the existence of distinctive (and irreducible) moral "values" – words that
in this conflict have been used to cover a variety of normative notions fundamental to moral and political theories – for example,
rights, duties, goods, and reasons for action. These philosophers
maintain that moral judgments that involve values can be true or
false, and that these moral facts cannot be reduced to the sort of facts
recognized by scientific theories. In that sense, they believe there are
value-laden, nonreducible moral judgments that are objective. On the
other side of this debate are the "naturalists," who insist that the
world, as our best scientific theories portray it, does not and cannot
contain values. Since values are the stuff of the theorizing of the
moral objectivists, it follows from the naturalists' position that there
can be no uniquely moral facts. Hence they deny the possibility that
there are value-laden, nonreducible moral judgments that are objective.

Many contemporary moral theorists, shaken by the naturalists'
challenge to the viability of their fields, have produced work that has

---

[1] See Frank Plumpton Ramsey (1931a), Epilogue ("There is Nothing to Discuss")
in Ramsey (1931, 291–2), quoted by Hilary Putnam (1990, 137).

1

been "dominated by a concern with the place of values in the natural world."[2] These theories have ranged from those that have defended the idea that moral values are real[3] to those that have sought to redefine the subject-matter of ethics so that it can be "naturalized" and thereby rendered acceptable given the ontological demands of science.[4]

This book offers the beginnings of a defense of, among other things, moral objectivity. But rather than constructing positive arguments defending the possibility or actuality of nonreducible moral facts, I will be defending moral objectivism by attacking the naturalists' position. In particular, I will attempt to show that the naturalists' argument against the moral objectivists' theory is self-defeating.

To see how this strategy will work, consider that there are four ways in which one might respond to the purported conflict between objective moral theories and the theories of science that the naturalists respect[5]:

1. One can believe that the commitments of science preclude acceptance of objectivist moral theory – and so much the worse for objectivist moral theory. Call this theory *moral anti-objectivism*. To be precise, it is the view that there are no irreducibly moral facts (facts that cannot be reduced to natural facts recognized by science) insofar as such irreducibly moral facts are not, and could not be, admissible by scientific criteria. Thus it is the denial of moral objectivism, as defined above, that insists that there are such irreducibly moral facts. There are a number of importantly different variants of this position: moral nihilists and skeptics (those who deny or doubt that there is any special domain of the moral, such as Quine), moral noncognitivists (who deny that there are irreducibly moral facts but explain morality as constituted by expressivistic assertions, such as Gibbard or Hare), and theorists who believe that "moral judgments can be analyzed into or reduced to factual statements of a sort clearly com-

<hr />

[2] Gilbert Harman (1984, 29).
[3] Such theories include those developed by "moral realists" – for example, Boyd (1988), Sturgeon (1984), Brink (1989).
[4] Such theories include those developed by Gibbard (1990), Blackburn (1984), Mackie (1977), and Gauthier (1986).
[5] My classifications are in certain respects comparable to those put forward by Brink (1989, 6). I am indebted to conversations with Mark Patterson about various possible classification schemes in this area.

patible with a scientific world view."[6] This latter group includes moral relativists such as Bernard Williams, who argue that morality is defined by different sets of social conventions in different societies.[7] It also includes those who put forward what I call "Hobbesian" contractarian moral theories, such as Gauthier (1986) and Mackie (1977), who, inspired by Hobbes (1651), attempt to reduce moral facts to facts of (instrumental) reason.

2. One can believe that the commitments of science preclude acceptance of objectivist moral theory – and so much the worse for science. Call this theory *moral nonnaturalism*. It is the view that there are irreducibly moral facts, and that because such facts are not and cannot be admissible by scientific criteria, those criteria cannot be exclusively used to establish what count as facts in the world. In short, it is the view that ethical inquiry is discontinuous with scientific inquiry.[8] G. E. Moore is perhaps the most famous exponent of this view[9]; the work of philosophers such as Thomas Nagel, Alan Donagan, Stephen Darwall, and Alasdair MacIntyre also falls into this camp.

3. One can believe that the commitments of science do not preclude the acceptance of objectivist moral theory, because, in the end, morality is like science after all. That is, both are objective, so that they both establish facts, albeit different kinds of facts. Hence this position not only insists that there are moral facts, but also that these facts are not reducible to natural facts. Most often, theorists who propound this position advocate what is called *moral realism*. Although that term is slippery, it is generally used to denote realist positions that insist that even though moral facts are not reducible to natural facts, they are fully compatible with science. For example, Brink denies the reducibility of moral facts to natural facts, and maintains that "moral facts and properties are no more *sui generis* than are the facts and properties of other higher-order disciplines."[10]

---

[6] Ibid.

[7] Harman has a distinctive, and not universally shared, conception of moral relativism. I will discuss it at length in Chapter 3.

[8] For more on this view, see Stephen Darwall, Allan Gibbard, and Peter Railton (1992, 130–1).

[9] See Moore's *Principia Ethica* 1903. Its nonnaturalism receives a nice discussion by Darwall, Gibbard, and Railton, ibid. See especially pp. 115–121.

[10] Brink (1989, 210).

Nicholas Sturgeon and John McDowell also put forward arguments of this type.

4. Finally, one can believe that the commitments of science do not preclude acceptance of objectivist moral theory, because, in the end, science is like morality – and not the other way around. In this view, science and morality are alike because even though morality has within it components that are not "scientifically admissible" given the traditionally understood criteria establishing scientific objectivity, on close examination the same components lurk in science too – albeit little recognized or admitted.[11] I call this position *sophisticated compatibilism*, and it can take two quite different forms. One form embraces a Feyerabendian view of science that disparages the pretense of objectivity in scientific discourse. And insofar as, in this view, scientific and moral discourse are basically similar, the view also dismisses the pretense of objectivity in moral discourse. I call this position *sophisticated anti-objectivism*. It has been advocated by, among others, Richard Rorty.[12] The second form insists that we can still see science as objective, but not in the traditional naive way, so that scientific objectivity is no different from the form of objectivity exemplified in the moral domain.[13] I call this position *sophisticated objectivism*.

In the last few years, most defenders of morality against the attacks of scientific skeptics have embraced some version of position 2 or 3 – that is, moral nonnaturalism or moral realism. But in this book, I shall advance a position on ethics and science that is motivated by position 4, and in particular, the sophisticated objectivist version of that position. Indeed, I shall go on to advance a thesis concerning normativity in general. Consider that moral objectivism is just an instance of a more general position that might be called *normative objectivism*, that holds that there are irreducibly normative facts. Moreover, each of the four positions just defined could be re-

---

[11] In this view, "although ethics cannot fit the commonsense view of scientific objectivity, this establishes nothing interesting about the objectivity of ethics, since science itself does not satisfy the commonsense view of scientific objectivity." Brink (1989, 6)

[12] See, for example, Richard Rorty (1980a, 1980b).

[13] To quote Brink, in this view, the "commonsense view of scientific objectivity is naive; once we understand the objectivity obtainable in the sciences, we can see that ethics is or can be every bit as objective as the sciences." (1989, 6)

cast as positions about the relationship between science and *any* normative theory—that is, there are:

1. Skeptical positions on normativity, including normative anti-objectivism, normative nihilism, normative relativism, and normative noncognitivism.
2. Normative nonnaturalist positions.
3. Normative realist positions.
4. Various possible versions of normative sophisticated compatibilism.

I will argue along sophisticated objectivist lines that in the same way a commitment to science does not preclude, in and of itself, the acceptance of moral objectivism, it also does not preclude, in and of itself, the acceptance of other types of normative theory. Indeed, I will make the stronger claim that science itself requires, and is undergirded by, a commitment to normative objectivism, meaning that any science-based argument against moral objectivism is ultimately self-defeating.

Of course, the values – I shall call them "norms" – relied on by naturalists and moral theorists aren't the same (although I shall also argue that there is much more overlap than the two groups have thought). Nonetheless, I hope to show that the naturalists' position requires the existence of normative facts that while largely (but not entirely) different from the sort of normative facts recognized by moral theory, are not metaphysically different either in their nature or in their operation from moral facts. Both moral theorists and naturalists therefore embrace two different forms of normative objectivity.

This argument cannot, by itself, vindicate moral objectivity. Naturalists can always claim that *their* kind of norms are sound, whereas the moral objectivists' norms are not. Few arguments defending the special soundness of the naturalists' norms exist in the literature, because naturalists tend not to want to acknowledge their own normative commitments. But those who do generally argue that the norms that undergird their position – for example, the norms of epistemology, or reason, or science – are sound because they can be "naturalized," whereas the norms of morality cannot.

I will discuss at length this argumentative move by the naturalists in order to show how it fails. As I shall explain, "naturalization" of the norms of epistemology or science tends, almost exclusively, to rely on instrumental reason. This form of reason is assumed to be metaphysically benign, unproblematic in naturalist terms, and yet the justificatory tool for legitimating the norms that the naturalist needs for the rest of his theorizing. Yet I hope to expose the "metaphysically occult" nature of instrumental reason. Not only is this seemingly benign conception of reason far more complicated than its adherents have realized, but it is also constituted by a variety of norms itself. Hence, using this conception of reason as a tool to naturalize other norms is just using another normative tool that is at least as "unnatural" as the norms it is intended to naturalize. It therefore cannot serve as the Archimedean lever for the naturalization of other norms, nor is there any other level by which it can itself be naturalized.

I shall take great pains to discuss the components of a theory of instrumental reason in order to show how many normative issues such a theory must take a stand on, and how many variants of such a theory are possible, depending on what stands a theorist of instrumental reason decides to take. Moreover, I shall also argue that part of what is involved in specifying a conception of instrumental reason involves taking a stand – a very minimal stand, but a stand nonetheless – on the nature of the good of a rational agent. If I'm right, even the most hard-core instrumentalist on reason can only theorize about reason by doing, in a small way, some theorizing that has normally been construed as "noninstrumental." The realization that a little of bit of ethics is required in order to develop a conception of reason on which a variety of sciences rely should, I hope, show both sides of the debate how much they have in common, not only in their acceptance of normative objectivity as an overarching thesis, but also in the kinds of norms they need for their theorizing.

Moreover, if I am right, naturalists are without any effective way of arguing that their normative commitments are any more defensible than the normative commitments of moral objectivists (simply claiming that naturalists' norms are "obviously" correct, clearly won't do, particularly in the face of controversy over what those norms are or how they should be specified). More importantly, naturalists are, at least thus far, without an effective way of defending their own form of normative objectivity. My arguments try to bring to the attention of philosophers an issue that has been insufficiently discussed – namely, how can we tell when a norm is sound? To answer this question, we require what I call a "theory of normativity." Such a theory tells us how to recognize which norms are sound and which aren't, and it tells us what it means to say that a norm is sound. There exist some models of what a theory of normativity should look like. These models have generally been developed in moral philosophy because of the widespread recognition that moral norms have been under attack. For example, the idea of using "reflective equilibrium" to test normative conceptions is at least part of such a theory of normativity.[14] I hope to show that philosophers in many fields beside moral and political philosophy – for example, epistemologists,· philosophers of science, and philosophers of language – need such a theory of normativity to defend their own normative commitments. Perhaps appreciating that all of us must develop ways of defending the norms on which our theorizing relies may help to break down barriers that presently divide different fields of philosophy.[15]

The final aim of this book is to persuade naturalists and moral objectivists to realize their kinship, and join forces in opposing what I take to be their real theoretical enemy – those radical normative skeptics – the sophisticated anti-objectivists, exemplified by many postmodernist thinkers – who reject the idea that there are any sound norms and who dismiss the idea that there is any universal and authoritative conception of reason that can be the foundation either for our attempts to understand the natural world or for our attempts to successfully structure the social one. It is the need for an effective philosophical answer to these thinkers that, as I shall now discuss, makes it imperative that naturalists and moral objectivists recognize their common commitment to normative objectivity and join forces to defend it.

There are a number of different kinds of theorists who fall into the category of radical normative skeptic, but in this book I am particularly interested in those who doubt or dismiss the authority of science. For example, many postmodernists argue that philosophical or scientific theories are merely expressions of culture (and of the

---

[14] The use of reflective equilibrium is familiar from Rawls's (1971) *A Theory of Justice*. Rawls cites Goodman (1955, 65–68) as employing a similar principle in nonmoral domains.

[15] Indeed, it may even make hiring easier if it helps to make those divisions less important!

ambitions of certain groups powerful in that culture), and there are sociologists of science who interpret the development of scientific theories in an entirely nonnormative way.[16] No naturalist these days can be unaware of the way that the history of science lends itself to such deconstruction. The history of biology or psychology, for example, is replete with examples of self-serving theorizing by members of culturally dominant groups that "just happen" to show that women are mentally weaker than men, that blacks are inferior, that homosexuality is unnatural, and so forth.[17] Only with the empowerment of these nondominant groups within the academy has such theorizing (at least somewhat) abated. The opponents of normative objectivity will draw one kind of lesson from this history – that theories that purport to rely on various forms of objective normative authority, whether in science, social science, moral theory, or politics, are in reality theories that manifest the culture of that society, and by and large serve the interests of that society's most powerful. Naturalists want to draw another lesson – that the theories in question are examples of *bad science*.

But if this is bad science, what is good science? On what does good science rely, such that we can trust it to give us something *sound* and such that we should take it to have authority over us?

The answer to these normatively charged questions generally given by philosophers is that good science is grounded in reason. But what is this reason? One of my purposes in spending so much time in this book explicating the conception of instrumental reason and discussing the extent to which science relies on it is to show naturalists how much their position depends on a normative conception of reason that cannot be naturalized, and whose authority is crucial if naturalists are going to be persuasive against their nonskeptical opponents.

Of course, moral objectivists have their own embarrassing history, which may be a major reason why there has been so much sympathy for the naturalists' attacks. In a variety of times and cultures, people

---

[16] This was explicit in the so-called "Strong Program" in the sociology of science advocated by the Edinburgh school. See for example, David Bloor (1976). For critical discussions and further references, see J. R. Brown, ed. (1984).

[17] The essays and bibliography of Tuana (ed.) 1989 provide one source for such examples, especially of the influence on science of sexual stereotypes.

who have claimed to know what is good for us, what unseen entities we ought to believe in (or else), and what political ideologies we must accept have been dangerous to the cause of freedom, using their particular brands of "normative truth" to license abuse. The hope of many modern naturalists, beginning with Hobbes, has been to find a way of philosophizing that relies only on what might be called "minimalist" conceptions of reason, in ways that will not only be consistent with the commitments of science, but that will also help to provide theoretical tools to block the fanatical dogmatists' attempts to impose their brands of truth on others, even while encouraging the creation of a peaceful and prosperous community life.

Today's moral objectivists say just what the naturalists say in the face of their bad history – that these fanatics are guilty of *bad* moralizing, or *bad* religious theorizing, or *bad* political ideology. The point, say the objectivists, is not to dismiss all such theorizing, but to demand that it be done well.

So once again, in the face of an embarrassing history, we see philosophers making an appeal to some conception of an ideal practice – in this case, ideal practices of morality, religion, and politics. Leaving aside what the ideal of religious theorizing must be (for I suspect there is a multiplicity of answers depending on the nature of one's faith), moral and political objectivists give roughly the same answer that the naturalists give to their skeptics to explain the foundations of good moral and political theorizing – that such theorizing must rest on reason. (And this is an answer that at least some religious thinkers will also give.[18])

Indeed, any theorist interested in discovering ethical truth by relying on reason must advocate modes of thinking and believing that are very different from those used by a fanatic. For example, an objectivist must eschew dogmatism and bias, insist on open-mindedness, and welcome (in Socratic fashion) challenges to current theory. Reliance on reason to determine ethical truth should no more encourage prejudice and dogmatism than reliance on reason to determine mathematical truth – or so the moral objectivist will argue. Dogmatism is the refuge of those who lack rational arguments, not those who are committed to them. As J. S. Mill has argued, close-minded prejudice is antithetical to, rather than characteristic of, any

---

[18] The journal *Faith and Reason* is one source for the writings of such thinkers.

reason-reliant objectivist in any field of philosophy – and particularly in moral philosophy.[19]

So both naturalists and moral and political objectivists are heirs of the Enlightenment by virtue of their commitment to reason as the tool for understanding and shaping our world. In particular, they agree that reason must govern the construction and operation of science, moral theory, or politics if the theorizing in these fields is to be properly authoritative over our beliefs, practices, and sociopolitical structures. And they share many of the same norms of reason – in particular, those norms that constitute a theory of instrumental reason – since this form of reason is fundamental to the projects and interests of each field. By clarifying components of the conception of reason on which both science, and moral and political theory rely, I aim to show not only how norm-driven these disciplines are, but also how we might construct a defense of this conception of reason in the face of present-day anti-Enlightenment attacks on it.

Aside from their implications for the debate between naturalists and moral objectivists, the arguments in this book have a number of other implications.

First, insofar as they involve extensive discussions of practical reason, these arguments may interest rational-choice theorists and other theorists of reason, even those who are not interested in the debate between the naturalists and objectivist moral theorists. For instance, I discuss at length expected utility theory and other technical notions of reason used by economists and social scientists in Part III of the book. And in Part II, I examine at length the components of instrumental rationality.

Second, because this project involves discussing the normativity required by science, at various points I spend a fair bit of time analyzing the methodologies of science and the sense in which science can inform us about what counts as "natural." I am particularly interested in portrayals of science that argue for its extensive reliance on instrumental reason, not only in its methodology, but also as a tool for justifying other values that scientists have thought it important to honor in their theorizing and experimentation. Hence, aspects of this book may be of interest to those who study the methodology

---

[19] See Mill (1859, 64). Christopher Hookway suggests the nondogmatical nature of the objectivist in his "Fallibilism and Objectivity: Science and Ethics" (1995). See especially p. 60.

of science and who are interested in the issue of whether or not scientific norms can be naturalized.

A DETAILED MAP OF THE ARGUMENT

There are two different ways in which one can argue for sophisticated objectivism. First, one can maintain that norms of the type that naturalists have attacked in other areas (such as morality and epistemology) are covertly present in science after all, despite the fact that scientists try to trade only in pure facts. This is the strategy J. L. Mackie commends to the moral objectivist. Mackie counsels his objectivist opponents that if they wish to reply to arguments that ethics is not acceptable to the naturalist, "the best move . . . is not to evade this issue, but to look for companions in guilt."[20] Second, one can maintain that the reason why theorists have thought there was a problem locating normativity in the world of facts is that they have incorrectly made a sharp distinction between facts and values, and then assumed that science operates from a concept of objectivity that disallows the idea that values can be identified with, or assimilated to, facts. According to this type of theorist, there is no real distinction between facts and values, because there is no such thing as a value-free fact, and thus science cannot pretend that it is insulated from evaluative material insofar as it trades only in "pure" facts. Putnam is well-known for this type of argument.[21]

As I shall eventually discuss, there might be a deep sense in which those who deny the fact/value distinction are right. But on the surface, there are plenty of reasons for believing that they aren't. Indeed, the debate between naturalists and nonnaturalists has raged this long in large part because both sides have been convinced that there is

---

[20] Mackie (1977, 39).

[21] But Putnam uses both strategies in his defense of ethics, despite the fact that they do not appear to be consistent. He argues for the "entanglement of facts with values" in *Realism with a Human Face* 1990, especially "Beyond the Fact/ Value Dichotomy" (135–141), "The Place of Facts in a World of Values" (142– 162), and "Objectivity and the Science/Ethics Distinction" (163–178), having been influenced by Murdoch (1970). On the other hand, he also embraces what he calls the "companion in the guilt" strategy, arguing that science contains values, such as coherence and simplicity, that cannot be eliminated and that are basic to the enterprise. See, for example, "A Defense of Internal Realism" (1990, 30–42), and *Reason, Truth and History* (1981).

something "different" about the evaluative material in morality – something that does not neatly fit into the world of scientific fact. Without wishing to deny the possibility that ultimately facts are inextricably entangled with values, I shall attempt to isolate and examine precisely what this "different" nonfactual element of morality is.

So in Part I of this book, I will be in sympathy with, and indeed welcome, the moral skeptics' suspicions about morality in my pursuit of (what J. L. Mackie calls) the "queer" nonnaturalist element within it, and I will be disagreeing with moral realists who insist that there is nothing strange or remarkable about moral discourse.[22] To be specific, I shall argue that the occult element in objectivist moral theories is the idea that there are moral norms generating reasons for us that have (what I will call) "objective authority" over us. By developing the suspicions of moral skeptics, I seek to confirm their view that morality doesn't fit into the scientific world view as that view has been *traditionally* understood.

However, in Part II, I will present a series of arguments designed to show that objectively authoritative norms are present in science as well, albeit not overtly. In particular, I will contend that they can and must appear in science because they are part of the conception of reason animating science. I will do so by concentrating on the notion of rationality relied on within science and social science – and in particular, our conception of instrumental reason. In Chapter 4, I will argue that our conception of instrumental reason is suffused with objective norms. Despite the widespread popularity of the instrumental approach to rationality, and despite widespread endorsement of the idea that hypothetical imperatives of instrumental reason are part of both science and morality, there has not been a precise definition of what instrumental reason is. I shall isolate a number of different possible instrumental theories of reason, and argue that none of them is a scientifically acceptable theory of reason, either because these theories collide with our (firmly held) intuitions about what a theory of reason is, or because they make an implicit appeal to objectively authoritative norms, and thus contain the same "queer" value element that naturalists have rejected in objectivist moral theory.

In Chapter 5 of Part II, I will argue that the instrumental concep-

---

[22] Mackie (1977).

tion of reason is also subtly informed by a variety of other normative commitments, including some commitments to the nature of the good of an instrumentally rational person, so that thinking about the best way to achieve our ends presupposes certain normative commitments about what our ends should be. This means, paradoxically, that instrumental reason can't really be construed as instrumental! This chapter is particularly important in the context of discussing theories in social science, which continually appeal to instrumental reason without realizing that such an appeal carries with it a commitment to a normative characterization of the good of a rational person. If I am right, theories of human reasoning in psychology and economics are suffused with covert normative appeals to (what might be called) the structure of a rational person's end, constituting, albeit in a very modest way, a kind of ethical theory of the good. Economists and other social scientists, particularly those who use or appeal to expected utility theory, have been (one might say) "doing ethics all along" – and it is time that this is explicitly realized.

Finally, in Chapter 6 of Part II, I will spend considerable time arguing that a conception of instrumental reason that is both laden with objectively authoritative norms and informed by a conception of the good animates and gives authority to the methodology of science, so that any use of science to attack the objective normativity of moral theory is self-defeating. In order to make this argument, I must tackle issues that are at the heart of defining the nature and practice of science. In a sense, this chapter is the heart of the book. It aims to show that since the methodology of science is defined in terms of good reasoning, it will turn out that science itself cannot be "scientific," and cannot accept its own conception of the "natural," making the naturalists' position self-refuting.[a]

Chapter 7 is a kind of introduction to Part III of the book, in which I shall pursue the nature of practical reasoning. One aim of Part III is to disparage the idea that there could be such a thing as a value-free or norm-free "science" of human reasoning, and to do so, I shall spend two chapters on the failures of the theory of reasoning many have thought was the most plausible – and scientifically acceptable – theory of reasoning around – namely, expected utility theory. More

[a] *Editor's note:* Tragically, Professor Hampton died before she was able to fulfill the promises of this paragraph. She left only the sketch of Chapter 6, which appears here.

generally in this part of the book, I am interested in exploring how "reasons" and "reasoning" fit together. If, for example, consequentialism is right, our reasons for preferring one action to another are and must be concerned only with the consequences of those actions. However, I will argue that human beings do not, and should not, engage in practical reasoning that only allows, as factors in the reasoning process, these consequentialist reasons. I shall argue that the actual practical reasoning we human beings use prior to decision-making has a nonconsequentialist structure, in a way that is responsive to reasons over and above those associated with consequences of actions. These arguments attempt to clarify what sorts of theories of morality and rationality can correctly capture the sources of our moral or instrumental reasons for action, and thus constitute a start toward developing an argument defending a nonconsequentialist view of both morality and rationality.

Having completed these arguments in Chapters 7 and 8, I will end the book in Chapter 9 revisiting the fact/value distinction by considering how distinct the supposedly "nonfactual" elements really are from the factual in the course of thinking anew about the nature of practical reasons.[b] However, it is nonetheless important throughout most of the book to emphasize the "queerness" of the former so as to dispel the illusion that there is any way to understand "facts" as "natural" in the way that 'natural' has been traditionally understood.[23] There is good reason to think that the world is stranger than most of us, reared in a culture animated by a narrow (and ultimately inadequate) conception of the natural, have wanted to admit. So those who have embraced moral realism have, in my view, adopted a bad strategy for reconciling morality with science. To make ethics "natural like science" is to deny these neglected aspects of our reality all over again, and to lose touch with important aspects of ourselves and our reality, some of which, in the end, I believe science itself covertly acknowledges.

---

[b] *Editor's note:* Jean Hampton was prevented by her sudden death from executing this project in Chapter 9, which appears later only in the form of her preliminary notes.

[23] I shall not be considering whether to categorize these queer facts as either supernatural (analogous to religious facts), or as *sui generis* as Moore argues [see Moore (1903), Chapters 1, 2, 4, and Brink (1989), pp. 222–24]. To undertake such categorization presupposes that one already has in hand a workable conception of "the natural," and that is precisely what I believe we do not have.

So if my arguments can puncture the hubris of those who, like Ramsey in the quotation that begins this introduction, think that they "know" what ultimate reality is like, then perhaps they can encourage philosophers to ponder anew what the "natural" might be. Perhaps such reflection will usher us into a more open and metaphysically flexible "postnaturalist" world. Or so I would like to hope.

Part I

Science and Objective Norms

Chapter 1

Naturalism and Moral Reasons

[computer file 3/24/96]

Back off, man – I'm a scientist.
— Peter Venkman (Bill Murray), *Ghostbusters*

Although this book seeks to show that the naturalists are wrong to criticize the normativity in moral theory, nonetheless in Part I, I shall be taking the naturalists' side, identifying what it is about the moral objectivists' norms that cannot, in the naturalists' view, pass "scientific muster." This involves explaining what "scientific muster" is supposed to be and why a theory is commonly thought to be disreputable unless it passes it.

Surprisingly, however, this is a difficult project. In this chapter, I will review a variety of ways that naturalists have tried to show the unscientific nature of objective moral norms, none of which I shall argue is successful. It is remarkable that objectivist moral theorists have been so much on the defensive in recent years, given that the naturalists' arguments against their theories have been incomplete, or imprecise, or have, in various ways, begged the question at issue.

I will then spend the next two chapters developing a more successful argument on behalf of the naturalists. Once we are clear about the unnatural component within objectivist moral theories, we will be in a position to look for it in the theories of the naturalists in Part II.

NATURALISM

To examine what makes a theory either scientifically acceptable or scientifically disreputable, we should begin with the concept of the "natural," because contemporary moral skeptics invariably invoke this concept to explain what science is committed to and what objectivist moral theories flout.[1]

We can locate two ways in which the concept of the natural informs theorizing in contemporary philosophy.[2] *Methodological naturalism* is the view that philosophy – and indeed any other intellectual discipline – must pursue knowledge via empirical methods exemplified by the sciences, and not by a priori or nonempirical methods. Quine is the preeminent example of a methodological naturalist: it has been a position attractive to those theorists "impressed by the fact that claims about the world which have, historically, been deemed by philosophers to be a priori true – the principle of sufficient reason, the Euclidean structure of space, the restriction of mechanical interaction to local contact, the nonexistence of vacua, and so on – have, with distressing regularity, been revised or abandoned in the face of scientific theories."[3] Nonetheless, it is a view that many find difficult to square with the apparently nonempirical methods employed by mathematicians, even in the face of arguments from some philosophers that logic and mathematics are empirical enterprises after all.[4] *Substantive naturalism*, in contrast, is the view that a given domain of inquiry can only yield true or false judgments if those judgments are identical with, reducible to, or supervenient on, factual statements of the sort that are normally allowed[5] by our best scientific theories. Hence those who are substantive naturalists can believe about any particular theory either (1) that the judgments of that theory supervene on or are reducible to such factual statements, or (2) that such a reduction or supervenience relation is not possible, so that the theory does not yield true or false judgments.[6]

---

[1] Gilbert Harman (1984, 29).

[2] Peter Railton (1989, 155–157).

[3] Ibid., p. 156.

[4] See, for example, John Stuart Mill (1895) *System of Logic*, especially Book III. Mill's position met with powerful counterarguments from Gottlob Frege, *The Foundations of Arithmetic* (see the edition translated by J. L. Austin, especially pp. 12–14).

[5] The phrase 'allowed by' here is ambiguous: Naturalists could make it precise in a number of ways. At one extreme, they could argue that it means merely "consistent with," which would yield a very broad conception of the natural; at the other extreme, they could argue that it means "explicable in terms of," which would yield a very narrow conception of the natural.

[6] I am following Harman in wishing to include moral nihilism among the possible naturalist positions in ethics. See Harman (1984), "Is There a Single True Mo-

Note that substantive naturalism is not the same as the view (which Railton calls "scientism"[7]) that holds all knowledge, and all meaningful language, comes (only) from science. Such a dismissal of the importance and worth of nonscientific activities and ways of knowing about the world, especially in art or literature, is in no way fundamental to the substantive naturalist, who is only committed to holding that true or false judgments must be in terms that are "allowed" by our best scientific theories – although how we should understand "allowed" here requires spelling out.

In general, most of the moral skeptics tend to be substantive naturalists (although many of them also embrace methodological naturalism), and this is, I suspect, because it is the more plausible of the two forms, insofar as it accommodates the successful use of non-empirical methods of mathematics and logic within scientific practice. Hence it is this form of naturalism that will primarily concern us. As we shall see, however, substantive naturalism is not fundamentally an ontological thesis (although it can involve ontological commitments), but a metaphysical one, deeply connected to a view about what counts as a satisfactory explanation of any event in the world.

Using the preceding definition of substantive naturalism, let us propose that any theory is acceptable from a scientific point of view, if it is a substantively natural position. Can objectivist moral theories qualify as substantively naturalist?

MACKIE'S ARGUMENTS

J. L. Mackie (1977) is a substantive naturalist who contends that much of the moral language of the Aristotelian, Kantian, rights-based, and utilitarian traditions violates substantive naturalism, and is thus irreconcilable with science, for two reasons. He argues, first, that such language refers to objects or properties that are metaphysically "queer" by virtue of being inherently prescriptive. Since the best scientific theories we have – in physics, chemistry, and bi-

---

rality?" Contrast Nicholas Sturgeon's use of the term, which would recognize only those positions that believe reduction or analysis of moral terms into scientifically acceptable statements count as naturalist theories. See Sturgeon (1984), "Moral Explanations."

[7] Railton, op. cit., p. 159.

ology – neither recognize nor require for explanation any such object or property, Mackie concludes that we are not licensed to believe that they exist. In Mackie's view, science requires us to understand the world both as "attitudinatively and motivationally neutral,"[8] and as "justificationally neutral" from a moral point of view. Second, Mackie complains that if such objects or properties existed, they would have to be discovered by an intuitive capacity unlike any recognized sensory capacity, almost magical in its ability to detect entities with objective "pull."[9] Since science recognizes no such special sense in human beings, not only does Mackie conclude that such a sense doesn't exist, but also that the objects or properties it would detect don't exist.

But how can Mackie be so sure that moral properties and objects are precluded from scientific acceptance? What exactly is this inherent "authoritative prescriptivity" (Mackie 1977, 39) that makes the objects or properties supposedly possessing it too queer to be believed? And what exactly does Mackie believe are the characteristics of those objects or properties that are "natural" or "real"? Mackie's arguments are clearly motivated by a substantive assumption about what kind of object or property can be natural, such that it is capable of being real, and recognizable by science. And yet he never clarifies what this substantive assumption is. Although we readers are sure to have some intuitive sense of what is scientifically problematic about moral prescriptivity, since Mackie explicitly defines neither it nor the conception of "natural" he is working with, he never conclusively demonstrates that moral prescriptivity is unnatural.

Mackie tries to suggest the problem he does not make explicit by using the term 'value' to describe the component within ethics that is supposed to be irreconcilable with science. It is a term that immediately calls to mind the fact/value distinction, and the traditional claim, made by many, that science does (and should) trade only in facts and not in values.

This claim needs refining, however, because a good look at science reveals that valuation is not something that is, or need be, excluded from our best scientific explanations, especially in fields such as biology.[10] It is perfectly acceptable, for example, to say that

[8] See John McDowell (1985), "Values and Secondary Qualities."
[9] Mackie (1977, 38–42).
[10] See, for example, Mohan Matthen and Edwin Levy (1984), "Teleology, Error

the snub-nosed guitar fish has adapted well to its ocean environment. Most biologists would regard the phrase 'adapted well' in this process as heuristic shorthand, entirely reducible to scientifically acceptable ideas. Indeed, we can rephrase the sentence to show this, as follows:

> The species named 'snub-nosed guitar fish' has genetically responded to its environment in the ocean (from date x to date y), given changes in that environment during that period, such that its numbers were more likely to remain steady or increase during that period.

There is nothing scientifically unacceptable in this sentence, demonstrating that the phrase 'adapted well' is merely a stand-in for the concept of inclusive fitness, and is thus useful metaphorical shorthand for a fundamental scientific concept. The conclusion seems to be that evaluative terms are acceptable to the naturalist, even when they occur in scientific investigations, if and only if they can be *reduced to* descriptive language permitted or recognized by, and/or used in, the sciences.

A more daring biologist might suggest that we can interpret the evaluative words in this sentence as more than mere metaphorical shorthand. For example, Dennett, following Darwin, argues that such ways of talking also show how biologists appeal to the concept of a "rational design."[11] In his view, modern biology is supposed to have shown us that we can appeal to the concept of design without anthropomorphizing nature or postulating a divine designer. But Dennett has an interestingly generous view of when and how we are justified in imputing intentions to an entity. If an entity is a type of complex system such that it is predictively valuable to impute intentions to it, then Dennett believes we are warranted in doing so. Intentionality is therefore a concept whose legitimacy is a function of its instrumentality for scientists. This position seems to imply that if it turns out we gain predictive power as scientists by thinking about species as "designed for the end of survival," we are warranted in imputing intentionality to some unseen natural force that

and the Human Immune System." See also Wesley Salmon on teleological explanation in "Four Decades of Scientific Explanation," in Kitcher and Salmon (1989, 26–32).

[11] See Daniel Dennett (1978), "Why the Law of Effect Will Not Go Away," p. 73.

has, as an intention, that end. So it seems that Dennett's position allows us to believe that just as you and I are intentional agents, so too is "Mother Nature"! (Or alternatively, just as the behavior of a particular homo sapiens can be better predicted by imputing intention to it, so too might the natural events on the earth be better predicted by imputing intention to it.)

The reader can decide the extent to which he or she is sympathetic to Dennett's views. Those who dislike the Dennettian view of intentionality can avoid it, and salvage the legitimacy of evaluative language in biology and other sciences, by insisting that intentionality talk (invoking words such as 'design') is literally false in these areas of inquiry, and should be reinterpreted as useful metaphorical shorthand for nonevaluative, nonintentional concepts.

With this discussion as a background, a supporter of Mackie's views would presumably maintain that he objects only to those forms of evaluation, of which ethical evaluation is an instance, which admit of no scientifically acceptable reduction. It is a hallmark of the fact/value distinction as it is made by theorists such as Mackie (who have been influenced by R. M. Hare) that an ethical evaluation will generally be thought to have two components – a descriptive component, and a prescriptive component that is in some way linked to the description. Hence, Mackie's view would seem to be that it is the prescriptive component that is problematic from a scientific point of view. Because the biological evaluation discussed can be reduced to entirely descriptive notions, it would seem to be scientifically acceptable insofar as it does not contain this problematic prescriptive element. But, alas, this reply merely restates the problem. Mackie never tells us what this prescriptivity is, nor why it is queer, and hence we can still complain that he has not conclusively established that it is unnatural or unscientific.

There is another problem with this reply. It is not always clear that one can make a sharp distinction between the descriptive and prescriptive components of a moral evaluation. The claim that one can is at least superficially plausible with respect to evaluations that rely on what Williams has called "thin" ethical concepts, such as *good, bad, right,* and *wrong*. If these concepts are used to apply to some component of the world (subject to a pure description), the naturalist would question what object or property these terms are meant to signify. But we also use terms in which the evaluation and the description seem thoroughly entangled,[12] such as *cowardly, mean-minded, manipulative,* or *cheerful*: Williams calls these "thick" ethical concepts.[13] A number of theorists (for example, McDowell) have denied that one can isolate a descriptive component of any of these terms, or provide synonyms for the "purely" descriptive component that is devoid of any evaluative content.[14] And on a more Wittgensteinian note, some of these theorists have charged that it is impossible to understand what these terms mean, unless one grasps them as evaluations.[15]

For reasons that I will not go into here, I am dubious about whether this position is correct. However, if it is, then the ethical is thoroughly entangled with the factual. And doesn't this show that value is as much a part of our world as anything scientific, and hence allowed by science, albeit perhaps not studied by science or used in any scientific theory? Indeed, since such evaluations are fundamental to our functioning in our social worlds, and used by us all the time in our dealings with other human beings, it would seem they are as central to our conception of the world in which we live as any scientific description. So why should they be regarded as problematic?

One can also reply to Mackie's queerness argument by noting the way it is overly indebted to G. E. Moore's open question argument, which purports to show that moral goodness must be understood as a "nonnatural" property. This argument plays into Mackie's hands. For if, as Moore wants us to conclude on the basis of that argument, moral goodness is supposed to be some kind of nonnatural property "out there" in the world, why should any naturalist believe it is real,

---

[12] Putnam uses the phrase 'entanglement of fact and value' in a number of places. See, for instance, his "The Absolute Conception of the World" in Putnam (1992).

[13] See B. Williams (1985), for example, Chapters 7 and 8.

[14] See John McDowell (1978, 1979). And see Williams (1985, 141–2); Hilary Putnam, "The Absolute Conception of the World," op. cit., and Iris Murdoch (1970).

[15] See Williams (1985). "An insightful observer can indeed come to understand and anticipate the use of the concept without actually sharing the values of the people who use it. . . . But in imaginatively anticipating the use of the concept, the observer also has to grasp imaginatively its evaluative point. He cannot stand quite outside the evaluative interests of the community he is observing, and pick up the concept simply as a device for dividing up in a rather strange way certain neutral features of the world." (pp. 141–2) Williams cites a number of discussions that trace the Wittgensteinian aspects of this claim. See pp. 217–8, fn 7.

or believe that human beings can have access to such a strange property? However, there are many moral objectivists who don't understand goodness (or rightness) in Moore's way. For example, Kantians who accept that there is a kind of moral proof procedure, analogous to, say, proof procedures in mathematics (which Kant himself calls the "Moral Law") utterly reject the idea that moral objectivity must be grounded in the existence of moral objects and properties that are "out there" albeit different in kind from any other sort of property or object recognized as natural. Mackie's queerness argument seems motivated by the assumption that the only way one can argue for moral objectivity is to be a moral Platonist of a Moorean stripe, but that is no more true than the claim that the only way to argue for mathematical objectivity is to be a mathematical Platonist who posits the existence of numbers as "nonnatural" objects.

Mackie also tries to undercut the idea of moral objectivity by pointing to the disagreements both within and across cultures about what counts as moral and immoral behavior. Once again, however, this sort of argument fails to persuade the opposition. There has been, and continues to be, disagreement among scientists about what counts as a satisfactory scientific theory, and disagreements between scientists and nonscientists about what kind of theory of the world is true (think of the controversy between evolutionary biologists and creationists), and yet the fact of that disagreement, in the eyes of scientific realists, does not show that there is no true theory of the world, nor that science cannot approximate it. Moreover, Mackie can't claim uncontroversially that our disagreements about moral matters is such that we do not expect to resolve them. In fact, the opposite seems true. People argue hard and passionately for their moral views, intent on persuading their opponents. They call them "wrong" or even "evil." They do not simply air their disagreements as if they were unresolvable, in the way that they might air their unresolvable disagreements over, for example, the best flavor of ice cream or the best printer font. So if the fact of disagreement doesn't signal the unreality of the objects being disagreed about, and if the nature of our moral disagreement seems to presuppose that all parties accept that there is a fact of the matter about who is right, why should we believe Mackie that moral disagreements undercut the idea that morality is objective? He can only persuade us if he specifies what it is about moral disagreement that makes it (permanently) unresolvable.

HARMAN'S ARGUMENTS

There is another well-known argument questioning the substantive naturalism of morality, put forward by Gilbert Harman.[16] Suppose, says Harman, we come upon a group of boys inflicting great pain on an animal just for the fun of it, and we say that we believe the boys' action is wrong. But it does not seem that the putative wrongness of the boys' action plays any role in explaining an onlooker's observation that the boys' action is wrong. The scientist in a laboratory sees a vapor trail, and explains it by positing a proton. The observation is evidence for this theory because the theory posits the proton, which explains the vapor trail, which explains the observation.[17] But in the case of the boys' hurting the animal, the onlooker's observation that their action is wrong is not evidence for the existence of the property of wrongness. Instead, we can best explain the onlooker's observation by appealing to the onlooker's *belief* (which probably has a cultural origin) that what the boys did was wrong. Moreover, even if the boys claim they hurt the animal "in order to do something wrong," we still need not explain their action by appealing to the putative wrongness of what they did. Again, we need only appeal to the boys' belief (most likely shaped by their society) that what they were doing was wrong. As Harman puts it, "The actual rightness or wrongness of their action seems to have nothing to do with why they did it."[18]

In general, Harman maintains that we can explain our moral (or immoral) beliefs or behavior by positing a societally shaped sensibility, or set of beliefs about what is right and wrong, and then saying that our moral judgment or our moral (or immoral) action simply originates from that societally shaped moral sensibility or set of beliefs.[19] If he is right, the truth or falsity of moral judgments is completely irrelevant to why we make and act on such judgments. Whereas in science our observations of the physical world are best explained by positing the existence of physical facts, Harman's view is that our moral observations are *not* best explained by appeal to

---

[16] See Harman (1977), especially Chapter 1, and his (1986) "Moral Explanations of Natural Facts – Can Moral Claims Be Tested Against Morality?"

[17] See Harman (1977, 6).

[18] Ibid. (1977, 9).

[19] Ibid. (1977, 4).

purported "moral facts" but merely to beliefs whose generation within us is largely a function of our psychology and the society we live in. Harman also argues that it is impossible to argue for moral facts by assimilating them to mathematical facts. The latter are also facts that we cannot perceive directly, but Harman maintains that these facts are real on the grounds that when they explain the observations that support a physical theory, scientists typically appeal to mathematical principles. And, according to Harman, "since an observation is evidence for what best explains it,"[20] and "since mathematics often figures in the explanations of scientific observations, there is indirect observational evidence for mathematics."[21]

Harman's arguments assume that science gives us two principles on which to argue for the existence of any facts:

1. A fact obtains if it figures in the best explanation of a putative observation of that fact.
2. A fact obtains if it figures in a physical theory that provides the best explanation of certain observations.

Since moral facts play no role in the content of scientific theories, it would seem that we cannot appeal to principle 2 in order to defend them. But is he correct to say that moral facts do not figure in the best explanation of observations of moral phenomena, such that principle 1 cannot be used to establish them?

It all depends on what one means by "best" explanation, and Harman doesn't explicitly tell us what he means by "best." Consider Jane, who sees the boys hurting the animal, and interferes in order to stop them because, she says, "what they're doing is morally wrong, and for that reason I have to stop them." Harman can offer (what I will call) a "psychological" explanation of Jane's action, but a moral objectivist will explain what Jane did in terms of the fact that she was (correctly) responsive to an objective moral obligation. Harman will think his explanation is better. But why? Some (such as Sturgeon[22]) have argued that, contra Harman, we often appeal to moral facts (which we take to supervene on natural facts) in our explanations, even if they don't tend to appear in scientific explanations, as when we say that Hitler's actions are explained by his

---

[20] Ibid. (1977, 10).
[21] Ibid. (1977, 10).
[22] Nicholas Sturgeon (1984), "Moral Explanations."

moral depravity (and when we say that we believe he was morally depraved because he *was* morally depraved).[23] So why doesn't principle 1, in conjunction with our actual explanatory practices, permit us to posit the existence of moral facts?

Harman's argument is incomplete, and thus ultimately unpersuasive, unless he can provide an answer to these questions. One answer he suggests, but never gives explicitly, is that even if we are prone to appealing to moral objects or properties in our everyday moral practices, in fact science does not and should not do so, because there is something about these objects or properties that disqualifies them from scientific recognition. This appears to be the point he is making when he says that there is no independent scientific way of verifying the existence of moral facts. It is, he maintains, "obscure how the rightness or wrongness of an action can manifest itself in a world in a way that can affect the sense organs of people."[24] How could such properties be sensed by us? How could they cause us to act?

But this response reveals that in the end, Harman is relying on something like Mackie's "queerness" idea to complete his argument against the existence of moral facts. That is, he is saying essentially that such facts are too different from the sort of facts that science recognizes to allow us to believe such facts exist, especially when we have a competing explanation for our moral judgments that is completely consistent with the physicalist assumptions of science. But we have already explored the queerness argument in our discussion of Mackie's views, and found that it has not, at least thus far, been successfully developed.

Might Harman argue that scientific explanations are more parsimonious than moral explanations? It would seem that all we need to explain Jane's action from a scientific point of view is an account of what she sees, and an account of how she categorizes what she sees in her mind, concluding with an account of how she makes a certain kind of negative projection on to the events she witnesses. In

---

[23] Sturgeon, "Moral Explanations," op. cit., discussed by Harman (1986). And see Sturgeon's (1986) "Harman on Moral Explanations of Natural Facts," commenting on this Harman article.

[24] See Harman (1986, 66); and also his (1977, 8) "there does not seem to be any way in which the actual rightness or wrongness of a given situation can have any effect on your perceptual apparatus."

contrast, an explanation from a moral objectivist point of view must include the additional appeal to moral facts that affect Jane in some (mysterious) way. So, on Ockhamite grounds, isn't the scientific explanation superior?

Not necessarily. Certainly Harman hasn't shown that it is. The only reason that the moral account might seem less simple than the scientific account is that Harman has not given us the full outline of what the scientific account would have to include to be genuinely explanatory. In particular, he has not told us how the idea of wrongness got into Jane's head, and how she came to learn to apply it to events such as malicious cat-burnings. The moral objectivist has the beginnings of an answer to this question, which of course Harman doesn't like – that Jane somehow had access to objective moral facts (for example, via something like a Kantian moral law) from which she learned that cat-burning was wrong. But the naturalist must also answer that question, not only by appealing to the influence on Jane of such things as cultural norms, sentiments and emotions, habituation and conditioning, but also by giving an account of how and why these norms arose, or why these sentiments came to be engaged in a certain way in Jane, or why she was conditioned to behave as she did (along with the identity of the conditioning agent). Is this second kind of explanation "simpler" than the first? Who knows? That question is hard to answer in the abstract, without concrete instances of the two kinds of theory in front of us. But more importantly, the explanations are so different, it seems to be beside the point whether one is "simpler" than the other. Certainly someone such as Harman, who is committed to naturalist explanations, will vastly prefer the scientific one, but the question is, why? Again, we are driven back to the idea that Harman must be implicitly assuming that there is something queer about the moral objectivist explanation, but it is a queerness that he does not articulate.

Mackie and Harman have plenty of company in this view that moral facts are in some way occult. In a lecture, Frank Ramsey once said:

> Most of us would agree that the objectivity of good was a thing we had settled and dismissed with the existence of God. Theology and Absolute Ethics are two famous subjects which we have realized have no real objects.[25]

---

[25] See Ramsey (1931a), in Ramsey (1931, 291–2). This passage and other parts of

So "we right-thinking people" are supposed to have concluded that both God and Good are fantasies, postulating objects that are, from a scientific point of view, simply unbelievable. But, alas, we still do not know precisely what it is about moral objects and properties that makes them too queer to be believed. Nor is such an account useful only as a support for the moral skeptic's position. Indeed, anyone who wants to be in a position to dismiss such things as demonology and astrology must be able to say what it is about these theories that makes them unscientific. So how do we go about doing so?

WILLIAMS'S VIEW

Another under the sway of the naturalists' view of the world is Bernard Williams, who distinguishes between "absolute" truths and "perspectival" truths. The former are what science gives us, the latter are what most human enterprises give us. Our everyday conceptions of objects, our ideas of color, and our moral values are based on our interests – either as a species, or, as is usually the case in morality, as members of a particular community, and they are *projected* by us on to the world. Thus they yield only perspectival truths – that is, truths given our interests and natures. But they do not yield absolute truths – that is, they do not tell us about the world to the maximum degree independent of perspective.[26] To understand this, admits Williams, is destabilizing to us. For once we realize that our ethical "truths" are perspectival and parochial, we recognize the "truth in relativism" that moral praise or condemnation of ways of life in social groups distant from ours loses all point.

But Williams's views amount only to another way of *stating* the naturalist's position, not a way of *justifying* it. Any moral realist will simply deny that moral values are projections, and demand to know why the recognition of these moral values as (in some way) existent independent of us is scientifically precluded. Williams does propose some possible answers. For example, he argues that in science we can hope for a convergence of belief guided by the way things ac-

this work are quoted by Hilary Putnam (1990) in "Beyond the Fact/Value Dichotomy."

[26] See Williams (1985, 138–40), discussed by Putnam (1990), in "The Absolute Conception of the World" and "Objectivity and the Science/Ethics Distinction."

tually are, whereas in ethics we cannot.[27] But from the objectivist's point of view, Williams's discussion overstates the degree of agreement in science, and fails to acknowledge or argue against what, from the objectivist's point of view, are better explanations for the disagreements in ethics – for example, the lack of a well-developed tradition of ethical research, and the relatively primitive stage of development of moral theorizing – problems that existed only a few centuries ago in science.[28]

Williams also notes that whereas the fallibility of its theories is a central assumption of science, it seems difficult to think of ethical theories as similarly fallible. A theory has to be able to be tested, and error located, in order for us to believe that it can be (or help us to pursue) the truth about the way things are. So if we cannot generate fallible theories in ethics, how can moral philosophy purport to be analogous to science, and a way to achieve moral truth?[29] Yet moral philosophers will insist that even given the relatively primitive state of ethical research, moral theories are tested all the time, and standardly found wanting. Think, for example, of the voluminous critical literature pointing out problems with John Rawls's *A Theory of Justice*. Here is an example of a moral theory put forward by a moral philosopher in order that it be tested by other rational enquirers. And we could give any number of other examples (choose your favorite moral and political theory). Of course, the testing in moral theory doesn't look anything like the testing in, say, physics, but this is also true of testing in mathematics and biology. Tests of theories differ from one field of inquiry to another (it would be silly to use spectrometers in economics). In addition, fields of inquiry will differ in the extent to which their theories survive the tests (arguably, theories in moral philosophy have not done as well as theories in other fields). But moral objectivists will insist that neither point detracts from the fact that in moral philosophy, theories are standardly tested using the tools of reason, and their errors exposed via these tools. Williams's mistake, they will say, is that he has confused "folk-moral

---

[27] For example, see Williams (1985, 136–7).

[28] See Hookway (1995), especially p. 49, who spends considerable time analyzing notions of convergence and disputing the idea that convergence is not possible in ethics. See also Jardine (1995).

[29] See Jardine (especially pp. 41–2) and Hookway (especially p. 66), both of whom discuss this worry and are sympathetic to it.

theories" of a culture with the reason-reliant theories of moral phi-losophers. But moral objectivists will insist that only the latter are analogous to the reason-reliant theories of scientists.

So the upshot of this discussion is that Williams gives us no de-cisive argument that separates "the absolute" from the "perspecti-val" and that locates scientific concepts (for example, those in physics) only in the former category, nor does he show decisively that moral concepts *must* be understood perspectivally, as projections generated by the interests of human beings living in societies. Hence he gives us no argument showing that we are precluded from ac-cepting moral objects and properties along with the other properties and objects that are recognized by the various sciences. As in the cases of Mackie and Harman, Williams's convictions are clearly an-imated by a deep-seated assumption that moral properties and ob-jects are somehow "unnatural," but that notion is neither explicated nor defended. Accordingly, Williams gives those skeptical of such a picture no reason to embrace it.[30]

Hilary Putnam complains, in virtue of Williams's remark in *Ethics and the Limits of Philosophy* that his viewpoint in the book constitutes the "contemporary" point of view, that Williams's book is "not a serious argument for ethical 'non-objectivism,' but rather the expres-sion of a mood"[31] – a mood that Putnam finds regrettably pervasive in philosophy today. The word 'mood' suggests that the views being expressed are groundless – amounting only to a kind of emotional patina that attends contemporary intellectual life. Yet Williams's "mood" is the same one that philosophical naturalists such as Ram-sey, Mackie, and Harman are in, and the "mood" that prevails among an enormous number of natural and social scientists gener-ally. If so many have it, it would seem there must be a reason for

---

[30] Williams (1995) admits this. Note that Putnam argues against Williams by at-tacking the metaphysical realism inherent in the view. But the quarrel between metaphysical realists and (what Putnam calls) "internal" realists (or idealists, broadly understood) is irrelevant to the debate about the relationship between science and ethics. One can be an internal realist, or an idealist, and still deny that there are ethical truths (imagine a Kantian who disavows the Second Cri-tique), or one can be an internal realist and accept such truths. Defending a certain metaphysics does not *by itself* save the idea that there can be ethical truths if there is something about the world – understood either in a realist, or an idealist way – that disqualifies ethical statements from being true or false.

[31] Putnam (1995, 107).

them to have it – indeed, an attractive (perhaps even irresistible) reason. But it is this reason that still escapes us.

Might that reason simply be that it constitutes a way of thinking about the world that strikes many as liberating? Williams argues that those who accept that "values are not in the world" – that "a properly untendentious description of the world would not mention any values, that our values are in some sense imposed or projected on to our surroundings" – may meet this belief with despair. But they can also view it "as a liberation, and a radical form of freedom may be found in the fact that we cannot be forced by the world to accept one set of values rather than another."[32] But clearly the fact that it may be (for some) a pleasing thought that values are not in the world does not constitute an argument for the idea. Regardless of whether this way of thinking about reality is pleasing or not, it is true.

OTHER THEORIES OF THE NATURAL

Given that moral skeptics have had trouble putting their fingers on exactly what it is about moral objectivist theories that preclude their being "naturalist," it is not surprising that theorists calling themselves moral realists have insisted that there is nothing scientifically questionable, from either a metaphysical or an epistemological point of view, about moral evaluation (see Brink 1989, p. 210; Sturgeon 1984). Such theorists defend the idea that there are moral facts by claiming that morality is, as an enterprise, allowed by, and (in many ways) no different than, science.

These theorists have two opponents: those, such as Mackie, Harman, and Ramsey, who are skeptical on naturalist grounds that there can be moral facts and moral knowledge, and those, such as myself, who think ethics is queer, but who believe that the same queerness is (covertly) present in science. These two opponents of moral realism are interesting bedfellows on this matter. Although they disagree with each other about whether or not there are moral facts, they join hands in opposing the moral realists because they insist, despite the realists' attempts to reassure them, that there is a genuine problem fitting ethics into the scientific world view. Yet these bedfellows find it remarkably difficult to pin down precisely what this problem is.

Part of the reason they have had such difficulty is that they are

---

[32] Williams (1985, 128).

working with a notion of "natural" that is not precisely defined. In fact, there are two ways in which this term can be defined, the first of which is insufficient to justify a rejection of moral objects and properties, and the second of which has never been developed satisfactorily to justify that rejection.

The first definition of 'natural' is that which is allowed and/or studied by science. I will call it the "science-based" definition.[33] This definition makes the current theories of science the ultimate arbiters of what counts as natural. In this view, science is not defined in terms of the natural, but rather the reverse.

The second meaning of the term 'natural' is substantive. In this view, 'natural' denotes a kind of object or property that is the opposite of nonnatural.[34] This distinction is supposed to be one that we grasp intuitively. What is natural, in this sense, is conceptually prior to our understanding of science, and (at least in part) determinative of the subject matter of science.[35] I will call this the "substantive" definition. (Note that those who endorse the science-based definition might be implicitly doing so because they accept the second sense – that is, they may regard science as the arbiter of the natural because science is committed to recognizing and studying what is natural, defined substantively.)

It must be the second, substantive sense of 'natural' that is driving the queerness arguments of theorists such as Mackie, Harman, and Ramsey, because the first sense is too weak to support such arguments. The most one could do, using the first sense, is to try to argue that right now we cannot say moral objects or properties exist, since right now, science does not recognize them. Now I am not at all sure

---

[33] For example, this definition is suggested by David Brink (1989, 22).

[34] Nominalists may use this term, meaning the opposite of "abstract." But nominalism and the physicalist ideas that underlie contemporary naturalism are not the same. Believers in universals can consistently deny or affirm that all properties or objects that exist are "natural," and nominalists may equally deny or affirm that all properties or objects that exist are "natural." See Tim Crane and D. H. Mellor (1990), "There is no Question of Physicalism," p. 185. For a discussion of nominalism, see Hartry Field (1980), Chapter 1. And see W. V. Quine (1960), Chapter VII.

[35] See G. E. Moore (1903), Chapters 1, 2, 4, and David Brink, op. cit., p. 22. And consider the following remark by Quine at the beginning of *Word and Object*, with respect to the word 'real': "It was a lexicographer, Dr. Johnson, who demonstrated the reality of a stone by kicking it; and to begin with, at least, we have little better to go on than Johnsonian usage." (p. 3)

that this argument is right. Exactly how do the commitments of present-day science to things such as quarks or DNA preclude commitments to rights and obligations? But even if it were right, this position does not allow one to say that we could *never* acknowledge that these objects and properties exist, since it would seem possible that science could evolve in a way that would require it to recognize their existence.[36] All that we would be licensed to conclude is that moral objects or properties seem queer from the *present* scientific point of view, but might one day be scientifically acceptable after all. However, theorists such as Mackie want to say that moral objects or properties are by their nature disqualified from existing, so that no credible science – either now or in the future – could ever recognize them. Hence theorists such as Mackie must be working from a substantive conception of what is natural. If we could pin down what that conception is, we would be able to determine the extent to which moral objects and properties fail to qualify as real given that conception, as well as the extent to which science is really committed to that conception.

But articulating that conception is no easy task. Part of the difficulty of doing so is that physics itself undermined in this century a popular and seemingly sensible conception of the natural that animated the thinking of many scientists and philosophers through the nineteenth century. Consider that starting in the seventeenth century, naturalists called themselves "materialists," insofar as they thought of the world as made up of "solid, inert, impenetrable and conserved" matter that interacts deterministically and through contact.[37] But twentieth-century physics has posited entities – and interactions between these entities – that do not fit the materialist characterization of the real. So what does the naturalist do? In the words of Crane and Mellor:

> Faced with these discoveries, materialism's modern descendants have – understandably – lost their metaphysical nerve. No longer trying to limit the matter of physics a priori, they now

[36] It may be that some of those who adopt the first definition are implicitly doing so because they have a substantive conception of what counts as natural, and insofar as they assume that scientific theories will always describe what is natural in this sense, they take it that these theories are a reliable guide to what actually exists.

[37] Crane and Mellor (1990, 186). See in reply Philip Pettit (1993), "A Definition of Physicalism."

take a more subservient attitude: the empirical world, they claim, contains just what a true complete physical science would say it contains.[38]

But why should we believe that the subject matter of physics will never involve the recognition of things (for example, norms, mental representations) that have standardly been dismissed as nonphysical heretofore – especially since this sort of thing has happened over and over again since the last century?

There is another problem with relying on physics to define what the natural can be. It is understandable why physics would be the arbiter of the natural – where the natural is supposed to cover all and only that which is real – if we have a well-founded conception of what counts as natural, and physics is understood to be designed to uncover and clarify all that is natural, and thus all that is real. But without that conception, what makes us think that the subject matter of physics, whatever it turns out to be at any given time, is licensed to define what is real? The metaphysical authority of physics is puzzling if reality is defined in terms of it, rather than vice versa. If it is true that the world is made up of all and only the sorts of entities that physics studies, then what physics tells us about the world should be authoritative for our beliefs. But if we don't have any way of knowing, or even characterizing, what is real independent of any particular theory, then for any of our favorite theories (take your pick), we have no particular reason to believe that (only) this theory depicts the real. Who says it does? Why should we believe what the physicists say is real (particularly when they keep changing their minds) and not, say, the pope or the dalai lama? How do the former constitute a reliable authority about the world in the way that the latter do not?

There are various explanations one could offer for that authority. For example, some readers might claim that the success of science – a success that has, among other things, enabled us to go to the moon – gives us reason to treat it as an authority about the world. Indeed, I believe that this account may well be useful in explaining why we take physics seriously, but not, say, numerology. But this account is insufficient to lend scientific explanations the authority to prevail over objectivist moral explanations, for two reasons. First, through-

---

[38] Crane and Mellor (1990), p. 186.

out history there have been many theories of all sorts – religious, political, and metaphysical – that have enabled people in various cultures to do things. But we do not think that this instrumental value is sufficient by itself to make them accurate descriptive accounts of the world. So why does the fact that our present-day theories have allowed us to make rockets, mobile phones, and camcorders show that they are reliable indicators of what reality contains? Second, such an argument claims to show more than it does. How has science been successful? We can't say it has been successful in giving us the only true description of the world, because that is precisely what is at issue. Of course it has played a role in enabling us to go to the moon, and develop all those rockets, phones, and camcorders, but such achievements are also (perhaps even mostly) a function of improvements in the capacity of human beings to cooperate socially, economically, and politically, since all these achievements have presupposed the operation of a liberal democratic society and a reasonably free market economy. So why aren't such achievements an argument for the truth of certain moral, political, social, or economic theories (for example, the moral thesis that "human flourishing requires treating individuals as free and equal") just as much as physical ones?

Another explanation one might offer for the authority of science has to do with the fact that scientific theories – in particular, physical theories about microparticles, understood as the fundamental constituents of the world – seem to have been highly successful as predictive theories. Hence, if predictive power is held to be an important goal of a theory (and, arguably, an indicator of the degree to which it is true), scientific theories would seem to meet that goal best, and accordingly be authoritative with respect to our beliefs. But even if it is true that scientific theories are predictively successful, they are predictively successful with respect to certain aspects of the world (for example, microparticles, chemical events, biological species). And why should their predictive success with respect to these things have any bearing on the reality of moral objects or properties? Only if one thought that all there is in the world is what science studies, would one believe (by virtue of the fact that moral objects and properties are not the subject matter of any scientific theory), that predictively successful scientific theories "show us" that moral objects and properties do not exist. But what justifies one in believing that all that exists is what science (at any given time) posits? This ontological faith is undefended, and difficult to know how to defend.

Indeed, is there even a particular ontology to which a defender of science is committed? There seems to be "a bewildering variety of alternative rational reconstructions" of theories in science with very different ontologies.[39] For example, at the level of commonsense objects such as stones, trees, and tables, we can say they are mereological sums of space-time parts, or mereological sums of field points (where these two positions are not consistent), or we can say that they are composed of different time-slices of particles in different possible worlds that cannot be identical with the mereological sum of time slices of particles. And at the level of physics, we can take space-time points to be individuals or mere limits.[40]

Perhaps the person who most brilliantly ridicules the idea that there is some obviously correct naturalist ontology to which all scientifically inclined people are committed is W. V. Quine, himself a committed naturalist. In the article, "On What There Is,"[41] Quine spends a great deal of time developing a semantics of existence claims. But having done that, he notes that he has not touched the issue of what there *actually* is:

> Now how are we to adjudicate among rival ontologies? Certainly the answer is not provided by the semantical formula "To be is to be the value of a variable"; this formula serves rather, conversely, in testing the conformity of a given remark or doctrine to a prior ontological standard. We look to bound variables in connection with ontology not in order to know what there is, but in order to know what a given remark or doctrine, ours or someone else's, *says* there is; and this much is quite properly a problem involving language. But what there is is another question.[42]

Quine goes on to say that in order to find out about reality, we need to rely on an ontological *standard*. A standard is a normative entity. An ontological standard tells us what sort of entities we ought to believe or disbelieve in. Now that's odd – how can this naturalist

---

[39] Putnam (1990, 170), "Objectivity and the Science/Ethics Distinction."
[40] Putnam (1990), "Objectivity and the Science/Ethics Distinction," pp. 170–1.
[41] Quine (1980), pp. 1–19.
[42] Quine (1980), "On What There Is," pp. 15–6.

rely on a normative object to define a naturalist ontology, if normative objects are problematic? But isn't asking which theory is "best" inevitably going to involve appealing to a standard? If Quine is right that ontological disputes, like any theory dispute in science, are adjudicated by appeal to certain norms thought to be appropriate in theory construction, then isn't it true that norms are "figuring" in science after all, not in the content of the scientific theories, but in their construction?[43] And doesn't that mean they should be acknowledged as the sort of thing that is real, according to Harman's second principle?

Never appearing to notice this oddity, Quine tells us his ontological standard – it is simplicity:

> Our acceptance of an ontology is, I think, similar in principle to our acceptance of a scientific theory, say a system of physics: we adopt, at least insofar as we are reasonable, the simplest conceptual scheme into which the disordered fragments of raw experience can be fitted and arranged.[44]

But the standard of simplicity, in Quine's view, doesn't pick out one unique ontology. Two that Quine regards as equally simple are the physicalist conception, which regards as real physical objects (to which our sensory apparatus responds), and the phenomenalistic conception, in which the values of bound variables are individual subjective events of sensation or reflection. What is striking about the phenomenalistic conception, especially with respect to Harman's argument against morality, is that it treats physical objects as "myths." Just as classes or attributes are dismissed as mythical Platonist objects by the physicalist, so too are physical objects themselves treated as mythical Platonist objects by the phenomenalist. Quine concludes, "The quality of myth . . . is relative; relative, in this case, to the epistemological point of view."[45] But if one person's myth is another person's reality, and there are only normative standards we can use to adjudicate their dispute – standards that may be themselves disputed and that may not decisively pick out one

---

[43] Hilary Putnam has often remarked on the oddity of Quine's reliance on a standard in the course of arguing that there are facts but not values. For example, see Putnam (1990), "Beyond the Fact/Value Dichotomy."

[44] Quine, "On What There Is," p. 16.

[45] Quine, ibid., p. 19.

view as best – how can any naturalist claim that there is a compelling reason to believe that (only) explanations that use a particular naturalist ontology (but which one?) are true? And how can he rule out the objectivity of moral norms by claiming that norms aren't real if he can only defend his own ontological theory by appeal to norms?

In a much later work, Quine develops an argument that essentially ridicules anyone who would attempt to define a naturalist ontology. The argument goes as follows: If the ultimate constituents of the universe are space-time regions, as contemporary physics can be interpreted to say, we can represent these as classes of quadruples of numbers according to an arbitrarily adopted system of coordinates. But the numbers in these quadruples can be modeled using set theory, and if these sets can themselves be constructed from the null set, then the null set is the ultimate constituent of the universe.[46] The argument portrays what Quine takes to be the foolishness of ontological speculation about the ultimate components of the world.[47] But if such ontological speculation is foolish, how can we show that moral objects or properties are disqualified as real? Without such an argument, theorists such as Ramsey, Mackie, and Harman (and indeed, Quine himself) would seem to be guilty of unjustified prejudice against these objects and properties.

However, Quine has a suggestion for the naturalist: Even if ontological speculation is foolish, he says that "structure is what matters to a theory, and not the choice of its objects."[48] So perhaps we can define the natural with reference to the physical sciences by defining the (authoritative) structure that is the hallmark of the physical sciences. But what is this compelling structure and how does it rule out moral objects and properties? Does "structure" refer to a certain kind of causal explanation in science that is not possible in objectivist moral theories? Perhaps, but it is an idea that is extremely hard to develop satisfactorily.[49] On the face of it, an appeal to causes ought to be troubling to the naturalist by virtue of Hume's attack on the idea. Didn't Hume give us good reason to worry that the idea of cause and effect is merely projected onto the world by the workings of the human mind? And if this is so, shouldn't a scientific portrayal

[46] See Quine (1981), "Things and their place in Theories," pp. 17–18.
[47] Ibid., p. 20.
[48] Ibid., p. 20.
[49] See Wesley Salmon, op. cit.

of the world be purged of such mind-dependent notions? This Humean attack has prompted many philosophers to try distancing science from the notion of cause (including Russell, who considered the notion anthropomorphic).[50] Moreover, replacing an appeal to causation with an appeal to the idea of "laws of science" is, at least arguably, even worse from a naturalist point of view, insofar as natural laws, were they to exist, would seem to presuppose some kind of mysterious necessity in the world. And if that necessity is real, why not also recognize the reality of moral norms?

One might think that the positivists had a way of characterizing the "structure" of scientific theories in a way that rules out morality understood objectively. According to the positivists, scientific statements are meaningful because they are publicly verifiable, and since ethical statements are not so verifiable, they are meaningless. Moreover, they are unverifiable *in principle*, along with sentences in metaphysics, religion, and poetry.[51] But aside from a few enthusiasts for positivism left in economics, positivism has largely been abandoned. Positivism requires that *single* propositions be verifiable, but many propositions in science cannot meet this demand. And if we say (as Harman suggests) that unverifiable propositions are nonetheless "indirectly" meaningful if they are part of a larger theory possessing observation sentences that are publicly verifiable, then we can no longer exclude the moral and metaphysical "nonsense" that as positivists we had originally opposed, since our larger theory might possess all sorts of values. As Vivian Walsh explains:

> To borrow and adapt Quine's vivid image, if a theory may be black with fact and white with convention, it might well (as far as logical empiricism can tell) be red with values. Since for [the positivists] confirmation or falsification had to be a property of a theory *as a whole*, they had no way of unravelling this whole cloth.[52]

That is, it would seem this whole cloth could now include "oughts" and "shoulds," standards and principles – just the material the moral objectivist needs. So once the positivist abandoned the idea that *each*

---

[50] See Bertrand Russell (1957), "On the Notion of Cause."

[51] See Putnam, "Objectivity and the Science/Ethics Distinction," p. 163.

[52] Vivian Walsh (1987), "Philosophy and Economics." Quoted by Putnam, "Objectivity and the Science/Ethics Distinction," p. 164.

sentence in a theory must be verifiable (an abandonment that science forces upon him), he lost his way of automatically disqualifying the meaningfulness of moral sentences.

Putnam notes with exasperation the persistence of the fact/value distinction in the face of the collapse of positivism.[53] I suspect that view as best n how can any naturalist claim that there is a persistence is due to the deep-seated grip on philosophers' minds of a certain conception of what counts as "natural" to which they believe science is committed. Positivism fails to articulate that conception. But the conception still survives, albeit in an inchoate form, and continues to influence philosophers under its sway, despite the fact that there now exists no articulation or explication of it.

CONCLUSION

So we return to our original question: What is it about moral objects or properties that precludes their scientific recognition? The fact that this question has not been satisfactorily answered reflects the extent to which naturalists hostile to morality have thought they occupied the philosophical high ground. But this discussion should show that they do not. It is remarkable that objectivist moral philosophers have been so thoroughly on the defensive for so many years about morality's standing and credentials as a realm of human knowledge when there exists no successful and widely accepted argument establishing that there is anything about such theories that makes them scientifically problematic.

Nonetheless, despite the plethora of arguments I've reviewed in this chapter against the naturalists' claim that irreducible moral values are in some way queer, I remain convinced that there is something strange about them from the standpoint of science. In the next two chapters, I will develop as precise a statement as possible of what this strangeness is.

[53] See Putnam, "Objectivity and the Science/Ethics Distinction," p. 165.

Chapter 2

The Anatomy of a Reason

[computer file 3/24/96]

Reason lies between the spur and the bridle.
              – Old English Proverb

If there is justification in the naturalists' dismissal of objective moral theories, it is something we still must search for. The goal of the next two chapters is to locate the nonnatural element in such theories. Ultimately I will argue that it is a certain thesis about norms and reasons for action to which naturalists object, but to which moral objectivists are committed.

To identify this thesis, however, I will need to do a lot of philosophical spadework. In Chapter 2, I will show that moral objectivism is characterized by a commitment to the idea that there are moral norms. I will then analyze the concept of a norm, showing how norms give us reasons of all sorts – to act, believe, feel, and decide, among others.[1] Finally, I will discuss the nature of reasons and the various philosophical issues that can be, and often have been, raised to understand, identify, and defend them. I will argue that the most important identifying characteristic of a reason is its "authority" – where this is something quite different from whatever motivational efficacy the reason might have.

Chapter 3 builds on this analysis by developing two theses about the nature of this authority, one of which moral objectivists accept with respect to moral reasons, and which is inconsistent with the commitments of naturalism, the other of which is acceptable to the naturalist, but incompatible with moral objectivism. I will also argue that the moral objectivists' views about the authority of moral rea-

---

[1] So, like Raz (1975/90, 9), I will maintain that the "key concept for the explanation of norms is that of reasons for action."

44

sons is just an instance of a more general view that accepts a certain kind of thesis about the authority of many sorts of norms and reasons, both moral and nonmoral. My ultimate aim is to clarify *normative* objectivism, of which moral objectivism is only a species. Hence, in both Chapters 2 and 3, I will be discussing reasons of all sorts, and I will argue that not only moral theory but *any* theory – in epistemology, cognitive science, or economics – that accepts what I will call the "normative objectivist thesis about reasons" is one that a naturalist is committed to rejecting.

WHAT IS MORAL OBJECTIVISM?

There is a currently popular conception of moral objectivism whose analysis I take to be instructive. As long as someone believes that this is what moral objectivism is, she will be unable to understand what it is about her theory that troubles the naturalist. In the end, I will argue that this conception of moral objectivism fails to capture what that theory is by leaving out an essential element of the theory, which also happens to be the very element that the naturalist finds troubling – namely, moral norms generating moral reasons that have what I call "objective" authority. More than likely this is no accident. It is understandable that a theorist might try to evade the attacks of his opponent by trying to leave out that part of his theory that appears most vulnerable to attack. So what this theory of moral objectivism leaves out is the best clue as to what is wrong with moral objectivism from the naturalist standpoint.

According to this theory, moral properties can and should be understood such that they are necessarily (metaphysically) identical with, or at least constituted by, natural properties by virtue of the fact that they supervene on these natural properties.[2] Philosophers who take this view believe it captures what is fundamental to moral objectivism, and they refrain from attempting to defend or analyze the idea that morality is about reasons for action. They also insist that this position can be developed in a way that allows morality to be consistent with naturalist scruples.

The key to this position is the notion of supervenience. I will follow Kim in understanding *weak supervenience* as follows:

[2] See Davidson (1970, 214); Blackburn (1971, 105–16); Wiggins (1980, 109–11, 214–5); Brink (1989), Chapters 6 and 7, and see, especially, p. 160.

A *weakly supervenes* on B if and only if, necessarily, for any x and y if x and y share all properties in B, then x and y share all properties in A – that is, indiscernability with respect to B entails indiscernability with respect to A.[3]

In contrast, *strong supervenience* is the view that there is a lawlike relationship between the supervening property and the base property. Again quoting Kim:

A *strongly supervenes* on B just in case, necessarily, for each x and each property F in A, if x has F, then there is a property G in B such that x has G, and *necessarily* if any y has G, it has F. [Kim (1984, 58); and see Brink (1989, 160–1)]

So whereas in the strong supervenience view, base properties necessitate the supervening properties, in the weak supervenience view, the supervening properties are only contingently related to the base properties.

There are, I believe, many reasons to be worried about the concept of supervenience [rehearsed, for example, by Blackburn (1985)]. In its strong form, it is particularly problematic, because of its twofold reliance on the idea of laws, and given the current climate of hostility to laws and appeals to necessity in philosophy of science,[4] it is ironic that defenders of morality have believed they could vindicate moral properties by appealing to a notion of necessity that advocates of science have come to conclude cannot itself pass scientific muster!

But let us grant for the sake of argument that one or the other form of supervenience is plausible and acceptable to the naturalist. The problem remains, however, that moral objectivism involves more than just a commitment to moral properties. It also involves a conception of normativity, which neither supervenience position addresses. This is a point that Harman essentially appreciates (1986, 62–3). Suppose that Jane sees Albert hitting a cat with a stick for the fun of it, and Jane believes Albert's act is wrong. Those who, like Harman, say moral norms are only culture-dependent will generally insist that Jane believes this because she has a (socially influenced) moral sensibility such that she *thinks* it is wrong. But those who are moral objectivists will insist that the actual wrongness of Albert's action *explains why* Jane believes it is wrong. That is, they will say

---

[3] Kim (1984, 58).
[4] See, in particular, van Fraassen (1989).

that there is a norm: "Human beings should not be cruel to animals"; that this norm gives us a metaphysically necessary reason not to be cruel to animals; that Jane knew about this reason; and that by virtue of that knowledge, she called Albert's action wrong.

Supervenience theorists don't include such norms in their analyses, presumably because they don't think a defense of moral realism requires norms.[5] Why do we need to make reference to norms to explain why Jane should believe Albert's conduct is wrong? Why isn't it sufficient to explain the conduct's wrongness by showing it to be a property that necessarily supervenes upon the natural facts of this event? If we do so, it seems we have explained everything we need to explain without reference to any (strange) norms.[6]

Yet, even though by leaving out norms these defenders of morality are encouraged to think that they have succeeded in showing how ethics can be entirely naturalistic, nonetheless they have left out the guts of morality. Consider that the idea of supervenience purports to explain the relationship between moral properties and natural properties. But nothing in this type of analysis explains the relationship between those moral properties and *us*, the moral agents. Even if morality is, in a lawlike way, related to objects in the natural world, it is also related to moral agents. Indeed, its relationship to moral agents is what we are attempting to understand when we ask about morality's authority over our lives.

Now supervenience theorists have most likely believed they have answered the question about morality's relationship to us by showing its relationship to the natural world. If someone asks, "Why does Jane believe that Albert's action was wrong?", she would presumably answer, "Because its wrongness necessarily supervenes on these natural events." But notice that this response has not really answered the question. "Yes," one might reply, "that may be true, but why does, and why should, *she* believe it?" Now the question specifically asks about her relationship to this event in the world, and it is this relationship that is at issue. As I shall discuss later, there is more than one way to answer this question. The supervenience theorist might naturally give the following reply. Jane believes (and should believe) this because it is true that the property of wrongness necessarily supervenes on this action, and she ought to believe what is

[5] Copp (1991).
[6] Sayre-McCord (1988b); Copp (1991).

true. But note that this answer appeals to a norm ("one ought to believe what is true") that relates her to these events in the world. And it is by virtue of this normative connection that we take it Jane has a reason to believe that Albert's action was wrong – a reason she herself appreciates.

Norms effect a connection between (various aspects of) agents and (various aspects of) the world, and perhaps this is most clear in the case of moral action. Consider that if Jane were a decent person and if she had the opportunity to do so, she would not merely label Albert's action wrong, she would try to stop him from persisting in it. A moral objectivist will argue that we ought to recognize not only that cruelty to animals is wrong, but also that we have a (necessary) reason to act so as to stop cruelty to animals, where this reason is decisive in certain circumstances. While the supervenience theorist gives us lawlike connections between moral evaluations and natural properties, he gives us no lawlike or necessary connections between these evaluations and the idea that certain activities are required of us when certain moral properties supervene on natural ones. As one critic of supervenience theory puts it, even if we accept the supervenience theory for moral properties, "we will at most have established that certain people, actions, and institutions have those properties we label 'moral.' We will not yet have shown that there is any reason to care about the properties or that some of the properties are better than others."[7] Yet surely what is at stake for the moral objectivists is this caring, that presupposes the recognition of an appropriate kind of conduct or belief in the situation, and that is supposed to precipitate action. If a moral theory does not include, defend, or explain reasons for action, it cannot incorporate the idea that there are beliefs, or forms of behavior with respect to events in the world, that "ought to be." But then in what sense is it a moral theory? Without reasons, such a theory lacks the essence of morality that is at stake in the argument.

The fact that supervenience theorists have failed to acknowledge that they need to answer the question about how we are connected to the moral properties in the world, and thus have failed to include reason-generating norms in their analysis, explains why many naturalists have been consistently unpersuaded by the arguments of supervenience theorists that theirs is a naturalized ethics. For ex-

---

[7] Geoffrey Sayre-McCord (1988a, 276).

ample, Harman complains that those, such as Sturgeon, who accept the idea that moral facts supervene on natural facts, say that Jane believes Albert's action was wrong, without ever explaining how the actual *wrongness* of Albert's act plays a role in generating Jane's belief that it is wrong (Harman 1986, 62). Harman is appreciating here that, on the moral objectivist view, moral theory must not only explain the relationship of morality to the natural world, but also the relationship of morality to moral agents. No matter how tightly the supervenience theorist identifies moral and natural properties, there is always that which directs *us* to make the identification, and as a result, act in certain ways, that eludes his analysis.

It is worth noting, however, that Harman is wrong to say that an objectivist *must* think that necessary moral reasons can *cause* our actions or choices. As we will discuss later in this chapter, it is a disputed question whether they also have motivational power. So, for now, we must allow that a moral objectivist might not have to explain the *motivational* power of a moral norm. Nonetheless, she is committed to giving an account of its directive authority over us – its guiding and commanding nature, as well as an account of how we come to know about that directive authority. (What would be the point of saying that it exists if we could never know about it?) So when I say the moral objectivist must explain the relationship morality has to us, I mean, most fundamentally, that the moral objectivist must explain the way in which morality is authoritative for us (in a way that we can come to know).

WHAT ARE NORMS?

To explain the authority of reasons, we must begin by understanding norms. Naturalists cannot be troubled by the bare idea of norms, for in their daily lives they are surrounded by them: rules of baseball, codes of etiquette, standards of good wine, and so forth. Such norms are accepted features of our social life. Nor would anyone want to deny that such norms play an important evaluative role in our lives. So it must be the objectivist's particular view about how some norms – in particular, the moral norms – generate reasons that are obligatory for us that naturalism seems to undermine.

In order to pursue what this view is, I will spend some time setting out what a norm is. As I use the term 'norm,' it will cover a number of different normative species – for example, rules, ideals, principles, and ends. I will say that a norm has four elements: a deontic operator; the norm's subjects – that is, the persons required to perform as the norm directs; the action that is required of them; and the circumstances in which its directives are required or permitted.[8] To begin, let us say, very generally, that a norm connects certain agents to the world by giving them a reason to engage in a certain action type (which can include believing, choosing, acting, intending, desiring, or feeling) as the norm directs, where this reason is decisive (that is, the right reason for determining how to act, choose, or believe no matter what other conflicting reasons or motives these subjects have) in certain circumstances.

This understanding of norms attempts to steer clear of any stand on their metaphysical nature. I aim to describe norms in a way that is neutral between rival conceptions of them, and in particular, neutral between a Platonist understanding of at least some norms as real objects "out there" in the world, and the view of some or all of them as (merely) psychosocial phenomena, connected to social practices or customs. I intend this understanding to accurately describe the norms with which we are all familiar in our daily lives, whatever their ultimate philosophical nature.

Note that I speak of norms being directed at "subjects," but we needn't suppose that these subjects are individual human beings. Norms may be applicable to nonhuman agents (for example, firms, animals), and they may be applicable to social groups (for example, nations, churches, schools, families) as well as to individuals. This definition therefore does not take any stand on who or what the subjects of norms are. It also leaves open the action types governed by norms, which might be anything from moral behavior to codes of dress to rules of belief formation.

On this conception of norms, fundamental to their operation is the production of reasons for engaging in any of these action types. So to understand norms, we must understand the reasons they generate.[9]

The term 'reason' has a number of different meanings, many of them well-explored in the literature on reasons.[10] For our purposes,

---

[8] See von Wright (1963), Chapter V; and see Joseph Raz (1975/1990, 50).

[9] I doubt that it makes sense to speak of reasons that are not norm-generated, but whether or not it does make sense is an issue that is not pertinent to my project in this book, and hence it is an issue that I will simply leave aside.

[10] In particular, by Raz, Brink, Baier. Baier's discussion is particularly nice; he

we must distinguish between two meanings of the notion of "a reason" that are easily confused. First, there are *explanatory reasons*, or "reasons why," which we refer to in order to explain some action or event, as in "The reason why the baby ate the geraniums was because she could reach them." These reasons are useful in explanation, but they do not purport to be "good" or "justifying" reasons. Second, there are what I will call *directive* reasons (after Baier, 1995). These are "reasons to," as in "He had a reason to take the baby out of the garden." Norms generate directive reasons to act, choose, or believe. Henceforth, when I talk of reasons generated by norms, I will always mean directive reasons. However, note that we often talk as if directive reasons can serve as explanatory reasons when the agent recognizes that he has such reasons, as in "John knew he had a [directive] reason to take the baby out of the garden, and that explains why he did." We shall have a great deal to say about whether directive reasons can serve as explanations in Chapter 4. For now, I wish only to note that the use of the term 'reason' in an explanation may have nothing to do with the idea of a reason as a justifying directive. Norms generate directive reasons, which may or may not also be explanatory.

So what are directive reasons? Let me start by proposing, quite simply, that "You have a (directive) reason to x" means, "It is a consideration for you in your deliberations, in certain circumstances, that you x." By this account, which is intended to match the commonsense way in which we think about reasons, we can have a number of different reasons to do something in a situation, one or more of which is/are the right one(s) to act on in the situation. But the fact that, say, only one of them is the correct or "decisive" reason in this situation doesn't distract us from the fact that the other reasons are still *reasons* for us, albeit not the ones which we should act on *now*.[11] We can further define this notion of decisiveness by using

distinguishes the following four categories of reasons: (1) explanatory reasons, reasons *why*, as in "the reason why the bottle burst"; (2) fact-linking reasons, reasons *that*, as in "a reason that John is not the father of Jill's son, Jack"; (3) directive reasons, reasons *to*, as in "a reason to believe that John is the father of Jill's son, Jack"; (4) directive explanatory reasons, "reasons *for which*," as in "the reason for which he subscribed." See Baier 1995, p. 44.

[11] One might adapt the terminology of W. D. Ross to make this point, distinguishing between "prima facie" reasons and "actual" reasons; but that terminology is potentially misleading. A reason that he would call "prima facie" is still a

Bernard Williams's notion of deliberative priority. According to Williams, a consideration has "deliberative priority" for us if we "give it heavy weighting against other considerations in our deliberations."[12] Thus we can say that a reason is decisive in a certain situation if its deliberative priority in that situation is *complete* – that is, if it has the heaviest weighting of all our reasons in our deliberation.

Regardless of whether or not a reason is decisive in a situation, to say that we have such a reason is to say that we have a consideration that is relevant to any deliberation we might want to engage in about what to do. By 'consideration' I mean something quite minimal – something like "action-directed mental element," or alternatively, something in the head that indicates a particular way of proceeding with respec˙ to some action type. Now there are many types of considerations of this sort that we don't believe provide us with reasons – for example, whims, cravings, phobias, obsessions. Hence, simply calling a reason for action a consideration in this minimal sense doesn't help us to distinguish reasons from these nonrational directive elements. Moreover, it doesn't seem as if something, to be a reason, *must* figure in an *actual* deliberation in order to count as a reason. To say one has a reason to act or choose in a certain way is to say that the reason applies to that person even if he doesn't actually perform a deliberation about what to do. (So when Mom says to her nine-year-old, "You have a reason not to say that sort of thing to your brother because it's rude," and her child replies honestly, "I never thought about that," the child's answer does not block the applicability of this reason to her, and certainly no parent has ever thought it did!)

So the fact that a reason can serve as a consideration in a deliberation doesn't help us as much as we would like in understanding what reasons are. In any case, deliberation is itself a norm-laden concept, meaning that we have reasons concerning how to engage in something that is appropriately called a deliberation (any old kind of thinking clearly won't do), along with reasons *to* engage in a deliberation in certain circumstances. Hence, trying to define norm-

real (and actual) reason – even if it is not decisive in the circumstances, because one can "have a reason" to do x and still conclude that one has a better reason to do y. Williams also has qualms about Ross's terminology, although they appear to be somewhat different. See Williams (1985, 176).

[12] Williams (1985, 183).

generated reasons by reference to a norm-laden notion of deliberation is circular.[13]

So we must do better in identifying the distinctive markers of a reason. This is the task of the rest of this chapter.

WHAT ARE REASONS?

In a well-known article, Bernard Williams (1981a) presents an account of what reasons are, which many have thought highly persuasive. I want to begin my attempt to identify the markers of reasons by considering his account. Although I shall argue that Williams's account fails to identify any necessary or sufficient conditions of something's being a reason, I regard it, nonetheless, as a highly instructive failure.

Williams distinguishes between "internal" and "external" reasons, and argues that only the former are real. Hence, if he is right, understanding the nature of a reason means, at least in part, understanding the way it is internal. An internal reason, according to Williams, is one that makes a "deliberative connection" between the performance of the directive of the reason, and some element in an agent's motivational set, or S, as Williams calls it. All the elements of S are motivationally efficacious by themselves, and Williams has a rather Humean conception of what can be in S (he would exclude things like Kant's Moral Law, and he would include all of the agent's desires). However, one could endorse the broad outlines of his account and have a more Kantian conception of S.[14] More expansively than Hume, Williams would also include in S, "dispositions of evaluation, patterns of evaluation, patterns of emotional reactions, per-

---

[13] Compare Kant's attempt to explicate the notion of reasons for action by appeal to the notion of *reasoning*. Kant's attempt to do so is an interesting failure. In contrast to a creature whose actions are determined by laws of nature – caused by nature operating through instinct – a human being, says Kant, has the "power to act in accordance with his idea of laws." (From Kant's *Groundwork of the Metaphysics of Morals*, Chapter 2 (1785, 80). And one might say that it is when acting "in accordance with his ideas" of that which "he ought to do" that a human being is acting from a reason. However, this way of thinking about reasons for action relies on the concept of a "law" understood as that which one "ought to do" – in other words, the concept of a norm.

[14] See Korsgaard (1986), especially p. 20.

sonal loyalties and various projects, as they may be abstractly called, embodying the commitments of the agent." (1981a, p. 103)

External reasons are, in contrast, reasons that make no deliberative connection with the agent's subjective motivational set. They are reasons that an agent is supposed to have, regardless of the contents of his subjective motivational set – reasons that a certain, special form of reasoning would reveal to an agent who had them. Can such external reasons exist?[15]

Williams argues that reasons can only be internal, and central to his argument is Henry James's story about Owen Wingrave. In that story, Owen's father argues that Owen must join the army, since all his male ancestors have done so, and family pride requires him to do the same. But Owen despises the idea of joining the army, and all his interests, desires, and projects require a nonmilitary life. Williams argues that if Owen's father said that Owen "had a reason" to join the army, he would be invoking an external reason, and Williams argues that it does not make sense to say that Owen has such a reason. Hence, in arguing for the thesis that all and only reasons are internal, he is arguing that *it is a necessary and sufficient condition of something's being a reason that it be deliberatively connected to some element of the agent's subjective motivational set S.* Henceforth I will call this the "deliberative connection with motives" requirement, or the DCM requirement for short.

Williams has a broad conception of deliberation (which we will discuss further in Chapter 4). Deliberation includes, in his view, not only the determination of means/end connections, but also reasoning with respect to consistency, time-ordering and priority (1981a, p. 104). He even proposes a form of "imaginative deliberation," in which we review our desires for objects. When we deliberate in this way, we get "a more concrete sense of what would be involved" in the satisfaction of a desire, so that as a consequence we might lose the desire, or appreciate new possibilities, and so gain new desires.

---

[15] There is an interesting reason to think that they can, which Williams doesn't discuss. Consider that we have reasons for belief, yet it seems very unlikely that such reasons can or should be deliberatively connected to motives. This leads one to wonder whether reasons for belief are external in Williams's sense. However, Williams never considers this issue, focussing exclusively on what are called "practical reasons" – reasons for actions, choices, and so on. I will leave this interesting issue aside here.

So Williams suggests that every determination of what is of value by the agent involves reasoning, and not merely desire. In any case, even if someone disagrees with Williams's substantive conceptions of deliberation or with what he takes to be the elements of a subjective motivational set (for example, if one has a more Kantian view of either one),[16] she can still accept the form of his position, as presented here, on what it is that makes something a reason for action – namely, that it is deliberatively connected to S.

Many readers have found Williams's internalist conception of reasons highly persuasive, and have believed that it follows from the DCM requirement that a reason is always *motivationally efficacious*. So in this interpretation of Williams's argument, it follows from the DCM requirement that a necessary (albeit not a sufficient) condition of something's being a reason is that it be motivationally efficacious. (Williams clearly rules out the possibility that motivational efficacy could be a sufficient condition for something's being a reason, by noting that there are motives that are nonetheless not reasons.[17]) Call this the "motivational internalist" requirement.[18] Someone who accepted it as a necessary condition of something's being a reason is requiring that reasons themselves be members of an agent's subjective motivational set.

However, on the basis of other things that Williams says, it is not quite accurate to say that he argues for the motivational internalist requirement as I have just defined it. Williams accepts that we can have reasons we do not know about, as when, for example, we have a reason to do something, but lack information that would reveal this reason to us. Since, clearly, what we do not know can't move

---

[16] Korsgaard (1986).

[17] Another way to see that motivational efficacy could only be a necessary and not a sufficient condition of something's being a reason is to imagine a variation of the Owen Wingrave story. Suppose that Owen actually joined the army because he was motivated by his father's arguments – even in the face of his knowing that his father had made no deliberative connection between joining the army and any element of his subjective motivational set. (Such irrational persuasiveness, and its potentially dangerous consequences, are the subjects of Jane Austen's novel *Persuasion*.) But in this case, Williams would surely not want to say that because, as a matter of fact, his father's words moved him, Owen now has a reason to go into the army, since these motivational words still established no deliberative connection between that action and any element in S.

[18] See Christine Korsgaard's "internalist" requirement, discussed in the next section.

us, a reason that is unknown cannot be part of our subjective motivational set. Hence, we can only attribute to Williams a modified motivational internalist requirement that I will call the "hypothetical motivational internalist requirement," which says that a necessary condition of something's being a reason for an agent is that it *would* be motivationally efficacious if it were known by that agent.

So Williams defines reasons as internal in two ways. First, all reasons are internal, in his view, in the sense that they satisfy the DCM requirement, such that they are deliberatively connected to an existing motive of the agent. Second, all reasons are internal in his view by virtue of satisfying the hypothetical motivational internalist requirement. The final picture that Williams paints is something like this: Practical reasoning is a process by which existing motives are channeled in profitable directions via instrumental reason, or some other deliberative process included among the reflections that Williams is prepared to count as practical reasoning. Because the existing motives of agents, insofar as they are distinctive and often quite specific, vary considerably among them, this channeling can take quite different forms for different agents, producing different sets of reasons.

This picture rules out the possibility that there could be such a thing as an external reason, defined as a reason whose applicability to an agent is not, and need not be explained by, its deliberative linkage to an occurrent motive of the agent. Therefore it cannot be true, as external reasons theorists say, that all people must have certain reasons to act in certain ways, regardless of their subjective motivational set. John McDowell paraphrases Williams's position as follows:

> [T]he external reasons theorist has to envisage the generation of a new motivation of reason in an exercise in which the directions it can take are not determined by the shape of the agent's prior motivations – an exercise that would be rationally compelling whatever motivations one started from. As Williams says (p. 109), it is very hard to believe that there could be a kind of reasoning that was pure in this sense – owing none of its cogency to the specific shape of preexisting motivations – but nevertheless motivationally efficacious.[19]

---

[19] John McDowell (1995, 71–2).

Accordingly, says Williams, only some sort of internalist Hume-like picture of reasons can be correct.

However, as I shall now explain, Williams fails to establish that all reasons are internal because his arguments fail to establish that the hypothetical motivational internalist requirement is a necessary condition of something's being a reason, and fail to establish that the DCM requirement is a necessary condition of something's being a reason. There are three reasons why his arguments fail: First, he assumes that the hypothetical motivational internalist requirement follows from the DCM requirement, when in fact it does not. Second, the arguments he gives fail to provide any independent proof of the hypothetical motivational internalist requirement, and in fact better support a denial of that requirement as a necessary condition of something's being a reason. Third, the way in which Williams argues for the DCM requirement commits him, ironically, to the existence of reasons that do not satisfy the DCM requirement, and are thus external as he understands that term.

I begin with the first point. Williams appears to assume that the hypothetical motivational internalist requirement follows from the DCM requirement because of the following argument: If reasons must be linked to an agent's S in order to count as that agent's reasons, then since the elements of S are motivationally efficacious, this makes the reasons themselves motivationally efficacious. But this is an illicit derivation. Just because the elements from which a reason is derived are motivationally efficacious, it doesn't follow that the reason itself is motivationally efficacious. Consider that by accepting that the DCM requirement gives us necessary and sufficient conditions for something's being a reason, we have accepted an answer to the question, "What makes something a reason for action?", but this answer does not take *any* stand on whether or not that reason is motivationally efficacious. While it is true that Williams's conception of reasons for action requires that there be a (deliberative) connection between the reasons' directives for action, and these motives, it does not follow, from the fact of that connection, that the reasons *themselves* are motivationally efficacious.

Thus, suppose that after a deliberation process, an agent arrives at the conclusion that she has a reason to do p in order to achieve her desired object q. This reason is related to S, and discovered in a deliberation process, so it would seem to be a reason that she *has*. But having said that, why does it follow, by virtue of the fact that it is a reason that she has, that she is also motivated to perform p? Why might not the reason be motivationally inert within her – that is, a reason that happens to have no psychological effect on her motivational structure, despite the fact that it is a reason that is related to one of her desires? And even if the reason is inert, isn't Williams committed to saying, by virtue of its connection with S, that it is still a reason for the agent?

Moreover, one can argue that it is, in a sense, still an internal reason, even if it is not motivationally efficacious, by virtue of its connection with S. To see this, let me distinguish between two very different kinds of "internalist" theses, one having to do with motivation, the other having to do with what I shall call "identification." *Motivational Internalism* is the view that reasons are – in some way to be specified – also motives. It adopts some version of the internalist requirement (either actual or hypothetical). *Motivational Externalism* denies that all reasons are also motives, and hence it rejects all versions of the motivational internalist requirement. But the issue of whether reasons happen to be motives need not be, and in Williams's case, is not, an issue about what it is that *makes* something a reason for action. While it is possible to answer the identification question by referring to a motive – for example, by saying that it is a necessary condition of something's being a reason for x that it be a motive, nonetheless, as we have seen, Williams actually rejects this answer – and indeed it is highly implausible. Instead, Williams puts forward a variant of what might be called *Identification Internalism* – the view that an agent has a reason to x if and only if x-ing is connected, via deliberation (presumably deliberation correctly performed) with an internal feature of the agent. Note that Williams's view specifies that this internal feature must be an element in the agent's motivational set. It is opposed by *Identification Externalism* – the view that an agent has a reason to x iff[a] x-ing can be connected, via deliberation, with an aspect of the world that in some cases is not an internal feature of the agent. However, note that by defending his version of identification internalism, Williams is not also defending any form of motivational internalism. Identification internalism, by itself, takes no stand on the issue of whether reasons are also motives. Hence one can be an identification internalist and a moti-

[a]*Editor's note:* Following standard practice, the phrase "if and only if" is abbreviated as "iff."

vational externalist, denying that the reasons we have (by virtue of their deliberative connection with certain of our internal features) must also be motives themselves. Most importantly, the identification internalist has not shown that reasons are also motives simply because he has shown the deliberative connection of these reasons with actual motives.[20] As Williams himself admits, the process of deliberation can have all sorts of effect on S, and it is also possible to believe that it might have *no* effect, in which case, the agent might have a reason to x, but no motive to x. Anyone who wants to insist that a motivational effect is in some way necessary or inevitable must provide an argument for that insistence – identification internalism does not, by itself, provide any argument at all with respect to the motivational efficacy of reasons.

Moreover, such an argument would appear difficult to construct. It seems easy to give examples of people who seem to know they have reasons, but for whom these reasons are not motives. Indeed, pick any example of irrationality that you like. Take, for example, the drug addict who desires to avoid contracting AIDS, and who thus has reason to stop shooting up with heroin using dirty needles. Although he may acknowledge this reason, he may also find that it has no motivational force for him. Nonetheless, we would still say that he has that reason. Even if it is motivationally "external," it is "internal" in the sense that it is related via means/end deliberation to one or more of his (acknowledged) desires, interests, and projects. Or imagine a variation of the Owen Wingrave story, in which Owen's father is right to argue that there is some element in Owen's S that can be deliberatively linked up with joining the army, such that Owen has a reason to do so, and yet Owen persists in stubbornly refusing to do so. (Perhaps he is self-deceived, or defiant of the dictates of reason in a way that makes him irrational.) By Williams's own account, the fact that Owen refuses to do what he has reason to do does not negate the fact that it is still a reason for him. The inertness of the reason in this case does not destroy the fact that it is a reason for him – and this is not only an implication of Williams's account, but also the way we think about reasons in everyday life.

A motivational internalist would likely want to dispute the pos-

---

[20] Jonathan Dancy also notes the way in which Williams's internal/external distinction comes apart from a more traditional motivational way of making that distinction. See Dancy (1993), Appendix I, pp. 253–7.

sibility of complete inertness, and argue that even in these two cases, there is some sort of hidden (and insufficient) motivational force within the reasons of Owen and the drug addict, but again, this is a thesis for which he must argue, and nothing in Williams's article provides such an argument. Certainly the plausibility of the DCM requirement alone does not generate such an argument.

This brings me to my second point. In the next section, I will discuss various ways in which one might develop an argument that links motivational efficacy to reasons for action. Suppose, for now, that such an argument could be developed. Would it show that motivational efficacy was a necessary condition of something's being a reason, such that all reasons, in order to be reasons, must satisfy the hypothetical motivational internalist requirement? No, it would not do so if we accept the broad outlines of Williams's own account of reasons, and in particular, the idea that the DCM requirement provides not only a necessary but also a *sufficient* condition of something's being a reason. To see this, consider again the Owen Wingrave example. Williams uses that story to argue that unless Owen's father can find an element in Owen's S to which he can deliberatively link a reason to join the military, Owen has no reason to do so. But note that this argument concerns how we are to identify the reasons that Owen has, where this identification process has *nothing to do with* the actual motivational efficacy of any of these reasons. Williams's point is not that Owen can't seem to get himself to go into the army unless his father's remonstrations can link up with some element in his S. It is, more fundamentally, that Owen *has no reason* to go into the army, despite everything his father could say, if there is no connection that can be made by deliberation between Owen's desires, interests, and projects (or any other element in S), and this activity. So accepting the DCM requirement means that regardless of whether reasons are motivational or not, what actually makes them reasons is the deliberative connection with S, and not any real or imagined motivational efficacy.

So the most persuasive interpretation of Williams's argument makes the motivational efficacy of Owen's father's words *beside the point*. Owen has a reason to go into the army iff there is a connection that can be made deliberatively between some element in S and that activity, and the actual motivational efficacy of that reason is neither a necessary nor a sufficient condition of its being a reason. Williams's argument is ultimately most persuasive as a thesis about how to identify the reasons we have on the basis of their relationship to our stock of motives, rather than as a thesis about any motivational efficacy that a reason must have.[21]

A careful reading of Williams's article shows that he never *explicitly* makes the mistake of saying that because there is a deliberative connection between a reason and a motive, this reason must also be a motive.[22] But in a comment on his article in another place, his

---

[21] Discussion of needs passage here? – for example, 1981b, pp. 105–6. It is also interesting to note that Williams's argument is consistent with the idea that all reasons are norm-generated. Consider that Williams never explains why or how deliberation (correctly performed) generates reasons. A natural way to make that explanation is to say that deliberation invokes norms. Take, for example, instrumental deliberation. When we deliberate about whether or not there is an instrumental connection between an action and a desire of ours, we are engaged not merely in cause-and-effect reasoning, but also in a *directive* process. That is, the results of this deliberation are not merely that a certain action will effect an end we desire, but also that we *ought* to take that action insofar as it is a means to what we desire. Hence, there is a norm implicit in instrumental deliberation, to the effect that we ought to do that which will be the best means to achieving what it is we desire. It would seem to be this norm, in conjunction with cause-and-effect information, that supplies us with what we consider to be instrumental reasons for action. Moreover, insofar as Williams recognized other forms of deliberation, one could argue that he is implicitly recognizing other kinds of practical norms that play a role in (what we call) a "reasoning" process. Suffice it to say here that Williams's defense of internal reasons is consistent with, and in certain respects supportive of, my definition of norms as generating reasons for action that are considerations in a deliberation about what to do, and that are *not* intrinsically motivational.

[22] I have been careful not to accuse Williams himself of making this error, since his paper suggests, but does not explicitly make, that error. Williams certainly accepts that one can have a reason to do some action x, where this reason is not a motive, insofar as one can fail to know about the reason. But it is not clear that Williams believes, once the reason is known, that the reason is also motivational. Consider the following passage:

> Does believing that a particular consideration is a reason to act in a particular way provide, or indeed constitute, a motivation to act? . . . . Let us grant that it does – this claim indeed seems plausible, so long as the connexion between such beliefs and the disposition to act is not tightened to that unnecessary degree which excludes akrasia. The claim is in fact *so* plausible that this agent, with this belief, appears to be one about whom, now, an *internal* reason statement could truly be made: he is one with an appropriate motivation in his [motivational set] S (1981b, 107).

It would seem from this passage that Williams does not believe the mere deliberative connection between reason and some motive in the agent's motiva-

account of his argument does commit him to this mistake. In that comment, he presents two statements[23]:

(R) A has a reason to φ
(D) If A deliberated correctly, he would be motivated to φ

Then he characterizes his argument for internal reasons as follows: Given a reasonable interpretation of the hypothetical in (D), every occurrence of D can be replaced by R.[24] But right here the mistake is made – to think that a reason about which we have correctly deliberated is something essentially *motivational*, is to mistakenly believe that just because a reason is derived from a motive, it is also itself motivational.

In making this mistake, Williams has plenty of company, for it seems to be a widespread and persistent error in contemporary philosophical literature on reasons. For example, note the error in the following passage from Samuel Scheffler's *Human Morality*:

> Hume held that, in general, only sentiments or desires are ultimately capable of moving a person to action. . . . Now when Hume's general view, or a sufficiently similar position is combined with the *internalist* principle that nothing can count as a reason for a person to act in a certain way unless it is capable of actually motivating him to do so, what follows is a form of the instrumental conception of rationality. According to the instrumental conception, any reason that an agent has to act in one way rather than another must derive ultimately from the agent's existing desires. (1992, 60–1)

tional set is sufficient to render that reason motivational since he is prepared to recognize a "gap" between knowing one has a reason and being motivated to act on it (which explains akrasia). Yet consider the following passage later in the paper:

> *What* is it that one comes to believe when he comes to believe that there is a reason for him to φ, if it is not the proposition, or something that entails the proposition, that if he deliberated rationally, he would be motivated to act appropriately? (1981b, 109).

Note the last sentence: Williams infers from the fact that one knows one has a reason to φ that one is motivated to φ. I am arguing that it is precisely this inference that is unjustified.

[23] Williams (1995, 187).
[24] Op. cit., p. 188.

Notice that the definition of the instrumental conception of reason in the last sentence does *not* follow from a Humean motivational thesis and Scheffler's internalist principle – which seems the same as what I called the "motivational internalist requirement" (not qualified with any hypothetical) – because, according to Scheffler's definition of instrumental reason, although an instrumental reason is "derived" from the agent's existing desires, there is no requirement that this reason *itself* be motivational nor "capable of motivating" the agent who has it. This conception of instrumental reason therefore *violates* Scheffler's internalist requirement, because it defines something as a reason for action without requiring that it also be capable of motivating, either in a Humean sense, or in any other sense. While someone who embraces this instrumental conception may believe that as a matter of contingent fact, it is usually true that when a reason is derived from a motive, it is also motivational itself, note that a further (empirical) argument is required to establish even this (nonnecessary) motivational effect – that argument is not provided by any defense of a conception of reasons as instrumentally connected with the agent's desires or sentiments. Moreover, note that if, as Scheffler suggests, the instrumental conception establishes that "any reason that an agent has to act in one way rather than another must derive ultimately from the agent's existing desires," that conception makes the *derivation* from existing desires the necessary condition of something's being a reason, and not that reason's motivational efficacy. This means the instrumental conception, so understood, rejects Scheffler's internalist requirement as providing a defining characteristic of something's being a reason. (I should also note here, although I will have to postpone a complete discussion of this point until Chapter 4, that Hume does not articulate any form of the internalist requirement, and never makes the mistake of confusing the justification of a reason with its motivational efficacy.)

If Williams's position on reasons is only a variant of identification internalism that subtly seems to exclude motivational internalism as part of what it is that makes something a reason for action, could we nonetheless revise his account so as to allow it to include some version of motivational internalism? More generally, is there some version of motivational internalism that is compelling, such that Williams should want to include the view into his account of reasons?

There are a number of positions that can qualify as motivationally internalist, relying on a number of different possible versions of the motivational internalist requirement. As I shall discuss in the next section, all of these positions are problematic, and they are particularly so for a naturalist. I suspect the relative popularity of internalism stems from the confusion between the authority of reasons and their motivational efficacy, so that philosophers have mistakenly believed that motivational efficacy had to be characteristic of a reason, if it was to be a reason. Nonetheless, once that confusion is cleared up, the problems with motivational internalism are much more evident. In particular, to the extent that philosophers such as Williams are sympathetic to naturalism, they should eschew any form of motivational internalism, and signs of positions that commit him to this eschewal are evident, as I shall also discuss, in Williams's article.

REASONS AND MOTIVATION

If there is no form of motivational internalism that can be derived from the DCM requirement, can we nonetheless append some form of the motivational internalist requirement to the DCM requirement, thereby creating what might be called a form of "double internalism," insofar as it embraces variants of both motivational internalism and identification internalism?

Before considering whether this is possible, we must think about the logic involved in this "appending." Given that motivational internalism doesn't follow from identification internalism, it must be a thesis that we adopt in addition to the latter. There are two ways that such a thesis could be added:

A. It could be added as another reason-defining condition – that is, as a condition that is jointly necessary, along with the DCM requirement, in order for something to be a reason. In this view, motivational efficacy would act, in concert with a deliberative connection with an agent's motives, as a reason-making feature. Hence the motivational internalism requirement would be a *reason-making* condition.

B. It could be added not as a reason-making feature, but as a contingent but invariably present feature of something's being a reason. In this view, motivational efficacy would be always something that a reason has, but not a characteristic that we believe makes it into a reason. This view accepts that the DCM requirement alone provides necessary and sufficient conditions of something's being a reason, but it also maintains that the set of reasons is a subset of the set of all motives. So being motivationally efficacious and being a reason is analogous to having a kidney and being a human. Just as "having a kidney" is a property that invariably accompanies, but is not the same as, those properties that make someone a human being, being "motivationally efficacious" is a property that invariably accompanies, but is not the same as, those properties of a reason that make it a reason.[25] So this view makes the motivational internalism requirement only what I will call a *reason-characterizing* condition.

However, I will now argue that neither way of appending motivational internalism to identification internalism will work, because there is no form of motivational internalism that is plausible, and hence no way to append motivational internalism to identification internalism that will work. To see why, we must review different forms of motivational internalism, and then determine whether any of these forms is plausibly appended to identification internalism in either of the ways I've just defined.

1. The simplest and most straightforward version of motivational internalism accepts the "actual" motivational internalist requirement that I discussed in the last section, which says that all reasons for an agent are motivationally efficacious. But as I noted in the discussion of Williams's argument, there are a number of reasons why this version of motivational internalism is implausible, many of which are actually suggested by Williams in his article. The problem with the actual motivational internalist requirement is that it would rule out recognizing that an agent can have a reason for doing something, of which she is not aware, on the grounds that what an agent isn't aware of, can't move her. And yet we think that we have many such reasons. For example, I can have a reason to avoid caffeine, and yet be ignorant of it, or I can deliberate with respect to my motives but do it badly, and thus fail to appreciate what my reasons actually are. In his article, Williams agrees, and thus rejects the identification of an agent's reasons with the reasons he believes he has, because an agent "may falsely believe an internal reason statement about himself" and because the agent "may not know some true internal rea-

---

[25] Except that they don't! Venturing into the realm of the necessary and what counts as defining is venturing into the problematic realm of the analytic, about which Quine has said so much [including the seminal essay "Two Dogmas of Empiricism" in Quine (1980)]. Such problems are not, however, pertinent to our work here, and thus I aim to avoid them.

son statement about himself" (1981a, 103). Thus, an agent "who believes this stuff is gin, when in fact it is petrol" (1981a, 102) has a reason not to drink this stuff, and yet he doesn't know about that reason, so that it cannot be a motive for him.[26] Similarly, suppose Owen Wingrave does not know that he has a reason to go into the military, because he has missed a deliberative connection between that action and some element in his S. What he doesn't know can't

---

[26] Such a use of the term 'reason' is not concerned with the "agent's rationality" (1981a, 102–3). This position is a little puzzling: If the agent had, for example, no way of knowing that the stuff was petrol, and every reason to think it was gin, why should his rationality be impugned by his mixing the stuff with tonic? To capture our commonsense usage of reasons in a way connected to the agent's rationality, it would seem we need to distinguish between negligent reasoners, like the rude nine-year-old girl in my earlier example, who could have (and we think should have) recognized her mistake in the situation, and reasoners whose mistake is not, in the same way, culpable because (for some reason) the mistake was "beyond catching" in the situation. As it stands, Williams seems to suggest a position of what is called in the law "strict liability" for reasoners – one that would hold all of us accountable for mistakes resulting in failures in recognizing our reasons, no matter how difficult such mistakes might be to detect (although perhaps I have misunderstood his intentions in this passage.)

[Editor's note: Professor Hampton concluded this footnote with the following notes to herself for possible future additions.]

Reasons for action as what we can reasonably expect people to have, as opposed to idealized statements of deliberative connections with motives, where these statements may be impossible for people to attain, or even understand? Gauthier on the Aztecs.

[The reference to Gauthier seems to be to the following passage:]

In some cases we may be able to infer what a person would have preferred, had she been correctly or fully informed about her circumstances. . . . But in other cases we may be quite unable to determine what persons would have preferred, since they will have formed no preferences in relation to the actual facts. We may relate the Aztecs' preferences for human sacrifice to their belief in the hunger of the gods for human blood, but how would their preferences have been altered had they held no such belief? We do not know and have no way of knowing. The preferences of the Aztecs were formed in the context of their beliefs; beyond that context they had, or need have had, no preferences. To suppose that each person must have a set of "real" or "true" preferences related to her actual circumstances, although often concealed by false or incomplete beliefs, seems psychologically implausible [Gauthier (1984, 29–30)].

move him, yet we still think he has a reason, in this situation, to join the military. Hence, if we believe, with Williams, that it is possible for an agent to have a reason to x about which he is ignorant, then we cannot accept that it is a necessary condition of something's being a reason for an agent that it actually be motivationally efficacious for him.

Indeed, it also seems that Williams is committed to saying that a reason exists even if no one has actually performed the deliberation, as long as it is true that the deliberation, *if* it were correctly performed, would effect a link between the reason's directive and an element of S. So, for example, even if neither the agent, nor any other person, established, say, an instrumental connection between a desire in the agent's set S and a certain action, it would still seem that the agent has reason to perform that action – a reason that, one hopes *someone* will uncover. Hence the (correct) deliberation need not be actual, but only hypothetical, so that this position would recognize the existence of reasons that an agent had, which she and everyone else nonetheless failed to know about because neither she nor anyone else had performed the correct deliberation to discover them. And to repeat, any reason that an agent has, but that she doesn't know about, can't move her (and can't be part of S).

To the extent that Williams's view is the commonsense view, then commonsense rejects this form of the motivational internalist requirement. This means there is a certain way in which Williams, along with commonsense, accepts that reasons can exist "outside" (dare I say "external to"?) an agent, in the sense that they need not in fact be part of the agent's current subjective motivational set, to be reasons that she has. Simple motivational internalism therefore violates our commonsense ways of thinking about reasons – ways that a naturalist such as Williams endorses.[27]

2. Suppose, therefore, that we try to append what I called earlier

---

[27] Another reason for denying the internalist requirement may be that reasons can apply to nonhuman individuals, or to human groups, within whom it can be difficult, perhaps impossible, to speak of any motivational efficacy of these reasons, given that such entities may not have any straightforward "motivational profile" to which we could be appealing in making such a remark. So for example, we might well say that "the U.S. has a reason to pull out of Vietnam," and be quite incapable of attributing any motivational efficacy to this reason, insofar as it may be impossible, in the circumstances to attribute any motivational capacities to the social entity called the U.S.

the "hypothetical" internalist requirement to identification internalism, so as to create a weaker, and seemingly more plausible form of motivational internalism. This is the form of motivational internalism that it seems Williams would most likely append to his DCM requirement. One who advocates this requirement says that a reason *would* be motivationally efficacious if it were known. A corollary to this requirement is that to *believe* one has a reason to x entails having a motive to x. (This is the position commended, for example, by Richard Price, who says "When we are conscious that an action is *fit* to be done, or that it *ought* to be done, it is not conceivable that we can remain *uninfluenced*, or want a *motive* to action."[28]) So in this view, all reasons, insofar as they are believed, are motivational, but not all motivationally efficacious considerations that we take to be reasons are genuinely reasons. Were Williams to adopt this view, he would believe that an agent, if she knew about her reasons (correctly defined through correct reasoning with accurate information), would *eo ipso* find the reason motivationally efficacious. Note that one who takes this position needn't say that the motive force that arises from a reason is always *sufficient* to move us (and note that Price does not say any such thing in the quotation just given). Theorists who accept this form of motivational internalism can therefore disagree about the sufficiency of the motives that reasons generate.[29]

---

[28] Cited by Brink (1989, 38), from Price (1787, 194). Brink finds similar sentiments in Stevenson, Falk, Harman, Mackie, and Blackburn.

[29] Note that theorists who embrace this form of motivational internalism can still acknowledge that the definition of the notion of a reason does not make reference to the idea of a necessary motive, even while maintaining that there is a necessary connection between reasons and motives. To put it another way, they will accept that what makes something a reason for us is something other than motive (so that its being motivationally efficacious is not a necessary condition of its being a reason for us), but they will believe that by virtue of its being a reason for us, a reason necessarily generates motives for us. Kant's defense of the moral law is of this form: The moral law provides reasons for us, and is ultimately authoritative for us, but its authority does not in any way *depend* on its motivational efficacy, although it is true that, by virtue of its authority, the moral law is (necessarily) not only motivationally efficacious but sufficient to move us. Thus Kant would reject Scheffler's internalist principle that something is a reason only if it is capable of being motivational, because he would reject the idea that motivational efficacy is part of what makes something a reason. Nevertheless, he would agree that moral reasons, as it happens, are also motivational.

However, it is very difficult to see how this form of motivational internalism could be plausibly appended to identification internalism. First, it simply doesn't seem true that motivational efficacy is an invariable feature of reasons – that is, it seems that there are many occasions when there are reasons that even when they are known, are nonetheless motivationally inert. (Remember the case of the drug addict who knew but was unmoved by his reason to use clean needles in order to avoid getting AIDS.) Suppose someone tried to claim, nonetheless, that, appearances to the contrary, a known reason always produces some kind of motivational effect. She would have to show proof to this effect (in the face of plenty of evidence to the contrary), and she would have to explain why this motivational effect was inevitable. I see no plausible way for either theory to be generated. Moreover, note that such an argument would still seem to be able to secure a merely contingent linkage between reasons and motivational efficacy; any attempt to make that linkage necessary seems too fantastic to be believable. For how can the world as we know it be such that there are reasons that *necessarily* create motives? Indeed, how are we supposed to elucidate the "necessary" in this position? Suppose we tried to do so using the notion of logical necessity, so that to believe or know that one has a reason to x logically entails one's having a motive to x. How can there be such a logical connection between reasons and the contingencies of our motivational structure? How is it that my psychology is under pressure by *logic* to respond to a (perceived) reason as motivational?

So a proponent might try to save this form of motivational internalism by arguing that even if a directive can be deliberatively linked with an agent's motives, that directive cannot be considered a reason if it does not have hypothetical motivational efficacy. Such a position treats the hypothetical internalist requirement as a necessary condition, along with the DCM requirement, of something's being a reason. But note that this position would accept that the contingencies of the agent's motivational psychology play a role in determining what counts as rational for him, and such a position seems highly implausible. Just because, say, Owen feels cold toward a course of action that deliberation has correctly connected with one of his motives doesn't mean that it isn't a reason for him. This view would permit an agent's obstinacy of self-deception with respect to the recognition of what his reasons were to influence what his reasons actually were – a view that would reward the irrational agent by letting him evade reasons he didn't like!

Nor can we appeal to some notion of *conceptual* necessity to explain the connection between believed reasons and motives. Whatever follows "necessarily" from our conceptions, it does not seem that (contingent) psychological *facts* follow from them. Accordingly, it doesn't make sense to say that it follows from the concept of having a reason to x that (as a matter of contingent fact) one also has a motive to x. Whatever our concepts are, they don't have control over the workings of the physical world. Nor does it seem that there is some kind of *physical* necessity between believing one has a reason and having a motive. In this view, the belief that one has a reason causes (with physical necessity) the creation of a motive. But such a thesis will be rejected not only by those who are skeptical of the notion of physical necessity, but also by those who are dubious that any such necessity could ever obtain between two elements of human psychology – that is, a belief (that one has a reason) and a motive. Even if we accept the fantastic hypothesis that (as it happens) it has always been true that those who have believed they have a reason to x, have also had a desire to x, that doesn't mean that such desires are *necessary* by virtue of these reasons.

Perhaps theorists such as Kant have had some sort of metaphysical necessity in mind when they have linked reasons and motives. But if so, they cannot have thought that reasons and motives are necessarily (metaphysically) the same, since there are many motives that aren't reasons. Instead, their position must be that there is some aspect of a reason for action that necessarily (metaphysically) also makes it motivational. But it is very hard to see how this position can be developed plausibly, since there seems nothing metaphysically necessary about any of our motives. Indeed, a naturalist would seem particularly committed to denying any such thesis of metaphysical necessity.

So the hypothetical form of the motivational internalist requirement seems too strong to be plausibly added to identification internalism, either as a reason-making condition or as a mere reason-characterizing condition.

3. So let us explore a new and even weaker type of motivational internalism that makes use of an idea that I will call *normative necessity*. One can believe that for an agent to have a reason to x is for him to have a motive to act on this reason to x *iff he is rational* – that is, iff he is (rightly) committed to acting on his (perceived) reasons. And to say that one *ought* to have a motive to act on a reason is to say that there is a higher-order norm, generating a reason to have a motive to act on reasons. So this form of motivational internalism rejects the idea that the motivational efficacy of a reason *must* (metaphysically) be experienced by the agent insofar as he knows about the reason. Instead, this view posits that if one has a reason to x, one *ought* (rationally) to have a motive to x. Or, alternatively, if one has a reason to x, one will be rational only if one is motivated to x. Note that one who takes this position will likely insist that the belief that one has a reason will only be motivationally efficacious, and *should* only be motivationally efficacious, if that belief is accompanied by a certain kind of warrant. Note also that in this view, even if this motive does not arise, one still has a reason to x. Hence this position assumes that what makes something a reason for action is something other than its motivational efficacy, meaning that this form of motivational internalism can only be appended to identification internalism as a reason-characterizing, but not a reason-defining, feature of something's being a reason. It is interesting that some theorists have assumed motivational internalism must be this third position, even in the face of statements such as Price's quoted earlier.[30]

To fully appraise this position, we would need to explore the idea of normative necessity, and we will do so at considerable length in the next chapter. It is a notion that will likely raise any naturalist's suspicions. Nonetheless, the position is full of problems. Most fundamental is the fact that appending a motivational internalism of this form, in this way, to the DCM condition, seems too weak to generate a position that could count as a form of motivational internalism at all. This view does not require that a motive *actually* accompany a reason, but only that it ought to do so. And those who are motivational externalists will likely not dispute this normative statement. Externalists are standardly thought to question the idea that motives *must* accompany reasons, not the idea that they ought

---

[30] See, for example, Christine Korsgaard (1986). Korsgaard calls the following the "internalism requirement": "Practical-reason claims, if they are really to present us with reasons for action, must be capable of motivating *rational* persons" (p. 11, my emphasis). The implication is that they may not be capable of motivating irrational persons, and thus, it cannot be the case that for an agent to know that he has a reason to x, he necessarily has a motive to x, since he may be irrational.

to do so. So it is not clear to me that the position counts as a form of motivational internalism at all.

Apart from this worry, this form of motivational internalism is too strong to satisfy either the demands of commonsense or the demands of the naturalists, even if it is added only as a reason-characterizing condition. It is too strong, because it is questionable whether we should *always* act *on* the reasons that we have. Joseph Raz has argued that even in a situation in which one has a decisive reason to x, it might still be the case that sometimes what motivates one to do x is something other than the reason one has to do x, and there is nothing wrong or violative of reason about this.[31] Raz gives several examples. Thus, consider the reason any of us has not to murder another human being.[32] I believe I have this reason, but the fact that I have thus far been motivated such that I never killed someone is not explained by the fact that I believe I have this reason. Nor can I reasonably be criticized because my motivation not to murder people does not derive from my belief that I have a reason not to murder people. Consider another example. It may be that a (Kantian-style) Moral Law directs parents to love their children, and yet if that love is going to be morally praiseworthy, it would seem that it would have to be motivated by something about the children themselves, and not by the law itself.[33] If this is right, then to do what the law requires, it is important that one *not* be motivated by the law to undertake the directed action.

Raz makes a distinction between *complying* with a reason and *conforming* to it to clarify this point about reasons and motivation.[34] To

---

[31] Joseph Raz (1990, 179–182).

[32] Ibid., p. 181.

[33] Ibid., p. 182.

[34] That distinction is from Raz (1990, 178–182). It is, of course, suggested in the well-known grocer passage in Kant's *Groundwork*, Chapter I. Raz's distinction is not quite sufficient. There is a difference between someone who is motivated such that he conforms to a reason, where the motivation has nothing to do with the reason, and someone who is motivated such that he conforms to a reason, where the motivation is different from the reason, but is in someone, chosen or selected because of that reason. For example, there is a difference between a Ulysses who doesn't sail toward the sirens, because, as it happens, he is assailed by a stronger opposing motive, and a Ulysses who doesn't sail toward the sirens because he has a stronger opposing motive that he has (somehow) arranged for himself to have because he knew he had a reason not to sail toward the si-

comply with a reason is to be moved to act in a certain way *by* that reason. To think such compliance possible is to take reasons for action to be motivationally efficacious. To conform to a reason, in contrast, is to do as the reason directs, but to be moved by something other than the reason itself. As we shall discuss at length in Chapter 4, for moral theorists such as Mill, only conformity and not compliance is possible with respect to many sorts of reasons (particularly moral reasons).[35] In contrast, for moral theorists such as Kant, compliance with moral reasons is always possible and morally required for moral agents, no matter what other conflicting motives they have.[36] Those who, unlike Kant, believe that the motivational efficacy of reasons is normatively necessary, will believe that (only) compliance with moral reasons is morally required for agents, but such compliance may not be possible if agents are not rational. Raz's position is intermediate between these extremes, because he argues that in understanding reasons for action, we need to accept that both compliance with and conformity to reasons are possible for us, and that sometimes one is required only to conform to, and not comply with, a reason.[37]

4. If Raz is right, we might develop an even more attenuated form of motivational internalism as the very weak position that to have a reason to x is to be rationally required to have a motive to x, but not necessarily a motive to act on (that is, comply with) one's reason to x. But note that this position is so weak that surely any motivational externalist should agree with it! This position requires only that the theorist recognize that reasons ought to be followed, whether or not the motive to do so comes from the reason itself. It is hard to believe that any theorist about reasons could possibly dispute such a position! Hence we have at last found a thesis that we can plausibly append to identification internalism, but it is a thesis that cannot be construed as a plausible form of motivational internalism.

This discussion therefore shows that it is difficult to formulate any

---

rens. The second Ulysses complies with that reason by arranging to conform to it. The first Ulysses merely conforms to that reason.

[35] Mill (1861).

[36] See Kant (1785).

[37] Raz's main motivation for making this distinction is to clarify the way in which we act from exclusionary reasons when we act from rules.

version of motivational internalism that is both plausible, and yet strong enough to be genuinely different from the motivationally externalist position. If this is so, why have so many philosophers claimed to be sympathetic to motivational internalism? I suspect, as I will now explain, that the answer to this question lies in their fear of directly confronting the normativity of reasons.

ARE THERE EXTERNAL REASONS AFTER ALL?

Given that in the end, Williams's arguments only support a form of identification internalism, we should appreciate just how uncontroversial that position is. For who, in the history of moral philosophy, hasn't been at least a partial identification internalist, understood as the position that an agent has a reason to x if x is connected, via (correct) deliberation, to some internal feature of the agent? Such a thesis is accepted by Kant (whose internal feature is the Moral Law), by Aristotle (whose internal feature is the desire for Eudaimonia), and by Jeremy Bentham (whose internal feature is the desire for pleasure). Although these philosophers disagree about which internal feature is morally relevant, and about the nature of the deliberation that connects internal features to reasons, they all accept the general idea that we can identify reasons by looking for deliberative connections with internal features of the agent. Arguably, even Plato can be considered an identification internalist in this sense, insofar as he too makes a connection between reasons for being virtuous and the desire for happiness. Moreover, all these moral theorists would agree with an even more specific version of identification internalism, which says that an agent has a reason to x if x-ing is connected via (correct) deliberation with an element in the agent's motivational set, since the internal features each of them recognizes as relevant to determining reasons happen also to be motives.

The fact that it is difficult to think of any moral philosopher who counts as an identification externalist (perhaps G. E. Moore is one, although this is arguable) likely reflects the fact that regardless of their theoretical differences, moral philosophers have in general believed that our reasons, and particularly our moral reasons, are connected to our natures as human beings. So the practical reasons they have recognized have been responsive to certain internal features (which have generally also been motives). Williams may well be right that most of these philosophers have been too ready to credit a certain universality to human nature and human motivational structure, thereby failing to realize the way in which reasons for action will differ from one individual to the next. And he may insist that their attempts to show that certain reasons (for example, moral reasons) are somehow *necessary* for people, in the face of their acceptance of some kind of internal identification thesis, are futile. To even try to establish any necessity to some of our reasons in the context of identification internalism, these philosophers would have to say (as, for example, Kant does) that some of the motives in people's subjective motivational sets are necessary for a rational being (for example, in Kant's case, the necessary motive is the Moral Law), so that all rational beings would, of necessity, have a reason that could be deliberatively linked to this motive. (So Kant argues that all rational beings, of necessity, have reasons to perform directives derived from the moral law.) Williams will surely reject this sort of (in his view) fantastic bit of psychologizing. Nonetheless, it is striking that the identification thesis is still a thesis that in its broad outlines, is accepted by his opponents. Does that mean that it provides us with at least the beginnings of a reliable theory of what reasons are?

Yes and no. While it may well provide accurate guidelines for identifying many of the reasons that we have, so that it succeeds as a sufficient condition of something's being a reason, it nonetheless fails to provide a necessary condition for identifying what a reason *is*. This is because, while it is true that many of our reasons *are* derived from a deliberation with respect to one or more elements of our subjective motivational set, there are also reasons that we have – indeed, reasons that Williams himself will want to say that we have – that cannot be deliberatively derived from our subjective motivational set. This means that the DCM condition fails as a necessary condition of something's being a reason (even if it survives as a sufficient condition of something's being a reason).

To see the DCM's failure, consider that any theorist, such as Williams, who wants to insist that a reason must be deliberatively linked with an element of S, will not believe that just any old thinking can qualify as deliberation. Only certain forms of thinking are deliberative, and these forms of deliberation can be done well or badly, correctly or incorrectly. Hence, deliberative processes of the sort that effect a linkage between motives and the directives of a reason are, for any identification internalist, including Williams, normatively defined processes. This means that there are norms defining correct, or well-done, deliberations. Indeed, it is via these (correctly performed) deliberations that normativity enters the reasons themselves, and such normativity must accompany a reason, in order for it to be a reason at all. As McDowell says of Williams's argument:

> Reason-giving explanations require a conception of how things ideally would be, sufficiently independent of how any actual individual's psychological economy operates to serve as the basis for critical assessment of it. In particular, there must be a potential gap between the ideal and the specific directions in which a given agent's motivations push him.
>
> Williams secures an independence that conforms to this abstract description . . . by his appeal to deliberation: what practical rationality requires of an agent is not simply read off from his specific motivations just as they stand (including, in Williams' example, a wish to drink some stuff which is in fact petrol), but is determined, from these motivations, by deliberation, whose capacity to correct and enrich the specific motivations one starts with is supposed to open up the necessary gap between actual and ideal.[38]

The idea is that the deliberation is the transforming device that channels mere motives into reasons and makes them "ideal" in the way we think reasons are.

However, if deliberation is itself a normative notion, the forms of reasoning that count as instances of deliberation (correctly done) are also defined by norms. Such norms generate reasons – including reasons directing how we are to deliberate, what counts as correct deliberation, and when we ought to deliberate. Are these reasons regarding deliberation internal or external? If Williams answers "internal," how does that answer make sense, given that, in order to use it, he would have to invoke the concept of deliberation he is trying to define?

This is not just a minor problem of clarification that requires tinkering with the identification account. It is a fatal flaw in the account itself insofar as it is presented as a theory of the necessary condition of something's being a reason. For it seems we have identified considerations that escape this condition, but that are nonetheless reasons.

---

[38] McDowell (1995, 76–7).

To better appreciate this point, consider in what ways Williams might try to argue that any of us has a reason to engage in a deliberation of a certain sort in a certain situation. He cannot, for example, try to equate that reason with an existing motive to do so. That motive may or may not exist in any given person (certainly there appear to be many people who seem to have no existing motive to reason at all, much less to reason well), and yet we think, even if the motive doesn't exist, that they still have a reason to deliberate. And if Williams tries to argue, like a Kantian, that there are motives to deliberate that exist "of necessity" in a rational being, then he would be invoking the same metaphysically and psychologically implausible idea with respect to nonmoral forms of reasoning to which he objects in Kantian theories. (Certainly it is an idea that seems inconsistent with the commitments of naturalism.) Nor can he argue that as a matter of fact, the forms of practical deliberation he recognizes just happen to be, given our nature as human beings, what we actually do. Not only is such a thesis descriptively dubious (since we "happen to do" all sorts of things, many of them involving reflection that seems irrational), more importantly, any attempt to leave the notion of what counts as "correct forms of deliberation" up to psychological contingencies fails to preserve the gap between mere proposals for action and genuine reasons – the latter being, to use McDowell's term, in some way "ideal." Indeed, reasons are derived only by "correct" forms of deliberation in Williams's view, which means that this view does not leave it up to individual agents to define what counts as a genuine deliberation.

Moreover, leaving up to the psychological contingencies of the agent not only the definition of what count as correct forms of deliberation, but also the force of any directive *to* engage in any of these forms of deliberation in certain circumstances, makes it impossible for Williams to require that *everyone*, no matter the elements of his subjective motivational set S, engage in deliberations in the right circumstances, and in the right way. Intuitively we, and Williams, believe that the question of how and when to use deliberation to derive internal reasons for action is not something that any agent can define based on what happen to be his motivations at the moment. Williams accepts this, which is why he requires that the motives in the agent's S be subjected to certain forms of deliberation in order to be transformed into genuine reasons, such that the agent who acts from them can be considered rational. But then it must be that the reasons to engage in deliberations of a certain form cannot be identified with mere motives. Nor can they be deliberatively defined without circularity.

So how do we commend to any agent – even an agent whose existing motivations are hostile to the idea – a reason to engage in a certain form of deliberation in a certain situation? To do so, it seems we need a way to "envisage the generation of a new motivation by reason in an exercise in which the directions it can take are not determined by the shape of the agent's prior motivations – an exercise that would be rationally compelling whatever motivations we start from."[39] But I have just quoted from McDowell's paraphrase of what the external reasons' theorist needs! Williams must generate a way to commend reasons to deliberate to even the most recalcitrant agent, no matter the motives of such an agent, *in just the same way* that an external reasons theorist needs to commend the external reasons she advocates, no matter the motives of such an agent. And that shows that Williams's account must treat reasons to deliberate as "external" in just the way that his opponents do – that is, these reasons must be regarded as external in the sense that they apply to, and rightly direct, an agent regardless of whether she likes the idea of their doing so or not. So while Williams may object to the sort of "eternal" reasons that have been proposed by moral theorists before him, it seems that he cannot object to the idea of there being external reasons, because his own account assumes them, insofar as it assumes that we have reasons to deliberate in certain ways, at certain times, no matter our existing motives. So the externalism that Williams's opponents endorse with respect to moral forms of practical reasoning is present in Williams's own account with respect to nonmoral practical reasoning.

Thus we have identified within Williams's own account external reasons for action – that is, reasons whose nature as reasons is neither explicable by their being motives, nor explicable by their being deliberatively connected to motives, where these reasons involve how to deliberate, and when to perform a deliberation in a certain way. These reasons escape the identificational internalist's net. What does that tell us about the reliability of that net in the first place?

---

[39] Ibid., (1995, 71).

THE EXTERNAL NATURE OF ALL REASONS FOR ACTION

Consider again the DCM requirement accepted by identification internalists. That requirement says that it is at least a sufficient condition of something's being a reason that it be deliberatively connected to a motive. Yet there is a sense in which any theorist who accepts this DCM requirement has embraced a certain way of thinking about *all* reasons that makes them external.

Recall Williams's definition of a reason as external if it is a reason that an agent is supposed to have, regardless of the contents of her subjective motivational set – and a reason that a certain, special form of reasoning would reveal to that agent were she to engage in it. Yet the phrase 'regardless of the contents of her subjective motivational set' is ambiguous. Of course, reasons that are deliberatively connected to an agent's motives are hers *because of* the contents of her subjective motivational set. That is, they "belong to" her because of their connection to S. But she needn't feel motivated to follow these reasons in order for them to be her reasons, and in that sense they are her reasons regardless of her motivational set. I will use the phrase 'belong to' to designate the way in which we can identify specific reasons for an agent because of their relation to the contents of her motivational set. In this sense, we must appeal to the motivational set to explain why certain reasons, rather than others, belong to an agent. Nonetheless, understanding how these reasons apply to her, such that she is directed by them – that is, understanding the nature of their authority over her – has nothing to do with the specific contents of her motivational set. Indeed, one would hope that a recalcitrant agent who failed to recognize one of the reasons that was deliberatively connected to a motive in her motivational set could be brought to do so via a form of "reason in an exercise in which the directions it can take are not determined by the shape of the agent's prior motivations – an exercise that would be rationally compelling whatever motivations we start from."[40] But note that once again I have invoked McDowell's paraphrase of the externalist's notion of a "compelling form of reason," which in this case would be a form of reason compelling this agent to recognize reasons that were deliberatively connected to the agent's S. Even "internal" reasons that satisfy the DCM requirement are external, in the sense that they di-

---

[40] Ibid (1995, 71).

rect the agent whether she likes it or not, and have a compelling rightness about them, whether she is willing to recognize that fact or not.

So there is a sense in which even the "internal" reasons that Williams recognizes have the externalist characteristics that he criticizes when they appear in, say, Kantian or Aristotelian reasons. But that is because reasons are "oughts" – prescriptive in their force, authoritative over us, whether we like the idea or not. Indeed, even instrumental reasons are "oughts," directing an agent regardless of whether she accepts them or not. Whatever internal story we want to tell about *why* they apply, these reasons have authority over an agent regardless of whether the elements in her S lead her to be motivated to follow them. Or so commonsense – and Williams – believe.

These ruminations have revealed one necessary condition that all reasons must have to be reasons, – namely, that they be "oughts" – that is, normative prescriptions that direct us to engage in a certain action type regardless of whether we are motivated to do so. Unlike mere motives that cannot be considered reasons (phobias, whims, obsessions, ill-considered cravings, and so on), reasons have a "rightness" about them. We speak of them using the language of "obligation" – as in "you ought not to drink that stuff because it's petrol" or "you ought to take better care of your children." For the time being, call this feature of reasons their "normativity." It is this normativity that is not indebted to the contingencies of S. Whether any of us understands the reason, likes the reason, feels moved by the reason – none of this matters with respect to the fact that it *is* a reason for us, such that it "rightly" directs or guides us.

In a way, this is a blazingly obvious characteristic of a reason! Why have theorists such as Williams failed to acknowledge it?

CONCLUSION

There are three lessons to be learned from this analysis of the problems with Williams's internalist theory. First, not all reasons are internal in the sense that they satisfy the DCM requirement – that is, not all reasons are deliberatively connected to existing motives – since reasons defining correct deliberation cannot be so defined, and the idea that we have such reasons is not only highly plausible intuitively but also required by even Humean accounts of reasons.

Hence, Identification Internalism, understood as a thesis about the necessary condition of something's being a reason, fails. Second, the cogency of reasons cannot be equated with or derived from their motivational efficacy, since reasons can be reasons without being motivationally efficacious or even hypothetically motivationally efficacious. Hence, these forms of Motivational Internalism fail. Third, reasons are normative, but that normativity cannot be explained simply by appeal to some sort of deliberative process by which reasons are formed because (1) not all reasons can be defined via an appeal to deliberation (in particular, reasons about when and how to deliberate in certain ways cannot be so defined), and (2) we need to explain the normativity inherent in deliberation – a normativity that reasons "inherit" – in order to understand what the normativity of all reasons consists in.

All these lessons may well seem dire for the naturalist. Indeed, I believe theorists such as Williams have worried that unless it is explained as natural, such normativity is highly suspect from a naturalist point of view. Hence, they have been motivated to "deconstruct" that normativity, so as to build it up from subjectively internal elements that insofar as they are natural, make the normativity itself seem acceptable. But in the end, Williams's internal reasons don't get their normativity from their connection with motives – that connection establishes, at most, the reasons' applicability to the agent who has them. (That is, it shows that because they are derived from her motives, they are *her* reasons.) Instead, that normativity is something they get from the deliberative process to which the motives are subjected. One might say that in this view, the reasons are supposed to somehow *inherit* the normativity that is in the deliberative process itself. And the problem with this attempt to render the normativity of reasons benign is that if normativity is what is distinctive about reasons, we don't get any further in understanding that normativity by appealing to deliberations, first, because the normativity within the deliberations (which the internal reasons inherit) remains unexplicated, and second, because the normative directives *to* engage in deliberations of certain forms in certain situations remain unexplicated.

If the internalist project fails, so that neither Motivational Internalism, nor Identification Internalism, succeeds, does that doom the naturalist project? No. Naturalists have instinctively worried about the normativity that is so nakedly present in the externalists' account of reasons and have sought to avoid it by appealing to occurrent (and contingent) motives in their theory. But this is the wrong strategy for the naturalist. Their best move is not to deny the normativity of reasons, nor to deny the way that it can be "external" to an agent's existing motivational structure, but to understand this normativity in a way that naturalistically "tames" it. There is, as we shall see, a way of acknowledging normativity that is completely acceptable from the naturalist standpoint.

However, there is also a way that is completely unacceptable. In the next chapter, I will pursue what I call the "authority" of reasons, which I will claim is the essence of what we consider their normativity. It is the distinctive marker of anything that we call a reason. I will go on to argue that it is a certain thesis about the authority of reasons that naturalists reject, but that is implicitly accepted by any moral objectivist.

Chapter 3

Reasons' Authority

[computer file 3/24/96]

> There is something in this more than natural, if
> philosophy could find it out.
> – William Shakespeare, *Hamlet*

Thus far we have still not located precisely what it is about ethics that appears to make it scientifically problematic. In this chapter, I shall argue, using the analyses of the last chapter, that it is a certain thesis held by moral objectivists about moral norms and the reasons they generate that fails to pass scientific muster. According to this thesis, there are norms that generate reasons whose authority over us is objective, and moral objectivists accept this thesis with respect to moral norms and reasons. However, moral objectivism is merely a version of normative objectivism, which is a general position that assumes this thesis with respect to one or more types of norms (which can be epistemic, political, and so on). One can be a normative objectivist but not a moral objectivist, and one can be a normative objectivist about morality but refuse to accept the thesis for any other type of norm. I shall argue that the consistent naturalist must oppose all forms of normative objectivism, where moral objectivism is just a particularly popular version of this more general view.

The first task is to develop a minimalist and metaphysically neutral theory of the normativity of reasons, since all parties accept that there are such things as reasons that oblige us. Thereafter, we will explain how this minimal and neutral conception of reasons is embellished and used differently in each partisan's metaphysical thesis about the nature of reasons. We will then be able to see exactly why the objectivist's thesis cannot withstand the naturalist's scrutiny.

COMPONENTS OF A THEORY OF REASONS

Suppose you wanted to develop what I will call a "theory of reasons" – that is, a theory telling you what reasons are and how they should be used to understand and/or explain certain kinds of behavior. You would need to develop answers to the following questions.

1. Who or what can have reasons? Only human beings? Also human institutions? Also certain nonhumans? Call this the *rational agency* question. It pursues what kind of creature is subject to reasons. It may or may not be true that to be subject to a reason, you have to be able to comprehend it.

2. How do we determine what reasons an agent that is subject to reasons actually has? This is the question that Williams tries to answer in his article "Internal and External Reasons." I call it the *identity* question; it pursues the issue of how reasons for any agent are identified or determined.

3. Of the reasons that an agent has, how do we determine which ones are relevant to a situation? I call this the *relevance* question; to define, in general, how to determine an agent's reasons is still not to define which of these reasons is applicable to any particular situation in which the agent finds herself.

4. Of the reasons that an agent has, and that are relevant to the situation in which she finds herself, which one(s) is/are decisive, if any? I call this the *decisiveness* question. It pursues how we do (or should) determine the reason(s) that "win out" if there is a contest between relevant reasons. It asks for the criteria for determining when any particular reason is mandatory in a situation, and criteria for determining when our reasons are such that acting on more than one of them is permitted. A "tie" between reasons needn't mean that both are equally permissible. It might instead mean that both of them are mandatory – so that you would be violating a decisive obligation no matter which reason you acted on. Someone who believes the latter is possible believes in severe moral conflict; someone who believes ties mean "equal permissibility" does not.

5. Once a reason has been determined to be one that an agent has, and one that is both relevant to a situation and either decisive or permitted in that situation, how do/should we explain action that is performed "because" of it? I call this the *motivational* question, and as I noted earlier, there are a variety of ways in which one might answer this question in an "internalist" way, none of which seems particularly plausible from a naturalist standpoint.

6. But there remains one more question – indeed, the most important question that should be asked about reasons. Even if we have a theory that answers all the preceding questions, it still doesn't explain what I called in the last chapter the "normativity" or "directive force" of reasons. Whereas it is an epistemological problem to know what reasons we have, it is a metaphysical problem to know what reasons are and how they affect us. In the last chapter, I argued that a necessary condition of something's being a reason was its having something I called normativity. But what is this normativity? Intuitively we understand it, and in response to it we say such things as, "This is a reason for you, so you ought to do it." But what is this "ought to"? Providing an answer to this question goes to the heart of a reason's normativity. Henceforth, I will call the compelling nature of a reason its *authority*. Understanding the nature of the authority of a reason is answering what I call the *authority* question. It is this question that will be central to our concerns in this chapter.

AUTHORITY

To begin to pursue the nature of the authority of reasons, we must begin by disambiguating the term 'authority.' There are three distinct meanings we can attach to that term, but, as I shall explain, only one of these meanings is associated with the metaphysical nature of reasons (and it is 'authority' in this sense that is presupposed by the other two meanings). It is also the meaning of authority that is associated with the thesis about reasons accepted by moral objectivists.

First, when we speak of a norm (or its reason) as authoritative, we may be referring to the circumstances in which its reasons are decisive, overriding other reasons. Call this 'decisiveness authority.' To say that a norm is authoritative in this sense is to say that you are now in a situation where its reason is the correct conclusion in a deliberation about what to do. Or to use Williams's phrase, it is to say that your reason has "deliberative priority."[1] In such a situation, we would say things such as, "You really ought to do x," by which we would mean that of all the reasons you have to do n – z, your reason to do x is decisive. We might also invoke the notion of "ne-

---

[1] Williams (1985, 183).

cessity" to talk about this reason, as in "You don't understand – it is absolutely necessary that you do x." We might say such a thing if we were, for example, trying to persuade someone that even if it were reasonable in the past to refuse to undergo a knee operation to repair a torn cartilage, such an operation is required now (that is, the reason to have the operation is now decisive). Note that this way of using the term 'authority' already presupposes that the reason being called authoritative is a (justified) reason for you. Some theorists have criticized what they believe is the tendency of moral theorists to think that all moral norms are decisive (and thus override) all nonmoral norms in any deliberation.[2] I shall not pursue this quarrel here because this is not the notion of authority that I want to focus on in this chapter.

Second, when we speak of a norm as authoritative, we can be referring to the way in which the agent has embraced it, or committed herself to it. Call this 'commitment authority'.[3] As Bernard Williams has discussed, there are times when we might talk about a reason for action as something that we believe we *must* act on. For example, a person who risked her life in France in World War II to save a Jew from being captured by Nazi sympathizers might say, "I had no alternative; I had to do what I could to save him."[4] Such a person is claiming that she has no capacity to act except on this reason (which, in such cases, is a decisive reason). As Williams notes, we can also have nonmoral reasons that we take to be necessary, such as "reasons of prudence, self-protection, aesthetic or artistic concern, or sheer self-assertion."[5] How do certain reasons come to be considered by us as "practically necessary"? Williams suggests that it is their deep-seated connection with a shared social life that can give them such power over us: "The agent's conclusions will not usually be solitary and unsupported, because they are part of an ethical life that is to an important degree shared with others"[6] But if the necessity of certain reasons (for example, moral reasons) is

---

[2] See Susan Wolf (1982), "Moral Saints," and Williams (1985), Chapter 10.

[3] Williams calls this notion of authority "practical necessity" (1981c; 1985, 188).

[4] In fact, that is exactly what many of the rescuers did say about their heroic behavior. See Neera Badhwar (1993), especially p. 97.

[5] Williams (1985, 188).

[6] And he complains that the system of morality tends to conceal "the dimension in which ethical life lies outside the individual" (1985, 191).

socially imposed, why do we think that action on these reasons is, to use Williams's own words, "discoveries about oneself," and "the very paradigm" of what we take responsibility for, and central to the constitution of our character?[7] I would maintain that even if there is a social component to the necessity with which these reasons grip us (and it is arguable that there is always such a social component – particularly if the necessary reason involves self-assertion), their importance to the agent is also (maybe largely) bound up with this agent's personal commitment to these reasons – a commitment that affects how the agent is motivated with respect to them. The "incapacity" to do other than the course of action that is being called motivationally inevitable would appear to be something that is willed by the agent, however much the reasons are also endorsed by his society. "Here I stand, I can do no other," proclaimed Luther; such a proclamation seems to rest on an agent's commitment to a norm in such a way that when its reasons are decisive, the agent conceives himself as literally (motivationally) unable to follow any other course. And what can be so embraced may be ignoble as well as noble, since nonmoral as well as moral norms can be ones to which we make this kind of commitment. (For example, an agent might be incapacitated to do anything other than pursue a life of greed, having embraced an ideal of personal wealth.) Hence, to talk about authority in this context, is to talk about the way in which an agent is motivationally related to a norm, by virtue of having made this special commitment. But once again, this is not the notion of authority that will enable us to understand the special significance of the deontic operator.

That significance can only be understood by pursuing a third sense of the notion of authority. It is this sense that we are ultimately interested in and that is presupposed by the other two conceptions of authority just explicated. Whether or not a reason is decisive for us, and whether or not we have committed ourselves to it such that we find our following it motivationally inevitable, it is still, by virtue of being a reason that we have, something that prescribes a course of action for us. This third sense of authority involves the idea of this prescriptivity.

In trying to get clear on this notion of authority, it is important to clarify the extent to which I'm *not* referring to the notion of "justi-

[7] See Williams (1981c), especially pp. 130–1.

fication" as it is often understood. Terms slip and slide in the theoretical discourse in this area so let me stipulate precisely what I mean by 'justification' here, so that it will be clearer how the notion of authority is different. To speak of a norm, or the reason it generates, as justified for an agent is to be saying something epistemological – that is, that there is warrant to believe that this is a reason for this agent. Or in other words, it is a way of saying that a norm specifying a reason for this agent has been correctly identified. It is to answer the question, "Is this a norm that gives us a reason to x?" Hence a theory of the justification of norms is one that tells us how to *identify* the norms that generate reasons for certain agents. So, for example, Williams's identification internalism identifies the reasons that we have by linking them, via deliberation (for example, instrumental deliberation) to motives.

But a theory of the authority of norms tries to explain *what it means* for a norm to be "applicable" to us. The word 'applicable' is a poor one, because norms don't merely "apply" to us, they *direct* us. Indeed, we use all sorts of words to elaborate on this applicability: besides "authority," we speak of a norm's "prescriptivity" or its "obligatory force" over us, its "compelling nature" or its "pull," its status as an "order" or a "command" (and not a mere "suggestion"). Note that all norms that are authoritative are also justified. That is, normative authority presupposes that the norm in question is justified in the sense that it is correct to say that it specifies a reason for x-ing for an agent.

Sometimes the word 'authoritative' in our normative talk mixes together what I have called "justification," "decisiveness," and "authority." Suppose you say to a friend, "Look, this is the principle applying to your situation – you've got to act in accordance with it, because it's authoritative for you." Here you are saying three things: first, that it is correct to say that the reason generated by this principle is one that your friend has (that is, it is a justified reason for her); second, that it is the decisive reason for your friend in this situation (that is, that it is a decisive reason for her); and third, that this reason "binds" your friend, such that she "has got to" follow it (that is, that it is a consideration about how to act that is authoritative – even if its force may be something that your friend resists, and fails to be motivated by). It is this last sense – the sense in which a reason is taken to be a directive for the agent – even if the reason has little or no motivational power – that I am interested in pursuing here.

We intuitively recognize this compelling quality to a reason – a quality that is quite different from what might be called the "drive" of a desire. There have been some attempts to characterize it in the literature. For example, Blackburn notes, "It seems to be a conceptual truth that to regard something as good is to feel a pull towards promoting or choosing it, or towards wanting other people to feel the pull towards promoting or choosing it."[8] Now if by "pull" Blackburn means something motivational, then the arguments against motivational internalism in the last chapter challenge the idea that there is any necessary connection, conceptual or otherwise, between such a pull, so understood, and moral reasons (certainly not conceptual necessity, since whatever is part of our concept of a reason, we are interested in determining what we *in fact* feel when we believe we have a reason). But we might understand the idea of "pull" in a nonmotivational way – for example, as some kind of inescapable attraction to the directive – some sense of its being compelling, which is nonetheless different from feeling moved to follow the directive. McDowell suggests a similar idea when he says that "explanation of behavior by reasons purports to show the favourable light in which an agent saw his action."[9] Again, there is the suggestion that a reason has a special kind of compellingness about it, so that to explain one's actions in terms of reason is to show them as compelling or attractive in this special sense.

This compelling quality of reasons is not, however, the same as the feeling of liking or approving the directive of a reason. It is easy to give examples of people who know they have a reason to x, and who not only do not like the action that the reason directs, but even despise it. For example, a person can have, and know that she has, a reason to go to the doctor, and thus feel the "pull" of doing so, and yet still despise the idea of doing so. In the garden of Eden, Eve knew she had a reason (indeed, the best of all possible reasons) not to eat the fruit of the tree of knowledge, and yet she was not positively disposed toward this reason, and in fact, defied it. Moreover, in order to account for the fact of immorality and irrationality, we would seem to have to recognize that human beings can take

---

[8] Blackburn (1984, 188), quoted by Brink (1989).
[9] John McDowell (1978), "Are Moral Requirements Hypothetical Imperatives?"

(highly) negative attitudes toward what they know to be their reasons.[10]

So there is something about the state of "believing one has a reason" that is distinctive. Being in such a state tends to involve a certain kind of "feel," even as being in a (mere) desiring state tends to have a certain (and quite different) "feel" to it. We experience reasons as "directives" – they "govern" us.

But complicating matters is the fact that not all reasons are authoritative in the same way, or to put it slightly differently, not all the directives delivered by our reasons have the same kind of directive force. In particular, some reasons command us, and thereby give us mandates, and others direct us in ways that indicate permissions, rather than commands. I may have a reason on Sunday to get my hair cut, but this reason will never have the kind of directive force of, say, my reason to care for my baby. Following Raz (1975/1990),[11] I will distinguish between *permissive* and *mandatory* reasons. Mandatory reasons are those whose directives are, in a certain situation, *necessary*, so that we say that in those circumstances, an agent *must* do as the norm directs. Later we will be trying to say more about what this necessity is. It is doubtful that there is any norm whose reasons are, in all circumstances, mandatory (even a moral norm is likely going to be outweighed by another moral norm in some circumstances).[12] There are also norms whose reasons are merely *permissive*. These reasons merely guide us – in the sense that they purport to give directives that it is a "good idea" to follow, such as the reason to get a hair cut on Sunday afternoon.

Such reasons lack the mandatory character of reasons that we think are "more important" (such as caring for one's children, or not murdering one's neighbor). So when we have a permissive reason, we are allowed, but not required, to act on it, so that we say in such circumstances that an agent may, but need not, do as any of these norms direct. (It is like the difference between saying that an action is a good idea and saying that it must occur.) In contrast, when we

[10] I discuss what I call the "defiance" of reasons, and consider it as an explanation of immorality and irrationality, in my "Mens Rea" (1990).

[11] Raz (1975/1990). The 1990 edition has a new postscript.

[12] It may even be outweighed by nonmoral norms. Susan Wolf (1982) suggests that this might be the case more often than moral theorists have wanted to admit.

have a mandatory reason, we say that the reason is sufficiently powerful that the action it directs is required, so that it is ordered in a strong sense. (Note, however, that even if we are free to choose between a number of permissive reasons in a certain situation, there may still be a background mandatory reason directing us to act from *some* permissive reason or other in this situation.)

Mandatoriness should not be confused with decisiveness. Decisiveness is a notion that has to do with the competition that can occur between reasons. Permissive reasons, for example, can compete against one another, and one of them can "win out" in our deliberations, making that reason decisive, as when, for example, I have to decide whether to get my hair cut on Sunday, or go to a new exhibition of nineteenth-century Japanese prints. In this situation, none of the reasons presents itself to me as a required order, and yet I can think of one of the reasons as decisive in the situation (so that we may speak of "decisive permissive reasons"). Some philosophers also believe that it is possible for there to be competition between mandatory reasons; in this case, we are forced to deliberate between two orders that present themselves to us as requirements. Deciding that one of them is the decisive reason would not, in this view, remove the mandatory nature of the reason not chosen, with the result that the agent would be in a tragic situation – forced to perform only one of the actions that are mandatory for him. Someone who believes such a situation is possible believes that human beings can face severe and irreconcilable moral conflict, and the possibility of such conflict has been explored in the recent literature.[13]

However, what permissive and mandatory reasons have in common, such that they are all *reasons*, is their authority – the sense in which they are supposed to have for us a "compelling rightness." As I noted in the last chapter, authority is not the same as motivational efficacy, but it does seem as if there is some kind of link between the two. Even if one is not some kind of motivational internalist, one will likely still believe that it is possible for human beings to be motivated by reasons. That is, one may reject the idea that motivational efficacy is either a necessary or a sufficient condition of something's being a reason, but one may believe, nonetheless, that a reason *can* be motivational, at least in certain circumstances. That is, both sorts of reasons have a pull, an attractiveness, a com-

---

[13] See, for example, Philippa Foot (1983) and Williams (1985, 176–7).

pelling quality, and it is this compelling quality that when we act on reasons, is that "for the sake of which" we act.

However, the motivational power of reasons is quite distinctive by virtue of the way reasons are something that we act "on," because of what we take to be their rightness. When we say that an agent acts "on," or "for the sake of" a reason, we are trying to say something about how this agent is "lured" to the action *by* the reason, as opposed to being driven or pushed into the action by some inner motivational force. The language of choice therefore fits with action from reasons, in a way that it cannot do with nonrational motivations. Think about how we act on a mere craving – the chocolate bar presents itself, and without thinking I grab it. I am driven by my craving, such that I not only act unthinkingly, but also in a way that is not directed by some sense of "what ought to be." The object of my craving does not present itself to me under the guise of "the right thing to have at this time"; it is merely something that I grab. (Analogously, the horse grabs the hay; he does not act on a reason to eat the hay.) While we can unreflectively act from a reason (as when we unthinkingly pull a drowning child from the river), we still think that this sort of action represents a choice of something that "ought to be" (in this case, an immediate and obvious choice of one course of action, where there were no serious competitors), whereas when we are "pushed" into an action by a craving or ill-considered desire, there is no such choice or decision. It is as if we are acting like animals.

Note that I chose the word 'craving' deliberately, because our use of the term 'desire' often coincides with or overlaps with our use of the word 'reason,' as in "she desired to benefit the battered women's shelter." The term 'desire' is therefore ambiguous, capable of covering both reasons and nonrational motivations. Moreover, intuitively we think that a motivation that is initially unreflective and visceral can become a reason if it is reflected on, such that its object becomes something we take to have this "compelling rightness" (either as a permission or as a mandatory command). Hence, in the literature, theorists such as Williams and Gauthier continually speak of ill-considered desires as not giving us reasons for action (although both acknowledge, because of examples such as the rescuing from drowning case noted above, that a reason need not be explicitly reflected on immediately prior to my acting on it in order for it to be my reason).

This distinction between, on the one hand, reasons that are compelling considerations on which we choose to act, and on the other hand, nonrational motivators as mere "drivers" of action, is at the heart of Kant's distinction between the difference between acting from reason and acting from desires. However, unlike Kant, I do not want to suggest that one can only act from a reason if one is acting, say, from some kind of moral law. Indeed, there are all sorts of reasons, many of them quite quotidian (for example, reasons to cut one's hair, mow the lawn, eat with the fork in the right hand, and so on) that cannot be left out of any complete analysis of the nature of reasons, and that have little or nothing to do with high-minded moral reasoning or moral action. Nor do I mean to suggest that this compelling quality must be understood as somehow "in the world," and thus a part of our reality. Having isolated the distinctive "feel" of reasons, and that which makes action from reasons quite different from actions generated by nonreasons, I now want to investigate what this "compelling rightness" is. Two theses are possible with respect to the authority of reasons, one of which is quite acceptable to the naturalist, the other of which is decidedly not.

TWO THESES OF NORMATIVE AUTHORITY

Suppose someone asked, "Why should Jane call Albert's harming of the cat wrong?" There are two kinds of answers to this question. One can say either, "That Albert's conduct is wrong is a (necessary) truth, and she has a (necessary) reason to believe what is true"; or "Given the physical structure of the world, the physical and psychological nature of Jane, and the effect on her nature by her society, she (merely) believes, in view of being taught a (societally invented) standard of wrongness, that it is 'wrong'." The first answer implicitly posits the existence of a norm "in the world" (somehow, someway) whose authoritative reason connects Jane to these events; in particular, the norm gives Jane a necessary reason to believe that which is true. The second answer instead implicitly posits a norm that is the (mere) invention of human beings in a society, and whose reasons are (merely) perceived or understood or felt as authoritative, given the nature of human psychology and the influence of culture. In elaborating these answers, we will develop two opposing theories of the authority of reasons.

The Psycho-Social Thesis

Consider a norm in the sport of dressage, requiring owners of horses performing dressage tests in a competition to present the horse in the show ring with its mane braided. It purports to give those who recognize it a reason to act in a certain way, where this reason is decisive in some circumstances (for example, it is not decisive if one's horse is an Arabian, but it is decisive if one's horse is a thorough-bred). We intuitively think that this norm is authoritative only for the people in the sport, and that its authority over them is explainable by reference to social and psychological contingencies. In particular, the fact that people who participate in this sport think they ought to obey it is explained by the social pressure on these people and their psychological response to this pressure when they take themselves to be subject to the norm. So to explain the authority of this or any similar norm, such as a rule in baseball, or a norm of etiquette, or a norm about taste in foods, we would tell a story locating the social forces that generated the norm, and the psychological responses to those forces by certain people that give these norms their power. In this view, the norm is the (mere) invention of particular human beings by virtue of their interests, and the sense such people have that a norm authoritatively applies to them (that is, that it is an "order" for them, such that they are directed to follow it) is entirely a matter of social and psychological contingencies. Or, alternatively, to say that norms are "obligatory" for certain people is to say that their society and their psychology are such that they regard these norms as governing them in an inescapable way. This sort of norm, which I will call culture-dependent, is ubiquitous, and includes norms of etiquette, rules of various sports, and ideals of physical beauty.

However, some theorists believe that *all* norms, including all moral norms, are culture-dependent. Those who believe this explain the authority of all norms as (what I will call) a "psycho-social" phenomenon. Of course, a sophisticated version of this account is going to want to explain why "common sense" tells us there is a difference between (what clearly seem to be) "artificial" norms such as monopoly rules, dressage standards, and codes of etiquette on the one hand, and moral norms such as "do not murder" and "treat all people as equals." There are a number of ways to construct such a sophisticated view, and each of these I take to be a variant of the psycho-social thesis about normative authority.

First, there is the "expressivist" variant of the psycho-social thesis, a version of which has recently been propounded by Allan Gibbard. In this view, the apparently "special" authority of moral norms is (in some way) a function of how people accept them. That is, our sense of their necessity is a product of our commitment to them (but not the other way around), and thus something that we understand by investigating human psychology (including, perhaps, its socio-biological origins) and the way it attracts us to the construction of and commitment to norms of a certain content. In this view, our sense that reasons emanating from norms have a certain compelling rightness that takes either a mandatory or a permissive form is a (mere) feeling that is attached to directives, such that we accept them, feel compelled by them, and are motivated by them. (The emotive nature of authority, on this view, allows the expressivist a natural link between authority, so understood, and motivational force.) Everything that I have said here about the authority of norms is therefore explicable in terms of theories of human psychology, sociology, and biology, which explain how our feelings become engaged by norms that are socially useful and perhaps also biologically inevitable.

Second, there is a cognitive version of the psycho-social thesis. Imagine a theorist who postulated the existence, in human brains, of a special kind of thinking. Call this "normative" thinking. In this view, characteristic of our mental life are not only desires and beliefs, but also norms and the reasons they generate. Hence, to think "I ought to do x" is to be in a distinctive cognitive state. In particular, one engages a part of the brain that "invests" normativity into a possible action, so that this authority is not a feeling but something more like a form of thought. Someone attracted to this view might also contend that usually (albeit not always) this normative state has a connection to our motivational structure, in a way that explains the sense in which we feel we can act *from* our belief that we ought to perform a certain action.

Third, there is what I will call the "error theory" variant of this view. This view, a variant of which is propounded by J. L. Mackie, explains the authority of reasons as deriving from people's acceptance of a certain kind of theory. As normative language develops, this view says that people come to develop a theory about what it means. The theory that has been current in our society is the objectivist's account of authority, as something that is independent of human psychology and culture. Because they accept such a theory, people in many cultures take what they identify as reasons to be innately compelling, such that they direct us (either via mandates or via permissions) to act in certain ways "objectively." But in fact this theory is in error, because there is no such objective authority, so that all norms and reasons are human inventions. Hence, in this view, people believe that the authority of many norms is objective because they accept a false theory – a theory whose acceptance may nonetheless be highly attractive to them (for psychological reasons). Because of this error, they behave as if they are compelled to follow what they take to be reasons, but they do so because of a deep-seated and metaphysical mistake.[14] Clearly, this version of the psycho-social thesis requires an explanation of why this mistake is so common across cultures, and why it seems to persist despite the efforts of so many naturalists (such as Mackie) to "expose" it.

All these versions of the psycho-social thesis accept the same basic strategy for explaining the authority of reasons – that authority is understood to be merely in the head (explicated as a feeling, or a cognitive state, or a theoretical belief), and its origins are explicable by virtue of human psychology, human biology, and/or human sociology.

The Objectivist Thesis

Those who are normative objectivists maintain that some norms (but not all norms – for example, not the norms of dressage) are examples of what I will call culture-independent or objective norms. The authority of these norms is supposed to be independent of social and psychological contingencies. Rather than explicating these norms' authority by reference to social and psychological contingencies, objectivists argue that such (independent) authority is the reason the society has (or ought to have) such norms as part of its culture, and they insist that no matter the facts of our society or our psychology, we ought to recognize, accept, and obey them.

Moral objectivists choose this account to understand the nature of

---

[14] See Mackie (1977), Chapter 1.

the authority of moral norms (perhaps also accepting it for other norms as well). They may also want to append to this view the supervenience theorist's analysis of moral properties. Recall that we said that norms give us reasons that are decisive in the circumstances. Specifying those circumstances might involve making reference not only to natural objects or events, but also (and more likely) to moral evaluations of these natural objects and events. The supervenience theorist offers an explanation of how these moral evaluations can be related in a law-like way to these natural objects and events. Even though his analysis does not explain – or justify – our beliefs, actions, or emotions with respect to these moral evaluations, it offers an account of how there can be a "moral world" to which (objectively authoritative) norms connect us.

The moral objectivist maintains that the authority of a moral norm does not merely consist in you or your society *thinking* that you have such a reason. Nor does she believe that you only "have" the reason if you happen to be aware of, or know about it. Instead, she will insist that its authority is "objective," which means that the reason it gives you in the circumstances that it specifies holds for you no matter the social or psychological conditions. Hence it is a reason applicable to your deliberations, a consideration relevant to your acting, choosing, and believing, and a decisive consideration in the circumstances it specifies. It is at this point that the objectivist resorts to the term 'necessity' to describe the nature of the authority of such a norm. To say that this reason holds, no matter the social or psychological contingencies, is, one might think, to say that it holds necessarily. To put it more precisely, for as long as we are moral agents – that is, subjects to whom moral reasons apply (leaving aside for now the criteria specifying moral agency) – the moral objectivist claims that the reasons given us by moral norms are reasons that we have necessarily, no matter the state of our psychology, our profession or interests, the views of our society, or our metaphysical or religious commitments. Whether or not we also have motives by virtue of knowing these reasons, whether or not they are decisive in the circumstances, and whether or not we have committed ourselves to them so thoroughly that we find it is impossible not to comply with them, these reasons direct us, or oblige us. Note that this thesis is separate from a thesis about motivation. When a moral objectivist says that someone "has" a moral reason, he is not saying that ipso facto this person has a motivation sufficient to move him to act from that reason if he knows of it. As I have discussed in the last chapter, moral objectivists can disagree on the extent to which reasons have motivational efficacy.

The necessity invoked by the moral objectivist to characterize the authority of moral reasons is not something unique to moral reasons. It is a necessity that attends any reasons generated by norms that are supposed to be "prescriptive" in a culture-independent way. Or, alternatively, it is a necessity by virtue of which a norm is supposed to be "objective," whether or not it is a moral norm. Traditionally, certain moral theorists, especially Kantians, have supposed that moral norms have a *special* necessity, unlike that of other norms, such that moral norms "obligate" us in a particularly powerful and undeniable way. But whether or not this is true, those who consider moral norms objective are assuming that they share with other (purportedly) culture-independent norms a certain "culture-independent prescriptivity" – and it is this prescriptivity that I am attempting to explicate here.

To understand this notion of objective authority, consider that it figures in a moral objectivist view in a number of ways. First, and most importantly, it appears in the theory's explanation of how it is that moral norms "apply" to us. For example, to say that we have moral reasons for action, in the objectivist view, is to say that these reasons, no matter what we may think or how we have been raised, have authority over us. Such authority is "outside" the agent, and that to which she is responding when she says that she understands that she ought to act from them. To speak of authority as "outside" the agent is perhaps a regrettably Platonist way of putting the point, but by using this word I mean to convey the objectivist's idea that the authority is not the invention of the agent, nor of human communities, but something to which agents and human communities respond.

Second, the moral objectivist assumes that the notion of authority is one that human beings can "see" or (in some way) discover. The fact that human beings are able to (in some way) sense or perceive this authority explains why they accept certain reasons and not others. And they will claim that when we do accept an objectively authoritative reason, we usually "feel" or "comprehend" its (objective) authority, which means experiencing a sense of its pull, such that we take it to be something that we are in certain circumstances bound to act upon.

Third, the moral objectivist claims that having felt this authority, it is – at least sometimes – an authority for the sake of which we can act, so that it is motivationally efficacious. However, as I've noted several times, the exact nature of the motivational efficacy of reasons, and indeed any psychological effects associated with believing that one has a reason, are issues about which moral objectivists can dispute.

So, to review, there are two kinds of authority that one can posit for norms, and in particular, for moral norms:

1. **Psycho-social authority:** A norm has this authority when the account of the obligatory force of its reason to act, choose, or believe in a certain way in certain circumstances makes reference (only) to certain contingent facts about the society and the psychology of the people who take themselves to be subject to the norm. Error theories, expressivist theories, and cognitive theories of normativity presuppose this conception of normative authority.

2. **Objective authority:** A norm has this authority when the account of the obligatory force of its reason to act, choose, or believe in a certain way in certain circumstances is that it is necessary – that is, that it holds regardless of social or psychological contingencies.

Since moral objectivism is the view that there are moral norms that have objective authority in the sense just defined, to evaluate the scientific acceptability of moral objectivism we must investigate the scientific acceptability of the thesis that some norms have objective authority.

HAVING REASONS

Is the idea of objective authority acceptable from a naturalist standpoint? I will argue that for two reasons it violates naturalist scruples: First, the idea of an authority that is objective is ineffable – that is, impossible to pin down in a way that seems to make sense. From a naturalist point of view, this ineffability militates against its being a real phenomenon in the world, and is instead a good indication that the authority of reasons is a psycho-social phenomenon. Second, central to moral objectivism is the idea that this authority is a kind of "compelling rightness" that exists independent of human psychology and culture, and that is that "for the sake of which" we act when we act morally. But I shall argue that explanations presupposing objective moral authority are instances of final cause explanations – a species of explanation that all scientific theories reject. Hence, basic to the scientific point of view is a repudiation of the idea that there is any compelling rightness in the world, or any entities that move or take action "for the sake of" something else.

The Ineffability of the Objectivist's Ought

When a moral objectivist says that moral reasons have objective authority, what precisely does she mean? One common way of explaining her meaning is to say that moral reasons are in some way necessary for the moral agent. The term "necessity" is frequently used by objectivists, figuring prominently, for example, in the moral writings of Immanuel Kant.[15] But what kind of necessity is the normative objectivist invoking, and how does this term convey the idea of the objective authority of the reasons that are taken to be objective, such as moral reasons?

Richard Boyd assumes that an objectivist must have *logical* necessity in mind, and on that basis argues that no naturalist can accept the objectivist's position. To quote Boyd:

> It might be held, for example, that the recognition that one course of action is morally preferable to another *necessarily* provides a reason (even if not a decisive one) to prefer the morally better course of action. Mere facts (especially *natural* facts) cannot have this sort of logical connection to rational choice or reasons for action. . . . It is of course true that the naturalistic moral realist must deny that moral judgments necessarily provide reasons for action.[16]

Boyd is saying here that it does not make sense for us to think that there is a logical implication between a sentence such as "Petting the cat has positive moral properties; beating the cat does not" and the sentence "The boy necessarily has a reason to pet the cat rather than to beat it." It is not just that science disallows such a logical implication; Boyd's point is that no believable theory of the world posits

---

[15] See, for example, Kant, (1785, 37).
[16] Boyd (1988, 214).

such a logical connection between facts and reasons for action. Hence Boyd is saying that if we were to understand the objective authority of moral norms in terms of such a logical connection, we would be violating the strictures of naturalism because facts cannot have this logical (or conceptual) connection to action. Indeed, in Boyd's view, naturalism simply amounts to the denial of a logical connection between an action's moral characteristics and a reason for performing it.

Boyd doesn't mind the concession because he believes that as a matter of contingent fact, our recognition of what is good and bad has a motivational affect on (almost) all of us. So, for example, he thinks that for most of us, to understand that cat-burning is bad leads to the triggering of motivations that lead us to try to stop cat-burnings if we see them. This, of course, isn't true of everyone – it isn't true, for example, for Albert the cat-burner, who may well be motivated to burn cats by the realization that it is wrong. So this contingent connection with our motivational structure explains, in Boyd's view, why moral knowledge doesn't always lead to moral behavior.

However, Boyd's view is not only a repudiation of motivational internalism. It is also a repudiation of the idea that moral knowledge gives rise to moral reasons. To see this, consider that Boyd's position not only separates Albert's knowledge that cat-burning is wrong from a motive not to engage in it; it also fails to locate any way in which Albert has a reason not to burn cats. Albert's labeling the activity 'wrong' is not only without intrinsic motivational impact on Boyd's view, but it is also without any authoritative impact. Albert is free to say, in Boyd's view, "Okay, cat burning is wrong, but what does that label have to do with whether or not I should do it? I want to do it, so I have no reason not to do so." In other words, there is no way to say that Albert has a reason not to burn cats if, as it happens, he would like to do so. Because Boyd refuses to recognize any necessary connection between the label "wrongness" and some form of human thought or behavior, his view fails to incorporate norms that link human beings (their thoughts, actions, feelings, and so on) with purported moral characteristics of the world. So, like the supervenience theorists discussed in Chapter 2, Boyd recognizes moral properties and motives, but has no room for (indeed, deliberately leaves out) reasons and the norms that generate them, so that they can only appear in this theory as contingent psychological responses to "moral facts" in his sense. I do not see, therefore, how Boyd can be a moral objectivist, if he is unable to secure, in his theory, the idea that is central to the moral objectivist's view – namely, that we ought not to kill our neighbors, neglect our children, be indifferent to the plight of the poor, and so forth. He gets moral properties, but leaves us free to do whatever we want with respect to these properties – and even more alarmingly, free to form any belief with respect to these properties.

The most that Boyd's position allows is that we can say that something is a reason for an agent if her psychology is such that she happens to regard it as such. Such a position would involve saying that whereas Jane and Albert both "see" that harming animals is wrong, Jane's psychology is such that she responds to this fact by taking herself to have a reason to refrain from harming them, whereas Albert responds to this fact by taking himself to have a reason to harm them. But note that there is *nothing* in Boyd's theory that would license us to criticize Albert and commend Jane (the most we could say is that Jane's response is the "more usual" – if that is even true). Moreover, in Boyd's view, Albert's harming the cat is perfectly consistent with Albert's understanding that this action is bad, for there is nothing in Boyd's theory that would give Albert a reason to stop burning the cat by virtue of its wrongness.

The fact that it fails to secure the sort of moral reasons that are basic to the moral objectivist's view means that Boyd's position fails as an elucidation of moral objectivism. Nonetheless, even if Boyd's positive views don't succeed as a way of securing the moral reasons that are necessary for a moral objectivist theory, he makes a powerful case that the appeal to logic won't work to explain the necessity of moral reasons. (And, indeed, logical necessity may simply be a species of the authoritative necessity that we are attempting to understand.)

So might we cash out the necessity of reasons (such as moral reasons) by saying that their authority is *metaphysically* necessary? To say that something is metaphysically necessary is to claim that it could not have been otherwise in certain respects.[17] Or in other words, metaphysical necessity is understood to follow from the essence of objects. It has been held, for example, that it is meta-

---

[17] See S. Kripke (1971, 1980) and H. Putnam (1977). But see also Putnam (1990), "Is Water Necessarily H$_2$O?" and Brink (1989), 165–6.

physically necessary for water to be identical with H_2O, or that a human being could not have been a mountain.[18] Using possible world analysis, we would say that in all possible worlds, water is H_2O or that Cicero is identical with Tully.

So if we say that moral reasons are metaphysically necessary, it seems we would be saying that the authority of moral norms is such that the reasons they generate hold in all possible worlds for all moral agents. As we have already discussed, a number of philosophers have invoked such necessity by proposing that moral properties are necessarily (metaphysically) identical with, or at least constituted by, natural properties by virtue of the fact that they supervene on these natural properties (for example, Davidson, 1970, 214; Blackburn 1971: 105–16; Wiggins 1980: 109–11, 214–5; Brink, Chapters 6 and 7, and especially 160), and they take such a position to be permitted by naturalism.

Whether such talk of metaphysical necessity is occult is a disputed question. Quine believes it is; many others do not. But that issue is beside the point for our purposes, because the necessity invoked by those who wish to capture the normativity of reasons is not the same as the necessity discussed by Kripke and others. The way in which moral reasons are supposed to be necessary for us is different from the way in which water is H_2O, and even different from the way in which the infliction of gratuitous suffering is wrong. Those who invoke metaphysical necessity speak of a "necessity *that*" as in, "It is necessary that water is H_2O." However, normative necessity is about the relationship between certain aspects of the world and *us*, linking us to these aspects of the world in a distinctive way. It is a "necessity *to*", as in "It is necessary to believe that killing the innocent is wrong" or "It is necessary to refrain from being cruel to animals." It is a necessity that has to do with us, in particular, with our beliefs, actions, choices, feelings, and intentions, and not a necessity that has to do with the way objects in the world are.

To see this, let us return to Harman's example of Jane's seeing Albert hitting a cat with a stick for the fun of it, and calling Albert's act wrong. As I noted earlier, there are two ways of explaining why Jane says this. One can say: "The wrongness of Albert's conduct is a (necessary) truth, and she has a (necessary) reason to believe what is true." Or one can say: "Given the physical structure of the world,

---

[18] See Kripke (1971; 1980, 97–105) and Putnam (1977; 1990).

the physical and psychological nature of Jane, and the effect on her nature by her society, she responds to these events by calling them 'wrong'." The first answer calls to our attention an objective norm that connects Jane to these events, in this instance a norm that gives her a necessary reason to believe that which is true. The second answer invokes no such norm, but only causal interactions between the world and Jane, such that she (merely) *thinks* Albert's action is wrong. But those who believe moral norms are culture-independent will say that there is a norm: "Human beings should not be cruel to animals"; that this norm gives us a metaphysically necessary reason not to be cruel to animals; that Jane knew about this reason; and that *by virtue of that knowledge*, she called Albert's action wrong. So the necessity invoked by the objectivist is involved in the relationship between moral properties and us, the moral agents, whereas, as I've noted, Kripke's metaphysical necessity concerns the *essence* of things, and not the relationship between us and various aspects of the world.

But although it may be easy to recognize this idea of normative necessity, it is certainly not easy to figure out what it is. Indeed, it isn't even clear that we should be talking about *necessity* here at all, insofar as it suggests the Kripkean idea of metaphysical necessity, and misleads us into thinking that we're talking about the essences of things. Perhaps a term such as "inescapability" would be better, since the idea seems to be that norms directed at us give us reasons (albeit reasons that are only decisive reasons in certain circumstances) that are ours "no matter what," for as long as we remain moral agents. But even this term is wrong and misleading because we all know that in a certain sense, moral reasons *are* (all too) escapable, in that many people do not act from them (even when they know them).

Indeed, it is part of our understanding of normative authority that it applies to creatures who can defy it. As Kant says, although we speak of an objective (moral) principle as "necessitating" the will, this does not mean that the will is of the sort that always acts from such a principle, and certainly not that it must do. In fact, the opposite is true:

All imperatives are expressed by an *'ought'* (*Sollen*). By this they make the relation of an objective law of reason to a will which is not necessarily determined by this law in virtue of its subjective constitution (the relation of necessitation). They say that something would be good to do or to leave undone; only they say it to a will which does not always do a thing because it has been informed that this is a good thing to do. The *practically good* is that which determines the will by concepts of reason, and therefore not by subjective causes, but objectively – that is, on grounds valid for every rational being as such. It is distinguished from the *pleasant* as that which influences the will, not as a principle of reason valid for everyone, but solely through the medium of sensation by purely subjective causes valid only for the senses of this person or that.[19]

There are a number of interesting points in this passage. First, there is the idea that moral reasons don't determine the will of human beings in the way that, say, they determine the will of a (perfectly good) divine creature (such as God or the angels). We are "necessitated" to act from these reasons, not determined (necessarily) to act from them. The "ought" expresses both the rightness of these reasons for us and the fact that we may not will to follow them. Second, there is the idea that if we do follow them, it is not because we are (merely) influenced to do so, in the way that the thought of the pleasant influences us to act so as to seek it. Instead, we follow them because we understand their rightness for us, or, as Kant puts it, because we understand that these are grounds for action "valid for every rational being." So we are moved to act from moral reasons *because we understand* their objective authority. It is by virtue of that authority that we can speak about these reasons as "necessitating," in the sense that their rightness inescapably governs us, such that when we know about that governance it can (but need not) motivate us (as moral beings) to act from these reasons. It is that "for the sake of which" we act.

Inspired by this Kantian passage, suppose we try one final way of understanding the nature of the "necessity" of moral norms that are held to be objectively authoritative. Let us say that moral reasons generated by objectively authoritative moral norms are necessary in the sense that their *governance* over us is inescapable. And by 'inescapable' here I mean that these reasons "apply" to us "no matter

---

[19] Kant (1785, 81).

what." According to this way of thinking about objective authority, no matter what we may do or think, we are directed by these reasons – either in the form of permissions or in the form of mandates. And this governance is inescapable or necessary because there is no way that we can throw it off, or change it by our actions, beliefs, or social systems. I will define a normative necessity operator (or NN) that works by operating on an action type of which a moral agent is capable (for example, believing, acting, intending, choosing, or feeling) connected with some propositional content related to that action type:

[NN operator] [(action type) + (propositional content)]

as in:

[NN] [(believing) (that gratuitous cruelty to animals is wrong)]
[NN] [(acting) (so that gratuitous cruelty to animals is stopped)]

So understood, normative necessity is still a metaphysical concept because it is supposed to hold regardless of whether or not we know about it or are aware of it. It is just not the metaphysical concept that is usually referred to by the term "necessity."

This way of thinking about authority is, I think, closest to the way that the authority of reasons *feels* to us – that is, it approximates what the experience of "having a reason" is like for those who understand and act from reasons. As I discussed earlier, reasons feel like orders – strong in the case of mandates, weak in the case of permissions, but directives nonetheless, with an inescapable rightness about them. Yet, as I will now explain, a naturalist critic will say that even if such a view correctly captures the phenomenology of "having a reason," it nonetheless fails to be plausible as a description of something real in the world because we have no coherent account of where these directives come from and no coherent account of why their governance is inescapable.

First, if reasons are directives, from whom or what do they come? There are two ways to answer this question: The first way appeals to God. The second way tries to avoid such an appeal by finding directive authority in human reason. We shall consider the viability of each answer in turn.

Suppose we regard reasons as emanating from a God who orders those whom she considers moral agents to believe certain things, act in certain ways, choose certain options, and so on. This view makes sense of reasons as, quite literally, orders, as well as the idea that these orders, whether in the form of permissions or mandates, are inescapable in that no creature under the purview of this God can escape them. No matter the people's interests, desires, concerns, or social structures, this God's orders "necessarily" apply to them – that is, these orders apply no matter the contingencies of their situation. Indeed, the necessity of the reasons that are supposed to be generated by culture-independent norms is so much like the necessity of inescapable divine "marching orders" that one might reasonably conclude that the notion of normative authority has, at least in part, religious origins. And, indeed, this has been suggested, – for example, by Anscombe.[20] (So the symbol representing the normative necessity operator might be a hand with an outstretched forefinger, representing the directive gesture of a supreme commander.[21])

There are, however, a host of problems with this way of explaining how reasons' authority is directive. First, many will insist that we do not have any evidence that such a divine commander exists. Second, even if we hypothesized her existence, we do not have any evidence that all and only the directives we consider reasons have been commanded by *her*. We lack stone tablets with commandments written on them these days. Third, the explanation sounds odd indeed as an account of the authority of permissive reasons. An all-powerful God would seem to have better things to do with her time than issue directives with respect to the best way to spend one's Saturday afternoon. Fourth, the view doesn't so much explain the nature of objective authority as it does move the mystery up a level. If reasons are directives that govern us because they are issued by some divine commander, then we understand their authority over us by virtue of the fact that this commander has authority over us. But such an explanation makes the divine commander conceptually prior to moral norms, and therefore explains their authority as de-

---

[20] G. E. M. Anscombe (1981).

[21] It might be thought that this idea makes the idea of moral commands lawlike, in the face of disagreement over whether or not this is the appropriate way to understand them. But I do not mean to suggest that *what* God would direct toward us should be understood as laws, but only that however we understand the nature of the moral norms directed at us (whether they be laws, principles, or something else), their authority over us is objective, and involves the idea of necessity just explicated. For a discussion of the development of the idea that moral norms are laws, see Gisela Striker (1986).

riving from her. But where did *her* authority come from? To say that it came from the fact that she is God is just a way of saying that you believe she has that authority, not a way of explaining its origin. So this explanation seems merely to have traded one mystery for another. Fifth, and finally, this explanation will be unsatisfying for those moral theorists who believe that even if God exists, she herself is subject to these commands (that is, God is moral because it is right to be so). Such theorists regard the necessity of moral reasons as conceptually prior to God, inasmuch as she is the subject of its "orders" just as we are. So if even God is governed by morality, then appealing to her doesn't help us to understand the nature of that governance.

So let us consider the second strategy, which explains authority as directive by appealing to reason. By this Kantian conception of objective authority, the commander that gives us orders is not some divine being but our own reason. Each of us, in her own mind, therefore carries the commander who issues these commands, but this commander is not some contingent psychological force within us, but something that transcends the particularities of our persons, and is even part of the world. (Indeed, this may be true if the world is itself partly the creation of reason – that is, if we believe that something like Kant's argument in his *Critique of Pure Reason* is correct.) But again critics will insist that we have traded one mystery for another, for what is this transcendent conception of reason? (It's clearly more than the contingent forms of cognitive processing that tend, albeit not universally, to characterize the thinking of human beings.) And why think that this mysterious faculty is possessed of authority? Again, the authority of reasons is being explained by appeal to something from which that authority is supposed to be derived, but where does its authority come from? And why should we believe there is something called reason that governs us inescapably? Who says? Why? On pain of what if we don't obey? (And why should we care about any of the sanctions? Suppose the sanction is "being irrational." Why should we care about such a label?) This view therefore not only fails to be convincing about the source of the authority of moral reasons, but fails to locate anything that makes the governance of these reasons inescapable. Reasons' governance appears toothless.

However, the naturalists will insist that all these problems and questions go away if we explain the phenomenology of authority such that it is a psycho-social phenomenon rather than something that is supposed to be, in some way real, and in the world. We have no evidence that there is any divine commander, nor any transcendent notion of reason, but we do know that human societies put pressure on their members such that they feel compelled to engage in certain forms of behavior at certain times. Human psychology is such that we feel "required" to do many sorts of things, given the mores (cultural, moral, and so on) that we are reared to accept. Thus, psychologists speak of super-egos, consciences, feelings of being obliged or under some sort of duty – but all such talk is based on the contingent and socially influenced nature of the human mind. In the end, the objectivist's inability to say anything that is as sensible and clear as this account of authority may be the most damning indictment of the view in the eyes of many naturalists, and a clear indication that authority is nothing more than a human phenomenon, a product rather than a cause of the operations of the human mind.

How the Objectivist's 'Ought' Violates the Strictures of Science

The last section argued that the objectivist's thesis about authority was sufficiently unclear that the naturalist's rival thesis seems superior to it. In this section, I want to make the even stronger argument that to the extent that the objectivist's thesis can be understood (and as I noted earlier, there are serious problems in clarifying it), as long as we commit ourselves to the metaphysical and methodological assumptions of science, we cannot consider that thesis even possibly true.

In Chapter 1, I discussed how difficult it was to pin down precisely what "naturalism" is such that one can explain why it excludes moral objectivism. Part of the problem is that those who call themselves naturalists do not all accept one conception of what counts as "natural." Nor have they been able to define the natural as that which is pursued by science, since there is no unified agreement on how to understand what science is. To make matters worse, there is also no definitive argument showing that only the entities recognized in scientific theories can exist, meaning that even if the "natural" could be defined more precisely, naturalists lack a decisive argument showing that only the natural is real.

As I noted, this makes it hard for the naturalist to give a decisive argument against moral objectivism. However, I want to propose in this section that we can at least define a very general and "minimalist" conception of science, one that all naturalists can agree with, however much they may disagree about a more substantive and detailed conception of the nature of the scientific enterprise. With that argument in hand, we will be able to see why someone who is a committed naturalist will object to any moral objectivist theory, for this minimalist conception of science rules out the legitimacy of any moral objectivist explanation that relies on the idea of objective authority. As I noted in the last section, the idea of objective authority is very unclear; but to the extent that we can get at least an intuitive sense of it, the commitments of science preclude such a thing from being real.

What does a moral objectivist have to say about reasons in order to have a theory that is genuinely objectivist? As I pointed out in the last section, she must say, first of all, that there exist norms generating reasons to act that are directives applying to her no matter the contingencies of her situation. Second, she must say that these reasons, along with their authority, can be known by agents (for what would be the point of a theory that recognized these reasons, but despaired of our ability to know them)? Third, she must say that it is at least possible for us sometimes to act "on" or "for the sake of" the reason, as when we say that "Elizabeth acted on her duty to visit Aunt Ethel in the Hospital" or "Jane interfered with Albert's behavior because she thought it was her duty to stop cruelty to animals." To quote Kant, "Everything in nature works in accordance with laws. Only a rational being has the power to act *in accordance with his idea of* laws – that is, in accordance with principles – and only so has he a will."[22] As Kant appreciates, acting on a (moral) law is not like being caused to act by a (physical) law. One might say that a reason is not a causal push, but a "compelling pull," which compulsion is nonetheless something that an agent can choose to resist or defy.

The second and third points are as important as the first. With respect to the second point, any moral objectivist must insist that the moral norms whose reasons link people with certain events, actions and so on, are accessible to them, such that they can be known –

---

[22] Kant (1785), Chapter 2, p. 80.

whatever stand they take on the issue of the motivational efficacy of these norms once they are known. Otherwise, what would be the point of appealing to such norms? (And indeed, how could the moral objectivist come to know them unless they were knowable?) With respect to the third point, moral objectivists are going to have to say that at least sometimes, people can (somehow) be moved to act on a reason, such that it is something for the sake of which they act – otherwise, moral reasons would be empty and useless in their directive force – somewhat like aesthetic characteristics of the world, rather than aspects of it that are important in understanding human behavior and belief.

So does science permit explanations that rely on the idea of objective normative authority? As I reviewed in Chapter 1, there is no consensus at all in the philosophical community on any substantive conception of the natural, nor any consensus on what science is, such that this enterprise, so defined, could be taken to define the natural. But I want to propose a very basic tenet that is at least a necessary (albeit perhaps not a sufficient) condition of a theory such that it can be considered scientific – which is that such a theory never invoke the Aristotelian idea of final causes in any way. The explanations of science, even though they can take many forms (sometimes causal, sometimes not, sometimes mathematical, sometimes not) nonetheless do not take, and cannot take (on pain of being unscientific), a form that relies on the idea that any object in the world acts for the sake of something else, or has a goal or proper place, to which it tends in its motion.

An explanation in terms of final causes has three components. First, it assumes that there is a certain place, state of affairs, or kind of motion that is appropriate or "fitting" for an object. This place, state of affairs, or movement is thought to have some kind of compelling rightness. The world is therefore conceived to be so arranged that there are states of being that are appropriate or right for various sorts of objects.

Second, this explanation assumes that the object whose movement or state is to be explained is in some way able to respond to this compelling rightness. This response needn't take the form of being conscious of that rightness, and thus does not assume any agency on behalf of the object. So, for example, the Aristotelians didn't think that when stones fell to the earth (which was thought to be their proper place), they consciously sought the earth because they understood that it was their proper place. Nonetheless, the fact that this was the place where they belonged was assumed to be something that the stones were constructed to be sensitive to. Similarly, planets were thought to be constructed such that they were sensitive to the requirement that their movement be circular, yet without being conscious of this requirement.

Third, a final-cause explanation assumes that the object's state or movement could be explained by appealing to its sensitivity to this compelling rightness. The object was thought to move or change, for the sake of attaining that state, or undertaking that movement, which was appropriate or fitting for it.

In rejecting all manifestations of Aristotelian science, naturalists in the modern era insist that we understand the behavior of any object in the world in a way that rejects the possibility of Aristotelian final causes. This eschewal is consistent with more than one way of conceptualizing the kind of explanation that is characteristic of science. Some will believe that it is an eschewal that is best understood in terms of a cause-and-effect model of scientific explanations (perhaps best realized in mechanistic explanations). Others (often for Humean reasons) dislike the idea of causation, and seek to understand scientific explanations so as to avoid this term (and in a way that will accommodate the strange and very nonmechanistic scientific theories of the twentieth century, such as quantum mechanics). *But both groups are committed to explanations that deny the possibility that an object moves for the sake of something else that compels it to do so by virtue of its "rightness" that it can somehow sense.* I take this to be definitive of the scientific point of view.

Indeed, it was because of their insistence on rejecting Aristotelian final causes that many continental thinkers in the early modern period (including Huygens) rejected Isaac Newton's theory of gravitational force. For these thinkers, the idea that a force called gravity acted on material objects was too close for comfort to the idea of a place for matter that "ought to be." Of course, the two ideas are not the same, and despite the smell of final causation to Newton's theory, thinkers in the Cartesian tradition were eventually won over to the Newtonian view because of its mathematical beauty and its theoretical unifying power. Nonetheless, this bit of history is instructive insofar as it shows just how much the rejection of final-cause explanations was central to a conception of what counted as science in the early modern era.

As I noted, this rejection is only a necessary and not a sufficient condition of something's being a scientific explanation. I will not attempt to articulate sufficient conditions here, nor is there any widely accepted list of such conditions extant in the literature at present. But this one necessary condition is enough to rule out any moral objectivist's explanations that rely on moral reasons held to have objective authority. This is because an explanation of an agent's behavior that appeals to objectively authoritative reasons is an instance of a final-cause explanation. Such an appeal assumes, first, that there is a course of action that "ought to be"; second, that the human being can sense the rightness of that course of action; and third, that she can act for the sake of this rightness. So, if to be scientific, one must repudiate final cause explanations, then one must also repudiate the moral objectivist's explanations that invoke the objective authority of moral reasons. Thus, if Sally visits Aunt Ethel in the hospital because, as she puts it, "I have a duty to do so," we cannot think that it is an adequate explanation of her behavior to posit a compelling rightness in the world for the sake of which she acted, any more than we could think that there was a compelling rightness to iron filings' being close to magnet that explained why they were attracted to the magnet.

This doesn't mean that naturalists have to give up the language of reasons. Given the serviceability of this language in our daily lives, naturalists will probably want to find a place for talk of reasons and goals, and "for the sake of" explanations. (They may or may not believe that such talk is compatible with the idea that human beings have free will; that depends on other philosophical commitments they have.) But to be consistent with the assumptions of science, such an accommodation has to be made in a way that rejects the idea that there could be culture-independent authoritative directives for the sake of which we act, since science rejects the possibility of final-cause explanations. (So, for example, reasons might be construed as a type of belief with a "felt" rightness traceable to the operation of psychology or culture, but they cannot be construed as directives whose authority exists independent of this psychology or culture.[23])

---

[23] The literature on the compatibility of reasons and causes is relevant to the issue of compatibility. See, for example, Keith Donnellan (1967). For arguments that

A moral objectivist might protest that science is only justified in rejecting final-cause explanations for the movement of objects other than human beings. By this view, human beings are different – uniquely nonmechanistic elements in an otherwise mechanized universe. The naturalist will, however, reject what he will regard as a hubristic picture, on the grounds that there are no reasons to justify treating ourselves as exceptions. Particularly because the science of biology struggled, and eventually succeeded, in ridding itself of the language of final-cause explanations in the nineteenth century, naturalists will argue that this exception is unjustified. If the operation of every other living creature on earth can be explained without resorting to final causes, why shouldn't such explanations suffice for human beings? The moral objectivist's plea to think of us as different and special looks like a plea for using an outmoded and ultimately unsuccessful pattern of explanation in the face of a new and far more successful way of conceiving of ourselves.

One last aside: The idea of objective authority also clashes with methodological naturalism. For how could such authority be detected by the empirical methods of science? We can probably explain how we could think such a thing, but how could we *find* it in the world? Using what tool or scientific device? It isn't difficult to understand this authority as *felt*, but the idea that there is something beyond what is felt, to which we are responding when we say we have a reason, presupposes that we have a tool by which to find it. But what tool or human sense could that be? Even those whose naturalism is purely methodological seem to have good reason to reject the idea of objective moral authority.

CONCLUSION

At last we have located the idea within the moral objectivist's theory that cannot pass scientific muster. It is the idea that there exist reasons

reasons are not (scientifically acceptable) causes, see G. E. M. Anscombe (1963) and Ludwig Wittgenstein (1958). For an argument that reasons are kinds of causes, see Donald Davidson (1963). Note, however, that this literature's relevance to the scientific acceptability of the moral objectivist's reasons is only tangential, both because it is controversial whether scientific explanations need be constructed in terms of causes, and because the concept of reasons tends to be insufficiently specified in a way that isolates out the particular thesis about reasons accepted by a moral objectivist.

with objective authority, about which we can know, and for the sake of which we can act. Such an idea cannot be developed with any precision, because neither the source of these directives nor their authority over us can be plausibly explained. Even more importantly, explanations that invoke the idea of objective authority violate science's strictures against final cause explanations. So for anyone who is committed to offering only explanations that are both consistent with the assumptions of science and rigorously intelligible in their own right, the moral objectivist's explanations will clearly not do.

Some readers may think that this chapter is somewhat suicidal for a moral objectivist to write. Haven't I killed off the position that I claim to be defending? Let me assure such readers, therefore, that I wouldn't have been so fervent in damning the idea of objective authority if I didn't have something up my sleeve. It's now time to reveal it.

APPENDIX

Editor's note: Professor Hampton removed the following material from her previous draft of Chapter 3 and saved it as a separate computer file, entitled CH34ADD and dated March 7, 1996. It had constituted the final section of Chapter 3 before March 1996, when she undertook what became her final revision of that chapter. The title of the file in which this material was saved suggests that she may have intended to incorporate some revised version of it into the manuscript. Since Chapter 3 in its final version appears self-contained, it may have been her intention to work some of the following material into a revised Chapter 4. Certainly the final revision of Chapter 3 does not lead naturally into Chapter 4 in what became its final form, suggesting that Professor Hampton had intended to substantially revise Chapter 4. Her premature death prevented her from undertaking that revision.

A POSSIBLE WAY OUT

At last we have in hand the "queer" element in the objectivists' moral theory that precludes its scientific acceptability, or to use Mackie's phrase, we have finally understood the "authoritative prescriptivity" that is too strange to be believed. It is the claim that there are moral norms that are "objectively authoritative" in the sense that they give us normatively necessary reasons for various human activities, including believing, acting, and desiring, which reasons we can (in some way) discover or detect, whose objective authority we can in some way "feel," and that may even play a role in motivating us to act as they direct us. But it is not just *moral* norms that have been supposed to possess this unbelievable "normative necessity" to which we are supposed to have access and (perhaps) respond motivationally. Epistemic, logical, and mathematical norms are also traditionally represented as giving us necessary reasons for belief. So might we acknowledge the reality of norms generating necessary reasons by saying that we detect them in something like the way we "detect" epistemic, mathematical, or logical truths? The problem with this proposal is that by doing so, we would merely be trading the mystery inherent in one normative realm, for the same mystery in other normative realms. So we need a way to naturalize the authority of *all* norms. How do we do it?

These days, there are many philosophers who follow Quine[1a] in rejecting the traditional notions of epistemic warrant in order to "settle for psychology."[2a] Although the naturalist may not be able to salvage the traditional conception of *justified* true belief with any of these naturalized theories, she can still offer an explanation of *when* our beliefs are true, and represent any norms of epistemic warrant as culture-dependent and reflective of our (natural) human interests. These psychological replacements for the old epistemology have taken a number of different forms, and still count as a "naturalized" epistemology. For example, as Goldman has suggested, the notion of a justification of a statement might be replaced by the notion of a statement's being the product of a reliable method.[3a] Such an account could be linked to an explanation of other epistemic norms as psycho-social creations, and the machinery of evolutionary biology seems tailormade to provide an explanation of how different cultures would come to develop highly similar epistemic norms (that appear to track the truth), by virtue of the fact that such norms allow us to satisfy interests that by virtue of our common human physiology, almost all of us have.[4a] Note that such a theory is consistent with a variety of metaphysical positions. One can eschew the objectivist's authority and be a realist, or an idealist, or as (to use Putnam's

---

[1a] Quine (1969).
[2a] Quine (1969, 78).
[3a] See Alvin Goldman (1979).
[4a] See Williams (1985) and Gibbard (1990) for arguments of this sort.

phrase) an "internal realist" (imagine a Kantian who rejected the Second Critique). No matter if one's theory of truth is the correspondence account, or some kind of coherence account, or even a Jamesian account, one can eschew the idea that any of these theories can be used to claim that we have necessary reasons for believing some proposition p.[5a]

The same moves made by naturalists in epistemology can be, and have been, made by those who are committed to developing a "naturalized" ethics. All of these theories have various ways of understanding norms such that their authority is construed as a psycho-social phenomenon, and their psychological effects understood consistent with standard causal models in science. Those who have developed such theories have shared the optimism of their counterparts in epistemology that this approach will be "good enough" to capture what we want a moral theory to explain and to do. This optimism is surely one reason why theorists in both areas of philosophy have thought they could afford to drop the idea of objective authority without significant loss. But is this optimism justified? And, in particular given our interests in this book, is a naturalized theory of normativity going to be able to yield what we think of as a theory of morality?

Consider, first, the noncognitivist form of naturalized moral theory, interpreting moral norms as expressive of certain states of mind. Such a theory explains the authority of moral norms in terms of certain emotions or psychological states that these norms generate in us, where this generation is explainable (at least in part) by our socialization or habituation in a culture.[6a] Most recently, Allan Gibbard

[5a] Hence Putnam's attempts to defend moral objectivism by attacking the correspondence theory of truth and defending internal realism are ineffective. The positions he attacks can be held in a way that is supportive of moral objectivism; the position he defends can be held in a way that is opposed to moral objectivism. Nor is Putnam right to think that the presence of intentional concepts in a theory helps the objectivists' cause, or that a causal theory of reference hurts it. What is important to objectivism is the idea of necessary reasons: as we'll see, the only way to show that the naturalist is the "companion in guilt" of the moral objectivist is to locate necessary reasons within the theories of science he accepts.

[6a] Putnam argues that moral relativism is really a variant of noncognitivism, because it represents moral norms as expressive of the interests of a *culture*. See Putnam (1990, 165): "Non-cognitivism has been rebaptized as relativism." In terms of my analysis, this would mean that the authority of norms is (at least

has developed a form of this theory, in which "accepting" a norm in "whatever psychic state, if any, gives rise to [a] syndrome of avowal of the norm and governance by it" (Gibbard 1990, 75). We shall discuss this theory at length in the next chapter. However, I want to note here a problem with Gibbard's analysis that critics have found in all variants of noncognitivist theories. As Gibbard himself admits, his analysis does not straightforwardly tell us what norms we ought to accept, but only what we mean *when* we accept a norm. To answer the former question consistent with his naturalist non-cognitivism, Gibbard says we must decide which norms are rational, which means settling "what norms to accept ourselves – for that is what it is to form an opinion as to the rationality of something" (Gibbard 1990, 47). So how do we settle on the rationality of a norm? As a naturalist, Gibbard rejects the idea that there are norms with objective authority that we are attempting to consult, dismissing the idea as implausible Platonism (although note that he doesn't clarify the way in which the problem is with the *authority* of these norms):

> On the Platonist picture, among the facts of the world are facts of what is rational and what is not. A person of normal mental powers can discern these facts. Judgments of rationality are thus straightforward apprehensions of fact, not through sense perception but through a mental faculty analogous to sense perception. . . .
>
> If this is what anyone seriously believes, then I simply want to debunk it. Nothing in a plausible, naturalistic picture of our place in the universe requires these non-natural facts and these powers of non-sensory apprehension (Gibbard 1990, 154).

So Gibbard aims to develop a form of noncognitivism that captures "whatever there is to ordinary notions of rationality if Platonism is excluded" (154). The problem with this proposal in the eyes of any moral objectivist is that what he calls "Platonism" is ultimately just the idea that there are objectively authoritative norms, and they will say that excluding this idea *is* excluding a central aspect of how we determine which norms – and in particular, which moral norms – to accept. Even Gibbard himself suggests that this is the case. In Chap-

---

in part) a creation of society, which has an interest in encouraging the behavior directed by the norms. For examples of noncognitivist positions in ethics, see Gibbard (1990); Stevenson (1937; 1944); Ayer (1936), Ch. 6; Hare (1952; 1963; 1981).

ter 15 of his book, in the course of setting out methods for assessing norms relevant to feelings, one of the methods he recognizes is "loosely intuitionistic"; when we use it we "take up the inquiry, think through examples, discuss together, confront puzzles and inconsistencies. Then see directly which norms for feelings strike us as plausible" (284). Gibbard concludes:

> We do not think we can peer into a special realm of normative fact, but we can act as if we thought we could (284).

Yet why should we act *as if* we could peer into such a realm, if we genuinely think no such realm exists? Gibbard leaves this question unanswered, and the reader can think of no answer other than the obvious one – namely, that it is part of our ordinary understanding that there are (necessarily) right answers in morality that we can, and should, attempt to *find*.[7a] So Gibbard's endorsement of the intuitionistic method for assessing norms indicates a reluctance on his part to give up the idea, implicit in this method, that there is something independent of our culture to which, in our moral life, we are attempting to (indeed, *ought* to) comply.

Mackie is an example of a naturalist who takes seriously the idea that in our moral language, we are appealing to an objective, culture-independent authority, and he rejects the noncognitivist analysis because it fails to acknowledge the reality of that appeal. He cites a remark by Bertrand Russell to demonstrate the commitment to objectivity in moral discourse. In the course of talking about his judgment that the introduction of bullfighting into England would be wrong, Russell says,

> In opposing this proposal, I should *feel*, not only that I was expressing my desires, but that my desires in this matter are *right*, whatever that may mean.[8a]

But though Mackie recognizes the appeal of objectivity in moral discourse, he goes on to deny that moral discourse can be true insofar as no such culture-independent authority exists. Mackie calls this the

---

[7a] Brink (1989, 26–31) has a nice discussion of the counterintuitive nature of the noncognitivist's proposal.

[8a] Cited by Mackie (1977, 34); from Russell (1944). Mackie notes that Russell concludes, however: "I can only say that, while my own opinions as to ethics do not satisfy me, other people's satisfy me still less" [Mackie (1977, 35)].

"error theory" of morality; it is the view that our moral language and practices are roughly as the objectivist describes them, but given that there are ultimately no objective moral norms to which they can refer, moral discourse is, strictly speaking, false, although perhaps socially useful for all that.

Mackie's position has drawn considerable criticism. To characterize this large and highly significant part of our daily lives as "false" has struck many as fantastic. Indeed, one might use Mackie's example of Russell's opposition to bullfighting to make the point that abandoning the idea that there are culture-independent moral norms that necessarily give us reasons for action can be difficult to do even for the most committed naturalist. It seems to rip the guts out of our ordinary moral practices.[9a] Outside of our philosophical study, we don't think we are in error when we upbraid our children for their inconsiderate behavior or when we call for social justice in our community, and we don't think we're merely "expressing our acceptance" of norms calling for mutual respect and social justice when we make (sometimes great) personal sacrifices in order to comply with these norms. We act as if we think the authority of these norms is not "in our heads" or traceable only to societal conventions and our (cognitive or affective) reactions to them, but "real" – and something to which individuals and societies should strive to conform.

Hence it would be exceedingly nice, from the naturalist point of view, if someone could figure out a way to talk about certain ethical behavior and beliefs as *right* without postulating the existence of such norms, or such necessary authority. A number of moral theorists have thought they had a way of doing so by basing the understanding of moral directives on the idea that they are hypothetical imperatives. This approach to morality, famously proposed by Hobbes and endorsed by theorists as diverse as Philippa Foot and David Gauthier,[10a] is an attempt to construct a moral theory that

---

[9a] Thus I believe we have reason to question the claim made by Boyd and Sturgeon that they are moral realists. While their theories explain how moral terms could be given reference, and how moral facts could figure in explanation of our observations, their conception of moral facts leaves out all normativity. In essence, they salvage the "naturalism" of morality by banishing its essential "queerness" from their theory. This strikes me as more of a capitulation to the Harman/Mackie argument, rather than an objectivist alternative to it (see Sturgeon (1992).

[10a] See Gauthier (1986); Foot (1972).

purports to salvage the objective authority of at least some moral norms, but in a way that is nonetheless naturalistically acceptable.[11a] It is a type of externalism – in Brink's sense of that term – and it answers the amoralist's question "Why be moral?" with an argument that appeals to ideas that *while justificatory in a certain way*, are still in terms that science would permit.

It does so by arguing at least some behavior traditionally called "moral" is instrumentally rational for all normally constituted human beings, given their desires, thereby representing the authority of morality as at bottom the authority of rationality, understood as a merely instrumental faculty. Insofar as instrumental rationality seems to be reducible to beliefs and desires – both of which are (arguably) natural parts of the world – then if at least *some* moral reasons can be explained and even justified by appeal to *them*, it would seem that we can show how morality still gives us reasons *in a sense* – albeit not necessary reasons generated by objectively authoritative moral norms – that rest on an entirely natural foundation, fully acceptable to any scientist. Using this strategy, this brand of naturalism gives us a moral theory that appears to posit no strange objects or intuitive powers, is entirely consistent with a physicalist metaphysics, gives straightforward, unmysterious answers to the question "Why be moral?", yet preserves the idea that at least some moral judgements are authoritative over us, apart from social or psychological contingencies.[12a]

Mackie's own commitment to this view explains why, after arguing in (1977) that ethics rests on false presuppositions, he goes on in later chapters to try to develop a moral theory anyway. Harman

---

[11a] But not all those who consider themselves neo-Hobbesians are naturalists. An example of someone who borrows heavily from Hobbes but eschews naturalism is Gregory Kavka, in his (1986). Those Hobbesians whose theories are naturalist include David Gauthier (1986); Gilbert Harman (1977); John Mackie (1977); Jan Narveson (1988); Christopher Morris (1990); James Buchanan (1975); and recent unpublished work by Ken Binmore.

[12a] It is worth noting that although he could admit that norms are generally socially recognized, taught, and reinforced, no self-respecting Hobbesian can take seriously an entirely societal account of *all* rational and moral norms (even if it might do for some of them), given that Hobbesians regard our sociality as tenuous at best and not fundamental to our nature as persons. Indeed, Hobbes believes he has to give a naturalistic explanation of one norm, mandating the establishment of the absolute sovereign, in order to explain how any cooperative human society is even possible.

is among many who have been puzzled by this: "It is almost as if [Mackie] had first demonstrated that God does not exist and had then gone on to consider whether He is wise and loving" (Harman 1984, 30). Harman concludes that Mackie must have thought ethics as it is normally conceived can be replaced by something else. But this "something else" is an approach to morality that although naturalistic, nonetheless gives us a way of seeing its directives as naturalistically acceptable reasons. If it works, it would seem to be the answer to the riddle of ethics.

Instrumental reasons are also fundamental to attempts to naturalize epistemic norms (for example, they would appear to be implicitly part of a reliabilist theory of epistemic norms). But if instrumental reasons are still *reasons*, don't we have to inquire after their authority over us? Are instrumental reasons any more "natural" than moral reasons or any other sort of reason if they are held to be authoritative over us, regardless of culture or psychology? And must they be held to be objectively authoritative in a naturalistically problematic way if we are to use them as justificational material in moral or epistemic theories? Indeed, must we consider them objectively authoritative in order for us to consider them genuine *reasons* at all? The next chapter pursues these questions as a way of beginning an inquiry into the coherence of a naturalist's dismissal of objective authority.

Part II

Instrumental Reason

Chapter 4

Instrumental Reasons[a]

[computer file 4/24/95]

Many philosophers and social scientists argue that the only acceptable theory of the nature of practical reason is what is called the "instrumental" theory, which says, roughly, that reason's only practical role is working out and recommending action that best achieves the end of the agent. Such theorists dismiss the idea that reason could ever play a noninstrumental role by dictating or determining ends themselves.

There are two general reasons why philosophers have been troubled by the noninstrumental view. First, it is a conception of reason that seems unacceptable from the standpoint of science. What special "sight" or access to normative reality can we realistically ascribe to human reason, such that it can tell us our ends in life? And how does a scientific worldview permit us to believe that there are unmotivated ends that we are rationally compelled to pursue? Science, after all, does not recognize such objects or properties with inherent prescriptive power. As we noted in Chapter 1, J. L. Mackie calls such

[a]*Editor's Note:* The break in continuity between the end of Chapter 3 and the beginning of Chapter 4 is due to the fact that Professor Hampton was in the process of revising the manuscript at the time of her unexpected death. She had not yet begun to revise Chapter 4 to bring it into line with her revisions of the earlier chapters, so although the version of Chapter 4 that appears here represents her latest revision, it had been written some time before. The manuscript it is based on is dated 5/95. Insofar as it was always her practice to record the date of the latest revision on a manuscript, Chapter 4 as it appears here is an edited version of work Professor Hampton completed in April or May 1995. Note in particular that while this chapter begins by discussing practical reason, that topic was not addressed under that name in Chapter 3, but only in Chapter 2.

objects and properties "queer" – indeed, too queer, given the strictures of science, for us to believe that they obtain.[1] Moreover, no scientific description of human beings has identified a rational capacity within us that can discover these objects. A second (and new) problem concerns motivation. Most theorists believe that whereas the question "Why be moral?" is deeply troubling, the question "Why be rational?" is not. Yet if reason is conceived along noninstrumental lines, it becomes so expansive, and its directives so wide-ranging and divergent from interests the individual is readily able to recognize, that the issue of behaving rationally, when rationality is defined like *that*, is now a real one.

For those who are committed to a "naturalistic" account of human beings, the motivational puzzles of the noninstrumental view, and the nonnatural role it accords reason, make this approach to reason unacceptable. Such theorists want a conception of reason that grants it no occult powers, and that presupposes a foundation that is utterly acceptable from a scientific point of view. The instrumental approach to reason seems to meet both criteria. Indeed, even the *normative* version of this approach seems to be able to explain the force and strictures of its rational directives in a way that is scientifically acceptable. This is because, in the instrumental approach, reason dictates only hypothetical imperatives, and these imperatives seem to be reducible to beliefs and desires (or if not desires then something like them – for example, preferences),[2] which are (arguably) allowed by, or reducible to, entirely natural phenomena. Henceforth in this chapter I will use the term 'desire' very broadly to mean a natural motivational feature of a human being that establishes an end that some course of action would seem to be able to "satisfy" or "achieve." The way in which hypothetical imperatives appeal to (or are based on) desires so construed seems to make them motivationally unproblematic, without the inexplicable "magic" that Philippa Foot and others say supporters of categorical imperatives have clothed them in.[3]

In this chapter, I shall argue that hypothetical imperatives, and the instrumental reasons that such imperatives generate, have what I call objective normative authority, and that this authority is just the

---

[1] Mackie (1977). See especially p. 38.
[2] See Harman (1983).
[3] Foot (1972, 167).

same as the authority that is supposed to make objective moral reasons scientifically unacceptable. I shall also argue that the psychological effects and motivational force of instrumental prescriptions of reason can only be explained in the same (apparently) nonnatural way as the psychological effects and motivational force of moral prescriptions. If these arguments are right, and instrumental reasons are no more acceptable to a naturalist than moral reasons, then insofar as the authority of science rests on the fact that its methods are responsive to instrumental reasons, science itself is just as nonnatural an enterprise as morality. And if science, given its commitments, is just as unscientific as morality, then to use J. L. Mackie's phrase, naturalists are the "companions in guilt" of any moral theorist.

HYPOTHETICAL IMPERATIVES

Conventional wisdom has it that there is nothing mysterious nor especially troubling about (what I will loosely call) the "force" of hypothetical imperatives issued by instrumental reason, in contrast to categorical imperatives, whose force is far from clear. But I shall now argue that the "ought" in a hypothetical imperative is just as puzzling as the "ought" in a categorical imperative.

J. L. Mackie probably speaks for most philosophers when he explains the force of a hypothetical imperative as follows:

> 'If you want X, do Y' (or 'You ought to do Y') will be a hypothetical imperative if it is based on the supposed fact that Y is, in the circumstances, the only (or the best) available means to X, that is, on a causal relation between Y and X. The reason for doing Y lies in its causal connection with the desired end, X; *the oughtness is contingent upon the desire.*[4]

But what *exactly* does it mean to say that the "oughtness" in a hypothetical imperative is in some way a function of the desire predicated by the imperative?

Most philosophers have not realized that this question about hypothetical imperatives needs answering. Consider the way Kant distinguishes between hypothetical and categorical imperatives; the former issue directives that are rational insofar as they achieve the satisfaction of some desire, whereas the latter issue directives that

---

[4] Mackie (1977, 28), my emphasis.

are taken to be authoritative no matter what our desires are. Whereas we are supposed to act on categorical imperatives (simply) because they are right or authoritative, Kant says that we act on hypothetical imperatives because their directives are a way to satisfy one or more desires that we have. This way of understanding the difference between them makes the hypothetical imperatives seem, from both a justificational and motivational standpoint, straightforward, and this is what philosophers such as Foot and Mackie have assumed.

But on closer examination, the contingency of the directives of a hypothetical imperative on a certain desire, does not, by itself, explain why we *ought* to follow the directive. While it is surely true that the "ought" statement in a hypothetical imperative should be withdrawn if the action that has been directed is not effective in satisfying an agent's desire, or if the agent does not have the desire,[5] nonetheless, if the agent has the desire and the action is effective, that ought statement "holds." But what does it mean to say this? Or to put it another way, how does this hypothetical imperative give the agent a reason for action that is different from the desire assumed by the imperative?

Moreover, how does the hypothetical imperative motivate us by virtue of the fact that it gives us this reason? Consider that action from a desire, and action from an imperative whose directives are contingent on a desire, are not the same. Nor is the appeal to the desire assumed in a hypothetical imperative sufficient to explain an agent's motivation to follow the imperative; unreflective action motivated by a desire is different, after all, from reflective, rational action on a hypothetical imperative assuming that desire.

These questions about hypothetical imperatives can be answered in four quite different ways, by theories that offer quite different accounts of the normativity of hypothetical imperatives. All these theories, however, sharply distinguish between what I have called in previous chapters the *authority* and the *motivational efficacy* of hypothetical imperatives and the reasons they give us. Consider that the question "Why should I be rational?" can have two quite different meanings: It can be a way of asking about the authority of a purported reason over me. That is, it can be a way of asking why I should take myself to be "ordered" to behave in this way. Or it can be a way of asking about what motivation I have to do that which

---

[5] See McDowell (1978, 13).

is assumed to be a justified, and hence, authoritative reason for me. Intuitively, we think that a reason generated by a hypothetical imperative is authoritative if it dictates an instrumentally effective way to act in the circumstances (where this reason may, or may not, override any other competing reasons in these circumstances – it can be a reason for us even if it is not a decisive reason to act in the circumstances). However, dictating the best action is not necessarily motivating that action. I will say that a reason generated by a hypothetical imperative is motivationally efficacious if it can, by itself, move us to act as it directs (albeit, perhaps with insufficient force to effect the action it directs).

Just because we know we have an authoritative instrumental reason to do some action x, it doesn't follow that this reason is motivationally efficacious. Alas, philosophers have persistently assumed that it is. As an illustration of this point, consider once more Williams's account of what makes something a reason for action analyzed in Chapter 2. By that account, in order for an agent to have a reason for acting, there must be a deliberative connection between the reason's directives for action, and an agent's motives. Williams calls such reasons "internal," and he denies that there can be any "external" reasons for action – that is, reasons that do not have this deliberative connection with our motives. Note, however, that this distinction between "internal" and "external" reasons concerns the issue of what it is that makes something a reason for action, and not the issue of whether or not a reason is also a motive.

Hence Williams puts forward a variant of Identification Internalism – the view that an agent has a reason to x if and only if x-ing is connected, via deliberation (correctly performed) with an internal feature of the agent. It is opposed by Identification Externalism – the view that an agent has a reason to x iff x-ing can be connected, via deliberation, with some aspect of the world that need not be, and sometimes is not, an internal feature of the agent. But identification internalism, by itself, takes no stand on the issue of whether reasons are also motives. In particular, identification internalism does not imply Motivational Internalism – the view that reasons are – in some way to be specified – also motives. Suppose that after a deliberation process, an agent arrives at the conclusion that she has a reason to do p in order to achieve some object q that would satisfy her desire s. This reason is related to a motive (her desires), and discovered by her in a deliberation process, so it would seem to be a reason that she *has,* and believes she has. But having said that, why does it follow, by virtue of the fact that it is a reason that she has and believes she has, that she is also motivated to perform p? To say that the motivation exists requires some further argument – Identification Internalism does not, by itself, provide any argument at all with respect to the motivational efficacy of reasons.

There are two general ways of constructing such an argument. First, one can put forward a variant of a motivationally externalist argument. In this view, an instrumental reason does not, by itself, motivate action. Hence, if after coming to the conclusion that she has a reason to x, an agent finds herself motivated to do x, that must be because of some inner (but contingent) psychological process causally effected by the deliberation, that has produced the motivation. The reason *by itself* is not motivational. Second, one can put forward a motivational internalist argument. In this view, an instrumental reason is something that can, by itself, generate a motivational force (although it is a further issue whether that motivational force is sufficient to produce the action in the circumstances). It is, in some way, "intrinsically" motivational. In this view, to know that one has a reason to x is also to feel motivated (at least to some degree) to do x.

An account of the "force" of a hypothetical imperative will consist of one of these theses about a reason's motivation, along with a view of the nature of the authority of that reason. There are a number of such accounts. In this section, I will describe the four accounts I take to be most promising.

1. First, there is what I will call the **Kantian** account – that is, the Kantian account of the normativity of *instrumental* reason. I am not referring to Kant's larger, noninstrumental conception of rationality. Kant is famous for the view that when we act morally we are acting on reason, and he contrasts such moral action with action that is (merely) caused by desires. This rhetoric, however, obscures the fact that he also recognizes a nonmoral component of reason, from which we act when we are motivated by hypothetical imperatives. And a careful look at his account of the force of hypothetical imperatives shows he believes that we are motivated to follow them *not* by the desires assumed by such imperatives, but by *reason* – that is, by the instrumental (and not the moral) component of reason. Although hypothetical imperatives are predicated on a desire, Kant maintains that they "present the *practical necessity* of a possible action as a means to achieving something else which one desires."[6] This "ne-cessity" is the substance of the authority of the imperatives, and it is *by virtue of that authority* that it has motivational effect on the agent: "Whoever wills the end, so far as *reason has decisive influence on his action*, wills also the indispensably necessary means to it that lie in his power."[7]

I have emphasized the phrase that shows that Kant believes, when we act from a hypothetical imperative, that it is not desire but (in-strumental) reason that moves us, just as, when we act morally, it is not desire but reason (in this case, moral reason, not instrumental reason) that moves us, by virtue of its authority. (That is, these im-peratives command us with "practical necessity.") And while Kant is aware that many human beings resist the means they ought to take to achieve their ends, his position is that by virtue of the fact that we *ought* to will means appropriate to our ends, we will do so for as long as "reason has decisive influence" on our actions. Kant also puts the same point in another way:

> .... it is an analytic proposition that, if I fully will the effect, I must also will the action necessary to produce it. For it is one and the same thing to conceive of something as an effect which is in a certain way possible through me and to conceive of myself as acting in this way.[8]

Kant's idea seems to be that it is "analytic" that if one wills an end, one must also will the means to it (or, if one doesn't will the means to it, cease willing the end), so at the very least, he is taking the hypothetical imperative to be demanding a kind of consistency be-tween ends and means taken to achieve them.[9] But what does he mean when he says this proposition is "analytic"? There are at least two possible interpretations of his remark.

First, it could be a kind of psychological thesis, to the effect that in fact one cannot desire the end without desiring the means to it. So interpreted, the proposition seems highly implausible. Not only does introspection seem to controvert it, more importantly, it is a

[6] Kant (1785), Chapter 2. Beck translation, p. 31.
[7] Ibid. Beck translation, p. 34.
[8] Ibid. Beck translation, p. 35.
[9] For the idea that there is a norm of practical coherence or consistency implicit in the hypothetical imperative, see Darwall (1983, 15 and 44–50), Greenspan (1975), and Hare (1971).

psychological thesis that would make irrational action impossible. That is, it would have us say about any agent who appeared to violate instrumental rationality that in fact he had not, because insofar as he wasn't motivated to pursue the best means to an end, he didn't desire the end either. So this interpretation has problems that are interestingly analogous to problems associated with the economists' conception of revealed preference. According to that conception, we can identify what a person prefers by looking at what he does (the action "reveals" the preference). Critics have complained that such a view makes it impossible to criticize a person's actions as mistaken given his preference; it rules out the possibility that preferences and actions could diverge. The same problem exists if we interpret Kant's "analytic" dictum as a psychological precept. If we saw someone who said he willed a certain end, but didn't pursue it, we would have to conclude, in this view, that he didn't will it after all. But this would mean it was psychologically impossible for willing with respect to ends and willing with respect to means to diverge, and such divergence is required in order for irrationality to be possible. Hence this interpretation rules out the possibility of instrumental irrationality. And a position that implies that human beings never violate instrumental rationality seems experientially invalidated! One must not argue too enthusiastically for the correctness of a normative thesis, lest one make it impossible for human beings to act contrary to it.[10] Note also how this interpretation flies in the face of the way in which Kant says that he wants to understand "ought" ("sollen") statements in the *Groundwork*. Such statements, he says, are directed at creatures who can, but need not, act from them; in particular, he specifies that both hypothetical and categorical imperatives may not be followed by those who know they are "subject" to them.[11] Hence, insofar as this interpretation fails to allow someone to violate an instrumental directive, it fails, in Kant's terms, to be adequate as an account of hypothetical imperatives. To

---

[10] It does not help to argue that this thesis establishes what human beings would will if they had full information. Irrationality isn't manifested if someone, because she lacked information about how to achieve her ends, fails to take the means to achieve them, but is manifested precisely insofar as she knows what she must do, but refuses to do it. See my "Mens Rea" (1990).

[11] See Kant (1785), Paton translation, p. 81, Beck translation, p. 30.

borrow a phrase of Kurt Baier,[12] this interpretation disallows Kant from treating a hypothetical imperative as a directive of practical reason.

Later in this chapter, I will suggest a way of thinking about this Kantian remark such that it can be taken to be both a directive of practical reason *and* descriptively plausible, even in the face of the reality of noninstrumental behavior. But we need to do a lot of work first before that interpretation can be constructed, and in the meantime, we can interpret Kant's remark quite straightforwardly as a normative proposition that nonetheless often fails to describe actual human reasoning or behavior. This interpretation fits with the view of the force of instrumental directives that I have just sketched on the basis of other passages in Kant's writing. In this interpretation, the analytic proposition is a kind of principle of "practical logic," analogous to logic principles such as DeMorgan's law, which people can violate, but which they ought not to violate. So although in fact there are agents who desire the end, but not the means to the end, this principle says that they ought not to do so, and will be condemned as irrational to the extent that they do so. The principle is analytic in the way any other logical principle (that human beings are also capable of violating) is analytic, and it is both authoritative over action, and motivational by virtue of that authority. This interpretation preserves the possibility that human beings can (and do) violate this "analytic" principle, but it establishes what, for a Kantian, would be a critical aspect of any appeal to instrumental reasons – namely, the fact that it has authority over agents in an objective, culture-independent way. No matter how human beings have been raised, nor the details of their psychology, it is normatively necessary ("analytic") that they ought to pursue means that are instrumentally effective in achieving their ends.

If we (at least provisionally) accept this second interpretation, then on the basis of this and previous passages, we can summarize the Kantian position on the force of hypothetical imperatives as follows: A hypothetical imperative is a norm that generates a reason for an agent to pursue an instrumentally efficacious action, whose authority over the agent is objective (she *must* follow this directive, or else be condemned as irrational). When a rational agent acts on a hypothet-

---

[12] See Baier (1995), Book One, *passim*.

ical imperative, she is not motivated to do so by the desire assumed in the imperative, but by the authority of the imperative (or alternatively the authority or "rightness" of the reason to action given by the imperative), so that the imperative is motivationally efficacious *by virtue of its authority*.[13]

So defined, the Kantian position is really a *family* of positions, and not a single view, for there are a number of ways of elaborating the idea that to be rational a person who acts from a hypothetical imperative is motivated by the authority of that imperative. For example, one can hold that the authority of hypothetical imperatives is *directly* motivational, in a way analogous to the direct motivational efficacy of the authority of a (moral) categorical imperative. Alternatively, one can hold that the authority of these imperatives motivates us indirectly – for example, by having an effect on our psychological structure such that a desire to do what the imperative directs is created.[14] Kant's view with respect to moral reasons is generally the former, but occasionally he suggests the latter.[15] The only difference between the two positions concerns how the authority of the imperative affects our motivational structure. Rather than taking it to be able to generate a motive directly, the second position understands the imperative to cause a desire, which in turn provides us with the motive. But both positions assume that the imperative's authority can have an effect on our psychology, and thus both preserve what is fundamental to the Kantian view – namely, the idea that our motivation to follow the imperative is derived from the authority of the imperative, so that we are appropriately said to be acting *for the sake of* the reason given us in the imperative.[16]

---

[13] It is the constant reference to the *necessity* of willing the means to a desired end that persuades me that Kant is not taking the view (suggested to me by J. Schneewind) that when we desire the end in fact (as it happens), we also desire the means (so that if we fail to perform the means to the end we are divided against ourselves). There can be no necessity to the formation of desires.

[14] Kant (1788) suggests this idea himself in the section, "The Incentives of Pure Practical Reason," Chapter 3 of his *Critique of Practical Reason*. See pp. 74–92.

[15] Ibid. See, for example, p. 82, where he seems to assume that the only way to explain how reason could be motivational is to credit it with the power to effect a desire in us to do the moral action. But note that this view still credits reason with the causal power to create a motive, even if it doesn't credit it with the power to directly motivate.

[16] If one holds the former view, one might argue that while it is possible for the authority of imperatives to work indirectly, it is better if it does not – that is, it

134

There can also be different Kantian positions concerning whether or not the authority of a hypothetical imperative always has motivational efficacy. One might argue, for example, that it always does, by virtue of the fact that the motivational effects of such authority are (in some sense) necessary. Or one can argue (only) that it sometimes does, so that these motivational effects of the authority are likely but neither inevitable nor necessary. And in situations where authority does have motivational effects, one can maintain, for example, that they always are present, even if at times they do not succeed in effecting action. Alternatively, one can maintain that while they always have some motivational force, that force may not be sufficient to motivate us to act on its directives in all circumstances. And one can maintain (as Kant did in the case of moral reasons) that the authority of these reasons is always sufficient to yield *some* motivation (albeit, perhaps, not enough to generate the action).

2. The second position on instrumental reason understands the prescriptive force of a hypothetical imperative as involving only one component, namely, normative authority. In this view, an imperative is authoritative, but *never*, by virtue of that authority, also motivationally efficacious. That is, it gives us objectively authoritative reasons for action just as Kant says, but those reasons cannot directly motivate us. They can, at best, be motivationally efficacious indirectly – for example, by causing the activation in us of certain desires (or any other motivationally efficacious psychological material) that motivate us to act as it directs; they cannot motivate us to act by themselves by virtue of their authority. Whereas Kantian instrumental reasons have what I will call "authoritative motivational force," this view attributes to instrumental reasons (at most) what I will call "causal motivational force." By virtue of the way in which Mill distinguished the "correctness" of a moral imperative from the motivation we have to follow that imperative, I am calling this position *Millian*, even though I am describing a position on the nature of

---

is better if we act directly from the reasons we have for acting. In contrast, one could maintain that reason does not demand that in all circumstances our motivation to follow its directives must come from its authority rather than, say, from our desires. For a defense of this latter view, see the work of Joseph Raz, especially his *Practical Norms and Reasons* (1975 / 1990), and the concluding postscript to the second edition.

instrumental reason, not moral reason. Mill distinguishes between authority and motivational efficacy in the context of presenting his moral theory in *Utilitarianism*. In Chapter 2, after setting out his principle of utility, Mill insists that we should not mistake the (compelling) meaning of a moral principle with the *motive* one might have to obey it.[17] In Chapter 3, he goes on to explore the motives we might have for following this principle, concluding that they are largely the feelings of conscience of those who have been raised to have them, and in Chapter 4, entitled "How Proved," he embarks on the task of constructing a proof to establish that only *this* principle constitutes all of morality. But that proof (which generations of students know is problematic) is *not* for Mill the source of our motive to follow the principle, nor do our motives justify the principle as the correct standard of moral action. So Mill sharply distinguishes what *gets* us to be moral from the content and compelling force of morality. A Millian position on instrumental reason distinguishes in the same way between what gets us to follow the directives of instrumental reason and the authority of instrumental reason.

The Millian position would license criticism of people who fail to act rationally by virtue of the way in which they do not act on the reasons supplied by instrumental rationality, even though their motivational structure is such that they have no capacity for doing so. Whereas the Kantian position is a thorough-going form of motivational internalism – that is, the view that to know that x ought to be done is to have a motive to do x – the Millian position embraces a form of motivational externalism, denying that it follows from knowing that I ought to do x that I have a motive to do x.[18] So although both the Kantian and the Millian positions insist that to know one ought to do x is to have a reason to do x, they differ in the positions they take on whether these reasons are motivationally efficacious. (Note, however, that in the Millian view, instrumental reasons are still "internal" in Williams's identificational sense, given that there is a deliberative connection between these reasons and an agent's motives.)

3. The third position on instrumental reasons, which I call *Humean*, agrees that cause-and-effect information can at most be only indirectly involved in getting us to act, by causing in us the devel-

---

[17] Mill (1861, 17). For a useful discussion of Mill's position, see Korsgaard (1986).
[18] See my discussion of this in Chapter 2. And for further discussion of different varieties of internalism and externalism, see Brink (1989, 38).

opment of desires to perform the instrumentally effective action; it cannot effect action by itself. This position is explicitly argued for by Hume (1739) himself:

> . . . reason, in a strict and philosophical sense, can have an influence on our conduct only after two ways: Either when it excites a passion by informing us of the existence of something which is a proper object of it; or when it discovers the connexion of causes and effects, so as to afford us a means of exerting any passion. (III, i, 1; p. 459)

But in this passage, Hume is saying not only that reason cannot move us to action *alone*, without any help from desires at all, but more importantly that it has a (merely) causal effect on action, and no motivational effect by virtue of any (supposed) authority over action.

However, what is striking about the Humean conception is that it also says that instrumental reason also has no authority over our actions![19] Consider Hume's (famous) remarks in Book II:

> 'Tis not contrary to reason to prefer the destruction of the whole world to the scratching of my finger. 'Tis not contrary to reason for me to chuse my total ruin, to prevent the least uneasiness of an *Indian* or person wholly unknown to me. 'Tis as little contrary to reason to prefer even my own acknowledg'd lesser good to my greater, and have a more ardent affection for the former than the latter. A trivial good may, from certain circumstances, produce a desire superior to what arises from the greatest and most valuable enjoyment; nor is there any thing more extraordinary in this, than in mechanics to see one pound weight raise up a hundred by the advantage of its situation.[20]

Note Hume's contention that one is not being irrational in preferring an "acknowledg'd lesser good" to a "greater" good. The meaning of these terms is somewhat obscure. In order for the phrase in which they occur to make sense, there must be some way that we can judge one good "greater" than another, apart from the strength of our preferences for either one. An appeal to instrumental reason gives us a way to make such a judgment. Suppose going to the dentist is a

---

[19] For discussions on Hume's position on reason, I am greatly indebted to Tom Christiano and Don Garrett.
[20] From *Treatise*, II, iii, 3 (1739, 416).

means to avoiding pain in the long term. Suppose further that an agent prefers avoiding long-term pain to spending an afternoon reading. Because going to the dentist is a means to the more preferred end, it is a greater good than spending the afternoon reading. And yet it makes perfect sense to imagine this agent saying that she prefers spending the afternoon reading to going to the dentist. Hume's position would be that *because* spending the afternoon reading is what one prefers to do, it is "not against reason" to do so. Our desires are not only the sole motivational force within us, they are the only force within us that can "tell us what to do." And a desire can act on us in a way that causes us to do something other than the course of action consistent with reason's information – for example, when it fails to cause within us a desire to perform the means that is sufficiently strong to counteract an opposing desire. (Remember Hume's mechanics metaphor: Sometimes a pound weight can raise up a hundred by the advantage of its situation.)

Of course, there can be some psychological process within us that is usually initiated by reason's instrumental deliberation, eventuating in a desire to do that which one has instrumental reason to do. In Hume's (1739) words:

> [R]eason, in a strict and philosophical sense, can have an influence on our conduct only after two ways: Either when it excites a passion by informing us of the existence of something which is a proper object of it; or when it discovers the connexion of causes and effects, so as to afford us a means of exerting any passion. (III, i, 1, p. 459)

In the latter case, reason has an "influence on our conduct" (perhaps it operates along the lines of what Hume calls a "general rule"), but note that this influence does *not* come about by virtue of its authority over our action. And its causal effect on the development of motives in us is a contingent phenomenon, derailed in certain circumstances.

> Men often act knowingly against their interest: For which reason the view of the greatest possible good does not always influence them. (II, iii, 4, p. 418)

If we interpret "interest" here as a person's greatest good, then when Hume admits that people act knowingly against it, he is saying that mere knowledge that some object or state of affairs is a greater good needn't be motivationally efficacious. But the fact that we fail to act so as to secure the greater good does not mean that we act against reason's authority because, to quote Hume:

> [A]ctions do not derive their merit from a conformity to reason, nor their blame from a contrariety to it; and it proves the same truth more *indirectly*, by shewing us, that as reason can never immediately prevent or produce any action by contradicting or approving of it, it cannot be the source of the distinction betwixt moral good and evil.... Actions can be laudable or blameable; but they cannot be reasonable or unreasonable. (III, i, 1, p. 458)

Compare this with Hume's remarks on character and action in III, i, 1, (p. 458) in which he once again insists that actions cannot be judged as rational or irrational:

> Reason is the discovery of truth or falsehood. Truth or falsehood consists in an agreement or disagreement either to the *real* relations of ideas, or to *real* existence or matter of fact. Whatever, therefore, is not susceptible of this agreement or disagreement, is incapable of being true or false, and can never be an object of our reason. Now 'tis evident our passions, volitions, and actions, are not susceptible of any such agreement or disagreement; being original facts and realities, compleat in themselves, and implying no reference to other passions, volitions and actions. 'Tis impossible, therefore, they can be pronounced either true or false, and be either contrary or conformable to reason. (III, i, 1, 458)

So for Hume, it is, strictly speaking, incorrect to call an action irrational, even if that action fails to achieve the stated aim of the agent.[21]

At the deepest level, Hume's position should be understood as a view of what reason *is*. Whereas philosophers such as Wollaston and Clark considered it to be a normative faculty with both authority and motivational efficacy over our actions, for Hume, reason is a purely informational faculty, working out relations of ideas and causal connections. Although he accepts that this information might play a causal role in the creation of a motive to perform a means to a desired end given the psychological processes of the human mind (and Book II is full of accounts of psychological processes generating various passions), he rejects completely the idea that it has any nor-

---

[21] While he notes that we sometimes call a passion irrational, strictly speaking it is the false judgment attending the passion that is irrational, and not the passion itself. See II, iii, 3, (1739, 416).

mative authority over action, or any capacity to move us by virtue of that supposed authority.

Contrast the Humean view with the Kantian and Millian conceptions of rational imperatives, both of which assume that reason can have normative authority. In the Kantian or Millian views, if you say about someone, "He ought to do y to achieve x in the circumstances," you are invoking what you take to be an objective norm to criticize him. I call this the "instrumental norm," which directs us to pursue those objects and perform those actions that will be the most effective means to a desired end. For the Kantian or Millian instrumentalist, to say that "reason has authority over us" is really to say that *this instrumental norm* has authority over us.[22] But Hume rejects the idea that there is such an objective authoritative norm. For Hume, acting on a hypothetical imperative does not involve accepting (or being motivated by) the authority of such a norm, but instead involves being caused to act in this way by a process that is affected by both one's desires and the information about how to satisfy them supplied by reason. That information, in conjunction with one's desires, might have the "feel" of an authoritative, natural norm, but in reality one is being directed by a conjunction of entirely natural (and scientifically-recognized) forces. And when those forces fail to direct us, Hume insists that we do not violate any authoritative code of reason applying to action – because no such code exists.

4. There is a fourth view of the force of hypothetical imperatives that one might consider a "naturalized" version of the Kantian view. Whereas the Humean view tries to purge from its theory of reason the problematic idea of normative authority altogether, this fourth view accepts that reason has such authority, but then attempts to explain it naturalistically by appeal to human psychology, and its psychological or biological origins. There are a number of different ways to "explain" normativity in a naturalized way, a few of which I will review here. But this general approach, which I will call the *naturalized Kantian* view, is to explain (to use the distinction introduced in Chapter 3) authority only as a "believed authority," and

---

[22] Note that the authority of this instrumental norm has to be understood noninstrumentally. Because it is the foundation of the idea that we ought to act on means appropriate to the achievement of our ends, it cannot itself be defended consequentially. Thus, understood as an imperative, it is categorical and not hypothetical (a delightful bit of irony in this story).

not offer an account of (objective) authority (as believed) on the grounds that the latter doesn't exist. This theory therefore traces out psychological or biological structures that generate in us the belief that something or someone has (something called) authority, but it refuses to try to find anything outside of our beliefs to which this authority could correspond, since it denies that any such authority, given its nonnatural character, could exist. I call it a "naturalized Kantian" theory because, like the Kantian theory, it takes normativity to be identifiable with a structure in the mind, but unlike Kant, the notion of "mind" used in this theory is one that is meant to be entirely natural, informed by our best psychological and/or biological theories (perhaps supplemented by an appeal to sociological influences).

Consider an example of such an explanation suggested by evolutionary psychology.[23] Suppose we have evolved as creatures who have the cognitive capacity to formulate imperatives that we take to be authoritative with respect to our behavior; in this view, normative thinking is a natural part of our mental activity. Suppose it is also true that we have evolved such that normatively authoritative imperatives have motivational effects on our behavior that cannot be assimilated or reduced to the motivations provided by desires. In that case, it would be true that these imperatives have a motivational effect on us *by virtue of their felt authority* – where this motivation is distinct from other (recognized) forms of motivation, and yet natural for all that. And we can explain the presence of this motivational effect in terms of the survival advantage it would have given our forebears. This story makes the normative, and the authority implicit in it, a kind of psychological category that is characteristic of human thought insofar as it has been evolutionary advantageous.

A story that is similar in its aim, but different in its details, is put forward by Allan Gibbard,[24] who argues that normative judgments express a psychological state, but a noncognitive one that is nonrepresentational in nature. This account doesn't so much explain normativity, and its attendant authority, as it does explain it *away*. A normative judgment only amounts to being in a certain kind of noncognitive state, and is not itself identifiable with a distinctive category of thought. But like the earlier evolutionary story, Gibbard's

---

[23] See Cosmides and Tooby (1989).
[24] Gibbard (1990).

story gives an account of norms and normative authority that draws entirely from psychology (whose structure he takes to be a product of our evolution as a species), and refuses to recognize anything "in the world" to which our psychology "answers."

We have no proof of either of these stories or of any similar story. Note, however, that if any such story is right, it is not only congenial to the naturalist, but also capable of being used to explain the motivational force of categorical imperatives just as much as hypothetical imperatives, thereby vindicating the motivational plausibility of noninstrumental conceptions of reason, every bit as much as the Kantian version of the instrumental conception.

So are any of these four positions successful? I will argue that although the latter three reject the idea that there is any motivational force deriving from the (supposed) objective authority of rational imperatives, none of these positions succeeds as a theory of *reason*. The only theory that succeeds as a theory of reason is the Kantian position, which, as we shall see, is manifestly unsatisfactory from a naturalist standpoint.

EVALUATING THE THEORIES THAT DISCARD OBJECTIVE AUTHORITY

A naturalist would, it seems, have to prefer either the Humean or Naturalized Kantian positions on instrumental reason, insofar as both the Millian or Kantian views accept the scientifically impermissible idea that instrumental reasons have objective authority. But I shall argue in this section that neither the Humean nor the Naturalized Kantian theory really provides us with (what we intuitively understand as) a theory of instrumental *reasons*. To be precise, each theory generates answers to the questions about the nature of reasons reviewed in the last chapter that do not fit our intuitions or our practices with respect to instrumental reasons.

The Humean View

To discuss the Humean position, I will employ a thought experiment I have introduced elsewhere.[25] Suppose there is a person who (as a matter of fact) only acts on his occurrent motives (where these mo-

---

[25] See Hampton (1992).

tives are defined either as desires or as whatever a Humean psychology takes to be a human being's motives), and knows this fact about himself. Such a person is unlike the notorious semimoral agents criticized by Hobbes and Hume. Whereas Hobbes's "foole"[26] or Hume's "knave"[27] believes "I should do that action which I can establish, using instrumental reason, it is in my interest to perform," this individual, whom I will call a "curmudgeon" (one who persists in acting "without reasons")[28] believes "I will [not I should] only do that action which is prompted in me by the strongest occurrent motive." Note that whereas the fool's and knave's remark is a prescriptive principle setting out what counts as legitimate reasons for action, the curmudgeon's remark has no prescriptive overtones (he is not saying that he ought only to act on occurrent motives), but is merely setting out what he takes to be an accurate descriptive statement about how he behaves as he does.

Given their statement, the fool and the knave believe that they can have reason on occasion to perform actions for which they need have no immediate occurrent motive if and when these actions will causally effect states of affairs leading to the satisfaction of desires or preferences that they have. However, the curmudgeon will believe no such thing. If he, say, has no occurrent motive to go to the dentist, he will not go, even if he knows that such a visit would enable him to satisfy highly important self-regarding desires. A Kantian might contend that were the curmudgeon to know such a thing, this knowledge would produce in him an occurrent motive to go to the dentist; but in order to illuminate aspects of the Humean view on instrumental reason, I will assume, as this view insists, that knowing that one has an instrumental reason is not sufficient to give one a motive to follow its directives. So the curmudgeon is someone who can know that he has a desire for x, and that y is a means to x, but will not, as a consequence of this knowledge, always have an occurrent motive to do y. And when he does not, he will not do y.

Now suppose you saw this curmudgeon refusing to do y even

---

[26] See Hobbes (1651), Chapter 15.

[27] See Hume (1751).

[28] According to the Oxford English Dictionary, a curmudgeonly person is greedy and churlish, and one who "knows no ties or obligations" (Foote, 1776). As I am using the word, it refers to anyone who pursues all and only what he wants, unconstrained in any way by norms (either rational or moral).

though he admitted to wanting x, and you issued a hypothetical imperative to him to the effect that he ought to do y to achieve x. If, as a Humean instrumental theorist would insist, you took your hypothetical "imperative" to be merely a statement of a causal connection between an action and an outcome you believe to be desired by the agent, then if he ignores you after you have uttered it, you would merely shrug and turn away. After all, you would believe you could give him neither a reason nor a motive for acting otherwise. But if you would mean your hypothetical imperative to be a real *imperative* and not merely a statement of the causal facts, you would charge him with making a *mistake* if he didn't follow it, calling him 'wrong' or 'irrational.' ("He *ought* to do y; he's irrational not to do it," you would insist.) But to respond to him this way is to attribute to him an objectively authoritative reason for action despite the fact that he refuses to recognize it, and to take yourself to be warranted to do so by virtue of the fact that you believe this reason applies to him whether he likes it or not.

So in essence you are maintaining that no matter the peculiar psychological or social facts that explain his curmudgeonly behavior, it is normatively *necessary* (objectively) that he do y in order to achieve x in these circumstances – a reason that, at the moment he does not recognize. To put it another way, when you say that he ought to do y to achieve his desired end x, then you believe, given that he wants x, and y is the means to x, that he has an objectively authoritative reason to do y. But this means you are judging him – and criticizing him – using a norm that you are assuming to be objectively authoritative (albeit perhaps not motivational by virtue of that authority) in just the way moral theorists take their moral norms to be valid. And as I said earlier, you are really appealing to the objective authority of what I have called the Instrumental Norm: "Act so as to perform the most effective means to a desired end." This norm is implicit in the fool's and knave's account of how they determine what action to perform, and it is the norm that you are using to attribute a certain reason for action to the curmudgeon, a reason that you believe he has necessarily, no matter his views about what actions he should, or will, take. If you believe – despite his disclaimers – that he is capable of acting from this norm, you are adopting the Kantian position on instrumental reason, attributing motivational efficacy to this authoritative instrumental norm. On the other hand, if you doubt its motivational efficacy, then you are embracing the Millian position, accepting the norm's authority, but admitting its motivational inadequacy in the circumstances. In either case, you will believe that no matter his occurrent motives, he has a reason to do y.

But the Humean instrumental theorist has no room for this instrumental norm in his theory, because such a norm permits us to do what the Humean says is impermissible – namely, criticize actions as irrational. Accordingly, a Humean's hypothetical "imperatives" are merely assertions of causal connections, which in *no* sense give "reasons" for an agent to act. There is nothing either authoritative or motivationally efficacious about the Humean's hypothetical imperatives. And a Humean (curmudgeon-like) agent only follows them if, as it happens, the agent has a preexisting motive to perform y, or if the agent is affected by the assertion such that she develops a motive to do y. In this case, the force of the 'ought' is explainable in terms of contingent psychological human responses.

The problem with such a theory of reason is that it can never convict someone of acting irrationally! Those who hear the imperative and don't perform y, *make no mistake* when they don't perform y. There are two ways in which the notion of mistaken action is lost on the Humean view.

First, many theorists, including Kant, will maintain that in order properly to be said to have made a mistake, we must not only have done something that we ought not to have done, but must also have been capable of performing the better action. In other words, we must have a reason to perform the better action, and that reason must also be motivationally internal – that is, capable of functioning as an occurrent motive. But in Hume's view, we do whatever it is that our desires dictate, and can do no other. Thus if, as Hume maintains, we can act only on our desires, and we have no desire to perform that action which is a means to our end, then we are not capable of performing it, and thus cannot be criticized along Kantian lines as wrong or mistaken when we fail to perform it.

Philosophers who subscribe to the Millian position on the nature of hypothetical imperatives will believe this is too strong a condition. They will believe that even in a situation where a person could not have done otherwise, criticism of his actions as irrational is still appropriate for as long as such criticism is interpreted as "external." According to this second position on what it means to call action mistaken, we can admit that a person may have no occurrent motive to perform the instrumentally mandated action, but nonetheless attribute to him (as Mill would do) a (justified) reason to perform that action if, as a matter of fact, he desires some end, and it is true that this action is a means to achieving that end. Our criticism of him as irrational would be based on this reason, which would function as a standard by which to measure his conduct, albeit a standard that, we would admit, he has no way to meet, given the facts of his psychology.

But the Humean position on hypothetical imperatives precludes even the Millian external type of criticism. As I noted in the development of the Humean view, it denies the idea that our determination of the best means to an end has any authority over us, and thus denies that instrumental reflection gives us a reason to act. This determination might have a *causal* effect on us, such that as a matter of (psychological) fact, we develop a desire to do that which is the best means to our ends. But the rational information about means to ends is not *itself* a reason for action. That is, when we determine that x is a means to y, not only is such information not, by itself, motivationally efficacious; more importantly, it isn't even authoritative. So someone who fails to act so as to achieve his ends, in a situation where he has no desire to perform the actions required to achieve those ends, does nothing wrong. This person quite literally *has no reason* to perform x to achieve y. And if he has no reason to do so, then he makes no mistake by not doing so. He violates no standards of action; and indeed, that's the point of this Humean view – *there are no standards of action*. Thus he cannot be criticized as irrationally mistaken.

Of course he can still be criticized, albeit not as irrational. Hume sanctions all sorts of criticisms in his discussion of natural vices, and the criticism of imprudence (that is, behaving in a way that is advantageous in the short-term but not in the long-term) might be thought to apply to at least some of the curmudgeonly people I am describing. However, not only is imprudent action not the same as instrumentally irrational action (for example, some imprudent actions can nonetheless be instrumentally rational, by virtue of the fact that they satisfy short term goals), more importantly, calling someone imprudent is *not* calling her mistaken. When, according to Hume, we criticize someone as vicious in some way, we are projecting onto her a property that is created from our displeasure at her actions, occasioned in us after sympathetic identification with her and/or others, where this projection is governed in certain ways by conventional rules generated by our society.[29] But on reflection, we must admit that this criticism is a function of how her actions strike us. It does not mean that by her lights, she made any mistake. And even if our criticism of her as (in some way) vicious is supposed to mean that she violated some (external) ideal, it is nonetheless a "projected" criticism that is based on certain emotions experienced by (many but not all) onlookers as they contemplate her behavior, and not a criticism of her behavior as irrational or in some way a mistake (given her motives).

So Hume's theory destroys the idea that people ever act irrationally, given that in his view, action is based on the strongest motivational force, and the "imperatives" of reason have no authority over, or motivational effect on, our actions. The Humean position must be that human beings can only act *nonrationally*, since reason is neither the standard nor the motivation (by virtue of being the standard) of human action. Of course, the Humean view admits that instrumental assertions, coupled with our preferences, might play a causal role in our performance of an action. But these assertions amount merely to psychologically efficacious ways of talking, and not normative prescriptions setting out what we *ought* to do if we wish not to be among those whose behavior violates the standards of reason. Any persistent tendency to interpret them in this latter way would have to be explainable by the Humean via some sort of Mackie-like "error theory" (which would credit us with a natural propensity toward such an interpretation, even while showing that it cannot be true).

But, remarkably, this means that the Humean view is actually inconsistent with the instrumental theory of reason as I have defined it above![b] In particular, it violates thesis 1 – that is, that "an action is rational to the extent that it furthers the attainment of an end."

---

[29] The importance of conventional rules determining the content of natural virtues and vices is an implication of Hume's discussion in *Treatise*, III, iii, 1 (1739, 581–2).

[b] *Editor's note:* Such a definition was indeed given in an earlier draft of the material that became Chapter 4. But this material had subsequently been rearranged by the author, so that no definition appears now until Chapter 7, in the following words:

The inclusion of that thesis in the definition of the instrumental approach is inescapable; for how could one endorse a version of the instrumental theory of reason but not criticize, for example, the man that wanted to cure his tuberculosis but refused to take the medicine that would do it, or the woman who wanted a college B.A. but refused to work to pass any of her classes? To say, as Hume does in the *Treatise*, that "actions do not derive their merit from a conformity to reason, nor their blame from a contrariety to it,"[30] is to refuse to allow reason to have *any* critical impact on human behavior at all. Yet isn't this exactly the position one is taking when one says, as Hume does, that reason only has a theoretical role? Ironically, that position is inconsistent with the instrumental theory of reason, un-

---

[30] From *Treatise*, III, 1, i, (1739, 458).

> "1. An action is rational only to the extent that it furthers the attainment of an end;
>
> *and* 2. The agent has followed a process of reasoning involving the determination of means to achieve ends, in a way set out by the theory (I will say, henceforth, that using reason to determine the extent to which action is a means to an end is an *instrumental* use of reason);
>
> *and* 3. The agent's ends are in no way fixed by reason operating non-instrumentally – that is, what makes them her ends is something other than reason operating noninstrumentally."

Professor Hampton gave closely related definitions of an instrumental theory of reason in her published essays Hampton (1995) and Hampton (1996). On pages 84–5 of the latter essay, the following definition of "an instrumental theory [of reason]" appears:

> "1. An action is rational to the extent that an agent believes it furthers the attainment of some end;
>
> *and* 2. The process of reasoning involves the determination of means to achieve ends, in a way described by the theory. (I will say, henceforth, that using reason to determine the extent to which an action is a means to an end is an *instrumental* use of reason);
>
> *and* 3. An agent's ends are in no way fixed by reason operating non-instrumentally – that is, what makes them our ends is something other than instrumental reason."

The essay goes on (p. 92) to distinguish among instrumental theories of reason between those that are descriptive and those that are normative.

"Instrumental theories of reason can be descriptive or normative. Both types of theory understand thesis 3 descriptively, so that a nor-

derstood as involving a certain kind of rational criticism of behavior, that is standardly attributed to Hume![31]

Suppose someone tried to explain the authority of instrumental reasons in a Humean way, consistent with naturalistic commitments, by appealing either to general or higher-order desires – for example, the general desire to act instrumentally, or else to a second-order desire to desire to act instrumentally, each of which might be thought to give something like "authority" to the first order desire, such that a person would believe he "ought" to act instrumentally by virtue of it.

There are a number of problems with either proposal. First, and most obviously, even if either one worked, it would work only for agents who happened to have the general or second-order desire, so that the "authority" of instrumental directives would be contingent on particular features of human psychology. But I take it that we do not believe that a person "ought" to take means appropriate to his ends only if, as it happens, he has a desire to desire to do so, or a general desire to do so.

Apart from this problem, neither proposal is acceptable for other

mative instrumental theory does not say that we *ought* to establish ends of action using something other than reason, but only that we *do* operate so that our ends of action are set by something other than reason. But these types of theory disagree about whether theses 1 and 2 describe how we actually operate or how we ideally operate. Descriptive instrumental theories say that as a matter of fact, when human beings engage in reasoning, they do so in an instrumental way (either at the operational or the meta-level), so that in our definition of the instrumental approach to reason, the details of thesis 2 set out the kind of mental functioning characteristic of members of our species. On the other hand, normative theories of reason are about how we *ought* to reason (at either the operational or meta-level); and their development of thesis 2 specifies the details of the ideal (albeit not always the actual) way to reason."

[31] For similar interpretations of Hume, see Darwall (1995) and Millgram (1995). However, it would seem that one could be a curmudgeon not only about reasons for action, but also reasons for belief – that is, resisting belief in (and in no way motivated to believe) that which (according to the imperatives of theoretical reason) one has reason to believe. What can Hume say to such a curmudgeon? Why should there be norms that are authoritative over belief when, according to Hume, there are no norms that are authoritative over action? I believe Hume seriously considers that there may not be authoritative theoretical norms either, which explains why he resorts so often to psychologizing talk in Book I of *Treatise*. See Owen (1994).

reasons. There are two problems with the appeal to second-order desires. First, suppose a curmudgeon has a second-order desire to desire to act instrumentally. Why should it be possible that as a result of this second-order desire, he comes to have the first-order instrumental desire? Isn't a theorist who believes in this possibility implicitly committed to the idea that the second-order desire is authoritative in a way that is motivationally efficacious with respect to desire-formation? Why should we believe such a motivational effect is possible? To desire to desire x may or may not result in desiring x; doing so is contingent on an individual's motivational psychology. Hence our curmudgeon may have this second-order desire, but *still* not have the first-order desire, and hence may still not see any point in doing x, given that he lacks the desire to do so.

Second, and more important, does this second-order desire really lend "authority" to anything? It is an assumption of those who appeal to hierarchies of desire that higher-order desires are authoritative with respect to the lower-order desires they are about. But why should this be so? What makes it the case that these desires are "more important than" any competing lower-order desire? Suppose the curmudgeon has a competing first-order desire not to do that action which, as it happens, is instrumentally efficacious in the achievement of an extremely important end; still if that competing desire is *stronger* than either the second-order desire or the first-order desire to behave in an instrumentally efficacious way, such that the curmudgeon fails to act in the instrumentally efficacious way, how has he done anything "wrong"? To say that he has is to attribute to the second-order desire an "importance" that is more than mere strength, and that would seem to involve the notion of objective authority that we have already seen a Humean cannot endorse, given his naturalistic commitments.

Initially it might appear that the appeal to a general desire would avoid this last problem. A general desire to act in an instrumentally effective way might be thought to govern the process of satisfying specific desires, so that a person with this desire would want to satisfy specific desires in an instrumentally rational way in order to satisfy this general desire. But why should an agent regard such a desire of hers as "governing" anything? A person may well have this general desire, but if it is weaker than another of her desires that will only be satisfied if she acts in an instrumentally irrational way, why should she take it that satisfaction of the general desire "ought" to take precedence, such that she has erred if she acts on the (stronger) desire? There is nothing in a Humean moral psychology that allows us to say that by virtue of acting against her weaker general desire she has acted wrongly, unless we attribute to that general desire some authority, which on the Humean view, we are unable to do. So the point is that the general desire to act instrumentally does not by itself generate that authority, and will only work to show that an agent has erred unless she acts instrumentally if this authority is (illicitly) added to the general desire.

The Naturalized Kantian View

The preceding argument against the Humean view stressed the way in which our normal reaction to irrational people presupposes that they have defied the authority of the instrumental norm. Although this presupposition appears to be problematic, the naturalized Kantian view proposes that we can accept our reliance on the idea of authority in our conception of instrumental reason, as long as we "naturalize" this idea. If such naturalization is possible, the naturalized Kantian can accept all the preceding criticisms of the Humean view, but nonetheless insist that they do not count in favor of any nonnatural view, such as the Kantian or Millian views, that rely on the idea of objective (nonnatural) normative authority.

The naturalized Kantian view of the force of hypothetical imperatives, unlike the Humean view, tries to accommodate the Kantian idea that those who violate these imperatives have "done something wrong," and it agrees with the Kantian position that to understand rational action, we must accept the way in which such action is taken "because of" the authority of the imperative. However, the naturalized Kantian position tries to naturalize the motivationally efficacious authority of these imperatives, understanding it as something "in the brain" – generating a distinct kind of motivational effect. This new naturalist position doesn't banish normativity from reason, but rather tries to "tame" it by naturalizing it.

I will argue, however, that this position still fails to capture the way in which we normally think about rational and irrational action. Consider that this position makes the normative authority of instrumental rationality a contingent feature of human biology, which may not be shared by all humans, and which may not persist as our evolution continues. In this view, different biologies are capable of producing different rationalities; means / end reasoning of the sort we are used to commending cannot be regarded as uniquely and objectively *right*.

Yet we *do* consider it uniquely and objectively right. Although it is common for people to believe that there are different conceptions of morality with different psycho-social origins, it is not common for anyone, and certainly not common for philosophers, to recognize the possibility that there can be different instrumental rationalities with different psycho-social origins.[32] A naturalized Kantian might explain this "prejudice" in favor of the instrumental conception as an inevitable part of the wiring of human beings insofar as members of our species could only have survived if they embraced it. But there are three reasons why this explanation won't suffice to explain our "prejudice."

First, any claim that there is some biological "inevitability" to our being instrumental reasoners is dubious. The survival of virtually every species on the planet is not contingent on its members thinking in this way (and many survive quite nicely without "thinking" at all). So why should we believe that the survival of our species has depended on its acceptance? Indeed, we have empirical evidence that it has *not* depended on it: If instrumental reasoning is an inevitable part of human wiring, why do so many human beings behave, at least sometimes, contrary to its dictates? To explain irrationality, the naturalized Kantian has to acknowledge that human brains are complicated, and contain structures that generate behavior at odds with instrumental rationality. Since these (well-entrenched) structures are also a product of evolution, and by hypothesis, contributory to human survival, they would seem to be every bit as important to human functioning as instrumental reason. Note that the temptation to say that they aren't because they aren't the *right* kinds of functioning has to be resisted by the naturalized Kantian; there is no objective biologically independent conception of rightness to which the naturalized Kantian can appeal to justify instrumental reasoning. The most this theorist can say is that many people (who regard themselves as "right-thinking") will regard such reasoning as correct, by

---

[32] Although this assumption is sometimes questioned [for example, by Stich (1990) and Kurt Baier (1995)] with respect to some forms of reasoning, I know of no one who has explicitly proposed that instrumental reasoning may be a social construction.

virtue of their psychology and the way it has been affected by their social milieu, but their (mere) sense of its rightness cannot be, by itself, an argument for the claim that instrumental reasoning is more important to the survival of the species than other forms of mental processing. Indeed, exactly what features of human beings have been contributory to the survival of the species seems to be more a matter of speculation than anything else. (For how can any theory that purports to answer this question be empirically tested?)

So someone who violated instrumental reasoning could claim that while the naturalized Kantian's view might explain why other people come to label her 'irrational,' it does not establish that there is anything "wrong" with her insofar as her reasoning and behavior is a product of her brain, and reflects the evolution of human beings, every bit as much as instrumental reasoning and behavior. Indeed, this theory allows *her* to label *them* irrational every bit as much as the reverse. Note also that the reality of extensive irrationality among the human population precludes the naturalized Kantian from arguing that those who violate the counsels of instrumental reason should not be included as members of the community of rational persons; that would be to exclude virtually all members of the human species! But even if such people were unusual, such exclusion is still not licensed by biology. Biologists do not exclude creatures from membership in a species simply because they display "unusual" features or features that they (for some reason) do not approve of or regard as evolutionarily unfit. Indeed, those features may be potentially important for the species' future survival if the environment selects for them in the future.

To see the second reason for the failure of the naturalized Kantian's position, let us put aside the preceding arguments for a moment, and suppose that the naturalized Kantian is able to define some minimal amount of instrumental rationality, which by hypothesis has been necessary for the survival value of the human species. Even granting the naturalized Kantian so much, however, does not allow him to salvage the idea that instrumental reasoning is more than just a kind of reasoning that (merely) "seems" right for some people. In particular, it does not give him grounds for commending those who possess at least this minimal amount of rationality or for criticizing those who do not. Members of this latter group would presumably be biologically different from the rest of us, but we could not consider them "wrong," or their wiring "defective" without treating the instrumental norm generating these evaluations as objective. We might "dislike" their wiring insofar as it differs from our wiring, but there is nothing in the naturalist's world that would permit us to conclude that our wiring is objectively *better* than theirs (we might *think* ours is better, but there is no objective value "out there" that our thinking can be based on). As we discussed in Chapter 1, the biologists' evaluative language does not involve appeals to any objective normative authority.

This brings us to the third, and most important, problem with the naturalized Kantian's view. Even if our species' survival were contingent on the acceptance of instrumental reasoning, the fact that a certain kind of (normative) reasoning is necessary for a species' survival given the contingent circumstances of its environment as it evolves does not make it *right*. Hence, even if it were true that human beings who are wired to think and behave instrumentally virtually all of the time have been able to survive better than those who did not have such wiring, *that* fact doesn't make their wiring intrinsically better than the wiring of any other person – the naturalist who repudiates objective normative authority cannot consider survival of a species an objective value by which to measure the traits of individual members of the species. Indeed, recall our discussion of the meaning of inclusive fitness in Chapter 1. To say that a certain trait has been good for a species is merely to say its environment has been such that this trait has allowed the numbers of this species to remain steady or to increase up to now. If the environment changes, the trait could cause those numbers to decrease. There is nothing in evolutionary biology that could make any trait – in particular, any reasoning procedure – intrinsically "right" or "good," and so nothing that we could say using evolutionary biology that could establish instrumental reasoning as (objectively) right and thus authoritative for all human beings.

So the naturalized Kantian story can at most explain the *felt* authority of the instrumental norm, but it can never explain how or why this norm "really is" authoritative independent of the contingent facts of human biology. In other words, the naturalized Kantian view can say that most of us may think it is authoritative because (for evolutionary reasons) we feel it to be so; but it can never say that we feel it to be so because it *is* so. Hence, given that we *do* think that there is a rightness to this sort of thinking, the naturalized Kantian's account is implicitly committed to a kind of Mackie-like error theory. It grants that people take the normative prescriptions of instrumental reason to be "objectively right" and not just a function of how they are made or how they think, and it grants that people act on them by virtue of what they take to be their objective authority, but it must deny that there is any such objective authority, and maintain that we mistakenly confuse the "feel" of the authority of these imperatives for this (unreal) objective authority.

Such an error theory is really a kind of skeptical position on practical reason analogous to moral skepticism. Compare Harman's position on moral thinking. Suppose we see boys pouring gasoline on a cat and we say "that is wrong." Harman's explanation of our evaluation is that we (merely) *think* it is wrong, where our having this thought can be explained by reference to natural facts about us (for example, our biology, psychology, or social influences). But there is no natural property of "wrongness" we are responding to when we make that evaluation. The naturalized Kantian position on the nature of instrumental reason is essentially the same. This position explains our evaluations of actions as instrumentally rational or irrational by pointing to the way our brains work, but it does not take it that our brains work this way because we are responding to something about actions that "really" makes them rational or irrational.

If this position is right, what effect would that have on our acceptance of norms, and in particular, the instrumental norm? Why wouldn't it undermine our sense of their authority, insofar as we now understand that such authority was merely "felt" and not "real"? A proponent of this position might insist that our wiring is such that we cannot (physiologically) reject certain sorts of norms – in this view, biology not only makes us normative reasoners, but also *wires in* the content of particular norms. But even if such substantive wiring makes sense, the fact that all of us are capable of acting irrationally seems to suggest that instrumental reasoning and action is *not* physiologically inescapable! So why should we persist in it? Why shouldn't we be curmudgeons? There are, it seems, Feyerabendian implications to this position that many of its proponents may find unwelcome. But I do not see any clear way of warding off such implications.

While these arguments are sufficient to show that the naturalized Kantian account does not capture the way in which we think about the authority of instrumental reasons, they are not sufficient to show that the naturalized Kantian position is *wrong*. I take it that many moral skeptics, including Mackie and Harman, may be distressed at the idea of accepting an error theory of the judgments of practical reason, insofar as they have standardly assumed that the judgments of instrumental reason could be naturalistically "grounded" in a way that makes them true, unlike moral judgments. But a naturalized Kantian may simply insist that, nonetheless, naturalists have no choice but to accept his view, insofar as there is no way to make those judgments come out as true in the way that we standardly understand them, and still remain naturalists. But later on in Chapter 6 we will explore why the naturalized Kantian position (and any error theory of the judgments of practical reason) is not good enough for a naturalist committed to the enterprise of science. If the naturalized Kantian view cannot provide a conception of rationality that is consistent with the commitments of science, then we will be left with the Kantian or Millian theory, and if my arguments earlier are right that the Kantian theory is the better of these two, then Kant's theory of reason is implicitly undergirding the practice of science. And if this is right, then science itself is grounded in the objective authority of a kind of "ought" statement – where that objective authority cannot be explained, or explained away, in psychological or biological terms. To put it another way, the methods of science are responsive to an authority that is taken by the practitioners of those methods to be "outside" of themselves (and "outside" of the society, or the culture, of which they are a part), to which they are responding (and to which anyone *could* respond) when they use these methods.

Ultimately I shall argue that this commitment to objective authority implicit in science makes self-refuting any science-based argument directed solely against the scientific permissibility of the objective authority of moral norms. Let me reiterate the point that I have not established that moral discourse (or, for that matter scientific discourse, or discourse that invokes instrumental reason) can be taken to be true; I have said nothing about how one determines the truth of any normative discourse, scientific or otherwise. So the naturalist might argue that scientific discourse is an example of a normative discourse that is true in a way that moral discourse can never be. Such an argument presupposes a theory of how one discerns the truth of a normative discourse—a theory that heretofore no naturalist has been interested in developing because no naturalist thought such a theory was necessary. ("We don't have unreduced norms in our discourse—only you moralists have them," they have said.)

What such a theory might look like, and whether it could successfully confirm naturalists' beliefs, will be the topic of Chapter 6.

EVALUATING THE THEORIES THAT RELY ON OBJECTIVE AUTHORITY

We're left with the Kantian and Millian positions on the "force" of hypothetical imperatives, both of which incorporate the troublesome notion of authority. But I shall now argue that only the Kantian position, which is the less naturalistic of the two, really succeeds as a theory of reasons.

The Millian View

Insofar as the Millian incorporates the Kantian conception of reason's authority, it is immediately problematic for the naturalist, who will object to the idea that such authority is real, whether or not that authority is taken to be motivationally efficacious. Hence the Millian understanding of the prescriptive force of hypothetical imperatives cannot be the underpinning for any naturalist, insofar as it would introduce the kind of nonnatural elements into that position to which naturalists have objected in moral theories. Nonetheless, for those non-Hobbesians who are willing to be more flexible about what they take to be "natural," the Millian position might seem to be plausible, and indeed a nice compromise between Kantian and Humean positions on reason, insofar as it combines a classic (and, for many, attractive) position on the nature of reasons with a naturalist theory of motivation.

But I shall now argue that this view is implausible precisely because of its naturalist motivational theory. Consider that for a Kantian, acting on the authority of an imperative is being moved to act by the reason given us by the imperative. Alternatively, the imperative's reason is that *for the sake of which* we act. In contrast, if a hypothetical imperative is a mere causal lever to action, it causes action, but not insofar as it gives us a reason. Its causal efficacy has to do with other features it possesses – for example, its rhetorical power, or its power on one's memory or aesthetic sense, and is not created by the (bare) idea (which may or may not be in our heads) that there is something for the sake of which we must act.

Consider the following examples of a hypothetical imperative that acts to effect action solely as a lever. First, there is Sally, who has a nasty sore throat. You tell her that she should go to the doctor to cure it. After hearing your imperative, Sally starts thinking about how much she dislikes the offices of the doctors she has seen in the past, then starts thinking about the doctors she has seen, then starts reflecting on the fact that her present doctor has done very well with his investments, and then develops a desire to see him so that she can get him to give her investment advice. Your hypothetical imperative was causally efficacious in generating a motive in Sally to see the doctor. But it is not true that she acted from the reason given her by the hypothetical imperative. That is, your imperative did not give Sally a reason, which, by virtue of its authority, created a motive in her to go to the doctor. Instead, the words you uttered conjured up ideas that initiated a line of thought that, as it happens (and it could have happened otherwise), eventuated in the generation of a desire to perform the action your imperative directed.

Second, consider a (science fiction) example of a tyrant who, whenever he gave hypothetical imperatives to his subjects, also gave these subjects injections of a serum that resulted in their developing a motive to perform the action prescribed by the imperative. Suppose that one subject, Tom, hated shots, and to avoid getting injected, would immediately develop a motive to do the action directed whenever he heard the tyrant's command. The command would therefore be responsible for Tom's motive, and yet it is not responsible for it *in the way* that would allow us to say that Tom's behavior was rational by virtue of the fact that he acted "from" the reason given him by the imperative.

Third, consider Rolf the dog, who has been trained to run to his meal dish to get his dinner whenever he hears the phrase, "Rolf, if you want dinner you must go to your meal dish." Rolf does not run to the meal dish because he is moved by the reason in the imperative – Rolf can't act from reasons. Instead, he runs to the dish because there is something about the imperative other than its reason for action that causally effects his action.

So, to say that in the Millian view, a hypothetical imperative can only affect us as a lever, is to say that *all* imperatives affect *all* of us in the way that Sally, or Tom, or Rolf the dog were affected by the imperatives given them. The Millian view precludes the idea that we can ever act *from* a hypothetical imperative, or *on* the reason given us by the imperative. Even if we agree with Raz that sometimes we conform to our reasons for action rather than comply with them, nonetheless we do not want a theory of reasons that says that this compliance is impossible. Capturing the phenomenon of compliance is part of what we want a theory of reason to do. Indeed, it is worth reflecting on the fact that even conformity to reason seems to involve in *some* sense, a responsiveness to the authority of that reason, even if acting on its directive is not directly motivated by that authority. Although I cannot pursue this idea here, consider that when we merely conform to, rather than comply with, our reasons, then insofar as this conformity is not accidental, it is nonetheless "for the sake of" the reason, and hence "from" the reason in a way that Sally's, or Tom's, or Rolf's actions were not. In general, "responsiveness to authority" is a hallmark of action from reasons, and that is precisely what the Millian view cannot accommodate.

So in the end, like the Humean position, the Millian view destroys the idea that we can ever act rationally or irrationally, and instead makes all action *nonrational*. Unlike the Humean view, it does so not because it says that there are no reasons for action, but because it insists that there is *nothing* that we can do *for a reason*. This is a subtle point. A person who acts rationally, as a result of your hypothetical imperative directed to her, will say that she is motivated *by* the reason in that imperative to do what she does; she does not say (or mean) that something about your articulation of the imperative (other than its giving you a reason) has (contingently) causally effected her motivational structure to effect a motive to act as the reason directed. In order to capture the idea that we can act rationally and irrationally, a theory of the normative force of instrumental reason must grant that hypothetical imperatives generate reasons for action that are by themselves motivationally efficacious, and not mere causal levers that usually (but contingently) have effect on our psychology.

Certain readers will wish mightily to resist this conclusion. Surely, they will insist, there is some way to see the hypothetical imperative as causal, and yet preserve the idea that we can act from it such that we are rational (or against it, such that we are irrational). But I would ask them how that imperative can be causal *in the right way* unless its causality works via the (authoritative) reason it gives us. If it is causally efficacious in any other way, then when we act as it directs we will merely be acting in accordance with that imperative, something that even an animal can do. Our action will be merely (fortuitously) according to reason, and not truly *rational*. To be causal in the right way, however, a reason must act on us in what seems to be a nonnatural way. As we discussed in the last chapter, the idea of action that is "responsive to authority" is troubling from a naturalist standpoint. Since explanations of action in terms of directive reasons involve an appeal to what Aristotle called "final ends" – the idea that someone is acting "for the sake of" something – a reason-based explanation is not a normal efficient cause explanation, because it posits the reason as that "for the sake of which" a person acted. To quote Kant, "Everything in nature works in accordance with laws. Only a rational being has the power to act *in accordance with his idea of* laws – that is, in accordance with principles – and only so has he a will."[33]

As Kant appreciates, acting on a (moral) law is not like being caused to act by a (physical) law. One might say that a reason is not a causal push, but a "compelling pull," which compulsion is nonetheless something that an agent can choose to resist or defy. How do any causal models of science allow us to capture this aspect of explanations of action that appeal to directive reasons from (authoritative) norms? Moreover, the pull that reasons exert is understood to be a function of their authority. It was the authority of the reason that prompts a rational agent's decision: "I knew it was the right thing to do, and that's why I did it." Or in other words, it is the *importance* of the reason that "causes" her to do it. Well, what could that mean? It is not the "importance" of the earth that explains why objects are (gravitationally) attracted to it, nor does it make sense to explain the attraction of iron filings to a magnet by appeal to any sense of importance. There is no explanation in science of any natural phenomenon that makes reference to anything like normative authority. The queer "inherent prescriptivity" that Mackie assumed to be, for any naturalist, beyond the pale is assumed by the objectivist to be (in some sense) responsible for a motive. But such a causation is, once again, unlike any causation recognized or studied by science.

The grain of truth in the Millian position is that we can have a reason that doesn't move us, insofar as we aren't aware of it, or don't understand it. We should not want to deny the reality of nonrationality, manifested by people who don't act rationally because they don't know what rationality demands. But an adequate theory of

[33] Kant (1785), Chapter 2. Paton translation, p. 80.

reason – one that preserves the idea that we can act rationally and irrationally – must preserve the idea that we can (and should) act from (and not merely according to) reasons.[34] The only theory of reason that preserves this idea is the Kantian theory. Ironically, the theory that has the least plausible and least naturalistic answer to the question "why be rational?" is, thus far, the most plausible account of how we think about instrumentally rational action.

The Kantian View

The Kantian view incorporates the idea that instrumental reasons are authoritative (regardless of our desires) and motivationally efficacious by virtue of that authority. Thus it fits with our intuitions about how we should think about the nature and effects of instrumental reasons. But the problem with the Kantian view is that by postulating the idea that a reason's motivational efficacy is necessary by virtue of its authority, all variants of the view accept both a conception of objective normative authority, and an account of motivation by virtue of this authority, neither of which is acceptable to a naturalist. We have already discussed the nonnaturalness of the idea of objective normative authority in Chapter 3. The idea that such an authority not only exists, but can move us to act, is even more fantastic to a naturalist. Whether or not the authority of the hypothetical imperative is taken to motivate action directly, or via some psychological intermediary such as a desire, all variants of the Kantian view take it that *this authority* can get us to perform the mandated action; and this kind of causal efficacy is neither recognized nor studied by science since the (objective) normative authority doing the causing is neither recognized nor studied by science. Indeed, we can use Kant's term 'willing' to describe this special motivation that reason

---

[34] I would suggest that this means Bernard Williams really defends a Kantian notion of reasons for action. Although Williams took his paper to be a defense of *Humean* understandings of reason and morality, Christine Korsgaard points out that, absent the addition of a substantive argument that rules the Kantian position out, Williams's defense of internal reasons is as much a defense of Kant's conception of reasons as it is of Hume's. See Korsgaard (1986). But I am pointing out here that since Hume's own position obviates the idea that there are reasons for action, and the Millian position is clearly externalist, Williams can only be defending a Kantian position on the *nature* of reasons for action, even if he has a Humean view of what the substance of those reasons can be.

provides; in the Kantian view, instrumentally rational people act so as to secure means to their ends not merely (and perhaps not at all) because they "want" to do so, but because they "will" to do so, where the substance and motivational force of this willing is provided by reason. Kant himself accepts this, and strives in his *Critique of Pure Reason* and in subsequent works on moral theory to develop a defense of the nonnatural motivational efficacy of this authority.

By virtue of understanding that authority, this willing of ends to means is supposed to be motivationally possible. The rational person thinks to herself, "I understand that this is the best end, and this action is the means to it, so I've got to do this action." So the authority of the instrumental reason is taken to motivate not merely the action, but the way in which a person sustains herself to the end, such that she performs the action. "Going to the doctor is awful, but I've got to do it if I want to be well, so I'll follow reason and carry through" says Harry, if he's rational. The binding nature of instrumental rationality doesn't merely prompt action, it does so by binding the agent to his (all-things-considered) end in these circumstances. In this sense, the agent "acts from" her reason to perform the action.

I take this to be an accurate account of how in fact we think about the dictates of instrumental reason and what we mean when we criticize those who violate them. So the Kantian account is the one that is assumed by our ordinary practice, informing our "commonsense" reactions to agents (a point I will pursue further in the next two chapters). And yet the idea of objective normative authority associated with reason that binds people to ends in a way that motivates their behavior seems to defy the common sense of any naturalist. As I've noted, the instrumental theory has been popular with naturalists and social scientists generally because it seems not only a highly plausible answer to the question "why be rational?", but also one that is acceptable to naturalists insofar as it does not appear to rely on some kind of "magical" force that human beings are supposed to have the capacity to sense and be motivated by. But the Kantian explanation of the motivational efficacy of a hypothetical imperative by virtue of its authority seems to make it just as magical as any categorical imperative. However contingent the hypothetical "ought" is on a desire, it is still *not* the same as a desire; to say, therefore, that its objective normative authority is what moves us to act rationally is to analyze the "prescriptive force" of hypothetical imperatives such that it is identical to the prescriptive force of categorical imperatives. If naturalists reject the plausibility of this analysis for categorical imperatives, they must do so for hypothetical imperatives.

There is another way to see both the attractiveness and the non-natural features of Kant's approach to practical reason, and this returns us to what Kant might have meant by referring to the "analyticity" of willing the means to an end if one wills the end. Precisely what is the mistake that irrational people are making, such that they deserve our criticism? Consider Harry, who is ill and desires above all else to be well, and therefore determines he should go to the doctor today, but instead he spends the day reading. Now there is a sense in which he is acting from an instrumental reason even when he avoids the doctor by reading, because the reason is a way of satisfying one of his ends. But, we say, it isn't the *right* end. Harry's reflection (which, for the sake of argument, we'll assume does not involve reason operating noninstrumentally) establishes that, all things considered, Harry's getting well is, in Harry's own view, the best or the right end in the circumstances, so that it must be the end that his reason serves. Hence, if Harry reads instead, we criticize him. So in a situation where someone such as Harry has a plurality of ends, we criticize someone who pursues an end that he takes to be less important as "irrational," not because he fails to sustain effective instrumental action at all, but because he fails to sustain effective instrumental action to achieve the "real" or the "right" end in the circumstances. So, to return to Kant's remark that "the proposition 'If I fully will the effect, I also will the action required for it' is analytic,"[35] we might say that our criticism of an agent who is irrational in the way that Harry is irrational offers us another way of interpreting Kant's remark – that is, to be instrumentally rational is to *will* the end that is in some way best or strongest in the circumstances, where willing means "sustaining a commitment to that end through action." The rational person is one who doesn't falter in her pursuit of the (best or strongest) end; she binds herself to it and remains committed to it in the face of a temptation to pursue a worse end that is nonetheless (in some respect) easier to achieve than the "better" end.

But this means, as Kant's remarks suggest, that our criticism of

---

[35] Kant (1785). Paton translation, p. 85.

someone as irrational is as much about ends as means. We're not just saying that the person performed the wrong means, but also that he failed to will (what he took to be) the better end in the circumstances. Although there may be some hypothetical imperative on which he can be said to have acted, he failed to act on the *right* hypothetical imperative, or the right instrumental reasons, insofar as he pursued the wrong *end*. As I've said, by "wrong end" I'm trying not to invoke the idea of an end dictated by reason understood noninstrumentally, so fill out that term in whatever nonrational and nonnormative way you like. The point is that even when we insist on thinking of reason as only instrumental in its role, it is still a conception of reason that is fundamentally concerned with ends – dictating not what they are, but rather the *way* we should be committed to them (or "will" them), where these dictates are understood as objectively authoritative, governing us no matter the content of our desires. Note that even if instrumental rationality doesn't tell you *what* to desire, it does tell you, following a decision regarding what you want, that you must remain committed to what you want by virtue of its being more important for you (according to your own lights) than other alternative ends.

This way of thinking about Kant's remark explains why it has a certain logical overtone. Instrumental reasoning is analogous to logical reasoning (which is another way in which we can consider it "analytic") by virtue of the fact that just as a rule of inference can mandate a conclusion, so too can willing an end that is the only or best or right end in the circumstances mandate an action, where "willing" here means, as I've said, a kind of reason-based commitment to achieving it. I am trying, on Kant's behalf, to make a conceptual point here about the nature of rational willing – that all and only instrumentally rational agents can be said to will ends, as opposed to merely "wanting" them – where willing is not only a distinctive psychological state but also a state that involves reason as a motive for action. Whereas we may merely "want" an end, but refuse to take what we regard as hateful means to achieving it, preferring action that will achieve some lesser good, if we are instrumentally rational agents then, via our reason, we will commit ourselves to that end – that is, "will" it, insofar as we regard it as the best or the only end in the circumstances – and thus will not become derailed by the temptation for lesser goods.

A Humean could, if he liked, admit the possibility of something like a psychological state of "commitment" to an end, triggered after performing some all-things-considered reflection, but he could not say that if this commitment failed – so that this psychological state somehow changed – he had in any way made a mistake. The charge that such a person made a mistake relies on a norm dictating the persistence of this state until the end is achieved. We might state the norm as something like, "Sustain action (or commit yourself to means) to achieve the end that your reflection has told you is most important in the circumstances." This norm clearly presupposes a commitment to some notion of reflection, which an instrumentalist theorist could try to flesh out in whatever (nonnormative, nonrational) way he liked, but it also mandates a way that the instrumentally rational person should be related to his reflectively best end that requires a commitment to sustaining the means to achieving it.

According to this way of interpreting Kant's remark, it is still normative, relying in particular on a norm directing us to behave in ways that we might defy, such that we are then appropriately considered irrational. Hence this way of construing Kant's remark leaves room for the reality of irrationality. Irrational agents fail to will the end that they acknowledge is the best end in the circumstances (they want it, but they don't will it), and for that reason we criticize them and call their behavior mistaken.

Willing is a psychological state, but if the Kantians are right, it is a psychological state that is responsive to the norm stated earlier commanding commitment. One might call it a "norm-responsive psychological state." And this norm is one that is objective – so the agent's responsiveness is to the norm and its (objective) authority; as a result of that authority, we bind ourselves to our all-things-considered end. (And if noninstrumentalists are right, we may also do so because there is something about this end that, using our reason, we've determined is important for us to follow.)

Note that this norm, which is implicitly involved in what it means to be instrumentally rational, is stated in a way that makes it categorical rather than hypothetical. Kant's position on the nature of hypothetical imperatives must be construed (contra his explicit wishes) such that understanding the bindingness of a hypothetical imperative is no easier than understanding the bindingness of a categorical imperative. My interpretation cannot save Kant's belief that the former is more straightforward than the latter; indeed, my argument is that Kant's belief is wrong. The only way to analyze Kant's analyticity claim is to do so in a way that locates in hypothetical imper-atives the same mysterious objective authority that attends the categorical imperative. Even more strikingly, I have argued that the force of hypothetical imperatives is dependent on, and *is at least in part constituted by*, the force of some antecedent categorical impera-tive that is in part definitive of instrumental rationality. I suspect Kant was influenced by the same myth as contemporary naturalists – that hypothetical imperatives are "easier" to understand and de-fend than categorical imperatives. The thrust of my remarks is that this is not so, *especially* if one takes seriously a Kantian-style view of the nature of hypothetical imperatives.

It is a testament to the free ride that the instrumental theory has enjoyed from philosophers in the modern era that hypothetical im-peratives were thought to be straightforwardly motivational in a way that categorical imperatives were not. But the upshot of the preced-ing arguments is that an "ought" is an "ought." And if we want to interpret instrumental oughts as prescriptive statements that apply to action and that we can act *from* (and not merely in conformity with), we must accept a Kantian account of the authoritative and motivational force of hypothetical imperatives. But as the next chap-ters will show, things get worse. Theorizing about the nature of in-strumental reason also requires taking a stand on the nature of the good, which means, paradoxically, that any theory of instrumental reason can't be "instrumental" after all.

Chapter 5

Why Instrumental Reasoning Isn't Instrumental

[computer file 1/22/96]

In Chapter 4, I aimed to show that instrumental rationality, as we standardly conceive of it, is informed by a notion of normativity that includes the idea of objective authority – just the idea that moral skeptics have claimed objective moral theories include, such that they are not acceptable from a naturalist point of view. The aim of that chapter was to begin the "companions in guilt" strategy for defending objectivist moral theory. That strategy is meant to disarm morality's skeptical critics, for if these skeptics presuppose in their conception of rationality the same occult element that they criticize in objectivist moral theories, then their criticisms indirectly defeat their own position.

This chapter continues the "companions in guilt" strategy by examining in more detail the nature of instrumental reasoning. Most theorists have taken it for granted that defining the nature of instrumental reason does not in any way involve developing a conception of the good, because figuring out the nature of instrumental reason is quite separate from the task of figuring out what the good is. This point of view is particularly critical for what I will call the "instrumentalists," who believe that the only role that reason plays in practical deliberation is an instrumental role.

However, in this chapter I will argue that any conception of instrumental rationality must involve at least *some* components of a conception of the good. To be precise, I will argue for two theses:

1. A critical component of instrumental reasoning, which I will call the theory of the "structure" of instrumental reasoning in situations where the agent has more than one end, is *the same thing as* a theory of the "structure" of that agent's good.
2. Different theories of instrumental reason are committed to

different theses regarding the source and nature of the preferences defining an agent's good. These theses are, as we shall see, minimally substantive, but they are substantive nonetheless. They define certain aspects of the content of the agent's good by setting out the sort of preferences that can or cannot be included in the agent's good-defining preference set.

If this is right, any conception of what it means to be "instrumentally rational" involves a certain conception of the good, and the criticism of a person as irrational involves objecting not merely to *how* the person pursues what she wants, but also to *what* she wants.

Most philosophers in our tradition have assumed this can't be right, arguing first that whatever a person's good happens to be, instrumental reason can be defined independently, such that it serves that good, and second that whatever a person's good is, a criticism of someone as instrumentally irrational does not involve a criticism of what she takes to be good. But while it is true that we needn't decide whether, say, Aristotle or Bentham had the better definition of the good for human beings in order to make progress in understanding the nature of instrumental reasoning, nonetheless I will show that understanding instrumental reason necessitates some reflection on how to understand our good. I will also argue that there currently exist in the philosophical literature theoretical quarrels about the nature of instrumental reasoning that are really quarrels about the conception of the good that a rational person should have. If this is correct, then there is no such thing as a conception of reason divorced from a conception of the good, a conclusion that vitiates the idea that reason can be defined as "merely" instrumental or divided into instrumental and noninstrumental components, that also shows the extent to which our conception of instrumental reason is built out of normative components that are taken to be objectively authoritative.

COHERENT PREFERENCES

To make my argument that theories of instrumental reason are not and cannot be instrumental, I must begin by "pulling a small thread" – a loose end – in the fabric of the standard conception of instrumental reason, in order to ultimately unravel it. So first we must locate that small thread.

As I will understand it, a theory of instrumental reason sets out the structure of that form of reasoning that aims to ascertain how best to achieve ends that an agent has. Many theorists believe that the only kind of practical reason that exists is instrumental reason; others think that there is a form of practical reason that actually defines the ends of action. But these theorists agree that reason at least plays an instrumental role. So an instrumental conception of reason attributes to reason *only* an instrumental role. Let me define an instrumental conception of reason more precisely. I will call something a "motivated end" if it is an end of action that an agent has because attaining it will serve, or help her to achieve, some other end of action that an agent has. I will call something an "unmotivated end" if it is an end of action that an agent has, but which is not itself a means to attaining or serving any other end (we might say that it is an end that is wanted for its own sake). An *instrumental conception of practical reason* says:

1. A fundamental component of practical reasoning is reasoning that determines the best means to an end (there may be other operations of practical reason, such as planning, but I leave this aside for now).
2. Practical reasoning plays no role in the setting of unmotivated ends of action.

Or we can define the instrumental conception using the following notion of a *preference*:

A preference of x over y is a kind of "disposition" that the agent has to choose x over y in a situation where one is offered a pairwise choice between them.

In this definition, nothing is said about where a preference comes from, so that it leaves open the possibility that the cause of preference may have something to do with reason (different theorists will take different stands on that issue). But an instrumental conception of reason will deny this. In particular it will say that

when an agent reasons prior to action, she reasons with respect to her preference set, which constitutes her "good," where what she prefers is not defined by her reasoning except insofar as that reasoning causes her to develop preferences by identifying motivated ends.

Henceforth, I will speak of an agent's good in terms of her preferences (either those she actually has, or those she ought to have). Note that even noninstrumental theorists have agreed with instrumental theorists that when it comes to defining reason's instrumental role, it is completely unnecessary to substantively evaluate what preferences count as good-defining.

But now we have found our loose end, because this definition of instrumental action is inadequate. Consider that tenets 1 and 2 make reference to instrumental action with respect to "an end" – that is *one* end. Yet instrumentally rational agents are always agents that have a plurality of ends. And it is surely relevant to what we should do with respect to one end that we have other ends. So this statement of instrumental rationality is not good enough to explain or prescribe how an end is or should be attained in agents (such as ourselves) that have multiple ends. We need to answer the question, "How should an agent reason so as to attain an end, when she has many ends at that time which she also wants to attain?" So I need a haircut, I want to go to the bank, and I feel sleepy. I could initiate action to satisfy any of these ends. What does the instrumentally rational agent do?

The standard instrumentalist answer is that the agent should figure out which end is "most important" – via some kind of "consideration" process – and then reason instrumentally with respect to that remaining end (for example, Brandt's "cognitive psychotherapy" or Gauthier's "consideration" idea).[1] Whether this consideration process is a form of reasoning or not is an issue that a theorist will have to resolve. Note that however she resolves it, that resolution won't threaten the instrumentalist position that reason's *only* role is instrumental as long as this consideration process, if it is a form of reasoning, is understood merely to be a process of *identifying* what the agent takes to be the most important preference, and plays no part in *making* any of these preferences "important." A mere identification role for reason does not implicate it in defining in any substantive way the character of the good, and it is this latter role that

---

[1] Brandt (1979), p. 13; Gauthier 1986, Chapter 2.

the instrumentalist refuses to grant reason. In any case, isn't this answer good enough?

Not quite. The problem is this. An agent who has many ends has preferences from which these ends are defined, but these preferences may not be coherent. Consider our (deliberately) spare definition of preference that tries not to assume any controversial or substantive psychological theory (so that, for example, it even eschews definition in terms of desire) but that is still mentalistic insofar as it takes preferences not merely to be behavioristically revealed through determinate choices, but also something "in the head" that is (in some way) causally responsible for the choices we make. By this definition, a preference of x over y is a kind of disposition, the cause of which we will not specify, to choose x over y in a situation where one is offered a pairwise choice between them. The set containing all a person's preferences, so defined, may not be "coherent." For example, the set may contain intransitivities. Or it may be incomplete – that is, there may be objects that the agent does not know how to compare such that she cannot formulate a preference between them. Such incoherence can make the process of reaching a determinate answer to the question "which end is more important?" impossible. Thus, many theorists, particularly in economics, assume that an instrumentally rational agent satisfies preferences only after she has insured that her set of preferences satisfies certain coherence conditions.

For now, let us leave aside what these coherence conditions might be – usually but not always they are identified with the axioms of expected utility theory. In Chapters 7 and 8, I will explore in great detail the nature of these axioms, in an attempt to evaluate expected utility theory as a theory of reason. For now, however, it suffices to say that even admitting that these axioms are relevant and necessary to instrumental action is a way of applying normative principles so as to define the agent's set of ends. But any such set is a specification of that agent's good. Hence, applying coherence principles to an agent's preferences such that her actions in satisfying those preferences are fully rational amounts to defining instrumental reason by using in part criteria defining what I will call the "structure of the good." Although specifying the nature of instrumental reason does not require specifying the content of the ends we ought to pursue, it does require specifying what might be called the "shape" or "structure" of the set of ends that we ought to pursue.

So now we see that defining an instrumentally rational agent involves saying something about that agent's good. Specifically, whether we believe that instrumental reason is the only form of practical reason, or one of many forms of practical reason, it seems we must define instrumental rationality in something like the following way:

> An agent is instrumentally rational in her reasoning and/or behavior iff she attempts, to the best of her ability, to determine and/or take the best means to an end that is the object of one of her preferences, where this preference is part of a set of preferences belonging to her that satisfies certain coherence constraints.

This definition makes clear that anyone interested in defining instrumental rationality is going to have to take a normative stand on what these coherence constraints are – a stand that, as I've said, simultaneously involves taking a stand on the structure of a rational agent's good. But the definition also suggests how many other normative issues must be resolved to specify a conception of instrumental reason precisely.

For example, we need a specification of what the "best" means to an end is ("best" here can refer to a number of different values – for example, most efficient, least expensive, most attractive, and so on, and will presumably involve some weighting of these values). Second, we need to know what it means to say that a preference "belongs to" an agent. (For example, does this notion require a conception of an "authentic" preference? Ought an agent be conscious or aware that she has a preference for it to belong to her? I do not see how one can avoid the realm of the normative if one wants to identify the markers that do or do not make a preference "really" one's own.) Third, we need to know what "to the best of her ability" means. What counts as an excused failure in instrumental reasoning or behavior is a highly disputable theoretical matter, just as defining the concept of excused failures in moral and legal reasoning or action is a highly disputable – and disputed – matter in these areas.

Fourth, and finally, we need to know what the coherence constraints in this definition *are*. There are many possible theories of coherence. Some of them (such as expected utility theory) imply that reasoning and rational action involve maximization, and they will offer different conceptions of what maximization is. For example, axiom systems that include the independence axiom offer a different conception of maximization than those that do not. Other axiom systems may have a nonmaximizing conception of optimal preference satisfaction (for example, those that exclude the continuity axiom). All these disagreements, however, underline the point that a conception of instrumental reason must take a stand (that will inevitably be controversial) on the right conception of coherence. And this conception will define the nature of instrumentally rational decision-making and behavior for an agent with a multiplicity of ends *by requiring something that concerns the agent's good* (defined by her set of preferences) – namely, that the preferences that together specify her good have certain characteristics that allow the set they comprise to satisfy these axioms.

There is another way to make the same point, using terminology that will be very useful later. Let us distinguish between three different sets of preferences. First is the *Set of all preferences* belonging to an agent, or for short, the *Total Preference Set*. Second is the *Set of all preferences that are the source of our good-defining preferences*, or the *Source Set* for short. Whether or not the *Source Set* is the same as the *Total Preference Set* is something that different theories of the nature of our good can disagree about; any theory that specifies that a preference must have a certain content in order to be even potentially good-defining, is recognizing the possibility that an agent can have a preference that is nonetheless not the sort of preference that *could* be good-defining, and thus not the sort of preference that could be part of the source set. Third is the *Set of Good-defining preferences*, or the *GD Set* for short. An agent's good is defined by the *GD Set*; the preferences that are members of the *GD set* are culled from the *Source Set*, where the latter set contains, as I said, preferences of the agent that *could* be, but need not be, in the *GD Set*.

Now, in general, a proponent of the instrumental theory of reason will want to identify all three of these sets. So, for example, whereas noninstrumentalists will argue that such things as whims or phobias are not and could not be good-defining, instrumentalists will insist that all preferences count as good-defining, no matter their strangeness or their strength, so that the total set of preferences is the same as the set of preferences that *could* be good-defining (that is, the source set) and the same as the set of preferences that *are* in fact good-defining. But the recognition of the need for coherence constraints in his theory forces the instrumental theorist to recognize at least the difference between the *Source Set* and the *GD Set*. After all, the *Source Set*, which includes all those preferences taken to be relevant to defining the agent's good, may or may not be coherent; the *GD Set* is created from the *Source Set* by applying coherence constraints to the preferences in the *Source Set*. If the *Source Set* is coherent, the resulting *GD Set* after these constraints are applied is identical to it. If the *Source Set* is not coherent, the *GD Set* will not be the same as the *Source Set*. The *GD Set* will be a proper subset if coherence is achieved just by deleting preferences. On the other hand, it may simply be a different set if preferences also have to be added. (It is an interesting issue whether adding preferences to the *Source Set* in this way amounts to, or involves, a noninstrumental use of reason.) Finally it will be the same size, but different in content, if, to achieve coherence, the agent is obliged to change some of the preferences in the original *Source Set*.

In any case, no matter how these normative issues are resolved, and no matter what the right theory of coherence turns out to be, the point is that defining the instrumental role of reason will involve taking a variety of normative stands, including most importantly, a normative stand with respect to what counts as a coherent structure of an agent's preferences. And that normative stand is simultaneously a way of defining instrumental reason, and a way of defining an agent's *good*.[a]

Reasons for action derive from the *GD Set*, but not from the *Source Set* or the *Total Set* (unless the latter two sets are identical to the *GD Set*). (Even if a preference belongs to me, if it is inconsistent with the rest of my preferences, I do not have a reason to act on it. Indeed, reason tells me I have a reason not to act on it.) Following Nagel,[2] I will call the reasons that we can derive from the *GD Set* "general reasons" to act. Such reasons are not tied to any particular situation that I am now in, or that I expect to be in, but they are the sorts of considerations that I do take into account in any deliberation prior

---

[a]*Editor's note:* At this point in the manuscript, the following note appears: "[RELATE FOLLOWING DISCUSSION TO CHAPTER TWO AND THREE DISCUSSION OF REASONS AND NORMS]." The author was unable to follow her own directive, thus leaving to the reader the task of relating the discussions as best he may.

[2] Nagel (1970), p. 35.

to action. (So, given that I prefer apples to oranges, I have a general reason to choose apples over oranges, which I would take into account if I were in a concrete situation where I had a pairwise choice between them.) In any particular situation, those general reasons that are deemed relevant to the situation, are what I will call (again following Nagel), my "prima facie" reasons in the situation. Finally, among my prima facie reasons, the reason that I conclude I ought to act on is the "decisive" reason in this situation. While it is sufficient for something to be a general reason that it be derived from a preference in the *GD Set*, there are a number of theories of practical reason that will insist that it is not a necessary condition of something's being a reason that it be a member of this set. I will take no stand on this particular issue in this chapter.

Theorists should have appreciated this connection between reason and the good simply by thinking about the form of expected utility theory. As I shall discuss in Chapter 7, von Neumann and Morgenstern proved that if an agent's preference set satisfies the EU (expected utility) axioms, she will act *as if* she were an expected utility maximizer. Note the "as if." The proof is not that, if someone's preferences satisfy the axioms, then we can provide further argument to the effect that she will, or should, be an EU reasoner. It is rather that satisfying preferences constrained by these axioms *is the same thing as* maximizing expected utility. The "reasoning procedure" of a rational person is represented as *identical* to that person's having a conception of the good with a certain structure. Indeed, someone who never "reasoned" at all but who had a set of preferences satisfying the EU axioms, would look just like an EU maximizer. And someone who was an EU maximizer would implicitly be "fixing" his preferences so that they had the structure the EU axioms require. This means that the procedure an agent uses when he is said to be "reasoning" in a certain way is conceptually identical to that person's conception of the good defined subject to certain coherence constraints. Whereas implicit in the instrumentalist position is a sharp distinction between the operation one uses to reason and that which one reasons *with*, these reflections show that no such sharp distinction can be made. What a person reasons with determines how she reasons. Or to put it another way: EU theory represents the structure of an agent's conception of the good, and her reasoning so as to achieve the good, as one and the same thing. And note that if one doesn't like the coherence constraints of expected utility theory, one can generate different constraints, and thereby get a different conception of reasoning. So conceptions of "instrumental" reasoning are essentially being generated by conceptions of the form and structure of the good. One might say that moving through life in a rational way is the same thing as developing a coherent set of preferences. A coherent structure of the good means instrumentally rational behavior in the pursuit of these goods, and vice versa. This analysis fits with what I suspect – and will argue in Chapter 7 – is a plausible way of justifying EU theory[3] – that is, in this view, EU theory partially articulates our (normative) conception of instrumental reason. While it does not articulate the entire conception (because, among other things, it does not articulate the principles of causal reasoning and probability formation that are relevant to determining the nature of means/end reasoning), it does articulate how an agent should respond to the fact that she has multiple ends so that she satisfies them effectively.[4]

Is this really a significant departure from the pure instrumentalist position? Nozick pleads that admitting coherence constraints on preferences into a theory of instrumental reason is "only one tiny step beyond Hume"[5] so why not allow them? As long as these constraints are only structural and not substantive, why should they be bothersome? Indeed, it seems that admitting them involves only a small modification of the idea that instrumental reason should be defined independently of the good: now we say that it must be defined independently of one's *substantive* conception of the good, but not independently of one's structural conception of the good. This is the sort of position that John Broome has dubbed *Moderate Humeanism*.[6] To be precise, it is the position that:

1. A fundamental requirement of practical reasoning is determining the best means to an end.
2'. Practical reasoning plays no part in the determining of unmotivated ends of action, except insofar as it provides principles of coherence that indirectly contribute to the deter-

---

[3] This strategy of defense was suggested to me by John Broome, who is convinced that this is the way most rational-choice theorists think of EU theory. See, for example, Jeffrey 1965.

[4] Hampton (1994). Discussion taken from p. 215.

[5] Robert Nozick (1993), p. 140.

[6] Broome (1991, 1993).

mining of such ends by providing constraints, which an agent's preference set (containing preferences defining both motivated and unmotivated ends of action) must satisfy in order for her behavior to be rational. (These principles define what I shall call the "structure of an agent's good.")

Alternatively, we can state the second tenet in another way:

alt 2′. Practical reasoning plays no part in the determining of unmotivated ends of action, except insofar as it provides principles of coherence that enable us to create, from the *Source Set*, the *GD Set*, some of whose members will define unmotivated ends of action.

Is this modified statement of instrumentalism good enough to qualify as a plausible theory of reason while capturing the essentials of the instrumentalist's intuitions? Alas, no. Let's pull the thread a little more.

FUTURE PREFERENCES AND RATIONALITY

EU theory is a theory of what the coherence constraints on a preference-set should be; it is one among many possible theories, and I will argue in Chapter 8 that it is not a particularly good one. Nonetheless, because it is well-known and popular, I will use it in this section as an example of what a theory of instrumental reasoning for an agent with multiple ends looks like. Does such a theory tell us all we need to know in order to understand the nature of instrumental reasoning?

No. There are two issues involving time that must be resolved by two different kinds of normative principles before we know how to use the theory to calculate rational action. First, there is the issue of the *satisfaction* of preferences relevant to the determining of costs and benefits of an action. And second, there is the issue of the time at which the preference occurs, such that it can be at least a potential member of an agent's *GD Set*.

In order to understand the first issue, consider that in order to determine which of two alternative actions is rational, we need to calculate the expected costs and benefits (in EU theory, the expected utility) of each action. To determine costs and benefits, we must determine how each action affects the satisfaction of our good-defining preferences. But to do this, we need to know *at what times* in our lives the satisfaction of our other preferences is relevant to the choice of these actions. All times? Only the immediate future? The immediate future plus the more distant future, which is added in at a somewhat discounted rate? If so, what rate? So, for example, if I am trying to decide on two courses of action, one of which gives me an expected benefit in five minutes, and the other of which gives me the same expected benefit in five years, is it rational not to be indifferent between them but to prefer the first action, just because its benefit is nearer? And, in general, when I am choosing, is it rational for me to be biased in favor of expected benefits to be received sooner rather than later?

Given that all of us seem to engage in reasoning that does not treat the benefits from all future times the same, and that does take nearer benefits more seriously than later ones, it seems to be true that rationality not only permits but may even require a bias toward the [immediate] future. (Indeed, if human beings simply cannot factor into their calculations benefits that are too far into the future, then we can infer from the maxim "ought implies can" that it is not rational for them to do so.) But there are many different forms of reasoning that permit such a bias. Is any one of them uniquely correct, or is one or more of them clearly incorrect, as a portrayal of instrumental reason?

There is in the rational choice literature some discussion of this issue, although in terminology that differs from my own. Consider, for example, Jon Elster's (1986) distinction between (what he calls) a "global maximizer conception of instrumental rationality" and a "local maximizer conception of instrumental rationality." Local maximizers do whatever they judge best at the time of choice; but this means they have a "myopic eye fixed to the ground" and cannot take into account "what happens behind the next hill" (p. 9). In contrast, a global maximizer can choose what is the worse option now, in order to be in a position to realize a far better outcome than the presently better option would yield. This maximizer doesn't just operate from the maxim, "always go up"; at any given time, she is able to go down rather than up if it will enable her to reach an even higher point later. The local maximizer may get stuck on a rather low hill; the global maximizer will be able to spot the mountains, and effectively head for them even if that means heading down valleys sometimes. Or, as Leibniz puts it, rational human beings will "reculer pour mieux sauter."[7]

However, note that Elster's local maximizer is essentially arguing that the time at which the satisfaction of preferences is relevant to choosing an action is only the immediate future. This is a reasoner whose bias toward [immediate] future benefits is extreme. If, for example, I have to choose whether or not to go to college, knowing that I will suffer significant short-term costs and few short-term benefits if I do so, and even more significant long-term costs and even fewer long-term benefits if I do not, then if I am a local maximizer, I will not choose to go to college. In this case, my "short-term" thinking reflects a strong bias in favor of benefits experienced sooner rather than later, and a strong fear of costs experienced sooner rather than later. To be precise, a *local maximizer*

> is one who chooses her course of action by consulting her present preferences, and calculating how well she expects those preferences will be satisfied by the performance of each alternative action in the "immediate future" (where this notion requires precise spelling-out).

In contrast, a *global maximizer*

> is one who chooses her course of action by consulting her present preferences, and then calculating how well she expects those preferences will be satisfied by the performance of each alternative action not only in the "immediate future" but also into the more distant future (where, again, this notion must be made more precise, and any proposed rate of discount for more distant costs and benefits must be defined and defended).

Note, as the definition of the global maximizer makes plain, there are actually many possible theories of global maximization depending on how far into the future the theory admits costs and benefits and at what discounted rate (if any) it admits them.

So which form of maximization is correct must be resolved by deciding (yet another) normative issue that involves the agent's good: How much, and in what way, ought an agent, in order to be instrumentally rational, to take into consideration the future costs

---

[7] Quoted by Elster (1986), p. 10.

and benefits of any alternative course of action? If instrumental action is about choosing the "best means to an end," this normative issue concerns how to specify precisely the ends that will be consulted during the reasoning process. As I noted earlier, the ends of action are defined by our preferences, so that when choosing an action, we must determine how those preferences that will be affected by the action in the immediate future will or will not be satisfied in the immediate future, thereby generating the "costs" and "benefits" of the action. But we must not only know the costs and benefits of the action, but the costs and benefits *when*. For if a rational person is not merely permitted but also required to be biased toward [imminently] expected future benefits, we must specify this "rational bias" precisely. In doing so, we further refine the nature of the ends that a rational agent pursues.

How would a pure instrumentalist respond to this argument? He could preserve his position that outside of specifying coherence constraints on preferences, defining instrumental reason does not involve defining the agent's good (or taking a stand on normative issues), by insisting that any bias toward the [immediate] future that we agents have is merely the result of our having a second-order preference concerning when we would like our first-order preferences satisfied. So what I have referred to as a "rational bias" is for this theorist merely the result of some preference we happen to have, and not a normative matter at all. (There's no way we ought to think about the future with respect to preference-satisfaction; there's only the way that we happen to do so.) So if an agent, in this view, happens (unlike most of the rest of us) to have an extremely strong preference for nearer pleasures, then she is rational to discount long-term pleasures in her calculation entirely, and reason as a local maximizer. (And if she doesn't have such a preference, then she is rational to factor into her calculations these long-term pleasures.) So what she is rational to do, in this view, is strictly a function of what kind of second-order preference she has with respect to the time of the satisfaction of her preferences. In this way, reasoning is represented as responsive to the preferences that we *in fact* have, just as instrumentalists have traditionally argued.

The problem is that our intuitions about what counts as instrumentally rational action do not support this response. Indeed, theorists such as Elster take it for granted that we regard the local maximizer as wrong – indeed as *irrational* (no matter what his preferences). Local maximizers strike us as lamentably stupid insofar as they will not choose courses of action (for example, having surgery, going to college) whose short-term costs exceed their long-term benefits, where these benefits are considerable. Local maximizers aren't, in a word, willing to *invest*, and wise investment seems to be one of the hallmarks of the instrumentally rational person. So our intuitions about what counts as "reasoning" turn out to select only those theories of reason that require the reasoner to take a long-term perspective with respect to the time of preference satisfaction.

This commonsense position convicts the local maximizer's second-order preference for short-term satisfaction of her first-order preferences as irrational. It therefore requires a very minimal substantive stand on the content of an agent's good-defining preferences, such that she can be declared rational. Not to take this is to have to accept the local maximizer as just as rational as the global maximizer. So in this case, if the instrumentalist refuses to take a normative stand on the nature of a rational agent's good, he is forced to admit into the realm of the rational a kind of agent who is normally banished from it.

Perhaps the instrumentalist will be willing to bite this bullet. But things get worse.

TENSED PREFERENCES

There is a second normative issue that instrumentalists must also resolve in order to develop in full their theory of instrumental rationality. This issue involves the time at which a preference occurs, such that it can be considered potentially good-defining.

Consider that standard theories of instrumental reason, such as expected utility theory, do not specify whether only preferences an agent has now, or also those preferences she has at other times, should be subjected to coherence constraints so as to produce a coherent set of preferences. Simply saying that one will use "all the agent's preferences" isn't good enough, because we need to answer the question "all of the preferences *when*"? Agents have preferences that change over time. EU theory says nothing about this phenomenon, hence it does not tell us whether the preferences that should be subjected to the axioms are only those an agent has at a time, or also include those she expects to have in the future. Indeed, some have interpreted the theory such that it condemns any change of preferences as irrational, insofar as preference changes introduce inconsistencies into the preference set.[8] But that's ridiculous: Human beings change their mind with respect to what they want all the time. There seems nothing wrong with such changes on the face of it; so why should we regard changing one's mind as bad or wrong? Indeed, to say that there is something wrong with changing your mind about what you want seems to be a quite serious violation of the principle that one's conception of instrumental reason should be independent of one's substantive conception of the good – because it seems to be motivated by the idea that "changing your mind is bad," or some such thing, which is a way of giving you a particular end (that is, the end of wanting only what you want now). So if we want to remain good instrumentalists, we need to come up with a way of using expected utility as a theory defining the coherence of preferences held by an instrumentally rational person that does not violate that principle by normatively precluding changes of mind altogether. This involves explaining how a rational agent should deal with the phenomenon of preference change. Should you include into your preference set only those preferences you have now, and make them consistent (and with each new preference change redoing your "coherence test" on the set), or do you include into that set both the preferences you have now, plus the preferences you expect to have, and then attempt to render this much larger set coherent? This is another way of asking which preferences at which time should be rendered coherent.

The first and perhaps the most obvious answer to this question is: Include only those preferences you have at any given time, so that changes of mind with respect to preferences involve new reflection with respect to the coherence constraints. This answer fits with the spirit of the instrumental idea: We might characterize it with the principle "serve whatever ends you have now, and if those ends change, serve the new ends." But this obvious answer is not so obviously correct once we appreciate the advantages of a second answer to this question. Instead of working from preferences that we have at a time, this second answer tells us to work from the preferences that we have now *plus* the preferences that we believe we *will* have in the future (although we don't have them now). That is, it tells us to include in the Source Set that will be subject to the co-

---

[8] Stigler and Becker (1977).

herence constraints not only the preferences we have now, but also those we expect we will have in the future (to the extent that we can determine them). Clearly this second answer will have to explain what it means to say that one "expects" to have a future preference, and what a "reasonable" expectation of this sort is, but for purposes of this chapter I shall leave aside this issue.

Let me explain further the details of both answers, using an example I owe to Michael Bratman.[9] Suppose there is a woman named Ann who on Monday morning prefers the state of affairs in which she reads after dinner all week to the state of affairs in which she has two beers at dinner and falls asleep after dinner without reading. However, Ann knows that this preference will change Monday evening, for the following reason. She knows that she will be offered a beer at dinner, which she also knows she will be inclined to accept (doing so is, after all, perfectly consistent with her present preferences, since she will be able to read that evening after only one beer). But she knows about herself that "she can't have just one," so that after having one beer, she will want a second. At that point, her preferences will be reversed, so that now she will prefer having two beers to having one beer and spending the rest of the evening reading. So how should Ann plan now, in the face of an anticipated preference reversal?

Each answer to the question of how to accommodate "changes of mind" that I reviewed above gives Ann a different strategy for dealing with her expected preference reversal. The first answer, which says "make the preferences you have at the moment coherent and satisfy those preferences," tells her to make plans to read during the morning, but after drinking one beer, make plans to sleep after dinner (and repeat this pattern the rest of the week). The second answer, which says "make coherent not only the preferences that you have now but also those you expect to have, then satisfy all these preferences," tells Ann to make plans that anticipate this preference change such that her set of present and future preferences can be considered coherent. Since an anticipated preference reversal is an anticipated incoherence in one's preference set (defined as extending over time, and not understood to refer only to the preferences one now has), this answer tells an agent like Ann to do something to fix this incoherence, either by changing her present preferences, or

[9] The example occurs in Bratman, forthcoming.

blocking or in some way ignoring her future preference change. Which action she chooses depends on her assessment of which preference is "better" – an assessment that she would make depending on the criteria of "betterness" that she accepts. (Note that a Benthamite expected utility theory generates one criterion of betterness. It tells Ann to fashion her preference set so that she includes in that set only those preferences that maximize utility understood in a Benthamite way as pleasure or happiness; but we can imagine other theories generating other criteria.) The point is that the second answer requires that she do something to insure that her present and future "wantings" cohere with one another.

What is really at stake in choosing between these two answers? At the very least, choosing between them involves deciding on yet another structural normative constraint on the conception of the good assumed by rational agents. But it's even more interesting than that. A choice between these two answers also involves specifying the *form* of instrumental rationality, and thus the procedure by which an instrumental agent reasons.

Preference reversal cases, such as Ann's, show us that there are actually two different kinds of global maximizers. There are the global maximizers who can accept short-term losses in order to reap long-term gains with respect to their *present* preferences; and there are the global maximizers who can accept short term losses to reap long-term gains with respect both to their present preferences *and* with respect to preferences they do not have now but expect to have later. Call the first sort "global maximizers from now" or NGMs; call the second sort "global maximizers from now and then" or TGMs.[b] To illustrate the point using the Ann example: The Ann who accepts the first answer is an NGM reasoner – that is, a global reasoner but one who only uses present preferences; whereas the Ann who accepts the second answer is a TGM reasoner – that is, a global reasoner with respect to both her present and future preferences.

We can use other preference-reversal examples besides the Ann

---

[b]*Editor's note:* Adam Morton has suggested more interesting names for one who reasons in accordance with a version of instrumentalism the author denotes here by one of these acronyms: NGM is the *grasshopper* because she's like the *cigale* in La Fontaine's "*La cigale et la fourmi*" who sings all summer and is then dismayed when winter comes. TGM is the prudent *ant*, for the same reason.

example to illustrate the phenomenon of preference reversal over time, and it is easy to construct these examples so that the right choice fits the TGM conception. A young woman who presently does not desire children but expects that in a few years she will want them, decides that it is rational to take action that does not preclude the future satisfaction of this preference – even though at the time she doesn't have the preference for children and the action involves suffering some costs that are not counterbalanced by any perceived benefits from the standpoint of her existing preferences. (Note that this is bearing a cost for the sake of a *belief* about what her preferences will be; it cannot be assimilated to the standard case of acting for the sake of an existing preference. I'll come back to this point later.) Whether we take her to be rational or not depends on how we think rational actors should define their set of source preferences, but I suspect that we would conclude that she was rational, and that conclusion presupposes a TGM conception. Or consider the person who has no present interest in drugs but who believes that were she to try cocaine, she would develop a strong desire for that drug. Let us suppose that her present preferences are consistent with drug use, but she is convinced that such drug use will not be consistent with satisfaction of her future preferences, so that she takes steps (perhaps costly) to insure that she does not try the drug. (The sheriff's department in my county is busy sending representatives to area high schools to commend to their students the rationality of this course of action.) And of course, there is the example of Ulysses and the Sirens, in which Ulysses anticipates a preference reversal and takes steps to insure that his present preferences ultimately prevail.

So we now have three different specifications of how people should reason – as local maximizers, as NGMs, and as TGMs. But it turns out that these three ways of specifying reasoning are really three different ways of specifying how to define the rational agent's conception of the good. Recall that I noted earlier that the set of source preferences was the set of preferences on which coherence constraints are applied so as to generate the set of preferences that define our good, or the GD Set. My argument above essentially amounts to this: Each of the three maximizing conceptions of reason is really just a specification of how to define either the Source Set or the GD Set. Whereas (as I have discussed) the local maximizer has a certain way of understanding the content of her GD Set (that involves the time of the satisfaction of the preferences in her set), the two global conceptions are different ways of specifying the source set of preferences from which the *GD Set* will be created. Both sets sharply distinguish between the set of all preferences the agent has, and the set of preferences that I have called the *Source Set*, and both make the latter a proper subset of the former.[c]

The NGM conception puts into the *Source Set* only occurrent preferences, which may extend either a short time or a long time into the future. The TGM conception puts into the set both occurrent preferences (whether long- or short-term) and preferences that the agent does not have now, but believes she will have. Both theories, after defining in different ways the *Source Set*, then advocate the application of various constraints (such as coherence constraints) to the *Source Set* to produce the *GD Set* of preferences. Note that a set of source preferences that includes future preferences that one does not have now but that one expects one will have is bound to be inconsistent because of the phenomenon of preference reversal that we have discussed. The TGM reasoner anticipates and plans for this preference reversal, whereas the NGM reasoner does not.

So if we want to answer the question, "which kind of reasoner is *really* the instrumental reasoner?", we must decide something about the *content of a person's good-defining preference set*, either directly, in the specification of how to generate, from the agent's source preferences, the good-defining preferences, or indirectly, in the specification of the set of preferences that belong in the *Source Set*, from which the *GD Set* of preferences will be generated. The latter operation involves, as I said, specifying the sort of preferences that are the *sources* of a person's set of ends defining her good. The former operation involves, as I said, specifying the constraints that one uses on the source preferences to determine those that are good-defining. These can include not only coherence constraints but also other principles such as the local maximizing principle "prefer what will get you the most now." So a quarrel about the nature of "reasoning" turns out to be a quarrel about how to understand or define the conception of the good that would be held by a rational person.

Indeed, we can even define two more forms of global reasoning. The first is a form of global reasoning that is intermediate between

[c]*Editor's note:* In fact, the *Source Set* will not be a proper subset of the set of all *actual* preferences unless the agent's expectations about his own future preferences turn out to be correct.

NGM and TGM reasoning. This form of reasoning requires only present preferences in the agent's *Source Set*, but she treats her future preferences as constraints on the satisfaction of her present preferences.[10] Any anticipated preference reversal is therefore treated like an obstacle to the satisfaction of present preferences, and thus (to the extent possible) warded off or blocked. This type of global reasoner does not merely satisfy her present preferences but also acts so as to *preserve* them. Call this a "preserve present preferences reasoner," or PGM reasoner for short.

Yet another kind of global reasoner is more extreme than the TGM reasoner. She factors into her *Source Set* not only present and future preferences, but also past preferences. This form of global reasoner is therefore able to act for the sake of preferences she *used* to have, as well as preferences she now has, or will have, and she creates her *GD Set* (for example, by applying coherence constraints) out of this (very large) *Source Set*. I will call this form of global reasoner a "global maximizer from now, then, and before," or a BGM reasoner. As I shall discuss later, Thomas Nagel seems to endorse the idea that BGM reasoning is the right portrayal of instrumental reasoning. It is the view that the preferences belonging in the *Source Set* need have no particular tense.

Having isolated these four forms of global reasoning (there may be more), the next question to ask is: Which one of these is correct? But note what this question appears to mean. If only one kind of reasoner is the real instrumental reasoner, the others are mistaken, and worthy of criticism as irrational. But selecting one of these reasoners as the right instrumental reasoner amounts to resolving a normative issue having to do with the nature of the good of the instrumentally rational agent. Note that appealing to expected utility theory doesn't really enable us to select which of these portrayals of instrumental reason is correct. That theory has usually been interpreted as working from preferences that one has at a particular time, and ignoring any possible preference changes that one expects to occur in the future (see Stigler and Becker 1977). But I see no reason

---

[10] I am indebted to John Broome for pointing out the possibility of this form of global reasoning to me. [Editor's note: Adam Morton's suggested mnemonics here are the *caterpillar* for the PGM reasoner, who looks ahead apprehensively to a time when she will be very different, and the *butterfly* for the BGM reasoner, who looks back fondly to a time when she was very different.]

why the theory could not assume any of the *Source Sets* I have defined earlier, where the axioms of the theory are applied to that larger set. How the theory should be understood depends on deciding how to structure this *Source Set*, and the theory simply doesn't answer that question. When we attempt to do so, we are indirectly theorizing about the good, and in particular, theorizing about its sources.

In the next section, I will examine arguments for each of these forms of global reasoning. But before proceeding to these arguments, I want to note that in this chapter I am less concerned about which of these conceptions is right than with making the point that defining instrumental reason must involve choosing one of them, which means taking a stand on certain issues about the nature of the good of a rational person. Recall our earlier discussion of the instrumentalist thesis – that reason should be defined independently of the good. Given the necessity of specifying coherence constraints on a set of ends, we modified this principle as follows: Reason should be defined independently of a substantive conception of the good. But the discussion of the relationship between global instrumental rationality and the possible ingredients of a person's set of ends defining her good seems to show that we need to modify this principle again, because now it seems that there are indeed substantive constraints on the good associated with instrumental reason that enter at the point of specifying the appropriate sources of good-defining preferences. To put it succinctly, the instrumental reasoner, in order to specify his conception of reasoning, has to say what a good-defining preference is, and doing so means that he must take a stand on the sources of the set of good-defining preferences. So it seems we must modify our statement of instrumental reason again, as follows:

alt 2": Practical reasoning plays no part in the determining of unmotivated ends of action, except insofar as it provides principles of coherence that enable us to create from the source preference set the good-defining preference set (containing preferences defining unmotivated ends of action), *and* except insofar as it provides principles that in part determine the kind of preferences that can be included in the *Source Set* from which the *GD Set* will be generated.

So even if we don't need to get involved in whether, say, Aristotle or Bentham is more correct about what is ultimately good for us, it appears that we do need to take a stand, in a minimal way, on a substantive issue involving the good in order to say what instrumental reason is.

The instrumentalist will want to resist the necessity of doing this. Will he be able to do so?

TWO THEORIES OF THE GOOD OF AN INSTRUMENTALLY RATIONAL AGENT

Although there is not much discussion among theorists about rationality about which preferences at which times belong in the *Source Set*, theorists have nonetheless argued for a particular one of these theories over the others. For example, David Gauthier defends NGM thinking in his *Morals by Agreement*, and an argument for what is essentially the BGM conception is put forward by Thomas Nagel in *The Possibility of Altruism*.[11]

In Gauthier's vocabulary, BGM or TGM thinking is the sort of reasoning we call "prudence" and NGM reasoning is the sort of reasoning we call "reflective heedlessness." Despite its name, Gauthier defends the latter:

> It is not rational, the defender of prudence claims, simply to maximize the fulfillment of one's present preferences, however considered they may be, if one does not take into account the preferences one will or may come to have. Of course one cannot have full knowledge of one's future, but one may form reasonable expectations, allowing for different alternatives with varying probabilities. The prudent person takes thought for the morrow and so, our objector claims, chooses rationally.

> An example will illustrate how prudence-based and preference-based accounts of rational choice differ. Winter will come, and when it comes Susan will prefer her home to be well-insulated. Is it not rational for her to insulate now, when prices are lower and workers and materials readily available? This would be the prudent course of action, but it is summer, and Susan is reclining by her pool without any care for winter. She

---

[11] Gauthier (1986); Nagel (1970).

believes that she will care, but right now she does not. The defender of the rationality of prudence insists that her present unconcern is irrational. But in our account, only a consideration
entering into one's present preferences can provide rational support for choice. If Susan's unconcern is fully considered, then she
has no reason to insulate now. (p. 36–7)

Note how Gauthier is arguing for a conception of the preference
source set from which good-defining preferences are supposed to
come. Don't put future preferences into that set, he says, and that admonition seems to be generated by a view of which preferences generate a person's good – that is, present preferences. Note also that his
position forces a sharp distinction between being prudent on the one
hand and being instrumentally rational on the other – that is, in his
view, prudence may be consistent with instrumental rationality, but
instrumental rationality does not imply prudence (and indeed, in his
example, Susan is instrumentally rational but not prudent).

Even more important, Gauthier's defense of NGM reasoning also
attempts to subsume all the other forms of global reasoning that we
defined. Although he uses different terminology, his defense of
NGM reasoning implies that TGM, BGM, and PGM reasoners are all
kinds of NGM reasoners, differing only in the type of second-order
preferences they have with respect to their past, present, and future
preferences. PGM reasoners have a present second-order preference
to satisfy only their present preferences, and they want to do so in
a way that preserves these preferences from change. TGM reasoners
have a present second-order preference to satisfy both present and
future preferences. BGM reasoners have a present second-order preference to satisfy past, present, and future preferences. Because all of
them have these present second-order preferences, all of them, on
Gauthier's view, would qualify as NGM reasoners. As he says in one
passage of *Morals by Agreement*:

To maximize on the basis of one's present preferences need not
be to ignore one's future preferences; one may take an interest
in one's future well-being now, preferring a satisfying life to
more immediate gratification. But also, one may not. Our view
is that prudence is rational for those who have a considered preference for being prudent, but not for those who on full reflection
do not. (p. 37)

On the basis of Gauthier's remark, we might propose the following position: All TGM reasoners are a *kind* of NGM reasoner – that is, a kind of reasoner who has, among some of her present preferences, second-order preferences that direct her to take account of what her future preferences will be. Of course, there may be NGM reasoners who do not have such second-order preferences, and these people will reason in a "reflectively heedless" way like Susan. Nonetheless, in this view, all global reasoners are NGM reasoners, so that we have no need to choose between different portraits of global reasoning and different conceptions of a good-defining preference set, because, in the end, there is only one kind of global reasoning and only one answer about what type of preference belongs in our source set of preferences – that is, present preferences.

Before considering the viability of Gauthier's position, I want to contrast it to the quite different theory of Thomas Nagel in *The Possibility of Altruism*,[12] which essentially defends what I have called BGM reasoning. Whereas Gauthier sharply distinguishes instrumental rationality and prudence, Nagel identifies the two. In his view, the instrumentally rational person acts so as to satisfy not only present preferences but also preferences that she expects she will have. Preferences give us reasons for action and, says Nagel, "reasons represent values which are not time-dependent" (p. 46). Hence, the expectation of some future desire itself provides a reason for planning to satisfy it. This is just another way of saying that the set of good-defining preferences (on which we have reason to act) includes more than just the preferences we have now, but also includes preferences we expect to have and perhaps also preferences we have had in the past. In Nagel's view, there is a "condition of timelessness on which prudential motives depend" (p. 47) that he takes to be "an aspect of the condition of generality which characterizes all reasons" (p. 47).[13] Nagel says his position is generated by the view that

---

[12] Nagel (1970).

[13] Nagel argues that if at t_1 we have an expectation that at t_2 we will have a desire to x, this means we will have a reason to x at t_2, which gives us a reason at t_1 to plan for x. So he derives the reason on which we act at t_1 from the reason we expect to have at t_2. But he could have developed his view more simply, without relying on the second, derived reason. That is, rather than saying we have a reason to plan to satisfy a reason we expect to have, he could have said that a future reason, like a present reason, is (quite directly) a consideration

to regard oneself as a being who persists through time, one must regard the facts of one's past, present and future life as tenselessly specifiable truths about different times in the history of a being with the appropriate kind of temporal continuity. And one must be able to regard the present as merely one of those times. (p. 62)

So this view of instrumental rationality involves not only a conception of what counts as our good, but also a conception of what counts as who *we* are. (Presumably Nagel's conception of our identity over time is one with which Gauthier would disagree.)

There is an obvious issue raised by Nagel's account: How do I make all my tenseless reasons coherent? While I may anticipate preference changes that do not pose any problem for my planning (for example, with food, as when I expect at age twenty that I will not like Big Macs at age forty although I like them now), there are other preference changes that do pose serious consistency problems. Nagel recognizes this, and does not know how to resolve the inconsistency:

It may happen that a person believes at one time that he will at some future time accept general evaluative principles – principles about what things *constitute* reasons for action – which he now finds pernicious. Moreover, he may believe that in the future he will find his present values pernicious. What does prudence require of him in this case? (p. 74)

Nagel doesn't know how to answer this question and doesn't even know if prudence should be relevant in this case. ("Why should one's future preferences prevail over one's present preferences in a case such as this?", he asks.) His quandary raises two issues: First, is instrumental rationality really identical to prudence? Can't a person be rational and prefer in certain circumstances satisfying present preferences over future ones? If so, then Nagel is, like Gauthier, committed to distinguishing prudence from instrumental rationality, even if there is substantial overlap between the two concepts. Moreover, this question is really connected to a second, which is larger

---

relevant to our deliberations about what to do. In this view, we don't need a derived reason to factor into our considerations a future reason; the future reason is directly applicable to those deliberations. This position would make the role of present and future reasons in our deliberation process identical. This second position fits well with Nagel's view of reasons as tenseless, which he spells out in Chapter 8.

and more basic: How does a rational person consistently pursue tenseless reasons? Does she apply consistency constraints to the whole set of reasons? If so, how does she do so? What constraints should she use?

If Nagel could answer these questions satisfactorily, he would be implicitly making a distinction between the set of good-defining preferences and the set of preferences that are sources for the good-defining preference set. And he would need a theory for how we derive the *GD Set* from the *Source Set*. We are not given such a theory, and it is not obvious how to generate one.

Given other remarks he makes, Nagel is also committed to making a distinction between all of the preferences a person has, and the set of source preferences: Some preferences are too trivial and whimsical to be even potentially good-defining. A desire to put parsley on the moon (p. 45) is an example Nagel gives of a whim that would amount to a preference that could not be put into the *Source Set*. Interestingly, it is a preference that Gauthier would certainly put in the *Source Set* as long as it was motivationally efficacious. The fact that Nagel would not do so shows that motivational efficacy is not a marker, in his view, that a preference must display in order to be placed in the *Source Set*. So if this isn't the right marker, what is? Nagel doesn't tell us, and he may well believe that determining the correct marker depends on determining the correct substantive theory of the good one embraced (for example, Aristotelian, Benthamite, or Kantian). If so, Nagel's view regarding how we are to identify members of the *Source Set* and the *GD Set* requires wholesale substantive reflection on the nature of the good, meaning that Nagel's theory of instrumental reasoning can only be filled out with a deeply contentful specification of what counts as good for an agent.

Both Nagel's and Gauthier's theory are incompletely developed, but can we determine which one of them is more nearly right? Nagel's position requires that a theory of instrumental reason take a stand on an aspect of the rational agent's good. Gauthier's position seems rather neatly to avoid having to take such a stand, and hence it would be preferred by any pure instrumentalist. If we can show that Gauthier's position is not viable, then we can show that either Nagel's view, or some other theory that takes a normative stand on the tense of the preferences belonging in the *Source Set*, must be appended to any theory of instrumental reason.

RATIONALITY RELATIVISM

What is the heart of the difference between Gauthier's and Nagel's positions? Consider, first, that all the reasoners whom Nagel calls rational will be called rational by Gauthier, because Gauthier will attribute to them a second-order preference to include in the *Source Set* preferences from the past, present, and future. However, many of the agents that Gauthier calls rational will be considered irrational by Nagel – for example, all the agents that Gauthier calls "reflectively heedless." Nagel will consider that they are wrong to leave out of their *Source Set* of preferences those that will occur in the future.

Nonetheless, Gauthier must admit that the "character" of the reasoning process – whether it looks like BGM reasoning, TGM reasoning, PGM reasoning, or simple NGM reasoning – depends on the substantive content of the source set of preferences, and in particular, the "tense" of the preferences in it. But these differences cannot, in his view, be normatively criticized. And that is the heart of his position: To avoid the normative issue, "what kind of preference should be included in the *Source Set*?" Gauthier answers, "whatever kind of preference the agent prefers to put in it." In this way, he hopes to keep his theory pure of normative stands, and in particular, pure of normative stands on the nature of the good of a rational agent. In contrast, Nagel takes a particular normative stand on the rational agent's good, such that he is able to call a wide variety of agents, such as the reflectively heedless Susan, irrational.

Commonsense seems to side with Nagel. It is usual to criticize people such as Susan as irrational, and unusual to allow as rational all the kinds of reasoners Gauthier allows. Just as the pure instrumentalist seems stuck accepting the local maximizer as rational, he also seems to be stuck accepting the heedless, imprudent, and reckless reasoners as rational. This position defies commonsense.

So why not just take a normative stand, as Nagel does? Why persist in advocating a pure instrumentalist position when it seems to lead to foolish results?

There are two reasons why an instrumentalist will want to refrain from taking the "sensible" normative stands that I've been advocating. First, any normative stand requires defending, and since instrumentalists are fond of criticizing normativity in the theories of others (particularly in the theories of moral philosophers), they are loathe to include it in their own theories. As I've noted, some normativity is inescapable – for example, with respect to the coherence constraints and with respect to defining such things as "excused failures" or "best" means to ends. But the instrumentalists will hope to argue that the normative stands they must take to define instrumental reason with respect to these issues is obvious, and in some way, metaphysically benign (in contrast to what they will regard as the poorly defended normative stands of the moral theorists).

Second, the instrumentalists will believe that in order to preserve the way in which our rational criticisms of others are meant to be motivationally efficacious, they must presuppose that our source set of preferences is made up only of present preferences. Only present preferences are motivationally efficacious in this view, so only these preferences can be in the *Source Set* if we are going to be able to expect our exhortations to others to "be rational" will succeed. In this view, telling the reflectively heedless Susan to be prudent is useless if you point to a future preference that has no occurrent motivational effect on her. Only if she has a present preference telling her to care about her future preference will it seem she will be motivated to listen to you, and if she does, then (as I've noted) she counts as a kind of NGM reasoner. Philosophers such as Nagel who believe that rational exhortation can have a motivational effect even on people, such as Susan, who do not have second-order preferences to satisfy certain future preferences, have this belief because they take the authority of reason to be motivationally efficacious. (We might say that in Nagel's view, reason can by itself generate a second-order preference to care about future preferences, and indeed, reason ought to do so, because prudent behavior is often, perhaps even usually, uniquely rational.)

But having located these central differences between Gauthier's and Nagel's position, I will now attempt to show that Gauthier's views, despite their initial attractiveness, are ultimately untenable.

Let me start with the insistence that preferences, to be good-defining, must be motivationally efficacious and hence must be present preferences. Now what makes something a "present" preference? Earlier, I defined a preference as a disposition to choose some x over some y. Now think about what are intuitively our "present" dispositions to choose some x over some y; are all of them motivationally efficacious *now*? It seems not. Consider that I have a disposition to sleep rather than to read whenever it is late at night; but as I am writing this, that disposition is inert, because it is indexed to a time and a condition of my body. Similarly, I have a disposition to choose chocolate over any other flavor when I am in an ice cream store, but that disposition is motivationally inert now, because I'm sitting at my computer. Despite their inertness, both dispositions are nonetheless *mine*, and the preferences they define can be considered part of my preference set. Indeed, if my preference set is going to be complete, such preferences must be included. But if we include those preferences that are motivationally inert, why not preferences that are indexed to a time a month from now, or a year from now, or a decade from now? If "present" preferences include some preferences that are motivationally inactive, then motivational efficacy can no longer be the defining feature for inclusion in a *GD Set*, and we might as well let in any disposition that we have good reason to believe we will have in the future, whether the future is five minutes from now, or five years from now. And if we insist that only motivationally efficacious preferences belong in the *GD Set*, then the number of preferences in that set at any given time is tiny. Any planning with respect to the future would in this view have to be accomplished only insofar as there existed in the *GD Set* all sorts of motivationally efficacious second-order preferences that told us to care about "future" preferences – not only the ones five years from now but also five minutes from now.

Note that if those motivationally efficacious second-order preferences didn't exist, this theory would have to accept that the agent was perfectly rational if he acted only with respect to the tiny set of motivationally efficacious preferences he happened to have at any given moment. Such an agent would be perennially imprudent; indeed, he would be incapable of planning. The instrumentalist might deny that such an agent would be possible among human beings. But the point is surely that his theory would be committed to considering such an agent *in principle* rational. Such a position flies in the face of common sense.

But what else can we do, says the instrumentalist? To call any such reflectively heedless agent irrational, when she has no occurrent second-order preferences to consider her future preferences, is not only motivationally useless but also normatively ungrounded.

Any defender of BGM or TGM reasoning will deny this. Such a theorist will maintain that reason can have direct motivational efficacy itself, and hence he will insist that a Nagel-like criticism of the reflectively heedless Susan is not only intuitively appropriate but potentially motivationally efficacious for her. Indeed, he will be suspicious of Gauthier's second-order preferences, given the way that they mimic the work that in his view, only reason itself is capable of doing. Consider that a person who has second-order preferences that direct her to take into consideration her first-order preferences will reason as a TGM or BGM maximizer; indeed, there is no behavioral difference between a person who acts for the sake of a present second-order preference to satisfy a future preference, and the person who directly acts for the sake of the future preference because reason demands it. But the fact that there is no difference is instructive. For what *is* a second-order preference to satisfy future first-order preferences? One plausible argument is that such a preference is generated by reflection on the good. In this view, the person who has a second-order preference believes that the future preference is part of her good – and indeed, *that is why she has the second-order preference.* Such a second-order preference is not like a preference for cheetos over corn chips; it's a preference that comes from reflection about how to understand and pursue her good. (So she thinks to herself, "I prefer a life in which I take into account my future preferences, to a life in which I do not.") So here the second-order preference is being driven by a belief about what she *ought* to consider part of her *Source Set* of preferences if she is to act rationally, so that it is this belief, and not the second-order preference it generates, that is fundamental to her thinking about what she has reason to consider. The second-order preference is in this sense "manufactured" by reflection on the good (in a way that seems to be an example of how reason can operate noninstrumentally in setting ends), resulting in conclusions that are at odds with Gauthier's claim that someone such as Susan could be rational. So in this view, any attempt to "assimilate" TGM or BGM reasoning to NGM reasoning works only by suppressing all of the reflection that recognizes the relevance of future preferences to good-determination and treating the results of that reflection merely as "just another present preference," albeit a second-order one. The assimilation disguises the very real difference between the *kinds* of considerations that are driving the reflectively heedless Susan and the prudent, planning Ann.

This discussion is meant to show that the sort of Humean psychology accepted by theorists like Gauthier who are attracted to the instrumentalist position is implausible, failing to take account of reasoning that is eminently recognizable in human life. Again, this implausible position is being driven by the instrumentalists' dislike of the inclusion of norms in their theory. For if reason were able to motivate us to change how we reasoned, it would do so on the basis of a norm directing us to operate one way rather than another. The Humean contention that reason is not motivationally efficacious is driven by the position that instrumental reason is a "minimally normative" theory, involving only "obvious" norms such as coherence and causal reasoning, but no other. Hence the pure instrumentalist tends to take it for granted that we can exhort our fellows, with some success, to make their preferences rational, where such success would show that an appeal to reason can be motivationally efficacious with respect to making our preference set rational. And he assumes that exhortations of the form "choose effective means to your ends" will be motivationally efficacious (as I discussed in the last chapter). But he is allergic to any other motivationally efficacious roles for reason because he does not wish to bring into the theory of instrumental reason any other norms.

Notice that pure instrumentalists therefore run from normative issues, meaning that they must accept that local maximizers, imprudently heedless people, and nonplanners must all count as "rational" because to say anything else involves taking a normative stand that is not obvious or metaphysically benign. But why should some norms be more metaphysically benign than others? Why should norms of coherence (which are hotly contested in the literature) be more acceptable than norms defining the content of the *Source Set* or norms defining the time of the satisfaction of our preferences? We get no answer from the instrumentalist, who seems inexplicably sanguine about some norms, and inexplicably frightened of others.

Moreover, the instrumentalists' tendency to run from normative issues makes one question the extent to which they will be able to sustain any kind of theory of instrumental reason once all the normative issues involved in developing such a theory are faced. Except with respect to coherence, we have shown in this chapter that instrumentalists, when asked "what forms of reasoning count as instrumentally rational," are prepared to answer, "All options, no matter how counterintuitive they may seem." But we may reasonably ask how they can develop any theory of instrumental rationality at all with such an answer. A theory of rationality is supposed to be a normative theory that can be used to criticize some agents. But instrumentalists seem prepared to advocate something that might be called *Rationality Relativism*, which is the view that apart from such things as the coherence of preferences, what counts as rational action is determined only by what an agent happens to prefer or desire with respect to such things as the content of the Source Set. It is a view that is exceedingly weak, and indeed would be vacuous were it not for the inexplicable stand that the instrumentalist takes on a few normative issues, emboldened by the belief that these stands are "obviously right" despite having no uncontroversial argument to defend them, nor any argument showing why the norms he assumes are metaphysically acceptable.

If these arguments are correct, a theory of instrumental reason is a theory that takes a variety of stands on a variety of normative issues in a way that attempts to successfully capture our intuitions with respect to the nature of instrumental action. The problem with the instrumental position is not so much that it is wrong as that it takes too few normative stands to be in the end plausible as a theory of reason.

THE TOXIN PUZZLE

There is another argument that shows the link between some contentful specification of the good and the formulation of a theory of instrumental reason. Consider Gregory Kavka's toxin paradox.[14] Suppose there is a millionaire who will give you a million dollars if, but only if, you form the *intention* to drink a toxin, which will make you sick for a day, but have no lasting detrimental effects. Note that the millionaire will give you the million dollars *before* you drink the toxin, as long as you form the firm intention (on which you will surely act) to drink the toxin after getting the money. What would the instrumentally rational agent do in this situation?

In the literature, there are two answers to this question. The first is what I will call the "traditional answer," and it is advocated by people such as Michael Bratman.[15] It says: Don't drink the toxin, because at the time prior to performing the action, you will already have the money, so that you cannot gain anything *now* by drinking it, and you will bear costs from doing so (getting sick for a day). And since it would not be rational to drink the toxin then, it is not

[14] Kavka (1983).
[15] Bratman (1987), pp. 101–106; Bratman, forthcoming.

possible rationally to form the intention to drink the toxin now. This last bit of reasoning is inspired by what Bratman calls the "linking principle," which says roughly that what you would find it rational to do at some time in the future must be, absent unforeseen circumstances, what you should find it rational to intend to do now.

The second answer to the toxin puzzle is what I will call the "resolute answer," and it is advocated by people such as David Gauthier and Ned McClennen.[16] In this view, the linking principle is thought to motivate drinking the toxin after all because, since it is rational to intend to drink the toxin (because one will get a million dollars by doing so), it is also rational to drink it when the time comes. So both sides accept the linking principle, but "run it in different directions" – that is, both accept the link, but one goes from rationality of intention to rationality of action, and the other goes from rationality of action to rationality of intention.

Now this is a quarrel about what an instrumentally rational person would do in this situation, and clearly it involves a quarrel about what instrumental reasoning is. But what is not so clear is that the quarrel is ultimately motivated by different conceptions of the good held by a rational agent, as I shall now explain.

One impediment to thinking about the toxin case and others like it is the worry that we are not able to commit ourselves via our intentions in the way that the resolute position requires. Let us put this issue aside by imagining that we can perform this commitment. In a way it is irrelevant if we cannot do so because if it would be rational to do it if we could, then the problem is only with the nature of human psychological architecture, and a fully rational agent would be constructed along resolute lines. So, to remove any psychological impediments to the possibility of being fully rational, imagine that we have available to us the architecture we need to reason in the way that the resolute position requires. Now we can ask: Would an ideally rational agent reason resolutely?

The first point to note is that answering this question depends on resolving the issue of whether or not those benefits that we get from the bare fact of forming an intention, which Bratman calls "autonomous benefits" (after Kavka's term 'autonomous effects') should be included in an agent's good. Autonomous benefits are different from what I will call "consequentialist benefits" – that is, benefits that

---

[16] Gauthier (1986); McClennen (1990).

come from the consequences of action, since autonomous benefits arise not from the results of action but from an intention to perform an action. A certain conception of consequentialist evaluation would preclude a consideration of autonomous benefits in the determination of what one ought to do, if it took the point of view that only consequences of actions are relevant to determining an agent's good, and an intention is not an action. If consequences alone are relevant to an agent's determination of her good, the autonomous benefits, insofar as they do not derive from consequences, should not be included in this determination. In my conversations with philosophers about this puzzle, I have often run across this way of reacting to it.[17] So the first substantive issue that must be resolved in deciding the quarrel between the resolute theorists and the traditionalists is whether the autonomous benefits deriving from intention-formation should be considered part of an agent's good. And clearly this is a substantive consideration about how to define what the good is.

So, yet again, defining rationality involves determining something about the good – namely, whether it includes only consequential benefits, or whether it may also include nonconsequential benefits such as autonomous benefits. No matter which answer you prefer to this question, the point is that you have to choose one of them in order to develop your theory of reason. And of course, this means that your development of a theory of instrumental reason requires you to take a stand on the good that has real substantive import. Here we're not dealing with issues of coherence or issues of time; we're dealing with issues about what *kind* of preference can be included in the *Source Set*, and thus in the *GD set*.

Suppose we resolve these issues in a way friendly to the resolute theorists, and allow autonomous benefits into the conception of the good (for example, by saying that the good should consist of whatever a person cares about, even if it isn't consequential in nature) in a way that allows them to trump consequentialist benefits. This still isn't sufficient to resolve the issue between the resolute theorist and

---

[17] I've heard this position advocated in conversation by philosophers as diverse as John Pollock and Philippa Foot in reaction to the toxin paradox, and initially it was Michael Bratman's reaction to the paradox (ref?). [Editor's note: Michael Bratman conjectures that the intended reference here could well be to Bratman (1987), p. 103 (in a point he credits to Dan Farrell – see his note 26). But Bratman thinks that he has been misunderstood here by Professor Hampton.]

the traditionalist, because the traditionalist's view is that despite considerable autonomous benefits, the toxin should still not be drunk after the money has been received, so the intention to drink it cannot, subject to the linking principle, be rationally formed. This means that the autonomous benefits are being trumped by something. But what?

Consider why traditionalists dislike resoluteness. In the name of these autonomous benefits, resolute theorists are telling an agent to bear the cost of drinking the toxin. Now suppose those autonomous benefits didn't exist. Then of course you wouldn't drink the toxin – you would only bear costs from doing so, and no benefits. The traditionalists say that the situation of the agent in the toxin case after the millionaire has dispensed his money is exactly the same: There are only costs, no benefits. Now one reason why he may come to this conclusion is that even if he decides to allow autonomous benefits into a rational calculation about what to do, if he also believes that "consequentialist" benefits that derive from action are more important than, or authoritative over, the autonomous benefits of an intention, then by virtue of the fact that the consequentialist costs of drinking the toxin are not only high, but also not in any way covered by consequentialist benefits of the action of drinking the toxin (since there aren't any), he may conclude that one should not drink the toxin. Note that this form of reasoning allows autonomous benefits to be factored into one's deliberation about what to do, *except* when there are consequentialist costs of doing so.[18]

But the resolute theorist approaches the case differently in a way that shows he has a different way of thinking about the agent's good. In particular, he asks the agent to directly compare the autonomous benefits with the consequentialist costs of drinking the toxin, even though the agent will experience the benefits before the costs. So not only do the consequentialist costs not negate the autonomous benefits, but also the time frame in which these costs and benefits are experienced is irrelevant to the agent's calculations. This is a way of having what I will call a "super global theory" of reason. (Nagel suggests the possibility of such a theory – see 1970, 54–6 – and his

---

[18] This argument is related to another argument I will make in Chapter 8 that the instrumental nature of reason has been thought about along consequentialist lines, and that doing so is really a way of specifying an agent's conception of the good in a way that I believe is normatively and descriptively implausible. See also Jean Hampton (1994).

tenseless view of reasons could be used to explain the plausibility of this theory.) The resolute theorist takes the traditionalist reasoner to be "too local" in his evaluation of the situation, allowing his evaluation of the rationality of an action given its immediate consequences to govern his evaluation of what to do in a larger situation that precludes him from getting more benefits. Indeed, in this situation we have the reverse of the situation in which Ann is a local maximizer. In that situation, Ann's commitment to doing what seems best on Monday night precludes her from developing a plan that carries over several nights so as to respond to other preferences that she might on reflection take to be more important than the preference to which she responds on Monday night. In the toxin case, the agent's commitment to doing what is locally maximizing subsequent to receiving any money from the millionaire precludes her from developing a plan that includes the earlier times associated with the events, in particular the time prior to forming an intention about whether or not to drink the toxin and the time subsequent to doing so in which she receives the autonomous benefits of the intention. One point the resolute theorist is making is that global reasoning should be understood sometimes to go in both directions – that is, not only forward into the future, but also backward, from the future to the present. So I suspect a resolute reasoner is an example of a *third* kind of global maximizer, which I have called a "global maximizer from now, then, and before," or a BGM reasoner. This sort of reasoner defines her *Source Set* to include not only present preferences and future preferences but also *past* preferences, and then she creates her *GD Set* (for example, by applying coherence constraints) out of this (very large) *Source Set*. (Again, Nagel's commitment to tenseless reasons would seem to commit him to endorsing this sort of view; see 1970, p. 72: "Regret is to the past as prudence is to the future; both are justified by timeless reasons.") Moreover, this kind of agent may believe not only that she *had* reason to do something (such that, if she did not, she justifiably feels regret), but also that she can be rational to act now for the sake of preferences she has had, but has no longer. I'll return to this point in a moment.

This discussion shows that resolving the quarrel between the resolute theorists and the traditionalists involves resolving the extent to which reasons to act are tensed or untensed, and resolving the relative priority and importance of different kinds of "goods" – consequentialist benefits versus intention-generated autonomous benefits. But both resolutions involve specifying something about the content of a person's good. Note that this specification is still minimal, but its "minimal" nature should not distract us from the fact that with respect to the admissibility and authority of autonomous benefits, it is still a contentful specification, and given that fact, we seem to have lost our instrumentalist principle entirely. Our pursuit of a conception of instrumental reason requires not only structural constraints on a conception of the good, and not only "source-defining" constraints on a conception of the good, but also content-defining constraints on a conception of the good.

WHAT IS A PREFERENCE?

I could give other examples of the way in which quarrels about the nature of instrumental rationality really turn out to be quarrels about the good. For example, rational-choice theorists have discussed endogenous preference formation, in which people change their preferences in response to their environment (rejecting preferences they can't satisfy – the sour grapes phenomenon) or developing preferences that they can satisfy (as the Crosby, Stills, and Nash song goes: "If you can't be with the one you love, love the one you're with"). Whether or not you take such preferences to be "legitimate" and genuinely good-defining, and whether or not you think that such preferences are themselves a rational response to an environment, will depend in part on the theory of the good you accept. And the theory of the good you accept with respect to this issue is going to affect what you take rationality to be. Someone who thinks that instrumental reason should essentially create a preference for one end over another (for example, by directing you to love the person who is here rather than the person who is not) is going to have a conception of "instrumental" rationality that allows it to define not only means but also ends themselves.

Or consider the fact that socialization can seem to "induce" preferences in a person. The issue of whether or not such induced preferences should be taken seriously by us (or by a political institution) as good-defining given how they came about raises a number of good-related issues. For example, it requires us to answer the question, "How is membership in a *GD Set* determined? By the agent, or by us (politically and morally savvy) outsiders?" It also raises the issue of whether good-defining preferences have to be "authentic," and theorizing about how to understand authenticity cuts to the heart of theorizing about the nature of the good.

Finally, consider the difficulty rational-choice theorists have had developing a theory of the "level of specificity" of preferences that the theory should use. Stigler and Becker[19] argue that one way for economists to deal with the phenomenon of preference change is to define preferences at an abstract enough level that such abstract preferences don't change (so, for example, my preferences for clothing styles might change over time, but not my abstract preferences to *be* in style rather than out of style). Their proposal, whatever the merits with respect to the definition of preferences that economists require, raises the issue of how to specify the level of abstraction of what we would count as a preference, or, in other words, it involves a theory of how to define our "ultimate" dispositions of choice. The fact that there is so little discussion of this problem among rational-choice theorists (who have tended to seek refuge in the behaviorist hope that preference can be "revealed" through actual behavior) is indicative of the fact that these theorists have been naive about the conceptual clarity of the notion of preference. Behavior certainly does not reveal what our preferences, understood mentalistically as dispositions, actually are (does my choice of a mystery novel over a CD show that I prefer mysteries to music, reading to listening, Conan Doyle to Tina Turner?). And more importantly, behavior doesn't help us to resolve the theoretical problem of the level of specificity of the preference (for example, this book over that CD, versus literature over music).

To put the point succinctly,[20] *what counts as a good-defining preference isn't self-defining;* hence to know what counts as a potentially good-defining preference one must have a theory that picks out such a thing, and this theory must take a stand (albeit perhaps a minimal one) on the nature of a good associated with rational action. This means that it is impossible to do "rational-choice theory" and avoid all reflection on the nature of the good, because in order to theorize about the "structure" of instrumental reasoning, one must take a whole range of positions regarding what a preference is, what the sources of good-defining preferences in a situation are, how to cope with preference change, whether or not it is rational to generate pref-

---

[19] Stigler and Becker (1977).
[20] This way of putting it was suggested to me by David Estlund.

erence change, and so forth. The underlying message of this chapter is that even the most positivistic rational-choice theorist has been, at least to a small degree, doing ethics all along – albeit without realizing it or (in general) wanting to admit it.

There is another moral implicit in the story I've been telling – that defining instrumental reason involves defining and defending a whole series of normative principles, so that a conception of instrumental reason is *constituted by* normative principles. That is, my arguments in this chapter implicitly suggest that *a conception of instrumental reason is only a set of normative principles, related to one another by other normative principles* that involve not only how to reason with respect to ends, but also how to define what one's ends are. This set will also include a conception of how these norms are to be applied to a person's deliberations, or her planning, or her preference set, so that she can be considered to be fully rational. (In the end, perhaps the essence of reasoning is inherent in the process of this "norm application.") So understood, any theory of instrumental reason is just as hip-deep in normativity as any moral theory, and therefore just as metaphysically problematic as any moral theory if, as many naturalists believe, normativity is metaphysically problematic. If this is right, some moral skeptics' attempts to rely on instrumental reason to generate a moral theory (most notably that of Gauthier, 1986) that is more metaphysically acceptable to the naturalist than standard objectivist moral theories turn out to be quixotic. And if even theories of reason violate naturalist scruples, we have good reason to wonder whether we should rethink any allegiance we might have to these scruples.

Chapter 6

Instrumental Reasoning and the Methodology of Science

[computer file 4/15/95]

Given that only the Gibbardian account is congenial to naturalism, shouldn't that be the account to prefer, even if, as I've discussed, it is an account that fails to accord with our intuitions and implies an error theory of our judgments of practical reason? In this section, I want to argue that this is not so, on the grounds that the naturalists' conception of science, as well as their argument against objective moral theory, actually assumes a Kantian conception of the authority of the imperatives of reason constitutive of its methods. If this conclusion is right, it will establish that any science-based argument against the idea of objective normative authority is self-refuting. For if we conclude on scientific grounds that such authority doesn't exist, we do so on the basis of the rational methods of science that turn out to assume this same authority. This refutation only works if it illicitly assumes what it claims to refute.

To begin, consider why naturalists are so convinced that we ought to believe what scientists tell us, rather than what, say, astrologers or magic-users or mystics tell us. What makes only the scientists authorities about the world, and these other people (at best) merely colorful and amusing cultural phenomena?

Is the only possible answer to this question one that makes reference merely to the way in which our culture has made us (and taught us) that scientists are "authorities"? Such an answer is Gibbardian in the sense that it explains our sense that "we ought to believe what scientists say" as deriving from a norm whose content is a cultural creation, and whose authority over us is (merely) a psycho-social phenomenon. The problem is that such a position is usually adopted by those who *attack* the authority of science, not those who defend it. Consider the following passage by Ian Hacking describing an article in *Nature* that lamented the way science was undermined by the writings of four prominent twentieth-century philosophers, Karl Popper, Thomas Kuhn, Paul Feyerabend, and Imre Lakatos:

> It was argued [in *Nature*] that this rogue's gallery of philosophers had destroyed a longstanding vision of science as finding out the truth about the world. The new philosophy did not present science as progressing from strength to strength. There was refutation and revolution, there were research programs that were mere successions of theories. At worst, there was the famous aphorism, "anything goes."[1]

Even more threatening than the writings of these rogues, in Hacking's view, has been what is loosely called the "social studies of knowledge," or SSK, the proponents of which argue that "the discoveries of science are determined by interests or the outreach of power networks."[2]

What all these roguish "demythologizers" of science have in common is the view that science is "just another" human enterprise, game, or social practice among many in a human society, determined by the interests, ambitions, or power-bases of those involved in it, so that any belief in a special authority of science within a culture must be explained as fostered by those committed to playing the game and holding power within it.

Note, however, that by robbing science of its foundation in the objective norms of reason, the demythologizers thereby rob it of its authority. There are no objective norms telling us that "we must find the truth" and "we must do it (only) this way, because only this way is rational and we must be rational." Instead, their view is that "anything goes" – and what will likely "go" in science will be determined by the interests, strategies, and power of those doing it.

Defenders of science (such as Philip Kitcher, Clark Glymour, Wesley Salmon, and John Earman) try to retrieve the authority of science by insisting that these objective norms be put back, although there is little explicit acknowledgment that this is what they are doing.[3] It

---

[1] Hacking (1994), p. 212.

[2] Ibid., pp. 212–3.

[3] See Kitcher (1993), e.g., pp. 172–3, discussed by Hacking (1994), p. 214. Kitcher insists there has been progress in biology, by virtue of the fact that people have developed "adequate" concepts of natural kinds and "correct" explanatory schema (or objective dependencies), p. 173. Science is taken to have gotten

is interesting that there is no uncontroversial statement of the rational methods of science, and the variety of ways in which scientific theories have been formulated makes it difficult (Feyerabend would say impossible) to rely on scientific practice to formulate them. But I am less interested in the details of the debate than of its implications for ethics. For *if* it is true that science is authoritative, then its authority is connected to the fact that its rational methods of enquiry and practice are authoritative for us. We ought to follow those methods and we ought to believe (at least provisionally – until a better theory comes along) the results of such methods.

These methods are rational in a number of ways, but most pertinent to our concerns is the way in which they incorporate instrumental reasoning. For example, in the design and performance of experiments, scientists are supposed to follow certain maxims of experimental design, so that the results of these experiments provide genuine confirming or disconfirming evidence for the hypothesis being tested. So we accept the results of experiments performed by, say, medical researchers only insofar as we are sure they accept the hypothetical imperative: "If you want to generate evidence relevant to the truth of a certain hypothesis, you ought to construct double-blind experiments." But here we have an ought – an ought of (practical) reason, one among many generated by a norm of (practical) reason on which science is based (if its defenders are correct). And our acceptance of the results of scientific experiments is not only based on our belief that scientists have followed such imperatives, but also on our belief that they *ought* to have done so. These imperatives are, we think, objectively authoritative for them, and the authority of their experimental results rests in part on their following these imperatives. If such objective normative authority "figures in" science, then Harman or Mackie or any naturalist cannot attack other theories, such as ethics, *simply* because they include norms, because science does so also.

If this is right, then even though objective norms are not the objects of scientific study, they are still "relied on" in the practice of science because objective norms of instrumental reason are fundamental to the practice of science, and basic to the claim that its theories about the world are "better" than nonscientific theories. But

things at least partly right by virtue of the fact that it incorporates the right ways of learning about the world.

doesn't this mean that objectively authoritative norms are just as scientifically acceptable as, say, mathematical objects? Recall that Harman allows that a fact obtains if it figures in a physical theory that provides the best explanation of certain observations. Doesn't the objective authority of instrumental reasons "figure in" any scientific theory that provides the best explanation of certain observations, not by virtue of being *in* the explanation but by virtue of the fact that it is what we are responsive to when we develop these theories and when we accept them?

The upshot of the preceding discussion is that naturalists who are committed to science and opposed to Feyerabend would seem to be up to their necks in objectively authoritative normative commitments, making them the "companions in guilt" of those moral theorists they have criticized. They may be companions in other ways insofar as their methods commit them to other norms (for example, the norm of simplicity – a particular favorite of Quine),[4] although I cannot pursue that here. Clearly, any commitment to norms whose reasons are thought to have objective authority makes the naturalists' science-motivated argument against objective moral theory self-refuting.

We can now see how dangerous the Gibbardian position is for the defenders of science. If the (elusive) methodology of science is informed by norms whose authority is something that we (merely) "express" when we engage in or support science, but not something that can be grounded in something outside our cultural practices or biological nature, then the same is true for all the ways of understanding the world (religious, mystical, magical) that compete with science. Each of these is as much the product of brain and culture as science, and the conviction that any of these is superior can only be explained as a psycho-social phenomenon. The Gibbardian view can explain why any person takes her methodology for understanding the world to be "right," but it cannot establish that one of them *is* right. And if this is so, science is only authoritative for those who accept it, and (as Feyerabend says) the enterprise of science as we know it cannot really undercut ethics, *because it has no objective authority to undercut anything.*[5]

---

[4] See, e.g., Quine (1990), passim.

[5] What if it were possible to establish, contra the claims of magic-users, religious people, and mystics, that only the methods of science are a reliable way of es-

Recall my comparison of Gibbard's analysis of norms of reason with Harman's analysis of moral norms. Harman's conception of a person's understanding of and commitment to moral norms as (merely) a psycho-social phenomenon is taken by Harman to vindicate the position of moral relativism. Given the varieties of human culture that human beings, given their natures, generate, we can expect to see, says Harman, the construction of all sorts of moral codes of conduct, as human beings interact with one another and work out (given their interests, relative power, and environment) moral norms that "make sense" to them. But we can adapt Harman's argument against ethics and use it to show that unless Harman is implicitly committed to scientific norms, it has Feyerabendian conclusions with respect to science. Harman implicitly gave us a choice to understand normative statements in ethics either objectively or psychologistically: Either we should believe that it really is true that burning cats is objectively wrong, or we should believe that (some but not all) people make such a judgment because of certain psychological facts about them and the kind of society they have grown up in. But we can insist that supporters of science have a similar choice to make: Either they can say that the norm of instrumental reason, along with other norms of practical reason implicit in science, are objectively authoritative, or they can say that we only say (or believe) that they are authoritative because of certain psychological facts about us and

tablishing the truth (see, e.g., Goldman 1986)? Would this provide sufficient grounding for science, such that in conjunction with a Gibbardian account of the authority of its norms, it could be taken to be better than its competitors? This way of naturalizing the epistemic practices of science is full of problems. First, the methods of science must be stated! And after they are stated, their reliability must be established – and established in a way that does not covertly rely on norms of rationality that are assumed to be objectively authoritative. Moreover, there must be an argument only the methods of science are reliable for getting at the truth. If (and this is a big if) all of this can be done, the defender of science will have established the truth of a hypothetical imperative of the form, "If you want to know the truth, then follow the methods of science." But why should the magic-users et al. be moved by such an imperative? If they refuse to follow it, why should they be taken to have "made a mistake"? Suppose they are accused of being inconsistent unless they do so; even if this accusation is correct, why should they care? This view gives us no objective standard by which to criticize nonscientific methods of learning about the world, but only standards that naturalists, by virtue of the norms they accept, can use to express their disapproval of such methods.

the (science-influenced) society in which we have grown up. And if Harman counsels that we must opt for the second choice in the case of ethics, he must also accept that the second choice is mandated in the case of science – leading to some kind of "roguish" view of science. For if moral norms, and the authority by which we take them to bind us, are psycho-social creations, then so too are the norms of science (such as the instrumental norm). And if that means that moral pronouncements cannot be taken as factual, then likewise pronouncements involving these "scientific" norms cannot be taken as factual.

The Gibbardian position yields the same results. If Gibbard is right, why shouldn't we accept relativism in other normative realms besides ethics? Not just moral norms, but norms of reasoning, epistemic inquiry, and practical action are a function of the interests, relative power, and environment of human beings who interact with one another in various cultures. Human cultures throughout history have generated a tremendous variety of explanations of the world, based on all sorts of different conceptions of how such explanations are to be formulated. How can a Gibbardian understanding of normative authority establish that any one of these explanations, or the methodology that generated it, is *right*?

Gibbardian naturalism exacts a high price from us. It robs us not only of the objective normative authority of moral imperatives, but of *any* imperative, even imperatives of instrumental reason. For many, the price will be too high. Moral skeptics claim to have no difficulty dismissing the idea that there is objective moral authority. But dismissing the idea that there is objective rational authority is much harder. Faced with curmudgeons, astrologers, and magic-users, naturalists believe they should be called irrational not because (given their culture) they cannot help but do so, but because such people *are* irrational – which is why naturalists believe they are justified in considering them so.[6]

---

[6] Perhaps a Kantian might explain our deep commitment to judgment via the instrumental norm by appeal to Kantian-style categories of thought to which we must adhere in order to understand, and live within, anything like a world. But such a Kantian way of construing the claims of the Gibbardian position is an attempt to find objective normative authority after all, albeit not in "the world" understood to exist apart from a rational person's construction of it. I am deeply sympathetic to this Kantian construal, but it does not sit well with the naturalist and realist assumptions of those who question objective normative authority.

But is Gibbardian naturalism, or indeed, any form of naturalist position that argues against the idea of objective normative authority even *coherent*? Consider that a naturalist's commitment to science is based, as I've discussed, on a deep-seated conviction that the results of science are authoritative, in part, because of the way in which science relies exclusively on reason in its attempts to understand the world. It is striking that naturalists such as Harman or Gibbard do not talk as if this authority is merely the product of some (contingent) cultural convention, nor something that is merely "felt" and that we merely "express." Moreover, such naturalists among us regard science as universally valid, and its method compelling for all. Why isn't this way of regarding science betraying a commitment to the idea that the rational methods of science rely on norms that are objective? Theorists such as Gibbard and Harman can only argue for reliance on naturalist assumptions in a way that undercuts the idea of objective normative authority if they also assume that these naturalist assumptions are universally and inescapably right, no matter our cultural convictions. But that assumption implies the falsity of their own conclusion.

Moral skepticism, in its modern science-influenced form, is therefore self-refuting, because in order to get off the ground, it has to presuppose the objective authority of one way of looking at the world in order to undercut the moral way. But rather than arguing that the scientists' norms are justified whereas the moralist's norms are not, modern moral skeptics have attacked the moralists' norms by attacking the idea of objective normative authority as unscientific. Yet this attack only makes sense if the norms of science are taken to be objectively authoritative with respect to belief.

The preceding arguments are intended not only as a way of defending objective moral theory from naturalist attack, but also as a way of pressing the naturalist to answer two central questions: "What is the ground of your position, such that any of us should be taken to believe it?" and "Why is that ground supposed to be incontrovertible, and authoritative for all, regardless of what they happen to (or like to) believe?" Unless that ground can be identified, naturalists must be taken themselves to be endorsing some culturally created "story" of the world, which all of us can enjoy on occasion, and which some of us might be particularly fond of, but which cannot be taken to be in some way *better* than any other (religious, mystical, or magical) story of the world. The only way of arguing for moral skepticism while avoiding such Rortian implications is to generate arguments establishing that all and only the norms posited by science have objective authority for human beings, and not the norms posited by morality. If such a position could be constructed successfully, critics of the idea of objective moral theories could still argue (consistently) that the only norms possessing objective authority are, as it happens, nonmoral. But I take it to be significant that no such argument has even been suggested, much less fully formulated. To formulate one successfully, a philosopher would have to provide us a way to determine when a norm was "really" objectively authoritative for us, and when it was just a mere cultural artifact. Philosophizing on the question of how to pick out objectively authoritative norms has generally been taken to be something unique to ethical theorizing, and, for many, a sign that this field of philosophy was "soft" insofar as it pursued "values" rather than "facts." But those who are scientifically motivated moral skeptics can only get their moral skepticism coherently off the ground if they engage in the same sort of theorizing in order to provide a justificational ground only for the norms that they take to be implicit in science. The moral is that all philosophy – indeed, all human thought that tries to be "well-grounded" and "justified" – is "soft."

Part III

Reasons and Reasoning

Chapter 7

Expected Utility Theory and Instrumental Reasoning

[computer file 4/23/95]

> Like all other arts, the Science of Deduction and Analysis
> is one which can only be acquired by long and patient
> study, nor is life long enough to allow any mortal to
> attain the highest possible perfection in it.
>   – Sherlock Holmes (Sir Arthur Conan Doyle), *A*
> *Study in Scarlet*

In the preceding chapters, I have argued that a theory of instrumental reason of the sort that science requires must be informed by norms that have objective authority, at least some of which concern the structure and content of human good. If these arguments are right, however, they still do not in and of themselves vindicate any objectivist moral theory. The moral skeptic can fall back on the following argument: Alright, I will accept that I have objectively authoritative norms lurking in my theory of rationality, but I do not believe that there are objectively authoritative *moral* norms. Norms of rationality are real; norms of morality are not.

This response raises an important question: how does one go about showing that any given norm is "real" – that is, a norm that genuinely has objective authority? Moral theorists have worried about this question in a variety of ways, but few outside of moral theory have done so, because, I suspect, they haven't believed that they had to do so. Objectively authoritative norms were supposed to be the fanciful wish of the objective moral theorist and not the stuff of scientifically acceptable theory. But if even science – and naturalist moral skepticism – require an appeal to norms with objective authority, then all philosophers need to start thinking about which norms actually have it and which don't. And if the moral skeptic wants to salvage his view that there is something illegitimate about objective moral theory, he must insist that even if there are norms of reason with objective authority, there are no moral norms with objective authority.

No argument for such a conclusion now exists – although I have talked with many moral skeptics who are convinced of that conclusion. What might moral skeptics do to vindicate their faith in the nonexistence of objectively authoritative moral norms – without threatening their commitment to objectively authoritative norms of reason?

In my view, the best bet for the moral skeptic is to think about the nature of *reasoning*. Norms generate reasons for acting, choosing, and believing, and reasons are supposed to be something that we figure out after reaso*ning*. As I proposed in Chapter 2, reasons can be defined as considerations relevant to a deliberation about how to act, choose, or believe in certain circumstances. Therefore, whatever a theorist takes "deliberating" or "reasoning" to be like will affect what kinds of reasons she believes we have. To make the same point in terms of norms: The structure of our reasoning process indirectly implies something about what norms can be taken to have objective authority because our reasoning process may function in a way that precludes the possibility of there being certain kinds of reasons (that is, certain kinds of considerations that are taken into account in this reasoning process), thereby precluding the possibility of certain kinds of (objectively authoritative) norms.

Let me give a concrete example of what I mean. Consider that traditional moral objectivists such as Kant take moral reasons to come from a kind of moral reasoning procedure that establishes that the agent has a decisive reason to make a certain kind of (moral) choice. But does such "moral reasoning" exist? Moral skeptics invariably assume that it does not, although most of them accept the reality of some kind of practical reasoning. The most popular theory of practical reasoning is the instrumental theory of reason, but even if, as I've argued, that theory assumes certain sorts of objectively authoritative norms, some of which involve defining the good, it does not require norms that mandate certain kinds of action (for example, actions such as "refraining from killing the innocent") that we normally consider "moral." Indeed, the only way "moral" action is rationally mandated by instrumental reasoning is if such action is a means to some end the agent has, but there is nothing in the instrumental theory (even given my arguments that it includes some specification of the good of a rational agent) that could mandate that the agent have ends for which moral forms of action are means. Accordingly, the moral skeptic can maintain that if practical reasoning is entirely instrumental in character, our specification of the norms implicit in this reasoning exhausts the objectively authoritative norms that apply to action, in a way that shows that objectively authoritative moral norms – that is, norms mandating certain sorts of "moral" action as required in certain circumstances – cannot exist.

I believe that many moral skeptics believe something like this argument against moral objectivity, over and above whatever metaphysical arguments they have against the idea of objective authority. Hence in this final part of the book, I want to try to refute this argument by considering in detail whether we have good reason to believe that our reasoning is such that it actually does accommodate moral reasons and is thus informed by moral norms that we take to be objectively authoritative.

I will undertake this task in two parts. First, in Chapter 7 I will spend more time reflecting on the nature of instrumental reasoning. There are still aspects of the structure of instrumental reason that remain to be revealed. In this chapter I want to further articulate the structure of instrumental reasoning by analyzing a theory often thought to be a detailed articulation of that structure – namely, expected utility theory (for example, by Gauthier 1986). On the other hand, there is the view suggested by Leonard Savage (1954/1972) (and see Anderson 1993) that the theory is a "formal" and noninstrumental characterization of our reasoning process. If EU theory is a theory of reason, which characterization of it is right? This confusion about the classification of the theory is important for us insofar as it exposes confusion about what an instrumental theory of reasoning is. Hence, in this chapter I will try to resolve that confusion and put forward an argument that shows how expected utility theory can be construed as an instrumental theory of practical reason.

How does such an argument help moral theory? In the next chapter I will evaluate the extent to which expected utility theory succeeds in characterizing the kind of reasoning people actually perform prior to choice. I will argue that it fails in interesting and characteristic ways. Let me stress that I'm not arguing against expected utility theory understood as a purely predictive theory, with no pretensions of describing or prescribing human reasoning. So interpreted, it may well be important to the functioning of economics. I am interested in showing that the theory fails, not as a predictive tool, but as a theory of what human practical reason is (a task that, as I will discuss, the inventors of this theory never intended it to undertake). Moreover, I shall also argue that its failure tells us something about what a successful theory of instrumental reasoning must look like. In particular, it tells us that a successful theory of instrumental reasoning must be *nonconsequentialist* in structure, where 'nonconsequentialist' here means something quite precise. This argument allows me to construe "instrumental" reasoning so as to make plenty of room for moral reasons and moral norms applicable to action of just the sort that moral objectivists believe exist. My arguments have implications for theories, such as those of Machina (1991) and Kahneman and Tversky (1990) that retain sufficient amounts of the structure and language of EU theory to make them modifications of the EU view rather than radically different theories. To the extent that they partake of certain central assumptions of the EU theory that I shall make explicit, these theories are every bit as problematic as the "mother theory" they aim to surpass. But I am mainly interested in the implications of these arguments for moral theory. As I will discuss, such arguments can be used to support the claims of objectivist moral theorists to the extent that these arguments suggest that human beings are able to engage in nonconsequentialist forms of reasoning – of the sort that moral reasoning is often said to be. Hence these arguments are supportive of nonconsequentialist theories of moral reasoning and nonconsequentialist accounts of moral reasons.

But in the end, these arguments (merely) "make room" for moral norms and moral reasons in a theory of practical reason, and thus they are still not arguments that *show* that these norms and reasons, understood as having objective authority, actually exist. Hence, although this book is designed to defend the assumptions of moral objectivism and ultimately, a nonconsequentialist form of moral objectivism, it does not give, or even try to give, a conclusive argument for either. Indeed, I will close the book with a discussion of what kinds of arguments remain to be developed in order to settle the plausibility of any form of moral objectivism. Such arguments attempt, in essence, to "get access to" the norms that have objective authority. In philosophy, we await new "theories of the normative." If this conclusion strikes advocates of objective morality as an insufficiently strong or forthright defense, at least I can say that it is an honest conclusion, accepting the reality that those of us convinced that objectively authoritative norms exist are still working from a kind of faith. Yet "faith" is also the right word to describe the convictions of the opponents of objective moral theory, which are no more informed by a well-developed theory of the normative than the convictions of the moral objectivists. The question, "On what theoretical ground are you standing, and why is it firm?", is one that all participants in this debate have reason to ask themselves.

DEFINING AN INSTRUMENTAL THEORY OF REASON

To further refine the structure of an instrumental conception of reason, we should begin by appreciating that such a theory can be developed in two very different ways. First, it can be developed as a theory of reason*ing* – that is, a theory that describes or prescribes the sort of human mental processing that we call reasoning. Second, it can be developed as a theory (only) about behavior, setting out what behavior counts as rational, with no application whatsoever to the kind of mental processing that may or may not have preceded such behavior. Call the first *Theories of Reasoning;* call the second *Theories of Rationale.*

Theories of Reasoning can be either descriptive or normative, and the normative variety can be used to judge an agent rational to the extent that she follows the specified reasoning process. Her actions, intentions, or preferences can be judged rational to the extent that they have been approved by this reasoning process, which, it is assumed, she should have used prior to doing or forming them. Theories of reasoning are (obviously) applicable only to agents, such as human beings, who have the capacity to reason as the theory specifies, and not to animals or institutions (such as firms).

Theories of Rationale, by contrast, can be used to judge the behavior (albeit not the reasoning process) of any kind of agent, human or nonhuman. There is no expectation that the agent performing the behavior could or did use the procedure specified by the theory to judge his behavior. Note that this sort of theory is *always normative* – that is, it always specifies a standard by which the behavior of an agent is judged. It is a common (and understandable) presumption of many that the procedure used to judge behavior should be the same as the procedure used to specify human reasoning. Nonetheless, it may be that the correct conception of (behavioral) rationale is one that given human constraints and limitations, is too difficult for us to use as a reasoning process.

What I shall call a *Purely Predictive Theory of Behavior* is unlike either type of theory of reason. Such a theory (only) predicts behavior capable of public observation. Although it may be linked with a theory of rationale, it is not itself a theory of reason because there is no necessary connection between what the theory uses to make its predictions and either the mental process used by the agent prior to selecting her behavior, or the (normative) theory of rationale appropriate for judging her behavior. Some might speculate that if a predictive theory made successful predictions of an agent's choices under uncertainty, then that success would provide evidence that the agent (in some way) mentally followed the procedure described by that theory to make those choices, so that it was (in some way) a description of the reasoning processes upon which the agent operated. But the success of these predictions doesn't require that one draw this descriptive conclusion, and might be explained in other ways.[1]

In Chapter 5, I developed what I took to be the main outlines of a theory of instrumental reason designed to conform to the instrumental conception of (practical) reason described there, which I will now review:

    1.   An action is rational only to the extent that it furthers the attainment of an end;

and 2.   The agent has followed a process of reasoning involving the determination of means to achieve ends, in a way set out by the theory (I will say, henceforth, that using reason to determine the extent to which action is a means to an end is an *instrumental* use of reason);

and 3.   The agent's ends are in no way fixed by reason operating noninstrumentally – that is, what makes them her ends is something other than reason operating noninstrumentally.

This theory allows that an agent may be wrong about whether or not an action will achieve her ends, and yet still be judged rational

---

[1] Satz and Ferejohn (1994) suggest explanations for the predictive success of expected utility theory other than its being a correct descriptive theory of mental reasoning. Note also that a predictive theory might be successful for an agent, e.g., an animal, that did not have the mental capacity to use it.

insofar as she has followed the correct procedures for making that determination (so she may be wrong because, say, she was supplied with faulty information but not because there was anything wrong with *her* reasoning). Note that all three theses are consistent with what might be called the "manifesto" of the instrumental approach to reason articulated by Hume – namely, that "Reason is, and ought only to be, the slave of the passions."[2]

I have been deliberately vague in defining thesis 1. Not all means to ends are rational; one must choose "effective" or "appropriate" means. Particular instrumental theories specify whether a means to an end must, in order to be rationally acceptable, be the "best" means given available information, or the "best" given perfect information, or simply "effective" (albeit perhaps not best) as established by certain criteria. Note also that the theory of instrumental rationality, as I am defining it, is not the same as "being prudent," which is commonly understood as performing actions to achieve long-term, rather than mere short-term, ends. There is nothing in instrumental rationality that would mandate us to prefer long-term ends over short-term ends – indeed, any such mandate would appear to involve a determination of our "proper ends" by reason, and thus be a violation of thesis 3.

Thesis 3 is defined so as to allow the possibility that reason can set goals by functioning instrumentally. That is, suppose we distinguish (following Nagel, 1970) between motivated ends – ends that are means to the attainment of other ends – and unmotivated ends – ends that are not means to the attainment of other ends. Some instrumental theories accept that reason can at least fix our motivated ends; others, such as Hume's own theory, deny even this possibility.[3] All of them, however, agree that our unmotivated ends are fixed by nonrational forces within us – for example, our passions. It is worth pointing out that this means all of them accept that our pursuit of unmotivated ends can have no rational basis – that is, no basis in *reason*.

All three theses require us to classify any theory that includes them as a theory of reasoning. This is because they all tell us about the reasoning process "in the head" of a rational agent – 1 tells us what an agent believes, 2 tells us what means/end reasoning is, and

---

[2] David Hume, *A Treatise of Human Nature*, II, iii, 3 (1739, p. 415).
[3] I discuss Hume's view at length in Hampton (1995, 1996).

3 tells us that there is no reasoning in the head that establishes un-motivated ends. Note, as I will discuss later, that a theory including 1, 2, and 3 needn't be committed to the claim that the *only* form of reasoning is means/end reasoning; there are other tasks that reason can perform consistent with thesis 3.[4] (Hence thesis 2 has been stated so as not to rule out this possibility.) It is only the noninstrumental fixing of ends that the instrumental theory forbids. Call the theory defined by all three theses above the *Instrumental Theory of Reasoning*.

However, the term 'instrumental' is sometimes understood in a much weaker way. Consider that we can define a variant of the in-strumental view that embraces only thesis 1, and hence applies only to behavior, and not to reasoning. Call this the *Instrumental Theory of Rationale*. On this theory, the behavior of an agent can only be called rational if it conforms to the results of a certain means/end proce-dure – which the agent needn't have used himself prior to acting. Such a theory is irrelevant to human reason*ing*, but is nonetheless supposed to be that which we use to evaluate the rationality of the behavior of any (human or nonhuman) agent. Because this theory provides a normative assessment of behavior, it is not a purely pre-dictive theory, although its normative prescriptions might be used for predictive purposes.

Finally, we can define a theory of reason that has within it an instrumental portrayal of reason understood as only one component of a multi-faceted human reason. Such a theory accepts modified versions of 1 and 2 but no version of 3. Hence it ascribes to reason both instrumental and noninstrumental roles, but contains a char-acterization of its instrumental role that would be given in theses 1 and 2. (To make it clear that instrumental reasoning is only one com-ponent of rationality, an adherent of this view might want to modify 1 and 2 so that they begin, "One way in which an action is rational is . . ." and "One form of human reasoning involves . . .") Call this a *Complex Theory of Reasoning*; its formulations of 1 and 2 can be either descriptive or normative. Once again, note that a complex theory will not portray its instrumental component as purely predictive in na-ture, but as a descriptive or normative portrayal of human reasoning (although, again, its descriptions or prescriptions might be used to make predictions). However, a complex theory of reasoning is not

---

[4] For a discussion of other tasks of reason that can fit within an instrumentalist theory, see Williams (1981b) and my 1996.

an instrumental theory as that term is standardly understood, even if it does admit that human reasoning has an instrumental component.

We now see that the question "Can EU theory be interpreted as an instrumental theory of reason?" is ambiguous. It can mean:

1. Can EU theory be interpreted as an implementation of the instrumental theory of reasoning, in either a descriptive or normative form?

or 2. Can EU theory be interpreted as an implementation of the instrumental theory of rationale (which is always a kind of normative theory)?

or 3. Can EU theory be interpreted as a conception of the instrumental theory that is part of a complex theory of reasoning, in either a descriptive or normative form?

This chapter is primarily concerned with the first question. But after completing the argument that EU theory cannot be interpreted as any kind of theory of reasoning, I will go on to show later in the chapter that EU theory fails both as a component of a complex theory of reasoning, and as a theory of (behavioral) rationale.

SPECIFYING WHAT INSTRUMENTAL REASONING IS

Insofar as instrumental theories are species of theories of reasoning, they can be developed along different levels. Such theories, whether descriptive or normative, come in two basic varieties. They can define the reasoning procedure on which we actually operate (or ought to operate) when we decide how to behave, or they can define the meta-reasoning we use (or ought to use) to *select* operational procedures for deciding how to behave. Theorists such as H. A. Simon[5] have argued for a theory of reason that defines reasoning at both levels. Simon and others have argued that because we are subject to constraints when we reason – in particular, constraints on information-gathering (for example, limited access, high costs of obtaining, and so on), and constraints on computational ability (for example, intellectual disabilities, the costs of taxing or intellectual work) – we often rely, when we are making decisions, not on reason itself (and

---

[5] See H. A. Simon (1955 and 1956). But it is not clear that Simon himself would accept my distinction between levels of analysis, and no such distinction appears in his work.

in particular, not on the expected utility calculation) but rather on shorthand rules and procedures. When we use such rules, they say we are "satisficing" in light of our "bounded rationality." So they understand the correct theory of reason to describe or prescribe the "meta-reason" that approves or disapproves operational reasoning procedures that given the constraints on human reasoning, are unlikely to be identical to meta-reason itself.[6] This meta-reason is in some sense what reason really is. By portraying it, we show how we calculate (or ought to calculate) when we select among various satisficing procedures that we hope will tend, over the long-term, to yield the same results as the impossibly hard calculations demanded by reason, and indeed have been selected and used by us for this reason.

Theories of reasoning can also differ in what they take the cognitive level of their descriptive analysis to be. They might take themselves to be describing the deliberation procedure that human beings do or should *consciously* follow when they are appropriately said to be reasoning. Or they might take rationality to be a less conscious, less deliberative affair, something more analogous to Chomskian "deep grammar," the structure of which is not consciously in view as we engage in it. How "unconscious" a theory of reason can be and still count as a theory of reasoning is an interesting question. Little discussion of this issue of the proper depth of mental analysis of rationality appears in the literature; I know of only one theorist to have pursued it.[7]

Most theorists, including Hume, treat their theories of reasoning as describing and prescribing the conscious mode of operation hu-

---

[6] Still, must I *know* that these shorthand rules are utility-maximizing in the circumstances and use them for this reason in order to be rational? Or is it enough that my actions merely accord with these rules, even if I don't understand them to be utility-maximizing in light of constraints? Just as with morality, the rationality of an agent may depend upon more than just the conformity of her actions to certain normative standards.

[7] That theorist is Alan Nelson, who first proposed the issue to me. See his (1990). Nelson suggests the grammatical analogy, and also proposes that "humans might have evolved specialized neurological structures that compute what the efficient courses of need-satisfying action are," and if this is correct, he notes, "there is a sense in which human minds or brains actually unconsciously compute utility maxima" (p. 131). But it is not clear to me the extent to which any nonconscious computation can count as *reasoning*, given that our conception of reasoning assumes it to be a conscious, deliberative affair.

man beings do or should follow. However, Kurt Baier is among those who see the instrumental theory as both an operational and a meta-decision procedure, evaluating not only particular decisions, but also rules or procedures for making these instrumental judgments. Baier says in Chapter 1 of *The Rational and the Moral Order*[8] that reason consists of a set of "guidelines" that enable us to "guide ourselves" in our attempts to attain our ends. Baier argues that these guidelines are social phenomena, "made available to us by our culture" so that we can guide ourselves toward attaining our ends. But he notes that these guidelines can be "flawed," and "in such cases, following reason means suitably departing from them."[9] So by understanding instrumental reason not only as an operating procedure but also as a meta-reasoning procedure, Baier tries to develop the theory along social rather than individualistic lines – that is, he conceives of the operating procedures we follow as reasoners not as private and internally wired, but as instrumentally defined by society. Indeed, Baier maintains that it is because the guidelines of rationality are social that we can have so much faith in them. Granted, he writes,

> these publicly available guidelines are not themselves the (infallible) guidelines for attaining these important ends, but merely what a culture has worked out to be the closest attainable approximation to them it could produce. But their generality, their public availability, and their widespread employment and revision, generation after generation, gives them a high likelihood that more errors have been eliminated than any single individual among us could eliminate by his own efforts, and therefore are normally our best bet. Of course, a detached comparison between the methods of different cultures may yield still better results. This seems to me the sound basis of the widespread conviction that reason is tied to universality.[10]

Readers are right, however, to detect an air of paradox in this passage. It cannot be the case that instrumental reason is *entirely* a social matter, otherwise the comparison of different culture's guidelines to see which yields "better results" could not take place.[11] To resolve

[8] Kurt Baier (1995). See pp. 49ff.
[9] Ibid. pp. 50–51.
[10] Ibid. p. 51.
[11] To quote Putnam (1983), "the 'standards' accepted by a culture or subculture,

the air of paradox, Baier can say that (only) the operational procedures of reason are products of a culture. The meta-procedure for
formulating, assessing, and modifying the operational guidelines
transcends culture (it is, after all, what we use to evaluate the ef-
fectiveness of different cultural guidelines) and thus must be universally available to all human beings as part of their human nature.

So were Baier to specify the details of the process of reasoning
that characterizes instrumental deliberation, those details would
likely be different at the two levels. At the operational level, specification of the reasoning process would make reference to culturally
defined guidelines, whereas at the meta-level, the guidelines could
not be culturally defined. Baier says much about the former and very
little about the latter.[12] But presumably specifying the latter involves
pursuing the way in which human beings (naturally?) engage in a
certain kind of practical reasoning prior to choice, regardless of their
culture or their socialization. Those psychologists and philosophers
who study reasoning "scientifically" might be understood as pursuing the operational guidelines implicit in our reasoning that tran-
scend culture and that in some sense have their source in our nature
as human beings.

Finally, instrumental theories can differ in the ways they take reason to function as an instrument. Even if reason is only a servant,
there is more than one way in which it can serve.

The most commonly recognized form of reason's servitude is
means/end reasoning, and the specification of this form of reasoning
is the hallmark of instrumental theories of reason. Hobbes's position
is typical in this regard. Although theorists such as Baier have accused Hobbes of rejecting the idea that there is any regimentation in
our instrumental reasoning,[13] Hobbes is in fact very concerned to
show that instrumental reasoning has a specific structure, involving
the "apt imposing of names" of objects and strict adherence to logical

---

either explicitly or implicitly, cannot *define* what reason is, even in context, because they *presuppose* reason (reasonableness) for their interpretation," p. 234.

[12] Sometimes Baier suggests that it might be possible to define the meta-level process of reasoning instrumentally. However, this idea is circular; in order to define
the instrumental reasoning process instrumentally, one must already have in
hand the instrumental reasoning procedure one is attempting to define. I discuss
this elsewhere, e.g., in my 1994.

[13] See Baier, op. cit., Chapter 1.

rules of inference.[14] Indeed, his *Leviathan* is a kind of massive exercise in instrumental reasoning, which is supposed to demonstrate to all that self-preservation requires the creation of an absolute sovereign and the eschewal of certain actions that although promotive of glory, will lead to a state of war and a short, miserable life. Subsequent instrumental theorists from Hume to the present day have developed various portrayals of the structure of means/end reasoning.

However, there is another task that an instrumental theory might assign to reason and still remain instrumental – that of discovering (but not defining) what our ends of action are. This means that an instrumental theory of reason could specify *two* different kinds of reasoning procedures. Nagel's distinction between motivated and unmotivated (or intrinsic) ends is once again helpful here. A theory of instrumental reason can specify a reasoning procedure for identifying each type of end: First, a procedure that determines causes of desired effects for the identification of motivated ends; second, a procedure for discovering (albeit not defining) what one's intrinsic ends really are. As long as the theory assigns to something other than reason the task of setting the intrinsic ends of human life, thesis 3 is satisfied, and the theory can remain instrumental even while granting reason the role of discovering these ends. If we invoke Hume's servant analogy, we can say either that reason's servitude can involve obeying orders from the master (for example, our desires, or our God) to take efficient means to achieving the end(s) set by the master, or it can also involve, at least on occasion, finding out who its master really is.

Because neither Hobbes nor Hume thinks that the objects of our desires are particularly difficult to determine, neither grants to reason the task of helping us to see exactly what it is that we want in life. Most likely this is because each of them takes it for granted that the goals established by desires or passions are sufficiently transparent that the agent would find it unnecessary to use reason to help identify those goals.[15] So when Hobbes characterizes the deliberative process someone would use in order to make up his mind about what to do, he says:

---

[14] See Part I of Hobbes's *Leviathan* (1651) and his *De Corpore* (1655).

[15] For a paper that criticizes this assumption in Hobbes's theory, see Paul Hurley (1990).

When in the mind of man, Appetites and Aversions, Hopes, and Feares, concerning one and the same thing, arise alternately; and divers good and evill consequences of the doing, or omitting the thing propounded, come successively into our thoughts; so that sometimes we have an Appetite to it; sometimes an Aversion from it; sometimes Hope to be able to do it; sometimes Despaire, or Feare to attempt it; the whole summe of Desires, Aversions, Hopes and Fears, continued till the thing be either done, or thought impossible, is that we call DELIBERATION. (1651: 6, 29, 28)

This passage is not about cause-and-effect reasoning; it is about deciding what to do when one has conflicting desires, either for unmotivated ends, or for motivated ends (driven by different desires for unmotivated ends). When we decide which end to pursue, Hobbes proposes that our deliberation does not in any real sense involve reasoning, but is rather the phenomenological weighing up of the strengths of these competing desires, which will proceed until the action is performed or until any action becomes impossible. Reason therefore plays *no* role in the process of selecting the desire that will prevail, and deliberation is merely a process in which the stronger desire finally manifests itself.

But we ought to wonder whether Hobbesian and Humean instrumental theorists should be so optimistic about the transparency of the unmotivated ends of human action. Contemporary instrumental theorists have been prepared to admit that our strongest desire-defined ends are not always clear to us. For example, David Gauthier insists that in order to be genuinely ours, the ends we pursue must be from "considered" preferences.[16] Although he does not describe this process of "consideration," it seems plausible to construe it as a kind of reasoning procedure, akin, perhaps, to Richard Brandt's "cognitive psychotherapy"[17] – a reasoning process that helps us to determine our "true" unmotivated ends. Similarly, Bernard Williams describes a form of deliberation involving one's imagination, whose function is the appraisal of old (unmotivated) desires and the generation of new ones:

[An agent] may think he has reason to promote some development because he has not exercised his imagination enough about

[16] See Gauthier (1986), Chapter 2.
[17] See Brandt (1979).

what it would be like if it came about. In his unaided deliberative reason, or encouraged by the persuasions of others, he may come to have a more concrete sense of what would be involved [if he had some object] and lose his desire for it, just as, positively, the imagination can create new possibilities and new desires.[18]

Because Williams, Brandt, and Gauthier fail to structure precisely their "desire discovery" procedures, it is unclear how different any of them finally is from Hobbes's unregimented "strongest desire manifestation" process, which Hobbes does not regard as a form of reasoning.[19] But because these modern theorists at least suggest the outlines of a reasoning procedure for discovering (but not defining) intrinsic ends, they can be understood to define reason's servitude broadly, to include not merely finding means to ends, but also discovery of the content of those ends.[20] Williams also suggests that there are other forms of deliberative reasoning, all of which could fit into a (suitably broad) conception of instrumental reasoning: ". . . such as, thinking how the satisfaction of elements in [an agent's subjective motivational set] S can be combined, e.g. by time-ordering; where there is some irresoluble conflict among the elements of S, considering which one attaches most weight to (which, importantly, does not imply that there is some one commodity of which they provide varying amounts); or, again, finding constitutive solutions, such as deciding what would make for an entertaining evening, granted that one wants entertainment."[21]

As will become clear, the fact that other forms of reasoning besides

---

[18] Williams (1981b), pp. 104–5.

[19] Baier points out that there is virtually no regimentation in Brandt's procedure, a fact that might lead us to wonder why it ought to be considered a "procedure" at all. See Baier, op. cit., Chapter 1.

[20] Whether or not such an "end discovery" reasoning procedure should be recognized is related to the issue of whether or not we should consider desires as, in themselves, reasons for action. Some theorists, such as Bond (1983), deny that they should be so considered. Bernard Williams (1985) says, in contrast, that "Desiring to do something is of course a reason for doing it," p. 19. However I would presume Williams means that we should consider desires as reasons only if they have been approved by the imaginative reasoning procedure he describes, since otherwise they might be deviant, misinformed, or ill-considered, and, hence not "justified" in the way we think reasons for action are supposed to be. For Williams's views on the way in which reasons must be justified, see his 1981b.

[21] Williams (1981b), p. 104.

means/end reasoning can be understood as "instrumental" if that term is construed broadly, will be important for us in appraising whether or not expected utility theory is an instrumental form of reasoning.

NON-INSTRUMENTAL THEORIES OF REASON[a]

In contrast to these variants of the instrumental approach to reason, noninstrumental theorists present reason not as a tool designed solely either to achieve or to discover the ends of our actions, but as something that, in addition to its instrumental functioning, quite literally, defines ends of action. For these theorists, reason *is* the master. There is more than one way of explaining its masterly role: One can say, as Plato suggests,[22] that reason is the *source* of ends of action, supplying to us the rightful content of our goals in life. Or one can say, following Kant, that reason is that which constrains what it is that we desire to pursue, so that desires propose the content of our goals in life and reason permits or excludes pursuit of these proposed goals (making reason a kind of limiting condition).[23] Those who believe in the existence of a distinctive kind of moral reasoning, by which we come to recognize or determine moral norms authoritative over our action, will generally embrace either a Platonic or Kantian conception of reason. Neither theory denies that reason has an instrumental role, but each insists that it also has a (direct or indirect) role in determining our ends, and that it provides the motivation to pursue the ends it determines. Hence, such theories of reason are generally the foundation of objective theories of morality.

There are three reasons why philosophers have been troubled by the idea that reason has either kind of noninstrumental role. First, it seems that such a theory unabashedly embraces the idea of objective authority to explain the force of the noninstrumental directives of reason, and all the problems with that idea that we reviewed in

---

[a]*Editor's note:* There is considerable overlap between this section and earlier sections of the manuscript – in particular the beginning of Chapter 4. The author would undoubtedly have minimized this duplication in subsequent revisions.

[22] But it isn't clear that Plato holds this view. I am indebted to John Armstrong for his discussions with me on this point.

[23] Herman (1985).

Chapter 3 would seem to argue against any noninstrumental theory that it seems would have to rely on it. Naturalists have therefore strongly preferred the instrumental approach to reason, which they have thought was capable of development along entirely naturalist lines, without reference to strange prescriptive objects or human capacities. Alas, however, the argument in the last chapter shows that they were wrong, so that there is no metaphysical reason for preferring the instrumental over the noninstrumental approach.

However, the instrumental approach might still be regarded as better insofar as the noninstrumental view has a second problem – namely, that its directives seem much more intuitively powerful than the directives of a noninstrumental theory. After all, what special "sight" or access to normative reality can we realistically ascribe to human reason, such that it can tell us our ends in life? How does a scientific worldview permit us to believe that there are unmotivated ends that we are rationally compelled to pursue? Moreover, no scientific description of human beings has identified a rational capacity within us that can determine these ends of life, respond to their inherent prescriptivity, and motivate action in compliance with their requirements.

The third problem facing those who say reason can function noninstrumentally concerns motivation. Most theorists share Baier's view that whereas the question "Why be moral?" is deeply troubling, the question "Why be rational?" is not.[24] Yet if reason is understood to operate noninstrumentally, it becomes so expansive, and its directives so wide-ranging and divergent from interests the individual is readily able to recognize, that the issue of behaving rationally, when rationality is defined like *that*, is now a real one.[25] Baier and others therefore believe Kant has gone down the wrong conceptual road; in their view, the normative form of the instrumental account of reason is the clear superior to the noninstrumental view, given that it appears capable of development in a way that avoids this motivational problem.

It is because of these difficulties with the noninstrumental conception of reason that many theorists have taken expected utility theory, construed as some kind of scientific conception of reason, to be an

---

[24] See Baier's *Carus Lectures*, Lecture I, "The Moral Order," p. 4. The lectures are published in expanded form as Baier (1995).
[25] Baier, op. cit, p. 19.

233

instrumental theory. In what follows, we will look into whether this can be so.

WHAT IS EXPECTED UTILITY THEORY?

Expected utility theory, developed by von Neumann and Morgenstern (1944/1947/1953) (hereafter vN/M), and Leonard Savage (1954/1972),[26] has its source in Daniel Bernoulli's (1738) discussion of the St. Petersburg Paradox,[27] and Jeremy Bentham's (1823) idea that in order to understand value as it originates in the subject, we require the concept of utility, understood as a cardinal (and interpersonal) measure of pleasure or happiness experienced by an agent when his desires are satisfied, and something that ought to be *maximized*.[28] However, von Neumann and Morgenstern substituted talk of preferences for talk of desires and developed a notion of "utility" that is deliberately *not* meant to refer to an experiential state.[29] There have been many subsequent axiomatizations of expected utility theory since vN/M, of roughly two types, first, those that follow vN/M and rely on objective probabilities, and second, those that follow Frank Ramsey's (1931b) idea, developed by Savage (1954/1972) that we can define probabilities subjectively from information about the agent's preferences. In my explication of EU theory in this section, I will use von Neumann and Morgenstern's original axiomatization, but I will discuss in later sections the Savage-type axiomatization.

Imagine a lottery ticket that has, as prizes, two of the most extreme extremes: Call these (after Baumol 1972) Eternal Bliss (e) and Death

[26] Savage's subjectivist approach to utility was anticipated by Frank Ramsey (1931b).

[27] Bernoulli argued that a rational and well-informed person prefers a to b if and only if a gives him at least as great an expectation of good (his word for good is 'emolumentum') as b, where the expectation of good is defined as the sum of the products one gets by multiplying the value of the quantity of each state by the probability of that state's occurring. For a brief discussion of Bernoulli's theory, see Broome (1991), p. 53 and 91ff. And see Bernoulli (1738).

[28] See Bentham (1823), in which he introduces utilitarian reasoning. For an overview of the development of expected utility theory, see Robert Sugden (1991).

[29] Or at least so they usually say. There are times in their development of the theory when they do resort to a more experiential interpretation of utility, which contradicts their official line. I note one such lapse later in this article; their inconsistency is criticized by Ellsberg (1954).

and Damnation (d). Let us assign the number 100 to u(e) and 1 to u(d):

u(e) = 100
u(d) = 1

And let us define the probability of receiving e as p and thus the probability of receiving d as 1−p. Call this lottery ticket: [p: e, d].

Now consider some prize a.[30] Depending on the value of a and the probabilities of e or d occurring, a person will prefer either a or [p: e, d]. If the probability of e is 1, the person prefers the lottery; if the probability of e is 0, the person prefers a. It is plausible that there will be some probability between 0 and 1, such that the person will be indifferent between a and the lottery. Call this p_a, and assign the number 0.3 to it. Now we can find the utility of a:

$$U \, [p: e, d] = p_a[u(e)] + (1-p_a)u(d) = 0.3 \times 100 + 0.7 \times 1$$
$$= 30.7$$

So the vN/M theory requires that we interview or observe a person in order to get him to (arbitrarily) assign utility numbers to certain *riskless* prizes: then, once we know how a person has committed himself, *and* once we know that this person's preferences satisfy certain seemingly weak axioms (to be defined more fully later), we can make the "von Neumann and Morgenstern prediction" – that is, "we need ask him no further questions in order to predict his ranking of any lottery tickets in which only these prizes are involved. We do not have to ask him how he feels about the odds involved in these tickets – this can be determined for him from our computation" (Baumol, 1972, 542). To put the vN/M result precisely:

> Given any two lottery tickets [p: a, b] and [p': a', b'] and a person whose preferences never violate the vN/M axioms, if we obtain (say, by observing his choices) the four probability numbers p_a, $p_{a'}$, p_b and $p_{b'}$ chosen so that: aI[p_a: e, d] and bI [p_b: e, d], etc.,

---

[30] I do *not* assume in the discussion that follows that prizes are money, or easily transferable into money. They are understood to be simply determinate outcomes, over which an agent has preferences, and hence may or may not be monetary. This appears to be the way Luce and Raiffa (1957/1985, 23ff) understand them, although they do not specifically say so.

then from these numbers it is possible to predict which of the two lottery tickets will be preferred.[31]

So starting from two defined end-points, an arbitrarily chosen scale, and questions regarding indifference between a sure thing and a lottery between the end-points, we can define the utility of the sure thing – albeit only as long as this person's preferences satisfy the vN/M axioms. And thereafter we will be able to predict what choice she will make among the relevant alternatives in any situation involving risk, again assuming her choices conform to the axioms.

Following is a brief statement of the vN/M axioms, which are based on Luce and Raiffa's well-known formulations of them [see Luce and Raiffa (1957/1985), Chapter 2.5, pp. 23–31]:

1. **Completeness (or Ordering):** For any prize a and any prize b, a>b or b>a or they are indifferent. (This axiom is what set theorists call "connectedness"; it specifies that all the objects over which we have preferences can be compared or ordered.)

2. **Transitivity:** For any prizes a, b, and c, if a>b and b>c, then a>c.

To define the next four axioms, suppose that $L^{(1)}$, $L^{(2)}$, . . . ,$L^{(s)}$ are any s lotteries that each involve a_1, a_2, . . . ,a_r as prizes, where $a_1 \geq a_i \geq a_r$.[32] If q_1, q_2, . . . ,q_s are any s nonnegative numbers that sum to 1, then $(q_1 L^{(1)}, q_2 L^{(2)}, \ldots ,q_s L^{(s)})$ denotes a compound lottery in the sense that one and only one of the given s lotteries will be the prize, and the probability that it will be $L^{(i)}$ is q_i. Thus:

3. **Reduction of Compound Lotteries:** Any compound lottery is indifferent to a simple lottery with a, b, c . . . as prizes, its probabilities being computed consistent with the ordinary probability calculus. That is, if

$$L^{(i)} = (p_1^{(i)} a_1, p_2^{(i)} a_2, \ldots ,p_r^{(i)} a_r) \text{ for } i = 1, 2, \ldots s,$$

then

$$(q_1 L^{(1)}, q_2 L^{(2)}, \ldots ,q_s L^{(s)}) \text{ is indifferent to } (p_1 a_1, p_2 a_2, \ldots ,p_r a_r),$$

---

[31] Based on Baumol (1972), p. 542.

[32] The axioms are stated assuming that the number of prizes of the lotteries is finite, but this is only for the sake of convenience. It is sufficient that the prizes are merely denumerable. The theory can be extended to deal with a nonfinite number of prizes.

where

$$p_i = q_1 p_i^{(1)} + q_2 p_i^{(2)} + \ldots + q_s p_i^{(s)}.$$

4. **Continuity:** Each prize a_i is indifferent to some lottery ticket involving just a_1 and a_r. That is, there exists a number p^i, such that a^i is indifferent to $[p^i a_1, (1-p^i)a_r]$.
5. **Substitutability (or Independence):** If A_i is defined as follows: $A_i = [p^i a_1, (1-p^i)a_r]$ (which is indifferent to a_i), then in any lottery L, A_i is substitutable for a_i – that is, $[p_1 a_1, \ldots, p_i a_i, \ldots, p_r a_r]$ $\sim [p_1 a_1, \ldots, p_i A_i, \ldots, p_r a_r]$. This means that the other alternatives that one could receive in the lottery must be irrelevant to the decision that A_i and a_i are indifferent. (This axiom is roughly equivalent to what is called, following Savage, the *"Sure Thing"* *Principle*, used in Savage's axiomatization of EU theory.[33])
6. **Monotonicity:** A lottery $[pa_1, (1-p)a_r]$ is preferred or indifferent to $[p'a_1, (1-p')a_r]$ if and only if $p \geq p'$. That is, between two lotteries involving only the most and least preferred alternatives, one should not prefer the one that renders the least preferred alternative more probable.

vN/M prove the following: If a preference relation R on the set of lotteries satisfies these axioms, there exists a function V representing R, where V assigns to a lottery, as its utility, the lottery's expected utility; moreover, any positive affine transformation V' of this function will also represent R. Call the function V and all its positive affine transformations "vN/M functions."[34]

The first point to note about this theory is that it was deliberately designed to be only a predictive theory of reason.[35] Many theorists (particularly philosophers) believe (and teach their students) that von Neumann and Morgenstern establish that *only* a vN/M function, or a linear transformation of that function, can represent the preference ordering of any person whose preferences satisfy the axioms. Many

---

[33] The "Sure Thing" Principle is similar to the Independence axiom, with the exception that the former does not assume objective probabilities, allowing for the determination of a decision-maker's subjective probabilities from his utilities.
[34] This formulation is based on Weymark (1991).
[35] Note that it has been a standard assumption among economists since the early 1950s that the term 'preference' in the theory should be understood behaviorally rather than mentalistically. A person's preferences are understood to be revealed by, or better yet, consist in, her (publicly observable) behavior.

of them therefore assume von Neumann and Morgenstern have shown that any such person *has a vN/M function in his head,* so that people whose preferences satisfy the axioms *actually are expected utility reasoners.*

Now this "leap" from mathematical proof to a conviction that EU theory is in the head of any human reasoner is completely unjustified. Why should a mathematical proof be taken to show us what is going on "inside the head" of any agent being studied, or have any descriptive or normative import concerning our reasoning processes? But this issue aside, it is simply wrong to say von Neumann and Morgenstern proved that *only* vN/M functions can represent preferences satisfying these axioms; instead, they have merely established that such functions *can* represent them. Non-vN/M functions also represent preferences that satisfy these axioms, and generate the same predictions, when such functions are monotonic but not linear transforms of the vN/M functions and when the decision rule attributed to a person using this monotonic transform is appropriately modified. Suppose, for example, that we represent a person's preferences using the cube of some vN/M function f. This new function f³ is a monotonic but not a linear transform of a vN/M function. By saying that he was acting *as if* he were seeking to maximize the expected value of the cube root of f³, any predictions we would make about his choices would be exactly the same as our predictions based on representing him as a maximizer of expected utility. So selecting this non-vN/M function to represent preferences also involves changing the way in which we think about the "decision rule" that a person follows when he makes a choice in a risky situation. But the predictions based on either function with either "rule" will be the same. (So one under-appreciated implication of the vN/M proof is that "decision rules" aren't fundamental to our decision-making. As long as our preferences satisfy the vN/M axioms, our "choice of rule" corresponds to a choice among any number of acceptable functions for representing our preference orderings.[36])

I am really making a mathematically trivial point that is nonetheless conceptually important. Kenneth Arrow (1951, 10) was worried enough about his fellow economists' tendency to believe von Neumann and Morgenstern had actually shown that intrapersonal cardinal measurement of preferences was possible to make the points I

[36] I am indebted to John Pollock for discussions on this point.

have just made. Despite Arrow's cautions, John Weymark (1991) felt that some economists and social scientists were still confused enough about this thirty years later to necessitate reiteration of the same ideas, particularly because economists such as Harsanyi have insisted on using expected utility theory as a foundation for utilitarianism. Weymark argues that a major reason why Amartya Sen objects to John Harsanyi's utilitarian theory is that Sen understands the way in which expected utility theory cannot yield *any* information about a person's (cardinally measurable) welfare, which means that, contra Harsanyi, expected utility theorems cannot be given a utilitarian interpretation. Philosophers and legal theorists are surely much more guilty of misunderstanding this point than economists, given the way economics enthusiasts in these fields standardly assume that expected utility theory gives us a way of "measuring" preferences that *reveals value*. For example, David Gauthier (1986, Chapter 1), citing Harsanyi as one of his authorities about expected utility theory, sets out EU theory insisting that "if utility is to be identified with value, it must be the measure [i.e. a cardinal measure] of considered preference," (1986, 48), and then goes on to "explain" how von Neumann and Morgenstern have shown us how to "measure" preferences.

But von Neumann and Morgenstern do no such thing. They have merely shown us how to *represent* preferences that happen to satisfy certain axioms on a cardinal scale, such that we can predict how a person with those preferences would choose under conditions of risk. So the conclusion of the vN/M proof is not that people *are* expected utility maximizers, nor that their preferences (even assuming that they satisfy these axioms) are generated by some psychological state whose structure is faithfully captured by a vN/M function. As Luce and Raiffa (1957) are at pains to explain, the numbers generated by a vN/M function aren't a "measure" of anything other than preferences, and certainly not something called 'utility' that can be identified with "welfare," which is supposed to underlie our preferences.[37] There is nothing more to utility than these numbers.

[37] But there are times when even Luce and Raiffa (1957/1985) stray dangerously from the right interpretation of the vN/M statement. For example, they say: "*Very roughly* von Neumann and Morgenstern have shown the following: If a person is able to express preferences between every possible pair of gambles,

This means that the theory as it was originally developed can only be understood as a purely *predictive* theory and not a descriptive or normative theory of human reasoning or a theory that provides a normative standard for judging behavior. In other words, nothing in von Neumann and Morgenstern's statement can be taken to establish, even if our preferences do satisfy their axioms, that we actually have vN/M functions in our heads driving our choices, or that our behavior or reasoning *ought* to conform to these functions when we make choices. All they establish is that such functions are a useful and easy way (albeit not the only way) to represent ordinal preferences satisfying these axioms such that we can predict behavior, which means that EU theory, as it was originally developed, cannot be taken to be any kind of theory of reason (it is neither a theory of reasoning, nor a theory of rationale). Indeed, as a predictive tool, EU theory doesn't even have to work for everyone at every time in order to be useful for the economist attempting to predict choice in large-scale market situations. This is the only interpretive conclusion supported by vN/M's conclusions.

There is good reason why von Neumann and Morgenstern would naturally develop a merely predictive theory of reason. They and other founders of EU theory wanted to avoid incorporating into the theory any psychological speculations about the fundamental springs of human behavior (since none of this would pass positivist muster), and so their theory officially takes no stand on what it is inside us that generates our preferences or on how our utility function "really" looks when it accurately represents the way we value something (and not merely how we are disposed to choose).

where the gambles are taken over some basic set of alternatives, then one *can* introduce utility associations to the basic alternatives in such a manner that, if the person is guided solely by the utility expected value, *he is acting in accord with his true tastes* – provided that there is an element of consistency in his true tastes" (p. 21). But what are true tastes? The sentence would be a tautology if they are supposed to be identical with preferences, so we can assume that they are not. And in fact the phrase conjures up welfarist ideas, despite the fact that there is nothing in von Neumann and Morgenstern's premises or in their conclusions that would enable us to link a person's (behaviorally expressed) preferences with his (welfare-conferring) tastes, much less his "true" tastes. This remark by Luce and Raiffa is evidence of how strongly decision theorists have wanted to link preferences, and the utility functions representing them, to welfarist ideas, in the face of a theory whose sparse premises do not permit such linkage.

To interpret EU theory as a normative standard applicable to behavior, or as a descriptive or normative account of what goes on in our heads when we are reasoning, is therefore to import "evidence" from outside that proof, involving in the former case, psychologizing about the reasoning process, and in the latter case, philosophizing about norms of behavior. I know of no philosopher or economist who has tried to develop or defend any such evidence. Those who blithely assume that von Neumann and Morgenstern's theory can be used as a theory of reasoning or rationale are therefore, without warrant, forcing the theory into roles that it was never designed to perform.

But before this section concludes, let me air one puzzle: Given that von Neumann and Morgenstern's EU theory is designed to be merely predictive, why does it rely on objective probabilities? Its predictions would appear to assume that the subjects are making decisions using these probabilities. But even if we accept the principle that "our subjective probabilities should be the same as objective probabilities," there is good reason to believe that many human agents' subjective probabilities fail to be identical to the objective probabilities, not merely because of irrationality, but also because of difficulties in information-gathering. Now perhaps reliance on objective probabilities is reasonable for a normative instrumental theory (although I do not think so, since one can reason well, and through no fault of one's own, still get the probabilities wrong), but it is clearly a mistake for any theory purporting merely to predict actual human choice behavior. von Neumann and Morgenstern's design of their theory does not match their conception of its proper role.

THE "OBVIOUS" NONINSTRUMENTAL INTERPRETATION

There are obvious reasons why proponents of EU theory should want to construe the theory as a kind of instrumental theory of practical reasoning. Theorists have been attracted to instrumental theories not only because they have held them to be plausible descriptive accounts of how human beings reason, but also because, as I discussed in Chapter 4, such theories have struck many as suitably "minimalist" in their normative forms, avoiding extensive appeals to values or norms inconsistent with the ontology and metaphysics of science (for example, see Mackie 1977). Thus, economists and philosophers alike have been attracted to (what they regard as) instrumental theories such as expected utility theory, or to close variants of the theory, because they have considered this kind of approach to be as "positive and wertfrei, that is, as scientific" as possible.[38] This is in part because instrumental theories reject the idea (implicit in most complex theories of reason) that in order to define our ends of action, we must appeal to values or norms that are recognized by reason operating in some noninstrumental way. But the eschewal of norms by some advocates of the instrumental theory goes even deeper, as I shall now explain.

Although EU theory was never intended to be any kind of theory of reason, the theory's supporters might still insist that by adding the right psychological and normative content to the theory, it can be readily transformed into a plausible descriptive or normative theory of reasoning. However, note that the addition of psychological content to the theory would mean it would no longer retain its positivist scientific credentials. von Neumann and Morgenstern developed EU theory taking no stand either on the nature of our reasoning prior to our behavior or on the source of our preferences. But that means their theory says nothing about the psychological forces within us that generate our preferences, meaning that all sorts of psychological phenomena – including reason operating noninstrumentally – could generate those preferences. Yet an instrumental conception of reason rules out the possibility that such a form of reason could generate preferences. So unless the expected utility theorist takes a stand on the source of our preferences, which means taking a stand on a particular issue of human psychology, he cannot insist that reason plays no role in the generation of unmotivated ends of action, or that its only role is instrumental as defined by this theory. To put the point succinctly, *as long as expected utility theory is psychologically neutral, it cannot claim to be an instrumental conception of human reasoning*. Economists have normally been intent on keeping psychological assumptions out of their theory, but ironically, doing so prevents them from embracing, from the naturalist standpoint, what many would take to be the most metaphysically acceptable theory of reasoning around.

Suppose that supporters of EU theory decided to "bite the bullet" and simply introduce this psychological content into the theory in

---

[38] This is M.D. Little's way of putting it (Little 1984). And see Cooter and Rappaport (1984) for a discussion of this idea.

order to make it an instrumental theory of reasoning. It turns out the structure of EU theory seems to argue against its introduction, for on the face it, there is a rather obvious noninstrumental interpretation of EU theory, which those who consider EU theory a formal and noninstrumental conception of reasoning likely have in mind. EU theory makes a subject's preferences the definers of the ends of that subject's action, and thus of what for that subject is valuable. However, the theory does not permit just any preference to be value-defining, but rather only those preferences that satisfy the axioms of expected utility theory explicated above. But this would appear to mean that the axioms play a role in fixing the ends of action by acting as a normative "sieve" through which our preferences must pass in order to be considered "value-defining." If this is right, reasoning using these axioms is noninstrumental in character, meaning that EU theory could not be considered an implementation of the instrumental theory of reasoning, insofar as, in this interpretation, it defies thesis 3.

A number of theorists who regard EU theory as a normative account of human reasoning characterize the theory in ways that strongly suggest this interpretation – and this even includes some who treat it as an instrumental theory of reasoning. For example, the philosopher David Gauthier (1986, 40), who considers the theory an instantiation of the instrumental theory of reason, nonetheless says outright that the transitivity axiom holds our preferences up to a standard, which is in effect a kind of consistency standard. And Leonard Savage (1954/1972, 20) claims that the axioms of rational-choice theory are analogous to rules of logic, which seems to suggest once again that these axioms function as noninstrumental consistency constraints on our preference set: "Pursuing the analogy of logic, the main use I would make of [the axioms] is normative, to police my own decisions for consistency and, where possible, to make complicated decisions depend on simpler ones."[39] I call this

---

[39] And yet consider Savage's own musings on the fact that he and others expressed preferences which violated the Independence axiom: "There is, of course, an important sense in which preferences, being entirely subjective, cannot be in error; but in a different, more subtle sense they can be" (1954/1972, p. 103). He is loathe to abandon the subjectivity of preferences which, it seems, is required by a theory which constrains our preferences with axioms of reason. Moreover, although Maurice Allais seems to adopt a purely Humean view about preferences when he says, "It cannot be too strongly emphasized *that there are no*

the *formal* interpretation of EU theory. In this view, the axioms of the theory are noninstrumental constraints on an agent's set of preferences that prescribe consistency on the set, analogous to logical constraints on an agent's set of beliefs.

But by accepting that desires can be subject to normative standards, one violates the Humean view that reason is a (mere) servant of the passions. One philosopher has argued that admitting these standards is only "one tiny step beyond Hume,"[40] but by taking this "tiny step" we not only invite the possibility that there are normative standards other than those of consistency (for example, moral standards) to which our desires ought to be subject (for on what grounds can we argue for some noninstrumental standards and against others?), but also end up with an interpretation of EU theory that can no longer be considered "wertfrei," and this will make some theorists uneasy about the theory's standing as a "scientific" conception of reason. Fortunately, those who desire to interpret EU theory as an instrumental conception of reason have a number of ways of arguing that this noninstrumental characterization of the theory is wrong.

ESTABLISHING THAT EU THEORY IS AN INSTRUMENTAL THEORY

One obvious way to try to counter the claim that EU axioms are noninstrumental constraints is to argue that these axioms can be *instrumentally justified*. In this view, the axioms are not noninstrumental constraints on preference because we have instrumental reasons for following them. This is because the EU axioms prescribe consistency, and agents must have consistent preferences if they are to achieve the maximal satisfaction of their preferences. So in this view, the EU axioms are defended *consequentially*, or to use a term of McClennen's (1990, Chapter 1), "pragmatically." In contrast, the previous inter-

---

criteria for the rationality of ends," nonetheless he goes on to add, "*other than the conditions of consistency*," showing that he understands the axioms as noninstrumental principles of reasoning constraining what can count as a "rational end" (quoted by Broome (1991), pp. 104–5, from Allais (1979b), p. 70). Finally, consider Richard Jeffrey's remark that decision theory should be understood as "a sort of Logic of Decision which individuals can use as an anvil against which to form and reform parts of their preference rankings" (Jeffrey 1971, pp. 647–56, quoted by Broome 1993, p. 71).

[40] See Nozick (1993), p. 140.

pretation assumed that the axioms would have to be defended in some nonconsequentialist way, either with a foundationalist argument, which would interpret the axioms as intuitively compelling and foundational to our reasoning, or with a coherentist argument, which would interpret the axioms as justified insofar as they cohered well with other intuitively compelling principles of reason.[41]

On the face of it, a consequentialist interpretation of EU theory has problems. Those who are committed to a pragmatic, consequentialist defense of the EU axioms must contend with arguments, such as those offered by McClennen (1990), that some of the axioms fail to be justifiable on these grounds. And they must deal with the issue of whether *only* these axioms are pragmatically defensible. Even if the principle "to satisfy ends, one must be consistent" is true, the EU axioms are not the only representation of consistency, so it seems one could satisfy the principle by using other reasoning theories with rather different axioms.

But there is a deeper and more devastating objection to this strategy for interpreting EU theory. As I shall now argue, *any* consequentialist defense of this set of axioms is conceptually incoherent.

Suppose you say the following to an agent who has inconsistent preferences: "If you retain a set of preferences that violate the EU axioms, then you won't maximize the satisfaction of your preferences." But of course the inconsistent agent will agree with you, because you have just uttered a tautology since these axioms define what it is to maximize the satisfaction of preferences. Or in other words, the EU theorem doesn't give people an instrumental reason to conform to the axioms; it gives them a precise statement of what they will be doing when they conform to the axioms. Moreover, an agent who violates these axioms is likely not to be an agent who has any interest in maximizing the satisfaction of her preferences (which explains her inconsistency). So how does your imperative give her a *reason* to follow these axioms? Note that you cannot appeal to her preferences to make this argument: When those preferences are in disarray, the concept of "maximizing" their satisfaction makes no sense.

The only way to make such an appeal is to "fix" at least some

---

[41] See McClennen 1991, Chapter 1, for a discussion. Despite his tendency to see the axioms as noninstrumental standards, this interpretation of some of the axioms (e.g., consistency) is also endorsed by Nozick (1993), p. 140.

substantial portion of those preferences so as to render them consistent, and defend the EU axioms with respect to these (consistent) preferences. But note that by so doing, you are essentially assuming the consistency (and the axioms effecting it) that you were supposed to be justifying.

To give an example, consider the "Money Pump" argument, a pragmatic defense of the transitivity axiom. According to that argument, if an agent has preferences over certain things – let's say they're over fruits – that are intransitive, a dealer could repeatedly offer the agent these fruits in exchange for the agent's money in a way that the agent would find attractive but that would result in his being "pumped" of money. Because, the argument concludes, the agent would regret losing money, he is pragmatically wise to make his preferences transitive and thereby render such pumping impossible. So the money pump argument purports to show that one has an instrumental reason for subjecting one's preferences to the transitivity axiom. But note that the argument relies on *two different kinds of preferences*: First, there are the agent's preferences for things (such as fruit in our example) that are intransitive, and then there are preferences for something (such as money in our example) that will be pumped if the other preferences (in our example, the fruit) are not rendered transitive. But the preferences over the objects being pumped (in our case, money) must already be either noncyclical, or transitive, in order for this argument to work. Hence the argument presupposes an ordering of preferences for money effected by either a transitivity or acyclicity axiom, and thereby *already assumes* the defensibility of one of these axioms effecting the minimal ordering. But such a defense *cannot* be consequentialist in nature – because whichever axiom is used partially defines the consequences. So whichever axiom is used must be defended using a foundationalist or coherentist (or, at any rate, nonconsequentialist) argument.[42]

---

[42] Suppose one were to mount a variation of the argument, in which the money pumper offers the agent not money, but one of the fruits over which his preferences are intransitive. In this case, the "fruit pumper" can pump the agent of all but 1 fruit. But if the argument concludes that the intransitivity of these preferences over fruit has been bad for the agent, it is assuming that the agent has (or ought to have) a preference for more fruit over less. And by what door did that preference come in? Moreover the argument presumes that the agent prefers 2 fruit to 1 fruit, 3 fruit to 2, 4 fruit to 3, and so forth. So not only is it assumed that the agent prefers more to less fruit, but also that his preferences

This means it is impossible to offer a consequentialist theory of human reason "all the way down." The instrumental model of reason – indeed, any consequentialist theory of reason – must rely on axioms of reasoning at least some of which are defended on nonconsequentialist grounds in order to be able to define what preferences count as value-defining for the agent, and thus to define the "good consequences" that the agent should be striving to maximize. But this means that to be able to reason instrumentally, we must be able to reason noninstrumentally (which is indeed what Savage might have been trying to say in the passage quoted here). Moreover, expected utility theory, interpreted as a theory of reasoning, seems to be designed in a way that fully respects this conclusion by virtue of the primacy it accords the axioms. Hence it appears that the theory can implement only what John Broome (1991, 1993) has called "moderate Humeanism," which interprets at least some of the axioms as noninstrumental constraints on the (otherwise subjectively defined) ends of action.

But such "moderate Humeanism" (which, as Chapter 4 has shown, cannot really be construed as literally Humean at all) need not be violative of the aims of those who intend to specify an instrumental theory of reason. Even if, as the preceding argument establishes, we do not have instrumental reason for adhering to the EU axioms, it still seems prima facie plausible to claim that if an agent's preference set satisfied these axioms, his reasoning on the basis of those preferences would perfectly realize what we *mean by* (ideal) means/end reasoning, and his action from those preferences would model what we mean by successful means/end action. The idea behind this argument is that we have a conception of means/end reasoning that EU theory articulates. While it may not be an articulation of the *entire* conception (insofar as it does not explicitly include principles of probability formation that are relevant to defining perfect means/end reasoning), it at least articulates an important component of that conception. It is a nice bit of irony that this argument admits (and relies on) the idea that the axioms defining means/end reasoning are not consequentially justified. Even if we

over quantities of fruit are connected and transitive. So once again this pragmatic defense of an axiom only works if some of the agent's preferences already satisfy one or more axioms, where these are defended in some kind of foundationalist or coherentist way.

think we ought to reason consequentially, in this view the tenets defining what good consequentialist reasoning is must be defined and defended nonconsequentially.

To appraise this strategy for defending EU theory as an instrumental conception of reason, we need to have some sense of what means/end reasoning is, so as to determine whether EU theory captures it. But if we use some kind of traditional Humean conception, EU theory will fail to represent it. Hume and his followers have tended to think of means/end reasoning as occurring with respect to a *particular* desire for a *particular* end, establishing what actions or objects are necessary for the attainment of that end. But EU axioms apply to a *set* of such desires or preferences; they concern the *relationship among* desires or preferences. Indeed, when one uses EU theory, one is unable to recognize when a preference is for an object that is a means, and when it is for an object understood as an end. Hence, ironically, *EU theory cannot be used to make any judgments about the instrumental rationality of a particular choice*, because it has nothing to say about how to identify a particular means to a particular end. Hence there is a sense in which EU theory has nothing to do with thesis 2 of an instrumental theory, which involves specifying what instrumental reasoning is.

There is another way to make this argument.[43] Consider that Savage structures his version of EU theory by taking actions to be functions that operate on events and yield outcomes, so that f(e) = o where f stands for an action, e for an event, and o for the outcome. It seems natural to construe the action (f) as the means to the realization of the outcome. But note that all of the reasoning needed to determine what consequences will follow from actions performed on a certain event is suppressed. By Savage's theory, it is simply assumed that we know this. Yet working out this information is, from the Humean standpoint, what means/end reasoning involves! So from a Humean standpoint, EU theory has nothing to do with means/end reasoning.

However, there is reason to think that the Humean way of thinking about instrumental reason is too narrow, and that effective instrumental action must be defined not only from the standpoint of any individual desire, but also from the standpoint of a *set* of desires. Even if EU theory does not include principles defining how to de-

[43] This was suggested to me by John Broome.

termine means to ends with respect to a particular desire, it does capture the principles that at least intuitively, many people believe one must follow in order to be said to be effectively satisfying as many of one's preferences as possible. And this might be the thought that is really behind the appeal to consistency discussed in the previous section – that is, it is not instrumentally rational to follow the axioms *in order to* satisfy one's preferences. It is rather that using these axioms to render one's preference set consistent, and then satisfying these (reformed) preferences, is part of what instrumental reasoning, and behavior, *consists of*.

In this view, EU theory captures at least a portion of what successful means/end reasoning looks like, because it offers us a *global* and not merely a *local* perspective on preferences satisfaction. The old-fashioned Humean perspective was merely local, only looking at each of our preferences piecemeal. Proponents of EU theory can argue that we also need a global conception of means/end reasoning that gives us a characterization of successful (or effective) means/end reasoning over our *set* of preferences, and in their view, this is what EU theory provides. So it seems we can defend EU theory as an instrumental theory insofar as we believe it successfully captures either how we actually reason so as to satisfy our set of preferences, or how we ought to reason so as to satisfy our set of preferences.

Note, however, that in this interpretation, the hope of interpreting EU theory as a "wertfrei" theory of reasoning is gone. A global theory of instrumental reasoning consists of axioms or principles to which our preferences are supposed to conform, and which therefore provide a sieve through which our preferences must pass before we can rationally act on them. But this means these axioms define ends of action indirectly in the same way as, say, Kant's noninstrumental (and moral) principle of reasoning (called the categorical imperative procedure, which acts as a kind of "moral sieve"). And since these axioms cannot all be defended consequentially, at least some of them must be defended with a foundationalist or coherentist argument, either of which precludes any Humean-style reduction of the normativity. Hence this interpretation destroys the supposedly "scientific" nature of EU theory so important to social scientists still working in the shadow of positivism.[44] Moreover, because this way

---

[44] But perhaps one might argue that insofar as our ends of action are being defined
by axioms constitutive of *instrumental* reasoning, they are still not the product

of interpreting EU theory involves specifying the structure of a person's good-defining preference set, it dovetails nicely with my argument in Chapter 5 that any instrumental theory must take a stand on the nature of the good of a rational agent. This interpretation of EU theory denies that an instrumental theory, to be instrumental, cannot take a stand on the structure of the preference set that defines the good of a rational agent. Instead, in this view, articulating this structure is part of the task of developing an instrumental theory to provide a way of ordering preferences, so that the theory can make clear how a rational agent satisfies the multiplicity of preferences, many of which compete with one another in various circumstances, in that set.

The upshot of these arguments is that EU theory survives as a theory of instrumental reason if and only if one accepts that developing a theory of instrumental reason involves and requires developing a theory of the good. Having arrived at that conclusion, can we also conclude that EU theory's way of defining the good and portraying instrumental action with respect to it is entirely satisfactory? Answering that question is the task of the next chapter.

---

of reason operating *non*instrumentally. Still, such a distinction might capture the letter, but not the spirit, of the Humean maxim that reason is only a slave of the passions.

Chapter 8

Expected Utility Theory and Consequentialism[a]

[computer file 4/24/95]

In the last chapter, I developed a strategy defending EU theory as a representation of a global instrumental theory of reason, which tells us how we ought to satisfy a preference in a situation where we have multiple preferences. Does that strategy succeed? Relevant to this question are counterexamples and experimental evidence purportedly showing that human beings consistently violate the EU axioms. That evidence appears to show that at the very least, EU theory fails as a descriptive account of our global instrumental reasoning. And the violations of some of the EU axioms seem so intuitively reasonable that EU theory also seems to fail as a normative account of our (global) instrumental reasoning. But not only does this evidence indicate that EU theory fails as a theory of instrumental reasoning, more importantly from the standpoint of moral philosophy, I will argue that this evidence shows EU theory fails because it is "too consequentialist" in structure.

The term 'consequentialism' was developed in moral philosophy.[1]

[a]*Editor's note:* Professor Hampton had presented arguments from this chapter in several places and received helpful comments from many people, including Richard Arneson, Michael Bratman, John Ferejohn, Paul Hurley, Frances Kamm, Debra Satz, Amartya Sen, Robert Sugden, and two anonymous referees for *Ethics.* She had planned to rework the arguments to take account of these comments and to make the arguments' structure more transparent, but was unable to do so. Here, as elsewhere in the book, it is important for the reader to bear in mind the preliminary nature of these investigations, and the consequent need to sympathetically develop and strengthen the arguments before evaluating them.

[1] G. E. M. Anscombe seems to have coined the term. See her 1958, reprinted in Anscombe 1981, where the term first appears on p. 36.

Indeed, moral philosophy has long been split between those who advocate a consequentialist portrayal of moral justification and those who advocate a nonconsequentialist, or deontological, approach to moral justification. There are a number of different kinds of consequentialist and deontological positions, and a variety of points of disagreement, but one of the most important concerns the nature of moral reasoning. The consequentialist says that we should choose the action whose consequences are best; the deontologist says that there are actions whose intrinsic moral rightness is such that at least in certain circumstances, these actions ought to be chosen over any alternative action even if their consequences are worse than those of the alternatives. However, if moral reasoning is understood to be a species of reasoning generally, this dispute can extend to the nature of *all* practical reasoning. When we reason practically, inside or outside a moral context, do we – should we – pay attention only to consequences of the actions or plans we are considering, selecting the action or plan that has the best (expected) consequences? Or do we – should we – attend to, and incorporate into our decision, evaluations of aspects of our choice problem other than these consequences, such as evaluations of the actions themselves?

In this chapter, I shall argue that we have plenty of evidence, gathered in the course of testing EU theory as a theory of reason, to conclude that the nonconsequentialists are right. As I will explain, this does not by itself constitute a victory for any of the positions that are normally classed as deontological moral views, because someone can believe that practical reasoning is nonconsequentialist, and still not be what we would recognize as a paradigmatic moral deontologist. Indeed, as I will explain, one can be both nonconsequentialist about the structure of practical reasoning and consequentialist about moral justification. So the nonconsequentialist nature of our reasoning process does not establish the soundness of certain deontological assumptions concerning the nature and authoritativeness of moral evaluations of actions that are normally taken to be central to any position denoted by that name. Hence the arguments in this chapter cannot (and are not intended to) convert people to some sort of Kantianism. However, they seek to show that at least with respect to the determination of the *rationality* (rather than the morality) of action, only nonconsequentialist models of our reasoning process are descriptively and normatively correct. And this argument at least leaves room for the possibility of Kantian portrayals of moral reasoning within the general structure of practical reasoning. Having gotten that room, I will consider the plausibility of Kantian-style portrayals of moral reasoning in the last chapter.[b]

Let me note before we begin that the following arguments do not take issue with the claim made by economists that EU theory is useful for purposes of predicting economic behavior in market contexts. *If* that is true (and there are many who would dispute it),[2] then economists should certainly use it. But even if EU theory is a predictive success, that success does not depend on its being like real human reasoning.[3] And the most obvious implication of my arguments will be that EU theory fails as a portrayal of our global instrumental reasoning. They also make highly dubious the claim that EU theory is a theory of rationale, applicable only to behavior and not to reasoning. It would seem the reasoning procedure that one would use to judge the global rationality of behavior should be based on the form of reasoning people do and should use, to make that determination themselves. So if there are violations of EU theory's axioms that seem reasonable, why should we judge any behavior that violates them as irrational? It is not the behavior, but the theory that condemns the behavior, that seems wrong. Finally, the preceding arguments show that any revision of EU theory (for example, that of Machina or Kahneman and Tversky) that is still driven by consequentialist assumptions and that therefore retains any of the problematic axioms assuming our preference formation is state-independent, will also fail as a portrayal of our global instrumental

---

[b]*Editor's note:* Professor Hampton did not live to fulfill this intention. The short draft of Chapter 9 contains no mention of Kantian-style portrayals of moral reasoning.

[2] To quote one philosopher of economics, "It is often asserted (more commonly in conversation than in print) that economics is terrifically good at prediction and explanation after all. I think that most scholars, even most economists, believe that this is wrong. Applications passed off as great successes usually turn out to be either post facto reconstructions of aggregate data from properties of imaginary representative individuals, or else things readily available to folk economists such as 'people buy smaller automobiles when gasoline prices are higher.' It is not clear how this disagreement can be resolved" Alan Nelson (1990). Nelson believes economics is "almost a paradigm case of a stagnating science" (p. 121). It is also worth asking what kind of science economics can be when the predictive success of its major theory is a matter of dispute. For more on economics as a science, see Alex Rosenberg (1983).

[3] See Satz and Ferejohn (1994).

reasoning, but they do not challenge they idea that any of these theories might have predictive value.[4]

CONSEQUENTIALISM

An important point of agreement between consequentialists and nonconsequentialists that makes their quarrel possible is that consequences can be conceptually distinguished from nonconsequential aspects of a situation. But what if no such distinction is possible? In particular, what if (something like) an action's "rightness" can be taken to be part of the consequences of a choice situation – for example, by being factored into the consequent state of affairs that would result from any particular choice? Then the consequentialist can insist that he *can* incorporate into his reasoning procedure the sorts of action-oriented evaluations that the nonconsequentialist defends. They will appear in the consequentialist's reasoning process as one among many consequences to be considered prior to choice, and will only determine that choice if, as it happens, they are more powerful consequential considerations than the others.

There are four possible positions with respect to the possibility of distinguishing consequences from nonconsequential aspects of a situation.[5] First, we can distinguish between *narrow consequentialism* and *narrow nonconsequentialism*, each of which insists that only one of these two aspects of a choice situation ought to be our focus while making our decision (the former insisting that we only look to consequences, the latter insisting that we only look to actions and/or processes). In contrast, *broad consequentialism* and *broad nonconsequen-*

---

[4] However, insofar as Machina drops the Independence Axiom, he abandons the most troublesome of the three axioms we considered. Hammond is particularly troubled by this abandonment: "In objecting to the independence axiom, one also objects to consequentialism, which is the best argument I know for the existence of preferences" (see Hammond 1988a, p. 514). But Machina can reply that independence is *too* consequentialist for EU theory, because (contra Hammond) EU theory does admit that preferences can be a function of at least one thing other than consequences – namely, attitudes toward risk. Nor do I understand why Hammond would deny that there can be such a thing as "nonconsequentialist preferences" – what I would call preferences over states in which consequences occur, especially given the violations of the EU axioms discussed here.

[5] This classification scheme is based on one proposed by Amartya Sen in his 1983.

tialism maintain that both consequences and attitudes toward actions are relevant in practical decision-making. Broad consequentialism denies that there is any real distinction between consequences and nonconsequential aspects of a choice situation, and advocates that we "include the actions into the consequent states of affairs and decide on the right action *exclusively* on the basis of the values of the respective states of affairs."[6] Broad nonconsequentialism admits that consequences can be relevant in the decision about what to do, but also insists that there are times when actions should be chosen, or resisted, because of the attitudes we have (attitudes that may or may not be moral) toward the actions themselves.[7]

The narrow versions of consequentialism and nonconsequentialism strike most of us as implausible. The idea that we should never take consequences into account seems blatantly silly. The idea that we should never choose actions on the basis of the attitudes we have to the actions themselves seems to fly in the face of what we actually do and what we believe we ought to do (at least sometimes), when we reason prior to choice. So it seems we must decide between the broad versions of these views. Which one is right?

If it is true that there is no real conceptual distinction between consequences and nonsequential aspects of a choice situation, this strengthens the hand of consequentialists considerably insofar as it makes it possible for them to accommodate what seems to be the plain fact that human beings *do* take into account attitudes toward actions (apart from their consequences) prior to choice. It also makes defending any sort of nonconsequentialist position – such as moral deontology – impossible, since it means there is in reality no such thing as a nonconsequentialist aspect of a choice situation. The best a deontologist could do would be to argue that one kind of consequence – the kind that includes the action – has some mysterious priority over other kinds.

However, if we could develop an argument refuting the claim that actions can be included in the consequent states of affairs and thereby factored consequentially into our decision-making, broad consequentialism is not a possible position, so that consequentialists are stuck with only the narrow version of their view. Since that ver-

---

[6] Sen (1983), p. 131.
[7] Ibid., pp. 130–1.

sion seems neither to describe how we reason practically, nor how we think we ought to reason practically, broad nonconsequentialism would remain as the only viable model of practical reason.

This chapter attempts the beginnings of such an argument. It does so by using expected utility theory as a kind of test case for the possibility of fitting actions into a consequentialist framework. A number of theorists, such as John Broome and Peter Hammond, have seen the way in which expected utility theory models a form of reasoning that is consequentialist.[8] Thus we can evaluate the extent to which this consequentialist model of our reasoning captures the way in which people actually reason practically. I will argue that the theory fails to describe how people make decisions about actions, and that it fails whenever people are responding to something other than the consequences of the alternative actions when they reason. Moreover, I will argue that there is no way to "consequentialize" these nonconsequentialist aspects of the choice situation, meaning that EU theory has no way to accommodate them satisfactorily. Because these departures from consequentialist evaluations will strike us as eminently reasonable, any insistence by the consequentialist that despite our nonconsequentialist practices we nonetheless *ought* to reason consequentially, will seem just wrong.[9] Hence this argument suggests both the reality and the reasonableness of nonconsequentialist modes of reasoning in our daily life.[10]

---

[8] See John Broome (1991); Hammond (1988a, 1988b).

[9] The arguments in this chapter are an extension of arguments I have made in Hampton (1994).

[10] Note that I do not consider here the possibility that our nonconsequentialist responses are derived *indirectly* from consequentialist reasoning. That is, perhaps we like or dislike certain actions because we have observed that they tend to have good or bad consequences (so that we tend to hate, say, cheating because we know that cheating, on the whole, produces bad consequences, and we have that attitude in our mind even in circumstances where we calculate that cheating would produce good consequences overall). But note that even if this explanation of our nonconsequential attitudes is correct, it does not affect the thesis that reasoning with respect to these attitudes is nonconsequentialist for as long as these attitudes persist.

CONSEQUENCES AND STATE-DEPENDENT UTILITIES

In order to concentrate on the nature of practical reasoning itself and not on the nature of any theories of moral value that nonconsequentialists and consequentialists generally disagree about, I want to see how far expected utility theory models our reasoning process prior to action in nonmoral contexts. While it may be true that no situation is completely free of moral overtones, nonetheless the situations we shall consider are about as free of these overtones as any situation can be! This means that we will be assuming that agents who have attitudes toward consequences or nonconsequential aspects of the situation are using nonmoral notions of good and bad, right and wrong. Indeed, in most of the examples I will discuss, these attitudes are best understood as informed by an "agent relative" notion of value. Such examples may make some readers uneasy if they are used to the debate between consequentialists and nonconsequentialists being carried out in moral contexts. But I am not concerned with the theory of value these theorists bring to their conception of practical reasoning, but rather with the structure of human reasoning designed to determine rational (as opposed to moral) action. Readers sympathetic to deontological theories of moral reasoning may also find certain assumptions made by EU theory to be either suspicious or offensive, particularly the idea that an interval measure of human preference is even possible. I ask them to play along with the assumptions of the theory so that we can use it to test its consequentialist thesis, particularly because doing so will lend credence to the nonconsequentialist representation of practical reasoning after all.

As Hammond has argued, the appeal of EU theory and its axioms rests on the consequentialist assumption that when an agent has taken into account the possible outcomes of the action under consideration, he has taken into account everything relevant to the issue of what preferences over action he should have in the choice situation. Indeed, the consequentialist character of EU theory is clearly seen in the Savage axiomatization, insofar as Savage actually defines an act as a mapping from states of the world into consequences.[11] Moreover, Savage also formulates two axioms that together specify that preferences over consequences are "state-independent,"[12] so that pref-

---

[11] See Savage (1954); and this point is discussed by Hammond (1988a), p. 504.

[12] As formulated by David Kreps (1988, 129–130), these axioms are as follows:

erences over actions can only be a function of preferences over their consequences and the risk involved in the action, and *not* a function of the particular states in which the consequences are received.

Hence the fundamental assumption of this theory is that "[t]o deliberate is to evaluate available lines of action in terms of their consequences, which may depend on circumstances the agent can neither predict nor control."[13] In particular, we can interpret EU theory as implementing the following two theses that jointly define what it means to say that reasoning prior to choice is consequentialist:

> 1. An agent's preferences over actions are solely a function of her preferences over the consequences of those actions;
>
> *and* 2. An agent's aim, as a reasoner, is to further the attainment of desirable consequences.[14]

EU theory is only one of a number of theories of reason developed by decision theorists that attempt to implement consequentialism.

Suppose that there is a set Z of consequences and a set S of mutually exclusive states of the world. Each $s \in S$ is a compilation of all characteristics about which a reasoner is uncertain and which are relevant to the consequences that will ensue from his choice. An action is a function F: S → Z, where f(s) represents the consequences of taking action f if the state of the world is s. A binary relation > gives the reasoner's preferences over the set F of acts:

Axiom 1:

> If $a \subseteq S$ and a is not null, and if f(s) = x and g(s) = y for all
> $S \in a$, then f > g given a iff x > y

Axiom 2:

> Suppose x, y, x', y', f, g, f ', g', a, and b are such that
> > y and x' > y'
> b) f(s) = x and f '(s) = x' on a, and f(s) = y and f '(s) = y' on a^c
> c) g(s) = x and g'(s) = x' on b, and g(s) = y and g'(s) = y' on b^c

Then f > g iff f ' > g'

---

[13] Jeffrey 1965/1983, p. 1.

[14] Peter Hammond (op. cit.) argues that consequentialism is the underlying idea behind EU theory, but defines consequentialism only with a version of my thesis 1. But to fully capture this position as it is normally understood, one must make explicit what Hammond clearly assumes – namely, that a reasoner's preferences over consequences are such that she wants as many *good* consequences as possible, and this is what thesis 2 says.

Indeed, we can think of normative decision theory as erecting "a superstructure of various possible axiom systems upon this basic 'consequentialist' hypothesis" (Hammond, 1988b, 25). These theories develop different conceptions of what it means to "further the attainment of desirable consequences." For example, EU theory gives us a maximizing conception, whereas an alternative theory that does not assume the continuity axiom would give us a nonmaximizing conception, insofar as it leaves open the possibility of lexicographic preferences.[15]

Whether or not EU theory can be understood as a *pure* consequentialist theory is a matter of controversy. On the face of it, the theory seems to allow our preferences over actions to be a function of both our preferences over their consequences and our preferences over risk. This would make the theory what I will call a Modified Consequentialist Theory, which holds that

1. One's preferences over actions are solely a function of one's preferences over the consequences of those actions *and* one's preferences over risk;
2. One's aim as a reasoner is to maximize the satisfaction of preferences over consequences and risk.

Or to paraphrase another economist, EU theory so interpreted says that what matter to an agent are both consequences and probabilities.[16] Note that it is an assumption of this modified consequentialist theory that reasoners are able to integrate preferences over consequences and risk so as to develop preferences over action. On the other hand, theorists such as Hammond argue that we can understand the consequences of the theory to be *prospects*, in which attitudes toward outcomes of action and attitudes toward risk are unified so the theory can be understood as purely consequentialist.[17] I shall not take a stand on which way of construing EU theory is right; even an interpretation that takes it to be only a modified consequentialism is sufficient for our purposes.

However, violations of EU axioms at least *seem* to occur when the reasoner's ultimate preference over the alternative actions is all or partly a function of the preferences over the state (for example, the

---

[15] See Hammond (1988b), pp. 29, 74.
[16] Kreps (1988), p. 52.
[17] See Hammond, op. cit.

gambling process, or the certainty, or the context of choice) in which the consequences are received. Call these preferences *state-dependent*; they are preferences that seem nonconsequentialist in that they are about aspects of the choice situation other than the consequences of the actions being considered. Following are counterexamples to each of the three axioms of EU theory stated earlier, each of which involves state-dependent preferences.

Independence Axiom

This axiom says, roughly, that if you're indifferent between a and b considered by themselves, you're indifferent between two lotteries that are the same with the exception that a is substituted for b. Now consider the following counterexample to this axiom[18]:

> Suppose a person is offered a lottery ticket T that gives her a .5 probability of $1000 or nothing at all. Let us say that she is indifferent between T and $200 (so that T is worth $200 or its equivalent in the utility scale). We imagine that it is not worth $500 (the expected monetary value of the lottery) because she dislikes the risk involved in the lottery. Now suppose she has a choice between two lottery tickets – in one the prize is T and x and in the other the prize is $200 and x. Should/will she be indifferent between these two lotteries? Maybe not! Since she is gambling anyway, maybe she will prefer the lottery with T (treating T as if the expected utility is now closer to the expected monetary value). So the negative impact that risk had on T before is now gone.

The work of Kahneman and Tversky (for example, see 1990) is replete with examples of violations of the Independence Axiom, and perhaps the most famous demonstration of the seeming reasonableness of its violation is Allais's paradox.[19]

Transitivity Axiom

In my view, the clearest example of a violation of the Transitivity Axiom, which is perhaps the most fundamental and seemingly plau-

---

[18] This is given by Baumol (1972), p. 546.
[19] See Maurice Allais (1979a, 1979b). Savage has an interesting discussion of the Allais paradox in his 1972 edition of *Foundations of Statistics*, pp. 101–3.

sible of all the EU axioms, is provided by Loomes and Sugden.[20] Suppose there is a situation in which an agent can take one of three possible actions. Each of these actions has three possible outcomes, all of which are equiprobable. The (cardinal) numbers in the matrix here correspond to the preferences an agent has over the outcomes of the actions, given these probabilities.

| | | Probabilities of consequences | | |
		1/3	1/3	1/3
	A	3	2	1
Actions	B	1	3	2
	C	2	1	3

Figure 1

According to EU theory, an agent should be indifferent between actions A, B, and C. But Loomes and Sugden argue, quite reasonably, that we can imagine a perfectly coherent reasoner for whom A > B, B > C, and C > A in view of what Loomes and Sugden call the reasoner's "regret aversion." This reasoner dislikes the experience of regret, and chooses actions so as to minimize its experience. Hence he chooses A over B (since, as we see in the first column, the experience of regret would be greatest if the first outcome occurred and he had chosen B), B over C (for the same reason, see the second column), and C over A (for the same reason, see the third column). But these preferences are intransitive.

Reduction of Compound Lotteries (RCL) Axiom

The assumption behind this axiom is that an agent will be indifferent between any compound lottery and any simple lottery that is equivalent according to the probability calculus. Although this axiom is explicitly stated in vN/M's formalization and is necessary to proving the EU conclusion, it is sometimes ignored in restatements of vN/M's proof,[21] because many theorists do not take it to be a concep-

---

[20] Graham Loomes and Robert Sugden (1982, 1984). And see Sugden (1991).

[21] For example, David Kreps (1988), pp. 51–2, calls it "axiom zero": "Our theory identifies any two lotteries that attach the same probabilities to the same prizes, even if the randomizing devices are different. The theory is a theory of choice among probability distributions – and when we seek to apply it to real phenomena that involve randomizing devices, or collections of randomizing devices

tually important or controversial axiom. Some readers may believe that its presence is only required in formalizations of EU theory that assume objective probability. However this is *not* so. In a Savage-style formulation, this axiom is proved as a theorem from certain more basic axioms (and assumes subjective probabilities), because once again it is necessary to proving the EU conclusion.

Yet human behavior seems to be in flagrant violation of this axiom[22] by virtue of the fact that many of us have some kind of attitude toward gambling that makes us either prefer or disprefer multiple gambles to single ones. For example, if an agent is a gamble lover, she will say "I prefer the compound lottery to the risk-equivalent simple lottery because I get more chances to gamble in the compound lottery than I do in the simple lottery, and I just love gambling!" Note that our gamble lover is acknowledging that the two lotteries over which she has a (strong) preference are *risk equivalent*. Her attitudes toward risk don't generate her preference, but rather her attitudes toward the *process* of gambling do. So attitudes toward risk, which EU theory does take into account, are not the same as an attitude toward gambling, which EU theory excludes via the RCL Axiom.

Interestingly von Neumann and Morgenstern recognized that such (non-risk-related) utilities over gambling would lead to viola-

---

used in sequence, there is an implicit axiom zero that all that matters to [the chooser] are the probabilities and prizes – the randomizing devices and their order are inconsequential to him."

[22] This is a charge that Daniel Ellsberg made in the 1950s. As he puts it, the RCL Axiom implies that the individual is indifferent to the number of steps taken to determine the outcome. On the contrary, a sensible person might easily prefer a lottery that held several intermediate drawings to determine who was still "in" for the final drawing; in other words, he might be willing to pay for the possibility of winning intermediate drawings and "staying in" even though the chances of winning the pot were not improved thereby. A longer time-period of suspense would usually also be involved, but it need not be. The crucial factor is "pleasure of winning," which may be aroused by intermediate wins even if one subsequently fails to receive the prize. Many, perhaps most, slot-machine players know the odds are very unfavorable, and are not really motivated by hopes of winning the jackpot. They feel that they have had their money's worth if it takes them a long while to lose a modest sum, meanwhile enjoying a number of intermediate wins, which go back into the machine to pay for the pleasure of the next win. See Ellsberg (1954), p. 543.

tions of the RCL Axiom, and on that basis, explicitly ruled them out. As Daniel Ellsberg notes in an early article on EU theory:

> Von Neumann and Morgenstern single out axiom 3: C:b [the RCL Axiom], which excludes this type of behavior, as the "really critical" axiom,[23] "that one which gets closest to excluding a 'utility of gambling'."[24]

But how can such an exclusion be justified? It looks as if von Neumann and Morgenstern argue for their axioms by excluding all and only the preferences that would generate violations of those axioms!

Now defenders of EU theory might respond that there is nothing wrong with such an exclusion precisely because von Neumann and Morgenstern intended the RCL Axiom to be about *riskiness* rather than utilities over gambling. Of course some people will love (or hate) the heightened suspense or the "gambling thrill," more of which is possible in the multistage lottery, and will prefer (or disprefer) it to a simple lottery. But since these preferences arise from utilities over gambling, which are quite different from "attitudes toward risk," these defenders might contend that they are not relevant in the context of the RCL Axiom that is interested (only) in the coherence of an agent's attitude toward risk. Since the risk in a multistage lottery and its equivalent single lottery is identical, then an agent who thought only about risk should be indifferent between them, and that is all the axiom requires.

And yet the fact remains that no matter how coherent an agent's attitude toward risk is, she will only instantiate this axiom for as long as she has no preferences over the number of stages in the gambling process. So since the mathematics of their proof requires that an agent instantiate this axiom in order for them to be able to prove that there is a utility function representing her preferences, von Neumann and Morgenstern "rule out" these preferences, insisting that simple and multistage lotteries be evaluated only in terms of their risk. But how can preferences over gambling be ruled out when they actually exist? Not only the risk in a gamble, but the gamble itself is something about which we can have an attitude, and therefore something that we can prefer or disprefer to something

---

[23] Here Ellsberg cites vN/M, p. 632.
[24] Here Ellsberg cites vN/M, p. 28. The quote is from Ellsberg, op. cit., p. 543.

else. So it would seem that a good predictive theory would have to take *whatever* feelings we have about it into account in order to be able to formulate an accurate prediction about how we will choose between it and another gamble. And a descriptive account would simply be inaccurate if it ignored it.

So the three counterexamples challenge the EU axioms by presenting instances in which agents appear – quite legitimately – to be reasoning in nonconsequentialist ways. The fact that in their defense of the RCL Axiom von Neumann and Morgenstern rule out preferences over gambling and interpret the axiom as being about preferences only with respect to the outcomes of lotteries shows that they did not want to allow into the theory preferences over the processes producing these outcomes. And this amounts to an attempt on their part to forbid nonconsequentialist forms of evaluation, which they realized would be inconsistent with the theory.

THE RESOLUTION STRATEGY

However, there is a popular way of defending EU theory against these sorts of counterexamples, which one might call the strategy of "loading up the consequences" and is akin to Sen's view, discussed earlier, that consequentialism can be defined so broadly that there is nothing that cannot be considered a consequence. In the case of EU theory, it involves reinterpreting the counterexamples so as to show that hidden in the examples are consequentialist attitudes, so that once these hidden attitudes are appreciated, there is no violation of any of the axioms after all.[25] If this strategy works, it would reinforce the broad consequentialist's claim that the distinction between consequences and nonconsequential aspects of a choice situation is not a real one since everything can be conceptualized as a consequence. Moreover, it would also support the claim that consequentialism is the right way to think about our reasoning process, insofar as it would help us to show that if we understand the consequences in any choice situation in an appropriately broad way, a human being in this situation will (almost invariably) conform to the (consequentialist) EU axioms in his choices.

Henceforth I will call this the *Resolution Strategy*, and I will now

---

[25] Both Broome and Hammond explicitly recommend this strategy as a way of saving the EU axioms from counterexample.

show how this strategy is supposed to rescue each of the EU axioms from counterexample. Each of these "rescues" is based on the idea that the initial sense that the axiom was violated derived from an inadequate conception of what the purported violator took the consequences of her actions to be.

The Independence Axiom

First, we will consider how the Resolution Strategy attempts to defuse Baumol's purported counterexample to the Independence Axiom. Given a choice between T and $200, an agent will likely explain that she chose the money rather than T by saying "I didn't like to take the risk by choosing T when I could have a lot of money for certain." Such a remark shows that her overall evaluation of T is effected by the pain she believes she will suffer by taking a risk in this situation. This "pain" *is generated by the context of the choice.* In what follows, let me define utility as *outcome generated* when it derives from preferences over objects and/or states of affairs that will follow from the selection of an action, and let me define utility as *state-generated* when it derives from preferences over the state in which the outcomes occur. (What I am calling state-generated utilities, some economists have referred to as "complementarities" – that is, interactions between the alternative states of affairs in the choice situation.[26]) In this choice situation, it is *because* the agent has a choice between a certainty and a risky option that the pain (associated with the fear of losing the gamble when she could have received a gain for certain) would be generated if she chose the risky option. Choosing T therefore involves dealing with a state-generated "bad," and a proponent of the Resolution Strategy would insist that our understanding of the consequences of actions should be broad enough to allow us to say that T's "utility yield" must be understood to include not only the money outcomes, but also that "bad."

Now suppose that the person goes on to explain, in the situation where she has a choice between two lotteries, that she would prefer lottery T because "if I know I'm going to have to take a risk anyway, I'd prefer the lottery with T because it has a higher expected monetary value." Here she's telling you that only the outcomes of the lotteries matter to her choice because there is no certain alternative.

[26] See Broome (1991), p. 96.

And her explanation tells us that she finds lottery T clearly preferable on this basis.

But note that according to this reading of the situation, *the Independence Axiom is not violated* because the utility of T *changes* in the two situations. It is wrong to say that the utility of T in the second choice situation is equal to the utility equivalent of $200 because the utility of T in the first choice situation subtly incorporates the possibility of experiencing painful regret if one loses the lottery after foregoing a sure thing. In the second choice situation, the utility of T incorporates no such pain – and hence should be higher than the utility of T in the first choice situation. So the resolution strategy insists that if the consequences of an action are understood to include both outcome-generated and state-generated utilities, there is no violation of the Independence Axiom.

The Transitivity Axiom

The resolution strategy gives us a way of arguing that regret-minimizers do not, after all, violate the Transitivity Axiom. It is because our original conception of consequences was limited to outcomes that transitivity seemed to be violated in Loomes's and Sugden's regret aversion counterexample. But if we understand consequences in a broadened way so as to include the importance to an agent of "minimizing regret aversion," it will no longer be the case that in Loomes's and Sugden's example the agent's preferences will satisfy A>B, B>C, and C>A. This is because for the agent that values not just A, B, and C understood as outcomes but also regret minimization, the B that is preferred to C is not the same as the B that is dispreferred to A; the latter B includes the possibility of experiencing more regret than the former B. The same is true for the two C's and the two A's. This way of presenting the example, however, makes it clear that there are different terms in each of the pairwise comparisons, and hence no violation of transitivity.

The Reduction of Compound Lotteries Axiom

With respect to the RCL Axiom, once again we can argue that if consequences are broadened in an appropriate way to accommodate a gamble lover's (or gamble hater's) preferences over the gambling process as well as the outcomes of that process, she would not violate the RCL Axiom by preferring, say, the multistage lottery over its equivalent single-stage lottery. The payoffs of the multistage lottery are incorrectly identified only with the prizes of the possible outcomes, but instead include the joy or displeasure occasioned by the multiple stages of the lottery. Since such joy or displeasure is not included in the single-stage lottery, the lotteries are not equivalent after all, and one who has a definite preference for one over the other is not violating the RCL Axiom.

Is this Resolution Strategy really a legitimate way of saving any of these three axioms? Some theorists have been uneasy about it.[27] As John Broome (1991, 98–9) explains, if we can save the axioms from counterexample by always finding in the context of choice some feeling or component that makes the seemingly identical choices different, then we will be able to rescue everyone from the charge of violating any particular axiom. That is, since some difference can always be found between two seemingly identical alternatives, one can always individuate alternatives sufficiently finely to save an agent from any charge of irrationality. So by this method, no agent could ever be accused of violating any of the axioms. Therefore, this interpretation, even while attempting to rescue the axioms from state-generated counterexamples, seems to render them vacuous.

Broome proposes that we save the strategy and the normative bite of the axioms by individuating alternatives over which preferences could be formed using what he calls "principles of rational indifference," which tell us when it is rational to be indifferent between two alternatives even when we could distinguish them (using fine-grained individuation procedures). But these "principles of reason" are essentially normative, defining our preferences by reference to what our ends *ought* to be, and were they to be inserted into expected utility theory, it would now be awash in intuitive appeals to an ill-defined, noninstrumental conception of reason that is highly problematic on metaphysical grounds, blatantly unscientific in content, and seemingly impossible to defend except by appeal to our intuitions – which may differ among individuals and among cultures, and which, in any case, have questionable justificational standing.

But we needn't embrace his extreme remedy because the resolution strategy is consistent with a nonvacuous understanding of the

---

[27] For example, see Mark Machina (1991), Paul Samuelson (1966), and Amos Tversky (1975).

axioms. The assumption behind the instrumental view is that preferences are subjectively defined. So a proponent of that view would reply to Broome that the preferences it is appropriate to assume, when testing the theory, are those each of us *actually has*. If we insist that the objects of preferences are individuated experientially – and *in the same way* that the agent being evaluated individuates them – then if her psychology is such that the experiential consequences of an action involve the feeling of regret, we should include that feeling; if this feeling is not present, we should not include it. There is a *fact of the matter* about what her preferences are insofar as there is a fact of the matter about what she will likely experience after choosing any particular alternative course of action. And while there may sometimes be epistemic problems in determining what these experiences are, we cannot solve these problems by making up "rational" principles that purport to tell us what her preferences *should* be.

If the Resolution Strategy worked, then on the basis of the argument, presented, I would regard it as a legitimate way of saving the axioms. However, as I shall now show, the strategy actually *fails* to save the axioms from counterexample, making any defense of its legitimacy moot.

HOW THE RESOLUTION STRATEGY FAILS[c]

To salvage EU theory from these counterexamples, it is not enough to develop a strategy that saves the agent from the charge that she

[c]*Editor's note:* Professor Hampton had intended to revise her formulations of the arguments in this section in the light of comments from readers, some of whom, she believed, had misunderstood their structure. The goal of each argument is to defend the claim that a set of rational preferences may fail to conform to some axiom of expected utility theory. To establish this claim for each of the three axioms considered, Professor Hampton *assumes* that an agent has a definite set of preferences that fail to conform to the axiom in question, and shows how such preferences would naturally result in choice behavior which itself *appears* to conflict with that axiom. The defender of EU theory may respond that this choice behavior may be interpreted as resulting from some set of preferences that actually conform to the relevant axiom, and so the choice behavior described does not in fact violate any axiom of the theory. However, that would refute the argument only if the proposed reinterpretation were the only correct interpretation of the agent's choice behavior. But the argument is that this cannot be the case, since

has acted irrationally by violating the axiom in question. We must also show that the agent with the sort of preferences postulated in the counterexample is able to act so as to instantiate the axiom in question. Otherwise, we will be unable to generate a utility function for her. However, I shall now argue that because there is no way to use the Resolution Strategy to redefine an agent's preferences in these counterexamples as preferences only for consequences, there is no way to show that the agent's preferences instantiate these axioms.

The Reduction of Compound Lotteries Axiom

Following is an argument to show that the resolution strategy fails with respect to the RCL Axiom.

1. We can only prove that an agent has a utility function if her preferences are such that they instantiate (and thus conform to) the RCL Axiom.
2. Let us define a "gamble lover" (GL) as someone who – for any two lotteries, one compound and one simple that are equivalent according to the probability calculus – strongly prefers the compound lottery. That is, someone is a GL just in case:

IF

- L (p,a) is a simple lottery in which there is some probability p that GL will win prize a

and

- L'(p',p'',a) is a compound lottery in which there is a probability p' that GL will win the chance of being in a lottery with probability p'' of winning some prize a
- p, p' and p'' are probabilities such that $p = p' \times p''$

THEN,
for GL:

$$L(p,a) < L'(p', p'', a)$$

3. Now initially it appears from this definition in 2 that a GL will never instantiate the RCL Axiom. But the defender of the

the proposed reinterpretation conflicts with the definite preferences the agent was assumed to have – preferences that by assumption fail to conform to the relevant axiom of EU theory.

axiom will say that it is naive to suppose that the prize of each lottery is the same since the "yield" of a compound lottery also includes a thrill from an additional gamble. Thus, suppose we attempt to accommodate GL's preference for compound over simple lotteries using the resolution strategy by factoring in the thrill of gambling to show that the effective prize of a compound lottery with prize a is actually greater than a. To do so, let us define prizes q and q' such that for the GL:

$u(q)$ = utility of getting a from L (p,a)
$u(q')$ = utility of getting a from L' (p', p'', a)
where $u(q') > u(q)$

4. According to EU theory, there are monetary prizes b and b' such that for a GL:

$u(b) = u(q)$
$u(b') = u(q')$
where $b' > b$

5. From 3 and 4, we can infer that for the GL:

L (p, b') I   L' (p', p'', b)

6. Suppose it is true that a GL sometimes instantiates the RCL Axiom; if so, then (consistent with the RCL Axiom), for a GL:

L(p, b') I   L'(p', p'', b')

7. But from our definition of a GL in 2 we know that:

L$(p, b') < $ L'(p', p'', b')

That is, by our definition of a GL, for any compound lottery and a simple lottery equivalent according to the probability calculus, the GL will strongly prefer the compound lottery. But 6 and 7 contradict each other. Therefore, our supposition in 6 is false, and a gamble lover will never be indifferent between equivalent compound and simple lotteries.

8. From 1 and the falsity of 6, we conclude that because a GL has preferences over compound and simple lotteries that never instantiate the RCL Axiom, there is no way that we can prove there is a utility function for a gamble lover.

This argument shows that the Resolution Strategy fails to salvage conformity to the RCL Axiom by the GL because it fails to fully "consequentialize" the agent's utility over gambling. In particular, it shows that we cannot get a GL to instantiate the RCL Axiom, by trying to make a GL's thrill from gambling *part of* the consequences that the person will receive if she chooses the compound lottery. In order to instantiate the RCL Axiom, a GL must be indifferent between some compound lottery and some probability-equivalent simple lottery. But any compound and simple lottery between which a GL is indifferent will not be so equivalent (see Step 5), and for any compound and simple lotteries that are equivalent, the GL will strongly prefer the compound lottery (see Step 7). And no matter how hard we try to capture as one of the consequences the utilities over gambling in the compound lottery, we can just repeat the argument given here, and do so again and again every time a new prize is proposed to try to represent the gambling utilities and embed them into the simple lottery in an effort to find a simply lottery that a GL will not disprefer to a probability-equivalent compound lottery. Hence the attempt to capture utilities over gambling *as a consequence* will lead to an infinite regress: Each time we think we've gotten the utilities over gambling factored into the situation as a consequence, we can represent the situation such that they resurface again as state-dependent.

The moral is that there is no way for a GL to instantiate the RCL Axiom. While we can use the Resolution Strategy to show that there is always *some* simple lottery such that she is indifferent between it and a compound lottery, these two lotteries will never be equivalent according to the probability calculus. And for any two lotteries, one simple and one compound, that are so equivalent, the GL will never be indifferent between them, and will always prefer the compound one.

But wait a minute, says the proponent of the Resolution Strategy. If our GL strongly prefers the compound lottery because it will give her an additional gambling utility, isn't she illicitly "double-counting" the utility of the gamble? So why don't we just decide (presumably by fiat) that once we have added in the utility to the prize in the compound lottery, we can't count it again?

There are two problems with this proposal. First, it salvages the idea that the GL is indifferent between the two lotteries in Step 6, at the price of forcing her to have a preference between the two lotteries in Step 5! For if she is indifferent between the lotteries in 6, then she must prefer the simple lottery in [5] since b' > b. But that is precisely what we know isn't true about our GL! Proponents of the resolution strategy haven't realized that if they "reinterpret" how to read these equations so as to explain how a GL could instantiate the RCL Axiom, they have to do so consistently, in which case they render nonsensical many of GL's other preferences.

Suppose they decide to sacrifice the indifference in Step 5 (and accept the nonsensical results of doing so, in ways that threaten the GL's satisfaction of the other EU axioms), and declare by fiat that any utility yield in any compound lottery should always be understood to be a function of *both* the utility of the prize that a person would win *and* the utility of the gamble, thereby insuring indifference in Step 6. Now have they shown that the RCL Axiom is instantiated by a GL?

No, for the second (and most interesting) problem with this proposal is that it misrepresents how GLs "factor in" their utilities over gambling. In the argument earlier, I was (deliberately) vague about specifying how the utility associated with the thrill of double gamble should be represented, and implicitly supposed, in my construction of the argument, that we could simply add it to the utility of the prize that would be received if the agent won the compound lottery. But clearly that can't be right, because the agent will enjoy the thrill of being in two lotteries, *even if she loses the prize*, as long as she wins the first lottery. Thus the additional gambling thrill in the (two-stage) compound lottery that she cannot experience in the simple lottery seems to be the value of some kind of function of the probability of winning (only) the first lottery – that is:

If x is the thrill of being in the second lottery and u(x) is the
    utility of x,
then

$$f(p') = x$$

Now it would seem that a person who has utilities over gambling evaluates the compound lottery by first computing the expected utility of the compound lottery (where the utility yield is only a function of the prize that would be won – that is, EU of L'(p', p",a)) and then adding to it the utility of the thrill of being in the second gamble, which is the value of some function of p' (that is, f(p')).[28] So u[f(p')] is the utility over gambling. And note that it does *not* represent what is standardly thought of as expected utility. I will come back to this important point later.

In any case, now we see that the value of this function cannot be considered part of, and thus added to, the utility of the prize in the lottery since getting the gambling thrill is possible even if the agent doesn't receive the prize. This means the GL can never instantiate the RCL Axiom because for any compound lottery, there will always be some value of f(p') the utility of which will be added to the expected utility of the compound lottery (as standardly calculated) and that *cannot* be added to the simple lottery that is its equivalent according to the probability calculus. Once again, note that a GL *will* be indifferent between *some* compound lottery and *some* simple lottery – the point is that this indifference can only occur in a situation where the two lotteries *are not equivalent according to the probability calculus*, in which case a GL can never instantiate the axiom!

So the Resolution Strategy fails, for two reasons. First, it is unable to show that a GL instantiates the RCL Axiom, and second, it misrepresents how a GL factors her state-dependent preferences into her calculations (implying that she adds them to the consequences, when in fact she does not and cannot do so). Remember the odd way in which we represented the thrill of gambling – as a value of a function of p'. Expected utilities are evaluations of consequences multiplied by probabilities, but a GL has utilities that are a *function of the process by which the consequences are produced*, which is why we had to represent them as derived from the value of a function of a probability associated with the process of producing the consequences in our discussion. But that representation itself is a marker for the fact that these utilities are a response to something *other* than the consequences that will be received from any of the actions under consideration.

Following are two more arguments, modeled after the argument just given, which make the same nonconsequentialist point by show-

---

[28] This seems to me the most plausible way of representing the psychology of the GL, but there are other ways of doing so. Suppose that our GL just liked being in multiple gambles and looked forward to them in a way that was disconnected from the probability of being in them. In that case, we might represent the utility he got from such gambles as f(1 + n), where n > 1.

ing that the Resolution Strategy fails to generate a way in which an agent in the counterexamples to the Transitivity and Independence Axioms can instantiate either axiom in any situation where they have certain state-dependent preferences. Having given them, I will discuss in the next section likely reasons why so many theorists have been convinced that the resolution strategy succeeds in saving EU theory.

The Transitivity Axiom

Following is an argument showing that an agent who is what I will call a "regret hater" has preferences that cannot instantiate the Transitivity Axiom. This is one of the most fundamental of the EU axioms. An agent who fails to instantiate *this* axiom is violating the foundations of sound consequentialist reasoning at the deepest level.

1. An agent can only be proven to have a utility function if her preferences are such that they conform to (instantiate) the Transitivity Axiom

2. Let us define a regret hater (RH) as a reasoner who, in situations described by the Loomes/Sugden matrix in Figure 1 (hereafter represented as M[U(A),U(B),U(C)], has preferences over the three actions A, B, and C such that A>B, B>C, and C>A. That is:

   For an RH: if M[U(A),U(B),U(C)]
           then A>B, B>C, and C>A

3. Suppose, consistent with the Resolution Strategy, that there are actions A', B', and C' yielding (with the same probabilities) the same possible prizes as A, B, and C *plus* the additional prize r, such that for the RH:

   B' I A

   C' I B

   A' I C

   and A' > B', B' > C', and A' > C'

(The idea here is that were we to find the right prize, we could make an agent indifferent between the actions in the Loomes/Sugden matrix in any pairwise comparison between them by adding

274

the prize to the payoffs of the action she would otherwise disprefer so as to neutralize any regret she might feel were she to choose that action.)

4. From 3 and the assumptions of EU theory we can infer that, for an RH:

    u(B') = u(A)

    u(C') = u(B)

    u(A') = u(C)

However, from 4 and our definition of an RH in 2, it follows that.

5. If M[U(A'), U(B'), U(C')]
    then
    A' > B', B' > C', and C' > A'

6. But 3 and 5 contradict each other. Therefore our supposition is false, and an RH in situations depicted by the matrix in Figure 1 (p. 261) has preferences that do not instantiate transitivity.
7. Hence, we cannot prove that a regret hater has a utility function.

Implicit in this argument is the point made by Sugden (1991, 762–3) that a Savage-style axiomatization is forced to incorporate a notion of consequences that precludes the interpretation of regret as a "kind" of consequence. It is tempting to think, particularly in light of Savage's very loose definition of a consequence (as "anything that may happen [to the person who is choosing]")[29] that decision theory has such a broad notion of consequence that *anything* can be considered a consequence. However, this turns out not to be so. In Savage's theory, we construct acts over which we have preferences by arbitrarily assigning consequences to states of the world such that every function from the set of all states of the world into the set of possible consequences is an act. To say a person has a preference between two acts f and g is to assume that it is possible to confront him with a choice between f and g. But if such a choice is to make sense, consequences must be defined "so that any assignment of consequences to states of the world is a meaningful act, and so that any

---

[29] Savage (1954), p. 13.

pair of such acts is a meaningful choice problem.''[30] This requirement prevents us from including as a consequence any reference to the *particular* choice problem, else the act, defined in terms of that consequence, cannot be meaningfully compared to any other act in the set of feasible acts. But this means that we are precluded from incorporating regret as a consequence in a choice problem: "Getting x and regretting not having chosen an option that would have given y" is a description of a state of affairs that includes a reference to a feature of the choice problem in which that state of affairs is embedded, and thus cannot be a consequence in Savage's sense (see Sugden, 1991, 763).

Hence, Savage's system makes it impossible for us to "consequentialize" regret, so that there is no way to incorporate it such that an agent who chooses actions so as to minimize it will instantiate the Transitivity Axiom. And what is particularly interesting about Sugden's discussion is the way that the (seemingly) broad leeway we have to understand something as a consequence in a Savage-style EU theory turns out not to be broad at all. As a result, this version of EU theory puts constraints on what attitudes we can have in a choice problem that prevent it from including the (state-dependent) attitudes we actually have. Unsurprisingly, given those attitudes, we violate its axioms.

The Independence Axiom

Finally, we can construct an argument to show that someone whom I will call a "certainty lover" will never instantiate the Independence Axiom.

1. An agent can only be proven to have a utility function if her preferences are such that they conform to (i.e. instantiate) the Independence Axiom
2. Let us define a "certainty lover" (CL) as someone for whom, if there is a simple lottery T and some q, such that she will be indifferent between them in a pairwise choice (where q is offered with probability 1), then if she has a choice between two lotteries, one of which offers T as a prize, the other of

---

[30] Sugden (1991), p. 762. And see Broome's 1991 discussion of this meaningfulness problem, Chapter 5.

which offers q as a prize, but which are otherwise identical, she will prefer the lottery with T – that is:

If q I T
then
L(p, x or T) > L'(p, x or q)

3. Suppose that there exists some prize y, such that for the CL:

   – q I T + y
   and
   – L(p, x or T + y)   I   L'(p, x or q)

   But according to our definition in 2, for a CL:

4. If q I T + y
   then
   L(p, x or T + y) > L'(p, x or q)

5. But 3 and 4 contradict each other. Hence our supposition is false, and we conclude that there is no y such that for our CL

   q I T + y
   and
   L(p, x or T + y)   I   L'(p, x or q)

6. From 5 it follows that the CL has preferences that do not instantiate the independence axiom.
7. Therefore there is no way to prove that a CL has a utility function.

Note that since an attitude toward certainty is an attitude toward risk, and an attitude that derails one of the EU axioms, this argument implicitly challenges the idea that EU theory can accommodate *all* attitudes toward risk within the framework of its consequentialist axioms. This has damaging implications for the claim made by Hammond, that EU theory can be conceptualized as a pure consequentialist theory for as long as consequences are defined as prospects.

These arguments are directed against consequentialism as it is represented in EU theory, so an advocate of consequentialism might maintain that a different theory (with a different rule of choice under uncertainty) might be able to represent consequentialism in a way that is immune from these attacks. But although there presently exist theories of rational choice that drop one of these axioms (for example, Machina drops the Independence Axiom, and Loomes and Sugden drop the Transitivity Axiom), thus far there is no rational choice theory that eschews all three axioms. So one or more of the preceding arguments apply to all existing alternatives to EU theory in decision theory. It is incumbent on an advocate of consequentialism, if he wishes to answer these arguments, to propose a theory that includes none of these axioms, but that also successfully captures both the nature of practical reason and the nature of consequentialism. It is beyond me how such a theory could be developed.

WHY THE RESOLUTION STRATEGY SEEMED TO WORK

The arguments speak for themselves, and yet I am sure that there will be readers who will kick against the traces. So in this section, I want to discuss why advocates of EU theory and consequentialist reasoning generally should have thought the Resolution Strategy was both plausible and successful.

Imagine that there are two rational creatures (whether or not they are like us human beings will, as we shall see, be a matter of controversy), one of which I'll call Harold and the other Maud. Harold has what I will call a perfectly Benthamite psychology – that is, he is the sort of individual who seeks to maximize a single experiential "substance." Following Bentham, I will call it "pleasure," but other Benthamites might have a different theory of what this single end of action is. In any such view, this single end of action is *experiential*, *homogeneous*, and, insofar as it comes in degrees, *continuous* (more or less) such that it *admits of measurement by a real number on at least an interval scale*. Harold is also a consequentialist reasoner because he is constructed such that consequences of action are for him the only causal source of pleasure. He is completely unaffected by the states in which these consequences are delivered (indeed, let us make him so pure that he doesn't even have attitudes toward risk). Hence he determines which action he should perform by (only) attending to the consequences of that action, and seeks to maximize those consequences he expects to be productive of pleasure (or the minimization of pain). So Harold is a creature whose preferences perfectly obey the EU axioms, such that we can prove that there is a utility function representing those preferences.

Maud is like Harold in one respect, but quite different in another. Like him, we will imagine that she has a perfectly Benthamite psychology as I have described it. But unlike him, she has two types of causal sources of pleasure – namely, the consequences of the actions that she is considering taking, and the states in which these consequences are delivered.

Now both Harold and Maud have psychologies that make them utility maximizers if we take utility in this case to denote pleasure (and the minimization of pain). But despite this, they do *not* reason in the same way prior to action. Harold's reasoning can be described by the expected utility theory; his preferences will instantiate the EU axioms. But Maud's will not; she experiences all sorts of state dependent utilities – for examples, utilities over gambling, attitudes toward certainty, feelings of regret, and so forth, and when she experiences these utilities her preferences fail to instantiate the axioms of EU theory – *and yet she is still a maximizer of utility*. We have all tended to identify a utility maximizer as someone who reasons in a way described by EU theory; but a utility maximizer can be someone for whom this theory fails, if the causal source of her utility is an aspect of the choice situation EU theory fails to recognize as a utility source. And when that happens, the theory cannot accommodate the way in which an individual such as Maud would (and should) reason prior to acting.

It is because the possibility that we might be Mauds has not been clearly seen that people impressed by the idea that we might be, in *some* sense (albeit perhaps not Bentham's sense), utility maximizers, have assumed that we must also be consequentialist reasoners. But we must distinguish the idea of "consequences" understood as determinate outcomes in the world, and pleasure (or whatever it is that utility is taken to measure) that is casually produced by these outcomes. And once we do so, it is easy to see that other things besides outcomes can cause pleasure if one has a psychology such as Maud's. The arguments in this chapter show that when this is true, we cannot represent a person's reasoning using a theory, such as EU theory, which implicitly assumes that the only causal source of pleasure or utility is outcomes.

What if we consider units of pleasure "consequences"? If we work with this notion rather than the notion of outcome, can we now describe someone such as Maud by the EU axioms after all? To see if we can, suppose that all the prizes in the axioms are actually paid off in terms of units of pleasure, which (we'll assume) Maud ultimately wants. Won't her preferences match the axioms now? Interestingly they will not. Take, for example, the RCL Axiom. Suppose that Maud has a choice between a compound lottery and a simple lottery that are equivalent according to the probability calculus and that will yield payoffs in pleasure. If Maud has utilities over gambling, she will not be indifferent between the two lotteries. She will prefer the compound lottery. And she will prefer it because the lottery itself is a causal source of pleasure for her, in a way that is neither acknowledged by nor allowed for by the EU axiom. That is, she will realize that she will not only get the pleasure payoffs as prizes, but also (if she wins the first lottery), the pleasure of the extra gamble. So we can repeat the argument given here with respect to the RCL Axiom with prizes paid off in utility, and show that Maud still does not instantiate the axiom. Moreover, if Maud is a certainty lover (regret hater), she will also violate the Independence Axiom (Transitivity Axiom) for the same reason – in particular, because the context of choice (the certainty, or the result that "could have been" if she chooses one action and not another) is an important component in the utility she experiences.

This discussion shows that we need to distinguish sharply between, on the one hand, how an agent reasons, and on the other, what I will call the agent's motivational psychology. Isolating the ultimate constituents of human beings' motivational structure does not yet help us to understand the nature of her reasoning unless we know how human beings respond to the world such that those ultimate motivational constituents are affected.

There is overwhelming evidence that in our world people are more like Maud than Harold, in the sense that states as well as consequences are important to them as they assess what to do in the world. Of course, whether or not they are utility maximizers is another matter. But at least with respect to *reasoning*, we have ample evidence that they do not, and should not, reason consequentially given that in fact they are sensitive to nonconsequential elements of a choice situation. We not only have preferences over gambling, feelings of regret, and attitudes toward certainty, but more importantly attitudes (some of which we call "moral") toward certain kinds of actions. Hence, in order to describe how practical reasoning actually works, we need a new theory of reason – one that is nonconsequentialist – even if it is true that we are in some sense creatures that are designed to "maximize utility." Indeed, formulating the kind of nonconsequentialism that Maud exhibits involves formulating functions of probabilities that yield utilities – where these utilities are *not* expected utilities – that are quite unrelated to any attitudes toward risk, and are not the product of some utility multiplied by a probability number.

FORMS OF NONCONSEQUENTIALISM

Recognizing that human beings are nonconsequentialist reasoners in a way that EU theory cannot capture does not yet mean embracing central tenets of deontological moral theory, for a number of reasons.

First, these arguments have only been concerned with representations of practical reasoning; they have not been concerned with the nature of moral justification. Moral consequentialism and moral deontology are positions about the latter, not the former. So it may be that even though we reason prior to choice in nonconsequentialist ways, what makes any act *morally* right is that it will produce the best overall consequences judged from some impersonal point of view. A moral consequentialist will insist that the theory of value that is appropriate for moral assessments of action is one that implies a certain kind of consequentialist assessment of those actions. Nothing in this chapter explicitly argues for the falsity of this position. Still, I suspect that moral consequentialism gets considerable purchase on the intuitions of philosophers because of the way in which its method of justification seems to match (what many take to be) the structure of our practical reasoning generally. If, as I have argued, our reasoning has a nonconsequentialist structure, that purchase is gone. And if our nonmoral evaluations of actions are not exclusively linked to the consequences of those actions, why should our moral evaluations of actions be exclusively linked to (morally relevant) consequences? Why can't there be morally relevant values associated with the actions themselves, which surface in the very real (moral) attitudes we have toward certain actions?

The second reason why the arguments in this chapter do not by themselves vindicate moral deontology is that as the example of Maud shows, one can be a nonconsequentialist practical reasoner and a utility maximizer with no interest in or ability to act from moral principles of the sort deontologists standardly defend. So just because Maud is sensitive to states as well as consequences doesn't mean that her nonconsequentialist reasoning is anything like the categorical imperative procedure! Contrast Maud with Thelma, who is sensitive to states as well as consequences, but who is not a utility maximizer, and who prefers certain actions to others because these actions instantiate certain principles (which she calls moral) to which she is committed. Whereas Maud's sensitivity to states in her practical reasoning is still driven by a concern for her own utility, Thelma's is not – her psychology is such that she can be driven by something other than utility, to which states as well as consequences are sensitive.

Let us return to the categories defined earlier in order to make this point clearer: The arguments in this chapter attempt to establish that there is no way we can construct a "broad consequentialism" that is broad enough to accommodate the variety of states in which we take an interest, but we can distinguish between what I will call *principled nonconsequentialism* (a category that includes a variety of moral deontological theories) which Thelma exhibits, and *nonprincipled nonconsequentialism*, a variant of which Maud exhibits. Nothing in this chapter argues in favor of one of these forms of nonconsequentialism.

Third, this chapter only attacks the idea that we are "consequentialists" in a certain quite specific sense of that term, and hence leaves unchallenged a sense of consequentialism that some who use that term to describe themselves might really be endorsing. In particular, it attacks what I will call *factor consequentialism* – the view that

> when deciding between two actions, choose by looking only at which action produces the best consequences.

Factor consequentialism can be developed into a number of forms, depending upon which rule of choice under uncertainty is built into it. In contrast, what I will call *weight consequentialism* is a view that permits a person to factor into her decision both how she feels about the consequences of an action and how she feels about the action itself – if she does value the action (she may not), but takes a position on *how* she should factor these things into her decision.[31] To be precise, it is the view that

> when deciding between two actions, factor into your decision your valuations of *both* the actions themselves and their conse-

---

[31] I am indebted to Amartya Sen, who suggested to me in conversation the idea of weight consequentialism as a distinctive version of consequentialist theory.

quences, where it cannot be the case that your valuation of the consequences of the action are irrelevant (that is, have no weight at all) in your reasoning about what to do.

Hence, weight consequentialism is opposed by some kind of "libertarian" or "radical Kantian" model of practical reasoning, in which actions present themselves to the reasoner as "right no matter what" – that is, commanded regardless of what happens. Weight consequentialism says that consequences are always relevant to determining the right thing to do, although it could also be that the agent's valuing of an action in its own right means he decides to weight it in such a way that he chooses it even if the action's consequences are bad. Consider Bernard Williams's famous example of a person named Jim who is forced to decide between killing one innocent person and thereby saving nine others, or not killing that person and thereby seeing all ten killed by another. Jim would reason as a weight consequentialist if, when he thought about whether he should kill the innocent person, he believed it relevant to his decision that he could save nine other people if he did so, but also took into consideration the fact that he valued the action of "my not murdering someone." But Jim would reason as a non-weight-consequentialist, if he thought that these nine deaths, however tragic, were nonetheless not relevant to his decision, insofar as murdering is always morally precluded – no matter the consequences of doing so. The latter is, one might say, "side constraint" thinking, or "actions as trumps" thinking, of the sort that a weight consequentialist believes doesn't make sense.

Weight consequentialism strikes me as being much different from, and in certain forms more plausible than, factor consequentialism. Indeed, factor consequentialism can be understood as only a special (and implausible) instance of weight consequentialism – that is, factor consequentialism is a species of weight consequentialism because insofar as the only factors it admits into practical decision making are consequences, it trivially satisfies the condition that the reasoner not value actions in such a way that they become trumps over consequences. But ultimately, as defined here, weight consequentialism is a position not about *what* the factors of one's decision-making are, but about *how* those factors are put together to make a decision.

For someone who is a weight consequentialist, the arguments in this chapter are irrelevant – nor does EU theory attempt to represent

weight consequentialism (except trivially, insofar as factor consequentialism, which is the conceptual framework motivating the theory, is an extreme instance of weight consequentialism). Hence a
(nonextreme) weight consequentialist will believe there is nothing
wrong with a person factoring into her decision not only how she
feels about the consequences of an action, but also how she feels
about the action itself – if she in fact does value the action.

Note something interesting about weight consequentialism. Not
only does it disallow someone from claiming that "the right is always prior to the good"; more fundamentally, it also does not permit
someone who endorses it to embrace the slogan "the good is always
prior to the right." That is, if "right" is the word we use to talk
about valuation of actions, and "good" is the word we use to talk
about valuation of consequences, then what one ought to do is going
to involve considerations of both the good and the right, where it
might be the case that in some circumstances, the right is weighted
more strongly than the good, and is decisive in determining one's
decision, whereas in other situations it is the good that has the
stronger weight. (Clearly, any weight consequentialist is going to
need a theory of weights, presumably generated by some theory of
valuation.) Weight consequentialists must therefore be prepared to
give up the "good over right" slogan, often thought to be the hallmark of the consequentialist position. Weight consequentialists will
disagree among themselves about the kind of theory of valuation to
embed in the theory. Some would want to endorse a theory that gave
certain sorts of actions very substantial weight; others would never
want to give actions much weight. It may well be that many people
who call themselves "deontologists" and many people who call
themselves "consequentialists" accept the same conception of practical decision-making that I have called weight consequentialism, but
are implicitly disagreeing only about the conception of value that
ought to inform how actions and their outcomes are weighted in a
moral decision.

How do we decide whether or not weight consequentialism is
true? Reliance on raw intuition is not really good enough against an
opponent whose intuitions clearly differ. One theory tells me that in
certain circumstances, I'm ordered to take into consideration only
actions no matter the consequences of those actions; the other tells
me I'm ordered to take into consideration whatever I value, which
can be both actions and consequences, and where it can never be the

case that my valuing an action can be such that its consequences are irrelevant to a determination of whether or not it is right to perform it. In both cases, I'm still represented as "ordered" – it's only that the orders are different. So which are the rational orders, or better, which orders does rationality dictate? Nothing in this chapter addresses this interesting question, and it argues neither for nor against weight consequentialism.

However, this chapter does argue that outside of moral contexts, only some form of factor *non*consequentialism, and not some form of broad factor consequentialism, is a correct representation of the way in which human beings do reason and ought to reason, given that there is ample evidence that we have state-sensitive preferences. Thus, if we are interested in understanding the nature of human practical reasoning, then even those who utterly reject deontological moral theory have reason to start taking seriously the idea that we can only do so successfully if we formulate a new conception of it. Theorists with different conceptions of how human beings function will presumably propose different models of practical reasoning that accommodate state-dependent preferences. But the arguments in this chapter indicate that philosophers and social scientists have good reason to reject their assumption that some kind of factor-consequentialist portrayal of human reasoning is correct. It is time to end their forty-year romance with decision-theoretic portrayals of practical reasoning that are factor-consequentialist in nature.

What would a successful nonconsequentialist global instrumental theory of practical reason look like? Answering this question is extremely difficult, making it understandable why theorists would have thought developing a consequentialist model of reason the obvious first choice, in large part because it would be so much *easier* to give prescriptions for the rational satisfaction of a set of preferences if those preferences were either for the same *kind* of thing, or else capable of being represented on one scale. Then we don't have to worry about developing prescriptions that presuppose (or dictate) the integration of preferences over very different sorts of things, and thus we don't have to tackle any issues of the normative importance of one sort of preference over another. All we need do is develop a theory that assumes that preferences over actions are (more or less) a function of preferences over consequences, and that each of us wants to maximize the desirable consequences. Such a theory straightforwardly generates a sensible general directive for satisfying a set of preferences – namely, satisfy preferences in the set so as to maximize desirable consequences.

But if human beings have preferences over actions that are not solely a function of their consequences, then this strategy won't work. State-dependent preferences and consequence-dependent preferences are fundamentally different; neither can be reduced to the other. There is no longer one type of "thing" that can be maximized, and prescriptions for how to satisfy a set of preferences can no longer avoid the problem of how to integrate different types of preferences. The problem is made particularly clear if we imagine that some of our state-dependent preferences have a moral basis, but it is also difficult to understand how to integrate nonmoral state-dependent preferences (for example, a preference for regret-minimization) with nonmoral preferences over the consequences of an action.

A truly effective global instrumental theory of reasoning will likely have to come to grips with this problem, and abandon the unsuccessful consequentialist route. The criticisms of EU theory in this chapter should therefore be linked to criticisms of utility theory made by theorists, such as Sen (1977), who argue that our preferences come in different "kinds," and may be created by reason operating noninstrumentally. Moreover, one might wonder whether the arguments in this chapter show that global "instrumental" reasoning has to be understood in the context of noninstrumental principles of reason that integrate different kinds of preferences. And if this is so, is the distinction between "instrumental" and "noninstrumental" reasoning really a useful one?

These remarks suggest that the formulation of a normative theory of reason whose axioms accommodate (what appear to be) the nonconsequentialist aspects of our global instrumental reasoning will likely have to include normative principles governing the integration of preferences. A defense of these principles – as well as some of the axioms in the theory – will have to rest on a foundational or coherentist argument (since, as we've seen, a consequentialist defense won't work), and this means not only that the objective authority of these axioms and principles will require a defense, but also that their (indirect) role in the formulation of our ends of action will be analogous to the role of noninstrumental principles of reason. We are a long way from the simple and straightforward conception of instrumental reason that moral skeptics have thought was "clearly" authoritative, in the way that moral norms and forms of reasoning are not. Part of the point of the last few chapters has been to show how enormously complicated our conception of reason – and particularly instrumental reason – actually is. Moral skeptics ought to start questioning the content and foundations of the conception of rationality they have long relied on uncritically.

Chapter 9

Toward a "Postnaturalist" Theory of Reasons

[computer file 9/14/95]

Thesis of this book: Naturalist moral skepticism, based on a naturalist theory of reasons, fails. Naturalizing the reasons that the naturalist requires for his own conception of practical reason and scientific methodology fails. The same nonnatural "authority" of moral reasons attends the naturalist's instrumental reasons; the same reflection on the nature of human good that is required in order to live a moral life is also required to live an instrumentally rational life. The naturalist-friendly conception of instrumental reasoning as consequentialist turns out to be inadequate. And if instrumental reasoning must be construed along nonconsequentialist lines in order to understand what we do, the claims by moral theorists that moral reasoning is nonconsequentialist become yet more plausible.

What do we do now? The death of one conception of reasons clears the way for the birth of another. The naturalist conception seemed simple, elegant, and commonsensical, but since it turned out to be none of these things, how do we construct a theory of reasons that is more successful? What are the criteria that we should use? What vestiges of the naturalist program, if any, should we remain wedded to?

There is, in my view, considerable virtue in the naturalist insistence on developing a theory that resists nonsense and flights of metaphysical fancy. But as we've seen, the conception of what is "natural" such theorists have used is much too narrow to allow them to develop a theory of their own conceptions of reasoning and scientific method. Suppose, therefore, that we try to remain true to practice – particularly scientific practice – and work out what we need to posit about practical reasons in order to explain that practice. If science is the arbiter of the real, and if what we mean by 'science' is defined not substantively but methodologically, then in addition to

288

any contentful specifications of scientific practice, we require a conception of the reasons that explain how that practice gets its authority. Once we have such a conception, we have the theoretical framework necessary to explain moral authority. Is that sufficient to show that there are moral reasons?

No. It is sufficient to show that there *could* be moral reasons, in the sense that there is nothing in the practice that we consider the arbiter of the real that rules them out. But it is not sufficient to rule them in. So how do we determine whether moral reasons are real? My hunch is that the naturalists are right to think that we need to start with less controversial reasons, figure out what makes them reasons, and then determine whether moral reasons have any of the same markers. One of the subtexts of this book, however, is that the naturalists have misunderstood why the sorts of reasons they accept as real, such as instrumental reasons, count as reasons. For example, there is a persistent tendency to advance what I have called the "internalism conception of reasons." Philosophers such as Gauthier and Williams try to argue that motivational efficacy is some kind of marker for a genuine reason, Gauthier doing so in the process of arguing that only present preferences can provide reasons for action (I discussed this position in Chapter 5), and Williams doing so in the process of arguing how it is that we know that a consideration regarding how we should act counts as a reason for us. But both theorists fail to show that the instrumental reasons they accept really are motivational. In Williams's case, it is the deliberative connection between an action and a motive that we have – where this connection can take a number of forms (an instrumental form being only one) – that gives us a reason to perform that action. But as I argued in Chapter 3, that deliberative connection does not *itself* make the reason motivationally efficacious. The fact that the reason is connected to a motive doesn't make *it* motivational. So there must be something about the deliberative connection that is the reason-making feature here, not anything motivational about the reason (since it need not have any motivational efficacy). Moreover, motivational efficacy is not only not necessary for something's being a reason in Williams's view; it is also not sufficient. If Owen in Williams's example is in a situation where he can determine no deliberative connection between the action and any element in his motivational set, and yet his father's pleadings push him to join anyway, we judge that there is something irrational about Owen's action. Clearly he was moved to join the military, but we also make a distinction between being rationally and irrationally motivated. In Williams's view, because there was no deliberative connection between this action and any element in the motivational set, we conclude that what Owen did was irrational, but in that case it is the deliberative connection with a motive, and not motivational efficacy itself, that is the marker for something's being a reason.

Where and why did Williams go wrong? As I discussed in Chapters 2 and 3, philosophers have persistently had trouble distinguishing between the authority and the motivational efficacy of a reason. In part because of the influence of Hume, who stressed the importance of motivation in any analysis of action, philosophers have tended to think that the authority-giving feature of a reason was its motivational efficacy. But just as commands can be right even if we don't want to follow them, a reason can be authoritative even if it fails to move us. And since we can make this distinction, we must be working with a notion of authority that is not informed by motivational efficacy (since we know it is possible for a reason to have the former, but not the latter, and we know that we can feel the latter, but still not have an authoritative reason).

This same point can be made in a different way by looking at Gauthier's misplaced reliance on motivational efficacy to explain why only present preferences are in what I called the good-defining preference set that gives us general reasons for action. As I discussed in Chapter 5, Gauthier probably makes this assumption on the grounds that only present reasons are motivationally efficacious. Again, motivation is suggested as the marker for something's being a reason. But there are, as I discussed in Chapter 5, plenty of preferences that seem to be ones that I "now" have, but that are motivationally inert (for example, my preference for mild salsa over hot salsa, or my preference for seeing a Tom Stoppard play over an Andrew Lloyd-Webber musical). Of course, in the right circumstances, these preferences will move me, but I do not know when that will be, and in the meantime, I am moved to sit here at my computer. So it is not that these preferences are motivational *now* that explains why they are in my good-defining preference set: Nor even that they would move me were I in the right circumstances, for couldn't I say that about virtually any preference that I could formulate, and isn't it also true about future preferences that they too will move me if I am in the right circumstances? (After all, I could think of circumstances in which I would rather see an Andrew Lloyd-Webber musical than a Stoppard play; and I could think of a situation where I would ask for hot salsa over mild.) Of course, some preferences are motivationally efficacious *now*, like the preference I have as I type this to continue typing rather than to stop, but if only motivationally occurrent preferences are in my *GD Set*, that preference set is extremely impoverished, and will have few of the characteristics that a theory of rational choice (of which expected utility theory is an example) requires if that set is going to be considered coherent.

What explains the persistent attraction of the idea that motivational efficacy marks something as a reason? I suspect it stems from philosophers' interest in avoiding postulating any "occult" reason-making markers. Motivational efficacy is clearly something real, something recognized by science, so why can't it serve as that which is at least a necessary (although perhaps not sufficient) criterion for something's being a reason? This idea, however, is attempting to skirt the reality that a reason has *authority*, and that authority cannot be identified with or in any way explained as motivational efficacy. And, alas for the naturalist, the notion of authority resists assimilation to anything that has traditionally been understood as "natural." Thus there is no way to posit a nonoccult conception of authority – unless of course, the line separating what counts as natural and what counts as occult is redrawn.

So how do we redraw the line, and stay well away from metaphysical flights of fancy?

Bibliography

Allais, M. 1979a. "The So-Called Allais Paradox and Rational Decision Under Uncertainty," in *Expected Utility Hypothesis and the Allais Paradox*, M. Allais and O. Hagen (eds.). Dordrecht: Reidel, pp. 437–681.

1979b. "The Foundations of a Positive Theory of Choice," in *Expected Utility Hypothesis and the Allais Paradox*, M. Allais and O. Hagen (eds.). Dordrecht. Reidel, pp. 27–145.

Altham, J. E. J., and Harrison, Ross (eds.). 1995. *World, Mind and Ethics*. Cambridge: Cambridge University Press.

Anderson, E. 1993. *Value in Ethics and Economics*: Cambridge, MA: Harvard University Press.

Anscombe, G. E. M. 1963. *Intention*. Ithaca: Cornell University Press.

1958. "Modern Moral Philosophy," *Philosophy 33*. Also in Anscombe 1981, pp. 26–42.

1981. *Ethics, Religion and Politics: Collected Papers, vol. III*. Minneapolis: University of Minnesota Press.

Arrow, K. 1951. *Social Choice and Individual Values*. New York: Wiley.

Ayer, A. J. 1936. *Language, Truth and Logic*. London: Victor Gollancz.

Badhwar, N. 1993. "Altruism Versus Self-Interest: Sometimes a False Dichotomy," in *Altruism*, E. F. Paul, F. D. Miller and J. Paul (eds.), Cambridge: Cambridge University Press, pp. 90–117.

Baier, Kurt. 1958. *The Moral Point of View: A Rational Basis of Ethics*. Ithaca: Cornell University Press.

1995. *The Rational and the Moral Order: The Social Roots of Reason and Morality*. Chicago: Open Court.

Baumol, A. 1972. *Economic Theory and Operations Analysis (3rd ed.)* Englewood Cliffs, N.J.: Prentice-Hall.

Bentham, J. 1823. *An Introduction to the Principles of Morals and Legislation*. 1982 edition, J. H. Burns and H. L. A. Hart (eds.). London: Methuen.

Bernoulli, D. 1738. "Exposition of a New Theory of Measurement of Risk." *Commentarii academiae scientiarum imperialis Petropolitanae 5*, trans. Louise Sommer in *Econometrica 22* (1954): 23–36.

Blackburn, S. 1971. "Moral Realism" in *Morality and Moral Reasoning*, J. Casey (ed.). London: Methuen.

1984. *Spreading the Word*. New York: Oxford University Press.

Bibliography

1985. "Supervenience Revisited," in *Exercises in Analysis: Essays by Students of Casimir Lewy*, Ian Hacking (ed.), Cambridge: Cambridge University Press.

Bloor, D. 1976. *Knowledge and Social Imagery*. London: Routledge and Kegan Paul.

Bond, E. J. 1983. *Reasons and Value*. New York: Cambridge University Press.

Boyd, R. 1988. "How to be a Moral Realist" in *Essays on Moral Realism*, G. Sayre-McCord (ed.). Ithaca.: Cornell University Press.

Brandt, R. B. 1979. *A Theory of the Right and the Good*. New York: Oxford University Press.

Bratman, Michael. 1987. *Intention, Plans and Practical Reason*. Cambridge, MA: Harvard University Press.

"Toxin, Temptation, and the Stability of Intention," in *Rational Commitment and Social Justice: Essays in Honor of Gregory Kavka*, Jules Coleman and Christopher Morris, (eds.), forthcoming from Cambridge University Press.

Brink, David O. 1989. *Moral Realism and the Foundation of Ethics*. Cambridge: Cambridge University Press.

Broome, J. 1991. *Weighing Goods: Equality, Uncertainty and Time*. Cambridge, MA: Blackwell.

1993. "Can a Humean be Moderate?" In *Value, Welfare and Morality*, R. G. Frey and Christopher Morris (eds.), pp. 51–73. Cambridge: Cambridge University Press.

Brown, J. R. (ed) 1984. *Scientific Rationality: the Sociological Turn*. Dordrecht: Reidel.

Buchanan, J. 1975. *The Limits of Liberty*. Chicago: University of Chicago Press.

Cooter, R. and Rappaport, P. 1984. "Were the Ordinalists Wrong About Welfare Economics?" *Journal of Economic Literature* XXII (2): 507–30.

Copp, D., and Zimmerman, D. (eds.). 1984. *Morality, Reason, Truth*. Totowa, N.J.: Rowman & Littlefield.

Copp, D. 1991. "Moral Realism: Facts and Norms," *Ethics 101*(3), 610–624.

Cosmides, L. and Tooby, J. 1989. "Evolutionary Psychology and the Generation of Culture: I. Theoretical Considerations," in *Ethology & Sociobiology* vol. 10(1–3), Jan, p. 29–49.

Crane, T., and Mellor, D. H. 1990. "There is no Question of Physicalism." *Mind 99*, April.

Dancy, J. 1993. *Moral Reasons*. Oxford: Oxford University Press.

Darwall, S. 1983. *Impartial Reason*, Ithaca: Cornell University Press.

Darwall, S., Gibbard, A., and Railton, P. 1992. "Toward *Fin de Siècle* Ethics: Some Trends," *The Philosophical Review 10*, No. 1 (January), pp. 115–89.

Darwall, S. 1995. *The British Moralists and the Internal 'Ought': 1640–1740*. New York: Cambridge University Press.

Davidson, D. 1963. "Actions, Reasons, and Causes," *The Journal of Philosophy 60* pp. 425–35. Reprinted in D. Davidson (1980), pp. 3–19.

1970. "Mental Events." Reprinted in Davidson 1980.

1980. *Essays on Actions and Events*. New York: Oxford University Press.

Dennett, D. 1978. "Why the Law of Effect Will Not Go Away," in *Brainstorms:*

Philosophical Essays on Mind and Psychology, Montgomery, Vermont: Bradford.

Donnellan, Keith. 1967. "Reasons and Causes," in *Encyclopedia of Philosophy*, Paul Edwards (ed.), New York: Macmillan, 1967, vol. 7–8, p. 85.

Ellsberg, D. 1954. "Classic and current notions of 'measurable utility'," *The Economic Journal* 64, 528–556.

Elster, J. 1986. "Introduction," in *Rational Choice*, J. Elster (ed), Oxford: Blackwell, p. 1–33.

Feyerabend, P. 1974. *Against Method: Outline of an Anarchistic Theory of Knowledge*. Atlantic Highlands, NJ: Humanities Press.

Field, Hartry. 1980. *Science Without Numbers: A Defence of Nominalism*. Princeton: Princeton University Press.

Foot, Phillipa. 1972. "Morality as a System of Hypothetical Imperatives," reprinted in Foot's *Virtues and Vices*. Berkeley: University of California Press, 1978.

1983. "Moral Realism and Moral Dilemma," *Journal of Philosophy* 80, pp. 379–98.

Frege, G. 1974. *The Foundations of Arithmetic*, trans. J. L. Austin. Oxford: Blackwell.

Gauthier, David. 1986. *Morals by Agreement*. Oxford: Oxford University Press.

Gibbard, Allan 1990. *Wise Choices, Apt Feelings*. Cambridge, MA: Harvard University Press.

Gillespie, N. (ed.). 1986. *Moral Realism: Proceedings of the 1985 Spindel Conference. The Southern Journal of Philosophy, Supplement* 24.

Goldman, Alvin. 1979. "What is Justified Belief?", in *Justification and Knowledge*, G. S. Pappas and M. Swain, (eds). Dordrecht: Reidel.

1986. *Epistemology and Cognition*. Cambridge, MA: Harvard.

Goodman, Nelson. 1955. *Fact, Fiction, and Forecast*. Harvard University Press.

Greenspan, P. S. 1975. "Conditional Oughts and Hypothetical Imperatives," *Journal of Philosophy* 72, pp. 259–276.

Hacking, Ian. 1994. Review of *The Advancement of Science: Science Without Legend, Objectivity Without Illusion* in *Journal of Philosophy*, April 1994 vol. 91, no. 4.

Hammond, P. 1988a. "Consequentialism and the Independence Axiom," in *Risk, Decision and Rationality*, B. R. Munier (ed.). Dordrecht: Reidel.

1988b. "Consequentialist Foundations for Expected Utility Theory," *Theory and Decision* 25, pp. 25–78.

Hampton, Jean. 1990. "Mens Rea," *Social Philosophy and Policy* vol. 7, pp. 1–28.

1992. "Rethinking Reason," *American Philosophical Quarterly* Winter, pp. 219–236.

1994. "The Failure of Expected Utility Theory as a Theory of Reason," *Economics and Philosophy* 10, pp. 195–242.

1995. "Does Hume have an Instrumental Conception of Practical Reason?", *Hume Studies XXI*, 57–74.

1996. "On Instrumental Rationality," in Schneewind (ed.), pp. 84–116.

Hare, R. M. 1952. *The Language of Morals*. Oxford: Oxford University Press.

Bibliography

1963. *Freedom and Reason*. Oxford: Oxford University Press.

1971. "Wanting: Some Pitfalls" in *Agent, Action, and Reason*. Binkley, Bronaugh and Marras (eds.), Toronto: University of Toronto Press, pp. 81–127.

1981. *Moral Thinking: Its Levels, Method, and Point*. Oxford: Clarendon Press.

Harman, Gilbert. 1977. *The Nature of Morality*. New York: Oxford University Press.

1983. "Human Flourishing, Ethics and Liberty," *Philosophy and Public Affairs* 12, p. 319.

1984. "Is There a Single True Morality?", in Copp and Zimmerman (1984).

1986. "Moral Explanations of Natural Facts – Can Moral Claims Be Tested Against Moral Reality?", in Gillespie (1986).

Herman, B. 1985. "The Practice of Moral Judgment." *Journal of Philosophy* 82, 414–35. August.

Hobbes, T. 1651. *Leviathan*, C. B. MacPherson (ed.). New York: Penguin, 1968.

1655. *De Corpore*, Vol. 1 of *The English Works of Thomas Hobbes*, W. Molesworth (ed.). London: John Bohn, 1840.

Hookway, Christopher. 1995. "Fallibilism and Objectivity: Science and Ethics," in Altham and Harrison (1995).

Hume, D. 1739. *A Treatise of Human Nature*, P. H. Nidditch (ed.). New York: Oxford University Press, 1978.

1751. *An Enquiry Concerning the Principles of Morals*. Indianapolis: Hackett, 1983.

Hurley, P. 1990. "The Many Appetites of Thomas Hobbes." *History of Philosophy Quarterly* 391–407, October.

Hurley, S. 1989. *Natural Reasons*. New York: Oxford University Press.

Jardine, N. 1995. "Science, Ethics, and Objectivity," in Altham and Harrison (1995).

Jeffrey, R. C. 1965. *The Logic of Decision*. New York: McGraw-Hill, 2nd rev. ed. Chicago: University of Chicago Press, 1983.

Kahneman, D., and Tversky, A. 1990. "Rational Choice and the Framing of Decisions," in *The Limits of Rationality*, K. Cook and M. Levi (eds.), pp. 60–89. Chicago: University of Chicago Press.

Kant, I. 1785. *Groundwork of the Metaphysics of Morals*. trans. H. J. Paton. New York: Harper & Row, 1956, and *Foundations of the Metaphysics of Morals*. trans. Lewis White Beck. Indianapolis: Bobbs-Merrill, 1959.

1788. *Critique of Practical Reason*. trans. Lewis White Beck. Indianapolis: Bobbs-Merrill, 1956.

Kavka, G. 1983. "The Toxin Puzzle" *Analysis* 43, 33–36, January.

1986. *Hobbesian Moral and Political Theory*. Princeton: Princeton University Press.

Kim, Jaegwon. 1984. "Concepts of Supervenience," *Philosophy and Phenomenological Research* 45:153–76.

Kitcher, Paul. 1993. *The Advancement of Science: Science Without Legend, Objectivity Without Illusion*. New York: Oxford University Press.

Korsgaard, C. 1986. "Skepticism about Practical Reason," *The Journal of Philosophy* 83, 5–25.

Kreps, D. 1988. *Notes on a Theory of Choice*. Boulder, CO: Westview Press.

Bibliography

Kripke, S. 1971. "Identity and Necessity," reprinted in Schwartz (1977).

    1980. *Naming and Necessity*. Cambridge, MA: Harvard University Press.

Little, I. M. D. 1984. "Comment," *Journal of Economic Literature* XXII (2): 1187.

Loomes, G. and Sugden, R. 1982. "Regret Theory: An Alternative Theory of Rational Choice Under Uncertainty," *Economic Journal* 92, pp. 805–24

    1984. "The Importance of What Might Have Been," in *Progress in Utility and Risk Theory*, Ole Hagen and Fred Westop (eds.). Dordrecht: Reidel, pp. 219–235.

Luce, R. D., and Raiffa, H. 1957/1985. *Games and Decisions: Introduction and Critical Survey*. New York: Wiley.

Machina, M. 1991. "Dynamic Consistency and Non-expected Utility Models of Choice Under Uncertainty," in *Foundations of Decision Theory: Issues and Advances*, Michael Bacharach and Susan Hurley (eds.). Oxford: Blackwell.

Mackie. J. L. 1977. *Ethics: Inventing Right and Wrong*. New York: Penguin Books.

Matthen, M., and Levy, E. 1984. "Teleology, Error and the Human Immune System." *Journal of Philosophy* vol. 81, no. 7, pp. 351–72.

McClennen, E. 1990. *Rationality and Dynamic Choice*. Cambridge: Cambridge University Press.

McDowell, J. 1978. "Are Moral Requirements Hypothetical Imperatives?", *Proceedings of the Aristotelian Society*, suppl. vol. 52, pp. 13–29.

    1979. "Virtue and Reason," *Monist*, vol. 62.

    1985. "Values and Secondary Qualities," in *Morality and Objectivity*, T. Honderich (ed.). Boston: Routledge and Kegan Paul.

    1995. "Might There Be External Reasons?", in Altham and Harrison (1995), pp. 68–85.

Mill, J. S. 1859. *On Liberty*. Indianapolis: Bobbs-Merrill, 1956.

    1861. *Utilitarianism*. Indianapolis: Hackett, 1979.

    1895. *A System of Logic*. London, New York: Longmans, Green.

Millgram, E. 1995. "Was Hume a Humean?" *Hume Studies* 21(1), pp. 75–93.

Moore, G. E. 1903. *Principia Ethica*. Cambridge: Cambridge University Press.

Morris, C. 1990. "Moral Standing and Rational Choice Contractarianism," in *Contractarianism and Rational Choice: Essays on Gauthier*, Peter Vallentyne (ed.). Cambridge: Cambridge University Press.

Murdoch, I. 1970. *The Sovereignty of Good*. New York: Schocken.

Nagel, T. 1970. *The Possibility of Altruism*. Princeton: Princeton University Press.

Narveson, Jan. 1988. *The Libertarian Ideal*. Philadelphia: Temple University Press.

Nelson, Alan. 1990. "Are Economic Kinds Natural?", in *Minnesota Studies in the Philosophy of Science* vol. 14: 102–35.

Nozick, R. 1993. *The Nature of Rationality*. Princeton: Princeton University Press.

Owen, D. 1994. "Inference, Reason and Reasoning in Book One of Hume's Treatise," *Southwestern Philosophical Review* 10 (1), pp. 17–27.

Petit, P. 1993. "A Definition of Physicalism," *Analysis* vol. 53, no. 4, pp. 213–23.

Bibliography

Price, R. 1787. *A Review of the Principal Questions in Morals*. Reprinted in Raphael (1969).

Putnam, Hilary. 1977. "Reference and Meaning" in Schwartz (1977).

1981. *Reason, Truth, and History*. Cambridge: Cambridge University Press.

1983. "Why Reason Can't Be Naturalized," in *Realism and Reason: Collected Philosophical Papers*, vol. 3. Cambridge: Cambridge University Press.

1990. *Realism with a Human Face*. Cambridge, MA: Harvard University Press.

1992. "The Absolute Conception of the World," in *Renewing Philosophy*. Cambridge: Cambridge University Press.

Quine, W. V. 1948. "On What There Is," *Review of Metaphysics*, 2, 21–38. September.

1960. *Word and Object*. Cambridge, MA: MIT Press.

1969. "Epistemology Naturalized," in *Ontological Relativity and Other Essays*. New York: Columbia University Press, pp. 69–90.

1977. "Facts of the Matter," in *American Philosophy from Edwards to Quine*, R. W. Shahan and A. R. Merrill (eds.). Norman: University of Oklahoma Press.

1980. *From a Logical Point of View* (2nd ed). Cambridge, MA: Harvard University Press.

1981. "Things and their place in Theories" in *Theories and Things*. Cambridge, MA: Harvard University Press.

1990. *Pursuit of Truth*. Cambridge, MA: Harvard University Press.

Railton, P. 1989. "Naturalism and Prescriptivity," *Social Philosophy and Policy*, vol. 7, no. 1, Autumn. pp. 151–74.

Ramsey, Frank Plumpton. 1931a. Epilogue ("There is Nothing to Discuss") in Ramsey (1931/1978).

1931b. "Truth and Probability" in Ramsey (1931/1978).

1931/1978. *Foundations of Mathematics and other Logical Essays*. R. B. Braithwaite (ed.). New York: Harcourt Brace, 1931. *Foundations*. D. H. Mellor (ed.). London: Routledge and Kegan Paul, 1978.

Raphael, D. D. (ed.). 1969. *The British Moralists*. 2 vols. New York: Oxford University Press.

Rawls, John. 1971. *A Theory of Justice*. Cambridge, MA: Harvard University Press.

Raz, Joseph. 1975/1990. *Practical Reason and Norms*. Princeton: Princeton University Press.

Rorty, Richard. 1980a. *Philosophy and the Mirror of Nature*. Oxford: Oxford University Press.

1980b. "Pragmatism, Relativism and Irrationalism," in *Proceedings and Addresses of the American Philosophical Association*, vol. 5. pp. 719–38.

Rosenberg, A. 1983. "If Economics Isn't a Science, What is it?", *The Philosophical Forum*, 14: 296–314, Spring-Summer.

Ross, W. D. 1930. *The Right and The Good*. New York: Oxford University Press.

Russell, B. 1944. "Reply to my Critics," in *The Philosophy of Bertrand Russell*, P. A. Schilpp (ed.). Evanston: Northwestern University Press.

1957. "On the Notion of Cause," in *Mysticism and Logic*. Garden City, NY: Doubleday.

Salmon, W. 1989. "Four Decades of Scientific Explanation," in *Scientific Explanation*, P. Kitcher and W. Salmon (eds.). Minneapolis: University of Minnesota Press, pp. 26–32.

Samuelson, P. 1966. "Utility, Preferences and Probability," in *Collected Scientific Papers, Volume I*, Joseph Stiglitz (ed.). Cambridge, MA: MIT Press, pp. 127–136

Satz, D. and Ferejohn, J. 1994. "Rational Choice and Social Theory," *Journal of Philosophy* 91(2):71–87.

Savage, L. 1954. *The Foundations of Statistics*. New York: Wiley, 2nd ed., 1972.

Sayre-McCord, G. (ed.) 1988a. *Moral Realism*. Ithaca: Cornell University Press.
    1988b. "Moral Theory and Explanatory Impotence," *Midwest Studies in Philosophy* 12, pp. 433–457.

Scheffler, S. 1992. *Human Morality*. New York: Oxford University Press.

Schneewind, J. B. (ed.) 1996. *Reason, Ethics and Society: Themes from Kurt Baier, With His Responses*. Chicago: Open Court.

Schwartz, S. P. 1977. *Naming, Necessity and Natural Kinds*. Ithaca: Cornell University Press.

Sen, A. 1977. "Rational Fools: A Critique of the Behavioral Foundations of Economic Theory," *Philosophy and Public Affairs* 6, pp. 317–344.
    1983. "Evaluator Relativity and Consequential Evaluation," in *Philosophy and Public Affairs* 12, no. 2 (Spring), pp. 113–132.

Simon, H. A. 1955. "A Behavioral Model of Rational Choice" *Quarterly Journal of Economics* 69, pp. 99–118.
    1956. "Rational Choice and the Structure of the Environment," *Psychological Review* 63, pp. 129–38.

Stevenson, C. L. 1937. "The Emotive Meaning of Ethical Terms," *Mind* 46, pp. 14–31.
    1944. *Ethics and Language*. New Haven: Yale University Press.

Stich, S. 1990. *The Fragmentation of Reason*. Cambridge, MA: MIT Press.

Stigler, G. J. and Becker, G. S. 1977. "De Gustibus Non Est Disputandum," *The American Economic Review* 67, no. 2.

Striker, Gisela. 1986. "Origins of the Concept of Natural Law," in *Proceedings of the Boston Colloquium on Ancient Philosophy* 2, pp. 79–94.

Sturgeon, Nicholas. 1984. "Moral Explanations," in Copp and Zimmerman (1984).
    1986. "Harman on Moral Explanations of Natural Facts," *The Southern Journal of Philosophy*, vol. xxiv, supplement, pp. 61–64.
    1992. "Nonmoral Explanations," in *Philosophical Perspectives, 6: Ethics*, Tomberlin, James E. (ed.).

Sugden, R. 1991, "Rational Choice: A Survey of Contributions from Economics and Philosophy," *Economic Journal* 101 no. 407 (July), pp. 751–85.

Tuana N. (ed). 1989. *Feminism and Science*. Bloomington: Indiana University Press.

Tversky, A. 1975. "A Critique of Expected Utility Theory: Descriptive and Normative Considerations," *Erkenntnis* 9, pp. 163–73.

van Fraassen, Bas C. 1989. *Laws and Symmetry*. Oxford: Clarendon Press.

von Neumann, J., and Morgenstern, O. 1944. *Theory of Games and Economic Behavior*. Princeton: Princeton University Press, 2nd ed. 1947, 3rd ed. 1953.

von Wright, G. H. 1963. *Norm and Action: A Logical Enquiry*, New York: Humanities Press.

Walsh, V. 1987. "Philosophy and Economics" in *The New Palgrave: A Dictionary of Economics*, vol. 3, J. Eatwell, M. Milgate, and P. Newman (eds.). London: Macmillan, New York: Stockton Press.

Weymark. 1991. "A Reconsideration of the Harsanyi-Sen Debate on Utilitarianism," in *Interpersonal Comparisons of Well-Being*, Jon Elster and John Roemer (eds.). New York: Cambridge University Press, pp. 255–320.

Wiggins, D. 1980. *Sameness and Substance*. Oxford: Blackwell.

Williams, B. 1981a. *Moral Luck*. New York: Cambridge University Press.

1981b. "Internal and External Reasons," in B. Williams (1981a), pp. 101–13.

1981c. "Practical Necessity," in B. Williams (1981a), pp. 124–31.

1985. *Ethics and the Limits of Philosophy*. Cambridge, MA: Harvard University Press.

1995. "Replies," in Altham and Harrison (1995), pp. 185–224.

Wittgenstein, Ludwig. 1958. "The Blue Book" in *The Blue and Brown Books*. New York: Harper & Brothers.

Wolf, Susan. 1982. "Moral Saints," *Journal of Philosophy* 79 (8), pp. 419–39.

Index